UNLOCKING THE LAW

UNLOCKING THE LAW OF EVIDENCE

4th edition

Dr Charanjit Singh

UNLOCKING THE LAW

Routledge
Taylor & Francis Group
LONDON AND NEW YORK

Cover image: putilich/Getty Images

Fourth edition published 2023
by Routledge
4 Park Square, Milton Park, Abingdon, Oxon, OX14 4RN

and by Routledge
605 Third Avenue, New York, NY 10158

Routledge is an imprint of the Taylor & Francis Group, an informa business

First edition published by Hodder Education 2009
Third edition published by Routledge 2016

British Library Cataloguing-in-Publication Data
A catalogue record for this book is available from the British Library

ISBN: 978-1-032-25275-9 (hbk)
ISBN: 978-1-032-25273-5 (pbk)
ISBN: 978-1-003-28243-3 (ebk)

DOI: 10.4324/9781003282433

Contents

Detailed contents

Guide to the book

Unlocking the Law of Evidence brings together all the essential elements for today's law students in a clearly defined and memorable way. Each book is enhanced with learning features to reinforce understanding of key topics and test your knowledge along the way. Follow this guide to make sure you get the most from reading this book.

AIMS AND OBJECTIVES

Defines what you will learn in each chapter.

SECTION

Highlights sections from Acts.

Definition

Find key legal terminology at a glance.

ARTICLE

Defines Articles of the EC Treaty or of the European Convention on Human Rights or other treaty.

CLAUSE

Shows a bill going through Parliament or a draft bill proposed by the Law Commission.

CASE EXAMPLE

Illustrates the law in action.

JUDGMENT

Provides extracts from judgments on cases.

QUOTATION

Encourages you to engage with primary sources.

ACTIVITY

Enables you to test yourself as you progress through the chapter.

KEY FACTS

Draws attention to essential points and information.

SAMPLE ESSAY QUESTION

Provides you with real-life sample essays and show you the best way to plan your answer.

SUMMARY

Concludes each chapter to reinforce learning.

Acknowledgements

To my Family and Friends, this falls far short of demonstrating the gratitude I have for the strength and peace that you reward me with daily. Thank you.

Dr C. Singh

Preface

Lawyers understand that litigation is underpinned by evidence; therefore an in-depth understanding of the law is of utmost importance. The rules on admissibility, relevance and weight will help you realise very quickly that a tactical use of such rules can facilitate success. Many cases are won, and lost, solely on the basis of a lawyer's command of the evidence and therefore whether or not and how they use it. The aim of this book is to provide you with a clear and comprehensive discussion of the law, and to reinforce your learning with diagrams, summaries and exercises. Evidence has a habit of presenting problems that often require immediate responses; for instance a witness may say something in their evidence the nature of which is so prejudicial that it would require a new jury to be sworn in. This book brings together the academic law with its more practical reality. The law is stated as at 1 March 2022. This fourth edition has been rewritten, edited and updated and includes new cases, commentaries and contemporary discussion. To all those students of evidence out there, and those that are refreshing their knowledge, '*the most savage of controversies are about those matters as to which there is no good evidence either way*' (Bertrand Russell, 1872–1970).

I would like to express my sincere gratitude to the staff at Taylor & Francis for their assistance in the completion of this edition. I would also like to thank all those who reviewed the fourth edition and made suggestions; full consideration was given those and, where possible, implemented.

Dr Charanjit Singh
Barrister-at-Law – Holborn Chambers, PhD
Assistant Head of School, University of Westminster

The emphasis of this book is to take a practical and tactical approach to the evidence all practitioners and students will encounter on a daily basis in their everyday professional lives. The book provides a clear and easily understood analysis of evidence. Without a solid comprehensive knowledge of what evidence actually comprises, and how it can be used to the benefit of a case, lawyers in all areas of the law will be at a disadvantage both in terms of the case and their clients. This book provides a guide to the knowledge and skills a lawyer requires in conducting a case so as to bridge the academic and practical skills divide. Dr Singh is a highly respected member of Chambers who has over the years combined his academic work with a busy practice and is therefore ideally placed to write this book which provides an invaluable aid to many.

Stuart Stevens
Head of Holborn Chambers, Barrister-at-Law

Figures

Table of cases

Table of statutes and other instruments

Statutes

1

An introduction to the substantive law of evidence

AIMS AND OBJECTIVES

The aims and objectives of this chapter are to:

- introduce the law of evidence to you through hypothetical examples and real case studies;
- help you understand the development of the law of evidence and its exclusionary approach through a brief historical overview;
- teach you, through examples, about the different categories of evidence that exist;
- highlight the importance of the rules on the admissibility of evidence through a discussion of the related rationale;
- aid you to contextualise the role of the judge and jury in assessing evidence through highlighting their relative functions;
- outline the general rules on the exclusion of evidence through a discussion of the principles upon which these are based.

1.1 Introduction

Studying the law of evidence requires a rigorous examination and understanding of the vast array of rules and exceptions, in both the criminal and civil law of evidence, set against the potential judicial decision to exclude. Having a thorough understanding of the core areas of law is also important. The rules of evidence and their exceptions co-exist, like the pieces of a complex jigsaw puzzle; they complement each other and recreate an image, a narrative or story in the minds of the triers of fact and/or law (including magistrates, judges and the jury) of what possibly happened within the greater context. The trial is an adversarial contest and therefore the parties will seek to present their case in the most persuasive manner that they can – this involves selecting the evidence that they will present. There are professional conduct rules that impact on a lawyer's ability to present evidence in particular circumstances. It is therefore fair to state that all lawyers, regardless of

DOI: 10.4324/9781003282433-1

whether they are solicitors or barristers, need to have mastered a sound appreciation of the substantive law of evidence. Tutors often remind their students that they can be tested on any part of the syllabus; this field of study is no different, with many assessments often turning out to be exercises of memory. One method of learning is to think about the rules of the substantive law of evidence as formulae – this can make recalling them much easier. There are three important things that you must remember – that the substantive law of evidence governs: (a) how *facts* are proven in court; (b) the rules on how evidence should be *put to and presented* in court; and (c) that these go along with the rules on which evidence *should be excluded from* the court altogether.

On that basis it is important that you appreciate that the parties to any action, whether it be a civil or criminal action, are not given blanket permission to put before the court all the evidence that may assist their case. An important point to note is that: the parties are only permitted to put before the court the evidence that is (a) *relevant* to a fact in issue in the case and (b) *admissible*; and even then a trial judge may decide to exclude it, for it is he or she who has the final decision on the matter. Although this sounds like a pretty tall order, as you read through the book you will begin to understand the context in which the law developed and *why*, for instance, the judicial ability to exclude evidence and give directions to the jury in relation to other types of evidence is so fundamentally important. The topics that are covered in this textbook include:

- burdens and standards of proof;
- competence and compellability of witnesses;
- the trial process (examination-in-chief, cross-examination and re-examination of witnesses);
- privilege and public interest immunity;
- adverse inferences and silence;
- hearsay;
- confessions and illegally obtained evidence;
- identification evidence;
- corroboration and care warnings;
- good and bad character evidence;
- doctrine of similar fact;
- opinion evidence;
- documentary and real evidence.

Although it has been some time since the similar fact doctrine was superseded by the rules in the Criminal Justice Act 2003 (CJA), the case law is still relevant for discussion purposes.

1.2 The exclusionary approach of the English law of evidence

In order to begin to explore and understand the substantive law of evidence it is pivotal that you appreciate what evidence is and how it works, so this is one of the main aims of this chapter and the textbook. The definitions that you will be introduced to in this chapter are those widely used in this field of study and they will remain consistent throughout this textbook. There are a number of infamous trials that exemplify the use of evidence and its impact on the outcome: the trials of Oscar Wilde (1895) and of Dr Crippen (1910) are two of the most notable. In the latter case the prosecution had the task of proving that the doctor had murdered Mrs Crippen (his wife). They alleged that he was having an affair and, because he wished to marry his mistress, he poisoned his wife. Whether the poison had in fact had the desired effect and killed her did not matter because they alleged that he had subsequently dismembered the body and then buried the chunks of flesh in the cellar of their marital home and burnt the bones – the head was never recovered. When his friends enquired about his wife's whereabouts he had simply told them that she was staying with relatives. When the police began enquiring into his wife's whereabouts Crippen changed his story, telling them that she had left him. He explained to the police that he had lied to his friends because he was too embarrassed to admit that that is what had happened. Shortly after this the doctor left England with his mistress. When the police dug up his cellar, to their horror, they discovered his wife's remains. Crippen was caught and returned to England, where he stood trial. One of the main evidential issues was the identification of Crippen's wife without the head. Evidentially, the head is one of the most useful parts of the human anatomy for identification purposes even when it is in a state that renders it difficult to make a physical identification; in such a case a dental record can be used for this purpose. Luckily, in the absence of the head the prosecution was able to use a distinctive scar to prove that the remains recovered belonged to his wife. Other prosecution evidence included that of Crippen's initial lies to his friends about the whereabouts of his wife and subsequently leaving England with his mistress. In answer to the question whether the prosecution could adduce this as evidence, they would have to prove that it was (a) *relevant* and (b) *admissible*.

Here is another scenario. Tim and Mary have been married for over twenty years, during which time Tim has been repeatedly physically, mentally and verbally abusive towards his wife. One day Tim returns from work drunk and starts to argue with Mary, shouting at her. He begins to walk towards her shaking his fists violently and Mary, fearing for her safety, picks up a frying pan and hits Tim on the head with it. Tim slumps to the floor in a pool of blood; unbeknown to Mary, he has a thin skull that is easily fractured. Tim subsequently dies in hospital. Mary is arrested and charged with murdering Tim. Scenarios such as this are not uncommon in assessments. The questions from a practical legal and evidential perspective include: what happens next procedurally? Can Mary prove that she was acting in self-defence? If she were to claim that her responsibility was diminished, how would she substantiate that claim? The job of Mary's legal counsel will be to advise her on:

- the case against her;
- any defences that she may raise; and
- the likely prospect of successfully defending herself against this allegation.

Counsel for Mary will want to challenge or test the evidence (the facts) that is stacked against her. This adversarial approach also seeks to ensure that any subsequent conviction is not unsafe. Appeals of decisions are often made where the proceedings have not been conducted in accordance with the rules of evidence (for example judicial misdirection) and process. In summary, evidence can be described as those *facts* that are used to either *prove* or *disprove* something.

There are many jurisdictions throughout the world that admit all relevant evidence. In contrast, the English law of evidence does not. Traditionally, the English system has adopted a far more cautious and arguably restrictive approach. This has, at first sight, resulted in the exclusion of what many would regard as important relevant evidence; for instance, a confession may be excluded because of the unlawful manner in which the police obtained it (discussed later in the book). The foundations to this approach lie in the concept of trial by jury. The widely accepted notion about juries was that they could not sufficiently analyse the evidence presented to them and that they were unable to allocate the appropriate amount of weight to certain types of evidence; for instance, they may give a sighting of the accused at the scene of crime more weight than it deserved. Finally, certain types of evidence were deemed risky because such evidence would more easily prejudice a jury if it were not excluded, even if it were highly relevant. There have been a number of changes in relation to this stance; for instance the UK now takes an inclusionary approach to some types of traditionally excluded evidence, such as hearsay in criminal proceedings, discussions surrounding the exclusion of juries in cases that are technically complex and allowing those who are legally qualified to sit as part of a jury. If you take a brief look at English criminal law you will notice how harsh certain penalties are that have been imposed on a defendant who had been found guilty (sometimes wrongfully) for the commission of a criminal offence. Thus, it was necessary to protect an accused from the inequity that would result from a jury mishandling the evidence.

Trial judges were vigilant in excluding evidence that they were suspicious of being concocted, fabricated or distorted. In addition to this, a series of public policy reasons evolved to exclude certain types of evidence from being disclosed. Legal professional privilege is a good example of the latter – this seeks to protect communications between the client and lawyer and promote candour in discussions (note, there are a range of new legal duties that qualify privilege, for instance the duty to report proceeds of crime or serious abuse of the vulnerable). Other examples include evidence that was not in the public interest to disclose because, perhaps, it would potentially damage national security – for instance certain types of military documents during wartime. Again, such documents, of which there are numerous examples, can be declassified many years later.

Lawyers analyse and prepare their client's case on the basis of a two-part test. The first limb of this test asks: is there any *relevant evidence* that proves the facts contended? If, the answer to this question is in the affirmative, then the next question is whether that relevant evidence is *admissible*. Only then can a lawyer determine how likely it is that a claim would be successful, i.e., to what level does the evidence meet the standard of proof, and subsequently advise the client. When you are undertaking an assessment question on the law of evidence you should begin by asking yourself these two questions because only evidence that is relevant and admissible can be put to the court. Whilst there is judicial discretion to exclude admissible evidence (discussed later), there is no judicial discretion to include inadmissible evidence. The test set out requires you to assess relevancy first – the following example will show you why. Consider this scenario: Sheetal is acting on behalf of Frank as legal counsel. She is presented with fifty pieces of evidence and, unbeknown to her, all fifty are technically admissible but only ten are relevant to prove Frank's case. Reflect on this: when determining what evidence could be used, should Sheetal assess the admissibility or the relevance of the evidence first? Should she choose to assess admissibility first, she would have to assess all fifty pieces of evidence and then determine relevancy. If, however, she chooses to test relevancy first, then she would only have to determine the admissibility of those ten pieces of evidence that were actually relevant to prove Frank's case. Thus, logically an assessment of relevancy first limits the exercise of testing admissibility to only relevant evidence, and it also helps prevent superfluous discussion on irrelevant evidence that may impinge on a conservative word count (coursework) or time constraint (exam). The analysis does not end there – as already outlined there are instances in which even relevant evidence is inadmissible; again, for example, it may have been obtained unlawfully such as a confession from a mentally disabled individual who is put under extreme duress through hunger, or evidence obtained by the police through an agent provocateur. The complexity of this subject is best demonstrated by its own rules; for example, there are occasions in which evidence obtained as a result of inadmissible evidence is independently admissible. Just because evidence A, which led to the discovery of evidence B, is inadmissible, it does not follow that evidence B is also automatically inadmissible. For instance, a piece of artwork is recovered as a result of Joel's confession, which the police obtained through duress – his confession may be rendered inadmissible by the duress but the recovered artwork from his home would remain admissible. In this scenario the prosecution would not be permitted to present to the court the fact that the artwork was recovered by reason of Joel's inadmissible confession.

It should be noted that, contrary to the belief of many, adversarial trials are not the search for the ultimate truth but to secure the safest conviction whilst safeguarding due process. This is underpinned by the fact that it is a fundamental rule of the English law of evidence that relevant evidence that is rendered inadmissible cannot be presented to the court for consideration regardless of its importance to the success of the case. This does not delimit subsequent argumentation regarding admissibility where appeals are concerned.

ACTIVITY

Why was the traditional approach in the English law of evidence an exclusionary one?

KEY FACTS

The English law of evidence was traditionally based upon an exclusionary approach; this is a position that changed with various statutes, for example the Criminal Justice Act 2003, more willing to promote an inclusionary approach.

Evidence can be described as facts that are used to prove or disprove something.

1.3 Types of judicial evidence

There are many types of evidence that can be put before a court; these will be discussed in due course. It is important to understand that a single piece of evidence can be admissible to prove a number of different things; for instance, a communication (a string of letters) between Nancy and Paul, where Paul denies ever knowing Nancy, can be presented to contradict Paul's lie (lies are discussed later). The same piece of evidence can also be presented as proof of what it contains. Perhaps the letter included a threat of some sort; therefore the contents of that same letter could be classed as hearsay. That same piece of evidence will also be susceptible to a number of rules. Thus, you must have a very good working knowledge of the various classifications of evidence (below), and the rules that accompany their admission, if you are to be able to successfully apply the substantive law of evidence to them. The following are common types of evidence studied:

- direct or percipient
- circumstantial
- hearsay
- original
- primary
- secondary
- presumptive
- conclusive
- oral testimony
- documentary
- real.

1.3.1 Direct or percipient evidence

Direct evidence, also referred to as percipient evidence, is that evidence which, if accepted by the court, does not require any further inferences to be drawn from it. Direct evidence will be a direct perception of a fact in issue by sight, sound, smell or taste: for example, Sachin's evidence of Martha singing a song is direct evidence of Martha's state; or Michael's evidence that he saw Jean shoot Adam with a sawn-off shotgun.

1.3.2 Circumstantial evidence

In contrast to direct or percipient evidence, circumstantial evidence is evidence that, if accepted by the court, does require further inferences to be drawn from it. For instance, Sachin's evidence that Martha was singing a song may be circumstantial evidence that she was intoxicated. Generally, the inference that should be drawn will be obvious; however, sometimes it is not so clear. Where it is unclear what inference should be drawn then that circumstantial evidence can be supported by other circumstantial evidence. The Crown Prosecution Service can decide to proceed with the prosecution of an offence on the basis of what is deemed to be wholly circumstantial evidence; thus, a conviction can be based on the same. When considering whether the evidence proves something circumstantially the jury will ask the following questions. Are the relevant facts, or some of them, proven by the evidence? If the answer to this is in the affirmative, then should the fact in issue be inferred by the existence of those relevant facts?

In *R v Exall* (1866) 4 F & F 922, Pollock CB formulated his famous analogy between circumstantial evidence and the strands of a rope, when he stated:

JUDGMENT

> '... one *single* strand of the cord may be insufficient to sustain the weight of something, but *three strands* stranded together may be of sufficient strength to do so'.

Looking at our earlier example again, Sachin's evidence could be further strengthened if he had also witnessed and stated that at the time Martha was singing she was clutching a half-empty bottle of Bombay gin. This will no doubt affect his evidence: Sachin's account of Martha singing would be considered to be direct evidence of her actions and his evidence of her clutching a half-empty bottle of Bombay gin is both direct evidence of her action and circumstantial evidence to support the inference that she may have been drunk at the time.

1.3.3 Hearsay

Hearsay
an out-of-court statement presented as proof of the truth of its contents.

Hearsay evidence is witness evidence of the fact that something is true. In contrast to percipient evidence, the witness will not have perceived it through their senses but will have learned something from another. This 'learning' can be either verbal, through another method of communication or through an actual document that they have seen. In summary, hearsay is a statement made by someone, on a prior occasion out of court, that in the present proceedings is tendered as proof of the truth of the contents therein. The courts were extremely cautious of such evidence and therefore had developed a general exclusionary rule. Equally, the rule was harsh in its application because it often resulted in the exclusion of otherwise relevant and admissible evidence, hence exceptions to avoid the rule were soon formulated under common law and statute. The current position is very different: the Criminal Justice Act 2003 takes an inclusionary approach to hearsay evidence. Hearsay is admissible in criminal cases where either one of the preserved common law exceptions within the Act applies or where the statute itself allows its admission. In civil proceedings, hearsay evidence has been statutorily admissible under the Civil Evidence Act 1995 for far longer.

1.3.4 Original evidence

Remember, hearsay evidence is *a statement made by someone, on a prior occasion out of court, which in the present proceedings is tendered as proof of the truth of the contents therein*. If, however, that same statement is tendered for a reason other than to prove the truth of its contents then it will become original evidence. A pattern begins to emerge at this stage: the classification of a single piece of evidence depends on, among other reasons, why it is tendered and therefore it may be classified as a variety of types of evidence. You will begin to understand how lawyers tactically use evidence to support their cases and undermine those of their opponents. It would be salient to mention at this stage that all lawyers are governed by rules of professional conduct and have certain duties imposed upon them by regulatory bodies such as the Bar Standards

Board for England and Wales. These rules are quite clear about the use of evidence such as an alibi where the lawyer knows it to be untrue and, while this textbook does not cover these rules, it would be to your advantage to review them at your own convenience.

The judge's reasoning in *Woodhouse v Hall* (1980) 72 Cr App R 39 provides a good example of how the rules of evidence work in practice. In this case the prosecution sought to adduce the evidence of a police officer that, whilst he was at a massage parlour, a masseuse employed by the accused had offered him sexual services in exchange for money. The accused argued that the evidence was inadmissible hearsay because it was in fact a statement that was allegedly made by the masseuse, on a prior occasion out of court that in the present proceedings was being tendered as proof of the truth of the fact that the massage parlour was actually a brothel. The court decided against the accused and held that the evidence was not hearsay evidence because it was not being tendered as to prove the truth of what the masseuse had said, i.e. that she would provide sexual services at a price, but to show that an offer for the provision of sexual services at a price had been made. You can see here how evidence of this incriminating statement was construed to avoid the hearsay rule.

1.3.5 Primary and secondary evidence

Primary evidence is considered to be the *best* type of evidence. For example, an original deed, contract, tenancy or lease agreement would be classed as primary evidence. In contrast, secondary evidence is considered to be its inferior counterpart. Examples of secondary evidence would include a photocopy of the original deed, contract, tenancy or lease agreement just mentioned or a statement as to the contents of the original document by someone who had seen it. There was a time when the law insisted that a claimant provide primary evidence as proof. This is not strictly the case anymore as many statutes make provision for the use of secondary evidence. It should be noted that the distinction between the two is important when it comes to evidential issues in relation to privileged documents, a matter that will discussed in Chapter 4.

1.3.6 Conclusive evidence

Conclusive evidence is evidence relating to something that cannot be contradicted by any of the parties to an action by operation of the law. An example is the doctrine of *doli incapax*, which presumes that a child under the age of ten cannot form the requisite *mens rea* (mental intention) required to commit a criminal offence, i.e. they cannot be held criminally responsible for their actions. Section 34 of the Crime and Disorder Act 1998 expressly abolished the application of the doctrine to children between the ages of ten and fourteen, but this has been questioned by the Court of Appeal in *DPP v P* [2008] 1 WLR 1005 where it stated *obiter* that only the presumption had been abolished and not the defence itself. Therefore, the defence may still be available in certain circumstances to children falling into this age bracket. Furthermore, s 34 does not have retrospective effect; for an example see *R v PF* [2017] EWCA Crim 983. Similarly, s 13 of the Civil Evidence Act 1968 provides that, in actions concerning defamation, proof that a person has been convicted of a criminal offence shall be 'conclusive evidence' that they committed the offence.

1.3.7 Presumptive or *prima facie* evidence

Presumptive evidence
presumptions that stand as evidence unless successfully challenged.

In contrast to conclusive evidence, the law provides rules known as **presumptive evidence** that apply unless successfully challenged. Where the law provides such a rule and it is challenged then it is for the court to decide whether or not the rule applies. For example, James walked out on his husband Philip seven years ago, and neither Philip nor anyone James knew, including his family, has heard from him since. Philip, James's mother Susan and her friends have made numerous enquiries as to his whereabouts but to no avail. In this instance, because James has been missing for over seven years he can be presumed dead. This rule is a presumptive rule of evidence because adducing evidence that James is still alive can challenge it.

1.3.8 Oral evidence or testimony

Oral evidence is also commonly referred to as oral testimony. This is the evidence that a witness, whether for the prosecution or defence, gives from the witness box. The point is that this form of evidence comes directly from the witness, at court, in their own words. Oral evidence includes evidence that is given as examination-in-chief, cross-examination and re-examination.

Although evidence that is tendered in the form of a document is normally classed as documentary evidence, in some instances the evidence will be treated as though it is oral evidence. For instance, the court may accept an affidavit (a form of a written statement) as oral evidence or allow the witness to give oral evidence outside of the courtroom by video link.

1.3.9 Real evidence

Real evidence is the evidence that people are most likely to have been exposed to at some time, either in a legal dramatisation on Netflix or television or in other forms of media. Real evidence is tangible evidence that the court, namely the judge and jury, can observe, inspect, perceive and draw inferences from. Commonly cited examples of this type of evidence include a murder weapon, for instance an axe, a gun, rope or even a knife. But this category also includes photographs of the scene of the crime and the actual appearance of a witness. To distinguish whether a piece of evidence is real evidence it must be something that is capable of making an impression on the court.

ACTIVITY

Explain what the terms *direct* and *percipient* evidence mean.
List three examples of *circumstantial* evidence.
Provide a short definition of *hearsay* evidence.
What is the difference between *presumptive* and *conclusive* evidence?
Is all relevant evidence admissible?
Give two examples of *primary* and *secondary* evidence.

KEY FACTS

The English law of evidence: an exclusionary approach

Evidence can be described as facts that are used to prove or disprove something.

Types of judicial evidence

Direct or percipient evidence – evidence that, if accepted by the court, does not require any further inferences to be drawn from it, i.e. a direct perception of a fact in issue by sight, sound, smell or taste.

Circumstantial evidence – evidence that, if accepted by the court, does require further inferences to be drawn from it; the inference drawn will be obvious.

Hearsay – a statement made by someone, on a prior occasion out of court, which in the present proceedings is tendered as proof of the truth of the contents therein.

Original evidence – a statement made by someone, on a prior occasion out of court, which in the present proceedings is not tendered as proof of the truth of the contents therein but as proof of something else.

Primary and secondary evidence – primary evidence is considered to be the *best* type of evidence, for example an original deed, contract, tenancy or lease agreement. Secondary evidence is considered to be its inferior counterpart, such as a photocopy of the original deed, contract or tenancy or lease agreement.

Conclusive evidence – evidence that, by law, cannot be contradicted by the parties to the action.

Presumptive evidence – rules of law that apply unless successfully challenged.

Oral evidence – evidence that a witness, whether for the prosecution or defence, gives from the witness box.

Real evidence – tangible evidence that the court, that is, the judge and jury, can observe, perceive and draw inferences from, such as the murder weapon.

1.4 Facts

Now having discussed the types of evidence that exist, it is also important to understand why evidence is adduced. Earlier in the discussion it was stated that in every case there are a number of facts that will be in issue; these are known as disputed facts. Where facts are disputed a party to the action will either need to prove or disprove the disputed fact through adducing relevant and admissible evidence. What follows is a brief discussion of the facts that are in issue in criminal and civil cases.

1.4.1 Facts in issue: criminal cases

Facts in issue facts that the prosecution must establish to prove guilt.

The facts that are in issue in criminal cases are mainly the facts that the prosecution must prove to establish a defendant's guilt, i.e. the elements of an offence. However, they also include those facts that constitute a defence raised by the defendant. Therefore, the prosecution will also have to adduce evidence in order to disprove any defence that the defendant has raised; for instance, the accused may be claiming provocation or diminished responsibility under the Homicide Act 1957 (as amended by the Coroners and Justice Act 2009). If the defendant pleads 'not guilty' then the entire prosecution case will be in issue, and the prosecution will have to prove the commission of the entire offence, proving, where required, that the defendant committed the *actus reus* with the requisite *mens rea*. If the prosecution fails to do this then the defence will succeed and the defendant will be acquitted.

1.4.2 Facts in issue: civil cases

In civil cases it is possible to ascertain which facts are in issue from a document known as the Particulars of Claim or Statement of Case, and perhaps even from the standard civil court claim form. This document contains a statement of material facts upon which the party claiming has based their claim. In short, the facts that are in issue in civil cases are *those facts that the claimant must establish in order to succeed* in their claim *and to disprove any defence* raised by the defendant, for instance the defence of contributory negligence or *volenti non fit injuria*, which concerns consent and translates as 'to a willing person injury is not done'. In civil claims, the adage 'he who asserts must prove' applies.

1.4.3 Facts in issue: formal admissions

A formal admission is an agreement between the parties indicating that the subject matter of the admission does not require proof.

An interesting question arises: what if a fact in issue, for example the existence of a duty of care, is formally admitted? The answer is straightforward: once admitted the fact is no longer a fact in issue. In that instance the party who has the burden of proving that fact in issue will not have to adduce any evidence to prove it and the court will not hear such evidence. The logic behind this is simple: there is no requirement to prove something that can be accepted as having been proven by a formal admission. To hear the evidence of this regardless would not only be an affront to common sense but also a waste of time and court resources. A defendant's guilty plea in a criminal case is a good example of an instance in which no facts pertaining to the commission of an offence remain in issue. Partial admissions are slightly less dramatic in their effect; for example, if Jayden is charged with murdering Olive but he states 'I was at the scene of the crime but I did not do it', then he has agreed the fact in issue relating to his presence at the scene, but his denial means that the fact of his having committed the offence still remains in issue and therefore the prosecution still has to prove that it was he who murdered Olive.

The prosecution or the defence can make such admissions at any stage before a trial. In civil cases, formal admissions are normally made in the Particulars of Claim. The main reason for making such admissions is the clarification of the actual issues; this helps speed up the time taken for an action to be completed and saves on resources – two things that are especially important in civil disputes (see the overriding objective of the Civil Procedure Rules, available at www.justice.gov.uk/courts/procedure-rules/civil/rules/part01). The effect of making a formal admission is that it is conclusive of the facts admitted, and evidence of such facts that are admitted is not admissible in those proceedings.

In criminal proceedings, formal admissions may be made by virtue of s 10 of the Criminal Justice Act 1967, which provides a self-contained code for the creation of formal admissions. The provision state:

SECTION

(1) . . . any fact of which oral evidence may be given in criminal proceedings may be admitted . . . by or on behalf of the prosecutor or defendant . . . and shall, as against that party, be conclusive evidence in those proceedings of the fact admitted.

(2) An admission under this section . . . [may be made before or at the proceedings and shall be in writing save when made in court] . . .

(3) . . .

(4) An admission . . . may with the leave of the court be withdrawn in the proceedings for the purpose of which it is made . . .

1.4.4 Facts in issue: collateral facts

It is also important to understand the definition of collateral facts and their effect. Collateral facts are those facts that affect the admissibility of evidence. For example: the police obtain a confession from Harry through oppressive means; in this instance the existence of oppression is a collateral fact because it will affect whether or not the court will allow the prosecution to adduce this evidence. Collateral facts also include those facts that affect the credibility of a witness or the weight that is given to a piece of evidence. Procedurally, collateral facts are normally put to the court before the evidence is presented; for example the defence may, in a *voir dire* (a trial within a trial), apply to have a confession obtained by oppression excluded.

1.4.5 Facts in issue: relevant facts

The next salient question concerns how facts in issue are proven or disproven. This is relatively unproblematic, *relevant facts* prove or disprove the facts in issue. In the case of *DPP v Kilbourne* [1973] AC 729 the court stated:

JUDGMENT

'. . . relevant i.e., logically probative or disprobative, evidence is evidence which makes the matter which requires proof more or less probable'.

The basic rule is as follows; only relevant evidence can be admitted (*see R v Turner* [1975] QB 834). Relevant evidence can be presented in the form of direct witness evidence or circumstantial evidence. Irrelevant evidence or evidence that is insufficiently relevant to a fact in issue will be rejected by the court (*R v Randall* [2004] 1 WLR 56). It is important that you understand that a court will not hear even sufficiently relevant evidence where a fact that was originally in issue has been admitted so that it is no longer in issue. The determination of relevance is dependent upon whether the evidence tends to prove or disprove a fact in issue, so counsel when coming to a reasoned judgment on the relevancy of evidence will normally ask this question: does this piece of evidence tend to prove or disprove a fact in issue? Alternatively, the same question can be posed in these terms: does this evidence have a probative effect? If the evidence does not tend to prove or disprove a fact in issue or does not have a probative effect then it is irrelevant and inadmissible. Contrast these two cases:

1. *Joy v Phillips, Mills & Co* [1916] 1 KB 849: evidence of a child being found with a halter and of their previous torment of a horse was admitted because it was relevant to this fact that was in issue: how the child was killed.
2. *Hart v Lancashire and Yorkshire Railway* (1869) 21 LT 261: the claimant alleged negligence when injured by a runaway train. His argument centred on the fact that the train company had recently changed the points on the track to avoid a repetition of the event that had occurred. The court decided that this change in practice occurred after the accident and was irrelevant to proving or disproving that the company was negligent; all it showed was they were improving their safety standards.

In *Joy v Phillips, Mills & Co* [1916] 1 KB 849 Lord Cozens-Hardy stated his reasoning for the admittance of this evidence was that not admitting it would be akin to 'shutting your eyes altogether to facts necessary for drawing the proper inferences'. In *Hart v Lancashire and Yorkshire Railway* (1869) 21 LT 261 the court commented that it was wrong 'to hold that, because the world gets wiser as it gets older, therefore it was foolish before'.

CASE EXAMPLE

R v Sandhu [1997] Crim LR 288

The Court of Appeal held that evidence that illustrated the defendant's state of mind at the time of committing a strict liability offence was irrelevant to prove the issue of the defendant's guilt. The logic is simple: reflect on your studies of criminal law and the fact that strict liability is imposed regardless of mental intention. Thus, the mental intent of the defendant is not a fact in issue and therefore evidence proving or disproving a guilty intention is irrelevant.

CASE EXAMPLE

R v Kearley [1992] 2 All ER 345 (HL)

The defendant was charged with being in possession of drugs with an intention to supply. During a search of the defendant's flat, and while he was absent, the police answered fifteen telephone calls – ten of which asked the defendant for drugs. Additionally, nine individuals came to the flat asking for the defendant, and seven of those nine requested drugs. At his trial, the officers were given permission to give evidence of the calls and exactly what was said. Kearley was convicted and appealed to the House of Lords on the basis that this evidence should have been excluded. The Law Lords decided that the evidence was inadmissible because it was (a) irrelevant and (b) inadmissible hearsay. The reasoning was as follows:

JUDGMENT

Lord Bridge stated that '. . . the fact that the words were spoken may be relevant for various purposes, but most commonly they will be so when they reveal the state of mind of either the speaker or the person to whom the words were spoken when that state of mind is itself *a fact in issue* or *relevant to another matter in issue*. The state of mind of the person making the request for drugs is of no relevance at all to the question whether the defendant is a supplier.'

Lord Ackner stated that '. . . each of those requests was, of course, evidence of the state of mind of the person making the request; *they* wished to be supplied with drugs and thought that *Mr Kearley* would so supply *them*. It was not evidence of the fact that the appellant had supplied or could or would supply the person making the request. But the state of mind of the person making the request was not an issue at the trial; accordingly evidence of his request was irrelevant and therefore inadmissible.'

Lord Browne-Wilkinson, dissenting, stated that '. . . the evidence was, in my judgment, relevant because it showed that there were people resorting to the premises for the purpose of obtaining drugs from the appellant. Although evidence of the existence of such would-be buyers is not, in itself, conclusive, the existence of a substantial body of potential customers provides some evidence which a jury could take into account in deciding whether the accused had *the requisite* intent to supply. The existence of a contemporaneous potential market to buy drugs from him, by itself, shows that there was an opportunity for the accused to supply drugs.'

Lord Oliver defined relevant facts thus: '. . . any two facts to which it is applied are so related to each other that according to the common course of events one either taken by itself or in connection with other facts proves or renders probable the past, present, or future existence or non-existence of the other.'

Therefore, it is fair to state that the relevance of evidence is not always clear-cut, and that the relevancy of a piece of evidence may change as the trial progresses – for example where new evidence emerges. When preparing for trial the prosecution will normally try to anticipate any defences that may be put forward and therefore produce evidence the production of which may not, at first sight, be clear. Normally, the judge will ask counsel to clarify the matter of relevance, and where the judge agrees, the evidence will be treated *de bene esse* or as being conditionally relevant. If, subsequently, the evidence then turns out to be irrelevant then the judge will direct the jury to ignore it. This is not as simple as it sounds, if, in the most extreme cases but not unlikely, the evidence turns out to be prejudicial then the jury will have to be discharged and a new trial ordered.

ACTIVITY

Define the roles of the judge and jury.
Give two examples each: facts in issue in criminal and civil proceedings.

KEY FACTS

Facts in issue: criminal cases – these are facts that the prosecution must prove to establish a defendant's guilt or disprove a defence.

Facts in issue: civil cases – these are facts that the claimant must establish in order to succeed in their claim and to disprove any defence raised.

Facts in issue: formal admissions – any facts in issue that are admitted do not have to be proven.

Facts in issue: collateral facts – these are facts that affect the admissibility of evidence, the credibility of a witness or the weight given to a piece of evidence.

Facts in issue: relevant facts – facts in issue are proven or disproven by what are known as relevant facts; that is, 'relevant, i.e. logically probative or disprobative, evidence is evidence which makes the matter which requires proof more or less probable'.

1.5 Admissibility, weight and discretion

Other than facts in issue there are a number of additional topics that must be understood. These are the admissibility and weight of evidence, and the judge's discretion to exclude evidence.

1.5.1 Admissibility

Although relevance is a prerequisite to evidence being admissible, it is not the sole requirement that needs to be satisfied before evidence can be put before the court. If the evidence is relevant because it proves or disproves a fact in issue, the admission of the evidence will then depend on whether or not it falls foul of any of the exclusionary rules in the English law of evidence. The design of these rules seeks to ensure (a) that the evidence is authentic and (b) its fairness.

It should be noted that evidence can be admissible for some purposes and inadmissible for others. For example, if Susie and Kenji rob a bank and Susie later confesses to the commission of the crime, her confession will be both relevant and admissible as evidence against her in court; however, it cannot be used as evidence against Kenji. In these instances, it is likely that the defendants will be tried separately because of the risk that the co-defendant will be prejudiced. It is salient to note some changes in jury trials under the CJA 2003: juries were to be excluded under s 43 in complex fraud (this is now repealed by s 113 Protection of Freedoms Act 2012); under s 44 juries were to be excluded where there is real and present danger of jury tampering notwithstanding any reasonable steps to prevent that (this is now in force). Please refer to the website accompanying this book for further updates.

1.5.2 Weight

Weight
whether the conclusion is evidentially proven or disproven.

Once it has been determined what facts in issue the evidence may prove or disprove (the evidence is therefore relevant and admissible), it is down to the court or tribunal of fact (jury) to decide what **weight** to attach to it. For some the weight of evidence can seem like an abstract notion; in the law of evidence weight simply refers to *whether the conclusion is proven or disproven by the evidence*. The weight that the jury give a particular piece of evidence will be subjective, drawing on both logic and common sense when they determine what they do or do not believe. There are two possible outcomes to this: the evidence may be given no weight and therefore disregarded completely or it may be given weight, thereby influencing the jury's decision concerning the extent to which they perceive its reliability, strength and truthfulness. Counsel cannot simply afford to concentrate on relevance and admissibility; they will inevitably have to consider the weight that is likely to be attached to the evidence. Considerations of the weight of evidence will have the following effect:

- the decision to prosecute or not;
- the advice given to the accused as to the prospect of successfully defending the allegation;
- whether or not there is a prosecution case for the accused to answer; and
- in civil cases, the weight of evidence will affect negotiation i.e., as a bargaining tool.

The courts, through their jurisprudence, have given quite specific guidance on the weight that should be attached to certain types of evidence. For instance, in terms of identification evidence take a look at the judgment from *R v Turnbull* [1977] QB 224 (discussed later) or, for a statutory example, take note of the Civil Evidence Act 1995.

1.5.3 Discretion

Traditionally the English law of evidence does not allow the judge the discretion to include *inadmissible* evidence. In contrast, the law does allow a judge the discretion to exclude *admissible* evidence. There are two notable provisions that must be considered when assessing the judicial discretion to exclude evidence:

- a court may, at common law, exclude prosecution evidence where its prejudicial effect outweighs its probative value: see *R v Sang* [1980] AC 402 and s 82(3) Police and Criminal Evidence Act 1984 (PACE); and
- s 78 PACE 1984 allows the court to exclude prosecution evidence if 'after having regard to all the circumstances, including the circumstances in which the evidence was obtained, the admission of the evidence would have an adverse effect on the fairness of proceedings'.

The CJA 2003 also resulted in further curtailment of judicial discretion; this is discussed later in the book with reference to hearsay.

ACTIVITY

Give two examples of facts in issue in criminal and civil proceedings.

KEY FACTS

Admissibility, weight and discretion

Admissibility – if the evidence is relevant, i.e. it proves or disproves a fact in issue, the admission of the evidence will then depend on whether or not it falls foul of any of the exclusionary rules of the English law of evidence.

Weight simply refers to whether the conclusion is proven or disproven by the evidence. The weight that the jury give a particular piece of evidence will be subjective, drawing on both logic and common sense when they determine what they do or do not believe.

Discretion – the court may, at common law, exclude prosecution evidence where its prejudicial effect outweighs its probative value; s 78 of PACE 1984 allows the court to exclude prosecution evidence if 'after having regard to all the circumstances, including the circumstances in which the evidence was obtained, the admission of the evidence would have an adverse effect on the fairness of proceedings'.

1.6 Judge and jury

The judge and jury play a vital role in the course of proceedings or the trial process, and in fact the English mode of trial procedure has its origins in trial by jury. Interestingly, the division of functions between judge and jury, and much of the procedure that exists today, was formulated by reason of this. The distinction is important because questions of law or fact may arise. The trial judge or magistrates will determine all questions of law. However, lay magistrates are not legally qualified, and therefore they will only determine questions of law on the advice of their clerk, who is normally a legally qualified solicitor or barrister of at least ten years' standing; see Practice Direction (Justices Clerk to Court) [1981] 1 WLR 1163. All questions of fact in the Crown Court will be determined by the jury, or by a single judge if sitting alone. In the magistrates' court, the magistrates will determine all questions of fact. Finally, it is the responsibility of the trial judge to sum up the case to the jury and to ensure, like a manager, that the trial runs as smoothly as possible. The following discussion highlights the difference between questions of law and those of fact.

1.6.1 Questions of law

Generally, questions of law will relate to the definition of an offence, elements of an offence and rules of evidence, i.e. admissibility and existence of sufficient evidence to allow the jury to consider an issue.

Where no evidence that the defendant has committed the offence exists or the evidence is so tenuous that no properly directed jury could ever convict on its basis, then counsel will make a submission that the defendant has *no case to answer* because the prosecution has failed to prove each and every element of the offence (facts in issue): see *R v Galbraith* [1981] 1 WLR 1039. This will be done after the prosecution has set out its case, at mid-time. The judge will then withdraw the case from the jury. In the magistrates' court the position is the same but governed by a 1962 Practice Direction issued by Lord Parker CJ in [1962] 1 WLR 227. In practical reality the prosecution may decide to withdraw the case by offering no evidence to the court at the start rather than wait and waste time and resource, and the accused will be acquitted.

Questions of admissibility are categorised as questions of law that the judge would decide in the absence of the jury. Sometimes problems arise in relation to admissibility. For instance, Sheetal (counsel A) objects to some of the evidence being tendered by Sabrina (counsel B). The procedure in these circumstances is as follows: Sheetal would inform Sabrina, who would avoid referring to the disputed evidence until the trial judge has ruled it admissible. Obviously, it is also likely that the judge may rule it inadmissible. The procedure for the judge ruling evidence admissible is as follows: the trial judge will hear the legal arguments of both sides on the rules governing the admissibility of the evidence in question and then make his or her decision.

Issues of admissibility of disputed evidence will normally be settled at the outset of a case because the progression of the case would otherwise be affected. Alternatively, it can be dealt with while the case is proceeding in a ***voir dire*** (trial within a trial), a procedure held in the absence of the jury. Witnesses are called to give evidence, and the admissibility of the evidence may be dependent on a factual situation, for example on the existence of oppression in obtaining a confession. Counsel that opposes the admissibility of evidence can do so in a procedure other than a *voir dire*. Strategically that may be the better option because the *voir dire* may, in counsel's opinion, allow the witnesses to rehearse their evidence in response to the defence argument. Where this is the case then counsel will normally attack the admissibility of the evidence after it has been put to the jury (see *Ajodha v The State (Trinidad & Tobago)* [1982] AC 204). The only time that this is not possible is where the law requires a *voir dire* to be held – where the admissibility of evidence that is disputed is that of a confession then s 76(2) of the PACE 1984 requires the procedure to be undertaken.

Voir dire

a trial within a trial to determine the admissibility of disputed evidence.

In summary, the trial judge would hold a *voir dire*, make a decision on admissibility of the evidence and then make no mention of it or the existence of the evidence in the presence of the jury. Where counsel does not object to the admissibility of disputed evidence at the outset of a trial or while the trial is proceeding then they can seek to appeal the decision. You should note, however, that the Court of Appeal has made it very clear that it is reticent to hear appeals based on the admissibility of evidence that remained unchallenged the first time around: see *The Tasmania* (1890) 15 App Cas 223. Where the trial judge makes an error while summing up, and accidentally mentions the evidence, then counsel will normally remain silent and appeal on the basis of a misdirection: see *R v Cocks* (1976) 63 Cr App R 79.

The position on admissibility is slightly more complicated when it comes to cases where no jury is involved because the person determining admissibility of the evidence (the judge) and the decision as to the outcome (normally the jury) are the same. The issue concerns the risk that where the evidence is inadmissible, even though the trier of fact seeks to put the evidence out of its mind, the subsequent decision will have been prejudiced. It may be that the evidence can be discussed generally, rather than specifically, but this does not solve the problems regarding admissibility after the evidence has already been heard. In non-jury trials a *voir dire* is basically redundant in preventing prejudice: see *F (an infant) v Chief Constable of Kent* [1982] Crim LR 682. Again, remember that if the evidence that is in dispute concerns a confession then a *voir dire* must be used. Lastly, it should be noted that the use of a *voir dire* might in fact be useful in a later appeal.

1.6.2 Questions of fact

Questions of fact are different beasts. To give a couple of examples, questions that relate to the weight of evidence or whether the evidence should be believed – i.e. is it credible? – and a defendant's fitness to plead are all questions of fact. For a discussion on the latter, reference should be made to the Insanity and Fitness to Plead Act 1991. The earlier discussion revealed, in the Crown Court the jury will decide questions of fact. There is an exception to the general rule; the judge will decide the following two questions of fact:

- the definition of unusual terms used in a contract;
- issues relating to foreign law.

What follows is a brief discussion of each of these points, starting with defining terms. The jury will decide a question of fact that relates to the ordinary meaning or usage of words (*Brutus v Cozens* [1973] AC 854). Such questions are subject to appellate control if the decision of the tribunal of fact is unreasonable and ought to be set aside. If the question of fact relates to the use of the word in an unusual context, then the judge will determine it. In contrast, the determination of the meaning or use of particular terms in a statute is classed as a question of law, and therefore it is a question for the trial judge. A good example of this is in an action for defamation, where the trial judge decides whether the words used are capable of bearing a defamatory meaning and the jury decides whether the words are in fact defamatory: see *Neill v Fine Arts and General Insurance Co* [1897] AC 68.

Furthermore, where the question relates to foreign law, the judge decides this issue as a question of fact. The law of other countries, including Scotland (for these purposes) and Commonwealth countries, is treated as foreign law. It is up to the trial judge to decide what foreign law is in issue based on expert evidence; the discussion of this is beyond the scope of this textbook, but reference may be made to s 15 of the Administration of Justice Act 1920. Finally, although the rule was substantially eroded, the trial judge was required to determine issues on the best evidence that was available. This was achieved by excluding evidence where better evidence was available: see *Omychund v Barker* (1745) 1 Atk 21 and *Garton v Hunter* [1969] 2 QB 37. The rule was not absolute and it seems that the final instance in which the rule applied, in relation to documents, has been finally laid to rest by the Court of Appeal's decision in *Springsteen v Masquerade Music Ltd* [2001] EMLR 654, where the court stated that '. . . the best evidence rule was recognized as no more than a rule of practice to the effect that the court would attach no weight to secondary evidence of the contents of a document unless the party seeking to adduce it *first accounted for not producing* the document itself . . . I would not recognize the continuing existence of the remaining instance of this old rule.'

1.7 Instances in which proof is unnecessary

Judicial notice
instances of notorious facts requiring no evidence to prove them.

There are a number of instances in which no evidence is required to prove something. To clarify, the general rule is that the court requires evidence in order to be satisfied that a fact in issue has been proven or equally disproven. There are, however, occasions in which absolutely no proof is required. We have already discussed one of them: formal admissions. The second instance concerns **judicial notice**. This allows the court to use its objective and general knowledge of the world. This sounds like a slight contradiction, especially when newspaper articles frequently highlight judges asking questions regarding facts that are generally considered common knowledge. For example, a personal instance I can recollect involves a Family Court judge enquiring what a treadmill was in the following terms: 'Is it like one of those things that hamsters run around on?' More famously, in an example cited by Roderick Munday in his textbook on evidence, a judge questioned what a 'Teletubby' was. Unsurprisingly this only seeks to propound the argument that some judges may exist in the metaverse.

Rest assured that this is not a common state of affairs, as the doctrine of judicial notice so eloquently proves; it allows the judge to dispense with the need for evidence regarding *notorious facts*. In *Lumley v Gye* (1853) 2 E & B 216 Coleridge J stated:

JUDGMENT

> 'Judges are not necessarily *ignorant in court* to what everybody else . . . out of court, are familiar with . . . we find in the year books *judicial reasoning* about the ability of knights . . . and gentlemen to maintain themselves without wages. . . .'

The point is quite simple: there are some facts that are so well known that requiring a party to prove them would be an affront to common sense and would only result in a waste of precious (and overstretched) court time. Furthermore, it would do little to enhance the image of the courts in the eyes of the public at large. Here are some examples of facts that are judicially noted:

- the rain falls (*Fay v Prentice* (1845) 14 LJCP 298);
- the postal system is not infallible (*Sloan Electronics Ltd v Customs and Excise Commissioners* [1999] unreported);
- countries such as Thailand, Jamaica and Holland are areas with drug trafficking, dealing and supply problems (*R v Crown Court at Isleworth, ex p Marland* (1997) 162 JP 251).

From these examples it should be obvious what types of facts are judicially noticed. The test is as follows: when facts are so notorious that it would be an affront to the common sense of judges and the dignity of the court to require proof of them they can be judicially noticed. There are two occasions when notice may be taken – automatically or after enquiry when the judge refreshes his or her memory. The difficulty with this principle concerns the limits of the doctrine. Some matters of 'common knowledge' vary with sections of the population, for example by particular age group or the educational upbringing of the individual. However, the test requires the judge to exercise an objective assessment of the popularity of the relevant facts. In *Hoare v Silverlock* (1848) 12 QB 624 the claimant had applied to a benevolent society for assistance and named the defendant as a referee. In supplying a reference, the defendant had said that 'her friends would realize the truth of the fable about the frozen snake'. The claimant sued the defendant for libel. The judge took judicial notice of the fable and that the words used by the defendant were defamatory. Erle J said: 'I may take judicial notice that the words "frozen snake" have an application very generally known indeed, which application is likely to bring into contempt a person against whom it is directed.'

Taking judicial notice after enquiry can be justified on the grounds that, although the fact is notorious, the details cannot readily be recalled. The judge needs to refresh his or her memory by consulting works of reference or considering the views of experts. In *McQuaker v Goddard* [1940] 1 KB 687 a camel bit the claimant while he was visiting the defendant's zoo. The question in issue, for the purpose of the law relating to liability to animals, was whether camels are *'ferae naturae'* (naturally fierce) or *'mansuetae naturae'* (naturally tame). The judge ruled that he would take judicial notice of the issue and listened to five expert witnesses who gave evidence on the subject. The judge decided that camels came within the latter classification.

JUDGMENT

'The judge takes judicial notice of the ordinary course of nature in regard to the position of camels among other animals. The reason why the evidence was given was, for the assistance of the judge in forming his view as to what the ordinary course of nature in this regard in fact is – a matter of which he is supposed to have complete knowledge.'

(Clauson LJ)

Likewise, in *DPP v Hynde* [1998] 1 All ER 649, the Divisional Court decided that a 'butterfly' knife in the possession of a person at Heathrow Airport was an offensive weapon under the Aviation Security Act 1982 partly because of consistency with the general offence under the Criminal Justice Act 1988.

On political and international matters, i.e. affairs of the state, the court may take judicial notice so that both the courts and the government may act in unison. For this purpose, the court will enquire from the Minister of Foreign Affairs about the relevant issues and a certificate, issued by that Department, will be conclusive of the information. In *Duff Development Company v Government of Kelantan* [1924] AC 797 the claimant company had obtained a judgment order against the defendant, the Government of Kelantan. The defendant applied for an order to set aside the judgment on the ground of sovereign immunity, i.e. that it was a sovereign independent state and not subject to British jurisdiction. The Secretary of State for the Colonies wrote to the judge, on request, to the effect that Kelantan was an independent state and the Sultan was its ruler.

JUDGMENT

> 'It is settled law that it is for the court to take judicial cognizance of the status of any foreign government. If there can be any doubt on the matter the practice is for the court to receive information from the appropriate department of His Majesty's Government and the information so received is conclusive. . . . Such information is not in the nature of evidence: it is a statement by the Sovereign of this country through one of his Ministers upon a matter which is peculiarly within his knowledge.'
>
> (Viscount Finlay)

An interesting question concerns the extent to which the personal knowledge of the adjudicator (professional judge or lay magistrate) may influence their judgment. Largely, the general knowledge of judges, juries and magistrates (i.e., professional lawyers or lay persons) plays a significant role in assessing the quality and weight of evidence adduced before a tribunal; for example the length of the skid marks, the type and age of the motor vehicle and the age of the driver may all combine in assisting the tribunal in determining by inference whether the vehicle was travelling at speed immediately before the collision. There simply is no way in which the tribunal may be prevented from drawing on their general knowledge in assessing the probabilities that exist.

But how far may an adjudicator use their specialist, non-legal knowledge in the judicial process? For example, can a judge or magistrate, who is also a medical doctor, use their medical knowledge in adjudicating on a related issue? The answer is that the tribunal (judge or lay magistrate) is never entitled to substitute its specialised experience for evidence. If the judge or lay magistrate has any relevant specialised knowledge, they are required to be sworn in and give evidence in the normal way. This principle was applied to a member of the jury who had specialised knowledge of the significance of the serial numbers on tyres in *R v Fricker* (1999) *The Times*, 13 July. The facts were as follows: the defendant was on a charge of handling stolen goods (a motor car tyre), and the juror in question used his knowledge to influence his fellow jurors in the jury room and cast doubt on the defendant's case. On conviction, the appeal was allowed because the juror was unlawfully using his knowledge as a substitute for the evidence that had been presented to him at court.

In addition, a judge (but not a lay adjudicator) is not entitled to rely on their specialised knowledge in a field other than law (e.g. medicine) in assessing the weight to be attached to evidence. In other words, a judge, who may be a surgeon or consultant, is debarred from using their medical knowledge in assessing the medical evidence admitted in court. Their legal training equips them to disregard their specialised non-legal knowledge and to rely on the evidence that has been admitted.

However, lay justices (and juries), although prevented from relying on their specialist knowledge as a substitute for evidence, are nevertheless entitled to rely on their professional knowledge in assessing the weight and quality of the evidence adduced. In this respect a lay magistrate (or a juror) is not entitled to force their views on other members of the bench.

The Divisional Court in *Wetherall v Harrison* [1976] QB 773 decided these principles. In this case, the defendant was charged with failing to provide a specimen without reasonable excuse, contrary to s 9(3) of the Road Traffic Act 1972 (since repealed and replaced). The defendant claimed that he could not give a blood sample because he had a fit. The prosecution claimed that he was simulating it. Sitting on the bench was a doctor who gave his opinion (without forcing his views) to the other magistrates. The defendant was acquitted and the prosecution appealed. The court held that there was no error in law and the appeal was dismissed.

JUDGMENT

'I do not think that the position of a justice of the peace is the same in this regard as the position of a trained judge. If you have a judge sitting alone, it is perfectly feasible and sensible that he should be instructed and trained to exclude certain factors from his consideration. Justices are not so trained . . . I start with the proposition that it is not improper for a justice who has special knowledge . . . to draw on that special knowledge in interpretation of the evidence which he has heard. I stress that last sentence because it would be quite wrong if he went on to give evidence to himself, still more is he not there to give evidence to other justices; but that he can employ his basic knowledge in considering, weighing up and assessing the evidence given before the court is I think beyond doubt.'

(Widgery CJ)

The concept of notoriety is the hallmark for judicial notice, but even this may change with time. For example, the fact that cats are domestic animals may change in years to come; therefore there is an element of speculation and cautiousness involved before a court will judicially notice a fact. A court may depart from the need for evidence to prove facts that are general knowledge. It must not, however, do so from subjective, personal knowledge, i.e. something that the trial judge has personal knowledge of. It has become increasingly difficult to distinguish between the two when on so many occasions *local knowledge* will have been judicially noted.

CASE EXAMPLE

In *Ingram v Percival* [1969] 1 QB 584, at first instance the justices used what seems their personal knowledge of tidal waters in a locality to judicially notice that netting of migrating salmon and trout was unlawful.

CASE EXAMPLE

Another interesting case is *Carter v Eastbourne Borough Council* (2000) 164 JP 273, where the justices judicially noted the age of some trees that an accused had uprooted, based on their personal knowledge of woodland.

In *Mullen v Hackney Borough Council* [1997] 1 WLR 1103, a county court judge took into consideration his personal knowledge of past breaches of repairing undertakings by the defendant council when fixing the penalty for a breach of an undertaking in question. The Court of Appeal held that the judge was entitled to take judicial notice based on his special local knowledge of how the council behaved.

The basic rule is that a fact must be notorious, and the decision to judicially notice it will be made on a case-by-case basis. Finally, there are a number of statutes that specifically provide for the taking of judicial notice on a number of facts.

Section 3 of the Interpretation Act 1978 requires the court to take judicial notice that an HM Government Stationery Office copy of a public Act of Parliament is accurate and complies with the official pronouncement of Parliament. In addition, all statutes are *prima facie* presumed to be public until the contrary is proved: see s 3 of the Interpretation Act 1978. Likewise, s 4(2) of the European Communities Act 1972 provides for judicial notice to be taken of treaties and community decisions.

ACTIVITY

Define the roles of the judge and jury.
What is meant by the terms *relevant* and *collateral* facts?
Outline who decides questions of law and questions of fact and why.
Give an example of the following: a *question of law* and *a question of fact*.
What does the term *weight* refer to in evidence?
Who decides issues on foreign law, the judge or the jury?
Summarise what is meant by *judicial notice*.
Outline the difference between *judicial notice* and *personal knowledge*.
Explain what the term *best evidence* means.

KEY FACTS

Judge and jury

The trial judge or magistrates will determine all questions of law. However, lay magistrates are not legally qualified and therefore they will only determine questions of law on the advice of their clerk. All questions of fact in the Crown Court will be determined by the jury or by a single judge if sitting alone. In the magistrates' court the magistrates will determine questions of fact. The trial judge is responsible for summing up the case to the jury and ensuring, like a manager, that the trial runs as smoothly as possible.

Questions of law – will relate to the definition of an offence, elements of an offence, and rules of evidence, i.e. admissibility and existence of sufficient evidence to allow the jury to consider an issue.

Questions of fact – include questions relating to the weight of evidence, whether the evidence should be believed – i.e. is it credible? – and a defendant's fitness to plead.

Instances in which proof is unnecessary

In general the court requires evidence in order to prove a fact in issue. However, there are instances in which no proof will be required: formal admissions and judicial notice. Judicial notice allows the courts to use their general knowledge of the world, allowing the judge to dispense with the need for evidence to prove notorious facts.

1.8 The binding nature of judicial findings

An interesting question arises in relation to judicial findings on issues previously litigated, i.e. where a judge has already decided on an issue. In that instance, because of the need for consistency and to prevent the continuous resurgence of issues, the English law of evidence sometimes requires such findings to be taken as binding a subsequent court of the same or lower jurisdiction. Further discussion on this point is beyond the scope of this book, but reference may be made to the topic of *estoppel*.

ACTIVITY

Explain how the English law of evidence treats judicial findings.

KEY FACTS

The binding nature of judicial findings

Judicial findings are binding as this promotes amongst other things consistency and prevents the continuous resurgence of issues, therefore the English law of evidence sometimes accepts judicial findings, i.e. in previous litigation, as binding a subsequent court of the same or lower jurisdiction.

1.9 Procedural rules: criminal and civil

Finally, the introduction of the Civil Procedure Rules (CPR) in 1998 and, more recently, in 2005, the Criminal Procedure Rules (CrPR), have had the effect of restricting the amount of evidence that is admitted for trial. The rules promote the fact that the trial judge has responsibility for *effectively managing a case* and thereby ensuring efficient use of court resources. The full range of CPR can be accessed at www.justice.gov.uk/courts/procedure-rules/civil/rules and the CrPR at www.legislation.gov.uk/uksi/2020/759/contents. In summary, both sets of rules promote what is known as 'active case management', which includes dealing with a case efficiently and expeditiously, minimising delay, ensuring that any evidence is presented in a logical way – i.e. short and clear – encouraging open communication and dealing with a number of issues at the same hearing, thereby avoiding pointless additional hearings. The full impact of the CrPR is not yet clear, but what is clear is that the presiding judge has considerable discretion to achieve the aims of the overriding object of the rules: see *R v K and Others* [2006] EWCA Crim 835.

ACTIVITY

Summarise how the Civil Procedure Rules and the Criminal Procedure Rules affect trial evidence.

SUMMARY

- The substantive law governs how *facts* are proven in court, the rules on how evidence *should be put to* and *presented in* court and the rules on which evidence *should be excluded from* presentation to the court altogether.
- The context in which evidence is presented is to allow the court to garner a greater understanding of what is alleged to have happened.
- The English law of evidence adopted a far more cautious approach to the admission of evidence, which often resulted in the exclusion of relevant evidence.

- Direct evidence is evidence that, if accepted by the court, does not require any further inferences to be drawn from it.
- Circumstantial evidence is evidence that, if accepted by the court, requires further inferences to be drawn from it.
- Hearsay evidence is witness evidence of the fact that something is true.
- Primary evidence is considered to be the *best* type of evidence, for example an original deed, contract, tenancy or lease agreement.
- Secondary evidence is considered to be the inferior counterpart of primary evidence; this can be a photocopy of the original deed, contract, tenancy or lease agreement.
- Conclusive evidence is evidence relating to something that cannot be contradicted by any of the parties to an action by operation of the law.
- Presumptive evidence is presumptions that stand as evidence unless successfully challenged.

SAMPLE ESSAY QUESTION

The law on judicial notice is a mess. Discuss.

Answer plan

Explain the difference between judicial notice and the use of local or specialist knowledge.
Highlight what can be judicially noted. Discuss the limitations on using specialist knowledge, and the point that according to the law the requirement is for evidence. Explore the fact that the law is underdeveloped and confusing.

Outline the strange relationship of judicial notice to evidence. Highlight the taking of judicial notice with and without enquiry, and whether the former is taken on the basis of some proof.

Discuss the variety of rationales that have been suggested for judicial notice and highlight how their effect is to undermine it. There are two theories: filtering out unarguable matters and as a labour saving device. The former is narrow and limited by notoriety and the latter is wider in application. Explore the cases relating to this point, for instance *Wetherall v Harrison* (1976) and *Bowman v DPP* (1990), where it was considered that magistrates were more like laymen because they could not exclude certain matters from their minds and therefore they were entitled to use local or specialist knowledge. Contrast this with *Mullen v Hackney LBC* (1997).

- In criminal cases the facts that are in issue mainly tend to be the facts that the prosecution must prove to establish a defendant's guilt and those facts that constitute a defence raised by the defendant.
- In civil cases the facts in issue are those material facts upon which the party claiming has based their claim.
- Weight relates to the extent to which the conclusion is evidentially proven or disproven.
- The English substantive law of evidence did not allow the judge the discretion to include *inadmissible* evidence but did allow them the discretion to exclude *admissible* evidence.
- Questions of law often relate to the definition of an offence, elements of an offence and rules of evidence, etc.
- Questions of fact often concern the weight of evidence or whether the evidence should be believed or not.
- Judicial notice is taken of notorious facts that do not require evidence to prove them.

Further reading

Cornish, W. R. and Sealy, A. P. 'Juries and the rules of evidence' [1973] Crim LR 208

Gallanis, T. P. 'The rise of modern evidence law' (1999) 84 Iowa L Rev 499

Munday, R. (2019) *The Law of Evidence*. Tenth edition. Oxford: Oxford University Press

Ormerod, D. and Birch, D. 'The evolution of the discretionary exclusion of evidence' [2004] Crim LR 767

Singh, C. (2014) *Beginning Evidence*. Oxford: Routledge

2

The law of evidence: The burdens and standards of proof

AIMS AND OBJECTIVES

By the end of this chapter you will be able to:

- comprehend and distinguish the various types of burdens of proof in civil and criminal cases;
- understand the principles concerning the different standards of proof;
- identify the incidence of the legal burdens of proof and the exceptions to the general rule;
- understand the function of the burdens of proof in litigation.

Incidence of the legal burden of proof
the identification of the party bearing a legal burden of proof.

Burden of proof
the obligation imposed on a party to prove an allegation.

Presumption of innocence
an automatic presumption in criminal cases that on a plea of not guilty, the defendant is entitled to be found not guilty until evidence to the contrary is proved by the prosecution;

2.1 Introduction

In legal disputes it is important to determine which party has the obligation to prove a point in contention; this is also called the **incidence of the legal burden of proof**. It is necessary to decide how much evidence is needed to prove the particular point in contention or the degree of cogency required of the evidence to satisfy the court on the point in issue; this is referred to as the standard of proof. The term **burden of proof** is connected with the general proposition that in legal proceedings, the axiom is: 'He who asserts must prove', i.e. a party who makes a positive allegation is required to prove their case. In addition, in criminal cases an automatic **presumption of innocence** is required to be drawn. Accordingly, on a charge of murder the accused is presumed to be innocent until the contrary is proven. It is therefore incumbent on the prosecution to prove that the defendant caused the death of the victim with the appropriate *mens rea*. Thus, the prosecuting authority – in the UK the Crown Prosecution Service (or the CPS/Crown) – will bear the legal burden of proof to establish all the elements of the offence. Similarly, in civil cases the party making the assertion is put to proof; for example in an action for negligence the claimant must prove that the defendant caused the relevant injuries in breach of a duty of care.

DOI: 10.4324/9781003282433-2

2.1.1 Several burdens

In many prosecutions or causes of action there may be a multiplicity of issues that the parties may wish to raise at court. On a charge of murder the defendant may wish to raise the defences of **provocation** and diminished responsibility. The following question arises: who needs to discharge the burden of proof and what is the exact nature of that burden? On the issue of provocation the defendant does not bear a legal burden but merely a duty to adduce **sufficient evidence** to raise the issue. The prosecution bears a legal burden to rebut such defence beyond a reasonable doubt. In other words, the defendant does not bear a legal burden to prove the defence of provocation but only an evidential burden to raise the defence. The defendant is only required to adduce sufficient evidence to raise the issue of provocation to the satisfaction of the judge. On the issue of **diminished responsibility**, by statute (see s 2 of the Homicide Act 1957, as amended) the accused bears a legal burden to prove the elements of the defence but only on the balance of probabilities and not beyond reasonable doubt. Thus, the phrase 'burden of proof' is ambiguous. It is generally accepted that there are two burdens of proof – 'legal' and 'evidential'.

the defence of **provocation** is now called the 'loss of control'. The defendant bears an evidential burden of raising the defence and, if so, the prosecution bears a legal burden of rebutting the defence; the defence of **diminished responsibility** imposes a legal burden on the defendant; the expression **sufficient evidence** refers to the quantum of evidence needed to discharge an evidential burden to the satisfaction of the judge.

2.1.2 Legal burden

Lord Denning crafted the phrase 'legal burden' and may be vindicated by the fact that its incidence is determined by substantive law. This appears to be the most popular expression and will be used throughout this book. Other expressions used include 'the burden of proof on the pleadings' (Phipson), 'the risk of non-persuasion' (Wigmore), 'persuasive burden' (Glanville Williams) and 'probative burden' (Lord Hailsham).

The legal burden of proof is the obligation to prove a point in contention, or fact in issue, in order to convince the tribunal of fact of the truth of the assertion. If a party fails to discharge a legal burden of proof to the satisfaction of the tribunal of fact they will, as a matter of course, lose the case. Thus, if the prosecution fails to prove the guilt of the accused beyond a reasonable doubt, the accused is entitled to an acquittal. Equally, in a negligence action, if the claimant fails to prove the elements of negligence, judgment will be given for the defendant.

The legal burden is fixed at the beginning of the trial and remains unchanged throughout the trial and never shifts to another party. Thus, in a criminal case, the various elements that constitute the offence are required to be proven by the prosecution. Failure on the part of the prosecution to prove one or more elements of the offence will result in an acquittal of the accused. The general rule regarding a fixed burden on the prosecution remains the same even though, exceptionally, a legal burden on a different issue may also be imposed on the accused; for example on a charge of murder the accused may raise the defence of diminished responsibility. In this case the prosecution will have a legal burden to prove the respective elements of murder, but the accused will have the legal burden of proving the elements of the defence of diminished responsibility. These are separate issues and consistent with the principle that the parties bear separate burdens.

2.1.3 Evidential burden

In addition, a party may bear an evidential burden. This is the obligation to put sufficient evidence of a point in contention before the court, to justify to

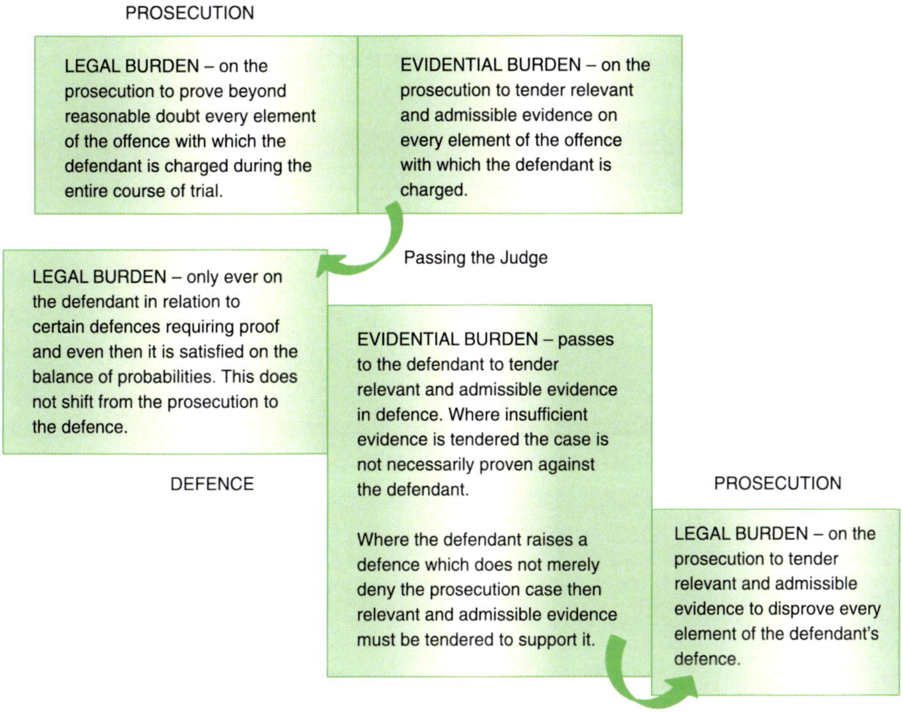

Figure 2.1 Distinction between legal and evidential burdens of proof

the court or tribunal considering the matter, i.e. a duty to raise a *prima facie* case or adduce sufficient evidence to the satisfaction of the tribunal of law that an issue ought to be considered ultimately by the tribunal of fact. The discharge of the evidential burden is for the judge to decide in a case tried by judge and jury.

2.1.4 Evidential burden of proof?

There is some judicial disquiet concerning the expression 'evidential burden'. Some judges do not regard this concept as a burden of proof as such. The reason is that a party with an evidential burden is not under an obligation to convince the tribunal of fact of anything. Such a party may rely on the evidence to suggest that certain facts exist; for example in a criminal case the defendant may rely on discredited evidence adduced by the Crown to argue that a reasonable doubt exists. Lord Devlin in *Jayasena v R* [1970] AC 618:

JUDGMENT

'. . . it is misleading to call it a burden of proof, whether described as legal or evidential or by any other adjective, when it can be discharged by production of evidence that falls short of proof.'

The issue here is whether a party with the evidential burden has a duty to raise the issue as part of its case or, more broadly, whether the issue exists on the facts of the case, and it is immaterial that the issue was not raised by a specific party.

In *R v Gill* (1963) 47 Cr App R 166, Edmund Davies J expressed himself as if the issue is required to be raised by the relevant party:

JUDGMENT

'The accused either by cross examination of the prosecution witnesses or by evidence called on his behalf or by a combination of the two, must place before the court such material as makes [the defence] a live issue fit and proper to be left to the jury. But once he has succeeded in doing this [and thereby discharged his evidential burden] it is then for the Crown to destroy that defence in such a manner as to leave in the jury's minds no reasonable doubt that the accused cannot be absolved on the grounds of the alleged [facts constituting the defence].'

Whereas Lord Tucker in *Bullard v R* [1957] AC 635 adopted the broader view to the effect that the relevant issue is not treated as the responsibility of a party:

JUDGMENT

'It has long been settled law that if on the evidence, whether of the prosecution or of the defence, there is any evidence of provocation fit to be left to a jury, and whether or not this issue has been specifically raised at the trial by counsel for the defence and whether or not the accused has said in terms that he was provoked, it is the duty of the judge, after a proper direction, to leave it open to the jury to return a verdict of manslaughter, if they are not satisfied beyond a reasonable doubt that the killing was unprovoked.'

It is submitted that the correct approach was that stated by Lord Tucker. It matters not how the issue was raised or indeed who raised the issue; provided that it was raised in the trial, the evidential burden may be discharged.

Lord Bingham in *AG's Reference (No 4 of 2002)* [2004] 3 WLR 976 refers to the phrase as a 'burden of raising' an issue in the trial as opposed to a 'burden of proof' *simpliciter*:

JUDGMENT

'An evidential burden is not a burden of proof. It is a burden of raising, on the evidence in the case, an issue as to the matter in question fit for consideration by the tribunal of fact. If an issue is properly raised, it is for the prosecutor to prove, beyond reasonable doubt, that that ground of exoneration does not avail the defendant.'

On the other hand there is judicial support for the expression 'evidential burden'. Clarke LJ in *DPP v Sheldrake* [2004] QB 487 declared:

JUDGMENT

'It is . . . sensible to continue to use it [evidential burden] provided that it is recognized that all that is required to discharge the burden is to identify evidence raising the issue.'

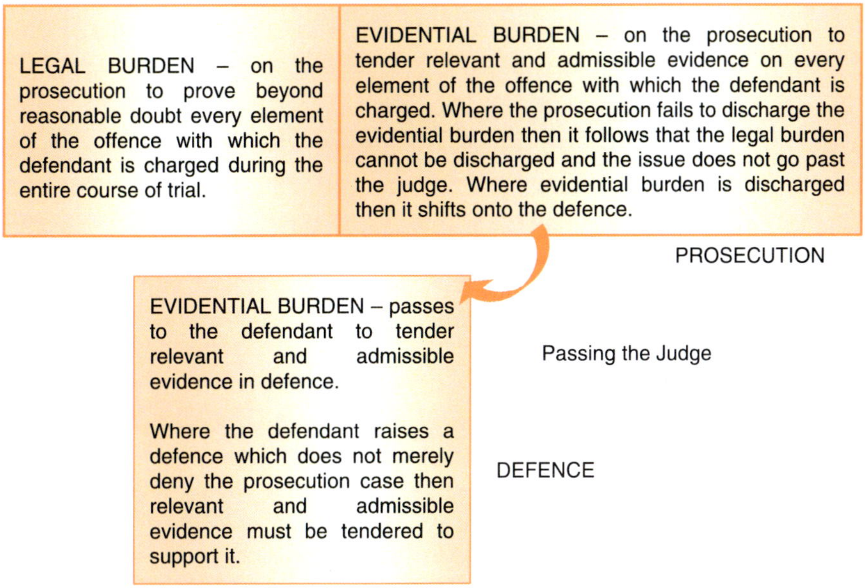

Figure 2.2 Party with both legal and evidential burdens of proof

2.1.5 Party with legal and evidential burdens

In addition, the party with a legal burden of proof also bears an evidential burden on that issue, subject to a few exceptions such as presumptions, formal admissions and judicial notice. Thus, the party with the legal burden has a duty to adduce sufficient evidence to raise the issue. This could be stated as being inevitable in the sense that the greater burden includes the lesser burden. At the same time, different tribunals decide on the different burdens. The tribunal of fact decides whether the legal burden has been discharged, whereas the tribunal of law decides whether the evidential burden is discharged. Moreover, the discharge of the evidential burden is determined before the discharge of the legal burden. The effect is that failure to discharge the evidential burden on an issue will mean that the judge will rule that there is insufficient evidence of the existence of the issue and must reject the allegation or withdraw it from the jury. On the other hand, the successful discharge of the evidential burden does not automatically mean that that party will discharge the legal burden. Discharging the evidential burden means only that the opponent runs a risk of an adverse finding by the tribunal of fact on that issue. In short, the court (tribunal of fact) is required to decide whether the party has proven their case.

2.1.6 Separate evidential burden

A party may bear an evidential burden without a corresponding legal burden; for example on a charge of murder the defendant may raise the defences of provocation or duress or self-defence. With respect to such defences the accused bears only an evidential burden without a corresponding legal burden. The obligation on the accused is to adduce sufficient evidence to convince the judge that the defence(s) ought to be considered by the jury. The defendant may convince the judge (discharge his evidential burden) but may or may not convince the jury of the existence of such defence(s).

2.1.7 Importance of distinguishing legal and evidential burdens

As a final introductory remark, it is essential that the legal and evidential burdens are distinguished for the following four reasons:

(a) To ascertain which party has the right to begin, i.e. to open the case and call the evidence. This is the party with the legal burden of proof. This burden is cast on the party at the beginning of the trial and stays with him until the end of the trial.

(b) When a party (perhaps the defendant) makes a 'no case' submission at the close of a claimant's or prosecution's case, the judge will rule on whether the evidential burden (cast on the party with the legal burden) has been discharged. A successful 'no case' submission would result in a failure on the part of the opponent to discharge the evidential burden.

(c) When the tribunal of fact is in doubt after all the evidence has been adduced. The issue here is whether the legal burden has been discharged. This in turn will depend on the type or degree of doubt that has been entertained by the tribunal of fact.

(d) When the appellate court is required to decide on the correctness of a summing up or judgment dealing with the burden of proof. The question here is whether or not the trial judge's ruling on the incidence of the burden of proof is accurate.

KEY FACTS

Key facts on legal and evidential burdens of proof

'Legal' burden of proof – definition – question of fact – party with the right to begin.

'Evidential' burden of proof – definition – question of law – duty to adduce sufficient evidence.

Party with the legal and evidential burdens – discharge of evidential burden – progression to tribunal of fact.

Party with the legal and evidential burdens – failure to discharge evidential burden – issue not considered by the tribunal of fact.

Party with the evidential but not legal burden – failure to discharge evidential burden – issue not considered by the tribunal of fact.

Party with the evidential but not legal burden – discharge of the evidential burden – issue may be considered by the tribunal of fact.

2.2 Incidence of the legal burden of proof

The incidence of the legal burden of proof involves the principles applied by the courts (and statute) to allocate the legal burden of proof on a party. The fundamental principle is based on the motto 'he who asserts must prove'. In criminal cases the basic principle is derived from the automatic presumption of innocence. It follows that in criminal cases the prosecution is required to prove all the elements of the offence.

2.2.1 Civil cases

In civil cases the party who substantially asserts the affirmative will bear the legal burden of proof. In any particular case this would depend on the circumstances in which the claim arises. This rule is adopted principally because it is fair that those who invoke the aid of the law ought to be put to proof and partly because a negative is more difficult to establish than an affirmative. The principle may be summarised in the Latin maxim *ei qui affirmat, non ei qui negat, incumbit probatio* (the burden of proof lies upon he who affirms and not upon he who denies).

In deciding which party makes an affirmative allegation, consideration is required to be given to the substance of the issue and not merely to the form in which the issue is presented. It is probably true to say that a positive assertion, in theory, can always be converted into a negative statement by appropriate linguistic manipulation; for example a claim for damages for breach of a repairing covenant may be expressed either that the defendant did not repair the house or that he allowed the house to become dilapidated. The mode of expressing the claim does not disguise the issue that, in substance, the legal burden is borne by the claimant for it is he who makes the assertion. A test laid down in *Abrath v NE Railway Co.* (1883) 11 QBD 440 is, 'If the assertion of a negative is an essential part of the plaintiff's case, the proof of the assertion still rests upon the plaintiff' (Bowen LJ). In this case the claim was for malicious prosecution. The court decided that the legal burden of absence of reasonable and probable cause rested on the claimant, *per* Bowen LJ:

JUDGMENT

'Whenever litigation exists, somebody must go on with it; the plaintiff is the first to begin; if he does nothing, he fails; if he makes a *prima facie* case, and nothing is done to answer it, the defendant fails. The test, therefore, as to the burden of proof or onus of proof, whichever term is used, is simply this: to ask oneself which party will be successful if no evidence is given, or if no more evidence is given than has been given at a particular point of the case, for it is obvious that as the controversy involved in the litigation travels on, the parties from moment to moment may reach points at which the onus shifts, and at which the tribunal will have to say that if the case stops there, it must be decided in a particular manner.''

In determining whether an affirmative allegation has been made and the nature of that allegation, and therefore the incidence of the legal burden of proof, the courts apply a number of principles. The principal issue involves rules of substantive law. If this principle is not decisive the courts will have regard to the statements of the case and, as a last resort, a balance of convenience. In practice, the determination of this question is based on precedent.

CASE EXAMPLE

Sutton v Sadler (1857) 3 CBNS 87

The heir at law claimed to be entitled to the deceased's estate as opposed to the devisee under the testator's will. The basis of the claim by the heir was that the will was invalid on the ground that the testator was insane. The trial judge decided that the legal burden of proof rested on the claimant, heir at law. On appeal, this was considered to be a misdirection. The devisee, defendant, bore the legal burden of proof, for it was he who was making the allegation that the will was valid. The devisee may discharge his evidential burden by relying on a presumption, namely, that the will appeared to be rational on the face of it.

Cresswell J:

JUDGMENT

'If, indeed, a will, not irrational on the face of it, is produced before a jury and the execution of it proved, and no other evidence offered, the jury would be properly told that they ought to find for the will, and if the party opposing the will gives some evidence of incompetency, the jury may, nevertheless, if it does not disturb their belief in the competency of the testator, find in favour of the will and in each case the presumption in favour of competency would prevail. But that is not a mere presumption of law, and, when the whole matter is before the jury on evidence given on both sides, they ought not to affirm that a document is the will of a competent testator, unless they believe that it really is so.'

CASE EXAMPLE

Joseph Constantine Steamship v Imperial Smelting Corporation
[1942] AC 154 (HL)

In this case the charterers of a ship claimed damages from the owners for breach of contract in failing to load the ship by a specified date. The owners defended the action on the ground that the contract was frustrated by the destruction of the ship owing to an explosion. In contract law, frustration is a defence to a claim for breach of contract, but only if the frustrating event occurred without the default of the defendant. The House of Lords held: the shipowners, having established the explosion had frustrated the commercial objective, did not need to prove that the explosion was not due to their neglect of default and they succeeded in their defence. The legal burden of proof on the issue of default rested with the claimant.

Viscount Simon LC:

JUDGMENT

'The question here is where the onus of proof lies, ie, whether, when a supervening event has been proved which would, apart from the defendant's "default," put an end to the contract, and when at the end of the case no inference of "default" exists and the evidence is equally consistent with either view, the defence fails because the defendant has not established affirmatively that the supervening event was not due to his default. I may observe, in the first place, that, if this were correct, there must by many cases in which, although in truth frustration is complete and unavoidable, the defendant will be held liable because of his inability to prove a negative – in some cases, indeed, a whole series of negatives. [. . .] The doctrine upon which the defence of frustration depends is nowhere so stated as to place this onus of proof on the party relying on it.' (at p 170)

In this case, the court considered that it would have been difficult for the defendants to prove the negative; that they were not at fault. Accordingly, the balance of convenience played a material part in deciding the incidence of the legal burden of proof.

In the case of a bailment contract, the duty of the bailee (recipient of the goods) is to return the goods in the same order and condition as when they were delivered to him. Therefore, in order to found a claim for breach of a bailment contract the bailor, the owner of the goods, needs only to establish receipt of the goods by the bailee in good order, and that the goods were short or damaged at the time of re-delivery to the bailor or at his direction. The bailor need not go further and show that the shortage or damage was preventable and ought to have been prevented. In *Milan Nigeria Ltd v Angeliki Maritime Co*, the High Court decided that an arbitrator had erred in imposing the legal burden on the claimant, bailor, to prove how the damage or short delivery of the goods had occurred.

CASE EXAMPLE

Milan Nigeria Ltd v Angeliki Maritime Co [2011] EWHC 892 (HC)

The claimant, Milan, was the owner of cargo (rice) to be shipped from Bangkok to Lagos, Nigeria. The defendants (bailees) were the owners of a vessel who agreed to ship the cargo. On arrival at the Nigerian port, a quantity of the goods was found to be in short supply and some of it was damaged. The arbitrator upheld the damage claim but rejected the short supply claim on the ground that the claimant had not discharged its burden of proof. The claimant appealed to the High Court.

Held

The court allowed the appeal and decided that the arbitrator had erred in imposing the legal burden on the claimant to prove how the loss occurred.

JUDGMENT

'The Tribunal clearly adopted the wrong approach to the burden of proof. It expressly, and on a number of occasions, identified the burden of proof of establishing the cause(s) of the damage as being placed on Milan, and it held that Milan was liable for such damage as it had failed to establish that the loss was due to Owners' defaults. In my judgment, the Tribunal's approach in this respect was wrong and not in accordance with the authorities.'

(Gloster J)

In respect of claims for breaches of contracts containing exclusion clauses the claimant is required to establish the existence of the contract, breach and resulting loss. The defendant will claim that the exclusion clause had been validly incorporated into the contract and protects him from the claim for breach of contract. In short, the party seeking to rely on a clause in a contract limiting their liability will bear the legal burden of proof. However, an allegation of a fundamental breach of the contract may have the effect of destroying the defence based on the exclusion clause. The issue that was raised in *Levison v*

Patent Carpet Cleaning [1977] 3 All ER 498 was, which party had the legal burden of proof with respect to the exclusion clause. It was argued that fundamental breach was part of the claim in respect of breach of contract. On the converse, it was argued that fundamental breach affects the enforcement of the exclusion clause and therefore required the defendant to bear the legal burden of proving that the loss did not constitute a fundamental breach i.e., a negative. The Court of Appeal decided that it was the defendant who bore the legal burden of proof.

CASE EXAMPLE

Levison v Patent Carpet Cleaning [1977] 3 All ER 498

The claimant deposited his expensive Chinese carpet to the defendants for cleaning. The contract, signed by the claimant, contained a clause exempting the defendants from liability for negligence. The defendants failed to return the carpet to the claimant on the ground that it was lost. In an action for breach of contract the defendants claimed that the exclusion clause protected them from liability. The claimant alleged that the non-delivery of the goods amounted to a fundamental breach of the contract by the defendants and deprived them of the benefit of the exclusion clause. The issue was, which party had the burden of proof regarding fundamental breach. The county court judge decided against the claimant, who appealed to the Court of Appeal.

It was held that the defendant bore the legal burden of proof to show that the loss suffered by the claimant did not amount to a fundamental breach:

JUDGMENT

'This brings me to the crux of the case . . . On whom is the burden to prove that there was fundamental breach?

'Upon principle, I should have thought that the burden was on the cleaners to prove that they were not guilty of a fundamental breach. After all, Mrs Levinson does not know what happened to it. The cleaners are the ones who know, or should know, what happened to the carpet, and the burden should be on them to say what it was . . .

'. . . I am clearly of the opinion that, in a contract of bailment, when a bailee seeks to escape liability on the ground that he was not negligent or that he was excused by an exception or limitation clause, then he must show what happened to the goods. He must prove all the circumstances known to him in which the loss or damage occurred. If it appears that the goods were lost or damaged without any negligence on his part, then, of course, he is not liable. If it appears that they were lost or damaged by a slight breach – not going to the root of the contract – he may be protected by the exemption or limitation clause. But if he leaves the cause of loss or damage undiscovered and unexplained – then I think he is liable, because it is then quite likely that the goods were stolen by one of his servants; or delivered by his servant to the wrong address; or damaged by reckless or wilful conduct; all of which the offending servant will conceal and not make known to his employer. Such conduct would be a fundamental breach against which the exemption or limitation clause will not protect him.'

(Lord Denning MR)

In this case the court gave due regard to the balance of convenience principle. If the legal burden of proving fundamental breach was imposed on the claimant, she would have found it difficult to discharge; whereas the defendants ought to have known what happened to the carpet.

In *The Glendarroch* [1894] P 226, the claimants brought an action for the non-delivery of goods shipped under a bill of lading. The goods had been damaged by seawater. The bill of lading exempted the defendants from liability for loss or damage occasioned by perils of the sea, provided that the defendants were not negligent. The Court of Appeal held that the claimants bore the legal burden of proving that the damage was caused by the defendants' negligence:

JUDGMENT

'When you come to the exceptions, among others there is the exception of perils of the sea. There are no words which say "Perils of the sea not caused by the negligence of the captain or the crew." You have got to read those words in by a necessary inference. How can you read them in? You have got the plain words, in their ordinary sense, that the ship-owner is relieved if the loss is a loss by perils of the sea in the ordinary sense of the word. But then you have to read in the other. You can only read it in, in my opinion, as an exception upon the exceptions. You must read in "Except the loss is by perils of the sea, unless or except that loss is the result of the negligence of the captain or sailors of the owner." That being so, I think that, according to the ordinary course of practice, each party would have to prove the part of the matter which lies upon him. The plaintiff would have to prove the contract and the non-delivery. If he leaves that in doubt, of course he fails. The defendant's answer is, "Yes, but my case was brought within the exception, within its ordinary meaning." That lies upon him. Then the plaintiff has a right to say there are exceptional circumstances – viz, that the damage was brought about by the negligence of the defendant's servants, and it seems to me that it is for the plaintiff to make out that second exception.'

(Lord Esher MR)

In *Munro, Brice and Co v War Risks Association* [1918] 2 KB 78, a claimant whose ship had been lost claimed under an insurance policy insuring it against loss by perils of the sea, subject to a proviso excepting loss by capture, seizure and consequences of hostility. The court held that the defendant bore the legal burden of proving that the loss fell within the proviso. The court took the view that once the claimant (assured) proved that its ship had been lost at sea he had made out a *prima facie* case under the policy against the defendants. The latter was required to prove that the loss was excepted under the hostilities clause.

A decision that was difficult to justify is *Hurst v Evans* [1917] 1 KB 352. The claimant, a jeweller, had an insurance policy in respect of loss or damage to his stock except where it was caused by any servant in his exclusive employ. He suffered loss and sued on the policy. The defendants claimed that the loss was caused by the theft of M, a servant in the claimant's exclusive employ. Evidence was admitted that M had been seen two days before the theft in a public house with three highly skilled safebreakers known to the police. The court held that the onus of proof was on the claimant to prove his loss was not due to one of the exceptions and he had not discharged his burden.

Incidence of the legal burden of proof – civil cases

Factors to be considered

- Rules of substantive law
- Statement of case (pleadings)
- Rules of convenience

Examples

- *Sutton v Sadler*
- *Constantine Steamship v Imperial Smelting Co*
- *Munro, Volcafe*

Figure 2.3 Party with evidential burden of proof

This case was disapproved in *Munro*, although not overruled. It was difficult to reconcile with *Munro*, save for the fact that the policy in *Hurst* was a special risks insurance policy. On a balance of convenience the decision could be justified because only the claimant could explain, or ought to be able to explain, how the loss occurred; but placing the legal burden on the claimant required him to prove a negative.

In *Volcafe Ltd v Cia Sud Americana de Vapores SA* [2018] UKSC 61 the action was against a carrier relating to loss/damage to a cargo of Colombian green coffee beans. The Supreme Court stated that it is the carrier who has the legal burden to disprove negligence i.e., that care was taken, both for the purpose of article III.2 and article IV.2 of the Hague Rules.

JUDGMENT

The Court of Appeal held: '(1) that where the cargo claimant established that goods which had been loaded in apparent good order and condition had been delivered in a damaged condition or lost, that gave rise to a sustainable cause of action for breach by the carrier of its obligation under article III, rule 2 of the Hague Rules properly and carefully to care for and carry the goods, not merely an inference of such breach; that, once there was such a sustainable cause of action, the carrier was under a legal burden, not merely an evidential burden, to prove on the balance of probabilities a defence based on one of the exceptions in article IV, rule 2; that, in order to discharge that burden, the carrier was not required to show that the damage had occurred without its negligence or notwithstanding that it had met its duty under article III, rule 2 properly and carefully to carry the goods; and that if the carrier established such a defence, it was for the cargo claimant to negative the operation of the exception by establishing negligence or a breach of the duty under article III, rule 2 (post, paras 35–36, 50, 112, 113).'

Thus, the court has overruled the decision in *The Glendarroch* and rejected the previous dicta by placing a legal burden on the carrier to disprove causative negligence. The carrier has the burden to prove what happened to the cargo if it is to avail itself to the defences under the Hague Rules, similar to the position of a bailee of goods, they, considering the balance of convenience, are best placed to explain what happened whilst the goods were in their possession. Therefore, the party that asserts an issue as part of their case will bear the legal burden on that regardless of whether it is proving the negative.

Parties may make provision in a contract for the legal burden on certain issues to lie on one or other of them. At common law such clauses are valid but will have to be clearly expressed. A contractual term that alters the normal rules on the burden of proof counts as an exemption clause for the purposes of the Unfair Contract Terms Act 1977: see s 13(1)(c).

ACTIVITY

Self-test questions

1. In civil cases, what factors are relevant in determining which party bears a legal burden of proof?
2. In an action by A for breach of contract for the carriage of a consignment of television sets by lorry from London to Manchester, the contract provided that B, a lorry owner, was not liable for loss caused by fire provided that the lorry owner's servants were not negligent. The lorry and its load are destroyed by fire in a service area on the motorway. B claims that he is not liable for the loss. A contends that B was facing bankruptcy and that the lorry has been deliberately set on fire so that B can claim on his insurance from the insurers of the lorry. Alternatively, A asserts that the fire was caused by the carelessness of the lorry driver.

   Consider the burdens and standards of proof on these matters.

2.2.2 Criminal cases – general rule – the 'golden thread' theory

In criminal cases the fundamental rule is that the prosecution is required to prove all the elements of the offence to the satisfaction of the jury or tribunal of fact. Another way of expressing the principle is that there is an automatic presumption of innocence in favour of the accused. This principle has been affirmed in Art 6(2) of the European Convention on Human Rights but it is also an integral part of the common law. The general rule, or 'golden thread' is illustrated by *Woolmington v DPP* [1935] AC 462.

CASE EXAMPLE

Woolmington v DPP [1935] AC 462

On a charge of murder by shooting, the accused raised the defence of accident. The judge directed the jury that once the Crown had proven the killing at the hands of the accused, it must be presumed to be murder and that it was for the accused to prove circumstances that would excuse the homicide as an accident. The accused was convicted of murder and appealed. It was held that this was a misdirection and the conviction was quashed:

JUDGMENT

'While the prosecution must prove the guilt of the prisoner, there is no such burden laid on the prisoner to prove his innocence and it is sufficient for him to raise a doubt as to his guilt: he is not bound to satisfy the jury of his innocence . . . Throughout the web of the English criminal law one golden thread is always to be seen that it is the duty of the prosecution to prove the prisoner's guilt subject to . . . the defence of insanity and [statutory exceptions]. If, at the end of and on the whole of the case, there is a reasonable doubt, created by the evidence given by either the prosecution or the prisoner, as to whether the prisoner killed the deceased with a malicious intention, the prosecution has not made the case and the prisoner is entitled to an acquittal. No matter what the charge or where the trial, the principle that the prosecution must prove the guilt of the prisoner is part of the common law of England and no attempt to whittle it down can be entertained. When dealing with a murder case the Crown must prove (a) death as the result of a voluntary act of the accused; and (b) malice of the accused. When evidence of death and malice has been given (this is a question for the jury) the accused is entitled to show, by evidence or by examination of the circumstances adduced by the Crown, that the act on his part which caused death was either unintentional or provoked. If the jury are either satisfied that this explanation or, upon a review of all the evidence, are left in reasonable doubt whether, even if his explanation be not accepted, the act was unintentional or provoked, the prisoner is entitled to [the benefit of the doubt].'

(Lord Sankey LC)

The *Woolmington* principle puts to rest any doubt as to the appropriate starting point in criminal prosecutions. This is the 'golden thread' theory that the prosecution bears the legal burden of proof. For the avoidance of doubt it must follow that if the prosecution fails to discharge its evidential burden, i.e. it fails to make out a *prima facie* case, the accused is entitled to an acquittal, for it would be clear that the prosecution will not be able to discharge its legal burden. The decision in *Woolmington* also classifies the exceptional circumstances when a reverse burden of proof will be cast on the accused. This will be considered later.

The effect of placing the legal burden on the prosecution results in the jury or fact-finding tribunal deciding whether the onus had been discharged. This is done at the end of the trial when all the evidence has been adduced. The governing principle also has the added advantage of assessing the risks of misdirection on the part of the judge. This involves a question of law for the courts to decide. The general principle is justified on the grounds that a high value is placed on the human rights of individuals, and the resources available to the Crown in the detection and presentation of the case against the accused far outweigh the facilities available to the individual.

In the infamous case of *R v Bentley (Derek)* (2001), the Court of Appeal decided that the trial judge's direction to the jury on the burden and standard of proof was inappropriate and flawed.

CASE EXAMPLE

R v Bentley [2001] 1 Cr App R 21

B was convicted of the murder of a policeman and sentenced to death in 1952. Following the dismissal of his appeal, B was executed in 1953. He was granted a royal pardon in relation to his sentence and execution in 1993, and B's niece appealed on B's behalf against his conviction by way of a reference by the Criminal Cases Review Commission. The appeal was brought on the grounds *inter alia* that the trial judge had given no direction on the standard of proof, his direction on the burden of proof had been unclear and misleading, he had made prejudicial and unfair comments suggesting that the police officers' bravery throughout the incident rendered the police witnesses more reliable than the defendant's and he had failed to present B's case adequately to the jury.

Held

Allowing the appeal, *inter alia,* that the many defects in the judge's summing up rendered B's trial unfair and his conviction unsafe.

JUDGMENT

'The jury must be clearly and unambiguously instructed that the burden of proving the guilt of the accused lies and lies only on the Crown, that (subject to exceptions not here relevant) there is no burden on the accused to prove anything and that if, on reviewing all the evidence, the jury are unsure of or are left in any reasonable doubt as to the guilt of the accused that doubt must be resolved in favour of the accused. Such an instruction has for very many years been regarded as a cardinal requirement of a properly conducted trial. The courts have not been willing to countenance departures from it. We cannot regard the direction in this case as satisfactory. By stressing the abundant evidence calling for an answer in support of the prosecution case, and by suggesting that that case had been "established", and by suggesting that there was a burden on Craig [Bentley] to satisfy the jury that the killing had been accidental (however little, on the facts of this case, the injustice caused to Craig thereby), the jury in our view could well have been left with the impression that the case against the appellant was proved and that they should convict him unless he had satisfied them of his innocence.'

(Lord Bingham CJ)

2.2.3 Exceptions in criminal cases

The definition of insanity has been laid down at common law by reference to the McNaghten rules.

Common law exception – insanity

The only common law defence in which the accused bears the legal burden of proof is **insanity**. The reason for this exception lies in the presentation of the rules in *McNaghten's Case* (1843) 10 Cl & F 200. It was assumed by the judges that the accused ought to bear the legal burden of proving insanity. Today, it is extremely doubtful whether there are any sound policy reasons for placing the legal burden on the accused, as opposed to an evidential burden.

The McNaghten rules are: 'The jurors ought to be told in all cases that every man is presumed to be sane and to possess a sufficient degree of reason to be responsible for his crimes, until the contrary be proved to their satisfaction; and that to establish a defence on the grounds of insanity, it must be clearly proved that, at the time of the committing of the act, the party accused was labouring under such a defect of reason from disease of the mind, as not to know the nature and quality of the act he was doing; or, if he did know it, he did not know he was doing what was wrong.'

Difficulty may sometimes arise where there is evidence of both insane automatism and non-insane automatism of the accused at the time of the alleged commission of the offence. It is imperative that the judge in his summing up to the jury distinguish between these two defences, for the incidence of the legal burden of proof differs. In respect of insane automatism raised by the accused, the defence will bear the legal burden of proof on a balance of probabilities. With regard to non-insane automatism the accused bears an evidential burden of raising the issue, but once there is sufficient evidence of the defence the legal burden to rebut the defence lies with the prosecution.

In *R v Burns* (1973) 58 Cr App R 364, Stephenson LJ said, 'It is not for the defence to prove automatism, it is for the prosecution to negative it once the defence lays a foundation for it. Nowhere does the judge draw that distinction. . . .'

In any event, *prima facie* evidence of the probable existence of the defence(s) must be established by the accused before the judge becomes duty bound to direct the jury of the incidence of the burden of proof regarding that issue. If there is insufficient evidence to support the defence of sane automatism, the judge is entitled to withdraw the issue from the jury. In short, if the defence fails to discharge its evidential burden, the issue may be withdrawn from the trial.

In *Bratty v AG for Northern Ireland* [1963] AC 386, Viscount Kilmuir said: 'Not only must automatism be expressly put forward as a defence, but also a proper foundation must be laid for it . . . In my view . . . it is necessary that a proper foundation be laid before a judge can leave automatism to the jury. That foundation is not forthcoming merely from unaccepted evidence of a defect of reason from a disease of the mind. There would need to be other evidence on which a jury could find non-insane automatism.' In this case the charge was murder and the accused raised defences of insane and non-insane automatism. There was insufficient evidence of non-insane automatism and the judge rejected the defence. The jury rejected the defence of insane automatism and found him guilty of murder. His appeal was dismissed.

Express statutory reversal of the burden

Lord Sankey in *Woolmington v DPP* referred to statutory exceptions to the general rule. These include both express and implied statutory exceptions or reverse burdens created by statute. There are a number of occasions when Parliament has expressly imposed a legal burden on the accused to prove a defence and sometimes the issue may concern an element of the offence.

Much depends on the wording of the statute. The statutory provision may expressly state that it is for the accused to prove the relevant defence such as s 2(2) of the Homicide Act 1957 in respect of diminished responsibility, which states 'on a charge of murder, it shall be for the defence to prove that the person charged is by virtue of this section not liable to be convicted of murder'.

Alternatively, the statutory provision may declare that an offence shall be 'deemed to be committed unless the contrary be proved'. The effect is the same as if the statute had declared that it shall be for the accused to prove to the contrary. On a charge under the Prevention of Corruption Act 1906, s 2 of the Prevention of Corruption Act 1916 enacts as follows:

SECTION

'Where in any proceedings against a person for an offence under the [1906] Act, it is proved that any money, gift or other consideration has been paid, given to or received by a person in the employment of HM Government or any Government Department . . . the money, gift or consideration shall be deemed to have been paid or given . . . corruptly . . . unless the contrary is proved.'

It may be noted that this provision concerns an element of the offence, namely, corruption or corrupt payments. A multitude of other statutory enactments have achieved the same. Many of these provisions will need to be reviewed in view of the approaches adopted by the House of Lords in *R v Lambert* [2001] 2 Cr App R 511 and *AG Reference (No 4 of 2002)* (2004); see later under the 'Impact of the Human Rights Act 1998'.

In those cases where the accused bears a legal burden of proof (either at common law or by statute), the standard of proof does not exceed a balance of probabilities: see *R v Carr-Briant*.

CASE EXAMPLE

R v Carr-Briant [1943] KB 607

The accused, a director in a firm, was charged under the Prevention of Corruption Act 1906 in that it was alleged that he gave or loaned £60 to an engineer employed in a government department. The defence was that the payment had not been made corruptly. The judge directed the jury that the standard of proof imposed on the accused was beyond a reasonable doubt. He was convicted and appealed.

The Court of Appeal allowed the appeal and decided that the judge had misdirected the jury as to the standard of proof that ought to have been on a balance of probabilities:

JUDGMENT

'In our judgment where, either by statute or at common law, some matter is presumed against the accused person "unless the contrary is proved", the jury should be directed that it is for them to decide whether the contrary is proved; that the burden of proof required is less than that required at the hands of the prosecution in proving the case beyond a reasonable doubt, and that the burden may be discharged by evidence satisfying the jury of the probability of that which the accused is called upon to establish.'

(Humphreys J)

However, in *R v Webster* [2010] EWCA Crim 2819, the Court of Appeal decided that the express statutory reversal provision in s 2 of the Prevention of Corruption Act 1916 was unreasonable, disproportionate and unjustifiably interfered with the presumption of innocence and will be read down so as to impose an evidential burden of proof. See later under the 'Impact of the Human Rights Act 1998'.

Implied statutory reversal of the legal burden

There are a number of cases where an enactment may be construed as impliedly imposing a legal burden on the accused. In other words the provisions may be treated as equivalent to occasions when Parliament expressly intended to impose a legal burden on the accused.

Section 101 of the Magistrates' Courts Act 1980 lays down the general principle in respect of summary offences. Similar provisions had existed long before the *Woolmington* case. Section 101 of the Magistrates' Courts Act 1980 states:

SECTION

'Where a defendant to an information or complaint relies for his defence on any exception, exemption, proviso, excuse or qualification, whether or not it accompanies the description of the offence or matter of complaint in the enactment creating the offence or on which the complaint is founded, the burden of proving the exception, exemption, proviso, excuse or qualification, shall be on him; and this notwithstanding that the information or complaint contains an allegation negativing the exception, exemption, proviso, excuse or qualification.'

The effect of the section is that where the conduct of the accused creates an offence but in circumstances where the statute creates a defence in respect of an exception, exemption, proviso, excuse or qualification, the burden of proving that the conduct comes within the exception, exemption, etc. is placed on the accused. The section makes it clear that it does not matter whether the provision relied on forms part of the clause creating the offence or whether it appears elsewhere in the statute. The principle originates partly from the notion that it is easy or easier for the accused to prove that they fall within the exception, exemption, etc. because of access to the relevant information and partly from the original provision enacted in s 39(2) of the Summary Jurisdiction Act 1879. In *Nimmo v Alexander Cowan & Sons Ltd* [1968] AC 107 (see later), Lord Pearson offered guidance on the approach to the construction of provisions incorporating principles similar to the predecessor to s 101 of the 1980 Act.

JUDGMENT

'An exemption or exception or proviso, and sometimes at any rate a condition, would be easily recognisable from the drafting of the enactment: to take the most obvious instances, an exception would naturally begin with the word "except" and a proviso with the words "Provided always that". Therefore points of grammar and drafting would appropriately be stressed in construing an enactment . . . [Likewise] the inclusion of [the expressions] "excuse or qualification" and . . . also the words "whether it does or does not accompany in the same section the description of the offence". All these show an intention to widen the provision and to direct attention to the substance and effect rather than the form of the enactment to which it is to be applied. There is no usual formula for an "excuse". "Qualification", if understood in a grammatical sense, might cover any adjective, adverb or adjectival or adverbial phrase. More probably it means some qualification, such as a licence, for doing what would otherwise be unlawful. There is no usual formula for a "qualification" in that sense. You have to look at the substance and effect of the enactment, as well as its form, in order to ascertain whether it contains an "excuse or qualification" within the meaning of the section.'

(Lord Pearson)

Section 101 is concerned with cases where the defendant is charged with doing an act that is not outright unlawful but becomes unlawful in certain circumstances, such as driving a motor vehicle on a public road without a valid licence: see *John v Humphreys* [1955] 1 WLR 325. In such a case, driving a motor vehicle on a public road is not an unlawful act *per se*, but becomes unlawful when the driver does not have a valid licence. The non-possession of a valid licence is not part of the offence requiring the prosecution to prove the negative but requires the accused, if he wishes, to prove the existence of a valid licence. The predominant application of such provisions is in respect of regulatory offences for which a licence or permission is required. The prosecution retains the legal burden of proving that the accused committed the prohibited act. If the prosecution fails to discharge the evidential burden that is attached to the legal burden, the accused is not put to proof and is entitled to be acquitted. In *Gatland v Metropolitan Police Commissioner* [1968] 2 QB 279, the accused had been charged that without lawful authority or excuse he had deposited a thing, namely a builders' skip, on a highway in consequence whereof a user of the highway had been endangered. It was held that, although it was for the accused to establish any lawful authority or excuse, and although he failed to do so, it was for the prosecution to prove, first, that the article in question had been deposited upon the highway and, second, that in consequence thereof a user of the highway was injured or endangered. As there had been no evidence that any user of the highway had been injured or endangered in consequence of the deposit, the prosecution had failed to discharge its legal burden and the conviction was quashed.

In *Nagy v Weston* [1965] 1 All ER 78, the charge was under s 121(1) of the Highways Act 1959 (now s 137(1) of the Highways Act 1980), which provides that it is an offence 'to wilfully obstruct the highway without lawful authority or excuse'. The court decided that this provision placed a legal burden of proof on the prosecution to prove a negative; namely, that the defendant did not have lawful authority or excuse. Section 101 (or its predecessor) was not applicable. The effect is that there has been little consistency in the approach to s 101 provisions.

In *Hirst v Chief Constable of West Yorkshire* [1987] Crim LR 330, the court endorsed the construction of the provision adopted in *Nagy*. In *Hirst*, the charge was under s 137(1) of the Highways Act 1980. The case concerned an alleged obstruction of the highway by protesting animal rights supporters. The court decided that the Crown bore a legal burden of proof to show lack of lawful excuse for the obstruction. It could be argued that these cases can be reconciled on the ground that in *Gatland*, to deposit an object, especially a large object, on the highway was *prima facie* capable of endangering life until the accused proves to the contrary; whereas, in *Nagy* and *Hirst*, being on the highway *per se* is not unlawful until the Crown proves to the contrary. Such cases have prompted J. C. Smith, in 'The presumption of innocence' (1987) 38 Northern Ireland Legal Quarterly, to state that:

> to deduce from this that Parliament intended to exclude the effect of s 101 from the obstruction offence, though not from another offence under the same statute, in respect of which Parliament has used exactly the same language, would seem to be to indulge in fiction of an arbitrary and undesirable kind.

It is a question of construction of the statutory provision to determine whether the prohibited conduct, the subject matter of the complaint, is to be treated as part of the offence imposing a legal burden on the prosecution, i.e. a negative pre-condition, or, whether the act is to be treated as a defence. In commenting on the predecessor to s 101 of the 1980 Act, in *Shehan v Cork JJ* [1908] 2 IR 1, Gibson J said:

JUDGMENT

> 'Does the section [creating the charge] make the act described an offence subject to particular exceptions, qualifications, etc., which, where applicable, make the *prima facie* offence an innocent act, or does the statute make an act *prima facie* innocent an offence when done under certain conditions? In the former case the exception need not be negatived; in the latter words of exception may constitute the offence.'

Much depends upon the wording of the statute in question, words such as 'unless', 'except', 'other than' or 'provided always' indicate that the offence is within s 101, but the section as a whole is required to be construed. In *Nimmo v Alexander Cowan & Sons Ltd* [1968] AC 107, the House of Lords took the opportunity to offer general guidance on the construction of provisions. It was an offence not to comply with s 209 of the Factories Act 1961. This section provided that a workplace should be a safe place for employees 'so far as is reasonably practicable'. In *Nimmo*, the court had to consider whether this provision created an 'excuse, exemption . . . etc.' causing the burden of proof to be placed on the defendant, or whether the prosecution continued to bear the burden. The House of Lords held that the burden was on the defendant. In determining this, it was necessary 'to direct attention to the substance and effect . . . of the enactment'. By a three to two majority, the House of Lords held that once the prosecution had established that the workplace was unsafe, it was for the defendant to excuse himself by proving that it was not 'reasonably practicable' to make it safe. The court was entitled to look beyond the linguistics of the section, 'at the mischief at which the Act was aimed and practical considerations affecting the burden of proof, and, in particular, the ease or difficulty that the respective parties would encounter in discharging the burden', and that 'exceptions are to be set up by those who rely on them'. In other words the question in *Nimmo* was, on construction of the provision, whether it was unlawful to provide an unsafe work place or whether it was only unlawful to fail to take all reasonably practicable steps to make it safe. Normal rules of statutory construction were required to be applied to determine what was prohibited.

In respect of trials on indictment s 101 of the 1980 Act has no direct application but the defendant may impliedly bear the legal burden of proof. Rule 6C of the Indictment Rules 1971 lays down that where the alleged offence is one for which the relevant statute provides a defence by way of exception, exemption, proviso, excuse or qualification, it is not necessary for any of these to be specified in the indictment. The effect is that it is well established at common law that the s 101 principle is applicable to both summary and indictable offences and must now be read subject to the Human Rights Act 1998 (see later). In *R v Edwards* [1975] QB 27, the Court of Appeal decided that there was a common law rule that was the same as s 101 of the 1980 Act, although it did not express the rule as clearly as the section. In addition, the court reviewed the leading authorities reversing the legal burden and decided it was a question of construction of the provision:

JUDGMENT

'. . . the common law, as a result of experience and the need to ensure that justice is done both to the community and to defendants, has evolved an exception to the fundamental principle of our criminal law that the prosecution must prove every element of the offence charged. This exception . . . is limited to offences arising under enactments which prohibit the doing of an act save in specified circumstances or by persons of specified classes or with specified qualifications or with the licence or permission of specified authorities. Whenever the prosecution seeks to rely on this exception, the court must construe the enactment under which the charge is laid. If the true construction is that the enactment prohibits the doing of acts, subject to provisos, exceptions and the like, then the prosecution can rely upon the exception . . . it is for the defendant to prove that he was entitled to do the prohibited act. What rests on him is the legal, or as it is sometimes called, the persuasive burden.'

(Lawton LJ)

In this case the defendant was charged with selling intoxicating liquor without holding a justices' licence, contrary to s 160(1) of the Licensing Act 1964. The prosecution proved a sale by the defendant of intoxicating liquor but omitted to adduce evidence that the defendant did not hold a licence, even though the register of licences was available to the police at any reasonable time. The accused was convicted and appealed. The Court of Appeal dismissed his appeal on the ground that, on construction of the Act, the legal burden was cast on the defendant to prove that he had a valid licence.

In respect of the construction of the statutory provision the court is not restricted to the four corners of the statute but may take into consideration extraneous factors. Such guidance had been given by Lord Griffiths in *R v Hunt* [1987] 1 All ER 1, where he said:

JUDGMENT

'. . . their Lordships were in agreement that if the linguistic constructions of the statute did not clearly indicate upon whom the burden should lie, the court should look to other considerations to determine the intention of Parliament such as the mischief at which the Act was aimed and practical considerations affecting the burden of proof and, in particular, the ease or difficulty that the respective parties would encounter in discharging the burden. I regard this last consideration as one of greatest importance for surely Parliament can never lightly be taken to have intended to impose an onerous duty on a defendant to prove his innocence in a criminal case, and a court should be slow to draw any such inference from the language of a statute.'

In this case the accused was charged with the unlawful possession of morphine, contrary to s 5 of the Misuse of Drugs Act 1971. Under the Misuse of Drugs Regulations 1973, it is provided that s 5 shall not apply in relation to any preparation of morphine containing not more than 0.2 per cent of morphine (a *de minimis* principle). The prosecution had adduced no evidence as to the proportion of morphine in the powder found in the possession of the accused. At the trial the defence made a 'no case' submission that was rejected by the judge and the accused changed his plea to guilty and appealed. The Court of Appeal dismissed his appeal, but the House of Lords allowed the accused's appeal and quashed his conviction on the following grounds:

- On construction of the statute, the case did not fall within the formula stated by Lawton LJ in *Edwards*.
- If, on construction of a statute, there is no indication that the burden of proof rested on the defendant, the court is entitled to have regard to policy and practical considerations – such as the mischief behind the passing of the statute, the gravity of the offence, or the ease or difficulty in discharging the burden of proof.
- In this case, if the accused had a burden of proof it would have been extremely difficult for him to discharge it. The substance was seized by the police and the accused has no statutory entitlement to a proportion of it for analysis; whereas it would be less inconvenient for the prosecution to discharge a burden of proving that the substance exceeded the prescribed limit of morphine.

Impact of the Human Rights Act 1998

Currently, all occasions involving reverse burdens of proof on the accused, whether at common law or expressly or impliedly imposed by statute, are required to be construed in compliance with the Human Rights Act 1998 (HRA), which incorporates the European Convention for the Protection of Human Rights and Fundamental Freedoms (ECHR). Article 6(1) of the ECHR states that 'In the determination . . . of any criminal charge against him, everyone is entitled to a fair and public hearing within a reasonable time by an independent and impartial tribunal established by law . . .', and Art 6(2) declares, 'Everyone charged with a criminal offence shall be presumed innocent until proved guilty according to law.' Section 3(1) of the Human Rights Act 1998 enacts as follows: 'So far as it is possible to do so, primary legislation and subordinate legislation must be read and given effect in a way which is compatible with the Convention rights.' Section 4(2) of the HRA declares: 'If the court is satisfied that the provision is incompatible with a Convention right, it may make a declaration of that incompatibility.' Section 4(6) enacts, 'A declaration [of incompatibility] under this section . . . (a) does not affect the validity, continuing operation or enforcement of the provision in respect of which it is given; and (b) is not binding on the parties to the proceedings in which it was made.' The appellate courts have, on several occasions, been faced with arguments that placing a legal burden of proof on a defendant in a criminal case contravenes Art 6(2) of the Convention. The essence of the argument is that if the defendant faces the possibility of a conviction on the basis that the specified offence presumes (or deems) certain facts to exist unless the defendant can prove to the contrary, this derogates from the presumption of innocence and is contrary to Art 6(2). The same argument can be advanced if a statute requires that a defendant be convicted unless he can prove certain facts as part of his defence. On these occasions the solutions that may be adopted by the courts are, first, to decide whether the provision imposing a legal burden on the accused (reverse legal burden) may be 'read down' within s 3(1) of the HRA to impose an evidential burden only on the accused. Second, if this is not possible, then the court may issue a declaration of incompatibility within s 4(2) of the HRA. The effect of such declaration is stated in s 4(6) of the HRA 1998.

The issue that was raised in *R v Lambert* [2002] 2 AC 545 was whether s 5(3) of the Misuse of Drugs Act 1971 compromised the presumption of innocence and whether s 3 HRA 1998 was applicable. In *Lambert*, the accused was charged and convicted of possessing cocaine with intent to supply contrary to s 5(3) of the 1971 Act. Section 28 of the Act afforded a defence if the defendant could prove that 'he neither believed nor suspected that the substance was a controlled drug'. The defendant possessed a bag but alleged that he was not aware of all of its contents. He was convicted and appealed. The House of Lords decided that the events occurred before the coming into force of the 1998 Act but in an *obiter* pronouncement declared that s 28 of the Act enacted that *prima facie* knowledge of the contents of the bag was not an ingredient of the offence which the prosecution was required to prove. In order to demonstrate lack of knowledge, according to the section, the defendant was required to prove this element and, in so enacting, the section had the tendency to undermine the presumption of innocence. However, in accordance with s 3(1) of the HRA 1998, it was possible to 'read down' s 28 of the Misuse of Drugs Act 1971 so as to impose only an evidential burden on the defendant. In other words, the 'reading down' of the section was because the court decided that the imposition of a legal burden on the defendant was a disproportionate means of achieving the justified aim of easing the difficult task of the prosecution in proving the defendant's knowledge in this type of case, namely, where the drugs are in a container. The court adopted the approach of the European Court of Human Rights (ECtHR) in arriving at its decision in *Salabiaku v France* (1988) 13 EHRR 379. The approach was:

- Member states were free to enact criminal rules and to define constituent elements of criminal conduct.
- Reverse burdens (or presumptions) operate in every jurisdiction. The European Convention does not prohibit such presumptions in principle but requires the reverse burdens to be kept within certain limits.

- The limits concerning such reverse burden provisions require the State to take into account the right of the defendant to a fair trial and to strike a balance between the interests of the State and the rights of the defendant. (Dickson CJC)

The tests laid down by Lord Steyn in *R v Lambert* concerning reverse legal burdens and the duty to ensure a fair trial were (a) whether the statutory reversal of the burden of proof interfered with the defendant's Convention rights under Art 6(2) and, if so, (b) whether there is objective justification of the legislative provision, i.e. the mischief at which the provision was aimed, and (c) the question of proportionality, i.e. the provision must not be greater than is necessary to deal with the mischief.

In the case of *Lambert*, regarding the first question the court decided that knowledge was an ingredient of the offence and therefore s 28 derogated from the presumption of innocence. The court adopted the reasoning of Dickson CJC in the Canadian Supreme Court decision in *R v Whyte* (1988) 51 DLR 481:

JUDGMENT

'If an accused is required to prove some fact on a balance of probabilities to avoid conviction, the provision violates the presumption of innocence because it permits a conviction in spite of a reasonable doubt in the mind of the tribunal of fact as to the guilt of the accused.'

(Dickson CJC)

In *Lambert*, Lord Clyde adopted a similar line of reasoning thus:

JUDGMENT

'It would be possible for an accused person to be convicted where the jury believed he might well be innocent but have not been persuaded that he probably did not know the nature of what he possessed. The jury may have reasonable doubt as to his guilt in respect of his knowledge of the nature of what he possessed but still be required to convict. Looking to the potentially serious consequences of a conviction at least in respect of class A drugs it does not seem to me that such a burden is acceptable.'

The test of justification or the pursuit of a legitimate aim involves Parliament enacting a provision (creating a crime) in order to 'free' society of a particular type of conduct, i.e. the relevant mischief. The mischief must be clearly identified. In *Lambert*, the mischief involved sophisticated drug dealers and couriers concealing drugs in containers, thereby enabling the suspect to claim that he was unaware of the contents, if apprehended. The test of proportionality requires the State to demonstrate that the imposition of the legal burden on the defendant meets the legitimate aims of the provision and does not exceed that goal and compromise the presumption of innocence (Dickson CJC).

The imposition of a legal burden of proof on the accused to prove the relevant issue on a balance of probabilities is a drastic measure. This may result in the conviction of the defendant if they are incapable of proving a relevant fact, even though there might be a reasonable doubt as to their guilt. In a way, it could be argued that *prima facie* reverse burdens compromise the presumption of innocence, subject to the justification and proportionality requirements.

JUDGMENT

> 'I am satisfied that the transfer of the legal burden in section 28 does not satisfy the criterion of proportionality. Viewed in its place in the current legal system section 28 of the 1971 Act is a disproportionate reaction to perceived difficulties facing the prosecution in drugs cases. It would be sufficient to impose an evidential burden on the accused. It follows that section 28 is incompatible with Convention rights.'
>
> (Lord Steyn in *R v Lambert*)

The impact of *Lambert* on the law regarding reverse burdens of proof may be summarised as follows:

1. Such provisions, without more, do not necessarily violate the presumption of innocence. In other words, some reverse burden provisions may be justified as legitimate.
2. States are required to keep such provisions 'within reasonable limits'.
3. The test of whether such provisions are within reasonable limits will depend on whether a proper balance has been struck between the interests of the public with regard to the issues at stake and the rights of the defendant.
4. A specific provision would be required to satisfy the test of proportionality. This involves asking whether there was a pressing need for the burden to be imposed on the defendant.
5. In appropriate cases a statutory provision that the defendant 'prove' an issue may be construed as imposing an evidential, as opposed to a legal, burden on the defendant, thus 'reading down' the provision.
6. These considerations apply equally to legal burdens impliedly imposed by Parliament on the defendant. Thus, the guidelines laid down in *R v Hunt* need to be read subject to Art 6(2) of the Convention.

Lord Steyn's opinion was elaborated on by Lord Nicholls in *R v Johnstone* [2003] 1 WLR 1736. In this case, the House of Lords upheld a provision under the Trademarks Act 1994 imposing a legal burden on the defendant to prove that 'he honestly and reasonably believed that there was no infringement of the registered trademark'. He was found guilty. The leading opinion was delivered by Lord Nicholls, who referred to a number of factors that are required to be taken into account in deciding whether a reverse burden of proof had been legitimately imposed on the defendant. These are:

- The serious nature of the offence and the punishment that may be meted out on a guilty defendant. The more serious the offence and punishment, the more compelling must be the reasons for imposing a legal burden on the defendant.
- The extent and nature of the factual matters required to be proved by the defendant and their importance relative to matters required to be proved by the prosecution.

- Whether the burden relates to facts that are readily provable by the defendant, such as matters within his knowledge.

Lord Nicholls added that in evaluating these factors the court's role is one of review. Parliament, not the court, is charged with the primary responsibility for deciding, as a matter of policy, what should be the constituent elements of an offence. The court will reach a different conclusion from the legislature only when the legislature has attached insufficient importance to the presumption of innocence. Of course, at the risk of stating the obvious, Lord Nicholls was dealing with a different statutory provision from Lord Steyn.

In *AG Reference (No 1 of 2004)* [2004] EWCA 1025 (there were five consolidated appeals concerning reverse burdens), Lord Woolf CJ observed that there was a significant difference in opinion between Lords Steyn in *Lambert* and Nicholls in *Johnstone* and suggested that Lord Nicholls's view ought to be followed. The Court of Appeal also laid down a number of guidelines for the benefit of the lower courts (see para 52 of Lord Woolf's judgment).

In *AG Reference (No 4 of 2002); Sheldrake v DPP* [2004] All ER (D) 169 (two consolidated appeals), Lord Bingham referred to Lord Woolf's guidelines (in *AG Ref (No 1 of 2004)*) and decided that the differences in emphasis by Lords Steyn and Nicholls were explicable by reference to the different subject matter in the two cases under consideration and rejected Lord Woolf's guidelines in so far as they are inconsistent with the guidelines laid down in the current case. The court is required to focus on the statutory provision and strike a balance between the interests of the community and the fundamental rights of the individual. Lord Bingham then reviewed the leading cases and proceeded to lay down a definitive set of guidelines (see para 21 of Lord Bingham's judgment):

1. The overriding concern is that the trial of the defendant should be fair.
2. The Convention does not outlaw presumptions or reverse burdens but requires these to be kept within reasonable limits.
3. It is the prerogative of each State to define the constituent elements of a criminal offence excluding the requirement of *mens rea*.
4. The substance and effect of any presumption adverse to the defendant must be examined and be reasonable. The test for compatibility with Convention rights is 'reasonableness' and 'proportionality'.
5. Factors that are to be taken into account to evaluate reasonableness include maintenance of the rights of the defence; flexibility in the application of the presumption; retention by the court of a power to assess the evidence; the extent and nature of the factual matters required to be proved by the accused, and their importance relative to the matters required to be proved by the prosecution; and the extent to which a burden on the accused relates to facts that, if they exist, are readily proved by him as to matters within his own knowledge or to which he has ready access.
6. Security concerns do not absolve member states from their duty to observe basic standards of fairness.
7. The justifiability of any infringement of the presumption of innocence may only be resolved by an examination of all the facts and circumstances of the particular provision, as is applicable in the particular case.
8. A sound starting point is to remember that if an accused is required to

prove a fact on a balance of probability to avoid conviction, this may permit the accused to be convicted in spite of the fact-finding tribunal having a reasonable doubt as to the guilt of the accused. This consequence of a reverse burden of proof should colour the court's approach when evaluating the reasons as to why the public interest will be served to an extent that justifies placing the legal burden on the accused. The more serious the offence and punishment that might flow from a conviction, the more compelling must be the reasons.

9. The interpretative obligation of the court under s 3 of the Human Rights Act 1998 is a very strong and far-reaching task and may require the court to depart from the legislative intention of Parliament. The court will reach a different conclusion from the legislature only when it is apparent that the legislature has attached insufficient importance to the fundamental right of an individual to be presumed innocent until proved guilty.
10. A Convention-compliant interpretation under s 3 HRA 1998 is a primary remedial measure and a declaration of incompatibility under s 4 of the 1998 Act is an exceptional course for the court to take. During the passage of the Bill (Human Rights) through Parliament, the promoters of the Bill told both Houses of Parliament that it was envisaged that the need for a declaration of incompatibility would rarely arise.
11. There is a limit beyond which a Convention-compliant interpretation is not possible, for it would change the substance of the provision completely. In these circumstances a declaration of incompatibility would be appropriate. This would be a measure of last resort.

JUDGMENT

'The overriding concern is that the trial should be fair, and the presumption of innocence is a fundamental right directed to that end. The Convention does not outlaw presumptions of fact or law but requires that these should be kept within reasonable limits and should not be arbitrary. It is open to states to define the constituent elements of a criminal offence, excluding the requirement of *mens rea*. But the substance and effect of any presumption adverse to a defendant must be examined and must be reasonable. Relevant to any judgment on reasonableness or proportionality will be the opportunity given to the defendant to rebut the presumption, maintenance of the rights of the defence, flexibility in application of the presumption, retention by the court of a power to assess the evidence, the importance of what is at stake and the difficulty which a prosecutor may face in the absence of a presumption. Security concerns do not absolve member states from their duty to observe basic standards of fairness. The justifiability of any infringement of the presumption of innocence cannot be resolved by any rule of thumb, but on examination of all the facts and circumstances of the particular provision as applied in the particular case.'

(Lord Bingham)

Lord Bingham then declared that the task of the court is never to decide whether a reverse burden of proof ought to be imposed on the defendant, but always to assess whether a burden enacted by Parliament unjustifiably infringes the presumption of innocence. This involves balancing the interests of the defendant to a fair trial with the needs of the public to be adequately protected.

Application of the principles to the facts of the cases

In *AG Reference (No 4 of 2002)*, the defendant was indicted on two counts under s 11(1) of the Terrorism Act 2000, namely being a member of the proscribed organisation 'Hamas' and professing to be a member of that organisation. Section 11(2) used the expression 'defence to prove', and this has the effect of imposing a legal burden on the defendant. At the conclusion of the case of the prosecution the judge ruled that there was no case to answer, and a verdict of not guilty was entered in respect of each count. The Attorney General took a reference and the issue was whether the defence within s 11(2) imposed a legal rather than an evidential burden on the defendant and, if a legal burden was imposed, whether it was compatible with the Convention. The House of Lords decided that s 11(2) of the Act *prima facie* imposed a legal burden of proof on the defendant. Adopting the 'justifiability' and 'proportionality' considerations, the statutory provision went beyond what was necessary for the protection of society and impinged on the presumption of innocence. The court decided that it may well be all but impossible for the defendant to prove that he had not taken part in the activities of such an organisation. Organisations that promote terror throughout the world, by definition, do not keep minutes of meetings, records or documents, and other members would be unlikely to come forward and testify on his behalf, while it is also possible that the defendant may have been a member before the organisation became proscribed (this eventuality was not provided for in the statutory provision). Applying s 3 HRA 1998, the interpretative function of the court was to adopt a construction that was compatible with Art 6(2) of the Convention. Accordingly, s 11(2) would be 'read down' and construed as imposing only an evidential burden on the defendant.

In *DPP v Sheldrake* [2004] QB 487 the defendant was convicted of being in charge of a motor vehicle in a public place after consuming so much alcohol that the proportion of it in his breath, blood or urine exceeded the prescribed limit contrary to s 5(1)(b) of the Road Traffic Act 1988. Section 5(2) enacted a defence for the accused to *prove* that at the time of the alleged commission of the offence there was no likelihood of his driving the vehicle while the proportion of alcohol exceeded the prescribed limit. The justices ruled that s 5(2) imposed a legal burden on the defendant and this did not interfere with the presumption of innocence. The defendant was convicted and appealed to the High Court by way of case stated. The High Court by a majority (two to one) allowed the appeal and decided that the provision will be 'read down' to impose only an evidential burden on the defendant. The House of Lords unanimously allowed the appeal and decided that s 5(2) created a legal burden of proof and was not incompatible with Art 6(2) of the Convention. The section pursued a legitimate aim and was proportionate. Lord Bingham expressed his opinion in the following manner:

JUDGMENT

'It may not be very profitable to debate whether section 5(2) [of the Road Traffic Act 1988] infringes the presumption of innocence. It may be assumed that it does. Plainly the provision is directed to a legitimate object: the prevention of death, injury and damage caused by unfit drivers. Does the provision meet the tests of acceptability identified in the Strasbourg jurisprudence? In my view, it plainly does. I do not regard the burden placed on the defendant as beyond reasonable limits or in any way arbitrary. It is not objectionable to criminalise a defendant's conduct in these circumstances without requiring a prosecutor to prove criminal intent. The defendant has a full opportunity to show that there was no likelihood of his driving, a matter so closely conditioned by his own knowledge and state of mind at the material time as to make it much more appropriate for him to prove on the balance of probabilities that he would not have been likely to drive than for the prosecutor to prove, beyond reasonable doubt, that he would. I do not think that imposition of a legal burden went beyond what was necessary. If a driver tries and fails to establish a defence under section 5(2), I would not regard the resulting conviction as unfair.'

In *R v Makuwa* (2006), a case on political asylum, the court decided that, on construction of the relevant statutory provision, an element of the defence involved the status of the defendant who bore the evidential burden of establishing her 'refugee' status, but the legal burden of rebutting this allegation rested on the prosecution.

CASE EXAMPLE

R v Makuwa [2006] EWCA Crim 175

The defendant was charged under s 3 of the Forgery and Counterfeiting Act 1981 with using a false instrument (a forged passport), presenting it to an immigration officer in an attempt to gain entry into the UK. She claimed that she fled the Democratic Republic of Congo out of fear for her safety. She raised the defence of political asylum under s 31 of the Immigration and Asylum Act 1999, relying on her refugee status. Section 31(1) enacts as follows:

> 'It is a defence for a refugee charged with an offence to which this section applies to show that, having come to the United Kingdom directly from a country where his life or freedom was threatened (within the meaning of the Refugee Convention), he (a) presented himself to the authorities in the United Kingdom without delay, (b) showed good cause for his illegal entry or presence, and (c) made a claim for asylum as soon as was reasonably practicable after his arrival in the United Kingdom . . .'.

The trial judge directed the jury that the legal burden of proving all the elements of the defence under s 31 rested on the defendant, including the fact that she was a refugee. The defendant was convicted and appealed.

Held

The Court of Appeal allowed the appeal and decided that the judge had misdirected the jury. The defendant bore an evidential burden to establish her refugee status but the Crown had a legal burden to rebut such an allegation. The remainder of the statutory defence was compatible with her Convention rights and imposed a legal burden on the defendant.

JUDGMENT

'The offences in respect of which s 31(1) provides a defence are those set out in Pt 1 of the Forgery and Counterfeiting Act 1981 (making, copying, possessing and using false instruments, including passports), offences under s 24A of the Immigration Act 1971 (obtaining or seeking to obtain entry by deception) and offences under s 26(1)(d) of that Act (falsification of documents and possession of a false passport for use for the purposes of that Act). In each case the prosecution is obliged to establish to the usual standard all the ingredients of the offence just as it would if the Defendant were not a refugee. The effect of s 31(1) is simply to provide a defence to a defined class of persons in prescribed circumstances. It does not therefore impose on the Defendant the burden of disproving an essential ingredient of the offence.

'The mischiefs at which these statutory provisions are aimed are many and various, but the principal mischief that Parliament must have had in mind when enacting s 31(1) was the use of false passports and other identity papers by those who are not entitled to enter the United Kingdom in order to obtain entry. It has been recognised both in Strasbourg and in this country that there is a legitimate public interest in the implementation of a lawful immigration policy which may provide a justification for measures that would otherwise involve an infringement of Convention rights, provided that their effect is not disproportionate to the aim which they seek to achieve.

'Having defined a refugee, the judge should then tell the jury (if the matter is disputed) that the burden is on the prosecution to prove that the Defendant is not a refugee. If they are sure that he is not, that is the end of the matter as far as this defence is concerned. However, if they think he may be a refugee, they must go on to consider the other matters that have to be proved. These should be separately identified and the jury should be told that it is for the Defendant to satisfy them of each matter on the balance of probabilities.

'In a matter of this kind the application of the appropriate test for refugee status and the correct burden of proof have a significant part to play in the protection of those seeking asylum from the imposition of penalties under the criminal law. We are satisfied that the judge's directions were defective.'

(Moore-Bick LJ)

The principles of justification and proportionality, as stated above, were applied by the Court of Appeal in *R v Keogh* (2007). The Court of Appeal reversed the decision of the trial judge and decided that ss 2(3) and 3(4) of the Official Secrets Act 1989, which purported to reverse the legal burden of proof, could be 'read down' so as to impose an evidential burden on the defendant. The reasons were that these provisions were incompatible with the presumption of innocence because they were unjustifiable and disproportionate and the 1989 Act may operate effectively without the imposition of reverse legal burdens.

CASE EXAMPLE

R v Keogh [2007] 1 WLR 1500 (CA)

The defendant was a civil servant, employed in the communications centre in Whitehall. He acquired possession of a highly confidential record in the form of a letter of a meeting on 16 April 2004 between the prime minister and the president of the United States. The meeting was primarily concerned with UK and US policy in Iraq. The defendant photocopied the letter and delivered it to Mr Anthony Clarke, a Member of Parliament and a strong opponent of the Iraq War. Mr Clarke reported the matter to No 10 Downing Street and the photocopy was delivered to the police. The accused was charged with offences under ss 2(3) and 3(4) of the Official Secrets Act 1989. These offences involve making a damaging disclosure of any information, document or other article relating to defence (s 2), or making a damaging disclosure of any information, document or other article relating to international relations (s 3). Defences were enacted requiring the defendant to prove that at the time of the alleged offence he did not know and had no reasonable cause to believe that the information, document or article in question related to defence (s 2) or to international relations (s 3) or that its disclosure would be damaging. At a preliminary hearing the trial judge ruled that the statutory defences imposed reverse legal burdens of proof on a defendant in respect of the mental element of the offences. The defendant appealed.

Held

The Court of Appeal reversed the ruling of the trial judge on the ground that an element of the offence lay not so much in disclosing the information, but in doing so when knowing or having reasonable cause to believe that it would be damaging. The reverse burden imposed on the defendant was arduous, disproportionate and without justification when all the relevant facts were more readily accessible to the prosecution than to the defendant.

JUDGMENT

'If the construction for which [counsel for the Crown] contends were correct, the defendant would be required to disprove a substantial ingredient of the offence. It is plain that this would constitute a significant infringement of the presumption of innocence. It would not be fanciful to conceive of a situation in which the jury would find a defendant guilty of an offence under s 2 despite entertaining reasonable doubt as to whether the defendant knew or had reasonable cause to believe that the document in question related to defence, or that its disclosure would be damaging. The same considerations apply in relation to a charge based on an alleged infringement of s 3.

'We have concluded that the 1989 Act can operate effectively without the imposition of the reverse burdens that ss 2(3) and 3(4) of the 1989 Act would impose according to their natural meaning. To accord them that meaning would be disproportionate and unjustifiable. Because those subsections, if given their natural meaning, are incompatible with art 6 of the convention, they should be "read down".'

(Lord Phillips CJ)

In *R v Webster* (2010), the Court of Appeal decided that the reverse onus of proof provision expressly created by s 2 of the Prevention of Corruption Act 1916 was no longer necessary and was unreasonable and disproportionate. Accordingly, it was 'read down' pursuant to s 3 of the Human Rights Act 1998 so as to impose only an evidential burden on the defendant.

CASE EXAMPLE

R v Webster [2010] EWCA Crim 2819

The defendant was charged under s 1(2) of the Public Bodies Corrupt Practices Act 1889 for making a corrupt gift to a public official. Section 2 of the Prevention of Corruption Act 1916 introduces a 'deeming' provision to the effect that a payment of money or a gift to a public official is deemed to be made corruptly until the contrary is proved. The trial judge directed the jury that the burden of proof was imposed on the defendant to establish that the payment was not made corruptly. The defendant was convicted and appealed. The Court of Appeal allowed the appeal, quashed the conviction and decided that the provision was disproportionate and unjustifiably interfered with the presumption of innocence. It would be read down pursuant to s 3 of the Human Rights Act 1998 so as to impose an evidential burden on the defendant to raise an issue as to whether a gift had been made corruptly and with the ultimate legal burden to prove that the gift was made corruptly imposed on the prosecution.

Likewise in the Scottish decision, *Adam (Derek) v HM Advocate* [2013] HCJAC 14, the High Court of Justiciary on appeal decided that a reverse legal burden under the Dangerous Dogs Act 1991 was not unreasonable and disproportionate and it was unnecessary to read down the provision. The reverse legal burden imposed an obligation on the defendant to prove that he had transferred control of the dog to a person whom he reasonably believed was a fit and proper person to have such control. The court decided that the legitimate aim of the provision was to address the mischief of dogs attacking members of the public, in particular children, in public places.

CASE EXAMPLE

Adam (Derek) v HM Advocate [2013] HCJAC 14

On 29 August 2010 two Rottweilers owned by the defendant attacked and mauled a ten-year-old girl in a public place. The defendant was charged with an offence under s 3(1) of the Dangerous Dogs Act 1991. Section 3(2) imposed a legal burden on him to prove that he had transferred control of the dog to a person who he reasonably believed was a fit and proper person to have such control. The defendant argued that the requirement under s 3(2) ought to be read down in accordance with s 3(1) of the Human Rights Act 1998. In rejecting this argument the court applied the principles in *Sheldrake v DPP* and decided that, having regard to the legitimate purpose of the provision, the imposition of the legal burden on the defendant was not disproportionate.

JUDGMENT

'One of the purposes of the Act was to prevent a serious danger to the public. To this extent it is analogous to the purpose of s.5 of the Road Traffic Act 1988, which was concerned with the prevention of death, injury and damage caused by unfit drivers . . . In light of this legitimate object of the 1991 Act, we see nothing objectionable in a requirement on a person accused of an offence under s.3(2) to discharge the legal burden of proving that at the material time the dog (or, in this case, dogs) was at the material time in the charge of another person, and that the accused reasonably believed that other person to be a fit and proper person to be in charge of the dog. The accused has a full opportunity to show that he had transferred control of the dog to another person at the material time, and that he had a reasonable belief as to the fitness of the transferee. In Lord Bingham of Cornhill's words in *Sheldrake*, these are matters so closely conditioned by his own knowledge and state of mind at the material time as to make it much more appropriate for him to prove them on the balance of probabilities, rather than for the prosecutor to prove beyond reasonable doubt that he had no reasonable belief as to the fitness of the transferee.

'In all the circumstances, balancing the interests of the public and the appellant's fundamental rights, we do not consider that the imposition of a legal burden in s. 3(2) of the 1991 Act is unacceptable, unreasonable or disproportionate. There is accordingly no need to read down the subsection so as to place only an evidential burden on the appellant.'

(Lord Menzies)

By the same reasoning the Court of Appeal in *R v Williams (Orette)* (2013) decided that on a charge of possessing a readily convertible imitation firearm, the imposition of a legal burden on the defendant to prove that he did not know or have any reason to suspect that the firearm was readily convertible satisfied the tests of justification and proportionality. The court decided that there were compelling reasons why Parliament imposed a legal burden on the defendant. Firearms offences have the effect of creating serious problems and compromising public safety. The defence created in s 1(5) of the Firearms Act 1982 involved facts within the knowledge of the defendant that may not compromise the presumption of innocence, but that the prosecution may have insuperable difficulty in proving.

CASE EXAMPLE

R v Williams (Orette) [2013] 1 WLR 1200 (CA)

The defendant was charged with possession of a prohibited weapon contrary to s 5(1)(a) of the Firearms Act 1968, as amended. The relevant weapon was an imitation firearm capable of firing blanks, but the prosecution alleged that the weapon was readily convertible into a live firearm. Section 1(5) of the Firearms Act 1982 created a defence to the effect that the defendant did not know or suspect that the weapon was readily convertible into a live firearm. The trial judge ruled that a legal burden was placed on the defendant and the jury decided that such burden was not discharged and he was found guilty. He appealed on the ground that the judge made an inaccurate ruling as to the incidence of the legal burden regarding the defence. The Court of Appeal dismissed the appeal and affirmed the conviction on the grounds that the imposition of the legal burden on the defendant achieved a reasonable and proportionate response to gun crime and afforded an acceptable balance between the protection of the public and the defendant's right to a fair trial. The defence turned on the state of knowledge of the defendant at the relevant time which would have been difficult for the prosecution to prove to the criminal standard.

JUDGMENT

'. . . where Parliament has, by section 1(5) of the 1982 Act, considered it appropriate that a defence of lack of knowledge or reason to suspect in such cases be available it is, in our judgment, justified and proportionate that the legal burden of such defence – a defence made available as an exception or modification to the strict liability approach – be placed on the accused.

'Further, the question of knowledge (or lack of it) involves facts readily available to the accused – he knows the circumstances in which and from whom he obtained the item. On the other hand, it could be very difficult indeed for prosecutors, and would be a real deterrent to prosecution let alone successful prosecution, if the burden were placed on the Crown to obtain the necessary evidence to disprove a case that the accused had neither knowledge nor reason to suspect.'

(Davis LJ)

Burdens of proof in criminal cases

Prosecution	**Defendant**
- elements of the offence	- elements of the defence
↓	↓
- evidential burden	- generally evidential burden
↓	↓
- decision of the judge (tribunal of law)	- decision of the judge (tribunal of law)
↓	↓
- sufficient evidence to justify a guilty verdict	- sufficient evidence to raise the issue
↓	↓
- legal burden of proof	- exceptionally a legal burden of proof may be imposed on the defendant
↓	↓
- decision of the jury or tribunal of fact	- decision of the jury or tribunal of fact
↓	↓
- beyond a reasonable doubt/	- balance of probabilities
- sure of guilt	

Figure 2.4 Discharge of the legal burden of proof

ACTIVITY

Self-test questions

1. Michael is charged with an offence under the Road Traffic Act 1988, s 12 which states:

   'A person who promotes or takes part in a competition or trial (other than a race or trial of speed) involving the use of motor vehicles on a public highway shall be guilty of an offence unless the competition or trial is authorised, and is conducted in accordance with conditions imposed, by or under regulations under this section.'

Consider the burden and standard of proof.

2. Consider whether each of the following directions to a jury represents a correct statement of the law:
   (a) 'Of course anyone may discharge a gun by accident and that would not be within the indictment of using a firearm with intent to avoid arrest. But it is for the prisoner, not the prosecution, to satisfy you that this happened accidentally.'
   (b) 'If you are to find the accused not guilty on this charge of reckless driving by reason of automatism he must persuade you of that on a balance of probabilities.'

2.3 Evidential burden

The evidential burden is the obligation to adduce sufficient evidence to raise an issue to the satisfaction of the tribunal of law. In a case tried by judge and jury, the discharge of the evidential burden is for the judge to decide. In contrast, the discharge of the legal burden is for the jury to decide. Thus, a party with a legal burden of proof is required to surmount two hurdles. First, he must adduce sufficient evidence to prevent the judge from withdrawing the issue from the jury to discharge the evidential burden. Second, the party is required to convince the tribunal of fact of the truth of the assertion, i.e. discharge his legal burden. If the evidential burden has not been discharged, based on a ruling by the judge, it follows that the legal burden attached to that issue will equally not be discharged. In addition, a party may bear an evidential burden without a corresponding legal burden, such as a defence of loss of control, self-defence or duress in a criminal case. In such a case, if the defendant fails to discharge the evidential burden, the issue will not be considered by the tribunal of fact; but if the evidential burden imposed on the accused has been discharged, a duty is imposed on the judge to leave the defence to the jury. Normally this will be done through the defendant actively asserting a defence, but the same result will be achieved if evidence emerges at the trial suggesting the presence of a defence even though not put forward by the defendant. In *R v Calvert* [2000] All ER (D) 2071, the Court of Appeal quashed the defendant's conviction for rape on the ground that, despite counsel for the defendant not positively raising the defence of consent, the existence of some evidence of consent required the judge to direct the jury on the evidence.

2.3.1 Shifting of the evidential burden

The burden of adducing sufficient evidence to justify a favourable finding may be distributed between different parties during the course of a trial. The concept of the 'shifting' of the evidential burden refers to the risk of an adverse finding run by an opponent when a party discharges the evidential burden; for example, where the prosecution has discharged its evidential burden by a rejection of a 'no case' submission by the defendant, the defendant runs the risk that the jury may find him or her guilty of the offence if they do not adduce any evidence. However, such a proposition may only be supported if it is assumed that:

(a) there is only one issue to be tried. In a criminal case there is a general issue of whether the defendant is guilty but there are multiple specific issues that involve the evidential burden that answer the general question; and
(b) that the evidence adduced by the prosecution in discharge of the evidential burden is sufficient to convict the defendant.

There is no such indication before the jury's verdict. On the contrary, there are multiple issues in a trial and the evidential burden on these issues does not shift as a matter of substantive law.

2.4 Standards of proof

The term 'standard' or 'quantum' of proof refers to the extent to which the judge and the jury, as separate bodies, are required to be satisfied that the proponent has made out their case. This applies to both the legal and the evidential burdens of proof. The expression 'standard of proof' refers to the quality of evidence adduced in support of the relevant allegation.

It follows that the party bearing the legal burden is required to adduce more persuasive evidence on a point than their opponent. If the evidence adduced on both sides is equally persuasive or credible, the proponent must lose the case. Similarly, if the opponent has raised a serious doubt about the accuracy of the facts as alleged by the proponent, the latter has not proved their case.

The question in issue is, by how much must the evidence of the proponent exceed the evidence supporting the opponent's case in order to justify a favourable result for the proponent? In other words, what is the proportionate amount and quality of evidence required to be adduced by the proponent? This varies with criminal and civil cases.

2.4.1 Criminal cases

The standard of proof imposed on the prosecution in order to discharge the legal burden of proof is 'beyond reasonable doubt'. This is the highest standard recognised in law and has been adopted for policy reasons, namely that it is better to allow guilty persons to be set free than allow an innocent person to be wrongfully convicted. The phrase 'beyond reasonable doubt' does not mean 'beyond a shadow of a doubt'. This is much too high a standard. Likewise, the phrase does not mean a 'preponderance of probability' or a 'balance of probabilities'. This is the civil standard of proof and is treated as too low to be used to rebut the presumption of innocence. Denning J in *Miller v Minister of Pensions* [1947] 2 All ER 372, explained thus:

JUDGMENT

'It [the criminal standard] need not reach certainty, but must carry a high degree of probability. It does not mean beyond a shadow of a doubt. The law would fail to protect the community if it admitted fanciful possibilities to deflect the course of justice. If the evidence is so strong against a man as to leave only a remote possibility in his favour which can be dismissed with the sentence, "Of course it is possible, but not in the least probable", the case is proved beyond reasonable doubt, but nothing short of that will suffice.'

There have been several mis-directions in the past because judges have adopted a variety of different phrases in place of the time-honoured expression 'beyond reasonable doubt', for example 'satisfied' in *R v Hepworth* [1955] 2 QB 600; the jury was told that they need to be 'satisfied, anything less will not do' in *R v Gourley* [1981] Crim LR 334; 'pretty certain' in *R v Law* [1961] Cr LR 52; 'reasonably sure' in *R v Head* (1961) 45 Cr App R 225; 'you must be satisfied so that you are reasonably sure' in *R v Sweeney* (1983) *The Times*, 22 October; 'reasonably satisfied' in *R v Kritz* [1950] 1 KB 82.

The phrase 'satisfied so that you can feel sure' of the accused's guilt is an acceptable alternative to the time-honoured formula. In *R v Summers* (1952) 36 Cr App R 14, Lord Goddard said:

JUDGMENT

'If a jury is told that it is their duty to regard the evidence and see that it satisfies them so that they can feel sure when they return a verdict of guilty, that is much better than using the expression "reasonable doubt" and I hope in future that that will be done. I never use the expression when summing up. I always tell the jury that, before they convict they must feel sure and must be satisfied that the prosecution have established the guilt of the prisoner.'

Lord Goddard's direction has found favour with the Judicial Studies Board, which has adopted it as part of its specimen direction for trial judges. The JSB specimen direction declares: 'How does the prosecution succeed in proving the defendant's guilt? The answer is – by making you sure of it. Nothing less will do. If after considering all the evidence you are sure that the defendant is guilty, you must return a verdict of "Guilty". If you are not sure, your verdict must be "Not Guilty".'

The courts have offered advice on many occasions to the effect that the criminal standard of proof is not a matter of some precise formula or particular form of words used by the judge, provided that the correct standard of proof has been conveyed to the jury. In *Ferguson v R* [1979] 1 WLR 94, Lord Scarman observed, '. . . though the law requires no particular formula, judges are wise, as a general rule, to adopt one'.

Moreover, it appears that not only the formula of words used by the judge will be examined by the appellate court, but the effect of the summing up as a whole to the jury, *per* Lord Goddard in *R v Kritz* [1950] 1 KB 82:

JUDGMENT

'It is not the particular formula that matters: it is the effect of the summing up. If the jury are made to understand that they have to be satisfied and must not return a verdict against a defendant unless they feel sure, and that the onus is all the time on the prosecution and not the defence, then whether the judge uses one form of language or another is neither here nor there. In the present case, [when] the judge told the jury that they must be reasonably satisfied and did not use the words, "satisfied beyond a reasonable doubt", he was not sufficiently stating the onus of proof.'

Occasionally, judges attempt to explain the type of doubt involved in the time-honoured formula, 'beyond reasonable doubt'. It is necessary to depict the type of doubt accurately. In *R v Stafford* [1968] 3 All ER 752, Edmund Davies LJ said:

JUDGMENT

'We do not agree with the trial judge when directing the jury upon the standard of proof he told them to remember that a reasonable doubt is "one for which you could give reasons if you were asked", and we dislike such a description or definition.'

In *R v Gray* (1974) 58 Cr App R 177, the trial judge inaccurately summed up to the jury thus:

JUDGMENT

'The standard of proof is sometimes said to be, beyond a reasonable doubt, and that means simply a doubt based upon good reason and not a fanciful doubt. It is the sort of doubt which might affect you in the conduct of your everyday affairs.'

The Court of Appeal held that this was a misdirection:

JUDGMENT

'If the learned judge had referred, for example, to the sort of doubt which may affect the mind of a person in the conduct of *important* affairs, then there could be no proper criticism . . . But in this case, the direction is open to legitimate criticism. The reference to "conduct of your everyday affairs" might suggest to a jury too low a standard of proof, because a doubt which would influence a decision on an important matter might sensibly be disregarded in a decision on some everyday affair.'

(Megaw LJ)

2.4.2 Discharge of the legal burden by the accused

In criminal cases the prosecution bears the legal burden of proof. In exceptional cases, as explored earlier, the accused may bear a legal burden of proof on a separate issue from the prosecution; for example the defence of insanity on occasions when Parliament expressly or impliedly imposes a legal burden on the accused. In these cases, the discharge of the legal burden requires the accused to prove the issue to the satisfaction of the jury or the tribunal of fact on a balance of probabilities.

CASE EXAMPLE

R v Carr-Briant [1943] KB 607

The accused, a director in a firm, was charged under the Prevention of Corruption Act 1906. In that case it was alleged that he gave or loaned £60 to an engineer employed in a government department. The defence was that the payment had not been made corruptly. The judge directed the jury that the standard of proof imposed on the accused was beyond a reasonable doubt. He was convicted and appealed.

The Court of Appeal allowed the appeal and decided that the judge had misdirected the jury as to the standard of proof which ought to have been on a balance of probabilities:

JUDGMENT

'In our judgment where, either by statute or at common law, some matter is presumed against the accused person "unless the contrary is proved", the jury should be directed that it is for them to decide whether the contrary is proved; that the burden of proof required is less than that required at the hands of the prosecution in proving the case beyond a reasonable doubt, and that the burden may be discharged by evidence satisfying the jury of the probability of that which the accused is called upon to establish.'

(Humphreys J)

It should be noted that on the authority of *R v Webster* (2010) (see earlier), the reverse onus provision under the Prevention of Corruption Act has now been 'read down' under the Human Rights Act 1998 to impose only an evidential burden on the defendant.

2.4.3 Discharge of the legal burden in civil cases

In civil proceedings the traditional standard of proof imposed on the party with the legal burden is a balance of probabilities or a preponderance of probability; the proponent is required to prove that their case is more probable than that of their opponent. It follows that if the probabilities are equally balanced the party with the legal burden will not succeed. The explanation of the phrase 'balance of probabilities' was made out in *Miller v Minister of Pensions* [1947] 2 All ER 372, by Denning J thus:

JUDGMENT

'If at the end of the case the evidence turns the scale definitely one way or the other, the tribunal must decide accordingly, but if the evidence is so evenly balanced that the tribunal is unable to come to a determinate conclusion one way or the other, then the man must be given the benefit of the doubt . . . The case must be proved on a reasonable degree of probability, but not so high as is required in a criminal case. If the evidence is such that the tribunal can say: "We think it more probable than not", the burden is discharged, but, if the probabilities are equal, it is not.'

Crime alleged in civil proceedings

There are many instances in civil proceedings where a crime is alleged to have been committed by a party, for example the allegation by the insurer that the insured created the loss by arson in respect of a claim under a fire insurance policy. The issue that will be considered here is the standard of proof that is imposed on the party making an allegation that the other party committed a crime. The current position, after a great deal of conflicting decisions, is that the standard of proof remains the traditional civil standard on the balance of probabilities.

CASE EXAMPLE

Hornal v Neuberger Products Ltd [1957] 1 QB 247

In this case, the claimant in an action for breach of contract alleged that one of the directors of the defendant company had made a fraudulent representation to the claimant. The alleged fraudulent representation was that a lathe sold by the defendant had been reconditioned. The county court judge had stated that he was satisfied that the allegations were proved on a balance of probabilities but would not have been satisfied if the criminal standard had applied. The Court of Appeal decided that the judge had applied the correct standard. The justification for the rule was stated by Denning LJ, as follows:

JUDGMENT

'If the learned judge had referred, for example, to the sort of doubt which may affect the mind of a person in the conduct of *important* affairs, then there could be no proper criticism . . . But in this case, the direction is open to legitimate criticism. The reference to "conduct of your everyday affairs" might suggest to a jury too low a standard of proof, because a doubt which would influence a decision on an important matter might sensibly be disregarded in a decision on some everyday affair.'

(Megaw LJ)

JUDGMENT

'I think it would bring the law into contempt if a judge were to say that on the issue of warranty he finds the statement was made and that on the issue of fraud he finds it was not made . . . the judge had reviewed all the cases and held rightly that the standard of proof depends on the nature of the issue. The more serious the allegation the higher the degree of probability that is required: but it need not, in a civil case reach the very high standard required by the criminal law.'

The reference by Lord Denning to 'the higher degree of probability that is required' where the allegation is more serious has the appearance of creating degrees of probabilities within the traditional standard with regard to more serious allegations, a sort of sliding scale. This is a contradiction in terms. Indeed, in the same case, Morris LJ explained that the issue does not involve a sliding scale of probabilities but rather the weight or credibility of the evidence needed to tip the balance of probabilities.

JUDGMENT

'Though no court and no jury would give less careful consideration to issues lacking in gravity than to those marked by it, the very elements of gravity become a part of the whole range of circumstances which have to be weighed in the scale when deciding as to the balance of probabilities.'

Perhaps the most serious criminal allegation in civil proceedings is murder and again the standard of proof is on the balance of probabilities: see *Re Dellow's Will Trust* [1964] 1 All ER 771. In this case, the issue was whether a wife (the beneficiary under a will) had murdered her husband, a testator. The court decided that the standard of proof was on the balance of probabilities, *per* Ungoed Thomas J:

JUDGMENT

'It seems to me that in civil cases it is not so much that a different standard of proof is required in different circumstances varying according to the gravity of the issue, but the gravity of the issue becomes part of the circumstances which the court has to take into consideration in deciding whether or not the burden of proof has been discharged. The more serious the allegation the more cogent is the evidence required to overcome the unlikelihood of what is alleged and thus to prove it. This is perhaps a somewhat academic distinction.'

CASE EXAMPLE

Re H (Minors) [1996] AC 563

An application for a care order was made by a local authority in respect of a girl who alleged that her stepfather had sexually abused her over a considerable period of time. The stepfather was charged with indecent assault on the girl and was acquitted at his trial. The issue before the court was, despite his acquittal, whether a care order ought to be made; in particular, the standard of proof to be imposed on the local authority. The House of Lords decided that the standard of proof is the traditional standard; on the balance of probabilities, but subject to the proviso that the more serious the allegation, the clearer should be the evidence:

JUDGMENT

'When assessing the probabilities the court will have in mind a factor that the more serious the allegation the less likely it is that the event occurred and hence the stronger should be the evidence before the court concludes that the allegation is established on a balance of probability. Fraud is usually less likely than negligence. Deliberate physical injury is usually less likely than accidental physical injury . . . Built into the preponderance of probability standard is a generous degree of flexibility in respect of the seriousness of the allegation.'

(Lord Nicholls)

In *Re S-B (Children)* [2009] UKSC 17, the Supreme Court affirmed the decision in *Re H* and decided that in care proceedings the standard of proof is a balance of probabilities. In this case M, a mother, appealed against a decision upholding care and placement orders made in respect of two young children, J and W. The judge directed herself on the standard of proof as being that 'a real possibility' that M had caused the injuries to J meant that there was a real possibility that she would injure W. The Supreme Court allowed the appeal and decided that it is now settled law that the test to be applied is a balance of probabilities. A prediction as to future harm had to be based on findings of fact made on the balance of probabilities.

The function of the appellate court in care and similar proceedings is not to determine whether it would have come to the same decision as the trial judge, for such courts do not hear oral evidence from all the witnesses. Instead, the function of the appellate court is to determine whether the trial judge made incorrect rulings on points of law. The Court of Appeal reiterated this principle in *Re D (Children)* (2012) concerning care proceedings involving allegations of multiple rapes by a brother, J, aged 13, of his sister, K, aged 11. The court so decided despite inconsistencies in the complainant's evidence at interviews and the acquittal of the defendant in a criminal trial. The Court of Appeal acknowledged that the trial judge had assessed the witnesses over a sustained period of time and following *Re S-B (Children)* (2009), accurately ruled and applied the burden and standard of proof in the case:

JUDGMENT

'As has often been pointed out, the function of the Court of Appeal is not whether it agrees with the judge or not, because it does not have any of the advantages that the judge has in the assessment of evidence, but whether it can be demonstrated that the judge was plainly wrong on the basis of the evidence that he had. I cannot begin to say that I am satisfied that he is plainly wrong.

'There is no doubt there was a time when the view was taken that the more serious the allegation the clearer the proof had to be. *Re B (Care Proceedings)* [2008] UKHL 35, lays that view to rest in the clearest possible terms and makes it clear that, however grave the allegation, it is the simple balance of probabilities that is to be applied and the justification for that advanced by Baroness Hale is that of course the implications and the consequences may be just as serious one way as they are the other and that the judge, required as he or she is to make findings, must do so without regard to the gravity of consequences but only to the question as to whether the local authority or those making the allegations have satisfied the court on the balance of probabilities that those allegations have been established.'

(Hedley J in *Re D (Children)* [2012] EWCA Civ 1584)

In *R (on the application of Maughan) v Her Majesty's Senior Coroner for Oxfordshire* [2020] UKSC 46, in its landmark ruling the Supreme Court held that the standard of proof in Coroners' Inquests is the 'balance of probabilities' when determining an unlawful killing or suicide. The decision is important because it departs from the position that an unlawful killing needed to be proved beyond reasonable doubt. This is a bold interpretation of the statute. The law on the standard of proof in Coroners' Inquests is set out in Schedule to the Coroners (Inquests) Rules 2013 Form 2, note (iii). The court stated that it is to be interpreted as 'other enactment' and concluded that the 2013 Rules were a statement of the common law that existed at the time and had therefore not been codified putting it within the court's reach.

Third standard of proof?

There appear to be a number of anomalous civil proceedings where a different standard of proof is required to be achieved. Some of these are:

- Claims for rectification of documents requires 'strong, irrefragable evidence', as in *Roberts v Leicestershire County Council* [1961] Ch 555.
- Proof of change of domicile requires the person who must prove that their domicile has changed to adduce 'clear and unequivocal evidence', as in *Re Fuld's Estate (No 3)* [1968] P 675.
- A party who intends to rebut the presumption in favour of the formal validity of a marriage is required to adduce 'strong, distinct and satisfactory' evidence, as in *Piers v Piers* (1849) 2 HL Cas 331.
- Contempt of court in civil proceedings must be proved beyond reasonable doubt, as in *Re Bramblevale Ltd* [1970] Ch 128.
- Proceedings before the Solicitors Disciplinary Tribunal for professional misconduct are required to be proved to the criminal standard, as in *Re A Solicitor* [1993] QB 69.

2.4.4 Discharge of the evidential burden

The discharge of the evidential burden is a question of law for the judge to decide. The question is whether the proponent has adduced sufficient evidence of the issue to justify the judge putting the issue before the jury or the tribunal of fact, thus making it a 'live' issue. No precise formula has been laid down concerning the standard of proof or the quantum of evidence needed to discharge this burden.

Alternatively, where the evidential burden cast on a party has not been discharged, the issue will not be put to the jury or considered by the tribunal of fact, for lack of sufficient evidence. The judge exercises a filtering power to distinguish occasions when there is some evidence to support an allegation and occasions when the allegation is unsupported by evidence. This judicial function concerns the evidential burden.

To ascertain the standard of proof required, it is necessary to distinguish five types of cases:

(a) the position where the accused bears the evidential but not the legal burden of proof;

(b) occasions where the accused bears both the evidential and legal burdens of proof;

(c) the situation where the prosecution bears the evidential and legal burdens of proof;

(d) in civil cases when a party bears the evidential and legal burdens of proof; and

(e) in civil cases when a party bears only the evidential burden of proof.

Accused bears solely the evidential burden

These are occasions where the accused bears only the evidential burden without the corresponding legal burden on the same issue; an example would be in raising a defence such as loss of control, duress, self-defence, etc. In these circumstances, it is only necessary for them to adduce sufficient evidence of the issue that, in the view of the judge, may create the possibility of a reasonable doubt as to their guilt.

Per Lord Morris in *Bratty v AG for Northern Ireland* [1963] AC 386 (on the issue of non-insane automatism):

JUDGMENT

'There was no sufficient evidence, fit to be left to the jury, on which a jury might conclude that the appellant had acted unconsciously and involuntarily or which might leave a jury in reasonable doubt whether this might be so.'

The point here is that only if the issue becomes 'live', or a triable issue, would the same be required to be put to the tribunal of fact. If it does not become a triable issue the tribunal of fact does not consider it. The defendant, either by cross-examination of the prosecution witnesses or by evidence called on his behalf, or a combination of the two, is required to put before the court the relevant issue (defence) before it is capable of being considered by the tribunal of fact. In essence, the tribunal of fact (jury) is required to come to a verdict on the whole of the evidence that has been put before them, and if they have a reasonable doubt as to the accused's guilt they are required to acquit. Lord Bingham in *Sheldrake v DPP* (2004) was prompted to question whether it is a misnomer to refer here to an evidential burden of proof.

JUDGMENT

'An evidential burden is not a burden of proof. It is a burden of raising, on the evidence in the case, an issue as to the matter in question fit for consideration by the tribunal of fact. If an issue is properly raised, it is for the prosecutor to prove, beyond reasonable doubt, that that ground of exoneration does not avail the defendant.'

(Lord Bingham)

Lord Devlin in *Jayasena v R* (1970) was more forthcoming in his criticism of the concept of the evidential burden and believed that it was confusing to call it a burden of proof.

JUDGMENT

'Their Lordships do not understand what is meant by the phrase "evidential burden of proof". They understand, of course, that in a trial by jury a party may be required to adduce some evidence in support of his case, whether on the general issue or on a particular issue, before that issue is left to the jury. How much evidence has to be adduced depends upon the nature of the requirement . . . It is doubtless permissible to describe the requirement as a burden, and it may be convenient to call it an evidential burden. But it is confusing [and misleading] to call it a burden of proof, whether described as legal or evidential or by any other adjective, when it can be discharged by the production of evidence that falls short of proof.'

Lord Devlin's comments were made in the context of the defence of self-defence, the point being whether an allegation of self-defence may be substantiated by reference to all the facts available to the court, as opposed to an obligation to prove the defence.

Accused bears both the evidential and legal burden

In the exceptional circumstances when an accused bears a legal burden (either in respect of the defence of insanity or a statutory reversal of the legal burden: see earlier) the discharge of the evidential burden is dependent on the accused satisfying the judge that there is sufficient evidence of the issue on which a jury might be convinced on a balance of probabilities. In short, the judge decides whether there is sufficient evidence of the defence to be put to the jury.

Whether the jury is satisfied on a balance of probabilities is a separate question from the discharge of the evidential burden (decided by the judge), and the former burden involves the discharge of the legal burden of proof. Whether the legal burden imposed on the accused has been discharged may sometimes be detected in the verdict; for example, on the issue of diminished responsibility the judge may decide that the accused's evidential burden had been discharged and puts the issue before the jury, but the jury may ultimately reject the defence and return a verdict of guilty of murder.

Where the prosecution bears both evidential and legal burdens

This involves the traditional case where the prosecution bears both the evidential and legal burdens. The discharge of the evidential burden is dependent on the judge deciding that there is a possibility of sufficient evidence adduced by the Crown that may convince the jury beyond reasonable doubt:

JUDGMENT

'The Crown is required to discharge the burden by adducing such evidence as, if believed, and if left uncontradicted and unexplained, could be accepted by the jury as proof.'

(Lord Devlin in *Jayasena v R* [1970] AC 618)

In this respect the judge acts as a barometer to determine whether the jury *may* convict on the evidence. A procedure to determine whether the prosecution has discharged its evidential burden involves the accused making a 'no case' submission at the close of the prosecution's case. A rejection by the judge of such a submission by the defence results in the discharge of the evidential burden by the prosecution.

The modern equivalent to the test for deciding whether the prosecution has discharged its evidential burden was stated by Lord Lane CJ in *R v Galbraith* [1981] 1 WLR 1039, thus:

JUDGMENT

'(1) If there is no evidence that the crime alleged has been committed by the defendant there is no difficulty – the judge will stop the case. (2) The difficulty arises where there is some evidence but it is of a tenuous character, for example, because of inherent weakness or vagueness or because it is inconsistent with other evidence. (a) Where the judge comes to the conclusion that the prosecution evidence, taken at its highest, is such that a jury properly directed could not properly convict upon it, it is his duty, upon a submission being made, to stop the case. (b) Where, however, the prosecution evidence is such that its strength or weakness depends on the view to be taken of a witness's reliability, other matters which are generally speaking within the province of the jury and where on one possible view of the facts there is evidence upon which a jury could properly come to the conclusion that the defendant is guilty, then the judge should allow the matter to be tried by the jury.'

In *R v Pryer* [2004] EWCA Crim 1163, the Court of Appeal decided that the *Galbraith* test involved the judge making an assessment of the whole of the prosecution case and not parts of it, such as the credibility of an individual witness. The test did not mean that the judge is entitled to 'pick out all the plums and leave the duff behind'. The credibility of individual witnesses does play a part in determining this question, but essentially the question concerns the case of the prosecution as a whole. In *Brooks v DPP* [1994] 1 AC 568, the Privy Council said that (in the context of committal proceedings) questions of credibility, except in the clearest of cases, do not normally result in a finding that there is no *prima facie* case.

Such submissions of 'no case' to answer are generally made at the close of the prosecution's case, although some attempts have been made by the defence to renew such application during the defence case. The position today, as clarified in *R v Brown (Davina)* [2002] 1 Cr App R 5, is that the judge has the power to decide that there is insufficient evidence to convict the defendant and consequently withdraw the issue from the jury. This is the position even after the close of the prosecution case, but it was said by the Court of Appeal that such a power should be exercised sparingly.

Civil proceedings where a party bears the legal burden

In civil proceedings, when a party bears a legal burden and a corresponding evidential burden, the discharge of the evidential burden is based on sufficient evidence being adduced to satisfy a reasonable trier of fact on a balance of probabilities. The judge (tribunal of law) is required to decide whether there is sufficient evidence to justify the tribunal of fact to make a finding in favour of the proponent. In the event of a 'no case' submission by the opponent the judge will postpone his ruling until all the evidence has been adduced.

Civil proceedings where the party does not bear the legal burden

In civil proceedings, where the party bears only the evidential burden, the obligation is to adduce sufficient evidence to leave the tribunal of fact in a state of equilibrium. This inevitably means that the party with the legal burden would be incapable of discharging it.

2.5 Tactical burden

Some commentators describe what has been referred to as the evidential burden as a 'tactical' burden. The notion concerns those occasions where a party does not bear a legal burden on an issue, but only an evidential or tactical burden. In these cases, strictly speaking there is no 'burden' cast on the party in the sense that they are not obliged to raise or prove an issue in order to succeed. Such a party may simply rely on the party with the legal burden not discharging the burden on a balance of probabilities; but, in doing so, they run a risk that the party with the legal burden may discharge it to the satisfaction of the tribunal of fact. Neither party has any decisive way of knowing before the end of the trial whether the legal burden of proof will be discharged. A party may merely speculate as to this possibility. Thus, the party without the legal burden, i.e. the party with a tactical burden, may reduce the risk of an adverse finding by adducing evidence of the issue. For example, on a charge of murder the defendant may sit back and rely on the prosecution failing to discharge its legal burden of proof, but he has no way of knowing if this possibility may materialise until the jury returns its verdict. To reduce the risk of an adverse finding he may adduce evidence that the deceased died accidentally. He is not obliged to do so, for this is not a fresh issue in the trial. The accused would be best advised to raise any defences available to him.

SUMMARY

- A legal burden of proof is an obligation to convince the tribunal of fact of the truth of the assertion.
- An evidential burden is a duty to satisfy the judge that there is sufficient evidence of an allegation to put the issue to the tribunal of fact.
- A party who bears the legal burden also bears the evidential burden of adducing sufficient evidence to raise the issue.
- A party may bear the evidential burden on an issue without bearing the legal burden of proof.
- The incidence of the legal burden of proof on an issue in civil cases depends on rules of substantive law, statements of the case and convenience.
- The incidence of the legal burden of proof in criminal cases is on the Crown, subject to the exceptions of insanity and express and implied statutory reversals of the burden: see *Woolmington v DPP*.
- Statutory reversals of the legal burden of proof are subject to the Human Rights Act 1998 and rights created under the European Convention on Human Rights: see *AG Reference (No 4 of 2002); Sheldrake v DPP*.
- The standard of proof in order to discharge the legal burden cast on the prosecution is 'beyond a reasonable doubt'.
- The standard of proof in order to discharge the evidential burden is 'sufficient' evidence.
- When an accused bears the legal burden the standard of proof is a balance of probabilities.
- In civil cases the standard of proof in order to discharge the legal burden of proof is a balance of probabilities.

ACTIVITY

Self-test questions

1. What do you understand by the expressions 'legal burden of proof', 'evidential burden of proof', 'tactical burden of proof', the 'incidence of the legal burden of proof', 'reverse legal burdens of proof' and 'standards of proof'?

2. In civil cases, what factors are relevant in determining which party bears a legal burden of proof?
3. To what extent is there clarity in the phrases 'beyond a reasonable doubt', 'balance of probabilities' and making out a '*prima facie*' case?
4. In criminal cases, what standard of proof is required to be discharged by the prosecution when the defendant makes a 'no case' submission?
5. In criminal cases, when would a defendant bear a legal burden of proof?
6. 'The real concern is not whether the accused must disprove an element or prove an excuse, but that an accused may be convicted while a reasonable doubt exists. When that possibility exists, there is a breach of the presumption of innocence' (*per* Dickson CJ, Canadian Supreme Court in *R v Whyte* (1988) 58 DLR 481). Discuss this statement in the light of the current judicial approaches towards reverse legal burdens of proof.

SAMPLE ESSAY QUESTION

Comment on each of the following rulings made in three separate trials:

(a) 'The claimant claims from the defendant the sum of £75,000 and the basis of this claim is a fraud alleged to have been perpetrated by the defendant. Fraud is a serious crime and it must not be lightly pleaded in a civil action such as this. Because of the seriousness of the allegation I have to apply an appropriate standard of proof which is higher than the usual civil standard. It cannot be as high as the criminal standard, but it must take into account the gravity of what is alleged and the improbability of its having been committed.'

(b) 'The defendant is charged with robbery and relies on an alibi for his defence. It is true that he does not have to prove this defence, but he does have an evidential burden to discharge in respect of it, which in my judgment he has failed to discharge. I cannot say that I have been persuaded on the balance of probabilities that his defence is one that the jury could be reasonably confident about. So I shall direct them to disregard any question of alibi.'

(c) 'The prosecution brings this case and it is for the prosecution to prove it. Unless, having heard all the evidence, you are satisfied on reasonable grounds that the defendant is surely guilty, he must be acquitted.'

Answer plan

- Define legal and evidential burdens of proof and briefly distinguish the concepts, highlighting which tribunal decides whether the appropriate burden has been discharged.

(a)

- Who is making the assertion? Consider the principles for allocating the incidence of the legal burden of proof in civil cases.
- The claim is based in contract or tort: we have not been told. Either way the allegation is most likely made by the claimant who therefore has the legal burden of proof.

- In the absence of a presumption, the imposition of the legal burden on the claimant requires him to initially discharge an evidential burden on the issues.
- What is the appropriate standard of proof applicable to each burden? See *Miller v Minister of Pensions*.
- Identification of the issue connected to a ruling on the standard of proof concerning a fraud.
- Does it make a difference to the standard of proof in civil proceedings that the claimant makes an allegation of a crime? See *Hornal v Neuberger Products; Re Dellow; Re H (Minors)*.
- Does the standard of proof vary with the seriousness of the crime?
- Is there any justification for the judge imposing a standard of proof higher than the traditional civil standard?

(b)

- Incidence of the legal burden of proof in criminal cases, see *Woolmington v DPP*.
- Does an alibi defence put forward by the defendant impose legal or evidential burden on the accused?
- The judge correctly identified that the accused bears an evidential burden of proof as this defence does not fall within the exceptions to the 'golden thread' theory stated by Lord Sankey in *Woolmington*.
- It could be argued that the absence of an alibi is part of the prosecution's case and therefore an element of the legal burden cast on the prosecution; the accused simply denies being at the scene of the crime.
- The judge correctly identified that he has the duty to decide whether an evidential burden has been discharged.
- What is the appropriate standard of proof imposed on the accused when he bears only an evidential burden?
- The judge has incorrectly ruled that the standard of proof is a balance of probabilities when the issue should be 'sufficiency' of evidence or creating a reasonable doubt as to his guilt. See *Jayasena v R*.

(c)

- The incidence of the legal burden of proof to prove the elements of the offence, see *Woolmington v DPP*.
- The issue here concerns the ruling by the judge as to the appropriate standard of proof to discharge the legal burden.

- Is the ruling correct that the standard is based on reasonable grounds of the guilt of the accused?
- Ultimately it is the effect of the summing up as a whole and the entire trial process that will be required to be considered by the appellate court and not necessarily one phrase, *R v Kritz*.

Further reading

Ashworth, A. and Blake, M. 'The presumption of innocence in English criminal law' [1998] Crim LR 306

Bennion, F. 'Statutory exceptions: a third knot in the golden thread' [1988] Crim LR 31

Birch, D. 'Hunting the snark: the elusive statutory exception' [1988] Crim LR 221

Bridge, C. 'Care proceedings: burden of proof' [2012] Family Law 1074

Coe, P. 'Justifying reverse burdens of proof: a tale of diminished responsibility and a tangled knot of authorities' [2013] J Crim L 360

Dennis, I. 'Reverse onuses and the presumption of innocence: in search of principle' [2005] Crim LR 901

Dingwall, G. 'Statutory exceptions, burdens of proof and the Human Rights Act 1998' (2002) 65 MLR 450

Douglas, G. 'Care proceedings: medical evidence – burden and standard of proof' [2012] Family Law 936

Fitzpatrick, B. 'Reverse burden and Art 6(2) of the European Convention on Human Rights: official secrets' [2008] J Crim L 190

Hamer, D. 'The presumption of innocence and reverse burdens: a balancing act' (2007) 66 CLJ 142

Hamer, D. 'Presumptions, standards and burdens: managing the cost of error' [2014] LP&R 221

Healey, P. 'Proof and policy: no golden threads' [1987] Crim LR 355

Hjalmarsson, J. 'The standard of proof in civil cases: an insurance fraud perspective' [2013] E&P 47

Lewis, P. 'The Human Rights Act 1998: shifting the burden' [2000] Crim LR 667

Lippke, R. 'Justifying the proof structure of criminal trials' [2013] E&P 323

Mirfield, P. 'The legacy of Hunt' [1988] Crim LR 19

Padfield, N. 'The burden of proof unresolved' (2005) 64 CLJ 17

Picinali, F. 'The threshold lies in the method: instructing jurors about reasoning beyond reasonable doubt' [2015] E&P 139

Roberts, P. 'Taking the burden of proof seriously' [1995] Crim LR 783

Roberts, P. 'The presumption of innocence brought home/*Kebilene* deconstructed' (2002) 118 LQR 41

Smith, J. C. 'The presumption of innocence' (1987) 38 NILQ 223

Stapleton, J. 'Factual causation of mesothelioma and statistical validity' [2012] LQR 221

Tavros, V. and Tierney, S. 'Presumption of innocence and the Human Rights Act' (2004) 67 MLR 402

Walchover, D. and Heaton-Armstrong, A. 'Reasonable doubt' (2010) 174 Criminal Law and Justice Weekly 484
Williams, G. 'The evidential burden: some common misapprehensions' (1977) 127 NLJ 156
Williams, G. 'Evidential burdens on the defence' (1977) 127 NLJ 182
Zuckerman, A. 'The third exception to the Woolmington Rule' (1976) 92 LQR 402

3

Testimony of witnesses

AIMS AND OBJECTIVES

By the end of this chapter you will be able to:

- appreciate the preparatory rules leading up to viva voce evidence in court;
- understand the occasions when a witness may give sworn and unsworn evidence in court;
- comprehend the test of competence and compellability of witnesses in both civil and criminal cases;
- recognise the occasions when special measures directions may be available to assist the witness in the presentation of his testimony.

3.1 Introduction

Viva voce
the technical expression used where a witness testifies in court; a **solemn affirmation** is an alternative to taking the oath and has the same effect as if the witness has taken the oath.

This chapter focuses on the most popular mode of proof of relevant facts, namely, live evidence (**viva voce**) or testimony presented in court in both civil and criminal cases. The witnesses may be encouraged or compelled to attend the proceedings. Once the witness has attended the proceedings, the primary question is whether they are competent to testify. Additional issues concern the presentation of their testimony on oath or subject to a **solemn affirmation**. Exceptionally, a witness may give unsworn evidence. Finally, the individual may require some assistance in order to testify. The judge has jurisdiction to make special measures directions that may assist the witness in this regard.

3.2 Attendance of witnesses at court

In both civil and criminal cases the parties will make arrangements with their witnesses to attend the court. Prior to the date of the trial, the witness would have made a witness statement in writing and it would be on the basis of such assertions that the party wishes the witness to testify. There is no general principle that the witness is not allowed to see their statement

DOI: 10.4324/9781003282433-3

a short while *before* testifying. The process of testifying is not designed to be a test of memory but an effort to present the truth in court, subject to rules of admissible evidence.

If a party is aware that there is a potential witness who is compellable, but unwilling to attend the court in order to avoid testifying, then that party may apply for a witness summons or order requiring the witness to attend on the relevant dates: see s 97 of the Magistrates' Courts Act 1980 and s 2 of the Criminal Procedure (Attendance of Witnesses) Act 1965, as amended. The following two conditions are required to be satisfied before a court will issue such a summons:

- that the person is likely to be able to give material evidence; and
- that their presence in court is necessary in the interests of justice.

If the person named in the witness order fails to attend the proceedings without lawful excuse, a warrant may be issued for their arrest in order to secure attendance. Where the witness, without lawful excuse, refuses to answer questions put to them, then they may be found guilty of contempt of court. The court has a range of powers for dealing with contempt, including imprisonment: see *R v Haselden* [2000] All ER (D) 56.

3.3 Order of presentation of evidence

The general rule is that it is the duty of the legal representative to decide what evidence is called and in what order to call the witnesses. The duty of the prosecution to call witnesses or read their statements under s 9 of the Criminal Justice Act 1967, involves a combination of rules of discretion and practice but subject to the overriding test of fairness in the proceedings. In *R v Russell-Jones* [1995] 1 Cr App R 538, the Court of Appeal laid down the following principles: the prosecution has an unfettered discretion to determine which witnesses they wish to call. Having made the decision as to their witnesses, they are required to serve witness statements on the defence and ensure that the witnesses attend the proceedings. To the same effect, the prosecution may tender the witness for cross-examination; i.e. the witness is called by the prosecution and, after the formal swearing in and identification, the defence is invited to cross-examine the witness. Where the prosecution has served witness statements it will have a limited discretion not to call one or more of these witnesses. The limitation on the discretion of the prosecution is that its omission to call a witness has to be exercised in the interests of justice. Witnesses called by the prosecution would be those who may give evidence as to the primary facts of the case, unless they form an opinion that such witnesses' evidence may be unworthy of belief. In this event, as the prosecution is required by law to inform the defence of all unused material, it would then be up to the defence to interview the witnesses and, if necessary, call them to testify on its behalf. Alternatively, the judge may call witnesses on behalf of the Crown in the interests of a fair trial. In *R v Mahmood* [2013] EWCA Crim 742, the Court of Appeal decided that the trial judge did not have the power to force the prosecution to call witnesses that the defence wished to question. The prosecution had properly exercised its discretion not to call the relevant witnesses and the defence had the option of calling these witnesses if they so wished.

In criminal proceedings, it is the practice to call the defendant before any other defence witnesses. Section 79 of the Police and Criminal Evidence Act 1984 has endorsed this practice.

Section 79 of the Police and Criminal Evidence Act 1984 enacts as follows:

SECTION

'If at the time of the trial of any person for an offence –

(a) the defence intends to call two or more witnesses to the facts of the case; and
(b) those witnesses include the accused,

the accused shall be called before the other witness or witnesses unless the court in its discretion otherwise directs.'

In civil proceedings, the practice is that the witness is entitled to remain in court before he or she testifies in the proceedings. This rule is subject to any orders made by the judge in his or her discretion to exclude a witness before they give testimony.

In criminal proceedings, the general practice is that all witnesses are excluded from the court until after they have given testimony. The purpose of the rule is that all witnesses should be examined out of the hearing of other witnesses who have yet to give their evidence. If a witness remains in court before testifying or after an order has been made to exclude the witness, and a party wishes to call the witness to testify, it appears that the judge has no discretion to exclude the testimony of that witness: see *R v Kingston* [1980] RT 51, *per* Edmund Davies LJ:

JUDGMENT

'No rule of law requires that in a trial the witnesses to be called by one side must all remain out of court until their turn to give testimony arises. This is purely within the discretion of the court. Indeed, if the court rules that witnesses should be out of court and a witness nevertheless remains in court . . . the judge has no right to refuse to hear his evidence.'

Of course the weight of the testimony of the witness may be severely affected, and it is a matter for the court to decide how credible such evidence will be. Moreover, in criminal proceedings witnesses are not permitted to discuss the case with each other while waiting in court during the course of the trial. This principle may be expressed by the judge following the conclusion of the testimony of each witness. If, despite this rule, the witnesses discuss aspects of the case during the trial, the judge is required to consider all the circumstances including the impact of their evidence in the trial, the subject matter of the discussion, whether any of the witnesses modified their testimony following the discussion and the stage during the trial when the discussions took place. In *R v Shaw* [2002] EWCA Crim 3004, on a charge of causing grievous bodily harm with intent linked to an incident of 'road rage' the victim had suffered severe injuries. The defendant raised the defence of self-defence.

The question in issue was the identity of the aggressor. There were two independent witnesses who testified for the prosecution, but while waiting in court they discussed the case with another prosecution witness. The witnesses made adjustments to their testimony. The matter was raised before the Recorder, who attempted to repair the damage by a direction to the jury. The accused was convicted and, on appeal, the Court of Appeal allowed the appeal and quashed the conviction in the interests of a fair trial.

JUDGMENT

'We accept that in many situations witnesses do have the opportunity to discuss and do discuss cases before a case ever comes to trial. Often they will know each other; and we accept that in many cases witnesses will know things or think they know things about defendants which reflect badly on such defendants. Nevertheless, it remains extremely important that witnesses do not discuss cases while waiting at court. There are a number of reasons for that. Witnesses may well meet who have not previously had any opportunity to discuss the case, as indeed was the situation here. If one or more of the witnesses is an independent witness, it is particularly important that their version of events is placed before the court uninfluenced by the views of others, and the imminence of giving evidence may give particular weight to what is known. In other words, we accept the trial of a defendant must take place in court before the jury and there must be no suspicion that he has been tried by witnesses waiting in their room.'

(Crane J)

In addition, no party has any 'property' in the evidence of a witness. Accordingly, if a party makes a contract with a witness, to the effect that the witness agrees to give their services exclusively to that party, that agreement is treated as being contrary to public policy and is unenforceable. Thus, such a witness is compellable to testify for the other party: see *Harmony Shipping Co v Saudi Europe Line Ltd* [1979] 1 WLR 1380. But, in criminal proceedings, once a witness has given evidence for the prosecution they cannot be called to testify for the defence: see *R v Kelly* (1985) *The Times*, 27 July.

3.3.1 Re-opening the prosecution case

As a general rule, the prosecution is not allowed to call further evidence after it has formally closed its case. Although, trial judges, including magistrates, still have a discretion to allow the prosecution to call further evidence after the close of the its case. There are limited circumstances in which this discretion has been exercised; the following occasions provide guidance on the exercise of that discretion:

(a) If a matter arises *ex improviso*, which no human ingenuity could have foreseen. This occurs where the prosecution applies for leave from the judge to adduce rebutting evidence to counter an allegation made by the defence. In *R v Blick* (1966) 50 Cr App R 280, the defendant was arrested following a police chase and charged with robbery. He testified that there was wrongful identification for, at the time of the chase, he was in a public lavatory. A juror who knew the area passed a note to the judge informing him that the lavatory was closed for repairs at the material time. The prosecution was given leave to call rebutting evidence to that effect. On appeal it was held that the evidence was properly admitted. No human ingenuity could have foreseen that access to a public lavatory would have been relevant to the case against the defendant. Likewise, as in *R v Milliken* (1969) 53 Cr App R 330, where the defence makes an unforeseeable attack on the credibility and honesty of police officers, the court in its discretion may allow the prosecution to adduce rebutting evidence that is likely to go some way to disproving the truth of the defence. Whereas in *R v Day* [1940] 1 All ER 402, this test was not satisfied. In this case the charge involved forgery of a cheque. The prosecution was granted leave to call a handwriting expert to compare the writing on the cheque with a sample of the defendant's handwriting. The conviction was quashed on the ground that the need to call the witness should have been anticipated by the prosecution.

(b) Where the prosecution inadvertently failed to lead evidence of a formal nature, the judge may permit the prosecution to re-open its case in order to repair the omission. In *R v Francis* [990] 1 WLR 1264, the court extended this exception beyond issues of a formal nature to cases of identification. It was stated that this discretion ought to be exercised sparingly. In this case the prosecution failed to prove that the person at a group identification was the accused and was given leave by the judge to cure the defect, even after the defendant made a 'no case' submission.

(c) There appears to be a general residual discretion retained by the judge to deal with any issues that may arise during the course of a trial. In *R v Munnery* (1992) 94 Cr App R 164, at the close of the case for the Crown, counsel for the appellant outlined the nature of the submission that he proposed to make, including a lacuna in the case of the Crown, and the matter was adjourned to the next day. By the next morning the Crown had obtained evidence rectifying the alleged lacuna. The prosecution was given leave to re-open its case and adduce this evidence. The Court of Appeal dismissed the appeal and confirmed the existence of the general discretion to permit the Crown to re-open its case, provided that this accorded with the interests of justice. In *James v South Glamorgan County Council* (1994) 99 Cr App R 321, the prosecution's main witness had arrived late, owing to transport difficulties and confusion as to the location of the court. The prosecution was given leave to re-open its case to call such witness.

The same principles of judicial discretion are extended to magistrates' courts. The discretion to allow the prosecution to re-open its case and call evidence is required to be *exercised sparingly and in the interests of justice*: see *Jolly v DPP* [2000] Crim LR 471. The discretion in the magistrates' courts to permit either party to adduce further evidence exists at any time before they retire, provided that no injustice was done. However, the position after they had returned to give their verdict was more restricted. The magistrates still had a discretion to receive further evidence but special circumstances were required if that discretion was to be exercised. In *Malcolm v DPP* [2007] 1 WLR 1230, the court decided that special circumstances exist by reference to the facts of each case. In *Tuck v Vehicle Inspectorate* [2004] EWHC 728 (Admin), Mackay J summarised the principles of re-opening the prosecution's case as follows:

JUDGMENT

'(1) The discretion to allow the case to be re-opened is not limited to matters arising *ex improviso* or mere technicalities but is a more "general discretion".
(2) The exercise of this discretion should not be interfered with by a higher court unless its exercise was wrong in principle or perverse.
(3) The general rule remains that the prosecution must finish its case once and for all and the test to be applied is narrower than consideration of whether the additional evidence would be of value to the tribunal. The discretion will only be exercised "on the rarest of occasions".
(4) The discretion must be exercised carefully having regard to the need to be fair to the defendant and giving consideration to the question of whether any prejudice to the defendant will be caused.
(5) The courts have in the past differed as to whether the mere loss of a tactical advantage can constitute such prejudice. The defendant, having spotted and drawn attention to a gap in the case by way of submission, as to which he could have remained silent, and taken advantage of that gap at the close of the evidence, was thought in *R v Munnery* (1992) 94 Cr App R 164 at 172 to be an important consideration. However, later cases take a discernibly different approach. A different view was expressed in *Khatibi v Director of Public Prosecutions* [2004] EWHC 83 (Admin) at 25 to 26 and in *Leeson* [2000] RTR 385 and 391F–G.
(6) Criminal procedure while adversarial is not a game and the overall interests of justice include giving effect to the requirement that a prosecution should not fail through inefficiency, carelessness or oversight.
(7) Of particular significance is the consideration of whether there is any risk of prejudice to the defendant.'

(Mackay J in *Tuck v Vehicle Inspectorate*)

3.4 Evidence: sworn/unsworn or solemn affirmation

The starting point is that the testimony of all witnesses in both civil and criminal cases is required to be presented in court after the witness has been sworn in or they have made a solemn affirmation. There is an exception with regard to the evidence of children. The justification for taking the oath is based on the reason that there was a divine sanction for speaking the truth. This remains the rationale today and the motivation for speaking the truth is purely subjective. If the witness wilfully tells lies under oath or having made a solemn affirmation, they may face perjury charges.

3.4.1 Oath

Section 1 of the Oaths Act 1978 declares the manner in which the oath may be administered. The witness taking the oath is required to hold the New Testament or, in the case of a Jew, the Old Testament, in his uplifted hand, and to say or repeat the words, 'I swear by Almighty God that the evidence which I shall give shall be the truth, the whole truth and nothing but the truth.' Unless the witness objects, the court officer is entitled to adopt the procedure as outlined above. The modern practice is that the appropriate officer enquires what oath the witness accepts as binding on him and he is then sworn in accordingly.

Section 1(3) of the Oaths Act 1978 enacts:

SECTION

'In the case of a person who is neither a Christian nor a Jew, the oath may be administered in any lawful manner.'

This procedure would involve the appropriate holy book being held by the witness, who then repeats a prepared oath similar to the one above but adapted to the tenets of the relevant religion. Whether the oath was administered in a 'lawful manner', as laid down in s 1 of the Oaths Act 1978, does not depend on the intricacies of the religion in question, but rather on whether the oath appeared to the court to be binding on the conscience of the witness and, if so, whether the witness themself considered the oath to be binding on their conscience: see *R v Kemble* [1990] 3 All ER 116. In this case, the witness, who was a Muslim, had taken the oath using the New Testament. On conviction, the defendant appealed contending that s 1 of the Oaths Act 1978 had not been complied with and that the witness was not properly sworn in. The Court of Appeal dismissed the appeal and laid down the test as stated above:

JUDGMENT

'We take the view that the question of whether the administration of the oath is lawful does not depend upon what may be the considerable intricacies of the particular religion which is adhered to by the witness. It concerns two matters and two matters only in our judgment. First of all, is the oath an oath which appears to the court to be binding on the conscience of the witness? And, if so, secondly, and most importantly, is it an oath which the witness himself considers to be binding upon his conscience?

'So far as the present case is concerned, quite plainly the first of those matters is satisfied. The court did obviously consider the oath to be one which was binding upon the witness. It was the second matter which was the subject so to speak of dispute before this court. Not only did we have the evidence of the professor, the expert in Muslim theology but we also had the evidence of the witness himself. He having on this occasion been sworn upon a copy of the Koran in Arabic gave evidence before us that he did consider himself to be bound as to his conscience by the way in which he took the oath at the trial. Indeed, he went further. He said, "Whether I had taken the oath upon the Koran or upon the Bible or upon the Torah, I would have considered that to be binding on my conscience" . . . that he did consider all of those to be holy books, and that he did consider that his conscience was bound by the form of oath he took and the way in which he took it. In other words we accept his evidence.'

(Lord Lane CJ)

There are special forms of oaths for jurors and interpreters.

3.4.2 Solemn affirmation

In alternative to taking the oath in both civil and criminal cases the witness may make a solemn affirmation. Section 5 of the Oaths Act 1978 lays down the principle that a solemn affirmation may be made if the witness objects to taking the oath or if it is not reasonably practicable without inconvenience or delay to administer the oath in accordance with the religious tenets of the appropriate faith. The solemn affirmation has the same force and effect as the oath. Thus, the witness may commit perjury if they wilfully lie from the witness box following their solemn affirmation.

Where the potential witness is incapable of taking the oath or making a solemn affirmation, their account may still be admitted in court as unsworn testimony, provided that they satisfy the overriding test of competence (discussed below).

3.5 Competence and compellability of witnesses

A witness is competent to give evidence if their testimony is receivable in court, subject, of course, to the rules of admissibility. A witness is compellable where they can be obliged to testify, even against their will. The sanction is a contempt of court for failing to testify without lawful cause. Likewise, it is a contempt of court for a witness to refuse, without lawful authority, to answer questions put to them.

The modern test for the competence of witnesses varies with the nature of the proceedings (civil or criminal) and the status of the witness (child, adult, accused, accused's spouse, person of defective intellect).

3.5.1 Civil cases

In *Omychund v Barker* (1745) 1 Atk 21 and a series of statutes, individuals were made competent to testify in civil proceedings. In *Omychund v Barker*, the court decided that non-Christians were competent to testify. The Evidence Act 1843 abolished the rule of incompetence on the ground that a person had been convicted or had an interest in the outcome of the proceedings. These are matters that are capable of affecting the weight of the evidence. The Evidence Act 1851 rendered the parties to civil proceedings competent and compellable to testify. The Evidence (Amendment) Act 1853 had the same effect with regard to the spouses of parties. The effect today is that all adults who do not suffer from defective intellect are competent and compellable to testify in civil proceedings. It should be noted that there are special rules created by statute that sovereigns and diplomats are not compellable to testify.

3.5.2 Sworn evidence

At common law the test for competence to testify involved the test for the giving of sworn testimony, subject to an exception created to accommodate the evidence of children. This test is known as the *Hayes* test, derived from the case *R v Hayes* [1977] 1 WLR 234. The rule was originally applicable to both criminal and civil proceedings and remains the test today for civil proceedings. The test for criminal proceedings is currently to be found in the Youth Justice and Criminal Evidence Act 1999: see below.

The *Hayes* test involves a cumulative two-tier requirement for the judge to decide whether:

- the intended witness appreciates the solemnity of the occasion;
- he is of sufficient intelligence to understand that the taking of the oath involves an obligation to tell the truth, over and above the ordinary duty of doing so. Knowledge or belief in God is not essential.

In *R v Hayes* the charges involved indecency with four small boys. The youngest, a nine-year-old, who testified, was ignorant of the significance of God and the existence of Jesus, but appreciated the necessity of speaking the truth while testifying. The question in issue was whether the child was competent to give sworn testimony. The Court of Appeal decided that he was capable of giving sworn evidence:

JUDGMENT

'It is unrealistic not to recognise that, in the present state of society, amongst the adult population the divine sanction of an oath is probably not generally recognised. The important consideration, we think, when a judge has to decide whether a child should properly be sworn in, is whether the child has a sufficient appreciation of the solemnity of the occasion, and the added responsibility to tell the truth, which is involved in taking an oath, over and above the duty to tell the truth which is an ordinary duty of normal social conduct.'

(Bridge LJ)

3.5.3 Unsworn evidence of children in civil cases

The current position of competence in civil cases is that the witness is required to give sworn evidence or make a solemn affirmation. An exception to this rule regarding sworn evidence was created by s 96 of the Children Act 1989, authorising the admissibility of unsworn evidence of children provided that they are incapable of giving sworn evidence.

The test for giving unsworn evidence in civil proceedings is enacted in s 96(2) of the 1989 Act, which states as follows:

SECTION

'The child's evidence may be heard by the court if, in its opinion –

(a) he understands that it is his duty to speak the truth; and
(b) he has sufficient understanding to justify his evidence being heard.

A child for these purposes is a person under the age of 18: see s 105 of the 1989 Act.'

The effect of this provision is that in civil proceedings a child may give unsworn testimony as a last resort, if they are incapable of giving sworn testimony.

3.5.4 Criminal cases

The test for competence of a witness in criminal proceedings is a cumulative, two-tiered test as laid down in s 53(3) of the Youth Justice and Criminal Evidence Act 1999, which states:

SECTION

'A person is not competent to give evidence in criminal proceedings if it appears to the court that he is not a person who is able to –

(a) understand questions put to him as a witness, and
(b) give answers to them which can be understood.'

The fundamental issue raised in s 53(3)(a) and (b) was one of understanding, namely whether the witness is capable of understanding what is being asked and whether the jury can understand the witness's answers. The words in s 53(3)(a), 'put to him as a witness', meant the equivalent of 'being asked in court' so that an infant who could only communicate in baby language with his mother would not ordinarily be competent but a young child who could speak and understand basic English with strangers may be competent to testify. In addition, questions of credibility and reliability are not relevant to the issue of competence but are significant as to the weight of the evidence. In *R v MacPherson* [2006] 1 Cr App R 30, the Court of Appeal decided that the additional common test of competence in *Hayes* has been modified by s 53(3) of the 1999 Act in the sense that there is no longer a requirement that the witness appreciates the difference between truth and falsity. In this case the court decided that a four-and-a-half-year-old victim of an indecent assault was a competent witness.

The trial judge who sees and questions the witness and makes a decision as to whether the witness is competent or not will very rarely be reversed on appeal, provided that the judge has correctly applied the test of competence. In *R v M* [2008] EWCA Crim 2751, on charges involving unlawful sexual behaviour with children, the victim (V) was aged nine years and had substantial learning difficulties. V was interviewed by the police and a report was prepared by a registered intermediary speech therapist who assessed her learning difficulties as medium. At the trial the judge viewed the video evidence of her testimony and questioned V and ruled that she was not competent to testify. The prosecution appealed and the Court of Appeal dismissed the appeal and declared that decisions of the trial judge on the issue of competence of witnesses will not lightly be interfered with by the appellate courts.

However, in *Re F* (2013), the Court of Appeal reversed the decision of the trial judge on the issue of competence on the grounds that, although she had set out the correct test, she excessively and inappropriately relied on the difficulties faced by the interpreter in communicating the information to and from the witness. The focus should have been whether the witness understands the questions put to her and gave answers that could be understood. In addition there was sufficient evidence on the facts of the case to indicate that the witness was capable of satisfying the competency test.

CASE EXAMPLE

Re F [2013] EWCA Crim 424 (CA)

The defendant was charged with sexual offences against H, the sister of his partner. H, aged 24, was profoundly deaf and suffered from learning difficulties. She had visited the defendant's flat in order to retrieve a pram for her sister. During her visit the alleged offences took place. The defendant pleaded not guilty and the matter proceeded to a trial. Special measures were issued to assist the witness and this took the form of an interpreter and a British Sign Language interpreter. In addition, H's ABE (Achieving Best Evidence) video interview had existed on the prosecutor's file and was expected to be played at the trial as part of H's examination in chief. The defence raised an issue as to the competence of the complainant to testify. This placed the burden of proof on the prosecution. Prosecuting counsel embarked on questioning H to point to different parts of her body. At this point the sign interpreter intervened indicating that any question posed would have to be leading in part because the interpreter would have to point to a body part as part of the question. After a discussion between the judge and the parties, the intermediary suggested that drawings or pictures might be used, but that suggestion was not taken up. The judge then asked questions from which it became clear that the witness had difficulty dealing with concepts of time and abstract matters. The judge then ruled that the witness was incompetent to testify. On appeal by the prosecution, the Court of Appeal decided that the judge's decision was seriously flawed. She had relied on the interpreter's difficulties in communicating in a non-leading manner between the witness and the court rather than the test for competence. In addition as there was additional evidence consisting of the ABE interview it was doubted whether the competency issue ought to have been taken at the initial stage. The trial judge could have proceeded on the basis that the witness was competent and review her decision at any stage during the trial.

JUDGMENT

'True it is that in her ruling the judge had set out the appropriate test, but she based her conclusion that H was not a competent witness firstly on the body parts issue. In relation to that the judge proceeded on the basis that the interpreter would have to point to the body part in question and that in doing so it would shed little or no light on the witness's true understanding of the question.

In our judgment, the judge substituted the issue of the interpreter's difficulties in communicating for the test of whether the witness could understand questions and give intelligible answers.

The second limb of the judge's reasoning related to difficulty with concepts of time and other more abstract concepts. In this respect the procedure adopted was for the reasons already mentioned an unsatisfactory way of testing the witness's understanding and ability to make herself understood. It did not represent, in our judgment, a valid or thorough test, and so the judge's conclusion in this respect is thereby undermined. We have found that the procedure was so flawed that the conclusions reached cannot be relied on as any fair test of competency.'

(Treacy LJ)

It should be noted that the general rule laid down in s 53(3) is applicable to all witnesses (including the defendant and his or her spouse) in criminal proceedings. When an issue concerning the competence of a witness is raised by a party in the proceedings of the court, the judge will rule on the issue in the absence of the jury. The legal burden of proof that the witness is competent to testify lies on the party calling the witness and the standard of proof is on a balance of probabilities. Interestingly, expert evidence may be called in order to determine the competence of the witness: see s 54 of the Youth Justice and Criminal Evidence Act 1999.

The decision as to the competence of a witness is a question of law for the judge to decide. Having initially made the ruling that the witness is competent, he retains a discretion throughout that witness's testimony to change his ruling and decide that the witness does not satisfy the test laid down in s 53(3) of the 1999 Act. The power to make such a ruling and exclude the evidence is laid down in s 78 of the Police and Criminal Evidence Act 1984 if the admission of such evidence would have 'an adverse effect on the fairness of the proceedings'. With regard to child witnesses the tender age of the child, inordinate delays between the date of the incident and the trial and the demeanour of the witness are factors that are required to be taken into consideration. In *R v Powell* [2006] EWCA Crim 3, the victim of a sexual assault was three-and-a-half years old at the time of the incident but some nine months later at the trial was initially treated as competent to testify by reference to her video-recorded interview. However, at the stage of cross-examination, via a live link, it became apparent that there were serious grounds for doubting her competence in that she failed to articulate many answers. The trial judge did not re-visit the question of competence, and on appeal against conviction the Court of Appeal allowed the appeal and decided that the trial judge should have considered exercising his discretion to exclude the evidence.

JUDGMENT

'Explanations can be found for each element of the delay in this case. However, the plain fact is that where a case depends on the evidence of a very young child it is absolutely essential (a) that the ABE interview takes place very soon after the event and (b) that the trial (at which the child has to be cross-examined) takes place very soon thereafter. As the expert evidence in this case showed, very young children simply do not have the ability to lay down memory in a manner comparable to adults. Looking at this case with hindsight, it was completely unacceptable that the appellant should have been tried for an offence proof of which relied on the evidence of a three-and-a-half-year-old when the trial did not take place until over nine months had passed from the date of the alleged offence. Special efforts must be made to fast-track cases of this kind and it is simply not an option to wait weeks for example for forensic evidence to become available.'

(Baker LJ)

In *R v Malicki* [2009] EWCA Crim 365, the Court of Appeal identified two problems arising from inordinate delays in trials involving witnesses of tender age. First, the child may not have an accurate recollection of the events that took place a significant period earlier and second, the child may recollect only what was said on the video recording and may not be capable of distinguishing what was said on the video and the underlying events. In these circumstances the judge may be entitled to exclude the evidence under s 78 of the Police and Criminal Evidence Act 1984. In this case the charge was indecent assault on a child aged four years and eight months at the time of the incident. The judge ruled that the child was competent to testify and she gave a consistent account of the incident in a video-recorded interview conducted by the police. The trial did not take place until some fourteen months after the alleged incident. There was a suggestion in cross-examination that although the victim claimed to remember the incident it was impossible to discern whether she was actually remembering the incident itself or was simply recalling her video, which she had just seen twice. At the end of the prosecution case the judge rejected the defence application to exclude the victim's testimony. The defendant was convicted and his appeal was allowed on the ground that there was a risk that the victim did not have any accurate recollection of events from fourteen months previously, as she was so young. There was an even greater risk that all the victim actually recollected was what had been said on the video, and that she was incapable of distinguishing between what was said on the video and the underlying events themselves.

JUDGMENT

'The video interview in the present case was prompt, but the overall delay until trial was much greater. The problem in such a case as it seems to us is twofold: first, the risk that a child so young does not have any accurate recollection of events 14 months previously (that is almost a quarter of her life ago); secondly, the even greater risk that if she is shown the video of her interview just before the trial and during the trial, as she must be, all she is actually recollecting is what was said on the video, and that she is incapable of distinguishing between what was said on the video and the underlying events themselves. It seems to us to be a near impossible task to undertake an effective cross-examination in those circumstances when the cross-examination must depend for its effectiveness on probing what actually happened in the course of the incident itself and immediately after it, not just going over what the complainant said in her interview. These problems go beyond the normal difficulties of recollection with an adult witness or an older child . . . We are satisfied that the judge ought in the particular circumstances of this case to have excluded the complainant's evidence and then to have stopped the trial for lack of any case to answer, and that the conviction cannot therefore stand. It follows that the appeal must succeed and the conviction be quashed.'

(Richards LJ)

In *R v B* (also known as *R v Barker*) [2010] EWCA Crim 4, the Court of Appeal reviewed the authorities concerning the testimony of children following delays between the time of the incident and the trial and issued a number of guidelines.

(1) The test of competence of all witnesses in criminal trials is declared in s 53 of the Youth Justice and Criminal Evidence Act 1999.

(2) The provisions laid down in the statute are clear and unequivocal and reinterpretation is not required.

(3) What is required under the section is not the exercise of discretion but the making of a judgment as to whether the witness fulfilled the statutory criteria.

(4) The test of competence is entirely witness specific. There are no presumptions or preconceptions. The witness need not understand the special importance of speaking the truth or understand every question or give readily understood answers to every question. Many competent adult witnesses would fail such a test. Provided that the witness could understand the questions put to him and could give understandable answers he is competent.

(5) The age of a witness is not determinative of his ability to give truthful and accurate answers. His credibility is to be assessed by the jury taking into account every specific personal characteristic.

(6) The competence test could be re-analysed after the witness has given evidence. If the child witness has been unable to provide intelligible answers to questions in cross-examination or a meaningful cross-examination has been impossible, the evidence may be excluded under s 78 of the Police and Criminal Evidence Act 1984.

In this case the defendant was convicted of rape of a child under three years old at the time of the incident. At the time of the trial the victim was four-and-a-half years old and gave evidence by way of a video interview. The judge considered expert evidence concerning the competence of the witness. The defence expert criticised the conduct of the interview and the use of leading questions but conceded that the child appeared to understand the questions put to her and was able to answer them. The judge ruled that the child was competent not only before she gave evidence but also afterwards. On conviction the defendant's appeal was dismissed by the Court of Appeal.

JUDGMENT

'The statutory provisions [under s 53 of the 1999 Act] are not limited to the evidence of children. They apply to individuals of unsound mind. They apply to the infirm. The question in each case is whether the individual witness, or, as in this case, the individual child, is competent to give evidence in the particular trial. The question is entirely witness or child specific. There are no presumptions or preconceptions. The witness need not understand the special importance that the truth should be told in court, and the witness need not understand every single question or give a readily understood answer to every question. Many competent adult witnesses would fail such a competency test. Dealing with it broadly and fairly, provided the witness can understand the questions put to him and can also provide understandable answers, he or she is competent. If the witness cannot understand the questions or his answers to questions which he understands cannot themselves be understood he is not. The provisions of the statute are clear and unequivocal, and do not require reinterpretation.

'We should perhaps add that although the distinction is a fine one, whenever the competency question is addressed, what is required is not the exercise of a discretion but the making of a judgment, that is whether the witness fulfils the statutory criteria. In short, it is not open to the judge to create or impose some additional but non-statutory criteria based on the approach of earlier generations to the evidence of small children.

'We emphasise that in our collective experience the age of a witness is not determinative on his or her ability to give truthful and accurate evidence. Like adults some children will provide truthful and accurate testimony, and some will not. However, children are not miniature adults, but children, and to be treated and judged for what they are, not what they will, in years ahead, grow to be. Therefore, although due allowance must be made in the trial process for the fact that they are children with, for example, a shorter attention span than most adults, none of the characteristics of childhood, and none of the special measures which apply to the evidence of children carry with them the implicit stigma that children should be deemed in advance to be somehow less reliable than adults. The purpose of the trial process is to identify the evidence which is reliable and that which is not, whether it comes from an adult or a child. If competent, as defined by the statutory criteria, in the context of credibility in the forensic process, the child witness starts off on the basis of equality with every other witness.

'The judge determines the competency question, by distinguishing carefully between the issues of competence and credibility. At the stage when the competency question is determined the judge is not deciding whether a witness is or will be telling the truth and giving accurate evidence. Provided the witness is competent, the weight to be attached to the evidence is for the jury.

'When all is said and done, the witness whose cross-examination is in contemplation is a child, sometimes very young, and it should not take very lengthy cross-examination to demonstrate, when it is the case, that the child may indeed be fabricating, or fantasising, or imagining, or reciting a well-rehearsed untruthful script, learned by rote, or simply just suggestible, or contaminated by or in collusion with others to make false allegations, or making assertions in language which is beyond his or her level of comprehension, and therefore likely to be derived from another source. Comment on the evidence, including comment on evidence which may bear adversely on the credibility of the child, should be addressed after the child has finished giving evidence.

'The competency test may be re-analysed at the end of the child's evidence. This extra statutory jurisdiction is a judicial creation, clearly established in a number of decisions of this court (*R v MacPherson: R v Powell: R v M: R v Malicki*).

'However, in cases involving very young children delay on its own does not automatically require the court to prevent or stop the evidence of the child from being considered by the jury. That would represent a significant and unjustified gloss on the statute. In the present case, of course, we have reflected, as no doubt the jury did, on the fact of delay, and the relevant timetable. Making all allowances for these considerations, we are satisfied, as the judge was, that this particular child continued to satisfy the competency requirement.'

(Lord Judge LCJ)

In *R v Sed* [2004] EWCA Crim 1294, the Court of Appeal decided that the test of competence was satisfied even though the witness did not have a one-hundred-percent understanding of the questions put to her and could not give answers which were one-hundred-percent understandable. The real issue is whether the witness was capable of giving a coherent account of the events for the benefit of the jury. The credibility and reliability of the evidence were matters for the jury to decide. In this case, an allegation of rape was made by an eighty-one-year-old woman suffering from Alzheimer's disease. The prosecution made an application to admit her evidence by means of a videotaped interview. The defence objected and called two psychiatrists who testified to the effect she was suffering from moderate to severe Alzheimer's disease and she was not competent to testify and her interview should not be admitted. The judge ruled that the taped interview was admissible. The Court of Appeal dismissed the appeal and decided that her evidence was sufficiently coherent to admit in the proceedings:

JUDGMENT

'It should be noted that s 53 does not, in terms, provide for 100 per cent mutual comprehension of material exchanges giving rise to potential evidence. And, in our view, depending on the length and the nature of the questioning and the complexity of the matter the subject of it, it may not always require 100 per cent, or near 100 per cent, mutual understanding between questioner and questioned as a precondition of competence. The judge should also make allowance for the fact that the witness's performance and command of the detail may vary according to the importance to him or her of the subject matter of the question, how recent it was (in this case the interview took place within two days after the alleged attempted rape) and any strong feelings that it may have engendered.'

(Auld LJ)

In *DPP v R* [2007] EWHC 1842 (Admin), it was decided that a thirteen-year-old complainant of indecent assault, and who was severely mentally handicapped, would be interviewed on videotape, which constituted her evidence in chief. She was unable to recall anything of the incident in cross-examination. The Divisional Court decided that she was competent to testify, despite her lapse of memory:

JUDGMENT

'The girl may have had learning difficulties. Her evidence may have needed treating with some care in consequence, but the problem at trial was not capacity to understand or to give intelligible answers, it was loss of memory. Recollection is quite different from competence.

'[This girl] could understand the questions and she could give intelligible answers. The problem was that her perfectly intelligible answer was, "I cannot remember." She was not incompetent. It may be that she could not, for lack of memory, give useful evidence by the time of trial, but that is a different question.'

(Hughes LJ)

In *R v Yacoob* (1981) 72 Cr App R 313 the court held that questions relating to the competency of a prosecution witness should be settled before the trial commences, prior to the witness being sworn or before they start to give evidence.

3.5.5 Sworn/unsworn evidence

In criminal proceedings the general rule, subject to two exceptions, is that only sworn witness evidence is admitted in court. The decision whether a witness is entitled to give sworn evidence is made by the judge: see s 55(1) of the Youth Justice and Criminal Evidence Act 1999.

The test for determining whether a witness may be sworn is laid down in s 55(2)(b) of the 1999 Act. This involves the common law, cumulative, two-tiered test that was known as the *Hayes* test (see above), namely whether the witness 'has a sufficient appreciation of the solemnity of the occasion and of the particular responsibility to tell the truth which is involved in taking the oath'. There is a presumption to the effect that the witness has a sufficient appreciation of the solemnity of the occasion and the duty to speak the truth, if he is able to give intelligible testimony: see s 55(3) of the 1999 Act. The test of 'intelligible testimony' is laid down in s 55(8) and is the same test for competence, namely whether the witness understands questions put to him and may give answers which can be understood. The legal burden of proof lies on the party calling the witness to testify and the standard of proof is a balance of probabilities: see s 55(4). The questioning of the witness is conducted in the absence of the jury, and expert evidence may be called by the party.

The two exceptions to the sworn evidence rule are stated in s 55(2) of the 1999 Act, thus:

1. The witness is under the age of fourteen.
2. The witness is incapable of satisfying the test for sworn evidence.

In respect of these exceptions the witness is entitled to give unsworn evidence. In respect of the first exception, i.e. the witness is under the age of fourteen, the witness is not permitted to give sworn evidence. The second exception (incapacity to give sworn evidence) involves a last-resort method of receiving the evidence of the witness. However, the legislation does not lay down a test to determine whether the witness may give unsworn evidence. This is a matter within the trial judge's discretion. Presumably, this is dependent on whether the witness is capable of giving a coherent account of the facts.

3.5.6 The defendant

In criminal cases the original rule at common law was that the defendant was not competent to testify, not even on their own behalf. The reasons commonly accorded for this incapacity were an interest in the proceedings and the overriding principle of not incriminating themself. However, the Criminal Evidence Act 1898 changed the law and made the defendant a competent witness for the first time, but only for or on behalf of the defence; that is for the defendant and any co-defendants. At the same time the defendant was not compellable to testify on their behalf and was accordingly entitled to refuse to testify. The common law rule of incompetence governed the defendant's capacity to be a witness for the prosecution.

The modern law concerning the competence of the defendant and other witnesses in criminal cases is laid down in s 53(1) of the Youth Justice and Criminal Evidence Act 1999. This Act repeals the Criminal Evidence Act 1898 and enacts the general rule in s 53(1) to the effect that all persons, irrespective

	Competence	Compellability	Sworn evidence (affirmation)	Unsworn evidence
Civil cases	*Hayes* test	yes	yes	Persons under 18
Criminal cases	s 53 of the 1999 Act	yes	yes	Persons under 14

Figure 3.1 Competence and compellability of witnesses

of age, are competent to give evidence. This principle includes the defendant, i.e. the person charged.

In addition, the defendant (or person charged) is not treated as a competent witness for the prosecution, whether charged solely or jointly with others. This is an affirmation of the common law rule as stated above. Section 53(4) of the 1999 Act declares as follows:

SECTION

'A person charged in criminal proceedings is not competent to give evidence in the proceedings for the prosecution (whether he is the only person, or is one of two or more persons, charged in the proceedings).'

Section 53(5) of the 1999 Act defines a person charged as not including 'a person who is not, or is no longer, liable to be convicted of any offence in the proceedings (whether as a result of pleading guilty or for any other reason)'.

The effect of this provision is that a 'person charged' is one who is currently on trial on indictment or summarily and pleads not guilty.

Moreover, the common law rule is applicable to the effect that the defendant is not compellable to testify in his defence. Thus, whether the defendant chooses to testify in his defence is a decision he will take after considering advice from his legal adviser. There is no compulsion on his part to testify: this is known as the defendant's right of silence (in court). The possible consequences of remaining silent will be considered later under the right of silence, but in a nutshell, if the defendant fails to testify in the circumstances enacted in s 35 of the Criminal Justice and Public Order Act 1994, the judge may direct the jury 'to draw such inferences as appear proper'.

Techniques available to the prosecution to call an accomplice

There are various devices available to the prosecution who may wish to call, as a witness, a person who has been allegedly implicated in the crime. In these circumstances the individual will be treated as an ordinary witness and may be competent and compellable to testify for the prosecution. These devices are:

- where a *nolle prosequi* is entered against a defendant;
- where a successful application is made for an order of separate trial; or
- where the defendant pleads guilty.

Nolle prosequi

This is a technique that is available to the prosecution where the defendant (D) is charged together with others (E and F) with the commission of one or more offences, and the prosecution wishes to call one defendant (D) to testify against other defendants (E and F). The prosecution may 'offer no evidence' against the defendant (D) and the judge or magistrates will formally acquit the defendant for the relevant offence. In these circumstances, D will be treated as an ordinary witness and will be both competent and compellable to testify for the prosecution.

Section 17 of the Criminal Justice Act 1967 provides as follows:

SECTION

> 'Where a defendant arraigned on an indictment or inquisition pleads not guilty and the prosecutor proposes to offer no evidence against him, the court before which the defendant is arraigned may, if it thinks fit, order that a verdict of not guilty shall be recorded without any further steps being taken in the proceedings, and the verdict shall have the same effect as if the defendant had been tried and acquitted on the verdict of the jury or a court.'

Although the section declares that the court 'may' enter a finding of 'not guilty', the word 'may' suggests that the court can refuse the prosecution application. In practice, however, the court is unlikely to reject the prosecution's application and force the prosecution to prove its case. Indeed, in *R v Grafton* [1993] QB 101, the Court of Appeal said that the decision whether or not to continue the prosecution had to be that of the prosecution, and the trial judge had no power to refuse to permit the discontinuance of the prosecution.

Application for separate trials

The trial judge retains a discretion to order separate trials of defendants who are accused of having jointly committed an offence. Factors which militate against separate trials are saving time and the convenience to witnesses in having one trial; the desirability of the jury having a full picture of the occurrence of the event in a single trial; and the risk of different verdicts being returned by different juries on similar facts in the event of separate trials: see *R v Moghal* (1977) 65 Cr App R 56. The decision is ultimately one for the discretion of the judge, and the Court of Appeal is unlikely to interfere with the decision of the judge provided that there is no miscarriage of justice.

Guilty plea by one defendant

In a trial with more than one defendant, if one defendant pleads guilty they are no longer treated as a 'person charged'. The effect is that such a person may be required to testify for the prosecution. In these circumstances, it is desirable that the guilty defendant be sentenced before testifying for the prosecution. The reason for the practice of sentencing the defendant before they testify is to avoid the temptation of the defendant colouring their testimony in the hope of receiving a lighter sentence. At the same time, if the judge is unclear as to the significance of the defendant's role in the commission of the offence, he or she may postpone sentencing until the conclusion of the trial of the co-defendant.

In *R v Payne* [1950] 1 All ER 102, Payne (P) and two co-defendants, A and B, were indicted on a charge of burglary. On arraignment on the first day of the trial, P pleaded guilty and the others pleaded not guilty. P was sentenced to two years' imprisonment and then testified for the prosecution. The two other defendants were found guilty the following day and were sentenced to twelve and fifteen months respectively. P appealed against his sentence. The Court of Appeal allowed the appeal and reduced P's sentence to fifteen months:

JUDGMENT

'It may be a very convenient course to sentence on the first day prisoners who plead guilty but that ought not to apply where two or more men are indicted together. If one pleads guilty and the other not guilty, the proper course is to postpone sentence on the man who pleaded guilty until the others have been tried and then to bring up all the prisoners to be dealt with together because by that time the court will be in possession of the facts relating to all of them and will be able to assess properly the degree of guilt of each. This man received a heavier sentence than the other two because he was tried in a different court on a different day. This is a most inconvenient practice and it ought to cease . . . But what I have said does not apply in the exceptional case where a man who pleads guilty is going to be called as a witness. In those circumstances it is right that he be sentenced there and then so that there can be no suspicion that his evidence is coloured by the fact that he hopes to get a lighter sentence.'

(Lord Goddard CJ)

3.5.7 The defendant's spouse/civil partner in criminal cases

Under the common law, in addition to the defendant, their spouse was also incompetent to testify in both civil and criminal proceedings. This rule has been abrogated in both civil and criminal cases by a series of statutory provisions. In criminal proceedings, the test concerning a witness's competence is enacted in s 53(3) of the Youth Justice and Criminal Evidence Act 1999. This involves a test that is applicable to *all witnesses* in criminal proceedings, i.e. whether the person understands questions put to him and may give answers which can be understood: see above. Also, the extent to which the spouse (including a registered civil partner) is compellable to testify in criminal proceedings is dealt with in s 80 of the Police and Criminal Evidence Act 1984. The principle enacted here is dependent on which of three parties involved in criminal proceedings calls the spouse of the defendant to testify. The three parties involved are:

- the defendant who is the spouse or civil partner of the witness;
- the spouse or civil partner of a co-defendant, who is charged in the proceedings, being called by the defendant;
- the prosecution who wishes to call the spouse or civil partner of any of the defendants.

It is important to understand that the rules concerning the compellability of the defendant's spouse applicable to the latter two categories are identical. In short, whether the defendant's spouse or civil partner is compellable to testify for the co-defendant or the prosecution is subject to the same principles as laid down in s 80 of the 1984 Act.

A spouse of the defendant has not been defined in the Act but is a person who, at the time of being called to testify, had contracted a valid marriage. The legislation was amended to include a registered civil partner of the same or opposite sex of the defendant. In both cases there is no requirement that the parties live with each other. However, persons living with each other without going through valid ceremonies of marriage or registered civil partnerships are not spouses etcetera for these purposes and will be treated as ordinary witnesses and compellable to testify for any party in the proceedings.

Spouse (civil partner) of the defendant

Section 80(2) of the 1984 Act lays down the rule that the defendant's spouse (or civil partner) is, subject to one exception, compellable to testify on his or her behalf in respect of *any criminal charges*. For example, Harry, who is married to Ann, is charged with common assault on Nuala. Ann is compellable to testify on behalf of Harry. The same principle applies if the alleged assault is on Ann.

The only exception to this principle of compellability at the instance of a spouse (civil partner) is the occasion when the spouse (civil partner) is also a defendant in the same proceedings: see s 80(4) of the 1984 Act. This is an obvious exception which would have been implied in any event on the ground that an accused person is never compellable to testify in criminal proceedings: see above.

Defendant calls the spouse (civil partner) of co-defendant / or accused's spouse (civil partner) being called by the prosecution

Where the spouse (civil partner) of a co-defendant is called by a defendant to testify on their behalf, the general rule is that the spouse etcetera of the co-defendant is not compellable to testify on their behalf. For example, where Hilary and Dominic are charged with theft from Boris, Carrie, the wife of Hilary, is not compellable to testify for the defendant, Dominic. The same principle is applicable where the prosecution wishes to call the spouse (civil partner) of an accused. In the example above, Carrie is not compellable to testify for the prosecution against Hilary or Dominic.

Exceptionally, where the charge in respect of the defendant is within a 'specified offence' identified in s 80(3) of the 1984 Act, the spouse or civil partner of the defendant is compellable to testify for either the co-defendant or the prosecution in the criminal proceedings: see ss 80(2A)(a) and (b) of the 1984 Act.

Section 80(3) states:

SECTION

'. . . an offence is a specified offence for the purposes of subsection (2A) above if –

(a) it involves an assault on, or injury or threat of injury to, the wife or husband or a person who was at the material time under the age of 16;
(b) it is a sexual offence alleged to have been committed in respect of a person who was at the material time under that age; or
(c) it consists of attempting or conspiring to commit, or of aiding, abetting, counselling, procuring or inciting the commission of, an offence falling within paragraph (a) or (b) above.'

Thus, the compellability of a spouse or civil partner of a defendant to testify on behalf of a co-defendant or the prosecution is dependent on the type of offence with which the defendant is charged. Section 80(3)(a) uses the expression 'involves', i.e. the offence 'involves' an assault, etc., which is much broader than 'against'. In other words, the spouse of the defendant or a person under the age of sixteen may be a victim of the assault, directly or indirectly. It is arguable that charges of blackmail and kidnapping against a spouse may involve an assault on that spouse and be within the definition of a 'specified offence'.

The difficulties surrounding the construction of s 80(3)(a) of PACE 1984 may be summarised as whether the words 'it involves' in the subsection in reference to 'an offence' mean that the involvement is required to be legal or alternatively whether the involvement is required to be factual. The legal involvement has a narrower construction and will be satisfied where the specified individual is the victim of assault, injury or threat etc. In contrast, a factual involvement has a broader construction and will be satisfied where, despite the victim of the assault not being the spouse etc., the factual evidence supporting the charge is connected with the spouse etc. The Court of Appeal in *R v A* (2012) adopted the narrower approach and decided that the compellability of the spouse of the accused to testify for the prosecution or the co-accused in respect of the 'specified offences' is determined by reference to the charge sheet or indictment.

CASE EXAMPLE

R v A [2012] 1 WLR 3378 (CA)

The defendant was charged with threatening to destroy or damage property, contrary to s 2(a) of the Criminal Damage Act 1971. The wife executed a pre-trial statement to the effect that a heated argument had flared up between the defendant and her at their flat and she had retreated to the children's bedroom. It was alleged that the defendant shouted out loudly that he would burn the house down and then entered the kitchen, pressed the portable gas igniter located there, turned on the hobs and the oven, and left the flat. At the trial the wife refused to testify and the judge ruled that she was not compellable to testify for the prosecution. On appeal the Court of Appeal dismissed the appeal and decided that the words within s 80(3)(a) are construed solely by reference to the legal nature of the offence as stated in the terms of the indictment.

JUDGMENT

'On the ordinary language of the provision . . . we can see nothing that points to a focus on anything other than the legal nature of the offence and not the specific factual circumstances in which the offence was committed . . . there are practical considerations that support this construction. It is essential in our view to be able to determine at the outset of the trial by reference to the nature of the offence and not the evidence which the prosecution intends to call whether the spouse is a compellable witness. If the evidence to be given about the factual circumstances of the offence could be taken into account, then it could not be determined at the outset of the trial whether the spouse was a compellable witness, as the evidence might not emerge in the way envisaged. Furthermore, if it were possible to look at the factual circumstances of the offence, then the range of offences caught by section 80 would be infinite. Looking therefore at the policy, language and practical considerations in a broad and purposive way, we consider that Parliament decided to strike the balance by reference to the nature of the offence and not by reference to the factual circumstances surrounding the offence.'

(Thomas LJ)

Unfortunately, the effect of s 80(3) is to give rise to anomalies; some of these were highlighted in *R v A*. The compellability of witnesses within s 80(3) is restricted to spouses and civil partners. It does not extend to partners living with each other, even for a considerable period of time. In addition, where a non-compellable spouse exercises his or her legitimate right not to testify, the judge in his discretion is entitled to admit his or her pre-court statements as an alternative to testimony and as evidence as to the truth, i.e. hearsay assertions under s 114(2) of the Criminal Justice Act 2003. Moreover, the witness's spouse may be charged with a series of offences, some of which may be included as specified offences within s 80(3), and others outside this provision. Strictly, this may mean that a reluctant spouse may be compellable for the prosecution or the co-accused in respect of only some of the offences charged, but not all of the offences. A possible solution to this dilemma may be that in respect of the offences to which the spouse is not compellable the out-of-court statements may not be admissible. In any event, the spouse or civil partner of a non-defendant is compellable to testify in all criminal proceedings.

A person may be understandably reluctant to testify against their spouse or civil partner; but there is strong public interest in favour of certain offences being prosecuted, and it will be difficult to secure evidence of these offences otherwise than from the defendant and/or their spouse or civil partner, hence the need to introduce an element of compulsion within s 80.

The decisive moment to determine whether a person is a spouse or registered civil partner of a defendant is at the time that the witness is called to testify in the criminal proceedings. A person who is no longer married to the defendant or where the civil partnership has been dissolved is not treated as being a spouse for the purpose of these provisions: see s 80(5) of the 1984 Act. Thus, an ex-spouse or ex-civil partner will be treated as an ordinary witness and will be compellable to testify for any of the parties. Once the individuals satisfy the legal tests for being spouses or civil partners, it is irrelevant that they are not living with each other at the time that the witness is called to testify.

In addition, a 'person charged in the proceedings' for the purposes of s 80 does not include a person who is not, or is no longer, liable to be convicted: see s 80(4A) of the 1984 Act. Thus, a defendant who has been acquitted or pleaded guilty is outside this definition and is treated as an ordinary witness.

Acaster warnings

Where a spouse (civil partner) of the defendant who is competent, but not compellable, to testify for the prosecution is called by the prosecution to testify on its behalf, the judge may be required to exercise their discretion to warn the potential witness, in the absence of the jury, that they are not compellable to testify. This is known as an *Acaster* warning, derived from the case *R v Acaster* (1912) 7 Cr App R 187:

JUDGMENT

'In any case where the spouse of the accused comes to give evidence against her husband, the judge ought to ask her, "Do you know you may object to give evidence?" . . . That I imagine is what other judges will do for the present, though there is no decision which binds us to do it. . . .'

(Darling J)

In *R v Pitt* [1983] QB 25, the Court of Appeal decided that although there was no rule of law to the effect that the judge should issue the warning, the matter would be treated as an exercise of the discretion of the judge. In this case, the defendant's wife, a competent but not compellable witness (as the law existed at that time), reluctantly testified for the prosecution against her husband. She gave answers that were inconsistent with her statement and was made a hostile witness and cross-examined by the prosecution. Her husband was convicted, but the Court of Appeal quashed the conviction on the ground that the wife did not appreciate that she was not a compellable witness and could not be taken to have waived her right not to testify without full knowledge of her rights:

JUDGMENT

'This case illustrates very powerfully why it is necessary for the trial judge to make certain that the wife understands her position before she takes the oath. Had that been done here, there would have been no difficulty . . . Up to a point where she goes into the witness box, W has a choice: she may refuse to give evidence or waive her right of refusal. The waiver is effective only if made with full knowledge of her right to refuse. If she waives her right of refusal, she becomes an ordinary witness . . . Once W has started upon her evidence, she must complete it. It is not open to her to retreat behind the barrier of non-compellability if she is asked questions that she does not want to answer. This makes it particularly important that W should understand when she takes the oath that she is waiving her right to refuse evidence . . . It seems to us desirable that where W is called as a witness for the prosecution of H, the judge should explain to her in the absence of the jury, that, before she takes the oath she has the right to refuse to give evidence, but that if she chooses to give evidence she may be treated like any other witness. . . .'

(Pain J)

In the event of a failure to warn a competent, but not compellable, witness that she is not required to testify for the prosecution of the co-accused, the Court of Appeal will take into consideration all relevant factors, such as:

- whether the witness was reluctant or enthusiastic to testify against her husband;
- whether she was called to testify for the co-defendant or the prosecution;
- the significance of her testimony.

Where the spouse exercises his or her right not to testify, the prosecution is not entitled to comment on their silence: see s 80A of the 1984 Act. This statutory restriction does not extend to the co-defendant and the judge. As far as the co-defendant is concerned, there is no restriction as to the presentation of their case, including the co-defendant's right to comment on the defendant's right of silence.

The trial judge has a restricted freedom to comment on the defendant's spouse not testifying in the case. The power of the judge to comment is dependent on the exercise of discretion, and the overriding duty is to ensure a fair trial. Indeed, in exceptional circumstances, the judge may use the summing up to rectify a breach by the prosecution. In *R v Naudeer* [1984] 3 All ER 1036, under the predecessor to s 80A, the court decided that, where the prosecution makes an unauthorised comment, the judge, subject to the circumstances of each case, is entitled to remedy the breach in their summing up.

3.6 Special measures directions

Sections 16 to 33 of the Youth Justice and Criminal Evidence Act 1999 lay down a number of provisions designed to assist young, disabled, vulnerable or intimidated witnesses to give evidence in criminal proceedings. These provisions have been substantially amended by the Coroners and Justice Act 2009. Procedural rules that govern the process of applying for a special measures direction have been created by the Criminal Procedure Rules 2011. In addition, the Criminal Practice Direction published at [2013] 1 WLR 3164, declares that the court is required to take 'every reasonable step' to encourage and facilitate the attendance of witnesses and to facilitate the participation of any person, including the defendant. This includes enabling a witness or defendant to give their best evidence and enabling a defendant to comprehend the proceedings and engage fully with his or her defence. The court is required to identify the needs of witnesses at an early stage and may require the parties to identify arrangements to facilitate the giving of evidence and participation in the trial. Ground rules may be drawn up by the judge after discussions with advocates and intermediaries before vulnerable witnesses give their evidence. When the witness is young or otherwise vulnerable, the court may dispense with the normal practice and impose restrictions on the advocate 'putting his case' where there is a risk of a young or otherwise vulnerable witness failing to understand, becoming distressed or acquiescing to leading questions. In *R v Jonas* [2015] EWCA Crim 562, the accused was charged with offences involving human trafficking and sexual exploitation. The trial judge drew up ground rules by imposing time limits and other restrictions on the cross-examination of two complainants. The accused was convicted and his appeal was dismissed on the ground that, applying the Criminal Procedure Rules 2011 and the Practice Direction 2013, the judge had a duty to control questioning. Excessive and repetitive questioning of vulnerable witnesses was required to be controlled by the judge. In the circumstances the trial was fair.

There are now five categories of witnesses who are eligible for assistance and in respect of whom special measures may be made by the judge or magistrates in criminal proceedings. These are:

- A witness who is under the age of 18 at the time of the hearing: see ss 16(1) and 21 of the 1999 Act. In the latter case, a special measures direction may be made in respect of a child witness who is in need of special protection, as defined. The special measures direction may take the form of presenting the witness's evidence by means of a video recording. Where this is not possible the evidence must be given by means of a live television link. In *R v Camberwell Green Youth Court* [2003] 2 Cr App R 257, the court decided that the presentation of evidence of a child witness in a room where the defendant was not present did not infringe the defendant's right to a fair trial. In addition there was an irrebuttable presumption that the presentation of evidence of child witnesses by way of video recording and live link, under the Youth Justice and Criminal Evidence Act 1999, was compliant with Art 6 of the European Convention on Human Rights. The defendant was not prevented from challenging prosecution witnesses who give their evidence by video recordings or live links. Further, there was nothing in the 1999 statutory provisions to hinder the trial court's discretion to do whatever is necessary to ensure a fair trial. Subject to amendments recently introduced to the 1999 Act (see later), child defendants were excluded from the statutory scheme.

- A witness who suffers from a mental or physical disorder or otherwise has a significant impairment of intelligence: s 16(2) of the 1999 Act.
- A witness whose evidence is likely to be affected on grounds of fear or distress about testifying: s 17(1) of the 1999 Act. Section 17(2) sets out a number of factors that the court should take into account in determining whether a witness falls within s 17(1), including the nature and alleged circumstances of the offence to which the proceedings relate. Section 17(3) also requires the court to consider any views expressed by the witness.
- The complainant as a witness in respect of a sexual offence is automatically eligible for assistance: s 17(4) of the 1999 Act.
- The use of a live link or intermediary for evidence given by certain accused persons under s 33A and s 33BA of the 1999 Act.

Section 18 authorises the making of a special measures direction, which may provide for any of the measures in ss 23–30 in the case of a s 16 witness, and for any of the measures in ss 23–28 in the case of a s 17 witness.

The prosecution or defence may apply to the court for a special measures direction or the court may, of its own motion, make such a direction: see s 19 of the 1999 Act. The court is required to determine whether any, and, if so, which, of the special measures available would be likely to improve the quality of the evidence of the witness: see s 19 of the 1999 Act. In deciding this question the court is required to consider all the circumstances of the case, including any views expressed by the witness and the extent to which measure(s) might inhibit effective testing of the evidence by a party to the proceedings: see s 19(3). Finally, the court is required to state in open court its reasons for giving, varying, refusing or discharging a special measures direction: s 20 of the 1999 Act. Section 21 makes special provision in the case of child witnesses. The effect is to impose a restriction on the discretion of the judge in deciding what special measures should be imposed. Measures such as the use of video-recorded evidence and live links are regarded as mandatory. Section 22 extends s 21 to certain witnesses who do not qualify on a strict application of the provisions, such as a witness who is eighteen at the time of the hearing but who was under eighteen when he made a relevant recording. Section 22A makes special provision in relation to proceedings for alleged sexual offences. Section 31 governs the status of evidence given by virtue of the provisions in this chapter; s 32 requires the judge to give the jury such warning (if any) as the judge considers necessary to ensure that the direction was given in relation to the witness does not prejudice the accused. The making of special measures directions by the judge will need to be considered in respect of a statement by a witness under s 116 of the Criminal Justice Act 2003 on the ground that the witness will not attend to give oral evidence through fear.

In *R v Watts* [2010] EWCA Crim 1824, the Court of Appeal declared that the parliamentary intention behind special measures directions is that witnesses who are eligible for assistance should testify with such assistance as is available; and that witnesses who lack sufficient communication skills should be able to give evidence with the use of an intermediary. Further, where evidence in chief has been given by means of video-taped evidence, such evidence may stand despite the absence of the opportunity to cross-examine the witness.

The 1999 Act lays down a variety of special measures that may be ordered by the court. These are specified in ss 23–30 of the 1999 Act and are as follows.

Screening witnesses from the defendant

The court may direct that a witness, while giving testimony, may be prevented by means of a screen or other arrangement from seeing the defendant. However, the witness must be positioned in such a way that he is seen by the judge (or justices), the jury, legal representatives and any court interpreters: see s 23 of the 1999 Act.

Evidence of witness (other than the accused) by live link

A special measures direction may take the form of giving evidence by a live link. Such a link has been defined as a live television link or other arrangement whereby the witness, while absent from the courtroom, is able to see and hear a person there and to be seen and heard by the judge (or justices), the jury, legal representatives and any court interpreters: see s 24 of the 1999 Act. The effect is that the witness is treated as being constructively present in the court. The Criminal Practice Direction, published at [2013] 1 WLR 3164, declares that this special measure direction may also provide for a specified person to accompany the witness. The presence of the supporter is designed to provide emotional support to the witness, helping to reduce the witness's anxiety and stress and contributing to the ability to give best evidence. The supporter may be anyone known to and trusted by the witness but who is not a party to the proceedings and has no detailed knowledge of the evidence in the case.

In addition, Part 8 (ss 51–56) of the Criminal Justice Act 2003 introduced similar provisions for witnesses other than the defendant to give evidence (examination in chief and cross-examination) through a live link. The court may make such a direction on the application of either party or of its own motion. If the witness is a child (under the age of eighteen), the court must give a special measures direction that provides for any evidence given by the witness that is not given by means of a video recording (s 27) to be given by means of a live link. This is known as the 'primary rule': see s 21(3). The primary rule does not apply if the court is satisfied that compliance would not maximise the quality of the witness's evidence or if the witness wishes to testify in court and the court is satisfied that this would not diminish the quality of the witness's evidence: see s 21(4). In this event, the court must direct the use of a screen pursuant to s 23 (see s 21(4A)); alternatively, the court may consider a different special measure. A 'live link' is defined by s 56(2) of the 2003 Act in a similar way as under the 1999 Act. Section 54(2) enacts that the judge (or magistrates) may give such direction as is necessary to ensure that the tribunal of fact 'gives the same weight to the evidence as if it had been given in the court room'.

Applications by the defendant for live link directions

Prior to the amendment of the 1999 Act, the question arose as to whether that Act empowers the court to issue directions permitting the accused to testify via a live link. In *R v Ukpabio* [2008] 1 Cr App R 6, the Court of Appeal decided that no such power exists under the Act, even where the accused is put in fear. The statutory provisions were based on the premise that the defendant's evidence should be given by him being present in court, subject to such protective measures, short of a video link, which the court considered to be appropriate in its inherent jurisdiction. The purpose was to ensure that the accused was able to give evidence properly and fully and in particular without fear. Section 47 of the Police and Justice Act 2006 introduced a new s 33A of the Youth Justice and Criminal Evidence Act 1999 authorising the court to permit the accused to testify (examination in chief, cross-examination and re-examination) by means of a live link. A live link is defined in s 33B to mean any technology that enables the accused to see and hear a person in the court room and to be seen and heard by the judge (or/and justices), the jury, any co-accused, the legal representatives in the proceedings and any interpreter or other person appointed by the court to assist the accused. The direction may be made on the application of the accused or by the court of its own motion, provided that a number of conditions are satisfied. In addition a number of prerequisites, laid down in s 33A(4) and (5), are required to be satisfied:

- section 33A(4) provides that where the accused is under the age of eighteen at the time of the application; and
- his ability to participate effectively in the proceedings as a witness is compromised by his level of intellectual ability or social functioning; and
- the use of the live link would enable him to participate more effectively as a witness; and
- the direction is in the interests of justice.

Alternatively, s 33A(5) provides that:

- where the accused has attained the age of eighteen at the time of the application; and
- suffers from a mental disorder (within the meaning of the Mental Health Act 1983), or otherwise has a significant impairment of intelligence and social function; and
- for that reason is unable to participate effectively as a witness in the proceedings; and
- the use of the live link would enable him to participate more effectively as a witness; and
- the direction is in the interests of justice.

Section 33A(8) enacts that the court is required to give its reasons in open court for making, refusing or discharging a live link direction.

In *R v Rahman and Others* [2015] EWCA Crim 15, the Court of Appeal considered the effect of s 33A(4) where a defence application was made on behalf of a fifteen-year-old accused. He was tried jointly with two co-accused charged with murder, unlawful wounding and aggravated burglary. The accused observed the cross-examination of his co-accused and had serious concerns about testifying because he was likely to lose his temper and because of his dislike of being challenged by authority. The defendant alleged that his level of social functioning may compromise his ability to testify and a live link may enable him to participate more effectively. In the absence of expert evidence his mother testified and supported his application. The trial judge refused his application and he failed to testify. On conviction he appealed on the ground that the judge had erred in refusing to grant the application. The Court of Appeal dismissed the appeal and decided that, although non-defendant witnesses under the age of eighteen are automatically eligible for special measures, defendants under the age of eighteen are required to satisfy additional criteria. The fact that the defendant was short-tempered and had a cynical disregard for authority were no justifications for issuing special measures directions and did not correspond with the intention of Parliament. The partisan nature of the testimony of the defendant's mother was insufficient to satisfy the test of impairment of the accused's intellectual ability or social functioning.

JUDGMENT

'It is clear that this is a case where the defence had no concerns whatsoever about the applicant's ability to participate effectively in the proceedings and to give evidence; they had no intention of applying for special measures until the applicant saw his co-accused being cross-examined. He began to fear he would respond aggressively to cross-examination. It is far from clear that, had the judge made a special measures direction, this would have allayed his fears to the extent that he would have chosen to give evidence.

The fact that the applicant may have a temper and does not like being challenged by authority figures does not justify an application of this kind. The same could be said of a large number of offenders, young and old. This characteristic is not what Parliament had in mind when it referred to 'social functioning' in s.33A. There was here no satisfactory basis for the assertion that the applicant's ability to testify would be compromised by his having to testify in open court. He was sufficiently mature to be able to stand a trial and to give instructions and he had no difficulty in understanding and answering questions, as was established when he was interviewed at length as a potential witness.'

(Hallett LJ)

Evidence given in private (in camera)

A special measures direction may order that a certain individual be excluded from the court while the witness testifies. The direction may not exclude the defendant, his legal representatives and interpreters acting for the witness. This direction may only be used where the proceedings relate to a sexual offence, or there are reasonable grounds to believe that the witness has or will be intimidated by any person other than the defendant: see s 25(4) of the 1999 Act.

Removal of wigs and gowns

A direction may be issued for the wearing of wigs and gowns to be dispensed with, while a witness gives their evidence: see s 26 of the 1999 Act.

Video-recorded evidence

Section 27 of the 1999 Act provides for a video recording of an interview of the witness to be admitted as the evidence in chief of that witness. However, the court is not entitled to make such a direction if, having regard to all the circumstances of the case, the recording ought not to be admitted in the interests of justice. In determining whether it would not be in the interests of justice to admit the whole, or part, of the recording, the court must consider whether any prejudice to the accused is outweighed by the desirability of showing the recorded interview. The prime consideration is the reliability of the video evidence. Where a recording is admitted, the witness must be called by the party tendering the recording in evidence, unless a direction has been made for the witness's cross-examination to be given otherwise than by testimony, or the parties have agreed to dispense with the witness's presence.

In a Practice Direction in criminal proceedings published at [2013] 1 WLR 3164, it is declared that where a video recording is to be adduced during proceedings before the Crown Court, it should be produced and proved by the interviewer, or any other person who was present at the interview with the witness at which the recording was made, subject to the parties agreeing to the contrary. In addition, the Ministry of Justice has published guidance on Achieving Best Evidence (ABE) on interviewing vulnerable and intimidated witnesses. It describes good practice in preparing for and conducting interviews with such witnesses, both adults and children, to enable them to give their best evidence in criminal proceedings.

The judge will initially make an assessment from the video recording as to whether the child witness is competent to testify. Where the child witness is not competent the video evidence will not be admitted. But if the child is competent, the judge will need to make an assessment as to whether the video recording complies with the ABE guidance and, if not, whether the breaches are so significant that the recording ought not to be admitted.

In *R v Pooley* [2015] 1 Cr App R 12, the Court of Appeal decided that the trial judge had erred in ruling that a vulnerable witness's testimony may be presented to the court by way of video-recorded interview but may not be cross-examined by defence counsel. The accused was charged on three counts with sexual assault on the complainant, aged eight. On the trial date the judge introduced himself to the witness in the absence of counsel representing the parties and, without warning, announced in court that the witness may not be cross-examined. Despite protests by defence counsel the judge was unmoved. The video evidence was played in court as the only evidence of the child, but the defence was allowed to prepare a document containing the questions he would have put to the witness and the trial proceeded. The accused was convicted and appealed on the grounds that the judge was in breach of a number of procedural points and the defendant did not have a fair trial. The Court of Appeal allowed the appeal on the grounds that it was unclear on what basis the judge made his ruling. If the witness was incompetent the judge ought to have informed the parties of his concerns and given them an opportunity to address the issues. In any event the clear requirement of s 27(5) of the Youth Justice and Criminal Evidence Act 1999 is that where the recording is admitted, the witness is required to be called, unless a special measures direction permits cross-examination by video recording or the parties agree not to cross-examine. In addition the trial was inherently unfair by preventing cross-examination of the main prosecution witness.

JUDGMENT

'With respect to the judge, who no doubt had the child's best interests at heart, we simply do not understand what he was saying as a matter of law, why he concluded the child could not be cross-examined and why he did not allow defence counsel to try a few sensitively phrased questions. It is not clear to us whether he had concluded the child was not competent to give evidence, not fit to give evidence, or it would not be good for her to give evidence. These difficulties might not have arisen had it been arranged for him to introduce himself to the witness at the same time as the advocates did.

'The judge's approach was wrong in a number of respects. If his visit was designed to assess her competence, he should have taken the parties with him or used the live link in their presence. He should not have questioned her alone: see section 54(6) of the Youth Justice and Criminal Evidence Act 1999. If his visit was merely designed to introduce himself properly to her and he unexpectedly began to question her ability to participate, he should have informed the parties of his concerns and sought their submissions, before making a ruling. He should have considered whether any other special measures such as the services of an intermediary might benefit the witness: section 54(3). Furthermore, he could have considered calling for an expert to assist him.

'If he had then concluded, on a sound basis, that the witness could not be cross-examined, he should have revisited the provisions of section 27 of the 1999 Act and the decision to allow the video recording to be played. He should have considered whether or not it was admissible where the prosecution could not tender the witness as required by section 27(5) of the 1999 Act (as amended). Finally, and most importantly, the judge should have openly and clearly given far greater consideration to the impact on the fairness of the trial of prohibiting the defence from testing the evidence of the main prosecution witness.'

(Hallett LJ)

In *G v DPP* [1997] 2 Cr App R 78, the Divisional Court decided that a failure to comply with the Memorandum of Good Practice (the predecessor to ABE) was a factor to be taken into account by a court in deciding whether to exercise its discretion to refuse to admit the recording.

In *R v Hanton* [2005] EWCA Crim 2009, the Court of Appeal decided that the correct test with regard to breaches of ABE guidelines involves the manner in which the interview was conducted and whether the questions asked were in accordance with the guidelines. What the jury had to assess was whether the videorecorded evidence was accurate and reliable. In this case the defendant was charged with indecent assault on two girls, aged six and eight years, who gave evidence by means of video recordings. The defence applied for the recordings to be excluded because of breaches of the ABE guidelines. The judge refused the application on the ground that the interviewer had acted in good faith and had done his best and left the matter to the jury without guidance. The Court of Appeal allowed the appeal and quashed the conviction on the ground that the judge had applied the wrong test.

In *R v K* [2006] EWCA Crim 472, the Court of Appeal affirmed the decision in *Hanton* and decided that the correct test for determining the admissibility of videorecorded evidence of a child was whether a reasonable jury, properly directed, could be sure that the witness had given a credible and accurate account on the videotape, notwithstanding any breaches of the relevant guidance for conducting interviews. It was possible for a court to consider other evidence that might corroborate the videorecorded evidence, but such consideration ought to be undertaken with considerable care. The Court of Appeal decided that the trial judge did not address the *Hanton* test specifically, although there were indications that he had that test in mind.

JUDGMENT

'The judge in the present case did not specifically identify the appropriate test, as in *Hanton*. If he had done, then the decision he reached would have been open to him. Although he did not address the test in terms, it is plain that what he had in mind throughout much of his judgment was whether the evidence might be relied upon by a jury such that any conviction by them of the defendant would be safe. Without expressly recognising the *Hanton* test as such, he was in practice adopting it. Although (in our view) he did not need to consider whether section 78 [of the Police and Criminal Evidence Act 1984] applied, he did so and came to the same conclusion. Although we cannot exclude the possibility that a different conclusion might be reached on a consideration of section 78 than would be on a consideration of section 27(2) of the Youth Justice and Criminal Evidence Act 1999, it is difficult to imagine the circumstances in which that would be so.'

(Hooper LJ)

In *R v Krezolek and Luczak* [2014] EWCA Crim 2782, the Court of Appeal applied the test in *R v K* and decided that on a charge of murder the video evidence of a six-year-old and a competent witness was admissible in the interests of justice. This was the position despite elements of fantasy and difficulties putting things in their chronological order. A certain element of leeway is expected to be made in respect of a child's account of events. Accordingly, evidence of child witnesses was not to be subject to the same forensic analysis as adult witnesses. The Court of Appeal reiterated the test as whether a reasonable jury, properly directed, may be sure that a witness has given a credible and accurate account on the videotape. But this cannot be reinterpreted to mean whether a reasonable jury, properly directed, may be sure that every aspect of the account is entirely credible and accurate. In any event the witness's account was supported in a significant way by other evidence.

As a general rule the jury is not entitled to have the evidence in a video recording of a child or vulnerable witness replayed in court to review its contents. The reason is to avoid the perception of an unfair advantage to be gained by the prosecution. However, in exceptional circumstances, where the jury makes a request to have a video replayed in order to review the manner in which a child witness had given his evidence (as distinct from the contents of the testimony), the judge is entitled to exercise his discretion and comply with the request, provided that he gives a balancing direction about the weight to be attached to the evidence. In *R v Mullen* [2004] 2 Cr App R 18, on charges of indecent assault on a girl aged ten, the complainant and her twelve-year-old brother presented their evidence in chief by means of video recordings. During their deliberations the jury asked to view the video recordings again. After establishing that defence counsel had no objection, the judge agreed. Halfway through the replaying of the complainant's recording the judge, after consulting *Archbold* (2003), interrupted the replay and established from the jury that the reason for the request was because they wanted to be reminded of the manner in which the complainant gave her evidence. They were then allowed to continue to view the recordings. The judge later gave a balancing direction to the jury. Following a conviction the defendant's appeal was dismissed on the grounds that the jury had requested to review the evidence for the purpose of seeing how the complainant gave her evidence, as opposed simply to being reminded of the content of that evidence. The judge had satisfied himself as to the validity of the reason for the jury's request and gave a balancing direction against attaching too much weight to the evidence.

JUDGMENT

'The authorities recognise that, if the purpose of the jury is to review the manner in which the complainant's evidence was given, then, despite its being a departure from the general position, the potential for prejudice as a result is something which may fairly be guarded against by an appropriate "balancing" direction. Thus, it is recognised that the potential for advantage to the prosecution is not in itself a matter which necessarily renders the trial unfair or an ensuing verdict of guilty unsafe. Provided that the judge satisfies himself as to the validity of the reason for the jury's request and gives the same type of balancing direction as in the case of a complainant, we consider that the judge's discretion similarly extends to the evidence of a supporting child witness.'

(Potter LJ)

Where the evidence in chief has been presented by way of a video recording, great care must be exercised by the judge before a jury may be allowed to see a transcript of the interview, even while the video recording of the interview is being shown. This may only be done in exceptional circumstances. The transcripts are only to be given to the jury following discussion between the judge and counsel in the absence of the jury. If transcripts are given, the judge is required to warn the jury then and there to examine the video as it was shown, not least to view the demeanour of the witness while giving evidence. The transcripts are to be withdrawn from the jury once the video evidence in chief has been given, except in very exceptional circumstances. If the jury were to retain the transcripts during cross-examination, the judge is required to positively exercise his discretion to permit the jury to do so and, if possible, to discuss this possibility, in the jury's absence, before the start of the evidence in chief. Further, if the transcripts were retained during cross-examination, they are to be recovered once the witness has finished giving evidence. Further, the jury may not be permitted to retire with the transcripts except in exceptional circumstances. Those exceptional circumstances would usually only be present if the defence positively wanted the jury to have the transcripts and the judge was satisfied that there were very good reasons why the jury should retire with the same, again after discussion with counsel. Finally, the judge is required to explain to the jury during the summing up why they were being allowed the transcripts and the limited use to which they could be put, namely to aid the jury to understand the evidence in chief of the relevant witness, and that the defence wanted the jury to retain the transcripts.

In *R v Popescu* [2011] Crim LR 227, the court laid down these principles in dismissing an appeal on a charge of rape. The complainant had a strong Romanian accent and gave her evidence in chief by way of recorded interviews. The jury was given transcripts of her evidence in chief in order to assist them in following the evidence. The cross-examination was conducted on the basis of the transcripts, which were retained by the jury for the remainder of the trial. The judge had warned the jury to consider the transcripts in the context of the whole of the evidence in the trial. The jury then retired with the transcripts. Following conviction, the defendant appealed. The Court of Appeal dismissed the appeal on the grounds that the defence wanted the jury to have the transcripts. The judge had used the transcripts in his summing up without objection from any counsel. Although the judge had not expressly considered whether it was right for the jury to retire with the transcripts, all the parties knew that it was going to happen and no one objected.

Videorecorded cross-examination or re-examination

Where a video recording has been admitted as the witness's examination in chief as stated above, a direction may provide for any cross-examination or re-examination of the witness to be recorded before trial by means of a video recording. Such a recording must be made in the presence of the judge or justices and legal representatives but in the absence of the defendant. The defendant, however, must be able to see and hear the examination of the witness, probably by use of a live link: see s 28 of the 1999 Act.

In *R v PMH* [2018] EWCA Crim 2452 the Court of Appeal outlined the best practice for pre-recorded cross-examination as follows:

- The judge should discuss, at a ground-rules hearing with counsel, how and when any limitations on questioning will be explained to the jury.
- Where this has not occurred, or where there have been changes, the judge should discuss, with counsel, how such limitations on questioning will be explained to the jury prior to the recording being played to them.
- Judges can give the jury a standard direction on special measures with a direction on any limitations that they may have imposed on cross-examination and the reasons for that prior to the recording being played to them.
- Judges should consider whether it is necessary to have another discussion with counsel before their closing submissions and prior to the summing up on any limitations that were imposed and the areas that those limitations may have had a material effect. This will assist counsel in identifying the areas on which they should address the jury.
- In summing up, the judge should remind the jury of any limitations imposed and the areas that have been identified upon which those limitations have had a material effect on the questions posed by counsel.

- Where written directions are provided to the jury the judge should include a standard special measures direction and a general direction outlining that limitations were imposed on cross-examination.

In *R v YGM* [2018] EWCA 2458 the guidance was clarified, where a judge agreed to give a direction on limitations imposed on cross-examination and where counsel was not given an opportunity for further comment in their closing speech:

JUDGMENT

'We believe that the following is best practice in a case involving cross examination of a vulnerable witness. First, the identification of any limitations on cross-examination should take place at an early stage. We assume that this will occur at the ground rules hearing where the judge will discuss with the advocates the nature and extent of the limitations imposed and whether they are simply as to style or also relate to content. Before the witness is cross examined, it is best practice, (as recommended by the Judicial College) that as well as giving the standard special measures direction, the trial judge also directs the jury in general terms that limitations have been placed on the defence advocate. If any specific issues of content have been identified that the cross examiner cannot explore, the judge may wish to direct the jury about them after the cross examination is completed. On any view, the judge should direct the jury about them in the summing-up. Finally, we should add that every advocate (and trial judge) is expected to ensure that they are up to date with current best practice in the treatment of vulnerable witnesses.'

Examination of witnesses (other than the accused) through an intermediary

This special measures direction provides for an examination of the witness to be conducted through an interpreter or other intermediary. The intermediary's function is to communicate questions put to the witness, and answers given by the witness to any person asking such questions, and to provide an understanding of the questions and answers to the witness or person in question: see s 29 of the 1999 Act.

Examination of the accused through an intermediary

Section 104 of the Coroners and Justice Act 2009 introduced a new provision in s 33BA of the Youth Justice and Criminal Evidence Act 1999. The new s 33BA entitles the accused to make an application to the judge for directions to be examined through an intermediary, subject to the following conditions:

Section 33BA(5) provides that:

- the accused is under the age of eighteen at the time of the application; and
- his ability to participate effectively in the proceedings as a witness giving oral evidence is compromised owing to his level of intellectual ability or social functioning; and
- the direction is necessary in order to ensure that he receives a fair trial.

Alternatively, s 33BA(6) provides:

- the accused has attained the age of eighteen at the time of the application; and
- suffers from a mental disorder (within the meaning of the Mental Health Act 1983), or otherwise has a significant impairment of intelligence and social function; and
- for that reason is unable to participate effectively as a witness in the proceedings; and
- the direction is necessary in order to ensure that he receives a fair trial.

Section 33BA(4) identifies that the function of an intermediary is to communicate questions put to the accused and, in reply, the answers to such questions including explanations of such questions and answers so far as is necessary to ensure understanding.

The examination of the accused is required to be conducted in the presence of the judge, jury and other persons stipulated in the direction: see s 33BA(7).

The court is required to give its reasons in open court for making, refusing or discharging a live link direction: see s 33BB(4).

Aids to communication

This special measures direction provides for any device, mechanical or otherwise, which will enable questions or answers to be communicated to or by the witness, despite any disability or disorder or other impairment that the witness suffers from: see s 30 of the 1999 Act.

Warning to the jury

Section 32 of the 1999 Act enacts that where evidence has been given in accordance with a special measures direction, the judge is required to give the jury such warning as he considers necessary to ensure that the fact that the direction was given in respect of a witness does not prejudice the accused.

Family proceedings and testimony of vulnerable witnesses

In care proceedings, prior to the sea-changing Supreme Court decision in *Re W* (2010), the court proceeded on the assumption that it was undesirable for a child to testify in the Family Court. In other words there was a presumption against children and other vulnerable persons testifying in care proceedings.

Witnesses under the age of 18	ss 16(1) and 21 of the 1999 Act
Witnesses who suffer from mental or physical disorder	s 16(2) of the 1999 Act
Witnesses who are intimidated	s 17(1) of the 1999 Act
The complainant of a sexual offence	s 17(4) of the 1999 Act
The defendant in special circumstances	ss 33A and 33BA of the 1999 Act

Figure 3.2 Special measures directions

The rationale for this presumption was the belief that a more direct involvement in court proceedings may increase the risk of a detrimental effect on the welfare of the child. Very often the disputed allegation of abuse on the complainant may turn on which party is to be believed. In the absence of the testimony of the complainant, substituted by a statement, there was a serious risk of injustice to the person against whom the complaint had been made. The Supreme Court in *Re W* unanimously decided that there will no longer be a presumption in family cases that a child will not give oral evidence. However, the court left it open to the Family Court to decide, on a case-by-case basis, when it would be appropriate for a child to testify and what assistance may be given to such witnesses. In deciding whether to allow a child to be called as a witness, the court is required to strike a balance between the interests of the child and the Convention rights of defendants.

CASE EXAMPLE

In *Re W* [2010] UKSC 12, care proceedings had commenced in respect of five children; four of these were the natural issue of F, who was the stepfather of C (Charlotte), the oldest child. C made serious sexual allegations against F, which also included the other four children. The care proceedings were founded almost entirely on these allegations. It was originally agreed that C would testify in the proceedings but the local authority changed its position and intended to rely on C's interview statement with the police. F's application for C to be called to testify was rejected by the judge and the Court of Appeal but upheld by the Supreme Court. The court decided the following: (1) the presumption of non-attendance of child witnesses was not reconcilable with the defendant's Convention rights; (2) striking a balance in care proceedings might well mean that the child may not be called in the great majority of cases, but that was a result, and not a presumption; (3) in considering whether a child should be called, a court will have to weigh the advantages that his or her presence will bring to the determination of the truth against the damage it might do to the welfare of that or any other child; (4) limb 1: in weighing the advantages of calling the child, the court would have to consider whether it could determine the case without making findings on particular issues; whether there will be anything useful to be gained from the child's oral evidence; the quality of any ABE interview; the nature of any challenge a party might wish to make, other than generalised accusations of lying or a fishing expedition, as distinct from focused questions putting forward a different explanation for certain events; the age and maturity of the child and the length of time since the events in question; (5) limb 2: in considering the risks of harm to the child, the court should consider the child's age and maturity, the length of time since the events, the support the child had from family and other sources, the child's wishes, as an unwilling child will rarely, if ever, be obliged to give evidence, the views of the child's guardian and those with parental responsibility, the risk of delay to the proceedings, and, where there were parallel criminal proceedings, the potential increased risk of harm from the likelihood of the child having to give evidence twice; (6) the court is required to factor in the steps to be taken to improve the quality of the child's evidence and at the same time to decrease the risk of harm.

JUDGMENT

'The presumption against a child giving evidence which requires to be rebutted by anyone seeking to put questions to the child . . . cannot be reconciled with the approach of the European Court of Human Rights, which always aims to strike a fair balance between competing Convention rights. . . . Striking that balance in care proceedings may well mean that the child should not be called to give evidence in the great majority of cases, but that is a result and not a presumption or even a starting point. When the court is considering whether a particular child should be called as a witness, the court will have to weigh two considerations: the advantages that that will bring to the determination of the truth and the damage it may do to the welfare of this or any other child.

'Several factors will be relevant for the court in considering the advantages of the child giving evidence; whether it needs to make findings on particular allegations; the quality of other evidence; the quality of any ABE interview and the nature of any likely challenge to it; the age and maturity of the child and the time elapsed since the events in question. Sometimes there will be nothing useful to be gained from the child's oral evidence. It is in regarding the second consideration, risk of harm to the child caused by giving evidence, that the extension of special measures could be significant. The court noted that it should look at levels of support the child has, the child's wishes and feeling about giving evidence and other views including that of the guardian and holders of parental responsibility, the risk of delay and whether the child may have to give evidence twice if there are criminal proceedings. In the instant case, it is significant that C was willing and indeed wanted to give evidence. There are many reasons why this will not always be so. We endorse the view that an unwilling child should rarely, if ever, be obliged to give evidence. The family court will have to be realistic in evaluating how effective it can be in maximising the advantage while minimising the harm to the child witness.'

(Baroness Hale)

Following this decision the Family Justice Council in 2011 issued *Guidelines in Relation to Children Giving Evidence in Family Proceedings*. These guidelines largely incorporate the tests in *Re W* and replicate the factors of which the court ought to have regard when conducting the balancing exercise.

The importance of the guidelines in *Re W* was considered by the Court of Appeal in *Re R (Children)* [2015] EWCA Civ 167. In care proceedings brought by a local authority, allegations were made against a father (F) that he had sexually abused his two children, GR, fourteen years old, and her younger, severely autistic, seven-year-old sister, RR. The local authority became concerned about the home conditions of the family and domestic violence between the parents. In addition, RR was observed by her teachers and social workers as showing inappropriate sexual knowledge. At school she was observed by staff saying and doing things that suggested that there had been sexual activity between her father and her and also with GR. This was supported by her ABE videoed interview. GR was not formally interviewed and did not make any allegations against her father. GR filed a witness statement denying the allegations made against her father and made an application to give oral evidence in support of that statement. The local authority opposed her application and the trial judge, in deciding against the application, adopted only the first limb of the test laid down in *Re W*, namely 'the fair and accurate determination of the truth'. He did not consider the second limb of the test, namely, 'the risk of harm to the child'. GR appealed and the Court of Appeal allowed her appeal and reversed the decision of the trial judge. The local authority and judge approached GR's application on the assumption that GR was not telling the truth in preparing her statement and her willingness to testify to that effect, and only paid lip service to the notion that there is no starting point that a child ought not to testify. The evidence suggested that GR was a mature, intelligent fourteen-year-old girl who had no specific vulnerabilities. She wished to give evidence and felt sufficiently strong about it to pursue the appeal. She may or may not be telling the truth, but her evidence went to the heart of the case. The second limb in the *Re W* test ought to have been considered, namely, the sense of grievance on GR's part, and injustice to the father, if the judge made a finding of sexual abuse contrary to GR's written statement.

JUDGMENT

'The "essential test" as identified by Baroness Hale [in *Re W* (2010)] and therefore the yardstick against which both limbs must be considered, is that justice must be done to all the parties when deciding whether permission should be given for a child or young person to give evidence. It is therefore axiomatic that consideration of each of the limbs of the test is carried out against the backdrop of a fair trial; it is only through the prism of a fair trial that justice can be done and be seen to be done to one or all of the parties. The judge considered only those factors which relate to Limb 1, that is to say the court's ability to determine the truth. [He] regarded the issue as having been settled and did not thereafter move on to consider the second limb of the test. It is accepted by all the parties that the learned judge erred. The test requires both limbs to be considered; that is because the test is not a simple evaluation of the marginal forensic value of oral evidence of a child witness. There may be cases where the contribution to the determination of the truth may be modest or even minimal but the child's welfare overwhelmingly requires her to be given the opportunity to be heard or, alternatively, the evidence may be pivotal, but the welfare indicators so adverse that there can be no possibility of subjecting the child to the trauma of giving direct evidence. It seems to me that a significant feature of the Limb 2 welfare evaluation, on the facts of this case, must be the justifiable sense of grievance that GR would have if, having filed her statement and expressed her willingness to speak to it, a judge having refused her permission to give evidence, nevertheless went on to disbelieve her and make findings of sexual abuse against her father.'

(King LJ)

3.7 Witness anonymity orders

Prior to the introduction of the Criminal Evidence (Witness Anonymity) Act 2008, which was repealed and replaced by Part 3, Chapter 2 of the Coroners and Justice Act 2009, witnesses who fell outside the five statutory categories as specified in the Youth Justice and Criminal Evidence Act 1999 could still be assisted through the court's inherent powers. These have been preserved by s 19(6)(a) of the 1999 Act. Under this head, prosecution or defence witnesses who have genuine fears concerning their safety and the welfare of others if their true identities were revealed may apply to the court for directions for anonymity orders. These are orders that may be made to protect the identities of witnesses. The measures that may be adopted by the judge can include the use of pseudonyms, a bar on asking questions that might lead to the identification of witnesses, the screening of witnesses and voice modulation of witnesses. This is an extremely complicated issue, and it is of paramount importance that the order, made by the judge, does not severely disadvantage the defendant to such an extent that it compromises a fair trial. In *R v Davis* [2008] 3 All ER 461, the House of Lords decided that the anonymity orders made by the trial judge in this case were not compatible with the defendant's human rights as laid down in the European Convention. In particular it severely restricted the defence's right to cross-examine the witnesses subject to such orders and violated Art 6(3)(d) and thus the right to a fair trial.

CASE EXAMPLE

R v Davis [2008] 3 All ER 461 (HL)

The accused was charged with murder by shooting. The defendant denied the shooting. The witnesses for the prosecution, who claimed to have identified the defendant as the gunman, claimed to be in fear for their lives if it became known that they had given evidence against him. Their claims were investigated and accepted as genuine. To ensure the safety of these witnesses and to induce them to give evidence, the trial judge made a variety of special measures directions: (1) they were each to give evidence under a pseudonym; (2) their addresses and personal details were to be withheld from the defendant and his legal advisers; (3) the defendant's counsel was prohibited from asking the witnesses questions that might enable any of them to be identified; (4) the witnesses were to give evidence behind screens; (5) the witnesses' natural voices were to be heard by the judge and jury but not by the defendant or his counsel. On conviction, the defendant appealed ultimately to the House of Lords. The Court allowed the appeal and quashed the conviction on the following grounds.

The protective measures compromised the long-established principle of English common law that the defendant in a criminal trial should be confronted by his accusers in order that he might cross-examine them and challenge their evidence. The directions adopted in this case were not compatible with the defendant's human rights. The conduct of the defence was unlawfully hampered to such an extent as to have rendered the trial unfair. It was not open to the courts to modify the common law rights of the defendant to the extent envisaged by this case. There was nothing in the Strasbourg jurisprudence that required states in their national law to balance anonymity against defendants' rights. In relation to the Convention, the use of anonymous evidence had not satisfied the requirements of Art 6. Not only had the evidence been the sole or decisive basis on which the defendant could have been convicted, but effective cross-examination had been hampered.

JUDGMENT

'To decide whether the protective measures operated unfairly in this case it is necessary to consider their impact on the conduct of the defence. For that purpose it cannot be assumed at the outset that the defendant is guilty and all that he says false. The appellant denied that he was the gunman. Why, then, did witnesses say that he was? His answer, on which his instructions to counsel were based, was that he believed the false evidence to have been procured by a former girlfriend with whom he had fallen out. Mr Swift duly sought to pursue this suggestion in cross-examination of the unidentified witnesses but was gravely impeded in doing so by ignorance of and inability to explore who the witnesses were, where they lived and the nature of their contact with the appellant. When, eventually, subject to the protective measures, a female witness was called whom the appellant believed to be the girlfriend it was at least doubtful whether she was or not, but this was a question that could not be fully explored. If the jury concluded that she was probably not the former girlfriend, they would also conclude that the defence had been based on a false premise. But this was an unavoidable risk if the defence were obliged to take blind shots at a hidden target. A trial so conducted cannot be regarded as meeting ordinary standards of fairness.

'I feel bound to conclude that the protective measures imposed by the court in this case hampered the conduct of the defence in a manner and to an extent which was unlawful and rendered the trial unfair. I would accordingly allow this appeal.'

(Lord Bingham)

'I do not believe that the Strasbourg court would accept that the use of anonymous evidence in the present case satisfied the requirements of Art 6. Not only was the evidence on any view the sole or decisive basis on which alone the defendant could have been convicted, but effective cross-examination in the present case depended upon investigating the potential motives for the three witnesses giving what the defence maintained was a lying and presumably conspiratorial account. Cross-examination was hampered by the witnesses' anonymity, by the mechanical distortion of their voices and by their giving evidence from behind screens, so that the appellant (and, since he was not prepared to put himself in a position where he had information that his client did not, his counsel) could not see the witnesses. Assuming that the sole or decisive nature of the evidence is not itself fatal, it is on any view an important factor which would require to be very clearly counter-balanced by other factors. Here there are none. The other factors are here very prejudicial in their impact on effective cross-examination.

'So, if the matter rested with the Strasbourg jurisprudence, I would allow the appeal. However, on the basis that there is in the present Strasbourg jurisprudence nothing that requires states in their national law to balance anonymity against defendants' rights, the primary question is whether English domestic law permits anonymous evidence in any circumstances. The defence would be precluded from knowing or asking questions disclosing the officer's [witness's] true identity and background; and it would become difficult to draw the line between this and more radical inroads into the basic common law rule.

'In this situation, I have been persuaded that any further relaxation of the basic common law rule, requiring witnesses on issues in dispute to be identified and cross-examined with knowledge of their identity and permitting the defence to know and put to witnesses otherwise admissible and relevant questions about their identity, is one for Parliament to endorse and delimit and not for the courts to create. Parliamentary legislation is the means by which common law principles regarding the admission of documentary evidence have been modified. It may well be appropriate that there should be a careful statutory modification of basic common law principles. It is clear from the Strasbourg jurisprudence discussed in this judgment that there is scope within the Convention on Human Rights for such modification. I would allow this appeal accordingly.'

(Lord Mance)

The immediate response by Parliament was the introduction of the Criminal Evidence (Witness Anonymity) Act 2008, which abolished the common law rules for issuing such anonymity orders. This Act was intended to be only a temporary measure and in turn it was repealed and replaced by Part 3, Chapter 2 of the Coroners and Justice Act 2009 (ss 86–93). Sections 86–93 of the Coroners and Justice Act 2009 re-enacted the provisions introduced by the 2008 Act, subject to minor amendments. It is a self-contained code for the making of anonymity orders in criminal proceedings.

The 2009 Act allows applications for 'witness anonymity orders' to be made to the court by the prosecution or defence. The relevant party is required to inform the court of the identity of the witness supported by any 'relevant material' but is not required to disclose the witness's identity or information to any other party to the proceedings: see s 87 of the 2009 Act. 'Relevant material' is defined in s 87(5) as any document or other material to be disclosed or relied on by the party. A 'witness anonymity order' is defined in s 86(1) as an order by the court that requires specified measures to be taken in relation to a witness to ensure that the identity of the witness is not disclosed in connection with criminal proceedings.

Kinds of measures

Examples of the types of measures that may be ordered are identified in s 86(2) as including:

(a) that the witness's name and other identifying details are withheld or removed from materials disclosed;

(b) that the witness may use a pseudonym;

(c) that the witness is not asked questions that may lead to the identification of the witness;

(d) that the witness is screened to a specified extent;

(e) that the witness's voice is subject to modulation.

Conditions for making the order

The conditions that are required to be satisfied before the order is made are laid down in s 88 of the Act. These involve three complementary requirements to be satisfied, namely conditions A, B and C.

Condition A is laid down in s 88(3) as follows:

SECTION

> 'The order is "necessary" –
>
> (a) in order to protect the safety of the witness, or another person or to prevent any serious damage to property; or
>
> (b) in order to prevent real harm to the public interest.'

In order to determine whether the order is 'necessary' the court is required to have regard to any reasonable fear on the part of the witness that the witness or another person would suffer death or injury or that there would be serious damage to property if the witness is identified (s 88(6)). A foundation for the witness's perception of fear will be required to be established by the party making the application. It is likely that the fear of the witness must satisfy the test of reasonableness and be genuinely held. The irrational, subjective perception of the witness of fear may not be enough.

Condition B is enacted in s 88(4) as follows:

SECTION

'Having regard to all the circumstances, the effect of the proposed order would be consistent with the defendant receiving a fair trial.'

This is an overriding requirement guaranteed by the European Convention on Human Rights and any order of the court will be measured by reference to this principle. This would include the power to conduct an effective cross-examination of the witness, highlighted in *R v Davis* (2008), *ante*.

Condition C is enacted in s 88(5) as follows:

SECTION

'The importance of the witness's testimony is such that in the interests of justice the witness ought to testify and –

(a) the witness would not testify if the proposed order was not made, or
(b) there would be real harm to the public interest if the witness were to testify without the proposed order being made.'

The issue here is the link between the importance of the witness's testimony and the witness's reluctance to testify without the protection of the order.

Relevant considerations

In deciding whether the central conditions A to C are satisfied the judge is required to have regard to a number of factors, laid down in s 89 of the 2009 Act, as follows:

SECTION

'(a) the general right of a defendant to know the identity of a witness in criminal proceedings;
(b) the extent to which the credibility of the witness would be a relevant factor in assessing the weight of his testimony;
(c) whether the evidence given by the witness might be the sole or decisive evidence implicating the defendant;
(d) whether the witness's evidence could be properly tested without his identity being disclosed;
(e) whether there is any reason to believe that the witness has a tendency or motive to be dishonest having regard to any previous convictions of the witness and his relationship with the defendant or associates of the defendant;
(f) whether it would be reasonably practicable to protect the witness by means other than by way of a witness anonymity order;
(g) such other matters as the court considers relevant.'

In exercising his discretion whether to issue the order or not, the judge will be required to apportion appropriate weight to the factors as stated above, but subject to the overriding requirement of ensuring a fair trial.

Warning by the judge

Where a witness anonymity order has been made, the judge is required to issue a warning to the jury to the effect that the issue of the order does not prejudice the defendant: see s 90 of the 2009 Act.

In *R v Mayers* [2009] 1 WLR 1915, the Court of Appeal reviewed the law on witness anonymity orders and gave guidance in the context of the of the 2008 Act. Although this Act has been repealed and replaced by ss 86–93 of the Coroners and Justice Act 2009, it is submitted that the principles laid down in *Mayers* are still relevant because the 2009 Act replicates the provisions of the 2008 Act. *Mayers* involved a conjoined appeal by three convicted defendants and an interlocutory appeal by the prosecution, concerning anonymity orders of witnesses and witness statements of undercover officers. In summary the court issued the following guidelines:

(1) The Act provides a self-contained code for dealing with applications for witness anonymity orders. The common law rules relating to such orders have been abolished.

(2) The ancient principle that the defendant is entitled to know the identity of witnesses who incriminate him is maintained.

(3) The issue of a witness anonymity order will only be issued as a matter of last resort.

(4) The Act seeks to preserve the delicate balance between the rights of the defendant, including his entitlement to a fair trial and the interests of the public in preventing crime and acquitting innocent persons accused of committing crimes.

(5) There is an element of impracticability in the suggestion that relocation of witnesses may be regarded as an alternative to witness anonymity orders. Relocation may only be considered in the rarest of cases.

(6) The common law principles relating to public interest immunity when such issues arise in the context of witness anonymity have been expressly preserved, and the obligations imposed on the prosecution in the context of a witness anonymity application go much further than the ordinary duties of disclosure.

(7) Nothing in the Act diminishes the overriding responsibility of the trial judge to ensure that the proceedings are conducted fairly.

(8) The judge is required to reflect both at the close of the prosecution case, and when the defence evidence is concluded, whether in the light of the evidence as a whole, the case can safely be left to the jury, notwithstanding that crucial incriminating evidence was given by an anonymous witness or witnesses.

(9) Section 90 of the 2009 Act deals expressly with a judicial warning to the jury, 'appropriate' to ensure that the defendant is not prejudiced by the 'fact' of the order. In general terms, the warning must be sufficient to ensure that the jury does not make any assumptions adverse to the defendant, or favourable to the witness, from the fact that an anonymity

order has been made and, in particular, must not draw an implication or inference of guilt against the defendant.

(10) Section 88 of the 2009 Act lays down the three conditions for making an order. All three conditions, A, B and C, are required to be met before the jurisdiction to make a witness anonymity order arises. Each is mandatory. In most cases, the most helpful approach would probably be to address condition C first. The interests of justice are undefined.

(11) Condition A involves the question of safety, and this may encompass the risk of personal injury or death, or a reasonable fear of either. In relation to property, however, the risk must be serious, and any harm to the public interest must be real. A specific problem arises in relation to police witnesses, particularly those working undercover. Such officers who have penetrated criminal associations can face death or very serious injuries. The reality is that there are often sound operational reasons for maintaining the anonymity of undercover police officers, and the court would normally be entitled to follow the unequivocal assertion by an undercover police officer that without an anonymity order he would not be prepared to testify. Although the credibility of a police or security operation may be challenged, it will be unusual for the defendant to be disadvantaged by ignorance of the true identity of the officer.

(12) Condition B is fact specific. The fairness of the trial process as a whole must be preserved, and it is a deeply entrenched principle of our criminal justice process that a safe conviction cannot be produced by an unfair trial.

(13) Section 89 of the 2009 Act lays down the considerations the court is required to take into account in analysing the conditions for making the order. None of the considerations outweighs any of the others, and the order in which they appear does not represent an order of priority or importance. They are not exhaustive or restricted to those expressly mentioned, and they leave open the possibility that in an individual case some further point may properly arise for consideration.

(14) A difficulty arose with regard to applications to admit hearsay evidence from anonymous witnesses. The stark reality is that the Act is entirely silent about the use of anonymous hearsay evidence, or evidence made in the form of a statement by an unidentified and unidentifiable witness which is simply read to the jury as part of the evidence. This procedure is not authorised by any express statutory provision. The Criminal Justice Act 2003 contains its own express limits on the circumstances in which a witness statement may be read. No surviving common law power to allow for witness anonymity survives the 2008 Act. The 2008 Act and currently the 2009 Act addresses and allows for the anonymity of witnesses who testify in court. This jurisdiction is governed by statute, and any steps to extend it must be taken by Parliament.

3.8 Miscellaneous

Persons of defective intellect

The competence of a person with defective intellect is determined in the usual way, by reference to the test laid down in s 53 of the Youth Justice and Criminal

Evidence Act 1999. In appropriate cases, in criminal law, expert evidence will be permitted to assist the court in determining the competence of the witness. The additional factor with mentally defective individuals depends on the exact nature of the mental defect, i.e. whether the witness may give a coherent account of matters not connected with their derangement.

CASE EXAMPLE

R v Hill (1851) 2 Den 254

On a charge of manslaughter, W, a witness and patient in a lunatic asylum, was called to testify for the prosecution. To counter the defence objection the prosecution called a medical officer at the asylum who testified to the effect that although the witness believed that a number of spirits spoke to him, he was quite capable of giving an account of any transaction that he experienced. The court held that the witness was competent to testify.

JUDGMENT

'It is for the judge to see whether the party tendered understands the nature and sanction of an oath and then if the judge admits him as a witness, it is for the jury to say what degree of credit is to be given to his testimony . . . but the witness may be *non compos mentis* and yet understand the sanction of an oath and be capable of giving material testimony. He had a clear apprehension of the obligation of an oath and was capable of giving a trustworthy account of any transaction which took place before his eyes and he was perfectly rational upon all subjects except with respect to his particular delusion.'

(Lord Campbell)

Temporary mental incapacity, due to transitory illness or intoxication, may lead to an adjournment of the proceedings.

Sovereigns and diplomats

Sovereigns and heads of states as well as diplomats and consular officials are competent but not compellable to testify in civil and criminal proceedings.

3.9 Training or coaching of witnesses/familiarisation

In *R v Momodou and Limani* [2005] 2 Cr App R 6, the Court of Appeal decided that there was a dramatic distinction between witness training or coaching, on the one hand, and, on the other hand, witness familiarisation. Witness training for criminal trials was prohibited but witness familiarisation was permissible. In *R v Bulat* [2014] EWCA Crim 165, the Court of Appeal decided that a trial was not unfair where the prosecution prepared a document headed 'list of predicted defence questions' and gave it to police witnesses. Although the heading was unfortunate, the contents of the document were in order. The prosecution witnesses were entitled to familiarise themselves with the information before testifying. Further, there was no underhand dealing by the prosecution. The document was disclosed to defence counsel before the officers testified.

The rule against witness coaching avoided the possibility that one witness might tailor his evidence in the light of what anyone else said, and, equally, avoided any unfounded perception that he might have done so. Those risks were inherent in witness training.

That principle did not preclude pre-trial arrangements to familiarise a witness with the layout of the court, the likely sequence of events when the witness was giving evidence and a balanced appraisal of the different responsibilities of the various participants. None of that, however, involved discussions about proposed or intended evidence.

In the context of an anticipated criminal trial, if arrangements were made for witness familiarisation by outside agencies, not, for example, that routinely performed by or through the Witness Service, the following broad guidance should be followed.

In relation to prosecution witnesses, the Crown Prosecution Service should be informed in advance of any proposal for familiarisation. The proposals for the intended familiarisation programme should be reduced into writing, rather than left to informal conversations.

If, having examined them, the Crown Prosecution Service suggested that the programme might be in breach of the permitted limits, it should be amended.

If the defence engaged in the process, it would be extremely wise for counsel's advice to be sought in advance, and again with written information about the nature and extent of the familiarisation.

In any event it was a matter of professional duty on counsel and solicitors to ensure that the trial judge was informed of any familiarisation process organised by the defence using outside agencies, and it would follow that the Crown Prosecution Service would be made aware of what had happened.

The familiarisation process should normally be supervised or conducted by a solicitor or barrister, or someone who was responsible to a solicitor or barrister with experience of the criminal justice process, and preferably by an organisation accredited for the purpose by the Bar Council or Law Society.

None of those involved should have any personal knowledge of the matters in issue and records should be maintained. If discussion of the current criminal proceedings began, as it almost inevitably would, it had to be stopped and advice given about precisely why it was impermissible, with a warning against the danger of evidence contamination and the risk that the course of justice might be perverted. No documents used in the process should be destroyed.

JUDGMENT

'There is a dramatic distinction between witness training or coaching, and witness familiarisation. Training or coaching for witnesses in criminal proceedings (whether for the prosecution or defence) is not permitted. This is the logical consequence of the well-known principle that discussions between witnesses should not take place, and that the statements and proofs of one witness should not be disclosed to any other witness: see *R v Richardson* [1971] 2 QB 484, *R v Arif*, *The Times*, 22 June 1993, *R v Skinner* (1993) 99 Cr App R 212 and *R v Shaw* [2002] EWCA Crim 3004. The witness should give his or her own evidence, so far as practicable uninfluenced by what anyone else has said, whether in formal discussions or informal conversations. The rule reduces, indeed hopefully avoids, any possibility that one witness may tailor his evidence in the light of what anyone else said, and equally, avoids any unfounded perception that he may have done so . . .

'This principle does not preclude pre-trial arrangements to familiarise witnesses with the layout of the court, the likely sequence of events when the witness is giving evidence, and a balanced appraisal of the different responsibilities of the various participants. Indeed such arrangements, usually in the form of a pre-trial visit to the court, are generally to be welcomed. Witnesses should not be disadvantaged by ignorance of the process, nor when they come to give evidence, taken by surprise at the way it works. None of this, however, involves discussions about proposed or intended evidence. Sensible preparation for the experience of giving evidence, which assists the witness to give of his or her best at the forthcoming trial is permissible.'

(Judge LJ in *R v Bulat* [2014] EWCA Crim 165)

SUMMARY

- Competence concerns the witness's capacity to testify.
- In civil cases the test of competence is laid down by the *Hayes* test.
- In criminal cases the test of competence is enacted in s 53 of the Youth Justice and Criminal Evidence Act 1999. The defendant is incompetent to testify for the prosecution.
- Compellability involves the obligation imposed on a witness to testify. At common law most competent witnesses are compellable, subject to exceptions in criminal cases concerning the defendant and his or her spouse or civil partner.
- The defendant is competent, but not compellable, to testify for the defence.
- In criminal cases the defendant's spouse or civil partner is compellable to testify for the accused – spouse or civil partner.
- In criminal cases the defendant's spouse or civil partner is generally not compellable to testify for the prosecution or his or her spouse's co-defendant except in the circumstances enacted in s 80(3) of the Police and Criminal Evidence Act 1984.
- Special measures directions may be issued by the court in criminal proceedings in respect of five categories of witnesses – witnesses under the age of eighteen, witnesses suffering from mental or physical disorder, witnesses who are intimidated, the complainant in an offence of a sexual nature, or the defendant whose ability to testify has been compromised by the level of his intellectual capacity or social functioning.
- A witness anonymity order may be issued by the court in accordance with the provisions of ss 86–93 of the Coroners and Justice Act 2009: see *R v Mayers* for guidance on the equivalent provisions that preceded the 2009 Act.
- Witness training or coaching, as distinct from familiarisation, is not permitted.

SAMPLE ESSAY QUESTION

Charles is charged with assaulting his son's schoolteacher, Jones. Jones testifies that after an altercation Charles struck her from behind as she turned away from him. Charles in his evidence denies striking her and says she tripped as she stepped backwards.

Brian, an intelligent six-year-old who saw the incident, has not received any religious instruction and has no belief in God. Is he a competent and, if so, a compellable witness for the prosecution? If Brian testifies for the prosecution are there any means that are available to assist him in the presentation of his evidence?

Answer plan

Provide a legal definition of competence of witnesses.
Is there a presumption of competence? See s 53(1) of the Youth Justice and Criminal Evidence Act 1999.

State and apply the test of competence as laid down in s 53(3) of the 1999 Act.

Lack of religious instruction or no belief in God are not relevant to determine competence.

Although Brian is six years old the court may assume that he is competent unless there is evidence to the contrary.

If there is an issue regarding Brian's competence, the party calling him (the prosecution) will bear the burden of proof on a balance of probabilities that he is competent; s 54 of the 1999 Act.

Give a legal definition of the concept of compellability.

If Brian is a competent witness then at common law he is compellable to testify.

Since Brian is under the age of fourteen he is required to testify by way of unsworn evidence; see s 55(2) of the 1999 Act.

As Brian is under the age of eighteen he becomes eligible for assistance for special measures under s 16(1) of the 1999 Act.

The court is required to decide which one or more of the eight statutory special measures is likely to improve the quality of Brian's evidence (s 19) and in particular the primary rule of evidence in chief of child witnesses by way of a video recording; s 21 of the 1999 Act.

The court is required to consider making a direction for the presentation of the cross-examination in the form of a video recording; see s 28 of the 1999 Act.

Provided that the trial is with a jury the judge is required to warn the jury that the fact that the direction was given does not prejudice the defendant; s 32 of the 1999 Act.

CONCLUSION

ACTIVITY

Self-test questions

1. In criminal cases, when is a witness competent to testify?
2. What is the test for competence of witnesses to testify in civil proceedings?
3. In criminal cases, when is a witness compellable to testify for the prosecution?
4. In what circumstances may an accomplice to a criminal charge be both competent and compellable to testify for the prosecution?
5. When may a defendant's spouse (or civil partner) be compellable to testify for the co-defendant or prosecution in criminal proceedings?
6. What are special measures directions? When may a judge make such a direction?
7. May a judge protect the anonymity of a witness and, if so, what conditions must be satisfied?

Further reading

Baki, N. and Agate, J. 'Too much, too little, too late? Draft CPS guidance on speaking to witnesses' [2015] Ent LR 155
Birch, D. 'Children's evidence' [1992] Crim LR 262
Birch, D. 'A better deal for vulnerable witnesses?' [2000] Crim LR 223

Brabyn, J. 'A criminal defendant's spouse as a prosecution witness' [2011] Crim LR 613
Cooper, D. 'Pigot unfulfilled: video recorded evidence under section 28 of the YJCEA 1999' [2005] Crim LR 456
Cooper, P., Backen, P., and Marchant, R. 'Getting to grips with ground rules hearings: a checklist for judges, advocates and intermediaries to promote the fair treatment of vulnerable people in court' [2015] Crim LR 420
Creaton, J. 'Competence to give evidence' [2007] Police Journal 356
Creighton, P. 'Spouse competence and compellability' [1990] Crim LR 34
Daniele, M. 'Testimony through a live link in the perspective of the right to confront witnesses' [2014] Crim LR 189
Doak, J. and Huxley-Binns, R. 'Anonymous witnesses in England and Wales: charting a course from Strasbourg?' [2009] 73(6) J Crim L 508
Gillespie, A. 'Compellability of a child victim' (2000) 64(1) J Crim L 98
Gillespie, A. and Bettinson, V. 'Preventing secondary victimisation through anonymity' [2007] 70 MLR 114
Henderson, E. 'Root or branch? Reforming the cross examination of children' [2010] CLJ 460
Henderson, E. 'All the proper protections – the Court of Appeal rewrites the rules for the cross-examination of vulnerable witnesses' [2014] Crim LR 93
Henderson, E. 'Communicative competence? Judges, advocates and intermediaries discuss communication issues in the cross-examination of vulnerable witnesses' [2015] Crim LR 659
Hoyano, L. 'Variations on a theme by Pigot: special measures directions for child witnesses' [2000] Crim LR 250
Hoyano, L. 'Striking a balance between the rights of defendants and vulnerable witnesses: will special measures directions contravene guarantees of a fair trial?' [2001] Crim LR 948
Hoyano, L. 'Coroners and Justice Act 2009: special measures directions take two: entrenching unequal access to justice' [2010] Crim LR 345
Hoyano, L. 'Vulnerable witnesses: manner of cross examination – witnesses young, female complainants' [2012] Crim LR 565
Hoyano, L. 'Reforming the adversarial trial for vulnerable witnesses and defendants' [2015] Crim LR 107
Jones, D. 'The evidence of a three year old child' [1987] Crim LR 677
Justice website – achieving best evidence www.cps.gov.uk/publications/docs/best_evidence_in_criminal_proceedings.pdf
Keane, A. 'Towards a principled approach to cross examination of vulnerable witnesses' [2012] Crim LR 407
Munday, R. 'Sham marriages and spousal compellability' [2001] 65(4) J Crim L 336
Ormerod, D., Choo, A. and Easter, R. 'Coroners and Justice Act 2009: the witness anonymity and investigation anonymity provisions' [2010] Crim LR 368
Ragavan, S. 'The compellability rule in England and Wales: support for the spouse of the defendant' [2013] J Crim L 310
Singh, C. 'Eliciting best evidence from a child witness: a comparative study of the United Kingdom and India' (2019) 17(1) Issues in Legal Scholarship 20190003
Smaller, E. 'Giving the vulnerable a voice' [2012] Counsel 25
Wurtzel, D. 'The youngest witness in a murder trial: making it possible for very young children to give evidence' [2014] Crim LR 893

4

The disclosure of evidence and protection from disclosure: Privilege and public interest immunity

AIMS AND OBJECTIVES

By the end of this chapter you will be able to:

- comprehend the rules relating to the disclosure of evidence through a brief historical overview of how they developed;
- understand the rules regarding privilege including the types of privilege, their basis and extent, and the instances in which privilege is lost;
- highlight how to identify the rules designed to protect documents from disclosure on the grounds of public interest immunity through case studies;
- evaluate, through hypothetical examples and for purposes of assessment, which public policy issues underpin public interest immunity.

4.1 Introduction

This chapter explores three related topics: disclosure, privilege and public interest immunity. They are presented together because all three affect the evidence that is adduced as part of litigation, whether that is through the application of rules that require the timely disclosure of specified evidence or its exclusion or restriction. The discussion starts with a brief overview of the rules on disclosure. Then the law on privilege is examined – this includes an investigation of the privilege against self-incrimination, legal professional privilege and journalistic privileges. The discussion in terms of these three categories includes an examination of their application; limitation and loss; statutory exceptions to them; and finally whether it is possible to waive them. The focus moves on to public interest immunity and

DOI: 10.4324/9781003282433-4

its application, whether it can be challenged and any restrictions that may be available with regards to it. In addition, the reasons that underpin public interest immunity, its greater role in terms of the detection of crime, whether it can be waived and if there are any statutory exceptions to it are also explored. These three topics are presented thematically in this chapter to highlight their interrelationship.

4.2 Disclosure

The general rule in both criminal and civil proceedings is that all relevant evidence is admissible unless the operation of any rule or statute renders it inadmissible. In criminal proceedings both the defence and the prosecution are required to make a disclosure of evidence at the pre-trial stage. This is a procedural area of evidence law and, prior to the Criminal Justice Act 2003 (CJA) introducing amendments to it, disclosure was governed by the Criminal Procedure and Investigations Act 1996 (CPIA), which had the following four main parts:

- a statutory duty on the investigating officer to record and retain information;
- a primary disclosure by the prosecution;
- disclosure by the defence;
- a secondary disclosure by the prosecution.

Section 23(1) of the CPIA provided for the Secretary of State to create a code of practice to accompany the Act, which included the requirement that all investigating police officers record and retain any information and material gathered or generated during the investigation of a criminal offence – this included crime reports, notebooks, custody records, interview records, communications and records that derived from tapes or messages. The requirement was for this information and material to be retained at least until a decision whether or not to institute proceedings against the accused had been made. You can download from the internet the 2020 version of the Code of Practice that accompanies the CPIA 1996 for the purposes of your own research. The new code requires investigators and prosecutors to take a 'thinking approach'. A significant change relates to the introduction of a rebuttable presumption relating to certain unused material that it meets the disclosure test. This unused material was, following the review, found to almost always assist the defence but which the prosecution consistently failed to disclose until significant correspondence between the parties had taken place, which was a waste of time and money. Therefore, the prosecution must now give reasons why it considers particular unused material does not meet the disclosure test.

The prosecution had an initial but limited duty to make a primary disclosure; this was far more restricted than it is under the contemporary requirements of the CJA 2003. Section 3(1)(a) of the CPIA required the prosecution to disclose *any material which in their opinion might undermine the case of the prosecution against the accused*. This then triggered the disclosure requirements of the defence, which required the accused to disclose in general terms *the nature of his or her defence – this would include outlining any alibi and issues that they wished to raise at trial*. Once this requirement had been satisfied the prosecution then, where necessary, would make a secondary disclosure: this time it would have to disclose *any material which might reasonably have assisted the defence.*

The Criminal Justice Act 2003 modified these requirements by amending the CPIA 1996 and introduced a single objective test for the disclosure of *unused* prosecution material. Thus, s 3(1) of the CPIA 1996 now reads:

SECTION

'. . . the prosecutor must (a) disclose to the accused any prosecution material which has not previously been disclosed to the accused and which might reasonably be considered capable of undermining the case for the prosecution against the accused or of assisting the case for the accused, or (b) give to the accused a written statement that there is no material of a description mentioned in paragraph (a) . . .

(2) For the purposes of this section prosecution material is material (a) which is in the prosecutor's possession, and came into his possession in connection with the case for the prosecution against the accused, or (b) which, in pursuance of a code operative under Part II, he has inspected in connection with the case for the prosecution against the accused . . .

(6) Material must not be disclosed under this section to the extent that the court, on an application by the prosecutor, concludes it is not in the public interest to disclose it and orders accordingly.'

Take some time to familiarise yourself with this provision. What will become clear is that there are now three (rather than four) clear parts to disclosure: a statutory duty on the investigating officer to record and retain information, prosecution disclosure and then a defence disclosure in the form of a detailed defence statement. Let us look a little more closely at the requirement for a detailed defence statement. Section 6A(1) was inserted into the CPIA 1996 by the CJA 2003 and the Criminal Justice and Immigration Act 2008 (CJIA) and states that:

SECTION

'. . . a defence statement is a written statement (a) setting out the nature of the accused's defence, including any particular defences on which he intends to rely, (b) indicating the matters of fact on which he takes issue with the prosecution, (c) setting out, in the case of each such matter, why he takes issue with the prosecution, (ca) setting out particulars of the matters of fact on which he intends to rely for the purposes of his defence, and (d) indicating any point of law (including any point as to the admissibility of evidence or an abuse of process) which he wishes to take, and any authority on which he intends to rely for that purpose.'

The prosecution has a duty to disclose, which continues from initial disclosure right through to the determination of the case.

Additionally, s 6A(2) provides the extent of disclosure required where the defence statement discloses an alibi, stating that:

'. . . a defence statement that discloses an alibi must give particulars of it, including (a) the name, address and date of birth of any witness the accused believes is able to give evidence in support of the alibi, or as many of those details as are known to the accused when the statement is given; (b) any information in the accused's possession which might be of material assistance in identifying or finding any such witness in whose case any of the details mentioned in paragraph (a) are not known to the accused when the statement is given.'

The Criminal Procedure Rules and Practice Directions (CrPR) as at October 2020 – govern the practice and procedure in criminal cases that are heard in the magistrates', Crown and appeal courts, and extradition hearings in the High Court. The Criminal Procedure Rule Committee sets out the rules, and their purpose is to assure that cases are dealt with justly. Part 15 of the CrPR lays down the practices and procedures that accompany the disclosure requirements under Parts I and II of the CPIA. For instance, under s 3 of the CPIA 1996 (discussed above) – where the prosecution discloses prosecution material to the accused or informs him or her that there is no such material to disclose, then the prosecutor must also inform the court officer at the same time (CrPR r 15.2(1)). The purpose, like its equivalent in the Civil Procedure Rules, is to help cases progress more efficiently. You can download these from www.gov.uk/guidance/rules-and-practice-directions-2020#disclosure.

In civil proceedings the requirements for disclosure are determined by the case management track to which the case is subsequently listed. The listing of a case to a management track normally takes place once the parties have completed what are known as the allocation questionnaires – this a procedure that is undertaken after particulars of claim and defence or counterclaim and counter-defence have been issued as part of the formal proceedings. Figure 4.1 outlines the basis upon which cases are allocated to a case management track for purposes of civil litigation:

Small	Cases valued at less than £5,000 in total value (or where the damages for pain, suffering and loss of amenity in personal injury claims are less than £1,000 and in housing disrepair where the claim is valued at less than £1,000). Costs follow the outcome, i.e. the winner can recover fixed costs.
Fast	Cases valued at between £5,000 and £15,000 in total value. A trial on this track will last no longer than one day. Costs follow the outcome, i.e. the winner can recover fixed costs.
Multi	All other cases and those worth less than £5,000 if complex and technical.

Figure 4.1 Case management track allocation

Part 31 of the Civil Procedure Rules (CPR) (as at January 2022) lays down standard disclosure requirements in cases listed on the fast and multi-tracks, while on the small claims track only that evidence that will be relied on at trial need be disclosed. CPR 31.6 states:

SECTION

'. . . standard disclosure requires a party to disclose only (a) the documents on which he relies and (b) the documents which (i) adversely affect his own case, (ii) adversely affect another party's case, or (iii) support another party's case, and (c) the documents which he is required to disclose by a relevant practice direction.'

In short, CPR 31.6 requires a party to make standard disclosure of the following documents:

- those on which they propose to rely;
- those that adversely affect their own or another party's case;
- those that support another party's case;
- any documents that are required to be disclosed by a Practice Direction.

Part 31 of the CPR is available to download freely at www.justice.gov.uk/courts/procedure-rules/civil/rules/part31#31.6. Check the website that accompanies this textbook for regular updates on current issues in this field of study. The discussion so far has concentrated on the general rules of disclosure; the focus now shifts to two related grounds (privilege and public interest immunity) upon which evidence may be excluded. However, this is not necessarily done by the court but by the person who wishes to suppress the evidence – remember this is evidence that is otherwise admissible.

ACTIVITY

Define disclosure and summarise its purpose.

True or false? The rules on disclosure in criminal and civil proceedings are the same. Give reasons for your answer.

What does standard disclosure in civil cases depend upon?

KEY FACTS

Disclosure

The *general* rule in both criminal and civil cases is that all relevant evidence is admissible.

In criminal cases, there are three parts to disclosure: a statutory duty on the investigating officer to record and retain information, prosecution disclosure and defence disclosure in the form of a detailed defence statement.

In civil cases, Part 31 of the CPR lays down the requirements for standard disclosure, that is, documents upon which the parties will rely, those that adversely affect their own or another party's case, those that support another party's case and those that are required to be disclosed by a Practice Direction – in these cases disclosure is dependent on track allocation.

4.3 Privilege

Privilege
legal protection, in certain relationships, that prevents a party having to forcibly disclose confidential communications.

The remaining discussion in this chapter focuses on the protection from the disclosure of evidence on the grounds that it is subject to **privilege** or it is immune from disclosure in the public interest (discussed at 4.6).

Where it is successfully claimed, privilege acts to protect evidence from being disclosed. Unlike public interest immunity, privilege attaches itself to evidence by reason of a justification with reference to an individual. The rationale that underpins privilege is as follows: to protect the interests of a party that, in limited circumstances surrounding the claim to privilege, the law recognises as being in need of protection. The privilege, when granted, belongs to the party in the proceedings that has claimed it either themselves or through his or her lawyers. If it is not claimed or the claim fails then relevant and admissible evidence will be subject to the normal rules on disclosure.

English common law contained the protection of evidence from disclosure on the grounds of privilege, but it is limited this to the following specified situations:

- against self-incrimination;
- legal professional or litigation privilege;
- without prejudice negotiations;
- journalistic privilege;
- matrimonial communications.

Note that privilege in relation to matrimonial communications was abolished in civil proceedings by s 16(3) of the Civil Evidence Act 1968 and in criminal proceedings by s 80(9) of the Police and Criminal Evidence Act 1984. In addition, journalistic privilege is not commonly featured in examination assessments in this field of study.

4.3.1 Privilege against self-incrimination

The common law provided that no witness was required to answer any question or produce any document in court proceedings where the answer or the document would incriminate themselves and expose them to charges of having committed offences in contravention of the criminal law. This privilege applied to both civil and criminal proceedings and forms part of the general right to silence, although in criminal proceedings an accused's silence can sometimes result in adverse inferences being drawn against them (s 34 of the Criminal Justice and Public Order Act 1994 is discussed later in the book). The rule in criminal cases is eloquently stated by the Latin maxim *nemo tenetur prodere se ipsum*, which translates into modern English as 'no one is obliged to give him or herself away'. Goddard LJ stated the rule in *Blunt v Park Lane Hotel Ltd* [1942] 2 KB 253 as:

JUDGMENT

'No one is bound to answer any question if the answer thereto would, in the opinion of the judge, have a tendency to expose the deponent to any criminal charge, penalty or forfeiture which the judge regards as reasonably likely to be preferred or sued for.'

Where a claim is successful then this particular type of privilege attaches itself to the witness; the result in terms of evidence is that a party may not be then able to obtain the relevant evidence through their cross-examination. The party seeking to adduce the evidence, or here the party opposing privilege, may prove the matter in another way if it has alternative relevant evidence or by a different method, for instance different witness. *Blunt v Park Lane Hotel Ltd* [1942] 2 KB 253 highlighted the traditional position in criminal proceedings as: any answers given by a witness can be used as evidence against them when determining their guilt in the proceedings and in relation to any future offences committed by them.

The Criminal Evidence Act 1898 (CEA) makes it clear that a defendant cannot refuse to answer incriminating questions in relation to the offence with which they are charged or in relation to their guilt that are put to them in cross-examination. However, this is now subject to s 101 of the Criminal Justice Act 2003, which concerns the admissibility of a defendant's bad character. Section 1(2) of the CEA 1898 states:

SECTION

'. . . a person charged in criminal proceedings who is called as a witness in the proceedings may be asked any question in cross-examination notwithstanding that it would tend to incriminate him as to any offence with which he is charged in the proceedings.'

An interesting question relating to whether a witness can be asked a question that may incriminate him or herself in respect of another criminal offence, namely one with which they do not stand charged, arises. The general rule is as follows: the privilege against self-incrimination applies unless the contrary is expressly stated. For example, statute may provide that the privilege has no application in relation to a specific circumstance – this is discussed later in this chapter. Where a claim for privilege against self-incrimination is successful the witness is entitled to leave unanswered the question that may incriminate him or her for the commission of an offence with which they are not charged. Where a witness answers such a question, then that answer in itself would amount to a confession – Chapter 10 reveals how confessions are admissible against their maker. Privilege will protect the individual from:

- the risk of future criminal proceedings;
- directly or indirectly incriminatory questions.

Additionally, the privilege against self-incrimination also protects the witness from the risk of future criminal proceedings or forfeiture in England, Wales and Scotland. This does not, however, include civil proceedings. The penalties that are covered include those provided for by the criminal law of the UK and the European Union. You should make reference to the European Communities Act 1972 – this can be freely downloaded at www.legislation.gov.uk/ukpga/1972/68/contents.

In *Rio Tinto Zinc Corporation and Others v Westinghouse Electric Corporation* [1978] AC 547, an American company called Westinghouse was sued in the US state of Virginia for an alleged breach of contract for the construction of nuclear power stations. Westinghouse contended that it could not perform its side of the contract for the following two reasons: (a) the shortage of uranium and (b) the steep prices and anti-competitive price-fixing by a cartel of international uranium producers. The latter included two UK companies, one of which was the Rio Tinto Zinc Corporation. On an application by Westinghouse, the judge in the Virginia court issued letters rogatory (formal request) to the High Court in London requesting it to order that certain named individuals (officers or directors connected with the two UK companies) appear at the US consular offices in London so that they could be examined on oath. The court also requested that the High Court order that the claimant produce certain documents or classes of document. The London High Court made the orders, but the individuals from the Rio Tinto Zinc Corporation contended that some of these documents were privileged because they would render it liable to be fined under the EEC Treaty, which had been enshrined into English law. The claim for privilege against self-incrimination was upheld in the UK, and the Virginian court judge also upheld the claim under the Fifth Amendment to the US Constitution. Subsequent to this the Virginian judge was informed by the US Department of Justice that it now required the evidence of the witnesses for a grand jury investigation into breaches of US anti-trust laws by the alleged cartel with the possibility of initiating criminal proceedings. The US Department of Justice applied to the Virginian judge for an order compelling the witnesses to give evidence under the US Constitution s 6002/2, which applies in the instance that the privilege against self-incrimination is claimed with the basis that any evidence cannot be used against the witness in a subsequent criminal case. The Virginian judge made the order and the individuals against whom it was made appealed to the UK Court of Appeal, which held:

JUDGMENT

'. . . that the master's order rightly gave effect to the letters rogatory in respect of the production of documents, subject to amendments to confine their operation to areas allowed by English law and further (Viscount Dilhorne dissenting) that the order rightly gave effect to them as regarded the witnesses sought to be examined but (*per* Lord Wilberforce) subject to the disallowance of certain witnesses . . . that the companies were entitled to claim privilege against self-incrimination under section 14(1) of the Civil Evidence Act 1968 in respect of the documents required to be produced, since production would tend to expose them to fines under Articles 85, 189 and 192 of the European Economic Community Treaty, which cover penalties imposed by administrative action and recoverable in England by "proceedings . . . for the recovery of a penalty" within section 14(1) . . . that, in accordance with the ruling of the judge of the Virginian court, upholding the right of the individual witnesses to claim privilege against self-incrimination under the Fifth Amendment to the US Constitution, they could not, in consequence of section 3(1)(b) of the Evidence (Proceedings in Other Jurisdictions) Act 1975, be compelled to give evidence . . . that the intervention of the Department of Justice, converting the letters rogatory into a request for evidence for the purposes of a grand jury investigation, changed their character, seeking to use the Act of 1975 for purposes for which it was not intended by extending the grand jury's investigations internationally in a manner which was impermissible as being an infringement of United Kingdom sovereignty, a context in which the courts were entitled to take into account the declared policy of Her Majesty's Government.'

In the UK, s 14(1) of the Civil Evidence Act 1968 clearly states that the privilege against self-incrimination does not extend to the exposure to the risk of proceedings in foreign civil or criminal court proceedings. For instance, if Judy Stench is charged with aggravated burglary in the UK she cannot claim the privilege against answering a direct or indirect question that may expose her to the risk of being charged with a criminal offence for smuggling drugs in Peru.

The privilege against self-incrimination also covers answers to questions that either directly or indirectly incriminate the witness – perhaps the answer is incriminatory or it leads to the recovery of evidence. In *Rank Film Distributors v Video Information Centre* [1982] AC 380, a case that concerned copyright infringement, the court decided that the defendant was entitled to claim the privilege against self-incrimination with regard to questions that concerned the sale and supply of counterfeit copies (see also *Tate Access Floors Inc v Boswell* [1990] 3 All ER 303).

What is clear is that the witness's assertion of privilege is not sufficient in itself to attract it: the judge is required to examine all the circumstances of the case and ascertain whether there is a *real and appreciable danger* that a prosecution may follow if the witness answers the question.

Impeached
charged for misconduct by calling into question the validity of a certain practice.

In the case of *R v Boyes* (1861) 30 LJQB 301, a witness declined to answer a question on the ground that the answer would incriminate him. He was then handed a pardon so that he could not be subsequently prosecuted; however, in theory he was still liable to be **impeached**. The Court of Appeal decided that the privilege was not available. Cockburn CJ stated that:

JUDGMENT

'. . . to successfully claim the privilege of silence, the court must see, from the circumstances of the case and the nature of the evidence which the witness is called upon to give, that there is a reasonable ground to apprehend danger to the witness from his being compelled to answer . . . the danger apprehended must be real and appreciable with reference to the ordinary operation of law in the ordinary course of things; not a danger of an imaginary and substantial character, having reference to some extraordinary and barely possible contingency, so improbable that no reasonable man would suffer it to influence his conduct. We think that a merely remote and naked possibility, out of the ordinary course of the law, and such that no reasonable man would be affected by, should not be suffered to obstruct the administration of justice.'

In *A&T Istel Ltd v Tully* [1993] AC 45, the House of Lords decided that where the Crown Prosecution Service (CPS) made an offer not to prosecute the defendant in respect of any frauds revealed, this amounted to sufficient protection and the defendant was not entitled to claim the privilege.

The application of the privilege against self-incrimination is not retrospective, and therefore if a witness has already been charged or has already provided the information, they cannot then assert the privilege.

The judge may warn a witness that he or she is not obliged to answer incriminating questions, but there is no rule of law to that effect. It follows that if the witness answers questions or produces a document in ignorance of his right to refuse to answer or produce the document the court may, nevertheless, rely on the evidence. An appeal cannot be maintained on this ground. However, where a witness is forced to answer questions in relation to which he was entitled to privilege, then the answer will be inadmissible as evidence against him in future proceedings, the reason being that his answers are treated as analogous to involuntary confessions: see *R v Garbett* (1847) 1 Den CC 236.

Statutory exceptions to the privilege against self-incrimination

There are a number of statutory exceptions to the privilege against self-incrimination. These include: s 31 Theft Act 1968; s 72 Senior Courts Act 1981; s 2 Criminal Justice Act 1987; s 98 Children Act 1989. Figure 4.2 summarises their effect:

Section 31 Theft Act 1968	A witness must answer questions relating to the recovery or administration of property – the answers cannot be used as evidence in subsequent proceedings under the Act
Section 72 Senior Courts Act 1981	The privilege is of no application to civil proceedings related to a dispute concerning intellectual property – the answers cannot be used as evidence in subsequent criminal proceedings unless they are for perjury or contempt of court
Section 2 Criminal Justice Act 1987	The DPP of the Serious Fraud Office has broad powers to investigate persons in respect of offences of serious fraud. Persons investigated may be required to answer questions or provide documentation
Section 98 Children Act 1989	A witness must answer questions in proceedings relating to the care, supervision or protection of a child – the answers cannot be used as evidence in subsequent criminal proceedings

Figure 4.2 The effect of the statutory exceptions to the privilege against self-incrimination

Privilege against self-incrimination and human rights

The European Court of Human Rights (ECtHR) has been unequivocal in stating that the privilege against self-incrimination is a fundamental part of the right to a fair trial, enshrined in Art 6 of the European Convention on Human Rights and Fundamental Freedoms. The text of this Convention can be downloaded from www.echr.coe.int/Documents/Convention_ENG.pdf (see also *Saunders v UK* (1997) 18 EHRR CD 23). This led to the amendment of the Companies Act 1985 (now the Companies Act 2006), and hence judges must consider the right to a fair trial when seeking to exclude evidence.

ACTIVITY

Summarise the nature of the privilege against self-incrimination.

What changes did s 101 of the CJA 2003 make to the CPIA 1996 in respect of the privilege against self-incrimination?

KEY FACTS

Privilege

This protects evidence from being disclosed by reason of a justification in reference to an individual. Evidence will be immune from disclosure on the grounds that it is privileged. Privilege is limited to specific situations that include the privilege against self-incrimination, legal professional privilege, without prejudice negotiations and journalistic privilege.

Privilege against self-incrimination

The general rule is that there is a privilege against self-incrimination unless otherwise provided. On occasion, statute may preclude such a privilege. In *Blunt v Park Lane Hotel Ltd* [1942] 2 KB 253 it was stated that the answers given by a witness in court could be used as evidence against them to determine their guilt in the proceedings and in relation to any future offences committed by them.

Section 1(2) of the CEA 1898 makes it clear that a defendant cannot refuse to answer incriminating questions in relation to the offence charged or their guilt put to them in cross-examination – see s 101 of the CJA 2003. The extent of the privilege includes protection from the risk of future criminal proceedings and direct or indirect incriminatory questions.

Section 14(1) of the Civil Evidence Act 1968 states that this privilege does not extend to the exposure to the risk of proceedings in foreign civil or criminal court proceedings.

Statutory exceptions to the privilege against self-incrimination

Section 31 of the Theft Act 1968, s 72 of the Senior Courts Act 1981, s 2 of the Criminal Justice Act 1987 and s 98 of the Children Act 1989.

4.3.2 Legal professional privilege

The discussion above reveals that the focus of the privilege against self-incrimination is the individual. In contrast, legal professional privilege concentrates on two issues:

- *communications between a lawyer and their client in the normal course of legal practice*, such as the giving or obtaining of legal advice; and
- *the communications between a lawyer (and/or their client) and a third party in contemplation of litigation*, for instance the report of an expert witness.

Communications that fall into either one of these two categories are privileged and immune from disclosure. The caveat is that it must be claimed by the party to whom the communication belongs, a claim that can be made regardless of the timing of the litigation. Taylor CJ explained the rationale behind legal professional privilege in *R v Derby Magistrates Court, ex p B* [1996] 3 WLR 681 as follows:

JUDGMENT

'. . . a man must be able to consult his lawyer in confidence, since otherwise he might hold back half the truth . . . he must be sure that what he tells his lawyer in confidence will never be revealed without his consent . . . legal professional privilege is thus much more than an ordinary rule of evidence, limited in its application to the facts of a particular case . . . it is a fundamental condition on which the administration of justice as a whole rests.'

Communication between a lawyer and their client that is in the usual course of legal practice will be privileged and immune from disclosure unless the client actually wishes it to be disclosed. The rule applies to communications between a barrister, solicitor, legal executive and paralegal so long as they are acting in the course of a professional relationship. Where such a relationship does not exist, then neither does this form of privilege. Consider this, Chun Yi writes to his friend Melania for one-off advice on buying shares in Metaverse Ltd and the related legal repercussions regarding tax. Melania also happens to be a barrister practising corporate law. This scenario presents a typical assessment issue as to whether this communication is privileged. The House of Lords made it clear in *Minter v Priest* [1930] AC 558 that the advice obtained must be legal advice that will be privileged even if Melania later refuses to act as Chun Yi's lawyer in the matter or if Chun Yi himself chooses to appoint Joe as his lawyer instead. As *per* Lord Buckmaster:

JUDGMENT

'. . . the relationship of solicitor and client being once established, it is not a necessary conclusion that whatever conversation ensued was protected from disclosure. The conversation to secure this privilege must be such as, within a very wide and generous ambit of interpretation, fairly referable to the relationship, but outside that boundary the mere fact that a person speaking is a solicitor, and the person to whom he speaks is his client affords no protection.'

Per Viscount Dunedin:

JUDGMENT

'. . . now, if a man goes to a solicitor, as a solicitor, to consult and does consult him, though the end of the interview may lead to the conclusion that he does not engage him as his solicitor or expect that he should act as his solicitor, nevertheless the interview is held as a privileged occasion.'

A claim for legal professional privilege will only be successful if the following is satisfied:

- the communication between the lawyer and their client is confidential in nature; and
- if not made in the course of a lawyer and client relationship, it must have been made with a view to establishing one.

The scenario concerning Chun Yi and Melania demonstrates this latter point. Where a party has been successful in claiming legal professional privilege they must continue to ensure that it remains intact. Generally, communications that are immune from disclosure by reason of legal professional privilege will remain immune unless the opposing party can prove that the communication was obtained to further a crime or perpetuate a fraud, or that the privilege has been waived. If the opposing party can prove that the communication itself was obtained to further a crime or a fraud, then the act of seeking legal advice will be considered to be a step taken in the furtherance of a crime or fraud and privilege will be lost. In *R v Central Criminal Court, ex p Francis and Francis* [1989] AC 346 the court confirmed that it is irrelevant who intended the crime or the fraud, and therefore the crime or fraud of the lawyer, the client themselves or a third party can cause the loss of legal professional privilege. This form of privilege also protects property from seizure: where the police have obtained a search warrant under s 8 of the Police and Criminal Evidence Act 1984 which allows them to enter, search and seize property, s 10 of the same statute prevents them from seizing anything that is protected under legal professional privilege, unless of course it is 'the thing' that is in furtherance of the crime or fraud.

Where a defendant obtains privileged information through trickery or by means of some fraud, then a claimant may seek an injunction preventing the defendant from using the information (see *Lord Ashburton v Pape* [1913] 2 Ch 469). Lawyers can often act for joint parties, and thus the requirement here is that all communications are disclosed to all those parties that are involved; only then can the parties claim legal professional privilege to prevent disclosure (see *Buttes Gas & Oil Co v Hammer (No 3)* [1981] 1 QB 223).

The personal nature of legal professional privilege means that the person entitled to it can waive it should they choose to do so. It is important to note that a wilful, ignorant or inadvertent disclosure of relevant evidence will render that evidence admissible.

Where a communication is disclosed by reason of the lawyer's professional negligence – perhaps, as does sometimes happen, they forgot to claim privilege – then privilege is lost unless of course the communication was obtained through a crime or a fraud. Consider this scenario; Midori decides to waive privilege in a document, which we will call A. Unbeknown to her that document also referred to documents B, C and D. The issue here concerns the extent of the waiver: does the consensual waiver of document A that contains references to documents B, C and D also result in the waiver of privilege in relation to documents B, C and D? The answer is in the negative – it does not. Often, where such waiver occurs then references to the other documents will be redacted (blacked out). Further, it should be noted that legal professional privilege does not end with the termination of the lawyer and client relationship. In *R v Barton* [1973] 1 WLR 115 and *R v Ataou* [1988] 2 All ER 321, the trial judge suggested that such privilege would end where communications in the lawyers' possession would have acquitted an accused who was actually innocent. The Court of Appeal was quick to overrule this, and therefore legal professional privilege continues regardless. Furthermore, privilege does not cease in relation to communications between a company and its legal advisors when the company is dissolved (see *Addlesee v Dentons Europe LLP* [2020] EWHC 238 (Ch)).

The following are important points to note before we move on to consider privilege and third-party communications. Where privilege has been lost or it has been waived and there is no injunction that restrains the use of the document then it can be used as proof so long as it satisfies the normal rules of evidence relating to relevance and admissibility (see *R v Tompkins* (1977) 67 Cr App R 181). In contrast to public interest immunity, legal professional privilege only attaches to an original document, the contents of which can be proven through the provision of a photocopy or by the oral testimony of a witness who has viewed it. Interestingly, it does not matter how the witness saw the contents, for instance through improper means (see *Calcraft v Guest* [1889] 1 QB 759).

Third-party communication attracts immunity from disclosure by reason of legal professional privilege if the dominant purpose, where there was more than one purpose, was either *pending* or *contemplated* litigation. Thus, where litigation is not pending or contemplated there can be no claim for this form of privilege (see *Wheeler v Le Marchant* (1881) 17 Ch D 675). Lord Wilberforce stated in *Waugh v BRB* [1980] AC 521:

JUDGMENT

'. . . while privilege may be required in order to induce candour in statements made for the purposes of litigation it is not required in relation to statements whose purpose is different – for example to enable a railway to operate safety. It is clear that the due administration of justice strongly requires disclosure and production of this report: it was contemporary; it contained statements by witnesses on the spot; it would be not merely relevant evidence, but almost certainly the best evidence of causation . . . if one accepts that this important public interest can be overridden in order that the defendant may properly prepare his case, how close must the connection be between the preparation of the document and the anticipation of litigation? On principle I would think that the purpose of preparing for litigation ought to be either the sole purpose or at least the dominant purpose of it: to carry the protection further into cases where that purpose was secondary or equal with another purpose would seem to be excessive, and unnecessary in the interest of encouraging truthful revelation. At the lowest such desirability of protection as exists in such cases is not strong enough to outweigh the need for all relevant documents to be made available . . . it appears to me that unless the purpose of submission to the legal adviser in view of litigation is at least the dominant purpose for which the relevant document was prepared, the reasons which require privilege to be extended to it cannot apply. On the other hand to hold that the purpose, as above, must be the sole purpose would, apart from difficulties of proof, in my opinion, be too strict a requirement, and would confine the privilege too narrowly: as to this I agree with Barwick CJ in *Grant v Downs* (1976) 135 CLR 674.'

The Court of Appeal further restricted this rule in *Three Rivers District Council v Governor and Company of the Bank of England (No 5)* [2005] EWCA Civ 933. The court stated that before communications can attract immunity from disclosure by reason of legal professional privilege, the following must be satisfied:

- a genuine prospect of litigation;
- the purpose, or dominant purpose, must be to obtain legal advice; and
- the communication must have a relevant legal context.

In this case, the claimants, creditors and liquidators (CCL) of the BCCI bank brought an action against the Bank of England in relation to its supervision of the bank before it collapsed for malfeasance in public office. CCL sought disclosure and inspection of the communications that had taken place during an inquiry into the bank's supervision between the bank's inquiry unit and its solicitors. The bank contended that this information was immune from disclosure by reason of legal professional privilege. The judge ordered disclosure, stating that only communications that had as their purpose seeking or obtaining legal advice in respect of legal rights and obligations were protected by legal professional privilege, and not those relating to mere presentation of evidence to the inquiry, for instance glossing over the evidence to attract the least criticism. The Court of Appeal dismissed the BCCI's appeal. Lord Scott stated that:

JUDGMENT

'. . . advice given by lawyers . . . for the purpose of enhancing the prospects of a successful outcome, from their point of view . . . would be advice given in a relevant legal context and would qualify for legal advice privilege.'

In *Jet2 (R. (on the application of Jet2.com Ltd) v Civil Aviation Authority (CAA)* [2020] EWCA Civ 35 the Court of Appeal confirmed the dominant purpose test for legal professional privilege. In this case the CAA, in 2017–18, published a press release on Jet2's refusal to join its consumer dispute resolution scheme; the former challenged this publication by judicial review. Jet2 applied for disclosure of emails concerning CAA's internal responses to its complaint after the publication and any drafts of the reply actually sent. The CAA claimed legal professional privilege and refused disclosure. The email correspondence involved multiple recipients, many of whom were in-house lawyers. A later witness statement by the CAA voluntarily disclosed a privileged email from that same period. Morris J, the judge at first instance, held that many of the documents or portions thereof were not privileged. He also stated that voluntary disclosure of the privileged email meant that CAA lost privilege in the rest by collateral waiver. The CAA appealed. The Court of Appeal held, *per* Hickinbottom LJ:

- LPP applies to in-house lawyers and to communications applying, considering or sharing legal advice internally;
- third-party information sent to a solicitor will not be privileged;
- 'client' has a narrow definition as those in the company authorised to seek and receive legal advice;
- material collected by a client from third parties with the purpose of instructing lawyers is not privileged; the *Three Rivers* House of Lords decision (above) is binding in this regard;
- legal advice must be given in a 'legal context (the first limb)' but is 'widely defined (the second limb)'; and
- LPP is subject to a dominant purpose test in English law, disagreeing with the *obiter dicta* from the Court of Appeal decision *in SFO v ENRC* [2018] EWCA Civ 2006, where approval of the dominant purpose test was refused.

This judgment provides clarity to what is a complex area of evidence law applicable to modern legal practice, where lawyers and non-lawyers are involved in litigation taking into account multi-chain emails with multiple recipients, and brings it into line with other jurisdictions such as Australia. In short, multi-chain communications that have the dominant purpose of instructing a lawyer will be privileged.

ACTIVITY

What does legal professional privilege cover?

Under what circumstances can this privilege be lost?

What was the significance of the House of Lords decision in *Three Rivers District Council v Governor and Company of the Bank of England (No 5)* [2005] EWCA Civ 933?

KEY FACTS

Legal professional privilege

This focuses on two issues: the communications between a lawyer and their client in the normal course of legal practice, i.e. giving or obtaining legal advice; and the communications between a lawyer or their client with a third party in contemplation of litigation, e.g. expert witnesses.

A claim for legal professional privilege will only be successful if the communication between the lawyer and their client is confidential in nature and, where not made in the course of a lawyer and client relationship, it must have been made with a view to establishing one.

The *general* rule is that communications that are immune from disclosure by reason of privilege will remain so unless it is shown that the communication itself was obtained to further either a crime or a fraud or the privilege is waived.

4.4 Journalistic privilege

English evidence law does not protect information just because it is 'confidential'. Journalistic privilege is the freedom from the disclosure of the source from which particular information came; it is considered by many to be a fundamental tool for democracy. This is because revealing the source would deter individuals from what can be termed as 'whistle-blowing' and could possibly lead to consequences of a serious constitutional nature. In *British Steel v Granada Corporation* [1981] AC 1096 the House of Lords stated that the court had an inherent jurisdiction to provide journalists with freedom from disclosure. The decision left the law in a state of confusion and in need of clarification. To this endeavour, s 10 of the Contempt of Court Act 1981 places journalistic privilege on a statutory footing, stating:

SECTION

'. . . no court may require a person to disclose, nor is any person guilty of contempt of court for refusing to disclose, the source of information contained in a publication for which he is responsible, unless it be established to the satisfaction of the court that disclosure is necessary in the interests of justice or national security or for the prevention of disorder or crime.'

The wording of the provision is clear: the person responsible for the publication, or the person responsible for any means of communicating with the public or a section of the public, does not have to disclose the source of their information. This is of course unless the law requires disclosure because it is in the interests of justice, national security or to prevent crime and disorder. An example of this is where the police raided a number of newspaper offices in relation to telephone hacking by journalists in the UK: the police undertook to preserve journalistic privilege and ensure that it was not compromised. Where a party to an action seeks disclosure of a document, then it must prove that it is in the interests of justice, national security or to prevent crime and disorder; in other words disclosure is necessary because it is essential and not just relevant. In *Secretary of State for Defence v Guardian Newspapers* [1989] AC 339 the court held that s 10 should be defined widely so as to include instances in which a source may be indirectly revealed: see *Maxwell v Pressdram* [1987] 1 WLR 298. Further protection is provided to journalistic material under the Police and Criminal Evidence Act 1984, which prevents seizure of such material without a warrant and court order authorising the same.

4.5 Negotiations without prejudice

The Civil Procedure Rules and Criminal Procedure Rules respectively encourage expediency that often results in the early settlement of disputes in civil proceedings and the efficient progression of criminal proceedings. In terms of the former, a number of pre-action protocols act to promote alternative dispute resolution (see www.justice.gov.uk/courts/procedure-rules/civil/protocol). On that basis, it makes sense that communications aimed at achieving the resolution of a dispute be protected from disclosure. Such communications, whether oral or in writing, are termed **without prejudice** communications and cannot be utilised as evidence of the admission of guilt. It is common practice to head any such communications, where in writing by letter or email, as being without prejudice. There is a common misunderstanding that the words 'without prejudice' serve to protect a communication from disclosure; privilege from disclosure is actually provided by the intention of the parties in making the communication: this is the act of writing the letter or email. In *Rush and Tompkins v GLC* [1989] AC 1280 the Court of Appeal clarified the misconceptions that existed in regard to 'without prejudice' negotiations, *per* Balcombe LJ:

Without prejudice
a legal term used in lieu of without abandonment of a claim, right or privilege, and without any implication as to the admission of liability.

JUDGMENT

'. . . this case had disclosed what appear to be some widespread misconceptions as to the nature of "without prejudice" privilege. In an attempt to remove those misconceptions, and to give guidance to the profession, we venture to state the following principles. (1) The purpose of "without prejudice" privilege is to enable parties to negotiate without risk of their proposals being used against them if the negotiations fail. If the negotiations succeed and a settlement is concluded, the privilege goes, having served its purpose. This will be the case whether the privilege is claimed as against the other party or parties to the negotiations, or as against some outside party. (2) It is possible for the parties to use a form of words which will enable the "without prejudice" correspondence to be referred to, even though no concluded settlement is reached, for example on the issue of costs . . . (3) In contrast, in our judgment, it might be possible for parties to use a special form of words which, at least as between correspondence even after a settlement has been reached . . . (4) The privilege does not depend on the existence of proceedings. (5) Even while the privilege subsists, i.e. before any settlement is reached, there are a number of real or apparent exceptions to the privilege. Thus: (a) the court may always look at a document marked "without prejudice" and its contents for the purposes of deciding its admissibility . . . this is not a real exception to the privilege, since the court must always be able to rule on the admissibility of a document, when a claim to privilege is challenged. It is under this head that the court can look at the documents to see, for example, if an agreement has been concluded and, if so, to construe its terms. (b) The rule has no application to a document which, by its nature, may prejudice the person to whom it is addressed. (6) The privilege extends to the solicitors of the parties to the "without prejudice" negotiations.'

Furthermore, 'without prejudice' letters may be written subject to an express limitation that if a compromise is not made, then the letter or offer can be referred to on the issue of apportioning liability for costs. In other words, a party to the proceedings may make an offer to settle, subject to a 'without prejudice' letter expressing a limitation that if the costs incurred in pursuing the original claim in court prove to be unnecessary or excessive, it may refer to the relevant offer in an effort to reduce the costs that the court may award against them. This procedure is called a *Calderbank* limitation, and it derives its name from a case concerning a matrimonial dispute called *Calderbank v Calderbank* [1976] Fam 93. This limitation has been extended to all cases. In *Cutts v Head* [1984] Ch 290 the court stated that the parties should be:

JUDGMENT

'. . . encouraged [to] fully and frankly put their cards on the table. The public policy justification for the privilege essentially rested on the desirability of preventing statements or offers made in the course of negotiations for settlement being brought before the court of trial as admissions of liability. Once, however, the trial of the issues in an action was at an end and the matter of costs came to be argued, it [the privilege] could have no further application.'

(Oliver LJ)

This form of privilege continues even when the parties have reached a settlement.

4.6 Public interest immunity

The remainder of this chapter will focus on public interest immunity. This is another popular choice for an essay or problem-based coursework assessment. Adversarial justice systems, like that of the UK, operate on the basis of bringing before the court all relevant admissible evidence. In criminal proceedings the prosecution has a duty to disclose; this emphasises the requirement for them to aid the court in reaching its decision and promoting the fair and efficient administration of justice. Contrast this with the duty in civil proceedings to make disclosure of evidence that takes a documentary form. For instance, the early exchange of witness statements means that now fewer hidden surprises exist, a tool used by some lawyers to spring evidence on the opposition so that they may be impeded in dealing with it because they are unprepared. This often resulted in heavy delays in litigation delaying the civil justice system. Sometimes the public interest requires that certain information be withheld from disclosure, perhaps because its release would pose a threat to national security. It may also be that withholding the information promotes the preservation of individual freedom or certain types of privilege, a point discussed later in this chapter.

In the instances where confidentiality must be preserved, then clearly access to that information must also be limited. A successful claim for public interest immunity, or PII as it is commonly called, permits a party to withhold information; this includes contents but can encompass the very existence of a document itself, on the basis that its disclosure would be prejudicial to the general good of the public. As case law demonstrates, government officials usually make most claims for PII; however, private individuals are also entitled to claim it (see *D v NSPCC* [1978] AC 171 or *R v Reading Justices, ex p Berkshire County Council* (1996) 1 Cr App R 239). The primary justification for establishing PII is based on the policy that the public interest in protecting certain pieces of information or documents outweighs the narrower concept of justice being accorded to a private individual in having all the relevant evidence available to them for presentation to the court. In *Rogers v Home Secretary* [1973] AC 388 Lord Pearson stated:

JUDGMENT

'The court has to balance the detriment to the public interest on the administrative or executive side which would result from the disclosure of the document against the detriment to the public interest on the judicial side resulting from non-disclosure of a document which is relevant to an issue in legal proceedings.'

Section 21 of the Criminal Procedure and Investigations Act 1996 (CPIA) governs the basis of public interest immunity in criminal cases. It provides:

SECTION

'(1) Where this Part applies as regards things failing to be done after the relevant time in relation to an alleged offence, the rules of common law which (a) were effective immediately before the appointed day, and (b) relate to the disclosure of material by the prosecutor, do not apply as regards things failing to be done after that time in relation to the alleged offence . . . (2) Subsection (1) does not affect the rules of common law as to whether disclosure is in the public interest.'

The CPIA 1996 normally requires full disclosure by the prosecution unless the common law rules apply. It should be noted that the Criminal Justice Act 2003, reference to which will be made in this chapter as and when necessary, has amended the 1996 Act. In addition, readers should check the website accompanying this book for further up-to-date information and crucial amendments.

From a historical perspective the decisions of the courts reveal that claims for PII by government ministers who sought to prevent disclosure of documentary evidence were conclusive in nature. Thus, the grant of the PII protection was almost automatic (see *Duncan v Cammell Laird & Co Ltd* [1842] AC 624). This was an untenable situation and quite rightly it was not long before it was placed under judicial scrutiny. It was challenged on the basis that left unchecked it was unreasonable and prone to technical abuse, abuse by individuals who held office or were in power and potentially a breach of Art 6 of the European Convention on Human Rights and Fundamental Freedoms (see *R v H* [2004] UKHL 3). PII is normally claimed in cases that involve 'affairs of state', for example the confidential workings of government or issues that relate to national security. In these instances the courts will normally preserve confidentiality, but there will be occasions on which the public interest requires disclosure of the evidence. In *Conway v Rimmer* [1968] AC 910 the House of Lords stressed that when a court is dealing with a claim for PII it should not grant protection automatically because any such claim is open to be challenged. In that case Lord Reid stated:

JUDGMENT

'. . . a Minister's certificate may be given on one or other of two grounds: either because it would be against the public interest to disclose the contents of the particular document or documents in question, or because the document belongs to a class of documents which ought to be withheld, whether or not there is anything in the particular document in question disclosure of which would be against the public interest . . . however wide the power of the court may be held to be, cases would be very rare in which it could be proper to question the view of the responsible Minister that it would be contrary to the public interest to make public the contents of a particular document . . . I would therefore propose that the House ought now to decide that courts have and are entitled to exercise a power and duty to hold a balance between the public interest, as expressed by a Minister, to withhold certain documents or other evidence and the public interest in ensuring the proper administration of justice. That does not mean that a court would reject a Minister's view: full weight must be given to it in every case, and if the Minister's reasons are of a character which judicial experience is not competent to weigh, then the Minister's view must prevail. But experience has shown that reasons given for withholding whole classes of documents are often not of that character. For example a court is perfectly well able to assess the likelihood that, if the writer of a certain class of document knew that there was a chance that his report might be produced in legal proceedings, he would make a less full and candid report than he would otherwise have done.'

Lord Morris continued:

JUDGMENT

'. . . it has been clearly laid down that the mere fact that a document is private or is confidential does not necessarily produce the result that its production can be withheld.'

The House of Lords (especially Lord Reid in *Conway*, see above) also made it clear that there are instances in which it would not be right to preserve confidentiality and that a court should order the disclosure of relevant documentation. The Lords also stated that there are other circumstances, for example where the documents are Cabinet papers, in which the preservation of confidentiality would be of utmost importance and therefore protection by PII should be provided. There is an ongoing discussion in relation to how long such a claim would endure, because transparency is a common tenet of democratic governance. In *Burmah Oil v Bank of England* [1980] AC 1090 the House of Lords stated that only a strong counterclaim would successfully challenge a claim for PII. In this case Lord Wilberforce pointed out that:

JUDGMENT

'. . . a claim for public interest immunity having been made, on manifestly solid grounds, it is necessary for those who seek to overcome it to demonstrate the existence of a counteracting interest calling for disclosure of particular documents. When this is demonstrated, but only then, may the court proceed to a balancing process.'

In both *Conway and Burmah Oil* their Lordships outlined that even though a minister who is claiming PII will be in a far better position to weigh up the implications that disclosure of a particular document may have, nevertheless the courts have the right to scrutinise his or her decision. The courts rarely scrutinise a minister's certificate where PII is claimed on the grounds of national security. Consider *Balfour v Foreign Office:*

CASE EXAMPLE

Balfour v Foreign Office [1994] 1 WLR 681

Mr Balfour was a member of the British diplomatic service and claimed that his former employer, the Foreign and Commonwealth Office, had unfairly dismissed him. He made an application for discovery of certain documents that were in the possession of the Office. The industrial (now employment) tribunal refused to order disclosure on the grounds that it had no jurisdiction to delve into the certificates issued by two Crown ministers that claimed public interest immunity on the grounds of national security. The ministers contended that the documents the claimant was seeking the disclosure of concerned the security and intelligence services. The claimant unsuccessfully appealed to the Employment Appeal Tribunal (EAT), which interpreted the original tribunal's decision as meaning that it was not able to carry out an evaluation of the validity of the national security reasons advanced.

In this case Russell LJ stated:

JUDGMENT

'. . . there must always be vigilance by the courts to ensure that public interest immunity of whatever kind is raised only in appropriate circumstances and with appropriate particularity, but once there is an actual or potential risk to national security demonstrated by an appropriate certificate the court should not exercise its right to inspect.'

4.6.1 Requirements on party seeking disclosure

Successful claims for disclosure and against immunity will prove that the interests of justice require the document(s) to be disclosed. Disclosure will depend on the nature of the PII claim, that is, whether it is a *class* or *contents* claim.

The court will take into account that claims for PII where the document concerned belongs to a class of documents may stifle the candour of those connected to it. In short, disclosure in this instance may prevent the individuals concerned from being open, frank and candid in future documents because they believe there may be a chance that it would be disclosed, for example frank disclosures within a document by government ministers. In support of this, Lord Scarman in *Burmah Oil* stated that:

JUDGMENT

'. . . the reasons given for protecting the secrecy of government at the level of policy-making are two . . . first is the need for candour in the advice offered to ministers: the second is that disclosure "would create or fan ill-informed or captious public or political criticism".'

Lord Reid in *Conway v Rimmer* [1968] AC 910, 952, thought the second of Lord Scarman's reasons to be 'the most important reason'. There will not, however, thankfully, be many instances in which such blanket secrecy is justified and thus the courts do not place much credence on this argument, especially when it comes to documents that are generic or routine, as was the case in *Science Research Council v Nassé* [1980] AC 1028. Where a claim for PII is made on this basis the presiding judge will decide as to what weight to give to the argument.

In contrast, a contents claim is one where a claim for PII is made on the basis that the document contains something that, if revealed, gives cause for concern because it would be prejudicial to the general good of the public. Claims for immunity on this basis are usually far more successful because it is far more certain, namely it is a specific document that would result in the alleged damage.

In most cases a court cannot, and often will not, order the disclosure of documents unless it is necessary to save costs or, far more importantly, for the fair disposal of a case. The party seeking disclosure must show that disclosure of the particular document or documents is necessary. This means that they must prove that, without the document their claim, which is a strong claim with good prospects of success, would be rendered weak or that they will definitely lose. The reasoning in cases often varies.

CASE EXAMPLE

Campbell v Tameside MBC [1982] QB 1065

The claimant was a teacher who was attacked by a student. She sought the disclosure of certain reports produced by the local education authority that showed that the student in question had a known violent past and should therefore have been placed in a special school. Without these reports the teacher had no evidence and therefore was almost certainly going to lose, hence the disclosure of the reports was considered necessary.

CASE EXAMPLE

Air Canada v Secretary of State for Trade (No 2) [1983] 2 AC 394

Air Canada sought the disclosure of documents relating to government policy concerning borrowing in the public sector. The Privy Council held that these documents were not necessary to determine a dispute that concerned landing charges and therefore protected them from disclosure.

In *Burmah Oil v Bank of England* [1980] AC 1090, the House of Lords held that '*after inspection*, none of the *documents* . . . contained matter of such evidential value as to make an order for their disclosure, in all the circumstances, necessary for disposing fairly of the case . . . that they were relevant but their significance was not such as to override the public service objections to their production; and that, accordingly, the appeal must be dismissed . . . *and* . . . where the court inspects a document for which crown privilege is claimed the crown should have a right to appeal before the document is produced.' The facts of the case are presented as *per* Lord Wilberforce:

JUDGMENT

'. . . the appellant the Burmah Oil Co Ltd sued the Governor and Company of the Bank of England for relief in respect of the sale to the Bank by Burmah Oil Co in 1975 of 77,817,507 ordinary stock units of £1 each of the British Petroleum Co Ltd . . . at a price of approximately £179 million. Burmah Oil Co claimed that the price represented ". . . a substantial undervalue of the stock and that the bargain was unconscionable, inequitable and unreasonable . . .". The present appeal arises out of an application by Burmah Oil Co for production of sixty-two documents listed in the list of documents served by the bank. The Bank, on the instructions of the Crown, objected to produce these on the ground that they belong to classes of documents production of which would be injurious to the public interest . . . they have put forward a certificate dated October 18, 1977, signed by the Chief Secretary to the Treasury supporting this objection. On the interlocutory hearing of the objection in the High Court Her Majesty's Attorney-General intervened in order to argue the case in support of it, and it was upheld by Foster J. On appeal by Burmah Oil Co to the Court of Appeal [1979] 1 WLR 473, the Attorney-General took a similar course, and that court, by majority, affirmed the judge . . . on a further appeal to this House, the Attorney-General was joined as a respondent and as such argued the case against production; the bank, as in the High Court and the Court of Appeal, took no part in the argument. But, I repeat, the only defendant in the action is the bank.'

In summary this case concerned a commercial transaction; the company claimed that the government had fixed an unfair price on stock that was sold to the Bank of England – the situation arose in an oil crisis during which the company had to be rescued. The House of Lords held, refusing to order disclosure, that disclosure of the documents was not in fact necessary for the fair disposal of the case and that they were relevant, but this did not override the fact that they were high-level policy documents.

4.6.2 Necessity of disclosure

At this stage the court will assess, having looked at the contents of the documents, whether it is actually necessary to order the disclosure of them for the fair determination of the case. In contrast to the earlier discussion, often the courts will refrain from examining documents that are argued as concerning high-level *national security* because such an exercise would be pointless; such documents are usually immune from disclosure at that time without much difficulty. On satisfaction of the necessity requirement, the court will conduct a weighing exercise. This consists of an assessment of the needs of the party seeking disclosure and the interest of the public in preserving confidentiality. Where necessity is shown, then the party seeking immunity will have a hard task of arguing against disclosure and must show that it is really necessary to withhold disclosure for the proper functioning of the public service.

The rest of the discussion will focus on the 'public policy' reasons commonly used to argue against disclosure.

4.6.3 Public policy

Claims for public interest immunity are mainly made on the basis that the documents are one of the following:

- documents concerning national security or high-level affairs of the state;
- national governmental policy documents;
- local governmental policy documents;
- confidential documents;
- documents relating to the detection and prevention of crime.

What follows is a brief look at each of these. National security is the most commonly pleaded argument by Crown ministers. Once again it is salient to state that the courts will not usually intervene to order disclosure of a document where immunity is sought on the grounds that it concerns the national security of the state or high-level state affairs. Most government policy will contain a significant amount of content that is political and therefore a claim for immunity from disclosure may be made on the grounds of public policy, as in *Burmah Oil* (above). Other areas of public policy that may result in claims for immunity include documents relating to the police complaints procedure: see *Neilson v Laugharne* [1981] QB 736 and *R v Chief Constable of West Midlands, ex p Wiley* [1995] 1 AC 274. In addition, where delegated legislation provides powers to a local authority or a statutory body to formulate and implement policy, then a claim for PII may be made because the state is not limited to national government (see *D v NSPCC* [1978] AC 171).

Another instance in which a claim for PII may arise concerns the detection or prevention of crime; for instance the identity of moles, police informants or whistle-blowers should not be disclosed because the system requires confidentiality in relation to the identity of these individuals so that it may continue to function effectively. This is unless, of course, the identity of the person is of utmost importance in establishing the accused's innocence, and thus the public interest that lies in the acquittal of an innocent person overrides the need for immunity from disclosure (see *Marks v Beyfus* [1980] QB 494). In *R v Rankine* [1986] QB 861 the same principles were applied to surveillance posts – although the Court of Appeal had already set guidelines in relation to the disclosure of this in *R v Johnson* [1968] 1 All ER 121.

Finally, confidential information was discussed earlier. Therefore, in summary: information provided in confidence will be privileged if it qualifies to be immune from disclosure under legal professional or journalistic privilege. Generally, there is no automatic preservation of confidentiality as a matter of public policy, and each case is decided on its own merits. For example, the court will weigh up the public interest in protecting confidential information versus an individual's need for disclosure each time: see *Alfred Crompton Amusements v Commissioners of Customs and Excise (No 2)* [1974] AC 405 and *Science Research Council v Nassé* [1980] AC 1028.

ACTIVITY

What assertion do claims for public interest immunity make?

Define the term blanket immunity.

Outline the main differences between a claim for legal professional privilege and public interest immunity.

KEY FACTS

Public interest immunity

A claim for *public interest immunity* permits a party to withhold information on the basis that its disclosure would be prejudicial to the general public good.

Section 21(2) of the Criminal Procedure and Investigations Act 1996 (CPIA) governs the basis of public interest immunity in criminal cases.

There are five main reasons that may be put forward as arguments in applications for PII: the documents concern national security or high-level affairs of the state; are national governmental policy documents; concern local governmental policy; are confidential documents; or they relate to the detection and prevention of crime (see *R v Franckevicius* [2017] EWCA Crim 1210). A full list of examples is provided in the CPIA 1996 Code of Practice 2020 at para 6.14.

The House of Lords has stressed on many occasions that in some instances it would be right not to preserve confidentiality and to order the disclosure of documents and in others not.

Where a claim is contested, the party seeking disclosure must show that the interests of justice require the document to be disclosed.

4.6.4 Waiver and objection

Waiver
the voluntary surrender or relinquishing of a right.

A series of co-related questions arise in relation to the existence of immunity. Questions regarding waiver – can immunity be waived and, if it can, on what basis – are but two. There are a number of conflicting authorities on this particular issue. The decision in *Rogers v Home Secretary* [1973] AC 388 suggested that immunity cannot be waived under any circumstance. Contrast this with the decision in *Alfred Crompton Amusements* (above) – here it was suggested that the person or persons that were protected could choose to waive it. Lord Denning in *Campbell v Tameside MBC* [1982] QB 1065 argued that waiver should be allowed in cases where the documents were not high-level but low-level policy documents and both maker and protected agreed with it:

JUDGMENT

'. . . in these cases the court can and should consider the *significance* of the documents in relation to the decision of the case. If they are of such significance that they may well affect the very decision of the case, then justice may require them to be disclosed. The public interest in justice being done – in the instant case – may well outweigh the public interest in keeping them confidential. But, if they are of little significance, so that they are very unlikely to affect the decision of the case, then the greater public interest may be to keep them confidential. In order to assess their significance, it is open to the court itself to inspect the documents. If disclosure is necessary in the interest of justice in the instant case, the court will order their disclosure but otherwise not.'

Parties to proceedings can also object to a document being disclosed. In this instance the item is listed as being 'subject to objection', and the argument in relation to the objection in civil proceedings is then heard at an alternative hearing and in criminal proceedings at a *voir dire*. Where the objection raised is by a crown minister, the minister will usually issue a certificate or affidavit confirming that they have seen the document and detail their objections on the basis of public policy grounds. If an objection is successful, then no reference can be made to it that may reveal the contents either directly or indirectly. At a European level, the European Court of Human Rights has recognised the need to withhold evidence from disclosure where it would not be in the public interest (see *Rowe v UK* (2000) 30 EHRR 1).

4.6.5 Contrasting privilege and PII

It is important that you understand the differences between privilege and public interest immunity. In terms of privilege the party entitled to claim this might choose to waive it, whereas it is doubtful whether PII can ever be waived and, if so, who can do this. As a corollary to the first point, no secondary evidence is admissible to prove the relevant document that is subject to PII. In other words, a copy of the prohibited document may not be admitted. In addition, an objection to the admissibility of the evidence may be taken by the judge, if not taken by the parties, witnesses or government department, provided that it is the subject of PII.

Figure 4.3 summarises the position:

Privilege	Public Interest Immunity
Privilege can be waived by the party claiming it	In the majority of cases immunity cannot be waived
Secondary evidence is admissible to prove a relevant document	Secondary evidence is not admissible to prove a relevant document
Only the party seeking to assert privilege can take objection to the document being disclosed	A judge, witnesses or a government department may take objection to the document being disclosed

Figure 4.3 The difference between privilege and public interest immunity

SUMMARY

- In criminal proceedings there are three parts to disclosure under the CPIA 1996. These are the statutory duty to record and retain information, prosecution disclosure and defence disclosure (detailed defence).
- The prosecution has a continuing duty to disclose from the start right through to the completion of a case.
- Part 31 of the Civil Procedure Rules (as at January 2022) lays down standard disclosure requirements in cases listed on the fast and multi-tracks; on the small claims track only that evidence that will be relied on at trial need be disclosed.
- Privilege, where successfully claimed, acts to protect evidence from being disclosed on the basis that in limited circumstances the law recognises it as being in need of protection.
- The main grounds upon which privilege may be claimed are against self-incrimination, legal professional or litigation privilege, without prejudice negotiations and journalistic privilege.
- The privilege against self-incrimination provides that no witness is required to answer any question or produce any document in court where it would incriminate them.
- Legal professional privilege seeks to protect from disclosure communications between a lawyer and their client in the normal course of legal practice or of a lawyer and/or their client with a third party in contemplation of litigation.
- Without prejudice negotiations seek to protect from disclosure communications aimed at achieving the resolution of a dispute – this ideally promotes candour.
- Public interest immunity permits a party to withhold information (evidence) on the basis that its disclosure would be prejudicial to the general good of the public.
- The five main grounds for PII applications are that the documents concern national security or high-level affairs of the state; are national governmental policy documents; concern local governmental policy; are confidential documents; or relate to the detection and prevention of crime.

SAMPLE ESSAY QUESTION

With case examples, analyse that the differences between privilege and public interest immunity are the same.

Answer plan

Highlight what privilege and PII are.
Define privilege and PII. Discuss the fact that both privilege and PII have the effect of excluding evidence that is relevant and admissible.

Outline the differences and similarities between them.
Discuss the arguments for and against each of these, showing the similarity in the way in which they produce the same result through different methods. Analyse the courts' balancing exercise in relation to privilege and PII and the considerations. Explore the contention regarding the interest of the public in having full disclosure and holding ministers to account for their decisions, etc.

Discuss who is entitled to claim privilege and PII, waiver and secondary evidence.
Highlight that privilege can be waived; however, the law is of mixed opinion where it comes to the disclosure in terms of PII. Discuss *Rogers v Home Secretary* (1973) and *Alfred Crompton Amusement Machines Ltd v Customs & Excise Commissioners (No 2)* (1974). Analyse how the courts have brought the operation of PII in line with that of privilege. Explore the fact that privilege only attaches to an original document and the proof of the contents of that document through secondary evidence. Mention that this is not the case with PII.

Further reading

Brown, S. 'Public interest immunity' (1994) PL, Win, 579–595

Chippindall, A. 'Expert advice and legal professional privilege' (2003) JPI Law, Jan, 61–70

Ettinger, C. 'Case comment' (2005) JPI Law 3, C114–117

5

Silence: the effect on an accusation

AIMS AND OBJECTIVES

By the end of this chapter you will be able to:

- understand the extent of an accused's right to remain silent and how the law historically developed;
- highlight how silence can affect an accusation through hypothetical examples and case studies;
- understand about silence under the common law and statute;
- outline the instances in which silence can adversely affect an accusation through highlighting contemporary changes in the way the silence is perceived;
- understand the inferences that can be drawn from instances in which an accused remains silent;
- appreciate the impact human rights law has on the accused's right to remain silent.

5.1 Introduction

The discussion in this chapter focuses on the silence of an accused person, a defendant who is faced with an accusation that they have committed a crime, and how that silence affects the accusation. The discussion will include a brief exploration of the common law and statutory rules on this issue and the instances in which the defendant remaining silent can lead to a jury drawing adverse inferences against them.

5.2 The historical development and significance of silence

In many legal systems worldwide it is recognised that someone might appear, as in film or in television series, to be found in a range of the most compromising or incriminating circumstances and, for reasons unbeknown

DOI: 10.4324/9781003282433-5

to those that discover them, they still choose to say absolutely nothing. Here is an example that comes to mind from a truly terrible film: Johanne walks in to discover that her husband Giles has stabbed Mark, with whom she was having an affair. Johanne sees that Mark is lying on the floor dying with a dagger still lodged in his chest and, while attempting to save him, she starts to pull the dagger out of his chest. Whilst in the act of pulling the dagger out of Mark's chest, Johanne is seen by Mark's husband Frank, who believes that what he is witnessing is Johanne killing Mark. On seeing Frank, a startled Johanne in an attempt to protect her husband Giles remains silent and does not utter a word or make any other gesture. The motive behind Johanne's silence in this instance is not to expose her husband's crime – what is interesting, and the topic of the discussion here, is where the law lies on this issue.

The discussion starts with a focus on the erosion of the right to silence in English law and the arguments for and against its existence are set out later in the chapter. The starting point is how an accused remaining silent generates suspicion because of the notion that an innocent person would instinctively react to protest their innocence.

To begin, a question for those of you who have shared a rental property with other people or who have friends who have done so. How often does someone ask: 'Who drank the last of the milk?' And in response, an often horrified set of flatmates in protest of their own innocence retorts, 'not me'. One assumption is that only those individuals who are 'guilty' and therefore have something to hide will say nothing. However, we can see from the example above that this is rather simplistic, and often people remain silent for many different reasons whether these are valid, noble or otherwise. Motive is often relevant to the mitigation of a crime but the law on the issue of a defendant's silence is far tougher in its stance.

The general rule is that an appropriately directed jury can draw adverse inferences where a defendant has remained silent during the investigation of a crime or at trial, for example questioning under caution. The law on this is set out in the Criminal Justice and Public Order Act 1994 (CJPOA), but before the consideration of the law it is important, for purposes of context at least, to take a brief look at the position of English law in relation to silence prior to its introduction. Before the 1994 statute was enacted the English law of evidence recognised that a defendant had a right to remain silent or had a privilege against self-incrimination, as discussed in Chapter 4. The rationale that underpins both these sets of principles has at its root the notion of fairness. The case of *R v Director of the Serious Fraud Office, ex p Smith* [1993] AC 1 explores this link and may be something for independent research in addition to that which is presented here.

The right to silence, which is now a qualified right because it is restricted by the CJPOA, used to mean that a defendant could say nothing during an interrogation by the police, give a no-comment interview, and did not have to give evidence at their own trial. This position allowed a defendant to stand back and require the prosecution to prove its case – some believed this to show that the law was weighted in favour of criminals who would use silence as a means of evading justice. In 1993 a report by the Royal Commission on Criminal Justice on the right to silence, chaired by Lord Runciman, declared that contrary to the above contention, high-flying criminals were not abusing the right to silence. In fact the Royal Commission's report stated that removal of the right could result in greater miscarriages of justice. The government chose not to follow the recommendations of the report, and the CJPOA 1994 was the result. Although a fairly simple statute, it was not long before it ran into problems with regard to fairness under Art 6 of the European Convention on Human Rights and Fundamental Freedoms (ECHR) – an issue discussed later in this chapter. Finally, when reading through this chapter keep in mind the *Lucas* direction; this directs the jury on any lies told by a defendant – that direction is discussed in Chapter 13.

5.3 Silence at common law

Section 34(5) of the Criminal Justice and Public Order Act 1994 (CJPOA) states that the Act does not affect the common law rules on silence.

Generally, under the common law an accused's silence when confronted about an incident is irrelevant. In exceptional instances, when an accusation is made in the presence of the accused, his or her silence may be construed as an adoption of the accusation or the charge, provided that the circumstances are such that an unequivocal denial or a reasonable explanation could be expected from them. One such circumstance is where the parties between whom a conversation is taking place are on equal speaking terms. Clearly, a conversation with a police officer would not fall into this category. In *R v Hall* [1971] 1 WLR 298 the Privy Council held that the silence of A (the accused) when faced with an accusation put by a police officer as to what B (the accomplice) had said did not amount to an informal admission by A. As *per* Lord Diplock:

JUDGMENT

'It is clear . . . that a person is entitled to refrain from answering a question put to him for the purpose of discovering whether he has committed a criminal offence. *A fortiori* he is under no obligation to comment when he is informed that someone else had accused him of an offence. It may be that in very exceptional circumstances an inference may be drawn from a failure to give an explanation or a disclaimer, but in their Lordships' view, silence alone on being informed by a police officer that someone else has made an accusation against him cannot give rise to an inference that the person to whom this information is communicated accepts the truth of the accusation . . . The caution merely serves to remind the accused of a right which he already possesses at common law.'

It is likely that this position might have been different had the accusation been made by the victim or a relation in circumstances requiring an explanation. In short, a defendant has the right to remain silent under the common law, but it is still difficult to try and reconcile this with the fact that they have stated nothing in response to accusations that incriminate them that are made in their presence.

As a result the following question arises; what, if any, instances are there in which silence under the *common law* can amount to the acceptance of an allegation, from which an adverse inference may be drawn. In the majority of instances silence *cannot* amount to such an acceptance (see *Hall v R* [1971] 1 WLR 298). However, in limited circumstances the opposite may be true; where an accused is faced with an allegation made by a person who stands on an equal footing with them and it is reasonable to expect them to reply. In such a scenario the decision in *R v Mitchell* (1982) 17 Cox CC 503 suggests that a lack of response may amount to an acceptance of guilt under the common law. The real issues to determine in this instance are (a) if the parties (accuser and accused) stand on equal speaking terms and (b) whether the circumstances require an unequivocal denial by an innocent person. This is a question of law for the judge to decide.

CASE EXAMPLE

Accusation
a formal criminal charge that is levied against a person for an alleged commission of a criminal offence.

R v Parkes [1976] 1 WLR 1251

A woman whose daughter had been murdered accused the defendant of having murdered her. In response to this the defendant remained silent. However, when she told him that she was going to call the police, he tried to stab her. In this case his silence amounted to an acceptance of the **accusation**. As *per* Lord Diplock:

JUDGMENT

'In the instant case, there is no question of an accusation being made by or in the presence of a police officer or any other person in authority or charged with the investigation of the crime. It was a spontaneous charge made by the mother about an injury done to her daughter. In circumstances such as these their Lordships agree that the direction given by Cave J in *R v Mitchell* is applicable:

"Now the whole admissibility of statements of this kind rests upon the consideration that if the charge is made against a person in that person's presence it is reasonable to expect that he or she will immediately deny it, and that the absence of such denial is some evidence of an admission on the part of the person charged and of the truth of the charge. Undoubtedly, when persons are speaking on even terms, and a charge is made, and the person charged says nothing, and expresses no indignation, and does nothing to repel the charge, that is some evidence to show that he admits the charge to be true" (As per Lord Diplock).

'Here Mrs Graham and the defendant were on even speaking terms. Furthermore, the defendant's reaction to the accusation was not one of mere silence. He drew a knife and attempted to stab Mrs Graham in order to escape when she threatened to detain him while the police was sent for.'

CASE EXAMPLE

R v Chandler [1976] 1 WLR 585

The Court of Appeal stated that a defendant's silence in the face of an accusation made against him while his solicitor was present had amounted to an acceptance of it.

JUDGMENT

'. . . we are of the opinion that the defendant and the detective sergeant were speaking on equal terms since the former had his solicitor present to give him any advice he might have wanted and to testify, if needed, as to what had been said. We do not accept that a police officer always has an advantage over someone he is questioning. Everything depends on the circumstances. A young detective questioning a local dignitary in the course of an inquiry into alleged local government corruption may be very much at a disadvantage. This kind of situation is to be contrasted with that of a tearful housewife accused of shoplifting.'

(Lawton LJ)

In *R v Jason and Hind* [2005] EWCA Crim 971, the Court of Appeal confirmed that a defendant's right to silence under the common law exists. In fact, in this case, the refusal of the defendant to leave his police cell to answer questions was merely an 'emphatic' way of exercising his right, which did not, under the common law, amount to an acceptance of the allegation from which an adverse inference could be drawn.

ACTIVITY

What is the extent to which an accused has a right to silence under the common law?

KEY FACTS

The common law and silence

The enactment of the CJPOA 1994 did not affect the common law rules on an accused's right to silence (s 34(5)).

An accused still has the right to remain silent under the common law. The difficulty lies in the accused reconciling the fact that they have stated nothing in response to allegations made in their presence that incriminate them with the related perception that only those who have something to hide remain silent.

Silence does not amount to an acceptance or admission of an allegation unless the accused is faced with an allegation that is made by a person on an equal footing where it is thus reasonable to expect them to reply. In these circumstances, the lack of response from an accused may amount to an acceptance of guilt.

5.4 Silence under the CJPOA 1994

Other than the rules under the common law, ss 34, 36 and 37 of the Criminal Justice and Public Order Act 1994 (CJPOA) provide specific instances in which a defendant's silence either at the time of being questioned by the police or when reasonably asked to explain themselves may lead to adverse inferences being drawn against them.

To recapitulate, under the common law a defendant's silence when being questioned by the police did not indicate an acceptance or informal admission that incriminated him or her of the crime they were alleged to have committed. The position is quite different under the CJPOA 1994 – a position partly brought about by the concern that criminals were using silence as a 'tool' or 'shield' with which to hinder the prosecution case by depriving the prosecution of essential evidence. The government, via the 1994 Act, even though this was contrary to the recommendations of the Runciman Report (1993), introduced a series of measures that were intended to dissuade a defendant from taking a course of action where he or she remained silent by producing, in appropriate circumstances, consequences if they did.

Interestingly, the CJPOA 1994 did not expressly abolish the common law on this matter but instead created a set of statutory rules that now run alongside them, and therefore it is important that you have a sound knowledge of both. Thus, an accused can still exercise his or her right to remain silent by refusing to answer questions or give oral evidence at court. The difference in

Section 34	Defendant fails to mention facts, when questioned, that are later relied on by them in their defence
Section 35	Accused fails to testify at court
Section 36	Defendant fails to account for incriminating objects, substances or marks
Section 37	Accused fails to account for their presence in an incriminating place

Figure 5.1 Silence and the Criminal Justice and Public Order Act 1994

the current position (post-CJPOA 1994) is that the otherwise unrestricted 'right to remain silent' has been eroded to become qualified by the requirement to 'speak up' in specified situations. An accused who seeks to exercise his or her right to remain silent risks the trier of fact (the jury) drawing adverse inferences against them. The remaining discussion in this chapter will focus on the following provisions of the CJPOA 1994:

To be successful in answering an assessment question on this topic students are required to have a good understanding of each of these provisions. Beware when assessing evidence that in addition to the defendant's failure to do one of the above that the method by which the evidence was collected was lawful because there may be an argument for its exclusion for unfairness under s 78 of the Police and Criminal Evidence Act 1984 (PACE).

Section 58 of the Youth Justice and Criminal Evidence Act 1999 has amended ss 34, 36 and 37, and thus the accused must be at an *authorised place of detention* when the failure or refusal arises. Authorised places of detention are police stations; the provisions do not apply where the accused is at an authorised place of detention but has not been afforded the opportunity to consult their lawyer. This area of the law has been further complicated by UK anti-terrorism legislation, a discussion of which is beyond the scope of this chapter. Finally, the Criminal Procedure and Investigations Act 1996 (as amended by the Criminal Justice Act 2003) allows an adverse inference to be drawn where there is a failure to comply with disclosure requirements (see ss 11 and 11(5)(b)).

ACTIVITY

What was the rationale for the enactment of the CJPOA 1994?

What effect did the CJPOA 1994 have on the common law rules on the right to silence?

KEY FACTS

Silence under the Criminal Justice and Public Order Act 1994

The CJPOA 1994 provides specific instances in which an accused's silence, either on being questioned by the police or when reasonably asked to explain themselves, may lead to the jury drawing adverse inferences against them.

The provisions of the CJPOA 1994 are in addition to the common law rules, as the 1994 statute did not abolish them.

The effect of the CJPOA 1994 is to qualify the right to silence; therefore an accused can still exercise their right to silence but it may in specified circumstances lead to the trier of fact (the jury) drawing adverse inferences against them.

5.4.1 Section 34 – failure to mention facts when questioned

The discussion on adverse inferences under the CJPOA 1994 starts with s 34. This provision has caused the courts a great deal of difficulty in terms of its interpretation and application: see *R v Bresa* [2005] EWCA Crim 1414. The aim of this provision is to try to discourage the accused from later fabricating a defence and to encourage them to disclose, early on, any defence or material fact that supports any defence that they may have: see *R v Roble* [1997] Crim LR 449. The wording of s 34(1) states:

SECTION

'Where in any proceedings against a person for an offence evidence is given that the accused:

(a) at any time *before* being charged with *the commission* of an offence, on being questioned *whilst* under caution by a constable trying to discover whether or by whom an offence had been committed, failed to mention any fact relied on in a defence in those proceedings; or
(b) on being charged with the *commission* of an offence or officially informed *of the possibility* prosecuted for it, failed to mention any such fact, being a fact which in the circumstances existing at the time the accused could reasonably have been expected to mention when being so questioned, charged or informed, as the case may be, subsection (2) applies. Subsection (2) allows the court or jury to "draw such inferences as appear proper".' (author's emphasis)

The Youth Justice and Criminal Evidence Act 1999 inserted s 34(2A) into the CJPOA 1994; therefore, a jury may only draw an adverse inference under s 34 where an accused has been given the opportunity to receive legal advice. Section 34(2A) states:

SECTION

'. . . where an accused was at an authorised place of detention at the time of the failure, subsections (1) and (2) of s 34(1) do not apply if *they* had *not* been allowed an opportunity to consult a solicitor prior to being questioned, charged or informed as mentioned in subsection (1) . . .'. (author's emphasis)

To clarify, s 38(2A) states that the reference to an authorised place of detention is a reference to a police station.

What follows is an examination of s 34(1) in a little more depth. The easiest way to deal with any provision of law, i.e. a section in an Act of Parliament, is to break it down into manageable parts. Often, textbooks will do this; however, it can be done by identifying the elements that make up the provision itself, but do not forget the relevant case law that accompanies each element. Here is how it works:

When broken down it becomes obvious that the drawing of an adverse inference under s 34 is dependent on the following elements being satisfied:

(a) before charge;
(b) questioning, in investigation, under caution;

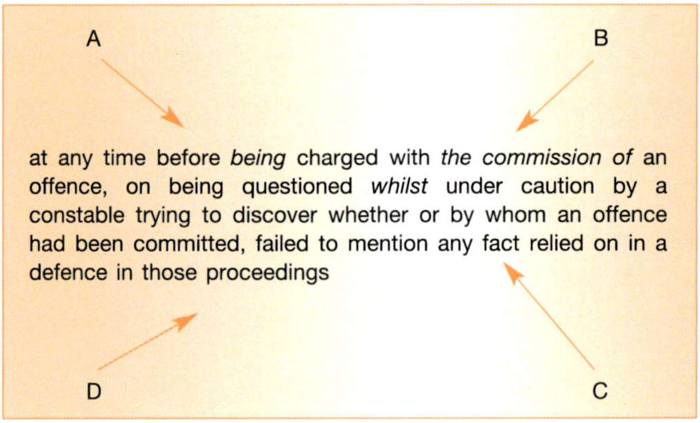

Figure 5.2 How s 34(1) of the Criminal Justice and Public Order Act 1994 works

(c) failure to mention any fact;

(d) subsequent reliance on the fact that the accused failed to mention in their defence.

This can be stated as follows; the accused fails to mention any fact, before charge and when questioned during investigation under caution, which they subsequently rely on in a defence. The first, element (a), is simple. The investigation and related questioning must take place before the defendant is charged with the commission of the offence. The aim of the provision is effectively to promote a differentiation between honest individuals who usually voluntarily proffer information from those that have something to hide.

Inference
the result of a reasoning process through which a logical deduction can be made.

Section 34 only applies once the suspect has been cautioned, as that is the point at which they will be made aware of the potential of adverse **inferences** that can be drawn from their silence. Under Code C, of the codes that accompany PACE 1984, the caution reads as follows: 'You do not have to say anything but it may harm your defence if you do not mention when questioned something that you later rely on in court. Anything you do say may be given in evidence.' Note the following three points:

- The suspect does not have to say anything.
- If the suspect fails to mention anything, when questioned, which they later rely on in court, it *may* harm their defence.
- Anything the suspect does say *may* be used in evidence.

Moving on to element (b), s 34 requires that the suspect is questioned in investigation; such questioning will normally take place at a police station in an interview room and be recorded. Where a suspect issues a significant statement, i.e. where questioning may be regarded as continuing although not taped, outside the interview room then that must be mentioned at the start of the next recorded interview. The suspect must be asked to confirm or deny the statement or be asked whether they would like to add anything to it.

On 2 February 2021, Case C-481/19 *DB v Commissione Nazionale per le Societe la Borsa (Consob), Intervener in the main proceedings Presidenza dei Consiglio dei Ministri* 2021, the Court of Justice for the European Union found that the Union's rules on insider dealing must allow an accused facing criminal penalties the right to remain silent during an administrative investigation; the accused cannot use the protection to justify delay, failing to appear at the hearing and not co-operating with an investigation.

The next elements ((c) and (d)) require the defendant (who is no longer a suspect and is now the accused, because they will have been charged) to run a defence based on the facts that they failed to mention at trial. Common examples of this may involve self-defence or perhaps an alibi. If the defence merely denies the prosecution case thereby requiring it to prove it, i.e. they do not raise a defence based on any fact, then s 34 will not apply, because the defence must be based on the facts that were not mentioned. Furthermore, the facts that the defendant failed to mention must be facts that could reasonably have been mentioned. This means that the defendant must know (a) what allegations are being levied against them and (b) the significance of the facts to the investigation of the offence.

The provision seeks to rectify the position where the defendant raises a positive defence or ambushes the prosecution at the last minute with a defence that it is unprepared to be able to counter.

In *R v Argent* [1997] 2 Cr App R 27 the Court of Appeal outlined the steps that have to be satisfied before an adverse inference can be drawn under s 34. They are:

- The proceedings must be against the defendant for the commission of a criminal offence.
- The defendant must have failed to mention the facts before they were charged.
- The failure must have occurred while the defendant was being questioned under caution by a police constable or another person charged with the investigation of criminal offences.
- The aim of the questions should be to ascertain (a) whether an offence has been committed and (b) by whom.
- The defendant must raise the fact or facts that they failed to mention in their defence.
- The fact or facts raised must be issues that could reasonably have been mentioned.

The legal test used to satisfy what amounts to a fact that could have been reasonably mentioned is *subjective and objective*, i.e. what could *that* defendant have reasonably mentioned (subjective) or what could reasonably have been expected of that defendant (objective). When considering this point it is important to understand that the position of the defendant at the time of questioning will be considered. The following factors can be taken into account in determining what could have been expected of a particular defendant at the time of questioning:

- personality
- physical and mental state
- age
- intelligence
- any language barriers, i.e. fluency in spoken English

- experience
- intoxication
- tiredness
- any legal advice received.

The Court of Appeal made it clear in *R v Parchment* [2003] EWCA Crim 2428 that before an adverse inference may be drawn, 'the jury must be sure that the prosecution's case was so strong that it clearly called for an answer [from the defendant]'. It was also stated that if the case against a defendant is weak, then the jury must be informed of the limited function of the 'failure to mention when questioned', otherwise the conviction would be unsafe, as it was in this case where the murder conviction of one of the accused was quashed because an appropriate direction had not been given to the jury.

In *R v Central Criminal Court, ex p S and P* (1998) 163 JP 776, the court refused to apply s 34 in relation to one of the accused by reason of his low IQ.

An issue arises where a defendant states that they did not mention a fact or facts after having received legal advice to that effect, that they should remain silent. Section 56 and Code C of PACE 1984 entitles an accused to legal advice before and during the interrogation and thus, although the fact that the accused may have remained silent after having received legal advice is a relevant consideration for the jury when deciding whether or not to draw an adverse inference, it does not in itself prevent the adverse inference from being drawn: see *Argent* (above).

CASE EXAMPLE

R v Condron [1997] 1 WLR 827

The defendant was a drug addict. He was advised by his solicitor to refrain from answering any questions on the basis that he was under the effect of drugs, even though the police doctor had deemed him fit for questioning. The court held that the fact that the defendant was acting on the legal advice given to him did not automatically mean that adverse inferences could not be drawn from his silence. If the defendant waived his legal professional privilege and gave evidence on the reasons for the advice, then that may prevent adverse inferences from being drawn. On appeal, the Court of Appeal decided that the judge's direction that the jury were entitled to draw adverse inferences from his silence was improper.

CASE EXAMPLE

R v Pointer [1997] Crim LR 676

The court held that an accused's silence would fall outside the provisions of s 34 if, at the time of questioning, the police had enough evidence to levy a charge.

The application of s 34 is dependent on an accused raising facts in their defence that were not mentioned in their interview. A regular bone of contention was 'what is *any fact relied on in defence*'. The Court of Appeal considered this question on many occasions and concluded that the term should not be narrowly construed. In *R v Milford* [2001] Crim LR 330 the court stated that the term *any fact* means 'something that is actually the case . . . a particular truth known by actual observation or authentic testimony, as opposed to what is merely inferred, or to a conjecture or fiction'.

A fact can be raised for the purposes of s 34(1)(a) by the accused in evidence, by a defence witness and even by a prosecution witness while giving evidence in chief or being cross-examined. Where the defendant puts a fact to a witness in cross-examination, then, so long as the other elements have been satisfied, that is enough for s 34(1) to apply, even if the witness refuses to accept the fact. It is clear from the wording of the provision that it applies to *any fact(s) relied upon* rather than *any fact(s) established*. Procedurally, this had the potential of having some impact on the way in which counsel, instructed by the defendant to act on their behalf, cross-examined witnesses. However, the decision of the courts in cases including *R v Weber* [2004] 1 Crim App R 40 confirmed that s 34 will not apply, because no facts will have been relied upon, where counsel's questions are designed to test or probe the prosecution case.

Furthermore, the provision will not apply where the defence offers nothing more than mere theories or speculation (*R v N* [1998] 1 WLR 153), nor will it apply if:

- the matters are too complex;
- they had occurred a long time ago so that an immediate response from the accused is not possible;
- the police fail to disclose relevant information to the accused's solicitor so that they are unable to appropriately advise the accused.

The case of *R v Roble* [1997] Crim LR 449 provides a further discussion of these points.

CASE EXAMPLE

R v McGarry [1999] Crim LR 316

In this case the defendant gave a no-comment interview to the police. Later on, after having received legal advice, he gave a written statement to them. At the trial the defendant was not cross-examined on his statement, and the trial judge directed the jury that they could draw an adverse inference from the facts. The Court of Appeal held that the judge had erred in law; the jury should have been directed not to draw an adverse inference.

CASE EXAMPLE

R v Ali and Others [2001] All ER (D) 16 (CA)

The three defendants (1, 2 and 3), who were from family A, had a long-standing feud with another family (B). During an altercation the defendants injured a member of family B and were charged with causing grievous bodily harm contrary to s 18 of the Offences Against the Person Act 1861. All three gave no-comment interviews; however, later on defendants 1 and 2 prepared and gave statements to the police; defendant 1 claimed that he was acting in self-defence. Defendant 3 gave an alibi. All three testified when it came to the trial. Consistently, defendant 3 maintained his alibi but defendant 1 added that he had heard the victim call to his family members for a knife. The trial judge directed the jury that they could draw adverse inferences against all three defendants for a failure to mention facts on which they were now relying. The defendants all appealed. The appeals of defendants 1 and 3 were dismissed; however, defendant 2's appeal was allowed because the facts on which he was relying were disclosed to the police in a written statement beforehand. The reason for this was that defendant 3 had made no pre-trial statement and defendant 1 had departed from his by the additional information regarding the knife. Defendant 2 had stuck to his statement.

The following question arises in relation to this: what if a defendant fails to mention a fact when questioned which they later rely on as a *sole* defence, and the case depends on the existence or non-existence of that fact. The Court of Appeal has decided that in such an instance the presiding trial judge should exercise their discretion and refrain from issuing a direction under s 34.

CASE EXAMPLE

R v Mountford [1999] Crim LR 575

The defendant (A) was staying at B's flat, which was searched by the police under warrant. During the search A was spotted dropping a package out of the window of the flat. When recovered it was found the package contained heroin that would have had a street value of £400. After arrest both A and B were taken to the police station. A made a no-comment interview; however, B plea-bargained, offering to testify against A. A was charged with possession of a class A drug with an intention to supply. A testified that B was the dealer, and it was he who had thrown the packet out of the window just before the search. Furthermore, he stated that he had not proffered this information at interview because he was unsure what B would have said and therefore did not want to 'grass' on him. The trial judge issued a direction under s 34 and A was convicted. The Court of Appeal allowed A's appeal on the basis that the trial judge had erred in directing the jury to draw an adverse inference and thereby prejudiced a fair trial. The *fact* that A had not disclosed during questioning and was now relying on was the sole basis of A's defence, and its existence was in question. What the judge should have done is directed the jury to consider the evidence without drawing an adverse inference.

Section 34 – inferences

The Criminal Justice and Public Order Act 1994 provides that a jury may draw 'such inferences *that may* seem proper'. Similar provisions had been running in Northern Ireland for a number of years prior to the enactment of the 1994 statute, and the jury is able to draw the inference that the defence put forward at the trial is a recent fabrication. In contrast, in England and Wales an adverse inference has the effect of casting doubt on any defence that is subsequently raised, although this may lead to an increased chance that the jury decide to return a **verdict** of guilty. You should bear in mind that no accused may be convicted solely on the basis of an adverse inference, and therefore silence alone is not enough for the jury to infer guilt (s 38(3)). In *R v Daniel and R v Montague and Beckles* [1998] Crim LR 148 the Court of Appeal confirmed that

Verdict
the formal decision or finding made by a jury, which it reports to the court.

the jury is not limited, under s 34, to draw an adverse inference of recent fabrication.

Where a judge gives a direction to the jury, then its effect is as follows:

- The legal burden of proof lies with the prosecution.
- The accused has a right to remain silent and can exercise that right.
- The silence of the accused may only be relevant after the prosecution has established a *prima facie* case to the jury's satisfaction.
- Silence alone is not enough to facilitate a guilty verdict.
- The jury may only draw an adverse inference from the accused's silence if they decide that the accused remained silent because of the belief that the story would not stand up when questioned, i.e. under investigative scrutiny.

When directing the jury the trial judge should also remind them of any reason an accused gives for failing to mention the fact(s) that they have now relied upon. Finally, two points to remember:

(a) Section 34(4) applies in those instances where an accused is questioned by the police, or another person who is charged with the investigation of offences.

(b) Section 78 of PACE 1984, discussed later in the book, applies to invest the judge with a discretion to exclude any evidence obtained improperly, i.e. through breaches of the PACE codes. For an example, see *R v Dervish* [2002] 2 Cr App R 105.

ACTIVITY

Section 34 of the CJPOA 1994 allows the jury to draw which adverse inference?

Outline the requirements that must be satisfied before an adverse inference may be drawn.

KEY FACTS

Failure to mention facts when questioned (s 34)

The drawing of an adverse inference under s 34 is conditional upon the accused having received legal advice.

The investigation and related questioning must take place before the defendant is charged with the commission of the offence.

The provision only applies once the suspect has been cautioned.

The jury may draw 'such inferences *that may* seem proper'.

5.4.2 Section 35 – a failure to testify

Section 35 of the CJPOA 1994 provides that adverse inferences can also be drawn where a defendant fails to testify at court.

Section 35 of the CJPOA 1994 states that:

SECTION

(1) . . . at the trial of any person . . . for an offence, subsections (2) and (3) apply unless (a) the accused's guilt is not in issue; or (b) it appears to the court that the physical or mental condition of the accused makes it undesirable for him to give evidence; but subsection (2) below does not apply if, at the conclusion of the evidence for the prosecution, his legal representative informs the court that the accused will give evidence or, where he is unrepresented, the court ascertains from him that he will give evidence.

(2) . . . where this subsection applies, the court shall, at the conclusion of the evidence for the prosecution, satisfy itself (in the case of proceedings on indictment . . . in the presence of the jury) that the accused is aware that the stage has been reached at which evidence can be given for the defence and that he can, if he wishes, give evidence and that, if he chooses not to give evidence, or having been sworn, without good cause refuses to answer any question, it will be permissible for the court or jury to draw such inferences as appear proper from his failure to give evidence or his refusal, without good cause, to answer any question.

(3) . . . where this subsection applies, the court or jury, in determining whether the accused is guilty of the offence charged, may draw such inferences as appear proper from the failure of the accused to give evidence or his refusal, without good cause, to answer any question.

CASE EXAMPLE

R v Kavanagh [2005] EWHC 820

In this case the defendant failed to give evidence in his defence, his solicitor had informed the magistrates of this; his mother gave evidence that he was suffering from depression. The magistrates decided that the defendant had no case to answer and they had not drawn an adverse inference because to do so would have been unfair by reason that he had been so depressed.

R v Kavanagh highlights the fact that the court has the discretion under s 35(1)(b) not to draw an adverse inference where it appears to it that the accused's physical or mental condition makes it undesirable for the accused to give evidence. In this case, the Divisional Court highlighted that supporting evidence of the physical or mental state of the accused that makes it *undesirable* to give evidence, other than an assertion to that effect from their advocate, must be provided. This decision reaffirms the Court of Appeal's earlier decision in *R v Friend* [1997] 2 Cr App R 231. However, this cannot be used as a strategic lawyering tool so that an accused that would do more damage to their case by giving evidence will not fall into this category.

The provision does not render the accused compellable to give evidence on behalf of themself. This means that they will not be guilty of being in contempt of court by failing to give evidence.

At this point it may be salient to revisit the instances in which a defendant may be competent to give evidence because this provision only applies to defendants who are both competent and mentally capable of giving evidence, i.e. testifying. Under Practice Direction (Crown Court: Evidence: Advice to a Defendant) [1995] 2 Cr App R 192 the trial judge has to ensure that the defendant is made aware of the consequences that entail in them not testifying. The Court of Appeal gave some guidance as to the operation and effect of s 35 in *R v Cowan* [1995] 4 All ER 939. In this case the court stated that the provision only applies once the prosecution has established a *prima facie* case. This means that the judge and jury must be satisfied that there is in law and fact a case that the defendant must answer.

It is also at this stage that the court will consider whether there is any evidence that shows that the defendant had a good reason for not testifying. The Court of Appeal stated that the instructed lawyer, a barrister or solicitor, cannot simply speculate as to the reasons why the defendant did not testify. Any reason put forward for not testifying must be supported by relevant and admissible evidence: see *R v Friend* [1997] 1 WLR 1433. Finally, the court also stated that the judge should remind the jury that it is for the prosecution to prove that the defendant is guilty beyond reasonable doubt and that they should remember that silence alone can never amount to an indication of guilt (s 38 CJPOA 1994). The trial judge will then direct the jury that *they can draw such adverse inferences from the defendant's silence that may be proper* if they are satisfied that:

(a) the prosecution has proven that there is a case that the defendant must answer; and

(b) there is no good reason why the defendant has failed to testify.

In terms of s 35, the main adverse inference that the jury may choose to draw is that the defendant does not have an answer to the allegations being levied against them, or that they do not have an answer that would stand up to the scrutiny of counsel's cross-examination. In summary, the effect of s 35 is to confirm (a) that the defendant is competent to give evidence, (b) that the defendant cannot be compelled to testify and (c) that their silence can confirm the case against them.

If the defendant gives evidence, then they must do so from the witness box. The questioning can go to the extent that the defendant may incriminate themselves or others. Prior to the Criminal Justice Act 2003 the defendant could not be questioned as to their previous bad character or convictions (s 1 Criminal Evidence Act 1898). Currently the position depends on whether that evidence is of a type that has already been admitted under the Criminal Justice Act 2003: see Chapter 12.

In this instance any evidence that a defendant gives, is evidence for all purposes. This means that it can be used against the defendant even if it incriminates them or others: see *R v Paul* [1920] 2 KB 183.

In *R v Rudd* (1948) 32 Cr App R 138 it was stated that:

JUDGMENT

'. . . a statement made in the absence of an accused person by *a* co-defendant cannot be evidence against the accused, *however*, if a co-defendant, *in the course of a joint trial*, goes into the witness box and gives evidence, then what *they* say becomes evidence for all the purposes of the case including being evidence against *their* co-defendant.'

Generally, where a defendant elects to testify, then, unless the court directs otherwise, they should do so before any other defence witness (s 79 PACE 1984).

ACTIVITY

What is the effect of s 35 on an accused's right to silence? Highlight case examples that substantiate your argument.

In *R v Cowan* [1995] 4 All ER 939 the Court of Appeal issued guidance on drawing adverse inferences under s 35 of the CJPOA 1994. Summarise this guidance.

KEY FACTS

A failure to testify (s 35)

This provision applies where an accused fails to testify at court.

In *R v Cowan* [1995] 4 All ER 939 guidance was given on the application of the provision:

- the prosecution must establish a prima facie case for the accused to answer and that there is no good reason why the accused did not testify;
- the instructed lawyer cannot speculate as to why the accused did not testify; and
- the trial judge should remind the jury that it is the prosecution that must prove that the accused is guilty beyond reasonable doubt and that silence alone is never an indication of guilt.

Reasons put forward by the accused for not testifying must be supported by relevant and admissible evidence.

5.4.3 Section 36 – failure to account for objects, substances or marks that incriminate the accused

The next instance that may give rise to an adverse inference relates to an accused's silence in failing to account for incriminating objects, substances or marks. Section 36(1) of the CJPOA 1994 states that:

SECTION

'Where a person is arrested by a constable, and there is (a) on his person, or (b) in or on his clothing or footwear, or (c) otherwise in his possession, or (d) in any place in which he is at the time of his arrest, any object, substance or mark, or there is a mark on any such object; and that, or another, constable investigating the case reasonably believes that the presence of the object, substance or mark may be attributable to the participation of the person arrested in the commission of the offence specified by the constable; and the constable informs the person arrested that he so believes, and requests him to account for the presence of the object, substance or mark; and the person fails or refuses to do so, then, if in any proceedings against the person for the offence so specified, evidence on those matters is given.'

In summary, s 36 requires the following to be satisfied:

- an arrest;
- an object, substance or a mark on any object;
- the object, substance or mark or any object with a mark on it must be on their person, in or on their clothing or footwear or in any place in which they are at the time of their arrest.

If all three are satisfied, then the constable who is arresting the person or investigating the case must:

- reasonably believe that the object, substance or mark may be attributable to the offence that the person is being arrested or investigated for;
- inform the person of this reasonable belief and ask them to account for its presence.

The procedure is quite simple. First, the suspect must be arrested and informed in ordinary language by the constable of their belief that the object, substance or mark indicates that the suspect was involved in a specified offence. This latter point is important: the provision will not apply if the constable very generally enquires into the suspect's involvement in *any offences*; it must be specified. The constable must then ask the suspect to account for the object, substance or mark and warn them of the consequences of failing to do so: see PACE Code C 2019, paras 10 and 10:10(b). The constable must ensure that they keep records of the entire process in the case as evidence that can be used in any subsequent trial.

Importantly, s 36 only applies where a suspect fails to account for incriminatory objects, substances or marks that are present at the time the suspect is arrested.

Example

Alia is arrested at the scene of a murder. Following her arrest, the constable asks her to account for (a) the blood on her blouse and hands and (b) the fact that she was seen by the victim's boyfriend with a dagger at the time at which the offence was committed. Section 36 would operate in relation to (a) but not (b), as she did not have the dagger on her person at the time of arrest.

CASE EXAMPLE

R v Compton [2002] ewCa Crim 2835

In this case the accused had proffered a bare statement when questioned about a number of drugs offences and a large amount of cash that had been discovered in his safe. The accused had stated that the cash came from a legitimate antiques business but was contaminated with heroin because he was a heroin user. In that instance the judge was entitled to leave the question to the jury whether the accused had failed to account under s 36(1)(c) or (d).

Evidence of the accused's failure to account is admissible against him. The difference between s 36 and ss 34, 35 and 37 (see later) becomes quite obvious: this provision does not need the question requiring the accused to account for the above to be put to them at an authorised place of detention, i.e. a police station, or after they have had the opportunity of having consulted their lawyer. This is because, referring to the rules on the *res gestae* (see Chapter 7), an innocent person would give information regarding the existence of an object, substance or mark or object with any such mark of their own free will. No adverse inferences may be drawn where the defendant has consulted their lawyer before a constable has put the question to them (s 36(4A)). Finally, s 36(2) states that a 'court or jury may draw such inferences from the failure or refusal as appear proper'. Once again you should remember that guilt cannot be inferred from silence alone (s 30(3)).

ACTIVITY

What are the requirements that must be satisfied for an adverse inference to be drawn under s 36 of the CJPOA 1994?

KEY FACTS

A failure to account for objects, substances or marks that incriminate the accused (s 36)

This provision applies where a *suspect* fails to account for incriminatory objects, substances or marks that are present at the time they are arrested.

A failure to account for presence in a place that incriminates the accused (s 37)

The final provision, s 37, allows the jury to draw an adverse inference for an accused's failure or refusal to account for their presence in an incriminating place. Section 37 states that where

(a) a person arrested by a constable was found by *them* at a place at or about the time the offence for which *they* were arrested is alleged to have been committed;

(b) that he or another constable investigating the offence reasonably believes that the presence of the suspect at that place and at that time may be attributable to *their* participation in the commission of the offence;

(c) the constable must then inform the suspect of their reasonable belief (as *per* s 36).

The suspect's failure or refusal to account will once again lead to the drawing of such adverse inferences as the jury may think proper. The procedure is as follows: s 37 only applies where the suspect is arrested either *at* or *near* a place that incriminates them. This means that the suspect cannot be asked to account for their presence at a particular place on a prior occasion, i.e. if Marjorie is arrested at the scene of a horrific murder, she cannot be asked to account for what she was doing there the previous week. Neither can the suspect be asked to account for their presence at other places, regardless of how much this may incriminate them.

Finally, three important points: (a) the inferences that are drawn will vary depending on the circumstances of the case; (b) silence alone cannot indicate guilt (s 38(3)), and (c) no adverse inference may be drawn from the silence of an accused where they were not permitted access to legal advice before the constable's request for the suspect to account.

ACTIVITY

Summarise the effect of s 37 on an accused's right to silence.

KEY FACTS

A failure to account for presence in a place that incriminates the accused (s 37)

Section 37 allows for the drawing of an adverse inference from an accused's failure or refusal to account for their presence in an incriminating place.

The failure or refusal to account will lead to the jury drawing such adverse inferences as it may think proper.

5.5 Human rights: fair trials and adverse inferences

Human rights are a common discussion in relation to the validity of the rules of evidence; this is especially true of the law that allows adverse inferences to be drawn from an accused's silence. It is common knowledge that everyone has the right to a fair trial that is protected by Art 6 of the European Convention on Human Rights and enshrined in national UK law by the Human Rights Act 1998. The text is available at www.echr.coe.int/Documents/Convention_ENG.pdf. On reform of the Convention, see also Reforming the European Convention on Human Rights: Interlaken, Izmir, Brighton and beyond, available at: https://edoc.coe.int/en/conferences-on-the-future-of-the-european-court-of-human-rights/7308-reforming-the-european-convention-on-human-rights-interlaken-izmir-brighton-and-beyond-a-compilation-of-instruments-and-texts-relating-to-the-ongoing-reform-of-the-echr.html.

The effect of the provisions of the CJPOA 1994 have been to undermine the common law, and thus the courts have not been shy in stating that the legislation should be interpreted in the manner in which it was originally intended to be interpreted: restrictively. The rationale behind this is simple: silence alone can never amount to an admission of guilt, nor can it form the sole basis upon which an accused may be convicted. Where adverse inferences play a large role in a prosecution case then, according to the European Court of Human Rights (ECtHR) in *Murray v UK* (1996) 22 EHRR 29 and *Condron v UK* (2001) 31 EHRR 1, it is more likely that an accused's right to a fair trial may have been undermined.

In *Condron* the ECtHR also stated that leaving the issue of silence to a jury does not in itself breach an accused's right to a fair trial under Art 6(1) or (2). For it is a relevant consideration:

JUDGMENT

'. . . that needs to be weighed when assessing whether or not it is fair to do so in the circumstances'.

The court went further in confirming that the right to remain silent, although regarded as an internationally recognised standard at the heart of the right to a fair trial, was not absolute.

The courts can ensure that an accused's right is not infringed by giving the jury accurate and fair directions to help them. These are standard guidelines that aim to ensure appropriate use of evidence. The direction would include the fact that silence alone can never amount to an admission of guilt. A failure to direct the jury will most probably result in any resulting conviction being rendered unsafe: see *Beckles v UK* (2002) 13 BHRC 522. In *Bristow v Jones* [2002] EWCA Crim 1571, the defendant, who was being prosecuted for carrying out a contract killing, had his conviction quashed because of a material irregularity in the way in which the judge had delivered the direction to the jury.

In summary, the right to silence has seen many changes and it is likely that it will continue to do so. No doubt the ECtHR and the domestic UK courts will continue to develop the case law in this area of the law of evidence. Keep up to date with current developments using the online resource that accompanies this book.

ACTIVITY

Do the provisions of the CJPOA 1994 on drawing adverse inferences from an accused's silence infringe the right to a fair trial under Art 6 of the European Convention on Human Rights? If not, what is the rationale behind your argument?

Outline one example in which an adverse inference may be drawn under each of ss 34–37 of the CJPOA 1994.

In what other ways may evidence be excluded?

SUMMARY

- An accused retains the right to remain silent at common law. Where an accused exercises this right they may be perceived as having something to hide.
- The common law rules on an accused's right to silence were not affected by the CJPOA 1994.
- Silence does not amount to an acceptance or admission unless the accused is faced with an allegation made by a person that is on an equal footing with them and where it is reasonable to expect them to reply.
- The CJPOA 1994 provides specified circumstances where an accused's silence may lead to the jury drawing adverse inferences against them.
- The CJPOA 1994 qualifies what used to be considered to be an unfettered right to silence.
- The circumstances in which the CJPOA 1994 allows a jury to draw adverse inferences include the failure of the accused to mention facts; testify; account for objects, substances or marks; and a failure to account for their presence at a place that incriminates them.

SAMPLE ESSAY QUESTION

The Criminal Justice and Public Order Act 1994 makes major reforms to an accused's right not to testify at trial. Discuss.

Answer plan

Outline the extent of the right to silence under the common law and the 1994 statute.
Define the right to silence under the common law and statute. Discuss the fact that the 1994 Act does not repeal the common law rules and its effect is to provide instances in which adverse inferences can be drawn from it.

Discuss the application of the common law rules on an accused's failure to testify.
State that under the common law the trial judge could comment on the accused's failure to testify at his trial but was required to emphasise that the jury could not infer guilt from this failure, mention the case of *Bathurst* (1968).

Highlight the changes made by the Act.
Discuss the fact that s 35 of the CJPOA 1994 allows a jury to draw adverse inferences from an accused's refusal to testify or, where they do testify, their failure to answer any question put to them without any good reason. Point out that this provision does not mean that the accused is compellable as a witness in his or her own defence. Explore the extent of the difference between this statutory provision and the common law: its effect is to allow the jury to infer guilt – mention *Murray v DPP* (1993).

Discuss how this takes the law back to the common law position as developed in R v Martinez-Tobon [1994] 1 WLR 388 where drawing adverse inferences was a matter of common sense when no explanation was provided by the accused in a situation in which he/she ought to have been in a position to give one.

Further reading

Redmayne, M. 'Rethinking the privilege against self-incrimination' (2007) 27(2) OJLS 209–232

Roberts, P. 'Modernising police powers – again?' (2007) Crim LR, Dec, 934–948

Singh, C. (2015) *Q&A Evidence 2015–2016*. Oxford: Routledge

Internet links

European Convention on Human Rights: www.echr.coe.int/Documents/Convention_ENG.pdf

Reforming the European Convention on Human Rights: Interlaken, Izmir, Brighton and beyond: https://edoc.coe.int/en/conferences-on-the-future-of-the-european-court-of-human-rights/7308-reforming-the-european-convention-on-human-rights-interlaken-izmir-brighton-and-beyond-a-compilation-of-instruments-and-texts-relating-to-the-ongoing-reform-of-the-echr.html

6

Course of trial

AIMS AND OBJECTIVES

By the end of this chapter you will be able to:

- understand the rules regarding refreshing a witness's memory and the effect of doing so;
- appreciate the distinction between and effect of unfavourable and hostile witnesses;
- understand the general rule of evidence concerning previous consistent statements and identify any exceptions to this rule;
- identify the objectives of cross-examination of witnesses;
- understand the rules laid down in ss 41–43 of the Youth Justice and Criminal Evidence Act 1999;
- appreciate the distinction and effect with regard to cross-examination as to issue and credit.

6.1 Introduction

Evidence in chief
the process in which the party calling a witness is allowed to present that witness's assertions of the facts.

Cross-examination
the process whereby parties in a trial are entitled to question a witness called by another party.

In both civil and criminal cases, proving a fact through witnesses requires the party calling the witness to present the facts to the court by following a number of strict rules. After the individual has been sworn in or has made a solemn affirmation, or exceptionally has been allowed to give unsworn evidence, the witness will be questioned by the party calling them. This process is known as the **evidence in chief**. No leading questions may be asked, and the object is to elicit evidence that is favourable to that party; in other words, to elicit from the witness facts that prove or support that party's case. On completion of this process the opposing party(ies) is/are entitled to question the witness. This is the **cross-examination** and its purpose is (a) to elicit facts that are favourable to the cross-examiner, and (b) to test the veracity of the witness or to discredit the witness. In contrast to examination in chief, leading questions may be asked by the cross-examiner. Finally, the witness may be re-questioned by

DOI: 10.4324/9781003282433-6

Re-examination restricted to the party calling the witness to deal with issues that arose in the cross-examination.

the party calling them in the **re-examination**. The purpose of the re-examination is to re-establish the credibility of the witness if this was shaken by the cross-examination. Re-examination will relate to matters that were raised in the cross-examination. Nothing more need be said about the re-examination. The same restrictions that limit the examiner in chief in the questions that they may ask apply equally to the re-examination; no leading questions may be asked.

6.2 Examination in chief

6.2.1 No leading questions

The traditional method of testifying in criminal cases requires the witness to take the oath or make a solemn affirmation and to testify from the witness box by answering questions put by the party calling the witness. This may be followed by cross-examination by the opposing party (parties) and a re-examination by the party calling the witness. Occasionally the witness's testimony may be presented in the form of a video recording and cross-examination may take a similar form. But in *R v Dutton-Wooley* [2009] EWCA Crim 811, the Court of Appeal considered that the unusual procedure adopted by the trial judge in the presentation of the evidence was wholly unacceptable but dismissed the appeal against the defendant's conviction under the Trade Descriptions Act 1968. The unusual practice concerned the evidence of seven firemen that the prosecution intended to rely on. Two of the firemen testified before the jury, and the judge proposed that the other five firemen be present in the courtroom while their colleagues testified. After the first two firemen had completed their testimony, the judge, in the presence of the jury, asked the remaining firemen whether they were of the same opinion. They spoke with one voice, saying 'yes'. The judge then asked the jury whether they had any questions for the firemen. One of the jurors called out a question for the witnesses. The response was in a manner adverse to the defence. The defendant's conviction was upheld owing to the strength of the evidence.

The process of the examination in chief is applicable only with regard to a party calling the witness. As a general rule, the party who calls the witness ought not to ask leading questions. A leading question is one that either assumes the existence of disputed facts or suggests the desired answer. It is also suggested that a leading question is one to which the answer is 'yes' or 'no'; for example, a question such as 'Did you see Arthur hit the victim, Femi?' The proper course would be to ask Arthur whether he recalls an incident on the relevant date. Where was he? He is then asked to narrate the incident.

If a leading question has been unfairly put by one party, the opposing party ought to intercede and object to the question. In the event of a dispute the judge will be required to make a ruling. However, the answers to leading questions are not inadmissible but relate to the weight of the evidence: see *R v Wilson* (1913) 9 Cr App R 124.

There are a number of situations where, exceptionally, leading questions are permitted. These include formal introductory matters on undisputed issues, such as the name of the witness, occasions when it is necessary to focus the witness's attention on a specific matter and, of course, cases where the opponent has consented to leading questions.

6.2.2 Refreshing the memory of witnesses

Very often a considerable time elapses between the occurrence of an event and the occasion to narrate that event in court proceedings. It would be unrealistic to expect the witness to recall every detail of the event with precision without assistance. Indeed, the process of testifying is not treated as a test of memory but is designed to test the honesty and reliability of the witness. At common law the witness was allowed to refresh his memory with documents, both in court and out of court. Reference to the 'in-court' refreshment of the memory of witnesses involves the occasion while the witness testifies from the witness box. The defining moment is the swearing in of the witness. Following this event the strict rules for refreshing the memory of witnesses operate, as distinct from the occasion where the witness wishes to refresh his memory prior to testifying in the proceedings.

Refreshing memory in court

Common law

At common law the rule was that a witness was permitted to refresh his memory in the witness box by reference to any document *made* or *verified* by him at a time when the matter was fresh in his mind. The authorship of the document was of immense importance. The requirement here was that the document was created by the witness himself when the facts were fresh in the witness's mind. This is a question of fact. Alternatively, if the document was made by a third party, the onus was on the witness to establish that he had endorsed or verified the document when the matter was fresh in his mind. Endorsement or verification may involve the process of the witness:

(i) reading the statement in the document at a time when the matter was fresh in his mind and adopting the information as accurate;

(ii) having the information read back to the witness, who then verifies the statement as accurate. In this event the person reading back the information to the witness is required to testify that the information that he read back was the information that he recorded: see *R v Kelsey* (1981) 74 Cr App R 213.

CASE EXAMPLE

R v Kelsey (1981) 74 Cr App R 213

Two men followed a car and one of them (Hill) made a mental note of its registration number. He repeated the number some 20 minutes later to a police officer, who wrote it down in his notebook and read it back. The witness (Hill) did not himself see the number that was written down by the police officer. At the trial the witness (Hill) testified but could not remember the number. The trial judge allowed the witness to refresh his memory from the officer's note, and the officer was called to say that the note produced in court was the one on which he had written the number. On appeal, the court decided that the document was properly used to refresh Hill's memory.

JUDGMENT

'In our view there is no magic in verifying by seeing as opposed to verifying by hearing. In the present case, a second witness is required. Hill dictated the number, heard it read back and confirmed its accuracy. But although he saw the note being made, he did not read it, so it was necessary for the officer also to be called to prove that the note he produced was the one Hill saw him making and heard him read back.'

(Taylor J)

The next requirement was that the document must have been executed at the time of the transaction or so shortly after the event that the facts were fresh in the mind of the maker of the statement. This is essentially a question of fact. An interval of four weeks was considered too long a delay to permit the witness to refresh his memory: see *R v Graham* [1973] Crim LR 628.

It was not essential that the witness should have had any independent recollection of the facts. Indeed, the witness's memory may be a blank when he sees the document. This is irrelevant because the rule only requires the witness to endorse the document as his own or accept the statement as being accurate. For example, an attesting witness may say that he is sure that he witnessed a document on seeing his signature on the document even though he has no recollection of the event. In *Maugham v Hubbard* (1828) 6 LJKB 299, a witness called to prove the receipt of a sum of money was shown an acknowledgement of the receipt signed by him. On seeing it, he said that he had no doubt that he had received it, although he had no recollection of the fact. The court held that this was sufficient evidence of the payment. Further, either the original document or a copy may be used by the witness to refresh his memory. Where a copy is used, it needs to have been made when the matter was fresh in the witness's mind.

The *aide-memoire* document is required to be produced to the opponent, on request, for inspection. There are no adverse consequences by calling for the documents for inspection. The opponent has a right to cross-examine on the document. If the cross-examiner confines his questioning to the parts of the document used to refresh the witness's memory the document will not be put in evidence. However, if the cross-examiner questions the witness on parts of the document beyond which the witness refreshes his memory, the party calling the witness is entitled to have the document put in evidence. In *Senat v Senat* [1965] P 172, Sir Jocelyn Simon said:

JUDGMENT

'The mere inspection of a document does not render it evidence which counsel inspecting it is bound to put in. Where a document is used to refresh a witness's memory, cross-examining counsel may inspect that document in order to check it without making it evidence. Moreover, he may cross-examine upon it without making it evidence provided that his cross-examination does not go further than the parts which are used for refreshing the memory of the witness.'

At common law, the effect of the note being put in evidence is that the document is treated as evidence of the consistency of the witness, i.e. the document bolsters the credibility of the witness's testimony as distinct from being evidence of the truth of the assertions. In short, the document becomes an exhibit: see *R v Virgo* (1978) 67 Cr App R 323.

Civil cases

In civil cases, in theory, the common law rules regarding the preconditions necessary to be satisfied concerning the refreshing of the memory of witnesses in court continue to apply, subject to two modifications:

1. The effect of the document being put in evidence is now admissible as an exception to the hearsay rule, i.e. the information is treated as evidence of the truth of the assertion; see s 6(4) of the Civil Evidence Act 1995, which declares as follows: 'Nothing in this Act affects any of the rules of law as to the circumstances in which, where a person called as a witness in civil proceedings is cross-examined on a document used by him to refresh his memory, that document may be made evidence in the proceedings.'
2. The judge has the power to allow the witness to refer to any document that he (the judge) considers reliable enough for such purpose.

Criminal cases

Criminal cases were governed by the common law rules until the enactment of the Criminal Justice Act 2003. Although the 2003 Act does not expressly abolish the common law rules as to the refreshing of memories of witnesses, it is submitted that the purpose of the legislation is that in due course it will supersede the common law in the majority of cases.

Section 139 of the 2003 Act provides:

SECTION

'(1) a person giving oral evidence in criminal proceedings about any matter may, at any stage in the course of doing so, refresh his memory of it from a document made or verified by him at an earlier time if –
(a) he states in his oral evidence that the document records his recollection of the matter at that earlier time, and
(b) his recollection of the matter is likely to have been significantly better at that time than it is at the time of his oral evidence.'

One analogy with the common law rule, s 139 allows a witness to refresh his memory from his own document or a document created by a third party, provided that in the latter case the witness verifies the document as reflecting a true record of the events. Verification for these purposes may take the form of reading the document or having the document read back to the witness and acknowledging its accuracy as in *Kelsey* (above). However, it should be noted that s 139 does not replicate the common law rule in requiring the judge to consider whether the document (*aide-memoire*) was made or verified by the witness *contemporaneously or when the matter was fresh in his mind*. Instead, the statute refers to the dual requirements in s 139(1)(a) and (b) in that the document records the witness's recollection of the events, and his recall of the events is likely to be significantly better at that time as opposed to the current moment in time while he is testifying. In *R v McAfee* [2006] EWCA Crim 2914, a witness was allowed to refresh his memory from a statement made some four-and-a-half months after the alleged incident. The Court of Appeal decided that there was no requirement of contemporaneity; once the statutory conditions were met, the judge's decision should be accepted unless it is obviously wrong, unreasonable or perverse. The witness's assertion is a factor to be taken into account, but it is not conclusive. However, the judge still has the discretionary power to decide that the document was executed after too long a period of time to permit the witness to refresh his memory with it. In *R v Mangena* (2009), the Court of Appeal decided that there was no requirement that a witness had to stumble in his evidence owing to a faulty memory before a direction could be made under s 139 to allow a witness to refresh his memory. The principle does not involve a test of memory but exists in order to promote justice.

CASE EXAMPLE

R v Mangena [2009] EWCA Crim 2535

The defendant and others were convicted on several counts involving fraudulent activities. The prosecution alleged that he had persuaded members of a church, with which he was involved, to entrust money to him, which he had then used in a Ponzi scheme. Over a thousand people had invested money in the scheme. The defendant denied culpability, blamed his co-accused and maintained that he had been operating a legitimate pyramid scheme. The trial judge had permitted several witnesses to refresh their memories from statements given to the police. On conviction the defendant appealed. The Court of Appeal dismissed his appeal and decided that once the two conditions in s 139(1) were satisfied it was a matter for the judge's discretion to permit the witnesses to refresh their memory by reference to their earlier statements. Given the lapse of time since the events in issue and the complexity of the issues it was obviously beneficial to allow reference to be made to the earlier witness statements.

JUDGMENT

'We consider that this judge was peculiarly well situated to exercise his discretion on this matter and we do not think that it is arguably possible to interfere with it. In this connection we would observe that for the most part the evidence of these witnesses, which had to be given over a distance of some four years or so between the events in question and the trial, in dealing with matters such as with whom they were having particular conversations and what monies they were investing and what money they were receiving back, were obviously matters on which an earlier witness statement would be a useful tool for the refreshing of memory. This was detailed factual evidence about their implication in an investment which the Crown's case said was a fraud, rather than the description of some particular event. In sum, for these reasons, we consider that this ground of appeal is not arguably correct.'

(Rix LJ)

Section 140 defines a document as 'anything in which information of any description is recorded, but not including any recording of sounds or moving images'. The effect is that a record of sounds or images, even in paper form, is not a document for criminal proceedings. In these circumstances s 139(2) permits the witness to refer to the recording.

Section 139(2) declares as follows:

SECTION

'Where –

(a) a person giving oral evidence in criminal proceedings about any matter has previously given an oral account, of which a sound recording was made, and he states in that evidence that the account represented his recollection of the matter at that time,
(b) his recollection of the matter is likely to have been significantly better at the time of the previous account than it is at the time of his oral evidence, and
(c) a transcript has been made of the sound recording, he may, at any stage in the course of giving his evidence, refresh his memory of the matter from that transcript.'

Thus, a witness may be allowed to refresh their memory from a transcript of a tape-recorded conversation they had with another person: see *R v Mills and Rose* (1962) 46 Cr App R 336. Indeed, Judge LJ in *R v Bailey* [2001] EWCA Crim 733 said:

JUDGMENT

'We can see no reason why the principle by which a witness is permitted to refresh his memory to the fullest extent should be confined to him looking at a piece of paper with writing on it. Common sense suggests that if modern technology provides a better or different means for the same purpose, it should be available for use in court.'

In conformity with the principle at common law (see above), the *aide-memoire* document may be surrendered for inspection to the opposing party without any adverse consequences: see *Senat v Senat* [1965] P 172. Likewise, the opposing party is entitled to cross-examine the witness on the document without it becoming evidence, provided that the cross-examiner restricts his questioning on the parts of the document used to refresh the witness's memory. However, if the cross-examiner questions the witness on parts of the document that were not used to refresh the witness's memory (excessive cross-examination), the party calling the witness is entitled to put the document in evidence, i.e. the document becomes an exhibit. By statute, the assertions in the document will be admissible as evidence of the truth of such assertions, i.e. as exceptions to the hearsay rule. See s 6(4) of the Civil Evidence Act 1995 for the position in civil cases. A similar result is achieved in criminal cases. Section 120(3) of the Criminal Justice Act 2003 enacts the effect of excessive cross-examination thus:

SECTION

'A statement made by a witness in a document –

(a) which is used by him to refresh his memory while giving evidence,
(b) on which he is cross-examined, and
(c) which as a consequence is received in evidence in the proceedings,

is admissible as evidence of any matter stated of which oral evidence by him would be admissible.'

Section 120(3) refers to a 'statement made by a witness' and makes no reference to third-party statements *verified* by the witness. Assuming that this was not an oversight by Parliament, it would appear that the effect of 'putting the document in evidence' varies with whether the witness refreshes their memory from their document or a third party's document. Where a witness refreshes their memory from a statement made by a third party but verified by the witness, and who is cross-examined excessively, the effect is that the document is evidence of the *consistency* of the witness only, as stated at common law. On the other hand, if there has been excessive cross-examination on *that witness's note*, the effect is as stated in s 120(3), namely that the statement is admitted as evidence of the truth.

At common law (see above) the courts did not draw a distinction between 'present recollection revived' and 'past recollections recorded'. Both concepts were generously treated as occasions where the witness's memory was refreshed. 'Present recollection revived' refers to occasions where the witness's memory is genuinely refreshed in the witness box by reference to the note made or verified by the witness, i.e. the witness recalls the events by referring to the note. On the other hand, the concept of 'past recollections recorded' refers to the situation where the witness's memory is blank even after referring to the note. The witness simply does not recall the event in question but is prepared to acknowledge the accuracy of the note or record executed at a time when the matter was fresh in his mind. See the common law position in *Maugham v Hubbard* (1828) above. The current position, under the Criminal Justice Act 2003, is that cases where past recollections are recorded are outside the purport of s 120(3), which is designed to deal with occasions where the witness's memory is genuinely refreshed by reading the note. The explanatory notes to the Act declare as follows:

SECTION

> 'This section [s 120] makes other previous statements admissible as evidence of the truth of their contents (not merely to bolster the credibility of the witness's oral evidence) in the following circumstances . . . subsection (3) applies to the situation where a witness is "refreshing his memory" from a written document. If he is cross-examined on the document and it is received in evidence, the *statement* will be evidence of any matter contained within it . . .'. (emphasis added)

The justification for this interpretation is that s 120(3) would otherwise have the effect of subverting the statutory regime enacted in s 120(4)–(6) without compliance with the conditions laid down in these provisions. In *R v Chinn (Michael)* [2012] EWCA Crim 501, Aikens LJ expressed his opinion as to the proper interpretation of s 120(3) thus:

JUDGMENT

> 'The wording of section 120(3) is a little difficult to follow. The opening words of it are "A statement made by a witness in a document". Then sub-paragraph (a) sets out the first condition – "which is used by him to refresh his memory while giving evidence". The word "which" in that paragraph must refer back to "a document", because it is the document which is used to refresh the witness's memory.

Moreover, it is clear that this sub-paragraph contemplates that *the document has to be used by the witness to refresh his memory while giving evidence in examination in chief, given the subsequent reference to cross-examination in sub-paragraph (b)*. Sub-paragraph (b) does not follow the old common law position in that it does not specifically stipulate that there must be cross-examination of a part of the document which was *not* used by the witness to refresh his memory. The sub-paragraph simply says "on which he is cross-examined ". The word "which" in that sub-paragraph must also refer to the document and, we think, to the whole document. Given the plain wording of that sub-paragraph there is no room for any implied limitation to a part of the document. We think that sub-paragraph (c) must be intended to reflect the common law rule that where there had been cross-examination then the document would become an exhibit in the trial; hence the words "[in] consequence is received in evidence in the proceedings". Thus, consistently with sub-paragraphs (a) and (b), the word "which" in that sub-paragraph must also refer to the document as a whole. The last part of section 120(3) refers back to the first words of the sub-section. So the thing that "is admissible as evidence of any matter stated of which oral evidence by [the witness] would be admissible" must be the "statement made by the witness in a document . . ." But if the document contains several "statements", plural, then those statements will be admissible as evidence of the matters stated in them of which oral evidence by the witness would be admissible, provided that those "statements" in the document were used by the witness to refresh his memory.' (emphasis added)

(Aikens LJ)

The effect is that where the *aide-memoire* document does not trigger the witness's memory it will constitute a species of hearsay evidence that may be admissible under s 120(4), (5) and (6) of the 2003 Act.

Section 120(4) enacts as follows:

SECTION

'A previous statement by the witness is admissible as evidence of any matter stated of which oral evidence by him would be admissible, if –

(a) any of the following three conditions is satisfied, and
(b) while giving evidence the witness indicates that to the best of his belief he made the statement, and that to the best of his belief it states the truth.'

Section 120(5) enacts that 'the statement identifies or describes a person, object or place.'

Section 120(6) provides as follows:

SECTION

'The second condition is that the statement was made by the witness when the matters stated were fresh in his memory but he does not remember them, and cannot reasonably be expected to remember them well enough to give oral evidence of them in the proceedings.'

These three provisions make no mention of third-party statements *verified* by the witness. The common law rule will apply in those circumstances. Provided that the note has been verified by the witness in the circumstances laid down in s 139(1) and the note being received in evidence, the effect is determined by the rules at common law, namely it is evidence of consistency only and not evidence of the truth. On the other hand, out-of-court statements made by the witness and that are used to refresh his memory whilst testifying, but the witness acknowledges that he has no independent recollection of the events, may be admitted as evidence of the facts stated in the circumstances laid down in s 120(4), (5) and (6). In other words, if the conditions laid down in s 139(1) to refresh the witness's memory have been satisfied and the witness, on reading the note in the witness box, admits that he cannot recall the events, wholly or partially, firstly, s 120(3) will not be applicable but, secondly, the circumstances may be governed by s 120(4)–(6), with the effect that the statement may be admitted as evidence of the truth. This was the position in *R v Chinn (Michael)* [2012] EWCA Crim 501. In this case, the defendant was charged with unlawful wounding following an incident in a nightclub where he was alleged to have thrown a glass bottle at a young woman. A few hours after the incident an independent witness, Inglis (I), made a statement to the police in which she described the defendant, the shirt he was wearing and the fact that he had thrown a glass bottle that had hit the victim. At the trial several months later, whilst testifying I said that she could not remember those details because it was so long ago, although she stood by what she had said in her statement. The judge granted the Crown's request for I to be shown a copy of her statement. I read her statement but maintained that she still could not remember the details. The judge then asked I what she had told the police when she gave her statement, and I replied that she had seen the defendant throw a bottle and it hit the victim. The defendant was convicted and appealed on the ground that the judge had erred in failing to discharge the jury because inadmissible evidence had been admitted during the trial. The Court of Appeal dismissed the appeal and decided that:

(i) I was entitled to examine her witness statement in an attempt to refresh her memory, since the conditions in s 139(1) of the 2003 Act had been fulfilled;

(ii) however, as her memory was not in fact refreshed by re-reading her statement, s 120(3) could not apply to make admissible the matters stated as evidence of the truth;

(iii) where the witness's memory was not refreshed by reading the note, the circumstances will be governed by s 120(4)–(6);

(iv) I's statement was admissible by virtue of s 120(4) and (5) of the Act to the extent to which it identified the defendant as the person who threw the bottle;

(v) but other parts of the statements were not admissible under s 120(4) and (6) because the proper procedure had not been adopted by the judge.

JUDGMENT

'We conclude that section 120(4)(5) can be used to admit parts of Ms Inglis' witness statement, but not the whole of it. The parts that describe the defendant and identify him as being the person who was in the nightclub and then threw a glass bottle that hit Ms Davies are, in our view, admissible under section 120(5). But other parts of the narrative in the witness statement that go beyond identifying or describing the defendant and the fact that it was him that threw the glass bottle, are not admissible under section 120(4)(5).

[With regard to s 120(4) and (6)] There was material in her evidence for the judge to have reached a conclusion that Ms Inglis could not reasonably have been expected to remember those matters well enough to give oral evidence of them at the trial. But we are not prepared to say that the witness statement of Ms Inglis was admissible under section 120(4)(6) because it is clear that no one at the time considered that subsection or its applicability or whether the two cumulative conditions in section 120(6) had, in fact, been fulfilled.'

(Aikens LJ)

Section 122 enacts that when a document becomes an exhibit, it must not accompany the jury when they retire to consider their verdict, unless the court considers it appropriate or unless all the parties agree.

Refreshing the memory of witnesses out of court

The rule is that a witness is permitted to refresh their memory out of court by any means that they consider necessary. This may be in the form of the witness's contemporaneous or even non-contemporaneous note of the event, a third party's account of the event, etc. The normal restrictions that are applicable to refreshing memory in court are not extended to this occasion because it is not possible to ensure that any strict rules will apply. In short, any prescriptive rules will be difficult to supervise. In addition, the trial process does not involve a test of memory but is a process of getting at the truth. The effect is that a line is drawn as to when no formal principles concerning the refreshment of the witness's memory applies, and this is up to the time that the witness steps into the witness box and takes the oath.

CASE EXAMPLE

R v Richardson [1971] 2 QB 484

On a trial for burglary and attempted burglary, four prosecution witnesses were shown statements they had made to the police. The defendant was convicted and appealed on the ground that these witnesses were allowed to refresh their memories before entering the witness box and that their evidence was inadmissible. The court dismissed the appeal.

JUDGMENT

'Testimony in the witness box would become more a test of memory than of truthfulness if witnesses are deprived of the opportunity of checking their recollections beforehand by reference to statements or notes made at a time closer to the events in question. In addition, refusal of access to statements would tend to create difficulties for honest witnesses but be likely to do little to hamper dishonest witnesses . . . It is true that by the practice of the courts a line is drawn at the moment when a witness enters the witness box, when giving evidence there he cannot refresh his memory except by a document which must have been written either at the time of the transaction or so shortly afterwards that the facts were still fresh in his memory . . . But there can be no general rule (which incidentally would be unenforceable) that witnesses may not before trial see the statements which they made at some period reasonably close to the time of the event. Indeed, one can imagine many cases, particularly those of a complex nature, where such a rule would militate greatly against the interests of justice.'

(Sachs LJ)

In *R v Westwell* [1976] 2 All ER 812, the Court of Appeal decided that there was no general rule that witnesses may not see their statements made at or near to the time of the events before giving evidence. In some cases the fact that a witness has read his statement before going into the witness box may be relevant to the weight that can properly be attached to his evidence, and injustice may be caused to the defendant if the jury was left in ignorance of that fact. Accordingly, as a rule of good practice, it is desirable but not essential that the opposing party should be informed when this has been done.

If a witness, having commenced their testimony, needs to refresh their memory out of court and not from the witness box, it would be for the judge to exercise his or her discretion to decide whether to allow the witness to refresh their memory and that the document to be used to refresh their memory was made or verified by the witness close to the time of the event. In *R v Da Silva* [1990] 1 WLR 31, the judge exercised his discretion to allow *aide-memoire* documents, provided that the following conditions are satisfied:

1. The witness indicates that he cannot recall the details of events because of a lapse of time.
2. The witness had made the statement much nearer to the time of the events and the contents of the statement represented his recollections at the time he made it.
3. The witness had not read the statement shortly before coming into the witness box.
4. The witness wished to have an opportunity to read the statement before continuing his testimony.

This principle was taken one stage further in *R v South Ribble Magistrates, ex p Cochrane* [1996] 2 Cr App 544. The court decided that the third condition laid down in *R v Da Silva* was not a requirement to be satisfied. Indeed, the conditions laid down in *Da Silva* were not prerequisites to be fulfilled. The question involved the exercise of discretion, and the real test is fairness and justice. In this case the witness had read his witness statement before testifying at the committal proceedings on a charge of conspiracy to pervert the course of justice. He then could not remember details of a conversation included in his statement that was made twelve to eighteen months earlier. The magistrate allowed him to look at the statement before continuing with his testimony. The defendant was convicted and appealed. The Divisional Court dismissed the appeal on the ground that the magistrates (or judge) had a strong discretion to decide whether to allow the witness to refer to the non-contemporaneous note before continuing his testimony.

JUDGMENT

'I do not understand the court there to be saying, as a matter of law, that once a witness was in the witness box he could only refer to his previous non-contemporaneous statement if all four criteria were satisfied. It was permissive, not expressed by way of invariable limitation. That, it seems to me, is supported from the tenor of the judgment when read as a whole.

'For example serious frauds require considerable preparation from witnesses who routinely have their own copies of their statements which may run to hundreds of pages. Clearly they will refer to them in the days or weeks they may spend in the witness box. They will have studied those statements both before and during their time in the witness box, and the course of justice is helped and not hindered by that because in complicated matters it is necessary that witnesses should be properly prepared, otherwise matters are reduced to a memory test and justice is not assisted. What is said there will apply equally to the confused, flustered and nervous old lady. Whether she has read her statement before she goes into the witness box or not, if she was confused and flustered when she first read it before giving evidence, she may very well need to read it again and the discretion should lie in the trial judge to allow her to do so.

'Finally, in relation to the relevance as to whether a witness has taken the opportunity to read their statement before going into the witness box, there can be no logical difference between someone who has read the statement and for some reason not taken it in properly and one who has never read it at all. It seems to me that the judge has a real discretion as to whether to permit a witness to refresh his memory from a non-contemporaneous document. By "real discretion" I mean a strong discretion, a choice of alternatives free of binding criteria. I do not mean the so-called weak discretion which is not a true judicial discretion at all, but simply a binding rule of law to be followed by the judge.'

(Henry LJ)

In *Owen v Edwards* (1983) 77 Cr App R 191, the issue arose as to whether a police officer, who used his notebook to refresh his memory out of court and did not refer to his notebook while testifying, may be cross-examined on the contents of the notebook and the consequences of this course of conduct. The Divisional Court relied on a paragraph from Archbold, *Criminal Pleadings, Evidence and Practice*, to the effect that the rules that apply to refreshing memory in the witness box should be the same as those that apply if memory has been refreshed outside the court, for 'It would be odd if it were otherwise.' The effect was that defence was entitled to cross-examine on matters in the notebook about which evidence had not been given by the officer subject to the risk of the material being evidence and the document being exhibited.

JUDGMENT

'The whole tenor of authority appears to indicate that the defence is entitled to see such documents, including notebooks and statements, from which memory has been refreshed subject, of course, only to the well-established rules that a witness can be cross-examined having refreshed his memory upon the material in his notebook from which he has refreshed his memory without the notebook being made evidence in the case, whereas if he is cross-examined beyond those limits into other matters, the cross-examiner takes the risk of the material being evidence and the document being exhibited and therefore available for use by the fact-finding tribunal.'

(McNeill J)

6.2.3 Unfavourable and hostile witnesses

The general rule is that a party calling a witness to testify in proceedings (civil or criminal) guarantees the witness's trustworthiness. The effect is that such a party is not entitled to impeach the witness's credit by questioning the witness as to their previous convictions or otherwise discrediting the witness or bringing out the witness's previous inconsistent statement. In other words, the party calling the witness is not entitled to conduct a cross-examination of their witness. In attempting to prove their case, they assume that the witness would testify on issues relevant to the facts in issue and in their favour.

The witness may disappoint the party in that they fail to prove the relevant issue or proves an issue prejudicial to the party calling them. Such a witness is treated as unfavourable. The witness may not have shown any animosity towards the party calling them but simply that the proof expected from them might have been exaggerated or overstated or the facts were not adequately perceived by them. Thus, an unfavourable witness is one who does not display any hostility to the party calling them but disappoints them in failing to prove the relevant issue.

At common law, the party may be allowed to contradict his witness by adducing contrary evidence from other witnesses in both civil and criminal cases without the leave of the judge. In other words, if W, a witness called by the claimant (in a civil case) or the prosecution (in a criminal case), fails to 'come up to proof', the claimant or prosecution may call another witness, X, to prove the relevant point.

In *Ewer v Ambrose* (1825) 107 ER 910, in an action in quasi contract (*assumpsit*) for money had and received, the defendant called a witness to prove a partnership; but he proved the contrary. The defendant called another witness to prove the partnership and, on appeal, the court decided that he was entitled to do so:

JUDGMENT

'Where a witness is called by a party to prove his case and he disproves that case, I think the party is still at liberty to prove his case by other witnesses. It would be a great hardship if the rule were otherwise, for if a party had four witnesses upon whom he relied to prove his case, it would be very hard, that by calling first the one who happened to disprove it, he should be deprived of the testimony of the other three. If he had called the three before the other who had disproved the case, it would have been a question for the jury upon the evidence, whether they would give credit to the three or to the one. The order in which the witness happens to be called ought not therefore to make any difference.'

(Littledale J)

'If a party calls a witness to prove a fact, he cannot, when he finds the witness proves the contrary, give general evidence to shew that that witness is not to be believed on his oath, but he may shew by other evidence that he is mistaken as to the fact which he is called to prove.'

(Holroyd J)

Hostile witnesses

A 'hostile' witness is one who shows animosity towards the party calling the witness. They are not desirous of speaking the truth, or they set out to sabotage the case of the party calling them. The judge in his or her discretion is required to make a ruling as to whether the witness is hostile or not. This decision is required to be determined in the presence of the jury, so that they can hear and see the answers given by the potentially hostile witness. It is only in exceptional circumstances that the decision may be made on a *voir dire*: see *R v Olumegbon* [2004] EWCA Crim 2337. In *R v Greene* [2009] EWCA Crim 2282, the Court of Appeal decided that the trial judge was best placed to assess the demeanour of the witness and their animus, and only in rare cases would the appellate court be minded to interfere with his or her decision as to whether or not the witness was hostile. Once the judge has made the ruling that the witness is hostile, then at common law, in both civil and criminal cases, the party calling the witness is entitled, subject to the discretion of the judge, to conduct a limited form of cross-examination of the witness. Such a party is entitled to ask leading questions and to reduce the impact of the witness's testimony by questioning them with regard to their memory, means of knowledge, etc. The purpose of the line of questioning is twofold:

(a) to persuade the witness to return to the details contained in their witness statement;

(b) to highlight inconsistencies between the witness's versions of events.

Whether the witness is merely unfavourable or is to be treated as hostile is a question of law for the judge to decide. If the witness gives evidence that is inconsistent with their out-of-court statement or fails to give evidence that is expected of them, the judge needs to consider whether the witness ought to be invited to refresh their memory as an alternative to considering whether the witness is hostile: see *R v Maw* [1994] Crim LR 841. Where a witness refuses to co-operate and refuses to answer questions put to him or her, the witness may be treated as hostile.

In *R v Thompson* (1976) 64 Cr App R 96, the defendant was charged and convicted with incest with his daughter (aged sixteen at the time of the trial). She had made a statement to the police implicating her father. At the trial, after being sworn in, she was asked by counsel for the prosecution about the merits of the case and said, 'I am not saying nothing, I am not going to give evidence.' The judge retorted, 'Oh yes you are.' The witness said, 'I'm not.' The judge said, 'Do you want to spend time in prison yourself?' The witness said, 'No.' The judge continued, 'You wouldn't like it in Holloway, I assure you. You answer these questions and behave yourself, otherwise you will be in serious trouble. Do you understand that?' The witness replied, 'Yes.' She then refused to answer the questions put to her. The judge then gave permission to treat the witness as hostile and she was cross-examined by the prosecution counsel; the accused was convicted and appealed. The Court of Appeal dismissed the appeal because the judge had correctly exercised his discretion to treat the witness as hostile.

It is unclear whether a party may re-examine his witness who was treated as hostile at the examination-in-chief stage. The argument here is that the witness remains the witness of the party calling them and, in theory, ought to be subject to re-examination by such party. However, a witness may be treated as hostile at the stage of the re-examination: see *R v Powell* [1985] Crim LR 592.

At common law, a hostile witness may, in addition to the limited form of cross-examination by the party calling him, be contradicted by the evidence of other witnesses and, with the leave of the judge, be contradicted by the witness's own previous statement.

Section 3 of the Criminal Procedure Act 1865 replaced s 22 of the Common Law Procedure Act 1854. Neither provision replaces the common law, which is considered to be broader than these statutory provisions. This was highlighted in *R v Thompson* above, where the Court of Appeal decided that the silence of the witness was sufficient to make her hostile at common law but that, strictly, the witness did not fall within the statutory definition of that term:

JUDGMENT

'We think this matter must be dealt with by the provisions of the common law in regard to recalcitrant witnesses. Quite apart from what is said in section 3, the common law did recognise that pressure could be brought to bear upon witnesses who refused to co-operate and perform their duties . . . The short question after all is: was the judge right in allowing counsel to cross-examine in the sense of asking leading questions? . . . it seems to us that he was right and there is no reason to suppose that the subsequent statutory intervention into this subject has in any way destroyed or removed the basic common law right of the judge in his discretion to allow cross-examination when a witness proves to be hostile.'

(Lord Widgery CJ)

Section 3 of the Criminal Procedure Act 1865 provides as follows:

SECTION

'A party producing a witness shall not be allowed to impeach his credit by general evidence of bad character; but he may, in case the witness shall, in the opinion of the judge, prove adverse, contradict him by other evidence, or, by leave of the judge, prove that he has made at other times a statement inconsistent with his testimony; but before such last mentioned proof can be given the circumstances of the supposed statement, sufficient to designate the particular occasion, must be mentioned to the witness, and he must be asked whether or not he has made such statement.'

Points to note with regard to this Act are:

- The 1865 Act, despite its unfortunate name, is applicable to both civil and criminal cases.
- The Act uses the expression 'adverse'. This expression has been construed as meaning 'hostile' only and does not include 'unfavourable' witnesses.

In *Greenough v Eccles* (1859) 28 LJCP 160, Williams J said:

JUDGMENT

'The section [s 3 of the 1865 Act] lays down three rules as to the power of a party to discredit his own witness: first, he shall not be allowed to impeach his credit by general evidence of bad character, secondly, he may contradict him by other evidence, thirdly, he may prove that he has made at other times a statement inconsistent with his present testimony . . . it is impossible to suppose that the legislature could have really intended to impose any fetter whatever on the right of the party to contradict his own witness by other evidence relevant to the issue – a right not only fully established by authority but founded on the plainest good sense . . . the section requires the judge to form an opinion that the witness is adverse, before the right to contradict or prove that he has made inconsistent statements is to be allowed to operate. This is reasonable and indeed necessary if the word, "adverse" means "hostile" but wholly unreasonable and unnecessary if it means "unfavourable".

'On these grounds, I think the preferable construction is, that, in case the witness shall, in the opinion of the judge, prove "hostile", the party producing him may not only contradict him by other witnesses, as he might heretofore have done, and may still do, if the witness is unfavourable, but may also, by leave of the judge, prove that he has made inconsistent statements. . . .'

- The section lays down the general common law prohibition on the party impeaching their witness.
- The judge in his or her discretion decides whether the witness is hostile in accordance with the definition as stated earlier, namely that the witness is not desirous of speaking the truth, and shows animosity towards the party calling the witness.
- The hostile witness may be contradicted by other evidence which is inconsistent with their testimony, such as the testimony of another witness (similar to an unfavourable witness).
- The hostile witness may be questioned by the party calling them about the inconsistencies in their statement.
- The hostile witness, with the leave of the judge, may be contradicted by their own previous out-of-court statement (oral or written), but before this is done the circumstances of the statement must be mentioned to the witness and they must be asked whether they made the statement.
- At common law, the evidential value of admitting the out-of-court statement is to establish the inconsistency in the testimony and thereby to discredit the witness. The out-of-court statement was treated as evidence of the inconsistency of the witness. It was a misdirection at common law to direct the jury that they may choose to rely on either the testimony or the statement. In *R v White* (1922) 17 Cr App R 60, on a charge of riotous assembly, a number of prosecution witnesses, who made unsworn statements to the police implicating the defendant, retracted their statements in court and declared that the defendant did not participate in the riot. In his summing up the judge directed the jury to choose between the sworn testimony and the unsworn statements. Following a conviction and an appeal, the Court of Appeal allowed the appeal and quashed the conviction owing to the misdirection.
- Where a hostile witness, on being questioned in cross-examination, adopts his out-of-court statement, this becomes part of his testimony and may be accepted by the court, subject to issues concerning his credibility: see *R v Maw* [1994] Crim LR 841.

- In civil cases, s 6(3) and (5) of the Civil Evidence Act 1995 declares that the out-of-court, contradictory statement shall be evidence of any fact stated therein. In other words, both the testimony and the contradictory statement will be put to the tribunal of fact, who will then decide accordingly.

Section 6(3) of the Civil Evidence Act 1995 provides as follows:

SECTION

'(3) Where in the case of civil proceedings section 3 . . . of the Criminal Procedure Act 1865 applies, which makes provision as to –

(a) how far a witness may be discredited by the party producing him,
(b) the proof of contradictory statements made by the witness, and
(c) cross-examination as to previous statements in writing,

this Act does not authorise the adducing of evidence of a previous inconsistent or contradictory statement otherwise than in accordance with those sections.

This is without prejudice to any provision made by rules of court under s 3 above . . .

(5) Nothing in this section shall be construed as preventing a statement of any description referred to above from being admissible by virtue of section 1 as evidence of the matters stated.'

- In criminal cases, s 119 of the Criminal Justice Act 2003 enacts that where the witness testifies and the out-of-court, contradictory statement is admitted in court, the latter will be treated as evidence of the facts stated, i.e. the effect is similar to civil cases: the statement is treated as an exception to the hearsay rule.

Section 119(1) of the Criminal Justice Act 2003 provides as follows:

SECTION

'If in criminal proceedings a person gives oral evidence and –

(a) he admits making a previous inconsistent statement, or
(b) a previous inconsistent statement made by him is proved by virtue of section 3, 4 or 5 of the Criminal Procedure Act 1865,

the statement is admissible as evidence of any matter stated of which oral evidence by him would be admissible.'

The effect of s 119(1) is that the judge may direct the jury to choose to rely on either the testimony of the witness or the out-of-court statement. This is a confirmation of the direction in *R v White* (see above). In *R v Joyce* [2005] EWCA Crim 1785, a decision under the 2003 Act, the Court of Appeal decided that the jury may be directed that they may accept what the witness asserts from the witness box or the out-of-court statement of the witness. The weight to be attached to the evidence varies with the facts of each case. In *R v Billingham* [2009] 2 Cr App R 341, it was decided that the jury was entitled to reject a statement in evidence because they did not consider it to be true. That could be because of its inconsistency with previous statements or other evidence, or simply its improbability or how it was given. Further, a jury should not be directed that the out-of-court statement is just as much evidence as the witness's testimony. The reason is that the jury may be confused into believing that equal weight may be accorded to both assertions.

JUDGMENT

'A jury is entitled to reject a statement in evidence, and to accord it no weight at all, because they do not consider it to be true. That may be because of its inconsistency with previous statements or because of inconsistency with other evidence or simply its improbability or the manner in which it has been given. For a jury to be directed that a previous statement is just as much evidence as the witness's testimony in court is liable to confuse them: the jury may take the direction to mean that they are obliged to give the previous statement the same evidential weight as the testimony (and vice versa).'

(Burnton LJ in *R v Billingham*)

In *R v Parvez* [2010] EWCA Crim 3229, the court decided that a statement was capable of being relied on by the jury as the truth despite being retracted by a hostile witness in his testimony. It was for the jury to determine whether its contents and the circumstances in which it was made were such that it could safely be relied upon, notwithstanding its retraction.

- In a jury trial s 122(2) of the 2003 Act enacts that a statement, in a document produced as an exhibit, should not accompany the jury when they retire, unless the judge considers that such a course is appropriate or the parties agree. In *R v Hulme* (2006), the Court of Appeal decided that the judge had erred in allowing the jury to retire with a witness statement made by a hostile witness who was extensively cross-examined on the statement. There were no special features of that document that made it necessary for the jury to be allowed to read it or take it into the jury room when they retired.

CASE EXAMPLE

R v Hulme [2006] EWCA Crim 2899

The accused was charged and convicted with committing grievous harm with intent contrary to s 18 of the Offences Against the Person Act 1861. The victim could not recall anything about the incident. The prosecution relied on two eyewitnesses, D and C. D did not come up to proof, was treated as hostile and had been cross-examined as to her witness statement. The second witness, C, had given an account that did not match that description of D as to how the blows had been delivered. Defence counsel had conceded that the jury was entitled to read D's witness statement before retiring and the judge had allowed them to take the statement into the jury room. The Court of Appeal dismissed the appeal but ruled that the defence had wrongly conceded in allowing the jury to read the statement, and the judge had been incorrect to permit the jury to retire with the document. There were no special features to be attached to the document necessitating the jury to have it with them. The reason for the general prohibition enacted in s 122 is to avoid the risk that the jury may attach disproportionate weight to the document. Had it been appropriate to allow the jury to retire with the statement, a robust direction would have been required from the judge.

JUDGMENT

'In our judgment the judge was wrong to allow the witness statement to accompany the jury when they retired to consider their verdict. The reason given by the judge that the document was needed in order to make sense of the case and for the evaluation of Miss D's evidence was in our view an insufficient reason to justify the course adopted. The jury would have been in a position to make sense of the case and to evaluate the evidence if the matter had been dealt with in the normal way by a reminder in the summing up of the contents of the witness statement and of what Miss D had said about that document and the circumstances in which it was made. There was no special feature of the document that made it necessary for the jury to have the document itself before them. The reason why we think that the matter should have been dealt with in that way rather than by giving them a copy of the document itself is the undoubted risk that the jury would place disproportionate weight on the contents of the document, as compared with the oral evidence.'

(Richards LJ)

- Where a party is aware before the witness is called to testify, that his witness wishes to change his testimony or is unwilling to assist the court, but the party nevertheless calls the witness to testify, it is a question of degree as to whether the witness ought to be treated as hostile if he does not come up to proof. In other words, the question that arises in these cases is whether the twin aims of persuading the witness to return to his original statement and drawing attention to the inconsistencies regarding the witness's version of events can be achieved. This is a question for the judge to exercise at his discretion.
- In *R v Dat* [1998] Crim LR 488, the variation in the witness's version of events was in the detail only and the prosecution witness had merely failed to give evidence supporting the Crown's case.
- On the other hand, in *R v Honeyghon* [1999] Crim LR 221, the Court of Appeal decided that where the prosecution was aware in advance of the trial that there was little hope of the witness returning to his original statement but the witness was called to testify, the judge should not have exercised his discretion to classify the witness as hostile. In a gang fight one person was killed. The defendants were charged with murder. There were a number of witnesses to the fight. Two witnesses agreed to speak to the police but refused to make written statements. A third witness made a written statement to the police implicating the defendant but refused to answer any questions at the committal proceedings. At the Crown Court trial the witness said that she could not remember anything. The prosecution counsel applied to treat these witnesses as hostile, despite defence objection. The witnesses were cross-examined by the Crown about their earlier statements. The defendant was convicted and appealed. The Court of Appeal allowed the appeal and quashed the conviction.

6.2.4 Previous consistent statements (self-serving or narrative statements or the rule against manufactured evidence)

The general common law rule against manufactured evidence, applicable to both civil and criminal cases, is that where a witness called by a party has testified in chief about an assertion:

- that witness may not be asked in chief whether they had made a statement repeating the assertion to another person;
- the party calling the witness is not entitled to adduce evidence of the assertion;
- the third-party recipient of the assertion may not be called to testify that the witness had narrated the assertion to them.

For example, Satinder, an eyewitness, has testified as to the facts that he perceived. Satinder may not be asked by the party calling him whether he repeated the assertion to Lucy. Likewise, the statement made to Lucy may not be adduced and Lucy may not be called to testify to the effect that Satinder had told her of the relevant facts.

The rationale behind the general rule of the prohibition of such evidence is to avoid the ease with which such evidence may be manufactured by merely repeating the assertion several times in order to admit the evidence several times. In addition, the general bar on adducing such evidence saves time and costs by shortening proceedings because such narrative evidence is superfluous in any event. The evidence has already been admitted through the original witness; the repetition of such evidence does not add to the accuracy or reliability of such evidence. Indeed, such narrative evidence has the potential to lead to a multiplicity of collateral issues that are capable of confusing the jury.

The general rule is sometimes referred to as the rule in *Corke v Corke and Cook* [1958] 1 All ER 224. In this case, H, a husband, who was separated from his wife, W, had petitioned for a divorce on the ground of W's adultery with the co-respondent, Mr Cook, a lodger. At about midnight, H and an inquiry agent confronted W in Mr Cook's bedroom and accused her of having recently committed adultery with Mr Cook. W denied this, and about ten minutes later she telephoned her doctor requesting that both she and Mr Cook be examined to ascertain whether they had recently had sexual intercourse. The doctor declined because such an examination could have been inconclusive. W was refused permission to adduce evidence of the request and refusal by the doctor and, on appeal, the court decided that the evidence was correctly excluded:

JUDGMENT

'To what issue does this item of evidence go? It does nothing to prove the condition of either the female or male organ respectively of the parties involved. It does nothing to disprove the intercourse that H alleged. The most that could be said is that W was showing a belief in her story and adding some reason why the court should believe her . . . W's conduct and statement cannot be regarded as revealing consciousness of innocence. They reveal at the most a consciousness that the doctor would not find any physical proof of guilt. I apprehend that the dishonest may be resourceful in giving an air of innocence to their transaction . . . Were it to be held otherwise, one wonders where ingenuity in bolstering up a witness's evidence would stop.'

(Sellers LJ)

This general rule is subject to a number of exceptions in both civil and criminal cases.

Complaints

The common law rule that was applicable to criminal cases only was that on charges of sexual offences the terms of a complaint that were made by the victim may be narrated by both the victim and the person to whom the complaint was made. For example, on a charge of a sexual nature, the victim, Victor, makes a complaint to Xena to the effect that David, the defendant, was responsible for a sexual assault on him. Obviously Victor may narrate the events at the time of the assault; Victor may also testify that he told Xena about the assault and that David did it; Xena may testify that she received the complaint from Victor and repeat the terms of the complaint, including the fact that Victor told her that David did it.

The terms of the complaint were admissible to prove the consistency of the conduct of the complainant with the testimony of the complainant and, where consent is in issue, to negative such consent.

CASE EXAMPLE

R v Lillyman [1896] 2 QB 167

The defendant was charged with attempted rape and indecent assault. The employer of the victim (a maid) was allowed to narrate the terms of the complaint made to her shortly after the incident. Following a conviction the defendant appealed and the appeal was dismissed on the ground that the complaint was correctly admitted in court:

JUDGMENT

'It is necessary in the first place to have a clear understanding as to the principles upon which evidence of such complaint, not on oath, nor made in the presence of the prisoner, nor forming part of the *res gestae* can be admitted. It clearly is not admitted as evidence of the facts complained of; those facts must therefore be established, if at all, on oath by the prosecutrix or other credible witness and strictly speaking evidence of them ought to be given before evidence of the complaint is admitted. The complaint can only be used as evidence of the consistency of the conduct of the prosecutrix with the story told by her in the witness box and as being consistent with her consent to that of which she complains . . . The evidence can be legitimately used only for the purpose of enabling the jury to judge for themselves whether the conduct of the woman was consistent with her testimony on oath given in the witness box . . . we think that it is the duty of the judge to impress upon the jury in every case that they are not entitled to make use of the complaint as any evidence whatever of those facts, or for any other purpose than that we have stated.'

(Hawkins J)

Two conditions are required to be satisfied in order to render the complaint admissible:

(a) The complaint must have been made at the earliest opportunity that reasonably presented itself.

(b) The complaint must not have been made in response to any threat or intimidatory enquiry or leading questions.

CASE EXAMPLE

R v Osborne [1905] 1 KB 551

The defendant was charged with indecent assault on a girl aged twelve. Evidence was given by another girl, aged eleven, to the effect that, shortly before the incident, she had left the victim with the defendant, arranging to return soon. On her way back, she met the victim running home and asked her, 'Why are you going home? Why did you not wait until I came back?' The answer from the victim incriminated the defendant. On conviction the appeal was dismissed.

JUDGMENT

'It appears to us that the mere fact that the statement is made in answer to a question in such cases is not of itself sufficient to make it inadmissible as a complaint. Questions of a suggestive or leading character will, indeed, have that effect and will render it inadmissible . . . In each case the decision on the character of the question put, as well as other circumstances, such as the relationship of the question to the complainant must be left to the discretion of the presiding judge. If the circumstances indicate that, but for the questioning there probably would have been no voluntary complaint, the answer is inadmissible. If the question merely anticipates a statement which the complainant was about to make, it is not rendered inadmissible by the fact that the questioner happens to speak first . . . it appears that in accordance with principle such complaints are admissible not merely as negating consent but because they are consistent with the story of the prosecutrix.'

(Ridley J)

Modern position: section 120(4), (7) and (8) of the Criminal Justice Act 2003

Section 120(4), (7) and (8) have made significant improvements to the common law in this context and created two radical changes to the law concerning complaints, without replacing the common law rule. The first is that the complaint concerns any offence with which the defendant is charged and is no longer restricted to offences of a sexual nature. The second major change is that if the complaint becomes admissible, the complaint shall be treated as evidence of the truth as opposed to merely being evidence of consistency.

Section 120(4) provides as follows:

SECTION

'A previous statement by a witness is admissible as evidence of any matter stated of which oral evidence by him would be admissible, if –

(a) any of the following three conditions is satisfied, and
(b) while giving evidence the witness indicates that to the best of his belief he made the statement, and to the best of his belief it states the truth.'

Section 120(7) provides as follows:

SECTION

'The third condition is that –

(a) the witness claims to be a person against whom an offence has been committed,
(b) the offence is one to which the proceedings relate,
(c) the statement consists of a complaint made by the witness (whether to a person in authority or not) about conduct which would, if proved, constitute the offence or part of the offence,
(d) [repealed] there is no longer a requirement that the complaint must be recent or as soon as can be reasonably expected after the alleged conduct,
(e) the complaint was not made as a result of a threat or a promise, and
(f) before the statement is adduced the witness gives oral evidence in connection with its subject matter.'

Section 120(8) enacts:

SECTION

'For the purposes of subsection (7) the fact that the complaint was elicited (for example, by a leading question) is irrelevant unless a threat or a promise was involved.'

In *R v O* [2006] EWCA Crim 556, the Court of Appeal expressed its opinion as to the relationship between the common law and the new statutory provisions laid down in s 120(4) and (7). The court identified that s 120(4) and (7) covered an area very similar to that dealt with under the old common law rules, but the statutory provisions are not limited to offences of a sexual nature. Indeed, the new statutory provisions apply to complaints made in respect of any offences. Moreover, the statutory provisions are not restricted to one hearsay statement as to a complaint made by an alleged victim. The statutory provisions were free-standing and provided their own criteria but they do not abolish the common law or codify the old law. The evidential value of the statement under the statutory provisions is that it is admissible to prove the truth of the matters stated and is not restricted to establishing the consistency of the complainant's account that exists at common law.

JUDGMENT

'Clearly the provisions of sub-sections (4) and (7) of the 2003 Act cover an area very similar to that dealt with by the old common law rules relating to "recent complaints" in sexual cases. The new provisions are not limited to sexual cases. The statutory test in s 120(4) is differently expressed, as indeed it is, in sub-section (7). The application to admit the evidence was made under the new Act. The learned judge, in our view, correctly concentrated on deciding whether the test of admissibility provided by the Act had been satisfied.

'It has to be remembered that a statement admitted under the new statutory provisions is admissible to prove the truth of the matter stated and not merely to demonstrate consistency of the complainant's account as was the case under the old law. There is obviously a need in fairness to restrict the evidence of "complaint upon complaint" which may merely be self-serving. The appellant sought to argue that the new hearsay provision as to complaints merely codify the old law of recent complaint and should be regarded as importing the restrictions inherent in some regards to that law. We disagree. The statutory provisions are freestanding and provide their own criteria.'

(McCombe J)

Additional points concerning these statutory provisions are:

- Section 120(7)(a) restricts the admissibility of the complaint to those made only by the victim of the offence. The provisions in s 120(4) and (7) are not intended to open the door to complaints by persons other than the complainant. In *R v T* [2008] EWCA Crim 484, the Court of Appeal allowed the appeal and quashed the convictions for sexual offences where the trial judge admitted complaints about the defendant's conduct by three prosecution witnesses other than the complainant.
- The witness is required to make the declaration laid down in s 120(4)(b).
- The complainant is required to testify in the proceedings. It is immaterial whether the complainant gives sworn or unsworn evidence.
- Section 120(7)(c) enacts that the complaint is required to involve conduct that, if proved, will 'constitute the offence or part of the offence'. The purpose of this provision is to ensure that only relevant complaints that focus on the offence are admissible. On a charge of assault, the fact that the victim states that an unfortunate event occurred to him, without indicating that he was assaulted, would not constitute a complaint. In the pre-2003 case, *R v Milner* [2000] All ER (D) 1163, the court decided that an unsent letter written by the complainant in a case of historic sexual abuse constituted a complaint. The letter was written when the complainant was sixteen years old about the abuse by her father and was framed in the nature of a complaint, as opposed to being a narrative. In the circumstances it could have been inferred that she intended to send it to someone. It is unclear whether s 120(7) has changed this rule. It must be stressed that the decision was based on exceptional facts. The trial judge has a broad discretion to determine whether the letter constitutes a complaint.
- The requirement that the complaint must be made recently, as laid down under s 120(7)(d), has been repealed by s 112 of the Coroners and Justice Act 2009.

- The condition laid down in s 120(7)(e) is the same as the common law, and s 120(7)(f) states the order of events regarding the statement that must follow the testimony of the complainant.
- The evidential effect of admitting the complaint by the witness is that it is evidence of any matter stated of which oral evidence by him would be admissible: see s 120(4) of the 2003 Act. In other words the complaint is evidence of the truth of the assertion (by statute) and also evidence of consistency of the complainant (as was the position at common law). The judge is required to direct the jury to this effect.

Statements forming part of the res gestae

The rule is that a witness's testimony may be confirmed by a repetition of the evidence by the same witness or a third party if it forms part of the same transaction or story or the *res gestae*. At common law, and under s 118(4) of the Criminal Justice Act 2003, such evidence was admissible as an exception to narrative statements and today is admissible as evidence of the facts stated. Section 118(4) provides:

SECTION

'Any rule of law under which in criminal proceedings a statement is admissible as evidence of any matter stated if –

(a) the statement was made by a person so emotionally overpowered by an event that the possibility of concoction or distortion can be disregarded,
(b) the statement accompanied an act which can be properly evaluated as evidence only if considered in conjunction with the statement, or
(c) the statement relates to a physical sensation or a mental state (such as intention or emotion).'

This subject will be dealt with in more detail in Chapter 7.

Rebuttal of a suggestion of a fabrication of testimony

At common law, the rule is that, under cross-examination, if it has been suggested that the witness has 'recently' (i.e. within a specified period) fabricated their story, the examiner in chief may rebut the suggestion under re-examination of the witness. In other words, in both civil and criminal cases, the party calling the witness is entitled to adduce evidence to rebut a suggestion made by the cross-examiner that the witness has fabricated their story.

But if the witness's testimony is attacked generally by the cross-examiner to show their unreliability as a witness, this exception to the rule against narratives will not entitle the examiner in chief to call rebutting evidence simply because a specific statement to the contrary may not be able to counter the allegation: see *R v Williams* [1998] Crim LR 494. In order to attract this exception, the nature of the cross-examination is required to be equivalent to a submission that the witness's story is a recent invention, i.e. at a specific time when the rebutting evidence that may exist will counter the allegation.

In *R v Oyesiku* (1971) 56 Cr App R 240 the defendant was charged with assaulting an officer in the execution of his duty. The defence was self-defence. The defendant's wife testified to the effect that the police officer was the aggressor. It was put to the defendant's wife that she had prepared her evidence in collusion with her husband (the defendant). The judge had refused to allow defence counsel to adduce evidence to show that the witness had made a consistent statement to her solicitor after her husband's arrest and before she had time to see or contact him. The defendant was convicted and appealed and the appeal was allowed because the judge had ruled incorrectly:

JUDGMENT

'Our attention has . . . been drawn to a recent decision in the High Court of Australia, *Nominal Defendant v Clements* (1961) 104 CLR 476. I desire to read only one passage from the full judgment of Dixon CJ. He said this: "The rule of evidence under which it was let in is well recognised and of long standing. If the credit of a witness is impugned as to some material fact to which he deposes upon the ground that his account is a late invention or has been lately devised or reconstructed, even though not with conscious honesty, that makes admissible a statement to the same effect as the account he gave as a witness, if it was made by the witness contemporaneously with the event or at a time sufficiently early to be inconsistent with the suggestion that his account is a late invention or reconstruction. But, inasmuch as the rule forms a definite exception to the general principle excluding statements made out of court and admits a possibly self-serving statement made by the witness, great care is called for in applying it. The judge at the trial must determine for himself upon the conduct of the trial before him whether a case for applying the rule of evidence has arisen and, from the nature of the matter, if there be an appeal, great weight should be given to his opinion by the appellate court. It is evident, however, that the judge at the trial must exercise care in assuring himself not only that the account given by the witness in his testimony is attacked on the ground of recent invention or reconstruction or that a foundation for such an attack has been laid by the party, but also that the contents of the statement are in fact to the like effect as his account given in his evidence and that having regard to the time and circumstances in which it was made it rationally tends to answer the attack. It is obvious that it may not be easy sometimes to be sure that counsel is laying a foundation for impugning the witness's account of a material incident or fact as a recently invented, devised or reconstructed story. Counsel himself may proceed with a subtlety which is the outcome of caution in pursuing what may prove a dangerous course. That is one reason why the trial judge's opinion has a peculiar importance."

'. . . That judgment of the Chief Justice of Australia, although technically not binding upon us, is a decision of the greatest persuasive power, and one which this Court gratefully accepts as a correct statement of the law.'

(Karminski LJ)

At common law, the effect of admitting the rebutting evidence was to establish the consistency of the witness. Today, these common law rules have been abolished, and in both civil and criminal cases the effect of admitting the rebutting evidence is to establish the truth of the matters stated. However, in both civil and criminal cases the preconditions for admitting the evidence are the same as the common law, except that in both cases the allegation by the cross-examiner need not involve a 'recent' fabrication: see *R v Athwal* (below).

The pre-2003 case of *R v Tyndale* [1999] Crim LR 320 indicates how careful the cross-examining counsel is required to be in order to avoid this principle.

The defendant (D) was charged with indecent assault on the daughter (V) of the woman with whom he was living. The alleged offences took place while D was living with V's mother and also after D separated from her mother. D left the girl's mother to live with another woman. V's mother told her and her other children that D had left her. V sent D an abusive note and, along with her brothers, stood outside D's house shouting abuse at him. V's complaint to her brothers of sexual abuse by D was ruled to be inadmissible as the law existed at that time. Defence counsel cross-examined V's mother and suggested that she had fabricated the basis of complaints to the police in order to get even with D. Prosecuting counsel was granted leave to adduce the earlier complaints in order to rebut a suggestion of fabrication. His appeal against conviction was dismissed on the ground that the complaints were allowed because they were made prior to the discovery of D's affair, which caused enmity between her mother and D. The principle that was laid down in this case remains the same after the 2003 Act.

Civil cases

In civil cases where rebutting evidence is admitted, the evidence is admitted under an exception to the hearsay rule.

Section 6(2) of the Civil Evidence Act 1995 provides as follows:

SECTION

'A party who has called or intends to call a person as a witness in civil proceedings may not in those proceedings adduce evidence of a previous statement made by that person, except –

(a) with the leave of the court, or
(b) for the purpose of rebutting a suggestion that his evidence has been fabricated.

This shall not be construed as preventing a witness statement (that is, a written statement of oral evidence which a party to the proceedings intends to lead) from being adopted by a witness in giving evidence or treated as evidence.'

Criminal cases

In criminal cases s 120(2) of the Criminal Justice Act 2003 lays down the modern rule.

Section 120(2) of the 2003 Act provides:

SECTION

'If a previous statement by the witness is admitted as evidence to rebut a suggestion that his oral evidence has been fabricated, that statement is admissible as evidence of any matter stated of which oral evidence by the witness would be admissible.'

The effect is that the statement is admissible as evidence of the truth of the assertion including evidence of consistency of the witness.

In *R v Athwal* [2009] EWCA Crim 789, the Court of Appeal decided that the principle in s 120(2), rebuttal of suggestion of fabrication, was outside the hearsay rules preserved by s 118 of the 2003 Act but became admissible hearsay under s 114(1)(a) and, in particular, s 120(2) of the Act. The judge misdirected the jury by telling them that the rebutting evidence is evidence of consistency of the witness. Section 120(2) makes it clear that the rebutting evidence is admissible as evidence of any matters stated of which oral evidence by the witness would be admissible. In other words, it is evidence of the truth of the assertion. In this case the defendants were a mother (B) and son (S) who allegedly murdered the son's wife (W). W disappeared on a trip to India with B and S. The prosecution relied on the testimony of B's daughter-in-law (D) to the effect that B had admitted to her that W was strangled and thrown into a river. Defence counsel cross-examined D and suggested that she had made up this story. The prosecution was granted leave to call rebutting evidence from two members of her family about the circumstances in which she had first told them of B's confession. The judge directed the jury that her rebutting evidence was limited to establishing the consistency of her testimony with her out-of-court statement and was not evidence of the truth. On appeal against conviction the Court of Appeal decided that this was a misdirection by the trial judge and the true position was that the jury was entitled to rely on the evidence as the truth of the assertion. The court also observed that the adjective 'recent' had not been replicated in s 120(2) in accordance with the recommendations of the Law Commission (1997). The omission of the qualification was a welcome simplification.

In *R v Wishart* [2005] EWCA Crim 1337, the court was faced with the difficulties that may arise in this context with the convergence of three separate principles – the privileges against self-incrimination and communications between the client and legal adviser (see Chapter 4), out of silence of the defendant and its effect under s 34 of the Criminal Justice and Public Order Act 1994 (see Chapter 5) and rebutting a suggestion of fabrication. Where the defendant relies on a defence in his trial that he did not reveal to the police when questioned, the jury may be invited to draw adverse inferences under s 34 of the Criminal Justice and Public Order Act 1994. To counter the risk of an adverse inference the defendant may call a third party to testify that he had communicated his defence to him at or about the time of the interview. If he calls his solicitor to testify on his behalf, he may run the risk of waiving his privilege regarding communications to his legal adviser. But if he is advised by his solicitor to remain silent, he may not have waived his privilege if that is the evidence in rebuttal. If the judge rules that the solicitor is required to disclose the reasons for the advice, and the defendant is cross-examined by the prosecution as to those reasons, the defendant may run the risk of not being able to defend himself and to retain his privilege.

CASE EXAMPLE

R v Wishart [2005] EWCA Crim 1337

The defendant (W) and others were charged with robbery. W made no comment when interviewed by the police. At the trial he relied on his defence of alibi. The prosecution alleged that the alibi was a fabrication. During cross-examination the judge enquired whether W had told his advising solicitor about the defence. W replied that he had. The judge directed that the solicitor should make available any notes of his conference with W before the police interview. The notes revealed that W had admitted his presence at the robbery. The judge then ordered disclosure and decided that W had waived his privilege. In his summing up the judge issued a s 34 adverse inference direction, and the defendant was convicted. On appeal, the court allowed the appeal and quashed the conviction on the ground that W was forced to give up his privilege, which cannot be treated as a waiver. A defendant against whom a potentially very damaging allegation of recent fabrication was made should be entitled to defend himself without running the risk that, in doing so, he would lose the protection of his privilege. But the defendant's bare assertion that he made a no-comment interview on legal advice did not of itself waive his privilege.

Previous statements of identification

The principle of law here at common law is that a prior identification of the defendant after the commission of the crime, but before the trial (perhaps at an identification parade), may be received in evidence either from the witness himself or another person who was present at the time of the identification.

It not infrequently happens that a witness who had made a prior identification of the defendant several months before the trial may have some doubt at the trial whether the defendant was the same person who was selected at the earlier identification, or the witness may have completely forgotten what took place earlier. In these circumstances, someone present at the prior identification is entitled to testify as to the facts. (It should be noted that this exception is distinct from the identification of the defendant at the time of the alleged commission of the crime, i.e. the *Turnbull* guidelines: see Chapter 13.)

CASE EXAMPLE

R v Osborne and Virtue [1973] QB 678

The defendants were convicted of robbery. Both defendants had been picked out at an identification parade four days after the robbery. Osborne was identified by Mrs Brookes; Mrs Head identified Mr Virtue. At the trial some seven-and-a-half months later, Mrs Brookes said that she could not remember having picked out anyone at the parade. Mrs Head first said that she thought Mr Virtue was the man she had picked out at the parade, but later said that she did not think that he was the same man who was charged. The police inspector in charge of the identification parade then testified that the women had identified the defendants. On conviction the defendants appealed. The Court of Appeal dismissed the appeal on the ground that the police inspector's evidence was admissible:

JUDGMENT

'All that Mrs Brookes had said was that she did not remember . . . that is very understandable after a delay of seven-and-a-half months . . . One asks oneself as a matter of common sense why, when a witness has forgotten what she did, evidence should not be given by another witness with a better memory to establish what, in fact she did when the events were fresh in her mind. Much the same situation arises with regard to Mrs Head . . . appearances can change after seven-and-a-half months . . . accused persons often look much smarter in the dock than they do when they are first arrested.'

(Lawton LJ)

Likewise in *R v McCay* [1990] Crim LR 338, a police officer present at an identification parade was called to testify that a witness had identified the defendant by saying 'it is number 8' when identifying the defendant at the parade from behind a two-way mirror.

Section 120(4) and (5) of the Criminal Justice Act 2003 enact that such identification is evidence of the facts stated; s 120(4) was mentioned earlier.

Section 120(5) states:

SECTION

'The first condition is that the statement identifies or describes a person, object or place.'

The effect is that the common law rule has been extended to 'objects and places'. In addition the testimony of the second witness is evidence of the matters stated.

Defendant's reaction when taxed with incriminating material

Evidence of the defendant's reaction when he is arrested or confronted with incriminating material is admissible in evidence as a relevant fact. Accordingly, a denial or exculpatory statement made by the defendant in such circumstances is admissible in order to establish the defendant's consistency: see *R v Storey* (1968) 52 Cr App R 334, below. (It should be noted that this rule exists as part of a wider principle involving the defendant's reaction generally. The defendant's reaction may be incriminating to the defendant, in which case the evidence may be admitted as an informal admission. In addition the defendant's reaction may be both exculpatory and incriminating. These are known as mixed statements. Both admissions and mixed statements are admissible as evidence of the facts stated under exceptions to the hearsay rule: see later.)

CASE EXAMPLE

R v Storey (1968) 52 Cr App R 334

The defendant was charged with possession of cannabis in her flat. When her premises were searched and the cannabis was found, she told the police that it had belonged to a man who brought it there against her will. This evidence was admitted. At the close of the prosecution's case the defence made a no case submission, which was rejected, and the defendant was convicted. She appealed on the grounds that as her explanation afforded her a complete defence to the charge, the no-case submission should not have been rejected. The Court of Appeal decided that the judge was correct in his ruling, for the evidence was only as to the consistency of the defendant's conduct and not of the facts stated. In short, the statement was admissible as to the credibility of the witness only:

JUDGMENT

'A statement made voluntarily by an accused person to the police is evidence in the trial because of its vital relevance as showing the reaction of the accused when *first taxed* with incriminating facts. If, of course, the accused admits the offence, then as a matter of shorthand one says that the admission is proof of guilt and indeed in the end, it is. But if the accused makes a statement which does not amount to an admission, the statement is not strictly evidence of the truth of what was said but is evidence of the reaction of the accused which forms part of the general picture to be considered by the jury.'

(Widgery LJ)

In *R v Pearce* (1979) 69 Cr App R 365, the principle was extended to cover exculpatory statements made to the police on subsequent occasions, although such statements may carry less weight compared with a statement made when 'first taxed'. However, it must not be assumed that the time for making the statement does not matter because if a carefully prepared statement is made by the defendant, the statement may lack weight in this context and may be excluded in its entirety. In *R v Newsome* (1980) 71 Cr App R 325, the defendant, prior to a third interview with the police, had conferred with his solicitor and drafted a statement which he submitted at the third interview. The judge excluded this self-serving statement on the ground that it lacked any weight, and the Court of Appeal upheld the decision of the trial judge. A similar result was reached in *R v Tooke* (1990) 90 Cr App R 417. The defendant was charged with assault. Immediately after the incident the defendant complained to the police that it was he who had been assaulted. He later went to the station and made a statement that was consistent with that version. The judge allowed the evidence of the first statement but not the second. His appeal against conviction was dismissed. The second statement added nothing to the first statement and was therefore of insufficient weight to be admitted in evidence at the trial.

The Criminal Justice Act 2003 does not modify this common law rule, with the effect that the principle is governed exclusively by the common law.

The related issues with regard to informal admissions and 'mixed' statements will be considered later. An informal admission is a declaration made by the defendant against his interests. These are admitted as exceptions to the

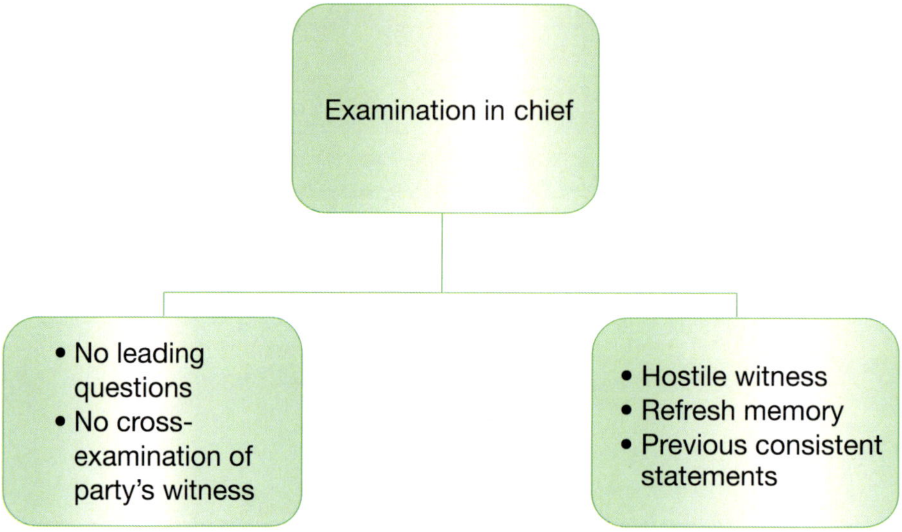

Figure 6.1 Rule against previous consistent statements subject to exceptions

hearsay rule and treated as evidence of the truth. A mixed statement is one made by the defendant, which contains both admissions and a denial of guilt. The entire statement, both inculpatory and exculpatory, is admitted with different levels of weight.

6.3 Cross-examination

Cross-examination is the process where the opponent's witness is subjected to questioning. The court may be given a version of facts that supports the case of the party calling the witness. It is possible that with clever cross-examination a different version of events may emerge. The cross-examiner will test the accuracy of the events presented to the court. The purpose of the cross-examination is twofold:

(a) to weaken, qualify or destroy the opponent's case, i.e. the case of the party calling the witness (broadly referred to as cross-examination as to credit);
(b) to elicit, through the opponent's witness, facts that are favourable to the cross-examiner (referred to as cross-examination as to issue).

Leading questions may be asked, and the witness is required to answer all questions put to them, except questions related to the following:

(i) Where the witness is entitled to claim and does claim a privilege, or the witness is protected by public interest immunity.
(ii) Where the evidence or information sought by the questioner constitutes inadmissible evidence. Clearly, cross-examination is subject to the rules of admissibility and, if the evidence is inadmissible, the need for the witness to answer the question, such as questions concerning the bad character of the witness or the defendant that are not admissible under one of the gateways laid down in the Criminal Justice Act 2003, is dispensed with (see later).
(iii) The judge has a discretion to excuse an answer to a question that he considers is not relevant to the issue or the witness's credit and is oppressive. The scope of this power will depend on the line of cross-examination, the style of questioning, the demeanour of the witness and the extent of repetition. This would vary with the facts of each case.

6.3.1 Sections 41–43 of the Youth Justice and Criminal Evidence Act 1999

A further exception to the requirement that a witness is required to answer questions put to him in cross-examination was originally enacted by s 2 of the Sexual Offences (Amendment) Act 1976, which has since been repealed and replaced by Part II, Chapter III or ss 41–43 of the Youth Justice and Criminal Evidence Act 1999. The Sexual Offences (Amendment) Act 1976 proved to be too restrictive. The Act was limited to rape charges only and prohibited the cross-examiner from adducing evidence or questioning the complainant in respect of any sexual experience with persons other than the defendant, except with the leave of the judge. The test for granting leave was based on a test of unfairness to the defendant to refuse leave. This was interpreted to mean whether the jury will consider the complainant's testimony in a different light: see *R v Viola* [1982] 1 WLR 1138. Omitted from the protection of the complainant under the 1976 Act was the cross-examination of the complainant regarding sexual experience with the defendant.

Part II, Chapter III of the Youth Justice and Criminal Evidence Act 1999 introduced provisions that are much broader and more comprehensive than its predecessor. The principles enacted in the 1999 Act are activated where four conditions are satisfied.

Condition 1

The defendant is charged with a 'sexual offence', as defined in s 62 of the Act. Such an offence is broadly defined in the Sexual Offences Act 2003.

Condition 2

There is a prohibition on the cross-examiner asking questions or adducing evidence about the 'sexual behaviour' of the complainant, except with the leave of the judge – the 'shield'.

Sexual behaviour

The definition of 'sexual behaviour' is laid down in s 42(1)(c) of the Act and means 'any sexual behaviour or other sexual experience whether or not involving the accused or other person. . . .' The effect is that any sexual activity of the complainant, either with other persons or on his or her own, will constitute sexual behaviour. The circumstances that may constitute 'sexual behaviour' or 'sexual experience' are varied and range from all forms of sexual intercourse to activities short of intercourse such as masturbation, romantic kissing, 'heavy petting', suggestive touching, and physical and verbal advances of a sexual nature. In *R v Ben-Rejab* [2012] 1 WLR 2364, the Court of Appeal decided that participation in an internet sexual quiz or questionnaire was held to fall within the subsection:

JUDGMENT

'It will be noted that "sexual behaviour or . . . experience" need not involve any other person. The expression is plainly wide enough, in our view, to embrace an activity of viewing pornography or engaging in sexually-charged messaging over a live internet connection. That being the case, the question for the court is whether an indulgence by answering questions in a sexually explicit quiz is "any sexual behaviour" within the meaning of the section. In our judgment it is. What motive can there have been when engaging in the activity of answering sexually explicit questions unless it was to obtain sexual pleasure from it?'

(Pitchford LJ)

However, allegations of previous false statements concerning sexual matters, whether against the defendant and/or a third party, are not questions about the sexual behaviour of the complainant and are therefore outside the protection of the 1999 Act. In *R v T* [2002] 1 All ER 683, the defendant was charged with indecent assault and rape of his niece between 1987 and 1989. The complaint was not made until 1999. The defence case was that none of the allegations had taken place. At a preparatory hearing, the defendant applied for leave to cross-examine the complainant about two occasions in 1987 and 1990 when she made false allegations of a sexual nature against other members of her family but not against the defendant. The judge refused to grant leave, and the Court of Appeal reversed the decision on the ground that the questions were not 'about' the sexual behaviour of the complainant but related to the veracity of her statements in the past:

JUDGMENT

'It seems to this court that normally questions or evidence about false statements in the past by a complainant about sexual assaults or such questions or evidence about the failure to complain about the alleged assault which is the subject matter of the charge, while complaining about other sexual assaults, are not ones "about" any sexual behaviour of the complainant. They relate not to her sexual behaviour but to her statements in the past or to her failure to complain.'

(Keene LJ)

The court also decided that defence counsel who makes the application for leave to cross-examine the complainant about his or her sexual behaviour is required to demonstrate a *proper evidential basis* for making the allegation of a false statement, and the judge is entitled to seek such assurances. The reason is to avoid an abuse of the process:

JUDGMENT

'It would be professionally improper for those representing the defendant to put such questions in order to elicit evidence about the complainant's past sexual behaviour as such under the guise of previous false complaints. But in any case the defence must have a proper evidential basis for asserting that any such previous statement was (a) made and (b) untrue . . . The judge is entitled to seek assurances from the defence that it has a proper basis for asserting that the statement was made and untrue.'

(Keene LJ)

A 'proper evidential basis', to be established by the defence, that the allegation of sexual behaviour of the complainant was false, means evidence on which a jury may be satisfied of the falsity of the allegation and does not involve the sexual behaviour of the complainant. This is a matter not for the exercise of the discretion of the judge but for his evaluation of the matter on the basis of the evidence. The decision of the judge is therefore 'fact sensitive' and little may be gained by examining the facts of other cases. In *R v M* [2009] EWCA Crim 618 the defendant appealed against his conviction for assault. The complainant, a neighbour, alleged that the defendant had sexually assaulted her in her flat. The defendant denied entering the complainant's flat on the relevant occasion and having any physical contact with the complainant. The defence sought leave to cross-examine the complainant about an allegation of rape against another person some years previously. There was evidence that she had done so in support of her application to be re-housed. She had asked the police not to investigate the allegation for fear of reprisals.

The trial judge refused the defence application for leave to cross-examine her as to this incident. The Court of Appeal allowed the appeal and quashed the conviction on the grounds that the previous complaint of sexual assault, which was said to be false, was not about her sexual behaviour but about her veracity. The judge should have concluded that s 41 was not applicable to the facts. The defendant had been deprived of a potentially valuable line of cross-examination.

The concept of sexual behaviour includes allegations of improper sexual activity with children who may be too young and lack the mental capacity to understand matters of a sexual nature. The lack of perception on the part of the victim does not alter that fact. In *R v E (Dennis Andrew)* [2004] EWCA Crim 1313 the Court of Appeal so held with regard to charges of indecent assault committed on two children, aged six and four. In addition the court upheld the ruling by the trial judge to the effect that the defence did not establish a proper evidential basis for making unsubstantiated allegations by the victims of sexual abuse against a large number of other persons some fifteen months after the incidents involving the defendant. None of the later allegations had been investigated and there was no evidence that they were untrue. In similar vein, in *R v All-Hilly* [2014]2 Cr App R 33, the Court of Appeal concluded that the trial judge had not erred in refusing defence counsel to cross-examine the complainant about previous allegations of sexual abuse by three men. Although previous false allegations of sexual abuse by parties other than the defendant may be construed as falling outside the definition of sexual behaviour, the defence is required to establish a proper evidential basis for such allegations, namely (a) that such allegations were made by the complainant and (b) they were false. In *R v All-Hilly*, on a charge of rape, the complainant in an ABE video interview alleged that she suffered historic sexual assaults on four previous occasions by three men. In two of these she reported the matter to the police but did not pursue them. In two other allegations she failed to report them to the police. Defence counsel was refused permission to cross-examine her as to these complaints. He was convicted and his appeal was dismissed. The Court of Appeal dismissed his appeal on the ground that the circumstances did not lead to an inference that the complaints were false. Failure to pursue a complaint did not inevitably mean that the complaint was false. An element of flexibility and understanding is required to be deployed on behalf of those who make allegations of sexual assault. A closer examination of the circumstances is required. The fact that complaints had been raised and not pursued more than once did not inexorably lead to the conclusion that they were false.

JUDGMENT

'The mere fact that a complaint is raised and is not pursued does not necessarily mean that a complaint is false. Courts should be ready to deploy a degree of understanding of the position of those who have made sexual allegations. Failure to pursue the complaint does not of necessity show that it is untrue. A rather closer examination of the circumstances is required. None of the individual matters raised begins to provide a basis for an inference or conclusion of a false complaint. In those circumstances there is no advantage to the defendant in seeking to rely on an accumulation of negative results. The fact that there is no instance which begins to show falsity cannot be converted into evidence of falsity by the fact that complaints have been raised more than once.'

(Treacy LJ)

In *R v Garaxo* [2005] EWCA Crim 1170, the Court of Appeal decided that the trial judge had incorrectly evaluated the significance of the two items of evidence that constituted the sexual behaviour of the complainant. On a charge of sexual assault, denied by the defendant, defence counsel wished to cross-examine the complainant about two previous incidents involving complaints about sexual assaults made against other men that were alleged to be false. The first involved a police report requested by the complainant for the 'Social' and in the second the complainant refused to co-operate with the police. The trial judge refused permission for defence counsel to cross-examine the complainant about these incidents. Following conviction the appeal was allowed on the ground that, once a proper evidential foundation for cross-examination had been established, it was wrong for the judge to prevent the defence from asking questions that may entitle the jury to draw an inference that the victim had fabricated her complaints.

Condition 3 Relevant issue

The evidence that the cross-examiner wishes to adduce or the questioning of the cross-examiner is required to relate to a relevant issue in the case. The test regarding a relevant issue is laid down in s 42(1) as an 'issue falling to be proved by the prosecution or defence in the trial'. This question requires a ruling by the judge as to the connection between the sexual behaviour of the complainant and the elements of the charge or defence. On the other hand, if the purpose of the defence is to impugn the credibility of the complainant, this would be outside the purview of s 42(1). Section 41(4) declares as follows:

SECTION

'No evidence or question shall be regarded as relating to a relevant issue if it appears to the court to be reasonable to assume that the purpose (or main purpose) for which it would be adduced or asked is to establish or elicit material for impugning the credibility of the complainant as a witness.'

In one sense any evidence that directly challenges the evidence of the complainant, or seeks to demonstrate a malicious motive, involves an attack on the credibility of the complainant. But note that the subsection refers to the 'purpose or main purpose'. This assumes that there may be more than one main purpose surrounding the defence counsel's application for leave, and if a main purpose is to impugn the credulity of the complainant, the application may be refused. This involves a question of law for the judge to decide how far the matter will be relevant to a fact in issue. The more general the allegation of sexual activity, the more remote the issue is likely to be. In *R v White* [2004] All ER (D) 103 the Court of Appeal decided that a general allegation that the complainant was a prostitute will be too vague to be directly related to the facts in issue of consent to sexual activity and is more likely to amount to evidence of impugning the credibility of the complainant.

In *R v Martin (Durwayne)* [2004] EWCA Crim 916 the Court of Appeal, in construing s 41(4) of the 1999 Act, decided that if one of the purposes for cross-examining the complainant as to her sexual behaviour, after a proper evidential foundation had been laid, was to add credibility to the defence case that he is innocent, then the restriction within s 41(4) may not operate, notwithstanding that a purpose of the cross-examination involves impugning the credit of the complainant. On a charge of indecent assault the defendant alleged that the complainant fabricated her allegation of indecent assault (non-consensual oral sex) because he rejected her advances for full sexual intercourse. The trial judge refused the defence application for leave to question the complainant about her instigating an act of oral sex on him. He appealed following a conviction and the Court of Appeal decided that the judge had erred and decided that one purpose of the questioning was to impugn her credibility but another purpose was to strengthen his case. On balance the judge should have allowed the questioning of the complainant.

JUDGMENT

> 'We consider that one purpose of the proposed questions clearly was to impugn the credibility of the complainant. However, it can also realistically be said that one purpose was to strengthen the defence case. We have come to the conclusion that the learned judge's ruling was wrong. The learned judge should, in our view, have permitted the questions desired. They were not questions which went solely to the question of credibility and it was for the judge to decide whether a refusal of leave might have the result of rendering unsafe a conclusion of the jury on any relevant issue in the case.'
>
> (Crane J)

In *R v Winter* [2008] EWCA Crim 3, on an indecent assault charge, the court decided that a declaration by the complainant that she had a loving and devoted relationship with her partner was not to be adjudged a lie merely because she also had a consensual sexual relationship with another man. In any event, if such statement was false, its relevance to the charge was so insignificant that the purpose is capable of being construed as an attempt to impugn the credibility of the complainant. In this case the complainant testified as to an incident involving indecent assault. The defendant unsuccessfully sought leave from the judge to cross-examine her on the issue that, despite telling the police that she had a long and devoted relationship with her partner, she also had a consensual sexual relationship with another man. On conviction, the Court of Appeal dismissed the appeal on the ground that the statement was not necessarily a lie. The effect was that the judge had correctly refused to grant leave to cross-examine her as the questions fell within s 41(4) of the 1999 Act.

Whereas in *R v P (R)* [2014] 1 WLR 3058, the Court of Appeal decided that the trial judge had erred in refusing to allow defence counsel to cross-examine the complainant as to her conduct in accepting the defendant's financial support and emotional succour concerning an abortion at a time when she was a young person. The court decided that such questioning was relevant because it contradicted the complainant's contention that she viewed him with distaste following the alleged sexual abuse by him and showed that the complainant may have confided in him on matters of an intimate nature. In this case, the defendant was charged with six counts of indecent assault on his stepdaughter (R) dating back to when she was eleven years old. The complainant testified to the effect that she viewed the defendant with distaste following the assaults. Defence counsel was refused leave to cross-examine her as to the support, both emotional and financial, provided by the defendant in procuring an abortion for the complainant. Following his convictions the defendant appealed. The Court of Appeal decided that the trial judge made an incorrect ruling for the questioning was relevant to a defence issue at the trial and, in any event, was not related to the complainant's sexual behaviour. However, on the facts of the case the convictions were safe.

JUDGMENT

'It seems to us that the initial inquiry must be as to the relevance of the proposed questions relating to the abortion. Relevance to an issue in the case is always a pre-condition to the admissibility of any evidence, whatever more technical rules may intervene thereafter with regard to particular types of evidence. In our judgment, this proposed questioning was relevant to the issue before the jury. It did tend to detract from her account that she viewed the defendant with distaste, because of his improper conduct, notwithstanding her continued dealings with him on less personal and intimate matters.

Were the proposed questions "about any sexual behaviour of the complainant"? It does not seem to us that to ask a person about whether someone has assisted her in and about the obtaining of a lawful abortion can be said to be a question 'about' sexual behaviour. Self-evidently, it is not. The fact that an abortion cannot result unless there has been antecedent sexual behaviour does not make the question about the fact of the abortion a question "about" any sexual behaviour. As Mitting J asked of counsel in argument, would a question asked of a mother whether she had been assisted by X during a pregnancy, when the foetus was giving signs of distress, be a question about sexual behaviour? The answer, we think, must be surely not. We recognise that a question about an abortion might in some cases be a way of asking about a person's sexual history, in which case it would be a question "about" sexual behaviour, but we do not see that a question asked of a formerly pregnant woman about events surrounding a termination of pregnancy would in itself amount to a question about sexual behaviour.'

(McCombe LJ)

Condition 4 Lifting the shield

The judge is required to grant leave to the cross-examiner only if the tests laid down in s 41(2) have been satisfied. Section 41(2) creates a two-tier test for the granting of leave to cross-examine the complainant about his or her sexual behaviour.

- Section 41(2)(b) enacts that 'a refusal of leave might have the result of rendering unsafe' the verdict of the jury on any relevant issue. The test here for the judge to decide is whether a refusal to admit the evidence or allow the questioning of the complainant would be to prevent the jurors from taking into account relevant material that may lead them to a different conclusion.
- Section 41(2)(a) refers to the relevant issue in sub-ss (3) and (5) of the Act.

Section 41(3)(a)–(c) of the 1999 Act identifies the tests as to whether the evidence or questions raised by the cross-examiner relate to a relevant issue in the trial.

Section 41(3) enacts as follows:

SECTION

'This subsection applies if the evidence or question relates to a relevant issue in the case and either –

(a) that issue is not an issue of consent; or
(b) it is an issue of consent and the sexual behaviour of the complainant to which the evidence or question relates is alleged to have taken place at or about the same time as the event which is the subject matter of the charge against the accused; or
(c) it is an issue of consent and the sexual behaviour of the complainant to which the evidence or question relates is alleged to have been, in any respect, so similar –
  (i) to any sexual behaviour of the complainant which (according to evidence adduced or to be adduced by or on behalf of the accused) took place as part of the event which is the subject matter of the charge against the accused, or
  (ii) to any other sexual behaviour of the complainant which (according to such evidence) took place at or about the same time as the event, that the similarity cannot reasonably be explained as a coincidence.'

Section 41(3)(a) of the 1999 Act

The test in s 41(3)(a) of the Act (see above) isolates and identifies the relevant issue as one that does not involve 'consent'.

The issue of consent is defined in s 42(1)(b) as 'any issue whether the complainant in fact consented to the conduct constituting the offence with which the accused is charged (and accordingly does not include any issue as to the *belief of the accused that the complainant so consented*)'. Thus, the 'issue of consent' involves an issue of factual consent and is distinct from the defendant's mistaken belief that the complainant consented. It would include a reasonable belief in consent or that the complainant was biased against the defendant and wanted to get even with him. Accordingly, an allegation of mistaken identity on the part of the complainant does not involve an issue of consent. Likewise, an allegation of a false complaint that the defendant had raped the complainant is not an issue of consent. In *R v F* [2005] 1 WLR 2848, on charges of rape of the defendant's stepdaughter between the ages of seven and sixteen, the defendant alleged that the complainant fabricated the allegations. The parties lived together as adults and shared a full consensual sexual relationship. The defendant alleged that the complainant was motivated by a desire for revenge following his decision to end the relationship. The trial judge refused to allow the defendant to adduce evidence or ask questions about the fact that the complainant had made sexually explicit video recordings during the course of their relationship. The Court of Appeal allowed the appeal on the ground that the evidence was relevant under s 41(3)(a) of the 1999 Act. The court also decided that once the criteria for leave were satisfied the judge does not have a discretion to refuse to admit the evidence:

JUDGMENT

'If the complainant enjoyed a full and happy adult relationship with the appellant, neither being raped nor dutifully submitting to his dominant control, although not amounting to positive proof that she had not been abused as a child, the relationship would have called into question how she could ever have brought herself into enthusiastic participation for a number of years with her former abuser.'

(Judge LJ)

In *R v Mokrecovas* [2002] 1 Cr App R 20 the charge was rape and the issue was consent, but the defendant wanted to cross-examine the complainant under s 41(3)(a) because she lied as to her allegation that she did not consent in order to mitigate the effects of being drunk and staying out late without permission when she returned to her home and was faced by her angry parents. The defendant wished to adduce evidence that the complainant had twice had intercourse with the defendant's brother within twelve hours of the disputed incident. The Court of Appeal decided that the trial judge had correctly exercised his discretion in refusing leave to cross-examine the complainant as to her sexual behaviour. There was no reason why the complainant could not have been cross-examined as to where she stayed that evening:

JUDGMENT

'We ask ourselves to what extent, if at all, is the defendant inhibited in suggesting that there was a motive for the complainant to tell untruths to her parents? How would the ability of the defendant to argue that the complainant had a motive to lie be improved if she were to be allowed to be cross-examined to suggest that the brother had had sexual intercourse on two previous occasions? In our judgment, the position of the defendant would not be improved in any way. The refusal of leave to ask the specific questions that Mr Owen wishes to ask will not result in any lack of safety or unfairness in the proceedings or in any relevant issue not being explored.'

(Lord Woolf CJ)

Section 41(3)(b) of the 1999 Act

Section 41(3(b) of the 1999 Act involves two criteria – the issue of *de facto* consent and the direct link in time to which the sexual behaviour of the complainant is related to the subject matter of the charge ('at or about the same time as the subject of the charge'). The explanatory notes accompanying the Act regard the expression 'at or about the same time' as used in the subsection as meaning not much longer than twenty-four hours before or after the alleged offence. This introduces an informal *res gestae* principle in interpreting the subsection. This subsection may include the complainant initiating consensual sexual activity with the defendant or third parties twenty-four hours before or after the circumstances constituting the charge in order to support the defence of consent.

Lord Steyn in *R v A* [2001] UKHL 25 said:

JUDGMENT

'An example covered by this provision would be where it is alleged that the complainant invited the accused to have sexual intercourse with her earlier in the evening. . . . Section 41(3)(b) acknowledges by its own terms that previous sexual experience between a complainant and an accused may be relevant but then restricts the admission of such evidence by an extraordinarily narrow temporal restriction.'

Section 41(3)(c) of the 1999 Act

Section 41(3)(c)(i) involves an allegation by the cross-examiner of *de facto* consent on the part of the complainant and a similarity in the sexual behaviour of the complainant as part of the event, the subject matter of the charge. Section 41(3)(c)(ii) involves consent and whether the complainant's sexual behaviour was similar to other sexual behaviour 'at or about the same time' (twenty-four hours before or after the event constituting the charge) such that the similarity cannot reasonably be explained as coincidence. Lord Steyn in *R v A* [2001] UKHL 25 provides an example, thus:

JUDGMENT

'An example [of the third gateway] would be the case where the complainant says that the accused raped her; the accused says that the complainant consented and then after the act of intercourse tried to blackmail him by alleging rape; and the defence now wishes to ask the complainant whether on a previous occasion she similarly tried to blackmail the accused.'

In *R v T (Abdul)* [2004] EWCA Crim 1220, the defendant was charged with rape that was alleged to have occurred on a triangular climbing frame in the children's play area in a park. The defence was consent. The Court of Appeal decided that the trial judge had erred in failing to allow the defendant to adduce evidence that the same parties had consensual sexual relations on the same triangular climbing frame a few weeks earlier. The striking similarities between the previous consensual acts of sexual intercourse and the alleged acts with which the defendants was charged were:

- sexual intercourse within the climbing frame, in a children's area and in the same park;
- the sexual positions taken up by the parties involved the complainant standing up and being penetrated from behind;
- oral sex had taken place.

JUDGMENT

'The effect of the ruling [by the judge] was to exclude evidence in relation to which there was no dispute, that the appellant and the complainant had had sexual intercourse within the climbing frame, consensually, approximately three to four weeks before 18 July. It excluded evidence which the appellant wished to give, which was that, on the occasion of that sexual intercourse, within the climbing frame, the same positions had been taken up, that is to say that the complainant and the appellant were standing up and that the sexual intercourse was taking place from the back. It also excluded what was in fact common ground that the oral sex, by consent, had taken place during the relationship. It is now accepted that the evidence relating to previous sexual intercourse within the climbing frame was similar within the wording of section 41(3)(c)(i). As it would seem to us, it is clearly arguable that the adoption of the same respective positions on that occasion as on the occasion the subject of the trial would also be similar within section 41(3)(c)(i). Indeed it is arguable that the consenting oral sex should be admissible, if not because it is similar, at least, in order to avoid there being an unfair trial.'

(Waller LJ)

In the leading case *R v A* [2001] 3 All ER 1, the House of Lords reviewed the provisions enacted in ss 41–43 of the Youth Justice and Criminal Evidence Act 1999 and considered the extent to which these provisions are consistent with the Human Rights Act 1998, in an attempt to seek compliance with the convention. In this case the charge was rape. The accused person's defence was consent, or alternatively, belief in consent. The defendant and the complainant had a consensual sexual relationship about three weeks before the circumstances that constituted the alleged rape. The defendant was prevented from cross-examining the complainant and adducing evidence as to her sexual behaviour. The House of Lords decided the following:

- The consensual sexual relationship between the defendant and the complainant three weeks before the alleged rape was admissible as to the belief in consent (within s 41(3)(a)) but not relevant as to the issue of consent itself.
- Further, a prior consensual sexual relationship between the defendant and the complainant is not irrelevant to the issue of consent, the subject matter of the proceedings.
- In addition, the test of admissibility under s 41(3)(c) is whether the evidence is so relevant to the issue of consent that to exclude it would endanger the fairness of the trial.
- Finally, the defendant is not allowed to cross-examine the complainant as to his or her sexual behaviour simply by raising the issue of belief in consent and consent as defences. Instead the judge is required to be satisfied that there is a proper foundation for pursuing leave to adduce such evidence or question the complainant.

JUDGMENT

'As a matter of common sense, a prior sexual relationship between the complainant and the accused may, depending on the circumstances, be relevant to the issue of consent. It is a species of prospectant evidence which may throw light on the complainant's state of mind. It cannot, of course, prove that she consented on the occasion in question. Relevance and sufficiency of proof are different things. The fact that the accused a week before the alleged murder threatened to kill the deceased does not prove an intent to kill on the day in question. But it is logically relevant to that issue. After all, to be relevant the evidence need merely have some tendency in logic and common sense to advance the proposition in issue. It is true that each decision to engage in sexual activity is always made afresh. On the other hand, the mind does not usually blot out all memories. What one has been engaged on in the past may influence what choice one makes on a future occasion. Accordingly, a prior relationship between a complainant and an accused may sometimes be relevant to what decision was made on a particular occasion.

'In order to assess whether s 41 of the 1999 Act is incompatible with the convention right to a fair trial, it is necessary to consider what evidence it excludes. The mere fact that it excludes some relevant evidence would not by itself amount to a breach of the fair trial guarantee. On the other hand, if the impact of s 41 is to deny the right to the accused in a significant range of cases from putting forward full and complete defences it may amount to a breach.

'It is possible under s 3 of the [Human Rights] 1998 Act to read s 41 of the 1999 Act, and in particular s 41(3)(c), as subject to the implied provision that evidence or questioning which is required to ensure a fair trial under Art 6 of the convention should not be treated as inadmissible. The result of such a reading would be that sometimes logically relevant sexual experiences between a complainant and an accused may be admitted under s 41(3)(c). On the other hand, there will be cases where previous sexual experience between a complainant and an accused will be irrelevant, e.g. an isolated episode distant in time and circumstances. Where the line is to be drawn must be left to the judgment of trial judges. On this basis a declaration on incompatibility can be avoided. If this approach is adopted, s 41 will have achieved a major part of its objective but its excessive reach will have been attenuated in accordance with the will of Parliament as reflected in s 3 of the 1998 Act. That is the approach I will adopt.

It is of supreme importance that the effect of the speeches today should be clear to trial judges who have to deal with problems of the admissibility of questioning and evidence on alleged prior sexual experience between an accused and a complainant. The effect of the decision today is that under s 41(3)(c) of the 1999 Act, construed where necessary by applying the interpretative obligation under s 3 of the 1998 Act, and due regard always being paid to the importance of seeking to protect the complainant from indignity and from humiliating questions, *the test of admissibility is whether the evidence (and questioning in relation to it) is nevertheless so relevant to the issue of consent that to exclude it would endanger the fairness of the trial under Art 6 of the convention. If this test is satisfied the evidence should not be excluded.'* (emphasis added)

(Lord Steyn)

Section 43 of the 1999 Act provides that where a party wishes to make an application under s 41 for leave to adduce evidence or question the complainant about his or her sexual behaviour, the application is required to be heard in private and in the absence of the complainant.

The court is then required to state in open court, but in the absence of the jury, its reasons for giving or refusing leave. If leave is granted, the court is required to direct the extent to which evidence may be adduced or questions asked.

Section 41(5) deals with evidence in rebuttal where the prosecution raises evidence of the sexual behaviour of the complainant. The evidence or question 'would go no further than is necessary to enable the evidence adduced by the prosecution to be rebutted or explained by or on behalf of the accused'.

The policy behind s 41(5) is that if the prosecution makes the decision to adduce evidence of the complainant's sexual behaviour as part of its case, the court is required to decide whether the defendant would be entitled to adduce evidence that would go no further than to rebut or explain the prosecution evidence. In *R v F* (2005) (see earlier) the court decided that if the rebutting evidence is relevant to a fact in issue in the trial and is therefore *prima facie* admissible, the judge does not have a discretion to exclude the evidence or to limit parts that may be heard in the interests of a fair trial.

In *R v Hamadi* [2007] EWCA Crim 3048, the Court of Appeal decided that the expression 'evidence adduced by the prosecution' within s 41(5) means evidence placed before the jury by a prosecution witness as part of the evidence in chief and of other witnesses in the course of cross-examination by the prosecution. The phrase did not extend to evidence given by prosecution witnesses under cross-examination. In other words, the expression accords to a deliberate and positive effort on the part of the prosecution to include the evidence as part of its case. In this case, on a charge of rape, the complainant's assertion under cross-examination that she had always been faithful to her partner constituted evidence of sexual behaviour but did not amount to evidence adduced by the prosecution within s 41(5). Accordingly, the judge was correct in exercising his discretion to refuse the defence to call rebutting evidence from a witness about a sexual relationship he had with the complainant.

JUDGMENT

'The starting point for the discussion is the natural meaning of the words used in subsection 5. In our view the expression "evidence adduced by the prosecution" naturally refers in this context to evidence placed before the jury by prosecution witnesses in the course of their evidence in chief and by other witnesses in the course of cross-examination by prosecuting counsel. It does not naturally extend to evidence obtained from prosecution witnesses by the defence in the course of cross-examination. We are unable to accept the submission that it extends to all evidence given by the prosecution witnesses, however it comes to be given.'

(Moore-Bick LJ)

In *R v Mitchell (Raymond)* [2004] EWCA Crim 3206, the Court of Appeal decided that on a charge of rape where the prosecution led evidence that the complainant was a prostitute but was no longer a prostitute on the night in question, which was disputed by the defence, the judge should have granted leave for the defence to cross-examine the complainant on this issue. The defence case was that she was actively engaged in prostitution minutes before the incident, they had consensual sex for which he paid and the prosecution had conceded the relevance of the issue under s 41(3)(c).

By virtue of s 41(6) the evidence or questions that may be put by the defence for the purposes of s 41(3) and (5) must relate to specific instances or questions of the alleged sexual behaviour of the complainant. The policy here is to restrict the line of questioning by the defence and not to permit him to simply blacken the character of the complainant.

KEY FACTS

Cross-examination of the complainant in sexual offences cases

- 'Sexual offences' – see s 62 of the Youth Justice and Criminal Evidence Act 1999
- General prohibition on evidence of sexual behaviour – s 41(1) of the 1999 Act
- Sexual behaviour – s 42(1)(c)
- No leave to discredit witness – s 41(4)
- Occasions to grant leave – s 41(3)(a), (b) and (c)
- Rebutting evidence of sexual behaviour – s 41(5)
- Permitted evidence or questions must relate to specific instances – s 41(6)
- Section 43 lays down the procedure for dealing with applications for leave.

ACTIVITY

Self-test questions

1. What constitutes sexual behaviour for the purposes of s 41 of the Youth Justice and Criminal Evidence Act 1999? Is there a need for young children and persons of defective intellect to understand the meaning of sexual behaviour?
2. On a charge for a sexual offence, would the defence be entitled to question the complainant about allegedly false allegations of a sexual nature made against other persons?
3. In what circumstances may the judge grant leave to the defence to adduce evidence or cross-examine the complainant about her sexual behaviour?
4. What is the procedure governing the defence application for leave from the judge to cross-examine the complainant about her sexual behaviour?

6.3.2 Chapter II – protection from cross-examination by the accused in person

Sections 34–39 of the Youth Justice and Criminal Evidence Act 1999 introduce a number of provisions designed to ensure that the defendant will not personally cross-examine the witness. In three types of case the defendant is not entitled to cross-examine in person certain witnesses. Section 34 of the 1999 Act enacts that in respect of sexual offences (as defined in s 62) the defendant is not entitled to cross-examine in person the complainant in respect of that or any other offence. Section 35 prohibits the defendant from cross-examining in person a protected witness (as defined in s 35(2)) on a charge as laid down in s 35(3). Section 36 creates a residual category of cases, namely occasions where the prosecutor makes the application or the court of its own motion raises the issue and makes the direction. The test to be satisfied is laid down in s 36(2) and the factors to be taken into consideration are specified in s 36(3) of the 1999 Act.

Where the accused is prevented from cross-examining a witness in person, the court must invite the accused to arrange for legal representation and notify the court within a specified time. If at the relevant time no legal representation is arranged, the court must consider whether in the interests of justice to appoint a qualified legal representative to act on behalf of the accused to cross-examine the witness: see s 38 of the 1999 Act.

Section 39 of the 1999 Act declares that where the accused is prevented from cross-examining a witness, the judge is required to give the jury a warning to ensure that the accused is not prejudiced by:

- any inferences that might be drawn from the fact that the accused was prevented from cross-examining the witness in person;
- the fact that the cross-examination was carried out by a legal representative appointed by the court.

6.3.3 Omission to cross-examine

As a general rule, if a party disagrees with, or does not wish to admit, a witness's version of events, they should test the witness's story under cross-examination.

Failure to cross-examine the witness generally will be taken to be acceptance of the witness's account and the party who did not call the witness will not be allowed:

- to attack the witness's testimony in his closing speech;
- to put forward explanations of the issue.

In *R v Bircham* [1972] Crim LR 430, defence counsel had failed to cross-examine the co-defendant (who testified) and prosecution witnesses on the issue of whether they were the perpetrators of the crime. He had attempted to make this suggestion in his closing speech when the judge intervened and disallowed him. The Court of Appeal decided that the judge was entitled to intervene in the interests of justice.

Occasionally, situations arise where an omission to cross-examine a witness on an issue was caused by inadvertence on the part of counsel. The advocate simply forgets to raise the issue. This difficulty may be overcome by having the witness recalled to the witness box in the exercise of the judge's discretion and in the interests of justice.

However, in exceptional circumstances a party may consciously refrain from asking a witness questions under cross-examination and, at the same time, dispute or disagree with the assertions made by the witness. These are occasions when the witness's story is incredible in itself and the advocate tactically omits to question the witness; likewise, where counsel indicates that they are refraining from asking questions for the convenience of the witness but does not accept the witness's assertions; for example young children in contentious family matters, or a distraught mother testifying as to the achievements of her deceased son.

6.3.4 Distinction between cross-examination as to issue and credit

A distinction is drawn by the courts as to whether a question asked by a cross-examiner relates to a fact in issue or the credit of a witness. The effect of the distinction is that in the former case, i.e. questions relating to an issue, the answers of witnesses are not final and contradictory evidence may be adduced by the cross-examiner. Such contradictory answers are subject to the rules of admissibility. A fact in issue is one that relates directly to the issue of guilt or innocence in criminal cases or to liability in civil cases, whereas the answers to questions related to the credit of the witness are final, subject to a limited number of exceptions. The credibility of a witness's testimony depends on their knowledge of the facts, their intelligence, integrity and veracity. All questions that tend to expose the errors, omissions, inconsistencies and exaggerations of the witness's story relate to their credit. In the civil case *Hobbs v Tinling* [1929] 2 KB 1, Scrutton LJ explained the nature of cross-examination as to credit, thus:

JUDGMENT

'When a witness has given evidence material to the issues in the case you can cross-examine him on matters not directly material to the case in order to ask the jury to infer from his answers that he is not worthy of belief, not a credible person, and therefore that they should not accept his answers on questions material to the case as true. This is cross-examination as to his credibility, commonly called cross-examination to credit. But as it is on matters not directly material to the case, the party cross-examining is not allowed to call evidence in chief to contradict his answers. To permit this would involve the Court in an interminable series of controversies not directly material to the case on alleged facts of which the witness had no notice when he came into Court, and which he or the party calling him might not be prepared without notice to meet.

'If the jury, hearing the answers given by the witness, do not believe him they are entitled to do so, and to use the view thus obtained as to his credibility in rejecting answers given by him on matters material to the case. But rejecting his denials does not prove the fact he denies, of which there is, and can be, no other evidence. It only destroys his credibility in respect of other evidence.'

Sankey LJ in *Hobbs v Tinling* expressed his opinion as to when such questions may be treated as related to credit. These principles relate to both civil and criminal cases:

JUDGMENT

'The Court can always exercise its discretion to decide whether a question as to credit is one which the witness should be compelled to answer, and in the exercise of its discretion the Court should have regard to the following considerations:

(1) Such questions are proper if they are of such a nature that the truth of the imputation conveyed by them would seriously affect the opinion of the Court as to the credibility of the witness on the matter to which he testifies.
(2) Such questions are improper if the imputation which they convey relates to matters so remote in time, or of such a character, that the truth of the imputation would not affect, or would affect in a slight degree, the opinion of the Court as to the credibility of the witness on the matter to which he testifies.
(3) Such questions are improper if there is a great disproportion between the importance of the imputation made against the witness's character and the importance of his evidence.'

The question of whether or not a fact is relevant to a fact in issue has important implications for the parties in terms of the admissibility of the evidence. Deciding relevance is a difficult question for the judge to decide.

CASE EXAMPLE

R v Funderburk [1990] 1 WLR 587

The defendant was charged with unlawful sexual intercourse with a girl under the age of thirteen. The victim gave a detailed description of the alleged act of intercourse including, during the incident, the loss of her virginity. The trial judge refused to allow the defendant to put questions to the complainant in cross-examination about an allegation that she told a potential witness that she (the complainant) had had intercourse with other men. The trial judge also prevented the defendant from calling rebutting evidence, namely the witness who heard the story. On conviction the defendant appealed, claiming that the questions related to the facts in issue and not the credit of the witness. The court allowed the appeal and quashed the conviction. The question was Intimately connected with the facts in issue:

JUDGMENT

'Having heard a graphic account from the child's evidence in chief as to how she had lost her virginity, the jury might reasonably have wished to reappraise her evidence and her credibility if they had heard that on other occasions she had spoken of experiences which, if true, would indicate that she could not have been a virgin at the time of the incident she so vividly described. Her standing as a witness might have been reduced. Unchallenged, the descriptive details could give the account the stamp of truth; detail often adds verisimilitude, and it seems to us that it certainly would have here. If a detail of such significance is successfully challenged it can destroy both the account and the credit of the witness who gave it. Therefore, it is submitted that this is not a challenge which goes merely to credit but that the disputed questions go directly to the issue and not merely to a collateral fact.'

(Henry J)

CASE EXAMPLE

R v Edwards [1991] 2 All ER 266

The defendant was charged with robbery. The prosecution evidence consisted of police officers who testified that the defendant made oral admissions. The defendant refused to sign the interview notes, claiming that the alleged admissions were fabrications. The defendant's counsel was prevented but wished to cross-examine the officers in respect of evidence given in a previous trial where the issue was again alleged fabrication of oral admissions. These defendants were acquitted, suggesting that the jury disbelieved the officers. On conviction the accused appealed. The court dismissed the appeal on the ground that the subject matter of the cross-examination was not sufficiently relevant to the officers' credibility (collateral issue) to be admitted under an exception. The significant issue was that the court decided that the matter was not directly related to issue but credit:

JUDGMENT

'The test is primarily one of relevance, and this is so whether one is considering evidence in chief or questions in cross-examination. To be admissible questions must be relevant to the issue before the court. Issues are of varying degrees of relevance or importance. A distinction has to be drawn between, on the one hand, the issue in the case upon which the jury will be pronouncing their verdict and, on the other hand, collateral issues of which the credibility of the witnesses maybe one. Generally speaking, questions may be put to a witness as to any improper conduct of which he may have been guilty, for the purpose of testing his credit.

'The limits to such questioning were defined by Sankey LJ in *Hobbs v Tinling & Co* [1929] 2 KB 1:

"The court can always exercise its discretion to decide whether a question as to credit is one which the witness should be compelled to answer . . . in the exercise of its discretion the court should have regard to the following considerations: (1) Such questions are proper if they are of such a nature that the truth of the imputation conveyed by them would seriously affect the opinion of the court as to the credibility of the witness on the matter to which he testifies. (2) Such questions are improper if the imputation which they convey relates to matters so remote in time, or of such a character, that the truth of the imputation would not affect, or would affect in a slight degree, the opinion of the court as to the credibility of the witness on the matter to which he testifies. (3) Such questions are improper if there is a great disproportion between the importance of the imputation made against the witness's character and the importance of his evidence."

'The distinction between the issue in the case and matters collateral to the issue is often difficult to draw, but it is of considerable importance. Where cross-examination is directed at collateral issues such as the credibility of the witness, as a rule the answers of the witness are final and evidence to contradict them will not be permitted.

'. . . The acquittal of a defendant in case A, where the prosecution case depended largely or entirely upon the evidence of a police officer, does not normally render that officer liable to cross-examination as to credit in case B. But where a police officer who has allegedly fabricated an admission in case B, has also given evidence of an admission in case A, where there was an acquittal by virtue of which his evidence is demonstrated to have been disbelieved, it is proper that the jury in case B should be made aware of that fact. However, where the acquittal in case A does not necessarily indicate that the jury disbelieved the officer, such cross-examination should not be allowed. In such a case the verdict of not guilty may mean no more than that the jury entertained some doubt about the prosecution case, not necessarily that they believed any witness was lying.

'That leaves the second question, namely, whether it would have been proper to allow the defence to call evidence to contradict any answers given by the police officers in cross-examination, in the unlikely event of those officers giving answers unfavourable to the defence? In our judgment this questioning would have been as to credit alone, that is to say, on a collateral issue. It would not have fallen within any exception to the general rule.'

(Lord Lane CJ)

CASE EXAMPLE

R v Nagrecha [1997] 2 Cr App R 401

The charge was indecent assault. It was alleged that the defendant, the complainant's employer, had indecently assaulted her on the first and only occasion that she worked for him. The defendant denied the assault. In cross-examination the complainant denied making unsubstantiated allegations of sexual impropriety against other men (and a previous employer). The trial judge refused to allow defence counsel to call rebutting evidence. On conviction the defendant appealed. The court allowed the appeal and quashed the conviction. The judge had erred in refusing to allow the rebutting evidence for the question related to issue. The jury may well have taken a different view of the complainant's testimony, including the alleged indecent assault:

JUDGMENT

'In our judgment, the answer to this appeal is, in the light of the authorities to which we have referred, that the judge ought to have permitted the defence to lead evidence from Mr Lee in the light of the complainant's denial in cross-examination. Such evidence went not merely to credit, but to the heart of the case, in that it bore on the crucial issue as to whether or not there had been any indecent assault. As to that matter, only the complainant and the appellant were able to give evidence. In our judgment, that being so, the learned judge ought to have permitted the evidence to be called because it might well have led the jury to take a different view of the complainant's evidence.'

(Rose LJ)

6.3.5 Sections 4 and 5 of the Criminal Procedure Act 1865 (previous inconsistent statements)

If a witness is challenged by the cross-examiner on the accuracy of their testimony and the witness repents, agrees with the cross-examiner and changes their testimony, this may constitute evidence on which the tribunal of fact may rely. In other words, the cross-examiner will succeed in getting the witness to testify in a way favourable to such party and the testimony may amount to evidence of the facts stated.

However, where the witness does not repent or does not admit making a contradictory statement, and the cross-examiner wishes to contradict the witness in respect of a matter in issue (as distinct from credit) by the witness's previous statement, they are entitled to utilise the provisions created by ss 4 and 5 of the Criminal Procedure Act 1865. This Act is applicable to both civil and criminal cases.

Section 4 of the Criminal Procedure Act 1865 provides:

SECTION

'If a witness, upon cross-examination as to a former statement made by him relative to the subject matter of the indictment or proceeding, and inconsistent with his testimony, does not distinctly admit that he has made such statement, proof may be given that he did in fact make it; but before such proof can be given the circumstances of the supposed statement, sufficient to designate the particular occasion, must be mentioned to the witness, and he must be asked whether or not he has made such statement.'

It is believed that this section is applicable in respect of a previous oral statement made by the witness and contradictory to their testimony. The subject matter of contradiction is required to relate to a fact in issue. The section refers to the witness 'not distinctly admitting' the statement. This is a broad expression that covers a variety of situations ranging from a denial of the statement to evasive or vague or equivocal answers, such that the witness does not remember the events or indeed silence. The procedure that has to be adopted by the cross-examiner prior to contradiction is that the circumstances concerning the particular occasion must be put to the witness.

Section 5 of the Criminal Procedure Act 1865 provides:

SECTION

'A witness may be cross-examined as to previous statements made by him in writing or reduced into writing relative to the subject matter of the indictment or proceeding, without such writing being shown to him; but if it is intended to contradict such witness by the writing, his attention must, before such contradictory proof can be given, be called to those parts of the writing which are to be used for the purpose of so contradicting him; provided always that it shall be competent for the judge at any time during the trial to require production of the writing for his inspection, and he may thereupon make such use of it for the purposes of the trial as he may think fit.'

The section deals with a statement of the witness in writing that is contradictory to his testimony. The section envisages two stages when the cross-examiner may resort to a previous inconsistent statement made by a witness in writing.

First, the cross-examiner may wish to retain the element of surprise, i.e. they may not wish to show that witness the previous statement. In order to achieve this tactical manoeuvre, they are entitled to cross-examine the witness about the statement without contradicting the witness. In other words, the cross-examiner will be entitled to ask questions about the authorship of an inconsistent statement and to explore the extent to which the witness is prepared to change their sworn evidence to correspond with their statement. If the witness changes their testimony, this may be relied on by the tribunal of fact.

The second tactical ploy envisaged by s 5 is with regard to the contradiction of the witness's testimony. Before the witness is contradicted, their attention must be drawn to the relevant parts of the document and they are given a last opportunity to explain the discrepancy in their sworn statement and the document.

The proviso to s 5 does not give the judge an absolute discretion to do whatever they like with the statement but entitles the judge to call for the document whenever he wishes. Accordingly, the cross-examiner is required to have the document in his possession even though he does not wish to contradict the witness.

At common law the effect of admitting the previous statement under s 4 or 5 is that it is evidence only as to the inconsistency of the witness and was not evidence of the truth. In civil cases, the evidential value of the contradictory statement has been changed by statute and it is now evidence of the truth of the assertion: see s 6(3) and (5) of the Civil Evidence Act 1995.

Civil proceedings

Section 6(3) of the Civil Evidence Act 1995 provides as follows:

SECTION

'Where in the case of civil proceedings section 3, 4 or 5 of the Criminal Procedure Act 1865 applies, which makes provision as to –

(a) how far a witness may be discredited by the party producing him,
(b) the proof of contradictory statements made by the witness, and
(c) cross-examination as to previous statements in writing,

this Act does not authorise the adducing of evidence of a previous inconsistent or contradictory statement otherwise than in accordance with those sections.

This is without prejudice to any provision made by rules of court under s 3 above . . .

Nothing in this section shall be construed as preventing a statement of any description referred to above from being admissible by virtue of section 1 as evidence of the matters stated.'

Criminal proceedings

In criminal proceedings, s 119 of the Criminal Justice Act 2003 has declared that the effect of the prior out-of-court statement contradicting the witness is evidence of the truth of the assertion. Thus, such statement may be put on par with the testimony of the witness.

Section 119 of the Criminal Justice Act 2003 provides as follows:

SECTION

'If in criminal proceedings a person gives oral evidence and –

(a) he admits making a previous inconsistent statement, or
(b) a previous inconsistent statement made by him is proved by virtue of section 3, 4 or 5 of the Criminal Procedure Act 1865

the statement is admissible as evidence of any matter stated of which oral evidence by him would be admissible.'

CASE EXAMPLE

R v Hayes [2005] 1 Cr App R 33

The defendant was charged with wounding with intent to commit grievous bodily harm contrary to s 18 of the Offences Against the Person Act 1861. Prior to the trial, the defendant's solicitor, with the permission of the defendant, wrote a letter to the Crown Prosecution Service (CPS) indicating that the defendant was willing to plead guilty to assault occasioning actual bodily harm contrary to s 47 of the 1861 Act. This was consistent with what the defendant had said to the police in interview. During cross-examination he denied having injured the victim, and the judge allowed the prosecution to cross-examine the defendant regarding the letter. On appeal, the court decided that the judge had correctly exercised his discretion. Such cross-examination did not involve unfairness to the defendant:

JUDGMENT

'It was relevant to his credibility in just the same way that it may be relevant to a defendant's credibility to cross-examine him about details in his alibi notice when his evidence at the trial has turned out to be different. Likewise, there is no objection, in principle, to a defendant being cross-examined on what is contained in his defence statement when it becomes relevant to an issue at the trial. We cannot see that there was any unfairness to the defendant in the admission of this evidence.'

(Scott Baker LJ)

6.3.6 Finality of answers to questions in cross-examination as to credit

The general rule is that under cross-examination a witness's answer to questions of a collateral nature or related to the credit of the witness is final. The rationale for this rule is that to allow the cross-examiner to adduce rebutting evidence on matters related to the credit of the witness may lead to a multiplicity of issues and unnecessarily prolong the trial. A collateral issue is one that is not directly related to the question in issue. The test for identifying collateral issues was laid down by Pollock CB in *AG v Hitchcock* (1847) 1 Exch 91, thus:

JUDGMENT

'. . . the test whether a matter is collateral or not is this: if the answer of the witness is a matter which you would be allowed on your own part to prove in evidence – if it has such a connection with the issues, that you would be allowed to give it in evidence – then it is a matter on which you may contradict him . . . [and the matter is not collateral].'

CASE EXAMPLE

AG v Hitchcock (1847) 1 Exch 91

The defendant was charged with having used a cistern for the making of malt whisky without a licence. A witness for the prosecution, having sworn that the cistern was so used, was asked if he had not said to one Mr Cook that Excise officers had offered him £20 to say the cistern had been used. The witness denied having made such a statement. The defendant's counsel proposed to call Cook and ask him whether the witness had told him so. The evidence was disallowed. On appeal the court decided that the witness's answer was final because what the witness told Mr Cook was irrelevant to the issue of whether the cistern was used for an illicit purpose. The answer was therefore collateral to the facts in issue:

JUDGMENT

'If the witness has spoken falsely he may be indicted for perjury. When the answer given is not material to the issue, public convenience requires that it be taken as decisive and that no contradiction be allowed. In the present case, the witness was asked whether he had been offered a bribe to say that the cistern had been used. This was not material, nor did it qualify what had gone before, for his being offered a bribe did not show that he was not a fair and credible witness.'

(Alderson B)

6.3.7 Exceptions to the *Hitchcock* rule

There are a limited number of exceptions to the rule in *Hitchcock*. These are occasions where, despite the questions in cross-examination being related to collateral matters, the party is nevertheless entitled to contradict the witness.

Section 6 of the Criminal Procedure Act 1865

The principle is applicable to both civil and criminal cases. It involves the answers to questions in cross-examination regarding the previous convictions of the witness not being final.

Section 6 of the 1865 Act provides as follows:

SECTION

'A witness may be questioned as to whether he has been convicted [of any offence], and upon being so questioned, if he either denies or does not admit the fact, or refuses to answer, it shall be lawful for the cross-examining party to prove such conviction . . .'

The various responses of the witness are included in the broad phrase, 'he either denies or does not admit the fact or refuses to answer' from the equivocal, evasive answer of the witness to a denial or the silence of the witness. Such responses permit the cross-examiner to contradict the witness without the leave of the judge.

In criminal cases, a witness may only be 'lawfully questioned' if the questions are permitted within ss 100 and 101 of the Criminal Justice Act 2003 and, in appropriate cases, the discretion of the judge. Assuming the question from the cross-examiner about the witness's previous conviction may be asked, the next hurdle to overcome is to ascertain whether or not the conviction is 'spent' under the Rehabilitation of Offenders Act 1974. Section 4 of the 1974 Act defines 'spent convictions'. Although this Act is applicable to civil cases only, in Practice Direction (Criminal Proceedings: Consolidation) para 1(6) issued in 1975 the Attorney General extended the Act to criminal cases.

Section 7(3) of the Rehabilitation of Offenders Act 1974 creates an exception to the non-admissibility of convictions when the judge decides to admit it in the interests of justice.

Section 7(3) declares:

SECTION

'If at any stage in any proceedings before a judicial authority in Great Britain . . . justice cannot be done in the case except by admitting or requiring evidence relating to a person's spent conviction or circumstances ancillary thereto, that authority may admit or, as the case may be, require the evidence in question . . . and may determine any issue to which the evidence relates . . .'

CASE EXAMPLE

Thomas v Commissioner of Police [1997] 1 All ER 747

The court decided that the judge has to weigh the degree of relevance of the spent conviction to the issues in question as against the amount of prejudice the admission of the spent conviction may have in respect of a fair trial. This is a balancing exercise that has to be conducted by the judge:

JUDGMENT

'Section 7(3) is expressed as a qualification to the general rule of exclusion in s 4(1), and its terms demonstrate that the evidence must be excluded unless judicial authority, i.e. the trial judge, is "satisfied . . . that justice cannot be done . . . except by admitting [it]". So there is a strong presumption against permitting cross-examination or admitting the evidence, but the section also emphasises that the discretion is a broad one. The judge may take into account "any considerations which appear to [him] to be relevant" and the overriding requirement is that "justice shall be done". In the context of civil proceedings, this means taking account of the interests of both parties, and justice requires that there shall be a fair trial between them.'

(Evans LJ)

Bias or partiality

A witness may be cross-examined with a view to showing that he was biased or partial in relation to a party or the relevant cause. If he denies the allegation, the cross-examiner will be allowed to adduce evidence in order to rebut the denial. The effect of admitting such evidence at common law is to discredit the witness. This rule is applicable to both civil and criminal cases.

CASE EXAMPLE

Thomas v David (1836) 7 C&P 350

The claimant sued on a promissory note. The defence was that the document was a forgery. An attesting witness to the defendant's purported signature was called by the claimant. This witness was asked in cross-examination whether she was the claimant's mistress. She denied the allegation. The defendant was allowed to rebut the denial. On appeal the court held that the evidence was correctly admitted:

JUDGMENT

'Is it not material to the issue whether the principal witness who comes to support the plaintiff's case is his kept mistress? The question is, whether the witness had contracted such a relation with the plaintiff as might induce her the more readily to conspire with him to support a forgery, just in the same way as if she had been asked if she was the sister of the plaintiff and had denied that. I think that the contradiction is admissible.'

(Coleridge J)

It is apparent that this exception is fairly broad-based, and much depends on the discretion of the judge as to what constitutes bias or partiality.

Another illustration of the principle is *R v Mendy* (1976) 64 Cr App R 4.

CASE EXAMPLE

R v Mendy (1976) 64 Cr App R 4

In this case Mrs Mendy was charged with assault. In accordance with the usual practice, all the witnesses were kept out of court prior to giving evidence. While a detective was giving evidence for the prosecution, a constable had noticed a man taking notes from the public gallery. This man was observed by the constable and a court officer leaving the court and discussing the case with the defendant's husband. Mr Mendy gave evidence and in cross-examination denied the incident (collusion). The prosecution was granted leave to call the constable and court officer to rebut the denial. The defendant was convicted and appealed, and the appeal was dismissed because the evidence was correctly admitted:

JUDGMENT

'. . . Was the evidence admissible? A party may not impeach the credit of the opponent's witnesses by calling witnesses to contradict him on collateral matters, and his answers thereon will be conclusive . . . Difficulties may sometimes arise in determining what matters are collateral, but no one seriously suggests that the issue in the present case was other than collateral. On the other hand, it seems strange, if it be the case, that the court and jury have to be kept in ignorance of the behaviour of a witness such as that in the present case. The suggestion which lay behind the evidence in question was that Mr Mendy was prepared to lend himself to a scheme designed to defeat the purpose of keeping prospective witnesses out of court . . . The truth of the matter is, as one would expect, that the rule is not all embracing. It has always been permissible to call evidence to contradict a witness's denial of bias or partiality towards one of the parties and to show that he is prejudiced so far as the case being tried is concerned . . . The witness was prepared to cheat in order to deceive the jury and help the defendant. The jury were entitled to be apprised of that fact.'

(Lord Lane CJ)

The issue may arise in connection with contesting police evidence. In *R v Busby* (1981) 75 Cr App R 79, the charges were burglary and handling stolen goods.

CASE EXAMPLE

R v Busby (1981) 75 Cr App R 79

Two police officers were called on behalf of the prosecution and were cross-examined by the defendant to establish *inter alia* that they were biased against the defendant. The cross-examiner questioned the witnesses to establish that they fabricated damaging remarks allegedly attributable to the defendant and that one officer, in the presence of the other, threatened a potential witness for the defence in order to stop him testifying. Both officers denied that the potential witness was threatened. The defence was prevented from calling the witness in question. The defendant was convicted and appealed. The Court of Appeal allowed the appeal and quashed the conviction on the ground that the evidence was admissible:

JUDGMENT

'It is not always easy to determine when a question relates to facts which are collateral only, and therefore to be treated as final, and when it is relevant to the issue which has to be tried . . . We are of the opinion that the learned judge was wrong to refuse to admit the evidence. If true, it would have shown that the police were prepared to go to improper lengths in order to secure the accused's conviction. It was the accused's case that the statement attributed to him had been fabricated, a suggestion which could not be accepted by the jury unless they thought that the officers concerned were prepared to go to improper lengths to secure the conviction.'

(Eveleigh LJ)

It must be emphasised that, in this case, the Court of Appeal decided that the questions put to the police officers were related to the facts in issue and were not concerned with the credibility of the witness. However, in *R v Edwards* [1991] 2 All ER 266 (see earlier), the court came to a different conclusion, deciding that the questions and evidence were related to the credibility of the witnesses and the answers were final in accordance with the general rule.

CASE EXAMPLE

R v Edwards (Maxine) [1996] 2 Cr App R 345

The police force featured was the Stoke Newington Drugs Squad. The members of this force had been the subject of an inquiry into planting of evidence and perjury. The accused was arrested on suspicion of possessing crack cocaine with intent to supply. The police alleged that when they searched the defendant they discovered eight foil wraps containing crack cocaine. They said that the defendant, while in the car on her way to the station, admitted that the wraps contained cocaine. She refused to sign a note of this admission. At her trial she said that she had never been in possession of the foil wraps. She alleged that the police found them in a parked car that she was standing next to. She was convicted. Following an inquiry into the Drugs Squad's activities and the acquittal of a number of persons arrested and charged by the Squad, the Home Secretary referred the case back to the Court of Appeal. This court allowed the appeal and quashed the conviction:

JUDGMENT

'Once the suspicion of perjury starts to infect the evidence and permeate cases in which the witnesses have been involved, and which are closely similar, the evidence on which such convictions are based becomes as questionable as it was in the cases in which the appeals have already been allowed. It is impossible to be confident that had the jury which convicted this appellant known the facts and circumstances in the other cases in which [the witness] had been involved, that they would have been bound to convict this appellant.'

(Beldam LJ)

The Criminal Justice Act 2003 has had the effect of restricting the discretion of the judge in deciding whether the questioning by the cross-examiner relates to credit or issue and involves bias. In criminal cases the issue today may involve an assessment of the admissibility of the bad character of the witness, or more particularly, 'evidence of, or disposition towards, misconduct on his part', within s 98 of the 2003 Act (see later). More specifically, the evidence and questioning may be focused on issues within s 100(1)(b) of the 2003 Act, namely:

SECTION

'. . . the bad character of a person other than the defendant is admissible if (b) it has substantial probative value in relation to a matter which –

(i) is a matter in issue in the proceedings, and
(ii) is of substantial importance in the context of the case as a whole.'

(See later.)

Evidence of reputation for untruthfulness

It has been a long-established practice that a party is entitled to call a witness (A) to testify to the effect that:

(a) from their (witness's) (A) personal knowledge, they are of the opinion that an opponent's witness (B) ought not to be believed on oath;

(b) the opponent's witness (B) has a general reputation for untruthfulness (this aspect of the test need not be based on personal knowledge).

This is an exceptional and perhaps outdated rule of admissibility but still has the force of law. This evidence is applicable to both civil and criminal cases and is solely related to the credit of the witness.

CASE EXAMPLE

R v Brown and Headley (1867) LR 1 CCCR 70

In this case, further to the close of the case for the prosecution, defence counsel applied for leave to call witnesses to prove that specific witnesses who testified for the prosecution had a reputation for untruthfulness. The judge allowed such evidence to be admitted but stated a case for the Court of Crown Cases Reserved. This court held that the evidence was admissible:

JUDGMENT

'It has been the practice to admit the evidence rejected in this case for centuries without dispute and we have personal knowledge of its existence during our time. So long a practice cannot be altered but by the legislature.'

(Kelly CB)

The rule was considered in a more modern case, *R v Richardson and Longman* (1969), and the court decided that the witness (A):

(a) is not entitled to testify in chief about his reasons for his opinion;

(b) may be entitled to state his reasons for his opinion in cross-examination.

CASE EXAMPLE

R v Richardson and Longman [1969] 1 QB 299

The defendants were charged and convicted of conspiring to pervert the course of justice by trying to influence a jury and suborning witnesses at a trial (of the brother of one of the defendants). The chief prosecution witness was Mrs Clemence. The defence called a witness, Dr Hitchens, in order to discredit Mrs Clemence. He was asked whether, in the light of Mrs Clemence's general reputation for veracity, he would be prepared to believe her on oath. He replied that in certain particulars she could not be believed on oath. The judge refused defence counsel to ask the witness further questions, which would have been whether, from his personal knowledge of her, he would have believed the prosecution witness. In addition, under examination in chief, the witness was not permitted to qualify his previous answer. The Court of Appeal held that although the judge was incorrect on his first ruling, he was correct on his second ruling. The proviso to s 2 of the Criminal Appeal Act 1968 applied and the appeal was dismissed:

JUDGMENT

'The legal position may be thus summarised:

"6.4.8 A witness may be asked whether he has knowledge of the impugned witness's general reputation for veracity and whether (from such knowledge) he would believe the impugned witness's sworn testimony.

"6.4.9 The witness called to impeach the credibility of a previous witness may also express his individual opinion (based upon his personal knowledge) as to whether the latter is to be believed upon his oath and is not confined to giving evidence merely of general reputation.

"6.4.10 But whether the witness's opinion as to the impugned witness's credibility be based simply upon the latter's general reputation for veracity or upon his personal knowledge, the witness cannot be permitted to indicate during his examination in chief the particular facts, circumstances or incidents which formed the basis of his opinion, although he may be cross-examined as to them . . ."

'It is clear from the transcript that defence counsel also desired to ask another question of Dr Hitchens and we were told (and accept) that it would have been in this form: "From your personal knowledge of Ms Clemence would you believe her on oath?" That question, in our judgment, he should have been permitted to put . . . Nevertheless, we are obliged to hold that the trial judge was technically wrong in ruling out that further question. As to whether he was also wrong in cutting short Dr Hitchens's attempt to qualify his earlier answer is far from clear; for it looks very much as though the witness was proceeding to adduce his reasons for qualifying it, and we know of no authority which permits that to be done . . .'

(Edmund Davies LJ)

Evidence of disability of opponent's witness

A party is entitled to call a witness (A) to testify to the effect that from his personal knowledge of a witness called by his opponent (B), such witness (B) was suffering from such a disability (mental or physical) as to militate against the truthfulness of his testimony, i.e. to discredit the witness. In addition, the witness (A) is entitled in evidence in chief to state reasons for his opinion. In a sense this principle of law was created out of the *Brown and Headley* principle. For example, a defence witness may be called to testify to the effect that a prosecution witness, who gave evidence of visual identification of the defendant committing the crime from a distance of 200 feet, was so short-sighted that he would have found it difficult to identify anyone from a distance exceeding fifty feet.

The law was settled in *Toohey v Metropolitan Police Commissioner* [1965] AC 595.

CASE EXAMPLE

Toohey v Metropolitan Police Commissioner [1965] AC 595

In this case the accused and two others were charged and convicted of assaulting a youth with intent to rob (today robbery). The defence was that they were merely trying to help him, but the youth became hysterical and accused them of hitting him and being after his money. A doctor was prevented from giving evidence for the defence to the effect that, on examination of the victim at the police station, he had formed the opinion that he was suffering from a disease of the mind and was prone to hysteria, and therefore regarded his testimony as unreliable. On conviction, the defendant appealed and the House of Lords allowed the appeal and quashed the conviction on the ground that the evidence was admissible:

JUDGMENT

'When a witness through physical (in which I include mental) disease or abnormality is not capable of giving a true or reliable account to the jury, it must surely be allowable for medical science to reveal this vital hidden fact to them. If a witness purported to give evidence of something which he believed that he had seen at a distance of 50 yards, it must surely be possible to call the evidence of an oculist to the effect that the witness could not possibly see anything at a greater distance than 20 yards . . . So too must it be allowable to call medical evidence of mental illness which makes a witness incapable of giving reliable evidence, whether through the existence of delusions or otherwise . . . *R v Gunewardene* [1951] 2 KB 600, was, in my opinion, wrongly decided. Medical evidence is admissible to show that a witness suffers from some disease or defect or abnormality of mind that affects the reliability of his evidence. Such evidence is not confined to a general opinion of the unreliability of the witness but may give all the matters necessary to show, not only the foundation of and reasons for the diagnosis, but also the extent to which the credibility of the witness is affected. . . .'

(Lord Pearce)

This principle is limited to occasions when the opponent's witness's credibility is attacked by adducing expert evidence in order to prove a scientific fact. In other words, expert opinion evidence is inadmissible in order to prove ordinary facts that are within the purview of the jury. The purpose of the rule is to avoid usurping the function of the jury. Thus, psychiatric evidence is not admissible in order to discredit a witness who is capable of giving reliable evidence. This is a matter for the jury to take into account in observing the demeanour of a witness and the content of his testimony.

CASE EXAMPLE

R v MacKenney (1981) 76 Cr App R 271

The defendant and another were charged with murder. A third defendant, Childs, had pleaded guilty and was returning Queen's evidence for the prosecution. The judge had ordered that Childs be examined by a defence psychiatrist, if he so consented. In the circumstances the witness refused to be examined. The defence attempted to secure the nearest alternative to an examination. Mr Irving, who held himself out as a psychologist, prepared a report for the defence after observing Childs testifying from the witness box. Defence counsel sought to call Mr Irving to testify on the basis that he was an expert and to prove that Childs was suffering from a mental illness; one of the characteristics was a tendency to fabrication. The judge, after considering the qualifications and experience of Mr Irving and the circumstances supporting his opinion ruled that his report was inadmissible and that he was not allowed to testify. On appeal following a conviction, the Court of Appeal dismissed the appeal on the ground that Mr Irving was not an expert, and in any event his report was not compiled after an examination of the witness:

JUDGMENT

'Counsel for the defence submitted to us that Mr Irving was qualified to diagnose mental illness. His training, he submitted, as a psychologist enabled him so to do. We do not agree. No doubt his training as a psychologist gave him some insight into the medical science of psychiatry. However, not being a medical man, he had of course no experience of direct personal diagnosis. He was thus not qualified to act as a psychiatrist.

'We agree with the learned judge that if a witness is suffering from a mental disability, it may, in a proper case, well be permissible to call psychiatric evidence to show that the witness is incapable of giving reliable evidence. We are prepared to accept that the mental illness need not be such as to make the witness totally incapable of giving reliable evidence, but it must substantially affect the witness's capacity to give reliable evidence. But this is very different from calling psychiatric evidence with a view to warning a jury about a witness who is capable of giving reliable evidence, but who may well choose not to do so. If the witness is mentally capable of giving reliable evidence, it is for the jury, with all the warnings from counsel and the court which the law requires to decide whether or not that witness is giving reliable evidence.'

(Ackner LJ)

Interventions by the judge

As a general rule the judge ought not to intervene in the cross-examination of witnesses. A feature of the adversarial system of justice is that the judge does not step into the arena and intervene in the questioning of witnesses, save when called upon to make rulings on disputed points of law. However, he is entitled to question witnesses in order to clarify matters for their benefit and the benefit of the jury. Exceptionally, the nature and frequency of the interruptions by the judge may have the effect of hampering the advocate's ability to adequately question the witnesses. In these circumstances there is a danger that a fair trial may be compromised. In *R v Sharp* [1994] 2 WLR 84, on a charge of obtaining property by deception contrary to the Theft Act 1968 (now fraud under the Fraud Act 2006), the judge frequently interrupted the defence advocate whilst he was conducting cross-examination of witnesses, including audible sighs and noises of disapproval by the judge when the defence was making his closing speech. He was convicted and appealed *inter alia* on the ground that the judge's interruptions amounted to a material irregularity. The Court of Appeal allowed the appeal and quashed the conviction on the basis that the cumulative effect of the grounds of appeal made the conviction unsafe.

JUDGMENT

'When a judge intervenes in the course of examination, or particularly cross-examination, a number of problems can arise depending on the frequency and manner of the interruptions. First the judge may be in danger of seeming to enter the arena in the sense that he may appear partial to one side or the other. This may arise from the hostile tone of questioning or implied criticism of counsel who is conducting the examination or cross-examination, or if the judge is impressed by a witness, perhaps suggesting excuses or explanations for a witness's conduct which is open to attack by counsel for the opposite party. Quite apart from this, frequent interruptions may so disrupt the thread of cross-examination that counsel's task may be seriously hampered. If the judge intervenes at a crucial point where the witness is being constrained to make an important admission, it can have an adverse effect on the trial.

'In general, when a cross-examination is being conducted by competent counsel a judge should not intervene, save to clarify matters he does not understand or thinks the jury may not understand. If he wishes to ask questions about matters that have not been touched upon it is generally better to wait until the end of the examination or cross-examination. But there may come a time, depending on the nature and frequency of the interruptions that a reviewing court is of the opinion that defence counsel was so hampered in the way he properly wished to conduct the cross-examination that the judge's conduct amounts to a material irregularity.'

(Stuart-Smith LJ)

However, in *R v Cameron* [2001] EWCA Crim 562, on a charge of rape, where a child complainant refused to answer questions under cross-examination and the judge, with the permission of the advocates, proceeded to question the witness on behalf of the defence, the Court of Appeal dismissed the appeal. The trial judge exercised his discretion in a correct manner, issued appropriate directions to the jury and carried out his overall duty to ensure a fair trial. The judge was faced with a choice of discharging the jury, inviting the prosecution to consider its position or taking the course that he did. In the circumstances the judge's decision was correct:

JUDGMENT

'Certainly, in the case of a child complainant in the trial of a sexual complaint, we do not consider that it should be regarded as beyond the judge's discretionary powers to adopt the procedure followed in this case, provided that he is satisfied that fairness can thereby be preserved, and provided that, once the procedure has been followed, he takes it into account in any subsequent ruling, and provided that in relation to the directions which he gives to the jury, he informs them of the unusual and less satisfactory nature of the procedure as a substitute for the traditional right of the defendant or his advocate to cross-examine prosecution witnesses.'

(Potter LJ)

In *R v O'Dwyer* [2014] EWCA Crim 2924, the Court of Appeal decided that the repeated interventions by the judge during the cross-examination of the main prosecution witness by the accused and the latter's examination in chief did not render the conviction unsafe. The accused represented himself and was convicted of false accounting and fraud. His appeal on the grounds that the judge intervened some twenty-four times during his cross-examination of the main prosecution witness and during his testimony was dismissed. The court decided that the judge had a duty to regulate the proceedings and the interventions as a whole were not too numerous or unwarranted and the fairness of the trial had been maintained.

To the same effect, in *Aujla v R* [2015] EWCA Crim 853 the Court of Appeal decided that, although a trial judge had been discourteous and rude to a defence advocate, in the circumstances the trial process was not rendered unfair by the judge's interventions and comments. The trial judge had a duty to actively manage cases justly, which included dealing with issues efficiently, expeditiously and proportionately. A judge's reprehensible conduct towards the defence advocate may only impact on the fairness of the trial if it interfered, in a material way, with the advocate fairly presenting his or her case.

JUDGMENT

'If a judge intervenes in a manner which is inappropriate – for example, if he exhibits annoyance, or suggests that he has a preconceived view, or is made in a way that belittles one counsel or another – that may risk rendering the trial unfair and any resultant conviction unsafe.

'Nevertheless, whilst it is unbefitting any judge, discourtesy in itself will not necessarily render a trial unfair or a verdict unsafe. Conduct of a judge will only lead to doubt with regard to a conviction if, looking at the matter as a whole, this court considers that, to let the conviction stand, risks an injustice being done or legitimately gives rise to a real perception that justice has not been done.'

(Hickinbottom J)

SUMMARY

Course of trial

- The purpose of the examination in chief is to present the evidence of a witness on behalf of the party calling the witness. This rule is applicable to both civil and criminal cases.
- No leading questions may be asked by the party calling the witness.
- While testifying, the witness may wish to refresh his memory. In civil cases the common law test is applicable. In criminal cases s 139 of the Criminal Justice Act 2003 specifies the test by reference to a document made or verified by the witness.
- The document is required to be surrendered for inspection to the opposing parties on request.
- The opposing parties are entitled to cross-examine the witness on the document, but if the cross-examination is on parts not used to refresh the witness's memory (excessive cross-examination) the document may become an exhibit at the instance of the party calling the witness. The exhibit is treated as evidence of the truth of the assertion. For civil cases see s 6(4) of the Civil Evidence Act 1995. In criminal cases the principle has been laid down in s 120(3) of the Criminal Justice Act 2003.
- A separate, relaxed regime is applicable to the witness refreshing his memory out of court.
- The party calling a witness to testify guarantees the witness's trustworthiness and may not be entitled to impeach the witness's credibility.
- The witness may prove to be unfavourable and may be contradicted by the evidence of other witnesses, if any.
- If the witness is treated as hostile he may be cross-examined to a limited extent by the party calling him and may be contradicted by the evidence of other witnesses, if any.
- In addition, with leave of the judge, the witness's out-of-court statement may be used to contradict the witness in both civil and criminal cases: see s 3 of the Criminal Procedure Act 1865.
- The effect of the contradiction in both civil and criminal cases is that the document becomes evidence of the facts stated therein.
- There is a general rule in both civil and criminal cases prohibiting the admissibility of evidence of previous consistent statements (narratives) of a witness, subject to exceptions.
- Exceptions to the general rule against narratives include complaints made by the witness to third parties in criminal proceedings, statements forming part of the *res gestae*, rebuttal of a suggestion in cross-examination of a fabrication of the testimony of a witness, previous statements of identification of the defendant, and the defendant's reaction when taxed with incriminating material.
- The effect of admitting evidence under the exceptions is that the out-of-court assertions are admissible as evidence of the truth.

- All witnesses who are called to testify may be cross-examined by the opposing parties.
- The purposes of cross-examination are to qualify the evidence of the witness given in chief and to discredit the witness, and leading questions may be asked.
- Special rules exist that create a 'shield' to protect a complainant as to his or her sexual behaviour who testifies on a charge involving an offence of a sexual nature.
- Charges of 'sexual offences' – see s 62 of the Youth Justice and Criminal Evidence Act 1999.
- General prohibition on the defence adducing evidence or cross-examining the complainant on his or her sexual behaviour, except with the leave of the judge.
- Sexual behaviour is defined in s 42(1)(c).
- Leave will not be granted if the purpose is to impugn the complainant's credibility: see s 41(4).
- Leave will be granted under s 41(2) and in the circumstances laid down in s 41(3)(a), (b) and (c).
- The prosecution may adduce evidence of the sexual behaviour of the complainant, and the court may grant leave to the defendant to adduce rebutting evidence: see s 41(5).
- When leave is granted to the defence to adduce evidence or cross-examine the complainant on his or her sexual behaviour, the evidence or questions must relate to specific instances.
- Section 43 lays down the procedure for dealing with applications for leave.
- Answers to collateral questions asked in cross-examination are final, subject to exceptions identified in s 6 of the Criminal Procedure Act 1865, bias of a witness, and evidence of the disability of an opposing witness.

ACTIVITY

Self-test questions

1. When may a witness refresh his memory (a) in court and (b) out of court, and what are the consequences of doing so?
2. What is meant by the expression 'hostile' witness, and how does this differ from an 'unfavourable' witness?
3. What exceptions exist in respect of the general rule against the admissibility of previous consistent statements?
4. How has the Criminal Justice Act 2003 improved the exceptions to the rule against narrative statements?
5. What are the traditional purposes of cross-examination?
6. What is the effect of the distinction between cross-examination as to issue and credit?

SAMPLE ESSAY QUESTION

Outline the provisions in ss 41 to 43 of the Youth Justice and Criminal Evidence Act 1999 relating to the cross-examination of the defendant about the sexual behaviour of the complainant, and consider whether they have the effect of prejudicing a fair trial.

Answer plan

The purpose of introducing a shield was designed to protect complainants in cases of sexual offences, to avoid gratuitous attacks on his or her credibility by introducing his or her sexual history.

Sections 41 to 43 of the Youth Justice and Criminal Evidence Act 1999 introduced provisions to protect the complainant from embarrassment or intimidation regarding his or her sexual behaviour.

The provisions are activated when the defendant is charged with a sexual offence as broadly defined in s 62 of the 1999 Act and the complainant testifies in the proceedings.

The nature of the 'shield' as laid down in s 41(2) involves a prohibition on evidence being adduced or the cross-examination of the complainant as to his or her sexual behaviour, except by the leave of the judge.

Sexual behaviour is defined in s 42(1)(c) of the 1999 Act and includes physical or verbal overtones of the complainant of a sexual nature.

There are five criteria by which leave may be granted or the shield may be lifted – ss 41(3)(a)(b)(c), 41(5) and 41(2)(b) of the 1999 Act. This requires the judge to make value judgments by reference to the facts of each case.

At the same time the judge is required to be satisfied that there is an evidential basis to conclude that the nature of the evidence or cross-examination is not to impugn the credibility of the complainant; see s 41(4) of the 1999 Act.

If the judge grants leave to the defence he is required to restrict the evidence or questioning to specific instances of alleged sexual behaviour; s 41(6).

The procedure for the application is laid down in s 43 of the 1999 Act.

Potentially the existence of the shield in some cases is capable of infringing the defendant's Convention rights.

In deciding whether any one or more of the above criteria for lifting the shield is satisfied the court will have regard to whether the sexual behaviour is connected with third parties or the defendant. In this regard the judge, in exercising his discretion, is required to consider whether the evidence or questions are so relevant to the facts in issue that to exclude it would endanger the fairness of the trial. Provided that judges approach the questions in issue by this method relevant evidence may not be excluded. [A consideration of the vast array of case law is necessary to answer this question.]

CONCLUSION

Further reading

Birch, D. 'A better deal for vulnerable witnesses?' [2000] Crim LR 223

Brennan, G. 'Sexual history evidence: the Youth Justice and Criminal Evidence Act 1999' (2002) 8 Queen Mary Law Journal 7

Brewis, B. and Stockdale, M. 'False allegations: the limitations of the "evidential basis" test' [2014] J Crim L 453

Buxton, R. 'Victims as witnesses in trials of sexual offences: towards equality of arms' [2015] Crim LR 679

Dein, A. 'Police misconduct revisited' [2000] Crim LR 801

Dennis, I. 'Sexual history evidence: evaluating section 41' [2006] Crim LR 869

Durston, G. 'Previous (in)consistent statements after the Criminal Justice Act 2003' [2005] Crim LR 206

Ellison, L. 'Cross-examination in rape trials' [1998] Crim LR 605

Henderson, E. 'Bigger fish to fry: should the reform of cross-examination be expanded beyond vulnerable witnesses?' [2015] E&P 83

Keane, A. 'The collateral evidence rule: a sad forensic fable involving a circus, its sideshow, confusion, vanishing tricks and alchemy' [2015] E&P 100

Keane, A. and Fortson, R. 'Leading questions – a critical analysis' [2011] Crim LR 280
Kibble, N. 'Judicial perspectives on the operation of section 41' [2005] Crim LR 190
Kibble, N. 'Judicial discretion and the admissibility of prior sexual history evidence' [2005] Crim LR 263
Kibble, N. 'Sexual offences: whether a rape complainant's false complaint "misconduct" is the result of personality problems?' [2011] Crim LR 818
Mirfield, P. 'Human wrongs?' (2002) 118 LQR 20
Munday, R. 'Calling a hostile witness' [1989] Crim LR 866
Munday, R. 'Athwal and all that: previous statements, narratives and the taxonomy of hearsay' (2010) 74 Crim JC L 415
Munday, R. 'Refreshing memory: previous statements that fail to revive witnesses' memories' [2012] CL&J 213
Ormerod, D. 'Evidence: previous inconsistent statements – admissibility' [2007] Crim LR 887
Ormerod, D. 'Hostile witness maintaining contents of prior statement not true' [2009] Crim LR 197
Ormerod, D. 'Previous inconsistent statements: directing juries in relation to previous inconsistent statements in view of effect and application of s 119 of the Criminal Justice Act 2003' [2009] Crim LR 529
Ormerod, D. '*R v Athwal*: evidence – hearsay – previous consistent statement – admissibility – rebutting fabrication' [2009] Crim LR 726
Pattenden, R. 'The submission of no case – some recent developments' [1982] Crim LR 558
Pattenden, R. 'Evidence of previous malpractice by police witnesses and *R v Edwards*' [1992] Crim LR 549
Pattenden, R. 'The hostile witness' (1992) 56 J C L 414
Seabrooke, S. 'Current topic: the vanishing trick – blurring the line between credit and issue' [1999] Crim LR 387
Singh, C. 'Eliciting best evidence from a child witness: a comparative study of the United Kingdom and India' (2019) 17(1) Issues in Legal Scholarship 20190003
Spencer, J. 'Rape shields and the right to a fair trial' [2001] Cambridge Law Journal 452
Stockdale, M. and Grubin, D. 'The admissibility of polygraph evidence in English criminal proceedings' [2012] J Crim L 232
Stockdale, M. and Jackson, A. 'Admissibility of previous statements of witnesses' [2012] CL&J 249
Temkin, J. 'Sexual history evidence – beware the backlash' [2003] Crim LR 217
Thomas, D. 'Sexual history evidence: whether the defendant charged with a sexual assault will able to cross-examine the complainant about previous false rape complaint?' [2010] Crim LR 792
Wolchover, D., Heaton-Armstrong, A., Hope, L. and Gabbert, F. 'Notebook challenge: no conferring: Pt 1' [2014] CL&J 224; Pt 2 [2014] CL&J 241; Pt 3 [2014] CL&J 266

7

Hearsay: the exclusionary rule

AIMS AND OBJECTIVES

By the end of this chapter you will be able to:

- understand the categories of hearsay evidence and how it developed;
- appreciate how the rules operate through hypothetical examples and real case studies;
- highlight how the Criminal Justice Act 2003 changed the approach to hearsay in the UK through a discussion of the changing perception of the risk attached to it;
- outline how the rules operate with discussion of real case studies;
- set out the common law exceptions to the rule through a discussion on how it developed;
- discuss the statutory exceptions in the criminal law through an exploration of their application;
- analyse the risk attached to such evidence via discussion of real case studies.

7.1 Introduction

The rule against the admission of hearsay evidence is one of the most fundamental rules in the law of evidence and is often unfortunately misunderstood. The Criminal Justice Act 2003 (CJA) introduced major changes to the admission of hearsay evidence in the UK. The basic rule in criminal proceedings is that both prosecution and defence witnesses should give oral evidence and be available to be **cross-examined** on the evidence that they give. Thus, Surinder is, in general, forbidden to give evidence on behalf of Francis. Later in this chapter the discussion will show you how Art 6(3)(d) of the European Convention on Human Rights and Fundamental Freedoms (ECHR) helps promotes the general rule by trying to place the accused and accuser on an equal footing. Part 20 of the Criminal Procedure Rules 2020 set out the process to be followed where a

Cross-examination
the process of questioning a party to proceedings in order to establish or undermine the truth of their testimony.

DOI: 10.4324/9781003282433-7

party to the proceedings wants to adduce hearsay for admission under the CJA 2003; in particular, see CrPR 20.2 (notice to introduce) and 20.3 (opposing the introduction).

Historically, there were two main issues attached to the admission of hearsay evidence. The first related to the potential distortion or error in recounting a statement. The second was the inherent difficulty in cross-examining a witness whose testimony relates to a hearsay statement because it was not percipient evidence i.e., they did not 'perceive' the events about which they are giving evidence themselves. In 1603, in his trial for treason, Sir Walter Raleigh cried out 'let my accuser come face to face and be deposed!' – his contention was that he had been deprived of his common law right to have his counsel cross-examine the witness that had given evidence against him. This common law safeguard helped protect the right to a fair trial – it prevented an accused being convicted on the basis of evidence that could not be tested. However, the existence of either of these two issues did not preclude hearsay evidence from being admitted – with many judges taking the view that the focus should be on the weight attached to this evidence rather than purely on its admission. Earlier in the book we discussed how such an inquiry is a factual one for the jury. In civil proceedings, the result of the Civil Evidence Act 1968 was to render most hearsay evidence admissible as evidence in civil cases – later the Civil Evidence Act 1995 completely abrogated the rule.

Before the changes that were brought about by the Criminal Justice Act 2003 the 'old' law attracted considerable criticism. In 1997 the Law Commission was instructed to conduct a full consultation on this area of the law of evidence, as a result of which it produced its report (no 245) titled 'Evidence in Criminal Proceedings: Hearsay and Related Topics'. The paper highlighted why there existed a need for reform to this area of law. The protagonists of the changes included Sir Robin Auld, of the Auld Report fame, who concluded that the rules in relation to criminal proceedings (remember that the civil rules on the admission of such evidence have always been far more flexible) should be made more flexible and that the jury should be allowed to assess the weight of the evidence and not have the decision made for them. The argument that the jury was unable to appropriately assess such evidence was one of the very arguments used against its admission. The Government White Paper titled 'Justice for All', which stated that justice could not be served where 'important information is excluded without good reason', further rationalised the changes. Finally, the rule against the admission of hearsay in criminal cases was seen to exemplify the disparity between the civil and the criminal law because the civil law had allowed admission of such evidence since 1968 (as above).

Before beginning our discussion it is important for you to understand that the provisions under the Criminal Justice Act 2003 (CJA) apply equally to the prosecution and defence, with the safeguard that the prosecution must prove the matters beyond reasonable doubt: the criminal standard of proof. The defence, in return, must only prove its matters to the civil standard of proof, on the balance of probabilities. At this point it may be helpful to refer back to the differences between the two standards of proof discussed in Chapter 2.

The Criminal Justice Act 2003 introduced the statutory admission of hearsay evidence – prior to this the rules governing admission existed in the common law, statute and general practice. The rule against the admission of hearsay evidence, and its exceptions, was of great importance in the English law of evidence. Murphy articulates the rule well, defining it as '. . . evidence from any

the evidence is that of a witness	it consists of that which someone else stated at some other time either verbally, in writing or using another method, e.g. hand movements	which is tendered to prove the truth of any fact stated by that person in that evidence

Figure 7.1 Defining hearsay

witness which consists of what another person stated (whether verbally, in writing or by any other method of assertion such as a gesture) on any prior occasion, is inadmissible if its only relevant purpose is to prove that any fact so stated by that person on that prior occasion is true. Such a statement may, however, be admitted for any relevant purpose, other than proving the truth of the facts stated in it.' Let us take a closer look at this definition and what it includes. In basic terms the definition has three elements (see Figure 7.1).

From this definition we can see that not all statements that were made on prior occasions are excluded; statements tendered to prove anything other than the truth of the facts stated are admissible, for example similar behaviour:

EXAMPLE

Gill hears that Ian has beaten Anna again. Gill's evidence could not have been admitted to show that Ian had beaten Anna; however, it could have been admitted to show that Ian had a violent disposition.

In *R v Blastland* [1986] AC 41, Lord Bridge of Harwich stated that the rule is very deeply rooted in the English common law:

JUDGMENT

'. . . hearsay evidence is not excluded because it has no logically probative value. Given that the subject matter of the hearsay is relevant to some issue in the trial, it may clearly be potentially probative. The rationale of excluding it as inadmissible, rooted as it is in the system of trial by jury, is a recognition of the great difficulty, even more acute for a juror than for a trained judicial mind, of assessing what, if any, weight can properly be given to a statement by a person whom the jury have not seen or heard and which has not been subject to any test of reliability by cross-examination. As Lord Normand put it, delivering the judgment of the Privy Council in *Teper v R* [1952] AC 480, at page 486: "The rule against admission of hearsay evidence is fundamental. It is not the best evidence and it is not delivered on oath. The truthfulness and accuracy of the person whose words are spoken by another witness cannot be tested by cross-examination and the light which his demeanour would throw on his testimony is lost." The danger against which this fundamental rule provides a safeguard is that untested hearsay evidence will be treated as having a probative force which it does not deserve.'

It applies to all instances of evidence in chief, cross-examination and re-examination, and it cannot be bypassed with questions requiring hearsay inferences or imputations. In summary, the rule was tough because such evidence was considered to be both unreliable and susceptible to the risk of being fabricated if not severely distorted. Technical issues were caused by its inconsistent application. Other problems lay with the fact that it could not be properly tested using cross-examination of the prior assertion, and juries tended to give such evidence more weight than was desirable. Although many arguments existed for its exclusion, the rule disadvantaged both the defendant and prosecution; there was never an argument that it should be included for fairness.

CASE EXAMPLE

Sparks v R [1964] AC 964

The victim, a four-year-old girl, gave her mother a description of her attacker as being a 'black male'. The girl did not give evidence herself, and her mother's statement of that description was ruled as being inadmissible hearsay evidence, even though it would have clearly shown the defendant, who was a white male, to be innocent.

CASE EXAMPLE

R v Turner (1975) 61 Cr App R 67

The issue concerned an admission of guilt in a case involving an armed robbery; the maker of the statement was not called as a witness. The question was whether the statement that was admitted was hearsay. The court decided that it was and therefore it could not be admitted as evidence, even though it showed that the defendant might have been innocent.

This rule against the admission of hearsay evidence operated for many years, and its harsh application resulted in the development of common law exceptions to it, something that was further strengthened by Parliament with statutory exceptions in both civil and criminal cases. There were many instances where hearsay evidence would have been of crucial importance, but it remained inadmissible if it did not fall into any of the exceptions (see *Sparks* above). It should be noted that exceptions to the rule against the admission of hearsay evidence in criminal proceedings developed in both the common law and statute. In 1965 the House of Lords in *DPP v Myers* [1965] AC 1001 laid the further expansion of these rules to rest by stating that any future expansion should only be undertaken by statute:

JUDGMENT

'It is difficult to make any general statement about the law of hearsay evidence, which is entirely accurate, but I think that the books show that in the seventeenth century the law was fluid and uncertain but that early in the eighteenth century it had become the general rule that hearsay evidence was not admissible. Many reasons for the rule have been put forward, but we do not know which of them directly influenced the judges who established the rule. The rule has never been absolute. By the nineteenth century many exceptions had become well established, but again in most cases we do not know how or when the exception came to be recognised. It does seem, however, that in many cases there was no justification either in principle or logic for carrying the exception just so far and no farther. One might hazard a surmise that when the rule proved highly inconvenient in a particular kind of case it was relaxed just sufficiently far to meet that case, and without regard to any question

> of principle. But this kind of judicial legislation became less and less acceptable and well over a century ago the patchwork which then existed seems to have become stereotyped. The natural result has been the growth of more and more fine distinctions so that it now takes even so concise an author as Professor Cross over 100 closely packed pages to explain the law of hearsay evidence.'
>
> (Lord Reid)

The rationale was the problems caused by ad hoc lawmaking, the result of which was to make the law uncertain because no consistent approach was being followed or principle being established. One final point to note before moving on to discuss the classification of hearsay evidence is that the old law was contained in a variety of statutes, including the Criminal Justice Act 1988.

ACTIVITY

Outline the elements of the hearsay rule.

True or false? Under the old law a hearsay statement could not be admitted to prove something other than the truth of its contents.

KEY FACTS

Hearsay

The definition of hearsay contains three elements:

- it is the evidence of a witness;
- it consists of that which someone else stated at some other time either verbally, in writing or using another method, e.g. hand movements; and
- it is tendered to prove the truth of any fact stated by that person in that evidence.

The *general rule* in civil cases is that hearsay evidence is admissible. In criminal cases the approach was exclusionary, unless the evidence was admissible by exception. The same evidence may be admissible if it is also classifiable as a different type of evidence and is therefore introduced for purposes other than as evidence of the truth of any fact it contains. The CJA 2003 takes an *inclusionary approach*, meaning that hearsay is admissible if it falls under one of the provisions of the statute.

7.2 Classifying evidence as hearsay evidence

A statement is defined in the CJA 2003 as 'any representation of fact or opinion made by a person by whatever means'; this includes a representation made by sketch, photo-fit or other pictorial form. When assessing whether a statement (or assertion) can be classified as hearsay evidence, you must be clear as to the definition of hearsay. This consists of (1) statements or assertions that are made on previous occasions, and (2) which are tendered as evidence to prove that their contents are true. Under the old rules the judge would determine whether a statement or assertion was hearsay evidence and whether it was inadmissible using a two-stage approach; the court would ask these questions:

(a) Is the evidence a previous statement or assertion that amounts to hearsay?

(b) What is the purpose for which it is being tendered?

The court would begin by asking itself whether the statement, assertion or gesture was made outside of court. If the answer was in the affirmative, it would move on to ask itself whether the statement, assertion or gesture was being tendered in court to prove the truth of its contents, i.e. the truth of the statement, the assertion or gesture itself. After this the court would ask itself a third and final question, whether the person making the statement, assertion or gesture intends that it be either believed or acted upon. Where all of these questions are answered in the affirmative, then the statement, assertion or gesture is hearsay evidence; if not, then the evidence is not hearsay evidence and *may* be admissible as original evidence. The golden rule still applies: only relevant evidence is admissible, and there is always a risk that the evidence is not relevant. Furthermore, it could be that the evidence falls under some other category for exclusion; remember, judges still have the discretion to exclude at common law.

7.2.1 Rationale for exclusion

Other than where admission was provided for by the common law and statutory exceptions, hearsay evidence was inadmissible for several reasons. These included:

- Hearsay did not satisfy the best-evidence rule: when the rules of evidence were going through their formative years, the courts became obsessed with admitting only the best evidence available. Hearsay evidence was considered a derivative of a secondary source, which ought not to be admissible because by this very reason it was untrustworthy:

JUDGMENT

'. . . hearsay evidence is not the best evidence and it is not delivered on oath. The truthfulness and accuracy of the person whose words are spoken by another witness cannot be tested by cross-examination and the light which his demeanour would throw on his testimony is lost.'

(Lord Normand in *Teper v R* [1952] AC 480)

- The very nature of the evidence meant that there was an absence of the opportunity to cross-examine (or test) it: as Lord Normand suggested in *Teper* above, the person from whom the source of the relevant fact had derived, by definition, is not available to be cross-examined with a view to testing the accuracy of the testimony.
- Hearsay was likely to be inaccurate because it was being recounted or repeated: it is a natural phenomenon that issues that are repeated without knowledge of the original facts are capable of being exaggerated, and this may result in inaccuracy. This accounts for the fear that had been experienced by common law judges in adopting an adversarial procedure of settling disputes.

7.3 A different (inclusionary) approach under the Criminal Justice Act 2003 – in outline

In 2003 the Criminal Justice Act 2003 introduced a brand new inclusionary approach to the admission of hearsay evidence that sought to modernise the law, *per* Rose LJ in *R v Joyce and Joyce* [2005] EWCA Crim 1785. Under the old regime the accepted rule was that hearsay evidence was inadmissible unless one of the exceptions applied; in the new approach the rule has changed to: hearsay evidence is admissible if it falls under one of the ways outlined in the CJA 2003 (each of which is discussed below).

Section 114 of the CJA 2003 provides that hearsay evidence, i.e. a statement not made in oral evidence in the proceedings, is admissible in criminal trials of any matter stated, if:

- any provision makes it admissible;
- any rule of law preserved by s 118 makes it admissible;
- all the parties agree to it being admissible;
- the court is satisfied that it is in the interest of justice for it to be admissible.

The effect of this on criminal trials has been profound because more hearsay evidence is now admissible than was the case under the common law. A key point to note is that admission of hearsay evidence in civil cases has been inclusionary and subject to safeguards for a number of years prior to this advent in criminal matters. The main provisions are enacted by the Criminal Justice Act 2003 and apply to all criminal proceedings. The statute came into force in April 2005. The provisions apply to *criminal proceedings*, and therefore the discussion begins with a brief explanation of this term. In *R v Bradley* [2005] EWCA Crim 20, a case concerning bad character, the Court of Appeal highlighted that the term 'criminal proceedings' under the CJA 2003 refers to any 'criminal proceedings to which the strict rules of evidence apply'. The effect of this is that the new rules apply to all stages in criminal proceedings where the strict evidential rules apply, and that includes trial and *Newton* hearings (*R v Bradley* [2005] EWCA Crim 20), and also preparatory hearings: see *R v H* [2006] 1 Cr App R 4, s 30 Criminal Procedure and Investigations Act 1996 and *R v H* [2006] 1 Cr App R 4. The definition also includes hearings pursuant to s 4A Criminal Procedure (Insanity) Act 1964 that are held to determine whether the accused committed the act or omission (see *R v Chal* [2007] EWCA Crim 2647), and committal proceedings (see *CPS v City of London Magistrates' Court* [2006] EWHC 1153 (Admin)). Figure 7.2 summarises the position.

The CJA 2003 regime also applies analogically to proceedings under the Proceeds of Crime Act 2002.

Newton hearings	A stage where a single judge hears the prosecution and defence evidence on disputed factual points in the case following a plea of guilty
Preparatory hearings	Hearings designed to improve the effectiveness of pre-trial preparation through early resolution of any pure evidential or admissibility of evidence issues. It also allows the judge to manage the trial more effectively
Trial hearing	This is when the actual trial takes place

Figure 7.2 The application of hearsay in all stages of criminal proceedings under the Criminal Justice Act 2003

ACTIVITY

What was the rationale that underpinned the exclusion of hearsay evidence?

KEY FACTS

Hearsay under the CJA 2003

The 2003 Act modernised the law: see *R v Joyce and Joyce* [2005] EWCA Crim 1785.

Section 114 of the CJA 2003 provides that hearsay evidence is admissible in criminal cases if:

- any provision makes it admissible;
- any rule of law preserved by s 118 makes it admissible;
- all the parties agree to it being admissible;
- the court is satisfied that it is in the interest of justice for it to be admissible.

Criminal proceedings include *Newton*, preparatory and trial hearings.

7.3.1 Previous statements or assertions – analysis of hearsay

The application of the rules to previous statements, assertions or gestures that are made by any person was discussed earlier. This includes any previous statements that may have been made by the witnesses themselves. Note that statements such as these might be admissible as evidence of a previous consistent or inconsistent statement. This is a good example of how a single piece of evidence may not be admissible as one type of evidence but may be admissible as another. This part of the chapter focuses on previous inconsistent statements. Previous consistent statements and statements used to refresh the memory of a witness were discussed in Chapter 6.

Prior to discussing previous inconsistent statements, the form that a previous statement, assertion or gesture can take must be determined. In general, the law accepts that a person may use a variety of methods to communicate information, i.e. orally, visually, spoken word, in a document or by gestures. Here are some examples of hearsay statements:

CASE EXAMPLE

R v Gibson (1887) 18 QBD 537

The defendant had a quarrel with the prosecutor's son at a public house in Wigan. After the defendant had left the public house the prosecutor, along with his son and some others, walked home along what happened to be the street where the defendant lived. Whilst passing the house the prosecutor was struck on the head by a stone that came from the direction of the defendant's home and suffered a serious injury. The defendant was seen entering his house shortly after the stone had been thrown. The prosecutor's son and a police officer broke down the door of the defendant's house, finding the defendant with his father, who was asleep in a state of intoxication. Shortly before the stone was thrown, witnesses had seen the defendant come up behind the prosecutor, passing him on the opposite side of the street. At the time the stone was thrown, there was no one except the defendant on the side of the street from where the stone came. The question was whether evidence that A had told B where C, the defendant, who had allegedly thrown a stone at the house, lived by pointing to a particular house was admissible. The court held that the oral statement and the actual gesture of pointing were both hearsay evidence.

CASE EXAMPLE

Chandrasekera v R [1937] AC 200

A woman had suffered her throat being cut and was thus unable to speak; however, whilst fully conscious she understood what was said to her and in response she was able to make signs and nod her head, after which she was asked whether it was the appellant who had cut her throat. She nodded her head and died shortly afterwards from asphyxia. The court held that the evidence of the signs she made in answer to questions that had been put to her whilst alive was admissible. However, the statements of witnesses as to their interpretation of the signs were not. In addition, the direct question as to whether it was the appellant who had cut her throat and her nod of assent amounted to a verbal statement made by her that fell within the meaning of s 32 of the Ceylon Evidence Ordinance 1895 and was admissible in evidence. Hence, there was proper and sufficient evidence in the form of a verbal statement by the deceased that implicated the appellant. Although this is a case from the Supreme Court of the Island of Ceylon (now Sri Lanka), it is a good example of hearsay statements.

CASE EXAMPLE

Myers v DPP [1965] AC 1001

Myers was charged on indictment on seven counts along with another man: conspiracy to receive stolen cars, conspiracy to defraud purchasers of the stolen cars and receiving five cars knowing them to have been stolen. The prosecution sought to prove that for each of the twenty-two stolen cars, Myers or his accomplice had purchased an identical wrecked car, the purpose of which was to transfer the identification and registration numbers from the wrecked to the stolen vehicle. The owners of each of the stolen cars were asked to identify it. Myers admitted to purchasing twelve of the wrecked cars and selling an equal number of cars bearing the same registration numbers as the wrecked ones, but his contention was that these were cars that had been rebuilt and repaired and thus were not in fact the stolen cars. In addition, he contended that in rebuilding and repairing the cars he had innocently removed the identification marks and plates from the wrecked cars and placed them upon the rebuilt cars so that the numbers corresponded. The prosecution sought to prove that Myers had actually disguised the stolen cars so that he could sell them; in doing so it sought to adduce the evidence of the employees of the car manufacturers who had built the stolen cars and kept detailed records of the engine, chassis and cylinder block numbers. The cylinder block number had been purposely moulded into a secret part of the block and thus was impossible to remove or replace. Counsel for Myers objected to the admission of this on the grounds that it was hearsay evidence, but the evidence was admitted and Myers was convicted. He later appealed and lost.

Myers (above) is quite a wide interpretation of a hearsay statement, which led the courts to seek to reclassify it not as hearsay evidence but evidence that had a special quality in its own right.

Even though the CJA 2003 covers previous inconsistent statements, they must still be admitted in accordance with the Criminal Procedure Act 1865. Section 4 states:

SECTION

'If a witness, upon cross-examination as to a former statement made by him relative to the subject matter of the indictment or proceeding, and inconsistent with his present testimony, does not distinctly admit that he has made such statement, proof may be given that he did in fact make it; *but before such proof can be given the circumstances of the supposed statement, sufficient to designate the particular occasion, must be mentioned to the witness, and he must be asked whether or not he has made such statement.'*

Only then may a previous statement be tendered as proof of an inconsistency. Prior to the enactment of s 119 of the CJA 2003, these statements were only admissible, and usually tendered, to undermine the credibility of the makers of them. Under the current regime, once the statement is admitted it becomes evidence of the truth of all matters that are stated in it, so long as those matters are admissible if the maker were to give oral evidence of them: see Chapter 6.

CASE EXAMPLE

R v Joyce [2005] EWCA Crim 1785

The defendant was identified by many witnesses, all of whom gave detailed statements as to why they were certain that it was he who had committed the crime. Once the trial commenced, contrary to their previous statements, they all claimed to be uncertain as to their identifications. This sudden change implied that the witnesses were in some way being forced to change their evidence. The trial judge allowed the admission of the previous statements under s 119, which served as evidence of original identification. The defendant was duly convicted on the basis that the statements were evidence of the truth of the matters that they contained, i.e. the identification.

What are the conditions for admitting hearsay evidence of a previous inconsistent statement under s 119 CJA 2003? The witness must be called to give oral evidence (s 120(1) CJA 2003).

Moving on to previous consistent statements (see Chapter 6): can such a statement be admitted to rebut a suggestion, made by the opposition, that a witness's evidence has been **fabricated** or concocted? The answer to this question is 'yes': in this circumstance the statement is admissible as evidence of the truth of any matter that is contained in it so long as oral evidence of the matter would have been admissible. This means that the admission of such a statement goes to more than just the credibility of the witness (s 120(2) CJA 2003).

Fabrication
a false or improper account of something.

Finally, if Abimbola (a witness), whilst in the process of giving oral evidence, uses a statement that he had made on a previous occasion to refresh his memory, and he has been cross-examined on it, that statement becomes admissible as evidence of the truth of the matters that it contains (s 120(3) CJA 2003). In summary:

- Abimbola (the witness) makes a statement outside court, i.e. in a police station;
- Abimbola uses that statement to refresh his memory whilst giving oral evidence in court;
- Abimbola is cross-examined on that statement.

Another interesting question arises relating to when such statements are admissible. The witness can, at any time, whilst giving oral evidence refresh their memory from a statement that they may have made on a prior occasion. Witnesses may feel the need to do this for a variety of reasons. How many people can answer a question relating to what they had for supper on this day last week? Often events that have taken place a while ago are difficult to remember, even more so when you consider that in reality it can take up to six months and usually longer before an accused appears in the Crown Court, and that means a similar period of time will have elapsed between the witness making the statement and coming to court to give evidence. Therefore, allowing the witness to refresh their memory avoids oral evidence becoming a test of memory. The American scholar Elizabeth Loftus has carried out extensive research on the fallibilities of eyewitness evidence that may be of some additional interest to some readers. The main question most students ask is, what are the instances, if any, in which a witness is permitted to refresh his or her memory from such a statement? The admissibility of the statement and the witness's ability to refresh his or her memory from it depends on the witness indicating that:

- to the best of their belief, they personally made the statement;
- to the best of their belief, it contains the truth; and
- *one* of the following three conditions is satisfied:
  - the statement either identifies or describes a person, place or object (s 120(5) CJA 2003);
  - the statement was made when the matters contained in it were fresh in the witness's memory but they cannot be reasonably expected to sufficiently remember or recall the facts in order to give oral evidence of those facts at the trial (s 120(6) CJA 2003);
  - the witness claims to be the victim against whom the offence was committed, the proceedings relate to it, the statement contains a complaint made by them regarding conduct that constitutes the commission of the offence or a part of it. The complaint was made as soon as was reasonably practicable and was not made because the witness was being threatened or promised something and, before the statement can be adduced in evidence, the witness must give oral evidence in connection with its subject matter (s 120(7)).

This provision restricts the ability of either party to automatically adduce evidence of a previous recent complaint and, in the worst-case scenario, from adducing it at all where the delay is substantial.

CASE EXAMPLE

R v Openshaw [2006] 2 Cr App R 27

A complaint was made four months after the commission of the conduct. Evidence of the previous complaint was admitted because the court decided that the concept of what is 'as soon as is reasonably practicable' will depend on the facts of each individual case, and to whom it is made.

7.3.2 The purpose of tendering the evidence

It is quite obvious that not all previous statements, assertions or gestures are admissible as evidence. Consider this scenario: Margaret is willing to tell the court *what* someone said, and her evidence is then tendered for that purpose. In terms of questions concerning admissibility, the correct answer is that it is not automatically admissible. The same would now be as follows: does Margaret's evidence fall under any of the provisions of the CJA 2003 or the common law? The discussion now moves on to consider the different types of hearsay statements and their position in terms of admissibility.

7.3.3 Statements relevant only to truth

In contrast to civil cases, the rule against the admission of hearsay evidence in criminal cases has been strictly applied. The basic position was that a hearsay statement was inadmissible unless it fell within one of the common law exceptions. Here are some case examples:

CASE EXAMPLE

R v Attard (1958) 43 Cr App R 90

The witness was a police officer who sought to give evidence of an interview that he had conducted through an interpreter with a non-English-speaking prisoner. His evidence consisted of telling the court that which the interpreter had told him. In this case his evidence was ruled to be inadmissible hearsay. In such cases it is usual practice to call the interpreter to give evidence.

CASE EXAMPLE

R v Marshall [1977] Crim LR 106

The defendant (A) confessed that the goods in his possession were stolen. This confession was inadmissible hearsay evidence because B had told him that they were stolen. In this case, had the confession been tendered to evidence A's belief that the goods were stolen then it would have been admissible, but it was inadmissible because it was tendered to evidence the fact that they were stolen.

CASE EXAMPLE

Jones v Metcalfe [1967] 1 WLR 1286

The defendant driver, charged with driving without due care and attention, had only been traced by reason of an eyewitness providing his registration number to the police. At the trial the eyewitness could not remember the number, nor were they allowed to refresh their memory. Therefore, the officer to whom the information of the registration number had been provided could not give evidence of that. It was in effect hearsay being tendered to prove the truth of what had been previously stated.

CASE EXAMPLE

Surujpaul v R [1958] 1 WLR 1050

Surujpaul was tried together with four others on a charge of murder. It was the prosecution's case that the murder had been committed whilst Surujpaul and his accomplices were carrying out their plot to steal money. This rested largely on the evidence of one of the accomplices, evidence that went to prove the existence of the plot. In addition, there was some material that would have led the jury to believe that the plan had been carried out by all or some of the accused and that it was in the course of carrying out the plot that the murder had been committed. The allegation against one of the accused was discharged and the other three were found not guilty as either accessories or principals. However, the jury found Surujpaul guilty as an accessory to murder. Surujpaul contended that the verdicts were inconsistent and contradictory because there could be no accessory without a principal. The Court of Appeal quashed the conviction on the basis that 'it was essential to the conviction of the appellant as accessory before the fact for the Crown to prove that he had counselled, procured or commanded one or more of the other accused to commit the murder and that such person or persons had in fact done so'.

Other interesting decisions on this point for research include *Comptroller of Customs v Western Lectric Co Ltd* [1966] AC 367 and *Wright v Doe d. Tatham* (Exch) (1937) 7 A&E 313. The rule also applies to statements made orally; a good example of this is *Teper v R* [1952] AC 480. In this case the defendant was accused of setting fire to his shop. He produced evidence of an alibi defence. In rebuttal, the prosecution adduced evidence that a woman was heard shouting at a motorist who had passed the shop; she had made a remark that implicated the motorist as the defendant. This evidence ruined his alibi defence and, on conviction, he appealed. The Privy Council allowed the appeal on the ground that the evidence was inadmissible hearsay:

JUDGMENT

'. . . no case is to be found which comes anywhere near this case, suggesting that the statement of this unidentified woman 230 yards away from the fire and 26 or more minutes after it started could be admissible on the authority of any known principle, or be said to be part of the *res gestae*'.

(Lord Normand)

Further, the House of Lords confirmed in *R v Kearley* (discussed later) that implied assertions were subject to the rule against admission of hearsay evidence. This has recently been set aside, and in *R v Singh* [2006] 1 WLR 1564 the Court of Appeal has stated that implied assertions no longer fall within the new CJA 2003 rule (see below). See also *R v N* [2006] EWCA Crim 3303.

7.3.4 Original evidence/non-hearsay statements

Not every statement is classifiable as hearsay evidence. Statements tendered for relevant reasons, other than as proof of the truth of their contents, are admissible as original evidence, i.e. evidence as to the making of the statement itself or evidence of the state of mind of the person making the statement or person hearing it. What follows is a brief review of this point.

Evidence that a statement was made

The discussion in Chapter 1 focused on the fact that only evidence relevant to a fact in issue may be admissible. Occasionally, the fact that a statement was made will be in issue; for example the existence of a contract, a previous consistent or inconsistent statement or a threat or defamatory remark may not constitute hearsay evidence.

CASE EXAMPLE

Subramaniam v Public Prosecutor [1956] 1 WLR 965

The defendant was charged with the unlawful possession of an offensive weapon and ammunition. He raised the defence of duress on the basis that terrorists had captured him and threatened him. At first instance the trial judge had ruled that this evidence was hearsay and inadmissible. On appeal the Privy Council decided that the court (jury) could receive such evidence so that it could establish (a) that threats had been made, and (b) the effect of them on the defendant.

CASE EXAMPLE

R v Chapman [1965] 2 QB 436

The evidence of a police officer that the police doctor had not objected to a sample being taken from the defendant was not hearsay evidence. It was original evidence by reason of there being consent and no objection. The court went on to state that this evidence would only be hearsay if it were tendered as proof of the defendant's health.

CASE EXAMPLE

Woodhouse v Hall (1980) 72 Cr App R 39

The defendant was prosecuted for acting in the management of a brothel contrary to s 33 of the Sexual Offences Act 1956. Evidence was given by police officers of various conversations they had had, in the absence of the defendant, in which immoral services had been offered to them by two women employed at the premises as masseuses. The evidence of the police officers showing that the women at the defendant's premises were offering sexual services for payment was admissible as original evidence. The statements were not being tendered as proof of their contents *per se*. The fact that services were being offered was circumstantial evidence of the point that the defendant's premises was a brothel.

Evidence of the state of mind of the maker

Although the exact state of mind of any person can never really be directly established, it can be proved through circumstantial evidence. This means that some statements may amount to original evidence of a person's state of mind and therefore be relevant for reasons other than the truth of their contents.

CASE EXAMPLE

R v Willis [1960] 1 WLR 55

The court decided that a conversation, between an employer and the defendant, that evidenced the innocent state of the defendant's mind should have been admissible because a statement showing the converse would have been admissible.

CASE EXAMPLE

Jones v DPP [1962] AC 635

This case concerned murder; here the defendant's false alibis were regarded as being original evidence of his guilty state of mind.

CASE EXAMPLE

Mawaz Khan and Amanat Khan v R [1967] AC 454

The defendants had suffered injuries that, they contended, had been sustained in a fight at a nightclub and not, as the prosecution case suggested, in the course of a murder. Although their alibis were identical, neither one of the two defendants gave evidence. The trial judge directed the jury that if they felt that any one of the alibis had been fabricated, then that fabrication would incriminate both defendants. The direction, on appeal, was held to be correct with the court stating that, *per* Lord Hodson, 'a statement is not hearsay and is admissible when it is proposed to establish . . . not the truth of the statement, but the fact that it was made . . .'. It went on to state that there would be no breach of the rule against admission of hearsay where it is tendered 'not for the purpose of establishing the truth of the assertions contained therein, but for the purpose of asking the jury to hold the assertions false and to draw inferences from their falsity'. The alibi statements showed that they were (a) acting in concert and (b) had common guilt.

CASE EXAMPLE

Ratten v R [1972] AC 378

The defendant shot his wife and pleaded accident. At his trial for her murder, evidence of a telephone call made by a hysterical woman five minutes before she was shot was admitted as circumstantial evidence of her terrified state of mind. Her state of mind was an issue before the court. The admission of the call collaterally evidenced whether or not the shooting had been an accident or murder.

CASE EXAMPLE

R v Blastland [1986] AC 41

Ratten should be contrasted with *Blastland*, in which the defendant (A) was accused of committing buggery with and murdering a boy (C). The defendant admitted that he had committed buggery with C before he had died but denied any involvement in the killing. In his defence he sought to adduce evidence that another man (B) had revealed the fact that the death had occurred well before this information had been made public, and appeared distressed and anxious. In fact, B had admitted to the killing but had later withdrawn his confession. The trial judge refused admission of this evidence on the grounds that it was hearsay. The House of Lords held a contrary view: the evidence was not hearsay as it showed B's state of mind, but because his state of mind was not in issue, it was inadmissible.

In the crucial decision of *R v Kearley* [1992] 2 All ER 345, the police intercepted calls made by unknown callers to the defendant's premises asking to buy drugs. Some of these unknown callers actually came to the premises in person. The question for the House of Lords was whether the evidence of the calls had been rightly admitted, even though the defendant was not present at the time they were made. The House decided that evidence of the calls, which was being tendered to show the use of the premises, was inadmissible hearsay, i.e. the truth of their content. Whether or not the callers thought that they would procure drugs was irrelevant. Therefore, it would be wrong to allow the negative inference that the premises were being used to distribute drugs to be drawn as a result of the assertions of the callers:

JUDGMENT

'I accept the proposition that, if an action is of itself relevant to an issue, the words which accompany and explain the action may be given in evidence, whether or not they would be relevant independently. But here the mere fact of the calls being made to the defendant's house was by itself of no relevance whatever, so we are back to the bare issue as to whether the implied assertion involved in the request for drugs should be excluded as hearsay. As English law presently stands, I am clearly of the opinion that it should.'

(Lord Bridge of Harwich)

In *Kearley* the House distinguished *Woodhouse v Hall* on the basis that in *Woodhouse* the fact of the existence of an offer made on the premises by an employee was sufficient evidence to establish that the premises were being used for the distribution of drugs. Likewise the House distinguished *Ratten v R*, because in that case the hysterical call was made from the premises and could be classed as (a) evidence of the attack on the victim as part of the *res gestae* and (b) relevant to the fabrication of the defence of accident. The House outlined that in *Kearley* it was not the state of the mind of the callers that was relevant to a fact in issue before the jury:

JUDGMENT

'. . . the first question then is whether the fact of the request for drugs having been made is in itself relevant to the issue whether the defendant was a supplier. The fact that words were spoken may be relevant for various purposes, but most commonly they will be so when they reveal the state of mind of either the speaker or the person to whom the words were spoken when that state of mind is itself in issue or is relevant to a matter in issue . . . the state of mind of the person making the request for drugs is of no relevance at all to the question whether the defendant is a supplier. The sole possible relevance of the words spoken is that by manifesting the speaker's belief that the defendant is a supplier they impliedly assert that fact.'

(Lord Bridge of Harwich)

CASE EXAMPLE

R v Gilfoyle [1996] 3 All ER 883

The defendant was accused of murdering his wife, and contended that she had committed suicide. In furtherance of this he tendered as evidence a note allegedly written by her about her depressed state of mind. The prosecution, in rebuttal of this, tendered evidence of remarks made by the wife to her friends in which she had told them how she had written the note at the request of her husband, and how she had found the whole thing highly amusing. The conversation was not hearsay evidence when tendered to show her state of mind, i.e. that she was not depressed.

Most recently the Court of Appeal has ruled in *R v Singh* (below) that implied assertions are no longer hearsay and therefore do not fall within the new CJA 2003 rule, because they are considered to be direct evidence as in *Kearley* (above): direct evidence that there was a market for the defendant to supply the drugs from his premises, i.e. people wanted to buy them from him.

CASE EXAMPLE

R v Singh [2006] 1 WLR 1564

The defendant was charged on indictment with conspiracy to kidnap. The prosecution alleged that the defendant had used mobile telephones to make and receive calls to and from his co-conspirators at the time of the kidnapping. The mobile telephone memories of the co-conspirators' phones contained the defendant's mobile telephone numbers. The trial judge ruled that this evidence was admissible to show that the defendant was a party to the conspiracy. The defendant was convicted and appealed on the ground that although s 115(3) of the Criminal Justice Act 2003 excluded implied assertions from the general rule against the admissibility of hearsay under s 114, such assertions remained inadmissible at common law. His appeal was dismissed: the court held that 'the effect of ss 114 and 118 was to abolish the common law rule against the admissibility of hearsay and to create a new rule against hearsay which did not extend to implied assertions . . . that the telephone entries were not "a matter stated" within the meaning of s 115(3) of the Act but were implied assertions which were admissible in evidence because they were no longer hearsay . . . that the judge had been right to allow the Crown to adduce the evidence'.

Other interesting cases include *R v Chrysostomou* [2010] EWCA Crim 1403 and *R v MK* [2007] EWCA Crim 310, which followed *R v Singh* [2006] EWCA Crim 660 – here the numbers stored in a mobile telephone did not fall under s 155 of the CJA 2003 as a matter stated but as implied assertions that were no longer hearsay and thus admissible. In *R v Twist and Others* [2011] EWCA Crim 1143, the Court of Appeal recommended that the concept of implied assertions should be avoided because the 2003 Act focuses on 'matters stated', and it suggested the following approach where the application of the hearsay rules was in consideration:

- identify the relevant matter that the hearsay seeks to prove and identify whether there is a statement of that matter in the communication;
- if the answer to this is negative, then no question as to hearsay arises;
- if the answer is in the affirmative, then the court should ask whether it is one of the purposes of the maker of the communication that the recipient (or another) believes that matter or acts on it as if it were true. If yes, then it is hearsay; if not, then it is not hearsay.

The court was quick to highlight that the application of the questions will depend on the facts of each case. For instance, sometimes a communication may be hearsay depending on the matter for which it is relied upon and what it is being tendered to prove.

Evidence of the state of mind of the recipient

Statements may be admitted to prove the state of the mind of the recipient; therefore the following question arises: is a statement that is tendered to show the effect on someone also admissible? Consider the following scenario: Maya receives a telephone call telling her to assault Adrian. She is told that if she refuses her family will be attacked. Two questions arise here in relation to Maya's defence. First, can the evidence of the telephone call be admitted to prove the truth of its contents (the fact that the family will be attacked); and, second, can evidence of the telephone call be admitted for any other purpose, for instance in aid of a defence of duress. The answer to the first of these questions is 'no' because it is inadmissible hearsay. However, the answer to the second of these questions is in the affirmative. In *Subramaniam v Public Prosecutor* (as discussed above) the court admitted evidence of terrorists' threats. These were tendered as evidence relevant to the defendant's defence of duress. They evidenced the effect that such threats had on his mind, and not of the truth of their contents.

Hearsay evidence relevant for a non-hearsay purpose

This is a particularly interesting area of the law of evidence and it has had its fair share of problems. Hearsay evidence may be tendered for a purpose other than as evidence of the truth of any matter stated. For example, Philip writes to Malcolm threatening him and demanding the return of the money he owes him. One week later Malcolm is found dead on the doorstep of his home having been bludgeoned to death. The letter, should it be available, may be tendered as evidence to contradict Philip's assertion that he did not know Malcolm. In *R v Rice and Others* [1963] 1 QB 857 the defendant was accused of conspiracy. It was alleged that he had, on a particular day, taken a flight with his co-defendant to Manchester. In support, the prosecution tendered an airline ticket for a flight to Manchester in the name of each of the defendants. The defence contended that this evidence was inadmissible because it was hearsay, i.e. the truth of the assertion that the defendants were on the flight. The Court of Appeal decided that the airline ticket was admissible since it was original, circumstantial evidence from which the jury could infer that the defendant had flown to Manchester. This was on the basis that if production of the ticket by the airline showed compliance with its normal procedures, then the inference that someone with the defendant's name had taken the flight could be drawn. The issue of whether or not the defendant had taken the flight was one for the

CASE EXAMPLE

R v Podmore (1930) 22 Cr App R 36

A document found in a particular place, partly written by A, who was deceased by the time of the trial, was admissible as circumstantial evidence of a dishonest relationship between the defendant and the deceased. The contents of the document were hearsay. However, the fact that it was found in a particular place was the relevant non-hearsay element that the party was seeking to adduce.

CASE EXAMPLE

R v Lydon (1986) 85 Cr App R 221

A car was stolen in Neasden, London, and then driven to Oxfordshire, where it was used in the robbery of a post office. Both the appellant, Sean Lydon, and his co-accused were charged with taking a conveyance without authority and robbery, charges to which the co-accused pleaded guilty. The issue was whether Lydon was the second person involved in the commission of the offences. Substantial identification evidence incriminated the appellant; a customer who had been in the post office when it was robbed, a part-time assistant who worked there, and the taxi driver who had driven both men to Neasden had accurately described the co-accused and had subsequently picked out the appellant from an identification parade (both of which could be undermined). Additionally, two women had described the car used, which was discovered in Nettlebed Road, the place where the taxi driver had picked up the two men. The trial judge allowed the admission of evidence relating to the discovery of a gun on a grass verge on the road the getaway car would have travelled along to get to Nettlebed Road. The gun was found in four pieces along with two pieces of paper on which was written 'Sean Rules' and 'Sean Rules 85'. On the gun was a smear in blue ink, which forensic evidence showed to be of a similar composition to the ink on the pieces of paper, and thus it was likely that both had come from the same pen. The only witness who had seen the gun described it as being brown when in fact the gun that had been found was black and silver. Lydon's only defence was an alibi. The trial judge permitted the prosecution to tender as original circumstantial evidence the pieces of paper and the gun. He appealed on the ground that the evidence about the gun was hearsay and thus that its prejudicial effect outweighed its probative value. Dismissing his appeal, the court decided that the reference to 'Sean' was no more than a statement of fact that involved no assertion as to the truth of the document and, if the jury were satisfied that the gun was the same as the one used in the robbery and that the pieces of paper were linked to the gun, then the reference to 'Sean' was but a further fact that would fit with the prosecution's allegation that it was the defendant who was the other person who had committed the robbery. Hence, admission of this evidence was not contrary to the hearsay rule because it was not unduly prejudicial.

jury to decide. In contrast to the labelling cases it seems that the safeguard in this instance is compliance with the airline's ticket and security procedures.

Negative hearsay evidence: lack of the record

Hearsay statements are adduced as evidence to prove the truth of their contents, namely that something exists or has happened. An interesting question arises in relation to the converse, that is those statements that prove the negative – something does not exist or has not happened; whether these be classed as hearsay too. The answer to this is in the affirmative; this was classed as negative hearsay. Under the common law the position was that both positive and negative records were subject to the rule against the admission of hearsay evidence, and either could be admitted if they fell under the exceptions to the rule.

In *R v Patel* [1981] 3 All ER 94, the prosecution sought to prove that a man named Ashraf was in fact an illegal immigrant. An immigration officer, whilst giving evidence for the prosecution, stated that Home Office Records did not show that a person, Ashraf, was entitled to enter the UK. The Court of Appeal decided that the records were hearsay, as was any oral evidence based on them. The court stated that the evidence could have been received by it if the person who had personal knowledge of the compilation of the records had given oral evidence of the absence of Ashraf's name on the record and the significance that this held. Although this would not have altered the fact that the records were hearsay, the court would have been prepared to hear an argument that they were in fact circumstantial evidence.

CASE EXAMPLE

R v Shone (1983) 76 Cr App R 721

The defendant had been charged with handling stolen motor parts after the goods were found on his premises. It was easily ascertained that manufacturer A had supplied the parts to company B, from which they had been stolen. Officials from company B testified as to their record-keeping process, stating that there was no record of these parts being sold or used. The absence of such a record of sale or use did not mean that their evidence was hearsay evidence as it was circumstantial evidence from which the jury was entitled to infer that they had in fact been stolen.

In criminal proceedings s 115(3) of the Criminal Justice Act 2003 now covers this area of the law. It is unlikely that the result in the above cases would have been any different on application of this provision. The issue centres on the intention of the person compiling the record: if an event has not been recorded it is unlikely that the person compiling the record would have intended that omission on the record to evidence the fact that an event had not occurred, as the Law Commission stated in its Report 245 1997 (see 7.10–7.11 and 7.41):

It seems that, if an inference is drawn from what a document says, the document is hearsay; but if an inference is drawn from what it does not say (or from the fact that no document exists), that is direct evidence.

Patel and *Shone* were authority, under the old law, for the requirement that evidence of an omission on a record must be given by the person who had personal knowledge and custody of the record itself. It is important for the court to be able to draw inferences, and it is likely that it will continue to require the aid of that person to do so; thus this requirement will remain intact even under s 115(3).

Other evidence: calculators, computers and other devices

The advances of technology have led to a greater increase in the use of electronic devices, such as computers and other machinery, to record or process information. This information is now widely used and presented in court proceedings, and therefore the classification or status of such information is important. The categorisation of this information depends on the nature and function of the electronic device involved. What follows is a look at this in more detail. Where knowledge or discretion is not required to be exercised by a device, i.e. it performs simple calculations that could be done manually, then that information is classified as *real evidence* and not hearsay evidence: see *R v Woods* (1982) 76 Cr App R 232. Information that is generated by the device, for example a computer may generate a list after someone inputs information into it, is classified as hearsay evidence. The general rule is that records produced by electronic equipment that relies on information supplied to it by a person is hearsay evidence. In criminal proceedings such evidence is only admissible in so far as it is accurate (s 129(1) of the CJA 2003, although sub-s (2) provides a presumption in favour of proper calibration of the equipment itself).

CASE EXAMPLE

R v Spiby (1990) 91 Cr App R 186

A device had automatically logged all telephone calls at an exchange and was a record. This amounted to real evidence because there had never been any human input into the recording process.

7.4 The common law exceptions to the rule

So far our discussion has focused on the strictness of the rule against the admission of hearsay evidence. It was exactly this rigidity that led to the development of a number of exceptions to the rule in the common law. Each authority that developed an exception attempted to overcome the hurdles of the documented unreliability and fabrication of hearsay evidence, and judicial reluctance to accept hearsay as good evidence. Additionally, a number of statutory exceptions to the rule also developed, the effect of which was to curtail the creation of further common law exceptions: see *Myers v DPP* [1965] AC 1001.

Section 114(1)(b) of the Criminal Justice Act 2003 has expressly preserved the common law exceptions to the rule against admission of hearsay in s 118, and s 118(2) has abolished those that are not mentioned. In summary, the hearsay exceptions that have been preserved by the Criminal Justice Act 2003 are:

- *res gestae*
- public information
- confessions
- other admissions (agents)
- reputation, i.e. character (the rule in *Rowton*)
- reputation or familial tradition
- common enterprise
- expert evidence.

The discussion that follows briefly explores each of the common law exceptions and the reasons that underlie their preservation or abolition.

7.4.1 The *res gestae*

The discussion begins with what can be said to be the most important of the common law exceptions to the rule against the admission of hearsay evidence, the *res gestae* rule. Sections 114(1)(d) and 118(1)(4) of the CJA 2003 expressly preserve this exception; to express a preservation also means that the principles surrounding this concept, including the case law, are also preserved. You should note two points: first, that such hearsay statements may also be admissible under s 116 of the CJA 2003; and second, that this common law exception applies only to criminal cases. The current law adopts the position that inadmissible hearsay statements are admissible if they form part of the *res gestae* – a term used to refer to the 'state of affairs'. Hearsay statements may form part of the *res gestae* where they are *spontaneous* and where they are an *integral part of the event*. Where they meet these criteria they will be admissible as evidence of the truth of their contents as part of the *res gestae*. The rationale behind this is that the statement is so mixed up with the event to which it relates or refers that it almost becomes part of it. Additionally, the spontaneity of the statement means that issues of unreliability and fabrication are mitigated, and that the risk of the same occurring is reduced. The rationale for this rule may be traced back to *Thompson v Trevanion* (1693) Skin 402, where, in an action for an assault on the claimant's wife, Holt CJ said that what the wife said immediately on the hurt received, and before she had time to devise or concoct a story to her advantage, might be given in evidence as part of the *res gestae*. The justification, therefore, for admitting this piece of relevant evidence is the spontaneity of such statement.

Here is a hypothetical example, Katharine is attacked whilst walking home from work at 1 a.m. in Holland Park. As she flees, she telephones the police in a hysterical state and informs them of what is happening. In this instance, it is likely that the statement will form part of the *res gestae* and be admitted as evidence of the truth of its contents. It may also be tendered to prove Katharine's state of mind at the time. Evidence of a contemporaneous and spontaneous outburst or statement made by the person doing an act, related to the act, will be admissible as evidence of what occurred, so long as there is no evidence to suggest that it has been calculated or made, knowing the effect that its admission will have; also see *R v Bliss* (1837) 7 A&E 500.

CASE EXAMPLE

R v Bliss (1837) 7 A&E 500

Evidence of a comment made casually by a man planting a tree to the effect that it was on the boundary was inadmissible as evidence of where the boundary was located. The comment would only have been admissible if the purpose of planting it there was to mark the boundary.

Where a bystander, observer or participant makes a statement relating to an event, then it will be of utmost importance to assess the facts of the case very carefully. For an interesting comparison take a look at the US version of the *res gestae* rule, which is aptly titled the 'excited utterances rule' (see the Federal Rules of Evidence (2015) rr 801–807; www.rulesofevidence.org/article-viii/). The term 'spontaneity' has a strict accepted meaning in the law of evidence, where it is defined as 'automatically or without an interval of time sufficient to enable the maker of the statement to devise a story': see *Thompson v Trevanion* (1693) Skin 402. The resultant effect of this test was that over the decades the courts had held that spontaneity could only exist if the statement was contemporaneous with the event, the latter part of which was strictly interpreted. The argument against such strict interpretation was settled in subsequent cases because spontaneity may certainly be included within that which is contemporaneous; however, contemporaneity with the event is not the only way of demonstrating that something is spontaneous. For instance, what happens if the statement is made before or after an event – does this render the statement inadmissible? Let us briefly explore the authorities on this issue:

CASE EXAMPLE

R v Bedingfield (1879) 14 Cox CC 341

The utterances of a victim who had just had her throat slit were inadmissible to prove the identity of her attacker because she had stumbled out of the room where the attack had taken place. Therefore her utterance was not spontaneous enough. Not surprisingly, the case was overruled and, although the decision has been ridiculed, it highlights the strict application of the rule and the resulting absurdity.

The issue of classification came before the Privy Council (PC) in *Ratten v R* [1972] AC 378 (discussed above), which concerned the admission of a hysterical telephone call from the defendant's wife who was shot shortly after making it. The question before the PC was whether the statement was classified as hearsay or circumstantial evidence. The PC held that the evidence was admissible as circumstantial evidence; even had it been classified as being hearsay, it would have in no doubt been admissible as part of the *res gestae*. The PC criticised the decision in *R v Bedingfield*. Lord Wilberforce stated:

JUDGMENT

'. . . regarding statements made after the event it must be for the judge . . . to satisfy himself that the statement was so clearly made in circumstances of spontaneity or involvement in the event that the possibility of concoction can be disregarded . . . the same must, in principle, be true of statements made before the event . . . if the drama, leading up to the climax, has commenced and assumed such intensity and pressure that the utterance can be safely regarded as a true reflection of what was unrolling or actually happening, it ought to be received.'

The effect of this approach is that the correct test for admission of such evidence was not based on a strict sense of timing or contemporaneity, but the unlikelihood of concoction or fabrication.

The decision in *R v Bedingfield* was overruled in *R v Andrews* [1987] AC 251. In this case, the victim of a robbery identified the robbers before lapsing into a coma and dying. It is obvious that this was clearly a hearsay statement, but could not be admitted as a dying declaration (see below). The question before the court was whether it formed part of the *res gestae*. The defendant argued that the identification was hearsay and it lacked contemporaneous spontaneity. However, the House of Lords re-stated that the real test for admission involved the lack of opportunity for concoction, and whether there was 'no real opportunity for reasoned reflection', that 'the mind of the *person making the statement* was still dominated by the event'. If there was any doubt as to the admission of the evidence, for instance the person making the statement was blind, then it should only be admitted where the possibility of error is excluded. On that basis the House of Lords felt that the telephone call was spontaneous as it was clearly part of the *res gestae* and therefore admissible as evidence. The case of *Andrews* is a prime example of the re-stated test from *Ratten* (above) that considered the time the statement was made on a more liberal basis.

A change in the approach adopted by the courts is evidenced by a number of subsequent decisions. In *R v Nye and Loan* (1977) 66 Cr App R 252 the court adopted a far more lenient approach to *res gestae* evidence by admitting a statement made by a victim of an assault several minutes after it had taken place. Similarly, in *R v Carnall* [1995] Crim LR 944 the court admitted a statement made one hour after a serious assault, once again as part of the *res gestae*.

CASE EXAMPLE

Tobi v Nicholas (1988) 86 Cr App R 323

X made a statement identifying Y as the defendant in a road accident. The statement was inadmissible hearsay evidence; the court held that the statement no longer formed part of the *res gestae* because X had left the scene of the crime to follow the defendant's car and had made the statement much later.

It is therefore important to demonstrate that the individual who made the statement had the state of mind outlined in *Ratten v R* and *R v Andrews* (above). Where the identity of the maker of the statement is unknown, it will not be possible to prove what their state of mind was when they made the statement: see *Teper v R* (above).

7.4.2 Statements evidencing the physical or mental state of the maker

This is a particularly interesting area of the law of evidence, as the following question arises: can a hearsay statement, where the maker of a statement refers to a particular state of mind such as fear or a physical state such as sickness, be admitted as evidence of that rather than the truth of its contents? The answer to this question is in the affirmative: the common law facilitated the admission of a statement that evidenced either the physical or mental state of the person making it, but not the cause of the physical or mental state: see *Gilbey v Great Western Railway* (1910) 102 LT 202. The condition is that the statement must refer to the health of the person making it and not that of someone else: see *R v Parker* (1960) 45 Cr App R 1. Here is a hypothetical example: Dirk complains that his husband, Tiago, has poisoned him. Dirk's statement will be admissible as evidence showing that he was feeling ill, but not to prove that Tiago poisoned him. The following two cases are good examples of this rule. In *R v Conde* (1868) 10 Cox CC 547, a child's complaint of hunger was admissible as evidence that he was hungry, but not that he had been neglected through the deprivation of food. And in *Shephard v US* (1933) 290 US 96, a wife's statement that her husband had poisoned her was admissible to show that she felt sick, but not admissible to show that he had poisoned her.

7.4.3 Statements by the deceased

Statements by the deceased sounds like a rather strange category. However, it does not refer to statements made by the dead, whether through a medium or otherwise, but to statements made by persons who have died since making them. The general rule states that an assertion that is made by a person who has since died, and cannot therefore give evidence, is admissible in certain instances. In short, the common law recognised the importance of this exception to the hearsay rule, statute subsequently limited it and the CJA 2003 finally abolished it. Now evidence of this type may be adduced under s 116(2)(a) (see above).

7.4.4 Declarations against an interest

This exception was an interesting one, even though it has now been abolished. Under this exception, where a statement of the maker went against their financial or proprietary interest, it was admissible as evidence.

The requirement was that the statement must have been made against the financial or proprietary interest of the person making it. The fact that the statement incriminated them for the commission of other criminal offences was insufficient.

CASE EXAMPLE

Higham v Ridgeway (1808) 10 East 109

The statement of a midwife, deceased by the time of the trial, indicating that she had been paid for the delivery of a child on a particular date, was admissible hearsay evidence of the date of the child's birth. Two points heavily favoured its admission: (a) the midwife had personal knowledge of the facts; and (b) her statement went against her own interests.

CASE EXAMPLE

R v Roberts [1942] 1 All ER 187

The defendant (A), charged with being involved in drug and gun crime, sought to rely on a statement that had been made by B to his wife that A knew nothing about the drugs or guns that B had intended to use. B died before the trial and his statement was therefore inadmissible under this heading.

7.4.5 Declarations in the course of a duty

This is another exception that has been abolished by the CJA 2003. However, a good appreciation of it is required because it exemplifies why and how the current law operates. Under this exception, hearsay evidence was admissible in certain circumstances where the person making the statement was under a legal, professional or moral duty to record information relating to the performance of their tasks. The condition was that there was contemporaneity in the creation of the record and the act being recorded. Here the issue of what amounted to 'contemporaneous' raised much discussion, but the requirement was not strictly interpreted. The courts agreed that it simply meant as soon as it was practicable to do so, and this was something that was dependent upon the facts of the case.

CASE EXAMPLE

R v Buckley (1873) 13 Cox CC 293

Evidence that a police constable had informed his supervising officer that he was simply going to observe a defendant to gather evidence of what the defendant was doing when he was killed, was admissible.

The condition also required the statement or declaration to be directly related to those matters that the person making the statement was under a duty to record. In *Mercer v Denne* [1905] 2 Ch 538, the records of a surveyor were inadmissible hearsay evidence because he was not under any duty actually to record that information. Contrast this case with *Mellor v Walmesley* [1905] 2 Ch 164, where it was far clearer that the surveyor was under a duty to record the information, and hence it was admissible as a declaration (or statement) made in the course of a duty.

7.4.6 Public documents containing facts

At common law the contents of a public document are admissible as evidence of the truth of its contents, even though there is always the risk that the opposition may disprove this. Strangely, this exception was created as a pure matter of convenience. Consider this scenario: Eddie requests a document and requires the person creating it to verify that it is accurate and true. He telephones the archives department and they tell him that an ex-employee called Sheetal created the record but that she emigrated to somewhere in New Zealand over two years ago and never left a forwarding address. This poses a problem for Eddie. Given the huge number of public records and the innate difficulty in trying to find the actual person who created them and then getting the creator to testify, it was far easier to allow the admittance of such evidence with the knowledge that the contrary could still be proven, i.e. it was not too onerous to admit it because of the safeguards, scrutiny and processes public records go through. The same applies under the current law: the exception is preserved by s 118(1)(b) of the CJA 2003, and this is alongside the other statutory exceptions that cover this (discussed below).

Prior to the CJA 2003 the common law rules required the document to satisfy the following requirements before it was deemed to be admissible:

- the document must have been created for the public record;
- it must have contained information of public interest;
- it should have been available for public inspection;
- it must have been created in contemporaneity to the events that it sought to record; and
- the person creating it has personal knowledge of the events recorded or has enquired into them.

The strict approach did not last long and the rules were relaxed as 'direct knowledge', such as the last of these requirements, continually diminished. Evidence of this type might also be admissible under s 117 of the CJA 2003.

7.4.7 Informal admissions

The remainder of this chapter focuses on another interesting common law exception, namely admissions. Under the common law a hearsay statement that is either entirely or partially adverse to the person making it is admissible as evidence of the facts contained therein. This is due to its negative nature. The rationale for this focuses on the fact that it may be incriminating; this, it is suggested, mitigates the likelihood that the assertion may be fabricated, is unreliable or untrue. The assertions can be oral, written or through conduct. However, the weight attached to the statement will vary according to the facts of the case. Furthermore, the assertion is read in the light of any other either exculpatory or explanatory remarks that may have accompanied it. What follows is a discussion on such admissions in both civil and criminal cases.

7.4.8 Binding admissions

An admission by a party either by themselves, or someone acting as an agent on their behalf, is admissible under the common law as an exception to the rule against the admission of hearsay evidence. This common law exception has been expressly preserved by s 118(1) of the CJA 2003. Let us explore these statements. Obviously, a defendant may be bound by an adverse statement that they themselves have made in their personal capacity or an admission that they have made whilst acting in a different capacity, such as a litigation friend or guardian.

Consider this: what happens if Jessie makes a confession that adversely implicates her and mentions Carol? The general rule is that an admission only binds the maker of it and not others. In the example, Jessie's confession will implicate only her. In civil cases, such evidence may be adduced by means of a statutory exception under the Civil Evidence Act 1995.

Here is another commonly posed question: is the position any different if a co-defendant makes the adverse statement or the confession? Hypothetically, we have a case that involves two defendants (Pam and Kath), and the allegation is that they jointly committed an offence, i.e. a common design. Pam admits the allegation. But does that admission also bind Kath? The issue here is as follows: if one accused admits guilt in relation to an offence with which they have been jointly charged alongside another person, does that then also implicate the co-accused? The answer is that it does *not* bind Kath unless the statement was made or words were uttered whilst carrying out the common design. The rationale for this is that the statement or words uttered, in this instance, become circumstantial evidence of a common design or, in other words, it is no longer classified as hearsay evidence. An interesting issue arises, whether Pam and Kath both bound a statement or utterance made by Pam after the common design has been carried out. The answer in this instance is different, as here the statement or utterance will only bind the maker (i.e., Pam). Figure 7.4 summarises the position.

Civil cases	Hearsay that is admissible under the Civil Evidence Act 1995
Criminal cases	Confessions (admissions relevant to guilt) subject to s 76 PACE 1984

Figure 7.3 Informal admissions in civil and criminal cases

Statement made, words uttered whilst carrying out common design	Bind both defendants
Statement made, words uttered after carrying out common design	Bind only the maker

Figure 7.4 Binding admissions

CASE EXAMPLE

R v Blake and Tye (1844) 6 QB 126

A1 and A2 were on trial charged with conspiring to evade customs duty. There were two books in which A1 had written. The first incriminated both of them, because it had been written in the pursuance of a common design, and was admissible against both of them. The second was a personal record by A1 and therefore only admissible against him.

Statements made by a co-accused outside a police station are considered to be outside of the common design and therefore are inadmissible as evidence against the co-accused: see *R v Governor of Pentonville Prison, ex p Osman* [1990] 1 WLR 277. Finally, common design can only be substantiated by evidence other than that of a co-accused.

Here is another interesting question: can an accusation that is made by an agent who is acting within the authority given to them by their principal bind the principal? The answer in this case is that it can. This raises serious ethical issues for lawyers and the spouse of a defendant. Consider this example: Peter is instructed to act as solicitor (agent) on behalf of David (principal) who has been accused of theft. Peter, as David's solicitor, has the right to make admissions on his behalf. Any admissions that Peter makes will bind David, so long as Peter makes the admission:

(a) whilst acting within his instructions;

(b) to the opposing party; and

(c) without any fraud.

If any one of these three factors does not exist, the admission will be rendered void and will not bind David: see *Ellis v Allen* [1914] 1 Ch 904. In terms of spouses, unlike the rules on competence and compellability and those in relation to that within the Police and Criminal Evidence 1984 (PACE), there are no special rules as to statements made by spouses. Gill and Sarah are spouses, so if Gill authorises Sarah to make an admission on her behalf, then that admission will bind Gill.

7.4.9 Substance: what can be admitted?

The general rule is as follows: if Ian makes an admission of fact, then that fact should be within Ian's knowledge and not based on hearsay: see *Comptroller of Customs v Western Lectric Co Ltd* [1966] AC 367.

CASE EXAMPLE

R v Chatwood [1980] 1 WLR 874

An admission by a severely addicted drug addict that the substance he was taking was a controlled drug was admissible as evidence because he had experience in the matter. The nature of the drug was ascertainable from the instruction of expert evidence. However, they were entitled to take the drug addict's admission into account.

7.5 Non-hearsay confessions

Once again the admission of a confession, i.e. a statement that incriminates the maker of it, tendered as evidence of the truth of its contents, is expressly preserved by s 118(1) of the CJA 2003. Confessions are admissible against their makers because the law accepts that they are reliable and carry more evidential or probative value than other hearsay statements; this is because they are only likely to be made if they are true. If a confession mentions or implicates another person, then that other person's lawyer will have to put forward the argument that the confession is inadmissible as hearsay evidence. This topic, along with the extensive rules introduced by s 76 of the Police and Criminal Evidence Act 1984, are discussed later in the book.

7.5.1 Other statements

Finally, what if Jenny makes a statement in the presence of Brian, who is a defendant? Then that statement may be admissible as evidence of the truth of its contents by reason that Brian accepted it as truthful, and as proof of his reaction: see *R v Christie* [1914] AC 545. Such evidence can now be admitted through a variety of available routes as a result of the CJA 2003. For example, the statement may be admissible as part of the *res gestae* under s 118(1).

ACTIVITY

Summarise what amounts to negative hearsay.

To what extent are records that are produced by mechanical devices admissible as evidence?

List the common law exceptions to the hearsay rule that are preserved by the CJA 2003.

Define the term *res gestae*.

KEY FACTS

Previous statements or assertions

Hearsay includes previous statements, assertions or gestures including information conveyed orally, visually, by spoken word or in a document.

The purpose of tendering hearsay

- Statements relevant to truth – the basic position was that the statement was inadmissible unless it fell into an exception.
- Original evidence – statements tendered for relevant reasons other than as proof of the truth of its contents are admissible; this includes:
  - evidence that a statement was made;
  - evidence of the state of mind of the maker;
  - evidence of the state of mind of the recipient.

The common law exceptions to the rule

The rule against the admission of hearsay evidence was strict, hence a number of exceptions developed in the common law that facilitated admissibility. These were expressly preserved by s 114(1)(b) and ss 118 and 118(2) of the CJA 2003 and include:

- public information – s 118(1)(b) preserves this exception – at common law the contents of a public document are admissible as evidence of the truth of its contents;

- reputation, i.e. character (the rule in *Rowton*);
- reputation or familial tradition;
- *res gestae* – ss 114(1)(d) and 118(1)(4) expressly preserve this exception and therefore the case law. The general rule is that inadmissible hearsay statements are admissible if they form part of the *res gestae* (state of affairs); spontaneous statements that form an integral part of the event;
- confessions – at common law the admission of a hearsay statement that was either entirely or partially adverse to the person making it was allowed;
- other admissions (agents) – this common law exception has been expressly preserved by s 118(1); therefore admissions by a party either by themselves or someone acting as an agent on their behalf are still admissible;
- common enterprise;
- expert opinion evidence.

SUMMARY

- Hearsay can be defined as the evidence of a witness consisting of something another person stated at some other moment in time whether verbally, in writing or using another method (e.g. hand movements) that is tendered as proof of the truth of any fact stated by that person in that evidence.
- In civil cases hearsay is admissible under the Civil Evidence Acts.
- In criminal cases the traditional approach was to exclude hearsay evidence, but a number of exceptions to this rule developed in the common law.
- Under the CJA 2003 the approach, which modernised the law, is now inclusionary, which means hearsay is admissible if it falls under one of the provisions of the 2003 Act.
- Previous statements, assertions and gestures, including information conveyed orally, visually, by spoken word or in a document can also amount to hearsay evidence.
- Hearsay evidence is tendered for a purpose other than as proof of the truth of its contents, i.e. evidence that a statement was made, evidence of the maker's state of mind or evidence of the recipient's state of mind amounted to original evidence and fell outside of the old rule.
- Many of the common law exceptions to the rule were preserved by s 114(1) of the CJA 2003, including public information (the contents of a public document is admissible as evidence of the truth of its contents), reputation (character – the rule in *Rowton*) or familial tradition, *res gestae* (statements that form an integral part of the state of affairs), confessions, admissions by others, i.e. agents, common enterprise and expert opinion evidence.

SAMPLE ESSAY QUESTION

Article 6 of the European Convention on Human Rights and Fundamental Freedoms (ECHR) and the Human Rights Act 1998 (HRA) had a major impact on the admission of hearsay evidence. Discuss.

Answer plan

State the effect of the ECHR / HRA 1998.
Set out the fact that as a signatory to the ECHR the United Kingdom has chosen to abide by the rights safeguarded within it. Define Art 6 and the right to a fair trial. State that Art 6 of the ECHR and the provisions of the HRA 1998, which makes the ECHR enforceable in domestic UK courts, afford the defendant an opportunity to test the evidence against them through the cross-examination of witnesses.

Outline the effect of Art 6 and the HRA 1998.
Highlight the fact that the ECHR does not abolish hearsay evidence but restricts its use, and that this applies to hearsay tendered by both the prosecution and defence (see *Thomas v UK* (2005)).

Explore the comments of the European Court of Justice (ECJ) in relation to Art 6.
Emphasise that the ECJ has made clear that Art 6 has a limited application and that the right under it is not absolute. It has also recognised that there must be a balance struck between the law of the European Union and the rights of an individual accused. Thus, the Court of Appeal concluded in *Xhabri* (2005) that the approach in relation to hearsay adopted by the Criminal Justice Act 2003 was not incompatible with the rights preserved by Art 6 of the ECHR.

Discuss Luca v Italy *(2003).*
Outline that in this case the ECJ highlighted that convictions based on evidence that the accused does not have the opportunity to test through cross-examination will not be compatible with Art 6. Mention that this is not the case where the witnesses are unavailable because of the accused or their agent's conduct, i.e. the witness has been threatened not to appear.

Further reading

Law Commission (1997) *Evidence in Criminal Proceedings: Hearsay and Related Topics*, Law Com No 245

Murphy, P. and Glover, R. (2011) *Murphy on Evidence*. Twelfth edition. Oxford: Oxford University Press

Singh, C. (2015) *Evidence: Question and Answers 2015–2016*. Eleventh Edition. Oxford: Routledge.

Worthern, T. 'Legislative comment: the hearsay provisions of the Criminal Justice Act 2003: so far, not so good?' (2008) 6 Crim LR 431–442

Resources

The Crown Prosecution Service Website provides a useful summary of the law on hearsay at: www.cps.gov.uk/legal/h_to_k/hearsay/ (2022)

Federal Rules of Evidence (2015) rules 801–807 at www.rulesofevidence.org/article-viii/ (2022)

8

Hearsay: admissibility in criminal cases

AIMS AND OBJECTIVES

By the end of this chapter you will be able to:

- identify the instances in which hearsay evidence is admissible in criminal cases and explore the law;
- highlight the statutory exceptions in criminal cases and discuss case study and hypothetical examples;
- outline the statutory safeguards provided by the Criminal Justice Act 2003 in relation to hearsay evidence and discuss how the law historically developed;
- set out the other exceptions to the hearsay rule and explore the rationale that underpins the law;
- discuss the impact that the European Convention on Human Rights has had on the admission of hearsay evidence in criminal cases and discuss the reasons why those rights are protected.

8.1 Introduction

The discussion in the previous chapter focused on the hearsay rule and what is classified as hearsay evidence under the current law. This chapter focuses on the admissibility of hearsay evidence in criminal cases. Starting with a brief look at the statutory exceptions that provide for the admission of hearsay evidence, the discussion then moves on to the various safeguards for admission of such evidence that are provided by the Criminal Justice Act 2003 and concludes with an exploration of how human rights have impacted on this area of the law of evidence.

8.2 The statutory exceptions and criminal cases

The Criminal Justice Act 2003 (CJA) has had the effect of limiting the scope of the rule against the admission of hearsay evidence in criminal cases.

DOI: 10.4324/9781003282433-8

Currently the position is as follows: hearsay evidence is statutorily *admissible* in criminal proceedings under s 114(1) of the 2003 Act. The statute specifically preserves the common law exceptions to admission of such evidence, by mutual agreement and under the safety valve, i.e. where the interests of justice so require it to be admitted.

In short, *hearsay* is defined by ss 114(1), 115(2) and (3) and 134 of the CJA 2003. Section 114(1) states that:

SECTION

'. . . in criminal proceedings *any* statement not made in oral evidence *at court* in the proceedings is admissible of any matter stated *if one of the four exceptions applies*'.

Under s 115(2) of the 2003 Act a *hearsay statement* is:

SECTION

'. . . any representation of fact or opinion made by a person by whatever means *including one made in* a sketch, photo-fit or other pictorial form'.

It is clear from this provision that the statement must be made by a person. The result of this is that the term 'statement' does not cover anything that is produced by mechanical process, i.e. audio or video recordings, or photographs. The rationale for this is based on the fact that such evidence is not classified as hearsay evidence and is admissible via other routes. This statutorily approves the decision in *Taylor v Chief Constable of Cheshire* [1987] 1 All ER 225.

Section 115(3) defines the term 'matter stated', which appears in s 114(1) as '. . . a matter stated is one [where the] . . . the purpose, or one of the purposes, of the person making the statement appears to the court to have been . . . to cause another to believe *it* or act or a machine to operate on the basis that the matter is as stated'. Section 134 of the Act defines 'oral evidence' as including 'evidence, *which* by reason of any disability, disorder or other impairment, a person called as witness gives in writing, by signs or by way of any device'. Figure 8.1 is a summary diagram of the definition.

This re-definition has caused some problems. In *R v Isichei* (2006) 170 JP 759, A and B, two female students, along with C, whom they did not know, were being ferried around Manchester late one night, looking for an open nightclub. Whilst at the club they came across C and D. A and B were robbed and assaulted; they subsequently identified D as one of the two assailants. The prosecution sought to adduce hearsay evidence that, whilst in the taxi, C had stated that he was going to call Marvin (D). The word 'Marvin', which happened to be the defendant's first name, was not a matter stated within the definition of hearsay under s 114(1). It was not made with the purpose of causing A or B to believe anything; therefore, evidence of the telephone call was admissible. On appeal Auld LJ stated that, although the judge may have

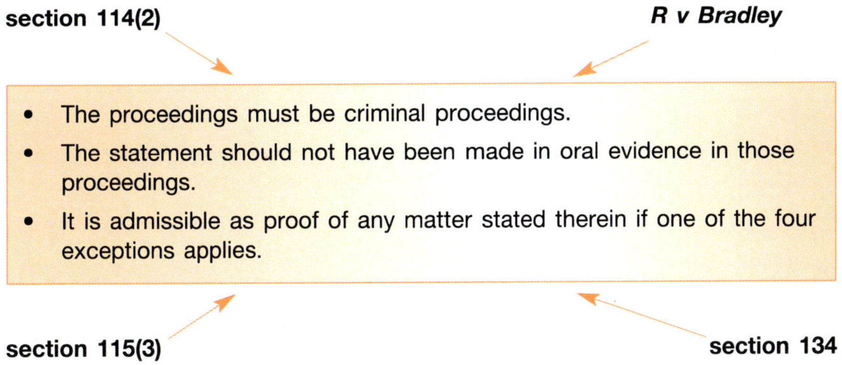

Figure 8.1 Definition of hearsay

erred, the evidence would have been admissible under s 114(1)(d) nonetheless (see below).

8.2.1 The interests of justice

For assessment purposes, knowledge of s 114(1)(d) and (2) is essential. Our discussion begins with the first of these. Under s 114(1)(d) of the CJA 2003, the court may admit hearsay evidence if, and only if, it is satisfied that it is in the interests of justice to do so. This wording of this provision means it is very wide and has therefore resulted in the admission of hearsay evidence where none of the other exceptions to the rule is applicable: see *R v Xhabri* [2006] 1 Cr App R 26. Section 114(1)(d) is supported by what is referred to as a 'safety valve', which outlines the factors that the court *must* consider before it can exercise its discretion to admit evidence under this provision – these are set out in s 114(2) and are:

- its probative value;
- the existence and availability of any other relevant evidence;
- the importance of the evidence in the entirety of the circumstances, i.e. considering the case as a whole;
- how the statement was made, i.e. circumstances;
- the reliability of the maker of the statement;
- how reliable the evidence relating to the making of the statement is;
- whether oral evidence of the matter can be given, and if not, why not;
- any difficulties the opposition would face in challenging it; and
- prejudice to any party resulting from its admission or facing a party challenging it.

It is important to note that the judge does not have to make a decision on each of these, and as Rose LJ stated in *R v Taylor* [2006] 2 Cr App R 14, '. . . what is required is *that the judge* give consideration to those factors . . . nothing in the wording of the statute requires *the judge* to reach a specific conclusion in relation to each or any of them'. Therefore, the trial judge is not under an obligation to reach a conclusion on each or any of these factors: their duty only extends so far as to require them to consider them and no more. One of the reasons for this relates to efficiency; one can only guess how long the enquiries would take and the likely appeals that would result in relation to their extent – all this would amount to delays in the proceedings and increases in costs. Another key point to note is that both the prosecution and defence can apply to have the evidence admitted. The court will always exercise its discretion cautiously to avoid potential miscarriages of justice: see *Sparks v R* [1964] AC 964.

ACTIVITY

Summarise the definition of hearsay under the CJA 2003.

Outline what amounts to a statement for the purposes of the CJA 2003.

What are 'matters stated'?

Explain the purpose of the safety valve.

KEY FACTS

The statutory exceptions to the rule

The CJA 2003 has had the effect of limiting the scope of the hearsay rule and the admission of such evidence in criminal cases.

Definition of hearsay under the CJA 2003

- Section 114(1) defines hearsay as any statement that is not made in oral evidence at court. In criminal proceedings this is admissible of any matter stated if one of four exceptions applies.
- Section 115(2) defines a statement as any representation of fact or opinion made by a person by whatever means, including one made in a sketch, photofit or other pictorial form.
- Section 134 defines oral evidence as evidence, including that by reason of any disability, disorder or other impairment, that a person called as a witness gives in writing, by signs or through any device.
- 'Interests of justice' is a catch-all term meaning that justice would be served if a certain measure is done or not done, even though it may not, strictly speaking, be permissible.

The admission of hearsay evidence

Interests of justice
a catch-all term that means justice will be served if something is done or not done. In evidence this is often found to broaden judicial discretion.

Section 114(1)(d) allows the court to admit hearsay evidence if it is satisfied that it is in the **interests of justice** to do so. This provision allows the admission of hearsay evidence where none of the other exceptions is applicable and is therefore supported by a *safety valve* under s 114(2), which outlines the following factors that the court must consider before it can exercise its discretion:

- its probative value;
- the existence and availability of any other relevant evidence;
- the importance of the evidence in the entirety of the circumstances, i.e. considering the case as a whole;
- how the statement was made, i.e. circumstances;
- the reliability of the maker of the statement;
- how reliable the evidence relating to the making of the statement is;
- whether oral evidence of the matter can be given; and, if not, why not;

- any difficulties the opposition would face in challenging it; and
- prejudice to any party resulting from its admission or facing a party challenging it.

In *R v Brown (Nico)* [2019] EWCA Crim 1143, the Court of Appeal considered the significance of the instance in which the maker of a statement cannot be identified where the hearsay is sought to be admitted under the residual power in the interests of justice per s 114(1)(d). The fact that the maker of the statement cannot be identified may lead the court to decide that the interests of justice are not satisfied and therefore the statement should not be admitted. The Court went on to state that this would not be a relevant consideration in cases where it is clear that there is no realistic scope to question the credibility of the maker of the statement if the identity were known. Thus, it cannot be then stated that the other party has been denied a material safeguard or subjected to possible prejudice.

8.3 Statutory exceptions and documentary hearsay

Documentary evidence is another type of hearsay: statements where any representation of fact, whether by words or otherwise (Sch 2 to the CJA 1988, which is replaced by s 115(2) of the CJA 2003 as above). Prior to the CJA 2003, ss 23–24 of the Criminal Justice Act 1988 provided that documentary hearsay evidence was admissible in limited instances, in criminal cases. The condition was that it was either impossible or impracticable to call the witness to give oral evidence. Both ss 23 and 24 only applied to documentary hearsay and not oral evidence. These provisions were respectively replaced by ss 116 and 117 of the CJA 2003; the first of these provides for the admission of first-hand documentary and oral hearsay statements, which was a major change for the statute books. The case law preceding this change has been used to interpret s 116 of the 2003 Act. Before the discussion of s 116 begins, note that neither s 23 nor s 24 of the CJA 1988 applied to confessions.

Section 116 replaced s 23(1) of the CJA 1988, which made first-hand documentary hearsay evidence admissible in criminal proceedings, so long as it is a 'statement made by a person in a document . . . as evidence of any fact of which direct oral evidence by *them* would be admissible' if the person:

- was dead, unfit due to mental or physical condition and thus unable to attend court (s 23(2)(a));
- was outside the UK and his or her attendance could not be reasonably and practicably secured (s 23(2)(b)); or
- could not be found where reasonable steps to find him or her had been undertaken (s 23(2)(c).

This was complemented by s 23(3), which provided for the admission of a hearsay statement made to a police officer or another person charged with either the duty of investigating offences or charging offenders where the person making the statement would not give oral evidence through fear or because they were kept out of the way, i.e. security issues. Therefore, the main effect of s 23 was to facilitate the admission of documentary hearsay evidence where the maker of such a statement was unable to give oral evidence.

Section 116(1) of the CJA 2003 allows the admission of first-hand hearsay statements where the witness is not available whether they are in documentary or oral form. However, it is not as simple as it sounds – prior to admission the following criteria must be satisfied:

- the evidence of the witness should have been admissible if they had been available to give evidence;
- the court is satisfied as to the identity of the maker of the statement; and
- the unavailability of the maker must be due to any one of the conditions in s 116(2).

Before moving on to discuss s 116(2), consideration of the first two of these conditions is required. Only relevant admissible evidence can be admitted. This means that the maker should be competent to give evidence. The evidence should be relevant to a fact in issue and it should be generally admissible, barring the fact that it is excluded by reason of it being hearsay evidence.

CASE EXAMPLE

Sparks v R [1964] AC 964

The court held that a three-year-old child was incompetent to testify. Her evidence was inadmissible because her oral evidence was also inadmissible.

CASE EXAMPLE

R v Macgillvray [1993] Crim LR 530

The victim, who had been set on fire, made a statement to a policeman whilst a nurse was present in which he implicated the defendant. However, he was too seriously injured to sign the statement that had been made. It was read back to him and he agreed its contents were true. The defendant contended that the statement was not made by the victim but was made by the police officer. The Court of Appeal held that the victim had made the statement since he had clearly indicated that the record was true when read back to him.

Second, the court must be satisfied as to the identity of the maker of the statement. For example, in *R v Teper* [1952] AC 480, a statement by an unidentifiable passer-by who suggested that the defendant was the arsonist was inadmissible. This example highlights why the court needs to be satisfied of the maker's identity. Consider this: the person against whom the statement is being adduced will not have the opportunity to have their barrister test or contradict the statement through cross-examination. This would result in an unfair advantage to the party adducing such evidence. Hence, the promotion of fairness in the proceedings requires satisfaction of the maker's identity. Finally, the unavailability of the maker of the statement must be due to one of the following factors outlined in s 116(2):

- the witness is dead (s 116(2)(a));
- the mental or physical state of the witness means that they are unfit to testify (s 116(2)(b));
- the attendance of the witness cannot be reasonably or practically secured because the witness is not in the UK (s 116(2)(c));

- after taking all reasonable and practicable steps, the maker of the statement cannot be found (s 116(2)(d)); or
- the witness will not give oral evidence or continue to give oral evidence in respect of their statement due to fear and, on that basis, the court gives permission for the hearsay statement to be given in evidence (s 116(2)(e)).

These conditions are clearly similar to those required under the previous law, s 23(2) of the CJA 1988. If any of the conditions, barring the final one, applies the admission of hearsay evidence will be automatic. What follows is an examination of this in a little more depth. The old case law proves useful here, where the hearsay statement is admissible under s 116(2)(a) or (b), but the witness does not testify by reason of mental or physical unfitness or death, then the old case law helps to determine that which is required to be proven if the statement is to be admissible. The requirement in this instance is similar to that in civil proceedings: 'he who asserts must prove'. The onus to prove the condition is on the party seeking to admit the evidence. On that basis, the prosecution must prove beyond all reasonable doubt that the maker of the statement is either dead or unfit, etc., and the defence has to satisfy the same on the civil standard of proof, namely on the balance of probabilities: see *R v Minors* [1989] 1 WLR 441 or *R (Meredith) v Harwich Justices* [2006] EWHC 3336.

The focus now shifts to s 116(2)(c) and (d). Often, it is not reasonably practicable to secure the attendance of the witness because the maker of the statement is outside the UK. If this is the case then the party that is seeking to have the statement admitted must prove that the maker of the statement is outside the UK by reason of their geographical location, e.g. they are in Japan. It is very clear that the practicalities in securing the attendance of the statement maker will depend on the facts of the individual case: see *R v Jiminez Paez* (1994) 98 Cr App R 239 or *R v Radak* [1999] 1 Cr App R 187, where the court has confirmed that attendance includes physical attendance and evidence by live link.

Questions often also arise in relation to the lengths to which the party seeking to adduce the evidence must go to secure attendance. This is a case of simple maths: the more important the witness and their evidence, the greater the number of steps that should be taken to secure their attendance: see *R v Castillo* (1996) 1 Cr App R 438. The party must also evidence the steps that they have taken whilst acting diligently (*R v Bray* (1988) 88 Cr App R 354) in trying to secure the witness's attendance (*R v Case* [1991] Crim LR 192 or *R v Henry* [2003] EWCA Crim 1296) *but* have failed to do so.

Section 116 is designed to secure the admissibility, as evidence, of hearsay statements where the maker of that statement is not available to testify. In *R v Adams* [2007] EWCA Crim 3025 the Court of Appeal stated that for the purposes of s 2(d) cursory steps would not satisfy the requirement to take 'such steps as it is reasonably practicable to take'. In this case the evidence of an important prosecution witness who had originally confirmed attendance and who had been left a voicemail the working day before the trial but who failed to attend court did not satisfy the requirements of the provision and should not have been admitted at first instance under s 116(2)(d).

Finally, consider the condition outlined in s 116(2)(e), where a witness does not give oral evidence in respect of their statement due to fear. Here the court has the discretion to allow the hearsay statement to be admitted, but only where the interests of justice so require. Fear is given a wide definition (see below). Section 116(2)(e) of the CJA 2003 is far wider than its predecessor, s 23(3) of the CJA 1988, because the current provision does not require the statement to have been made to an officer of the police service. The implication of this change can be demonstrated as follows: if Xin makes a statement to her barrister, Roberta, then Roberta can apply to the court for leave to adduce the statement, a situation that was not covered by s 23(3).

Arguably, this has clarified the law on this matter. Section 116(3) of the CJA 2003 acts to clarify and widen the definition of fear by including within its definition the personal or collateral fear of death, injury and financial loss: see *R v Davies (Anita)* [2006] EWCA Crim 2643. This means that the definition includes fear of injury to oneself and even to a relative, for example to Bob's Aunt Jemima. Thus, it follows that the fear experienced does not have to be wholly personal. Furthermore, like its predecessor and barring a few exceptions, there is no requirement for the fear to be caused by any particular person. If, however, it is the prosecution that causes the fear, then the trial judge may exclude the evidence under s 78 of the Police and Criminal Evidence Act 1984.

CASE EXAMPLE

R v O'Loughlin [1988] 3 All ER 431

The court decided that the very fact that the witness is absent through fear of some sort must be proven through means of admissible evidence. In this instance threats and pressure by terrorists was enough.

It was argued that it was not good enough for an individual to state that they had feared something. The fact that the person had feared something should only be accepted if it could be objectively justified, i.e. that a reasonable person would also have apprehended such fear as a result of the threat that was made, for example, to his pet cat. In *Acton JJ, ex p McMullen* (1991) 92 Cr App R 98, the court refused to accept that it did, but stated that the party seeking to prove that the witness was in fear as 'a consequence of the commission of the material offence or of something said or done subsequently in relation to that offence and the possibility of the witness testifying as to it'.

CASE EXAMPLE

R v H, W and M (2001) *The Times*, 6 July

The statement of a witness who was absent through the fear of death was admitted even where no one connected with the case had actually made contact with him. The admission was technically incorrect and the conviction was quashed.

CASE EXAMPLE

R v Martin [1996] Crim LR 589

The court suggested that there was no need to limit the fear to that which arises from the crime or the defendant.

CASE EXAMPLE

Neill v North Antrim Magistrates' Court [1992] 1 WLR 1221

Two boys made statements after having witnessed an offence take place. After this, their mother informed the police that the boys were frightened to give evidence. At the trial the prosecution called the officer to give evidence of what the mother had said to him, but his evidence was not admissible in order to establish the fear that the children may have felt. This evidence was hearsay because it had come through their mother. The officer should have interviewed the boys so that he could then have presented the court with evidence of their state of mind. The rule is as follows: evidence of fear, i.e. the state of mind, must be established through admissible evidence.

The provision applies equally to those witnesses who begin to give evidence but do not continue giving evidence through fear: see *R v Ashford Justices, ex p Hilden* [1993] QB 555.

The formalities for admission under s 116(2)(e) are clearly defined. The party seeking to adduce the evidence must obtain leave from the court to do so, persuading it that it is in the interests of justice to admit the evidence. The court must be satisfied of this and consider the factors outlined in s 116(4) of the CJA 2003, which are:

- the contents of the statement;
- the risk of any unfairness to the party seeking to adduce the evidence if it is excluded;
- the risk of any unfairness to the party against whom the evidence is being admitted;
- the fact that the evidence cannot be challenged through cross-examination; and
- the availability of special measures protection under ss 17 and 19 of the Youth Justice and Criminal Evidence Act 1999.

For good examples on this, see *R v Doherty* [2006] EWCA Crim 2716. The discussion now moves briefly onto special measures protections under ss 117 and 119 of the CJA 2003, starting with s 117. Note: **special measures** are a series of provisions that help vulnerable and intimidated witnesses give their best evidence in court and help to relieve some of the stress associated with giving evidence. Special measures apply to prosecution and defence witnesses, but not to the defendant. This provides for the admissibility of a hearsay statement that is contained in a document so long as:

Special measures
provisions that are designed to aid vulnerable or intimidated witnesses give evidence. The rationale is to relieve the stress associated with giving evidence so that best evidence may be elicited.

- oral evidence of the information contained in the statement would have been admissible; and
- the conditions outlined in s 117(2) of the CJA 2003 are satisfied.

The conditions outlined in s 117 are very similar to those in s 24 of the CJA 1988, which permitted the use of documentary hearsay in a range of circumstances, including those instances in which the document itself was created or received in the course of a trade or business; and where the maker of the statement could be assumed to have had personal knowledge of the facts contained in it. Section 24 provided that:

SECTION

'. . . any statement in a document shall be admissible in criminal proceedings as evidence of any fact of which direct oral evidence would be admissible if . . . (i) the document was created or received by a person in the course of a trade, business, profession or other occupation, or as the holder of a paid or unpaid office and (ii) the information contained in the document was supplied by a person (whether or not the maker of the statement) who had, or may reasonably be supposed to have had, personal knowledge of the matters dealt with.'

Subsections 117(2)(a) and (b) mimic those previously contained in s 24(1)(i) and (ii). The effect of this on the law is generally positive. The case law that went with s 24 also remains relevant. In the greater context it is clear that s 117(2) does not require the document to form part of a record. However, it still needs to be created or received in a business or professional context. This is because the latter ensures that the document still has some degree of reliability because of the supposed business checks it would go through, i.e. for accuracy. Furthermore, the maker of the statement is no longer required to be under a duty of any sort; they simply need to create or receive the document in a business or professional context.

The criticism surrounding this provision centres on the fact that although satisfaction of business or professional requirements means the document is more likely to be reliable, these requirements may also act as safeguards where the information is being created or simply compiled. However, this is not really adequate where the information is merely received in such a context. The requirement for some personal knowledge mitigates the potential inaccuracy or unreliability of such a document. An interesting fact about this provision is that the person supplying the information and creating or compiling the record can be the same as the party seeking to adduce such evidence. Additionally, such party still does not need to show that the supplier of the information is unable to give evidence: see *R v Foxley* [1995] 2 Cr App R 523.

Once the conditions in s 117(2)(a) and (b) are satisfied, the final consideration is s 117(2)(c). Only if all *three* conditions are satisfied can evidence under this provision be admitted. Once again this subsection is similar to its predecessor, s 24(2) of the CJA 1988. Section 24(2) provided that where the information was indirectly supplied, then '. . . each person, through whom the information was supplied, who received it must act . . . (a) in the course of a trade, business, profession or other occupation, or (b) as the holder of a paid or unpaid office'. This meant that every person that received the information should have done so in either a business or professional context; it did not, however, state whether or not the person was required to communicate it in that context too.

Regarding statements prepared for the purpose of pending or contemplated litigation, i.e. criminal proceedings or investigation, s 117(4) of the CJA 2003 replaced s 24(3) of the CJA 1988, which provided that such evidence could not be admitted unless the maker of the statement:

- was dead or not fit enough to attend;
- was outside the UK and it was not reasonably practicable to secure their attendance;
- could not be found after all reasonable steps had been taken to trace them; or
- was in fear or being kept away and the statement was made to an officer of the police service.

Students of the law of evidence often wonder why this provision was revoked and an almost identical one re-enacted. The problem with this provision was that it was inherently unclear whether it applied to the original eyewitness of a crime or to the actual person who incorporates the information in the document; s 117(4), albeit in an almost similar provision, rectifies this issue. For an example of the functioning of the old law, see *R v Bedi* [1992] Crim LR 299 and *R v Carrington* (1994) 99 Cr App R 376, which should be contrasted with *R v Derodra* [2000] 1 Cr App R 41.

Finally, s 117(5) requires the party seeking to adduce the evidence to provide a statutory reason (see s 116(2) CJA 2003) as to why the supplier of the information cannot or does not attend to give evidence. This provision also allows for an additional reason for non-attendance: it states that such evidence will be admissible where the supplier cannot reasonably be expected to have any recollection of the matters in the statement due to the time that has elapsed, taking into account all the circumstances, including the interval of time between the making of the statement (supply) and now (trial).

In support of these changes s 117(7) of the CJA 2003 has given the court the discretion to exclude evidence it believes to be unreliable. This may mean that the contents or source of the information is unreliable or the method by which it was created, supplied or received rendered it so.

8.4 The safeguards: ss 124–126

In adversarial proceedings, such as those in England and Wales, the method used rigorously to test any evidence in court is cross-examination, the purpose of which is to ensure that a miscarriage of justice does not occur, i.e. no one is convicted on a weak evidential basis. Think about the effect on that opportunity where the evidence of an absent witness is admitted. The opportunity is tragically lost and this is sometimes at the expense of the opposing party. This fact is considered very seriously because of the resultant unfairness that could arise, giving rise to grounds for an appeal.

Section 124 of the CJA allows the admission of evidence that relates to the credibility of the witness who is absent, and it includes any issue or relevant matter that could have been put to the witness in cross-examination. It also includes evidence of a previous inconsistent statement tendered as proof of any contradiction (s 124(2)). In addition, the opposition may adduce (lead) additional evidence in rebuttal of any allegation made in the absent witness's statement (s 124(3)). This allows the evidence of an absent witness to be rigorously tested in balancing fairness to the defendant.

Section 125 gives the court the discretion to direct an acquittal or to discharge the jury after the close of the prosecution case. The court may do this in a number of situations. Consider this, what if the whole or a substantial part of the evidence against a defendant was purely hearsay evidence? Remember, it is still important that the prosecution secure a case against the defendant that is based on relevant and admissible evidence, that is, not purely hearsay or circumstantial in nature. This is because securing a conviction on the basis of potentially unreliable evidence would result in an unsafe conviction that would eventually be quashed, because the evidence is not considered, in essence, to be strong enough. The increased risk of unfairness and a miscarriage of justice outweighs the need to secure a conviction. Section 125 of the CJA 2003 only applies to jury trials, because on summary trial in the magistrates' court the magistrates would direct themselves to acquit the defendant.

Under s 126 of the CJA 2003, the court can also exclude hearsay evidence if it is satisfied that the case for excluding it substantially outweighs the case for admitting it. This may be done after considering the danger that to admit it would result in undue waste of time and the value of the evidence to the entire case. This means that the court, after assessing the value of the evidence in relation to the case as a whole, can exclude hearsay evidence where it considers that its admission would result in a waste of time. The discretion is a broad one and the consideration of the value of the evidence to the case as a whole is not usually the only factor taken into account. Finally, the court retains the discretion to exclude any prosecution evidence, including hearsay evidence, where its admission would adversely affect the fairness of the proceedings under s 78(1) of PACE 1984. An equal discretion to exclude defence evidence now, arguably, exists under s 126(1) of the CJA 2003.

In *R v S* [2018] 4 WLR 24 it was confirmed that the courts have a specific power to exclude hearsay evidence under s 126(1)(b) of the CJA 2003, where it is satisfied that 'the case for excluding the statement . . . substantially outweighs the case for admitting it, taking account of the value of the evidence'; this takes into account any risk if admitted it may result in an undue waste of time.

ACTIVITY

Outline the four exceptions in which hearsay is admissible under the CJA 2003.

KEY FACTS

Statutory exceptions and documentary hearsay

Documentary hearsay is a statement containing any representation of fact whether by words or otherwise. Prior to ss 116 and 117 of the CJA 2003, ss 23–24 of the CJA 1988 provided that documentary hearsay was admissible in criminal cases in limited instances.

- Section 23 is superseded by s 116, which allows the admission of first-hand hearsay statements where the witness is not available whether they are in documentary or oral forms if:
  - the evidence of the witness should have been admissible if they had been available to give evidence;
  - the court is satisfied of the statement maker's identity;

- the unavailability of the maker must be due to any one of the conditions in s 116(2) which require that:
  - the witness is dead (s 116(2)(a));
  - the mental or physical state of the witness means that they are unfit to testify (s 116(2)(b));
  - the attendance of the witness cannot be reasonably or practically secured because the witness is not in the UK (s 116(1)(c));
  - after taking all reasonable and practicable steps, the maker of the statement cannot be found (s 116(2)(d));
  - the witness will not give oral evidence or continue to give oral evidence in respect of their statement due to fear and on that basis the court gives permission for the hearsay statement to be given in evidence (s 116(2)(e)).
- Section 24 is superseded by s 117, which allows the admission of a hearsay statement that is contained in a document so long as:
  - oral evidence of the information contained in the statement would have been admissible;
  - the conditions outlined in s 117(2) of the CJA 2003 are satisfied.

Sections 124–126 safeguards

To prevent miscarriages of justice these provisions provide safeguards where the evidence of an absent witness is admitted:

- Section 124 allows the admission of evidence that relates to the credibility of the witness that is absent.
- Section 125 gives the court discretion to direct an acquittal or discharge the jury after the close of the prosecution case.
- Section 126 allows the court to exclude hearsay evidence if it is satisfied that the case for excluding it, after considering the danger that to admit it would result in undue waste of time and the value of the evidence to the entire case, substantially outweighs the case for admitting it.

8.5 Further exceptions to the hearsay rule

In addition to the exceptions outlined in the CJA 2003, there is also a series of exceptions to the rule against the admission of hearsay evidence in other statutes. Let us take a brief look at the status of some of these. They include:

- Children and Young Persons Act 1933
- Criminal Justice Act 1967
- Criminal Justice Act 1988
- Bankers' Books Evidence Act 1879
- Youth Justice and Criminal Evidence Act 1999.

Sections 42 and 43 of the Children and Young Persons Act 1933 provide for the admission of statements made by child witnesses in cases concerning sexual offences, assaults and murder. The condition is that the court must be satisfied that if the child was forced to give oral testimony in court, then there would be serious danger to his or her health. In practice, it can be difficult to argue admission under these provisions by reason of the fact that the Youth

Justice and Criminal Evidence Act 1999 (YJCEA) facilitates the presentation of such evidence. The court may permit such a child witness to give evidence by means of a video recording or a television live link. It is salient to note here is that s 30 of the YJCEA 1999 repealed s 69 of PACE 1984, which provided for the admission of computerised documentary evidence. This is now subject to s 129(1) and (2) of the CJA 2003.

Section 9 of the Criminal Justice Act 1967 provides for the admission of depositions, i.e. hearsay statements, with the consent of the parties. Section 30 of the Criminal Justice Act 1988 provides for the admission of expert reports but only where the evidence was admissible and the expert would have been competent to give it. This is discussed in more detail later in the book. Finally, ss 3 and 4 of the Bankers' Books Evidence Act 1879 provide for the admission of any entry in a banker's book of any matter that is recorded in it.

ACTIVITY

List the other statutes under which hearsay evidence may be admissible barring the Civil Evidence Act 1995 and the CJA 2003.

8.6 Other issues

Multiple hearsay
information that is relayed through more than one person before it is recorded.

The final topic of discussion in relation to hearsay evidence in criminal cases concerns hearsay evidence in retrials and **multiple hearsay**. The discussion begins with hearsay at a retrial. In summary, a retrial occurs when an appeal against conviction is successful and, in the interests of justice, the appeal court orders the case to be retried. Section 131 of the Criminal Justice Act 2003 amended the Criminal Appeal Act 1968, thus, any oral evidence that was given at the original trial must also be given orally at the retrial. Consider this, if oral evidence was given in the original trial, and then that evidence was tendered as a written statement in the retrial, it would be hearsay and therefore potentially inadmissible. Section 131 allows such evidence from the original trial to be tendered in a way, other than orally, where all the parties to the case agree or it falls under ss 114(1)(d) or 116: see *R v Lang* [2004] EWCA Crim 1701, where the transcript of evidence given by A at the original trial was admitted, under s 116, as evidence in the new trial.

Those who have played the game of 'Chinese whispers' understand that its purpose is to get a set of information from person A through to person Z without it being altered. What normally happens is that when the information has reached person Z, it has gone from being 'I like eating jelly babies' to something along the lines of 'John's dog has rabies'. The same can happen to evidence when it is shunted from pillar to post. Consider this scenario, Midori witnesses a robbery; he tells her brother, Kenji, who tells his friend, Bryan, who finally tells a police officer, Davinder. The question here relates to the classification of this evidence. When evidence, such as that of Midori, filters through more than one individual before it is recorded, it is referred to as multiple hearsay. This type of hearsay is only admissible in the following instances:

- under s 117 of the CJA 2003 as a business document;
- under s 119 of the CJA 2003 as a previous inconsistent statement;
- under s 120 of the CJA 2003 as another previous statement;
- where all parties to the case agree to it being admissible; or
- where the court decides to exercise its discretion, under s 121 of the CJA 2003, to admit the evidence on the basis that the interests of justice require it to be admitted. This may be due to its value and reliability in the context of the overall case.

The test under s 121 of the CJA 2003 is more stringent than that under s 114(1)(d) of the CJA 2003 because multiple hearsay is more likely to be infected and unreliable than first-hand hearsay evidence.

8.7 The impact of human rights on the admission of hearsay evidence

Students, practitioners and researchers of the law – more specifically for current purposes the law of evidence – soon realise that human rights law is a pervasive topic, i.e. it crops up everywhere. This section of the chapter will take a brief look at the human rights issues that have arisen and those that are likely to arise as a result of the changes brought about by the CJA 2003. Whether or not the admission of the hearsay evidence of an absent witness breaches the right to a fair trial provided by Art 6 of the European Convention on Human Rights and Fundamental Freedoms (ECHR) is a continuing debate; the concern lies in the fact that admission of such evidence may breach the right of the defence to cross-examine prosecution witness evidence (see Art 6(3)(d)). It is clear that the safeguards provided by ss 124–126 of the CJA 2003 mitigate the issue of unreliability, and the courts have confirmed that the CJA 2003 is generally compliant with the ECHR.

The European Court of Human Rights (ECtHR) through its jurisprudence suggests that no consistent approach is being taken on this matter. For example, in *Kostovski v The Netherlands* (1990) 12 EHRR 434, the court decided that a defendant is entitled to 'adequate and proper' opportunity to 'challenge and question' any witness giving evidence against them. In contrast, in *Asch v Austria* (1993) 15 EHRR 597, the court stated that the right provided by the ECHR is only breached if the prosecution case is substantially based on the evidence of a witness who is absent. Another useful example is *R v Thomas and Flannagan* [1998] Crim LR 887. The problem with these judgments is twofold: a case-by-case approach, albeit desirable because each is decided on its own merits, results in inconsistency of application and, as a result, there is no guidance or standard on which to base any practical reality. What is clear from the judgments is the following:

- the defendant has the right to examine or have examined the evidence of a witness that stands against them;
- where a case is not solely based on the hearsay evidence of an absent witness, i.e. evidence other than that of the absent witness, then the requirement that the defendant be given an 'adequate and proper' opportunity to 'challenge and question' it will be satisfied; and

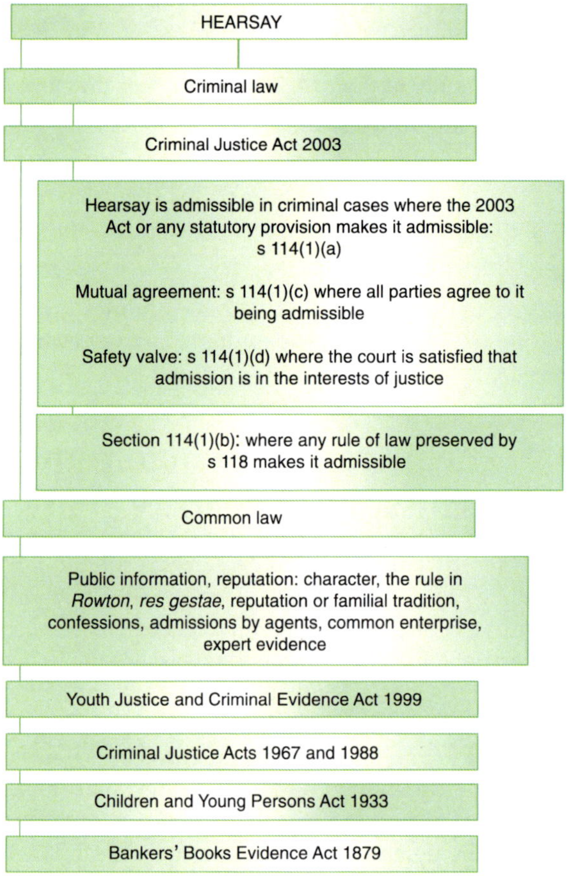

Figure 8.2 Summary diagram of the ways in which hearsay evidence may be admitted

- where a case is wholly or substantially based on the hearsay evidence of an absent witness, i.e. there is not any other or much other evidence apart from that of the absent witness, then the defendant will have grounds on which to lodge an appeal, i.e. the trial was unfair and the conviction was unsafe.

Other issues in relation to this are more than likely to crop up, and I recommend frequent visits to the website that accompanies this book for updates.

Figure 8.2 shows a summary diagram of the ways in which hearsay evidence may be admitted.

ACTIVITY

Define multiple hearsay, providing at least one example.

Are there any human rights issues that affect the use of hearsay evidence?

SUMMARY

Classifying evidence as hearsay evidence

Hearsay evidence consists of statements or assertions that are made on previous occasions, which are tendered as evidence to prove that their contents are true. Under the *old* rules, determining whether evidence was hearsay evidence and whether it was inadmissible was a two-stage approach. The court would ask: does the evidence consist of a previous statement or assertion, which amounts to hearsay, and what is the purpose for which it is being tendered?

The CJA 2003 and a new approach to hearsay evidence

The Criminal Justice Act 2003 introduced a brand new inclusionary approach to hearsay evidence modernising the law. Under the new approach the rule in s 114 of the CJA 2003 provides that hearsay evidence, i.e. a statement not made in oral evidence in the proceedings, is admissible in criminal trials of any matter stated. The occasions are when any provision makes it admissible, any rule of law preserved by s 118 makes it admissible, all the parties agree to it being admissible, or the court is satisfied that it is in the interests of justice for it to be admissible.

Previous statements or assertions

The hearsay rule applies to previous statements, assertions or gestures that are made by any person; this includes a previous statement that may have been made by the witness themselves. It is accepted by the law that a person may use a variety of methods to communicate information, i.e. orally, visually, spoken word, in a document or by gestures. The CJA 2003 covers previous inconsistent statements that are admitted in accordance with the Criminal Procedure Investigations Act 1865 (CPIA).

Statements relevant only to truth

In criminal cases the rule against the admission of hearsay evidence has been strictly applied; the basic position was that a hearsay statement is inadmissible unless it falls within an exception.

Original evidence/non-hearsay statements

Statements tendered for relevant reasons other than as proof of the truth of their contents are admissible as evidence, i.e. to evidence the making of the statement itself, or to evidence the state of mind of the person making the statement, or the person hearing it.

Circumstantial evidence: lack of the record

Normally a statement will amount to a hearsay statement if it is tendered to prove the truth of its contents, i.e. something exists or has happened. If tendered to show the opposite, the statement still falls under the same rule.

The common law exceptions to the rule

Section 114(1)(b) of the Criminal Justice Act 2003 (CJA) expressly preserves the common law exceptions to the rule against hearsay in s 118, and s 118(2) has abolished those not mentioned. In summary, documents admissible as evidence of facts stated therein, that have been preserved, are:

- public information
- reputation, i.e. character (the rule in *Rowton*)
- reputation or familial tradition
- *res gestae*

- confessions
- other admissions (agents)
- common enterprise
- expert evidence.

Further exceptions to the hearsay rule

In addition to the exceptions outlined in the CJA 2003 there are a series of exceptions to the rule against the admission of hearsay evidence in other statutes, including:

- Children and Young Persons Act 1933
- Criminal Justice Act 1967
- Criminal Justice Act 1988

SAMPLE ESSAY QUESTION

The Criminal Justice Act 2003 provides for an inclusionary approach to the admission of hearsay evidence in criminal proceedings. It has been argued that, as a result of the CJA 2003, the hearsay rule now achieves its aim far better than before. Discuss.

Answer plan

Outline the main factors.
Begin by stating that there was a collection of reasons why hearsay evidence was inadmissible; refer to *Teper v R* (1952) and discuss the fact that hearsay evidence cannot be tested by cross-examination etc. Discuss *Sparks v R* (1964) and *Myers v DPP* (1965), and the inequity that resulted from a strict application of the rule.

Highlight the exceptions to the rule and the decision in Kearley.
Mention the exceptions to the rule and the effect of the decision in *R v Kearley* in finding a further form of hearsay: the implied assertion. State that the rationale for the rule was now somewhat obsolete.

Discuss the effect of the reforms by the CJA 2003.
Explore how the provisions of the CJA 2003 on hearsay evidence may infringe the European Convention on Human Rights (ECHR) but mention the limited right to a fair trial under Art 6 and the varying approach of the European Court of Justice (ECJ) on this matter, referring to *Al-Khawaja v UK* (2009). Highlight that the CJA 2003 removed the concept of implied assertions through a definition of matters stated; explore the case of *Singh* (2006). Finally, analyse the safety valve under s 114(1)(d).

- Bankers' Books Evidence Act 1879
- Youth Justice and Criminal Evidence Act 1999.

Other issues

Section 131 of the Criminal Justice Act 2003 amends the Criminal Appeal Act 1968, which means that any oral evidence that was given at the original trial must also be given orally at the retrial. In addition, multiple hearsay is only admissible in the following instances:

- under s 117 as a business document;
- under s 119 as a previous inconsistent statement;
- under s 120 as another previous statement;
- where all parties to the case agree to it being admissible;
- where the court decides to exercise its discretion, under s 121, to admit the evidence on the basis that the interests of justice require it to be admitted because of its value and reliability in the context of the overall case.

Further reading

Choo, A. L. T. and Nash, S. 'Evidence law in England and Wales: the impact of the Human Rights Act 1998' (2003) 7(1) International Journal of Evidence and Proof 31–61

Ormerod, D. 'Case comment: *Ali v Revenue and Customs Prosecutions Office* [2008] EWCA Crim 1466; (2008) 172 JP 516 (CA (Crim Div)) – Criminal Justice Act 2003 s 114 – judge's refusal to admit document based on information as to its contents derived from PII hearing' (2009) 2 Crim LR 106–109

Singh, C. 'Eliciting best evidence from a child witness: a comparative study of the United Kingdom and India' (2019) 17(1) Issues in Legal Scholarship 20190003

Worthern, T. 'Legislative comment: the hearsay provisions of the Criminal Justice Act 2003: So far, not so good?' (2008) 6 Crim LR 431–442

9

Hearsay: civil cases

AIMS AND OBJECTIVES

By the end of this chapter you will be able to:

- understand the reasons behind the inclusionary approach to hearsay evidence in civil cases and discuss the rationale that underpins the law;
- highlight the instances in which hearsay evidence is admissible in civil proceedings through a discussion of the Civil Evidence Act 1995;
- outline the issues relating to the competence, compellability of witnesses and weight that is attached to hearsay through hypothetical and case examples;
- understand the relative procedural requirements.

9.1 Introduction

The discussion so far has mainly centred on hearsay evidence and its admission or use in criminal proceedings; in this chapter the focus shifts to hearsay and its admissibility in civil proceedings. The discussion begins with a brief look at the use of hearsay evidence in civil proceedings and its admission according to the Civil Evidence Act 1995 (CEA).

9.2 The use of hearsay evidence in civil cases

Tried
tested or legally evaluated for guilt or innocence in a court of law.

In this final chapter on hearsay evidence the discussion focuses on the rules on hearsay evidence in civil cases. In short, civil cases tend rarely to involve juries, in that they are **tried** by a judge sitting alone, therefore the attitude towards the admission of hearsay evidence has been far more relaxed than its counterpart in criminal proceedings. This is partly attributable to the fact that lawyers, judges and politicians all believed that juries

DOI: 10.4324/9781003282433-9

were not able to appropriately assess hearsay evidence, and therefore the risk that they might attribute more weight to the hearsay evidence than should have been attributed needed to be mitigated. The lack of jury trial in civil proceedings meant that this issue was duly avoided.

In *Carmarthenshire Council v Y* [2017] EWHC 36 (Fam) the Commercial Court stated that '. . . oral evidence given under cross-examination is the gold standard because it reflects the long-established common law consensus that the best way of assessing the reliability of the evidence is by confronting the witness.' Judicial criticism also extends to witnesses: in *Naziyah Ismail v Ciaran Joyce* [2020] EWHC 3453 (QB) the court commented on the 'inherent unreliability of memory' of witnesses, given evidence may be given several years after the event.

The definition of hearsay in relation to civil cases and criminal cases is slightly different. Hence, the realignment of the rules in these two separate areas of law is not exact.

9.2.1 The Civil Evidence Act 1995

The very first set of statutory exceptions to the rule against the admission of hearsay evidence in civil cases was formulated in the Civil Evidence Act 1968. These were not without their critics. The provisions were very far-reaching and unduly complex. The Civil Evidence Act 1995 (CEA) sought to rectify these complexities, with the effect that hearsay evidence is now generally admissible in civil cases. The rule in civil proceedings is that hearsay evidence is admissible under the CEA 1995, the Children Act 1989 and the Child Support Act 1991. You should also refer to Practice Direction 33 – Civil Evidence Act 1995 and Part 33 of the Civil Procedure Rules (Miscellaneous Rules About Evidence) that refers to the procedure that must be followed should a party wish to rely on hearsay in civil proceedings: see: www.justice.gov.uk/courts/procedure-rules/civil/rules/part33.

9.2.2 Section 1 CEA 1995

Section 1(1) of the CEA 1995 states that in civil proceedings 'evidence shall not be excluded on the ground that it is hearsay'. Thus, evidence cannot be excluded simply because it is hearsay but the provision does suggest that 'procedural' requirements must be satisfied. Section 2 deals with these requirements and that will be discussed later. Civil proceedings are defined in ss 11 and 12 of the CEA 1995 as any proceedings in a court or tribunal, or in arbitration, where strict rules of evidence apply whether by law or agreement between the parties.

Hearsay statements in civil proceedings are not the same as those in criminal proceedings. Statements in this instance include any representation of fact or opinion, regardless of how it is made (s 13 CEA 1995). The definition of hearsay is outlined in s 1(2)(a) of the CEA 1995 as 'a statement made otherwise than by a person *whilst* giving oral evidence in the proceedings which is tendered as evidence of the matters stated *therein*'. The CEA 1995 applies to all types of hearsay evidence (s 1(2)(b)).

It has been held in *Gubarev v Orbis Business Intelligence Ltd* [2020] EWHC 2912 (QB) that it is not satisfactory to use hearsay to establish important facts; it is best used for those facts that are peripheral or uncontroversial.

9.2.3 Section 2 CEA 1995

Any party wishing to rely on hearsay evidence must comply with the requirements of s 2 of the CEA 1995; that is, give notice of their intention to rely on such evidence. In addition, the opposition must be provided with, if they request them, details of the hearsay evidence so that they may overcome any practical difficulties that arise from the admission of it (s 2(1)). In support of the admission of such evidence, s 2(2) gives power, usually to the relevant government minister, to make rules of court, i.e. what hearsay issues are excluded from the notice requirement and any time limits for the serving of notice on the opposition, etc. This allows the functioning of the law. Consider this scenario: Davinder gives notice to the opposition barrister, Sachin, of her intention to rely on hearsay at trial on 25 July 2022. However, she gives Sachin that notice on 24 July 2022. This situation would be absurd, it would inevitably lead to increased expenses and a waste of court time where proceedings are subsequently delayed. The overriding objective is contained within the Civil Procedure Rules, available freely to download at www.justice.gov.uk/courts/procedure-rules/civil/rules/part01. These rules lay down the considerations that are taken into account in the conduct of civil proceedings.

If a party fails to comply with either s 2(1) or (2), then s 2(4) of the 1995 Act makes it clear that any such failure does not render the evidence inadmissible but affects the weight that will be given to it, with potential costs penalties for the party in default. The general study of civil litigation and practice, which often forms part of an LLB Honours degree, shows that the general rule in civil proceedings is that costs follow the event, i.e. the loser pays the other side's costs. There are instances in which no notice is required, for example where the evidence is given by affidavit, i.e. sworn, or the maker of the statement is dead and his or her estate is subject to probate, then no notice has to be given.

In relation to the courts approach when dealing with hearsay, in *Harb v HRH Prince Abdul Aziz* [2015] EWHC 2195 (Ch), Aziz (defendant) chose to rely on hearsay evidence rather than attend court to give evidence-in-chief, his legal team argued that he was prevented from doing so by Saudi Arabian law. The court found that this point was not proven and made an order requiring Aziz to attend trial which he failed to do. Thus, his evidence was treated and weighted as hearsay evidence, this affected his defence. Aziz appealed; the Court of Appeal held that the trial judge had failed to test the evidence. Furthermore, that the judge surmising that Aziz failed to attend court to avoid being cross-examined may have adversely affected that assessment. In contrast, in *Mohidin v Commissioner of the Police of the Metropolis* [2015] EWHC 2740 (QB) the court held that the decision to not require a witness to attend court and instead tender it as hearsay evidence was a tactical decision to avoid the witness being cross-examined deprived that evidence of its weight.

9.2.4 Section 3 CEA 1995

The provision under s 3 of the CEA 1995 is peculiar to civil cases, and no equivalent exists in relation to criminal proceedings. Where party A proposes to tender hearsay evidence against party B, without calling the maker of the statement as a witness, then party B may, under s 3, be allowed to call the maker of the statement to give evidence. What follows is a discussion of this in more detail. Sarah, acting on behalf of Benjamin, gives notice to Jayden, who acts on behalf of Chanelle, of her intention to tender the hearsay evidence of Daniel at the trial. Jayden can, under s 3, apply to the court for leave to call Daniel to give oral evidence. The purpose of this is so that Jayden may cross-examine Daniel on his hearsay statement, even though Daniel has not given any evidence-in-chief. This is because his hearsay statement will stand as evidence-in-chief.

9.2.5 Section 4 CEA 1995: weight

In civil cases the court has the discretion to allocate appropriate weight to hearsay evidence; s 4(1) sets out the criteria the court can use to assess the weight of such evidence, including any circumstances that may reasonably lead the court to infer that the evidence is unreliable or reliable. Within this, there is a possibility that absolutely no weight will be attached to it. Section 4(2) states that the court may have regard to the following:

- how reasonable and practicable it was for the party tendering the evidence to produce the maker of the statement at court as a witness;
- whether the statement was made contemporaneously in relation to the occurrence or matters stated;
- whether the evidence is multiple hearsay;
- whether anyone involved has a motive to either hide or conceal the matters contained in the evidence;
- whether the hearsay statement is a first-hand hearsay or an edited account;
- whether the statement was made jointly with another person;
- whether the statement was made for a particular purpose; and
- whether the evidence is presented as hearsay to prevent the court apportioning the appropriate weight to it.

Hence, where a witness can easily give oral evidence at trial but fails to do so, then the weight attached to the hearsay statement can be substantially reduced. Once again reliability is dealt with by a requirement that the statement be produced as close as possible in time to the event occurring.

It is possible to advance a case on uncorroborated hearsay alone, the court can give that evidence weight – there is no rule of law prohibiting that. However, the court confirmed in *Gubarev v Orbis Business Intelligence Ltd* [2020] EWHC 2912 (QB), citing *Welsh v Stokes* [2007] EWCA Civ 796 and *Polanski v Conde Nast Publications Ltd* [2005] UKHL 10 that it will be careful before attributing any weight to that evidence and will only give it such weight that it deserves in all the circumstances.

In *Shagang Shipping Company Ltd (in liquidation) v HNA Group Company Ltd* [2020] UKSC 34 the Supreme Court considered the issue of admitting hearsay evidence and the general rules on admissibility and set out the following:

- It is logical, but not mandatory, for a court to consider admissibility before deciding on matters of weight and impact of hearsay evidence.
- When considering hearsay evidence, it would be helpful for judges to address the question of weight and s 4 CEA 1995 considerations in detail. A failure to do so does not mean that the question has not been addressed.
- The assessment of weight is not binary in that a fact is proven or not, the court should have regard to 'any circumstances from which any inference

can reasonably be drawn as to the reliability or otherwise of the evidence' per s 4(1) and those circumstances need not be proven to the civil standard of proof.

9.2.6 Section 5 CEA 1995: competence and credibility

It may be advisable to refer back to Chapter 3 and the discussion on competence and compellability at this point. In civil proceedings, hearsay statements made by anyone considered to be incompetent as a witness cannot be admitted (s 5(1)). That includes anyone who is mentally ill or those who do not understand the nature of the proceedings and children who do not satisfy the test under s 96(1) of the Children Act 1989.

In addition to this, the credibility of the maker of the statement can be attacked under s 5(2). The extent of this attack would be to use any evidence that would have been admissible had the witness given oral evidence, i.e. previous inconsistent statements. This restrictive approach is taken because it prevents the issues from being bogged down by collateral issues, i.e. things not relevant to the facts in issue. Any party wishing to attack the credibility of the statement maker must give notice of the intention to do so within 28 days of receiving the s 2 notice from the party intending to use the statement.

9.2.7 Section 6 CEA 1995: previous statements

Section 6(1) allows, with the leave of the court, the admission of the previous statements of any witness called to give evidence. Where a party is seeking to adduce a previous statement to rebut an allegation of fabrication, then they can do so without first obtaining the leave of the court. Both previous consistent and inconsistent statements are evidence of the matters stated therein. For purposes of further reading, reference should be made to ss 3–5 of the Criminal Procedure Act 1865 and to Chapter 6.

Finally, it should be noted that s 6(4) and (5) preserves the instances in which memory-refreshing documents become evidence: see Chapter 6 for further discussion.

9.2.8 Section 7 CEA 1995: common law

Common law
judge-made law that applies on the basis of customs or legal precedent that has developed of hundreds of years in the UK.

Section 7(1) of the 1995 Act preserves the **common law** rules on civil evidence. Section 7(2) provides that the following documents are admissible as evidence of facts stated therein:

- published works, i.e. histories, dictionaries or maps;
- public documents, i.e. registers;
- records, i.e. court records, treaties and crown pardons.

Section 7(3) preserves the common law rules that allow the court to find certain evidence as proving or disproving matters where:

- evidence of reputation is admissible to prove good or bad character;
- evidence of reputation or familial tradition is admissible;
- the purpose is to prove or disprove pedigree;
- the purpose is to prove or disprove the existence of any person or thing;

- the purpose is to prove or disprove the existence of a marriage;
- the purpose is to prove or disprove that any public or general right exists.

Notice under s 2 is not required where any of these common law exceptions applies.

9.2.9 Section 8 CEA 1995

In civil cases, any statement that is contained in a document can be proven using either an original or an authenticated document (s 8(1)), or even a copy of a copy of a copy (s 8(2)). It becomes quickly obvious how relaxed these rules are in comparison to those in the criminal law.

9.2.10 Sections 9 and 10 CEA 1995

Sections 9 and 10 of the 1995 Act make admissible any records that are shown to form part of either a business or a public authority record. What normally happens is that an officer from the business or public authority will give a signed certificate confirming that they are part of the records (s 9(2)). A record is defined in s 9(4) to include records in any form, i.e. paper or electronic. The same provision also defines business and public authority. Where an entry is missing from the record then this is referred to as an instance of negative hearsay. This can be rectified by the officer producing an affidavit to establish its absence. Finally, it should be noted that the court could dispense with any formalities that are required under s 9.

Section 10 of the 1995 Act states that the Ogden tables are admissible for the calculation of future financial loss based on actuarial sciences. A useful discussion on these tables is available to download freely from the Government Actuary's Department internet website at www.gad.gov.uk/services/Other%20Services/Compensation_for_injury_and_death.html.

ACTIVITY

What is the difference between the definitions of hearsay in the Civil Evidence Act 1995 and the Criminal Justice Act 2003?

Summarise the requirements, as set out in s 2 of the CEA 1995, that the party seeking to adduce hearsay evidence must comply with.

Does the CEA 1995 allow the party against whom hearsay evidence is tendered to call the witness to give evidence?

Summarise the effect of s 4 of the CEA 1995.

Which, if any, rules of the common law rules relating to the admission of hearsay evidence does the CEA 1995 preserve?

KEY FACTS

Hearsay in civil cases

The *general rule* in civil cases is far more relaxed than in criminal cases because of the lack of a jury; trial lawyers are far more competent to assess appropriately for purposes of weight this type of evidence.

The law is contained in the CEA 1995:

- **Section 1** states that evidence in civil proceedings shall not be excluded on the ground that it is hearsay.
- **Section 2** requires the party intending on relying on the statement to give notice of its use.
- **Section 3** allows the party against whom the hearsay was adduced to call the maker of the statement to give evidence.
- **Section 4(2)** sets out the criteria the court must use to assess the weight and reliability of the hearsay. This includes:
  - how reasonable and practicable it was for the party tendering the evidence to produce the maker of the statement at court as a witness;
  - how contemporaneously the statement was made in relation to the occurrence or matters stated;
  - whether the evidence is multiple hearsay;
  - whether anyone involved has a motive to either hide or conceal the matters contained in the evidence;
  - whether the hearsay statement is a first-hand hearsay or an edited account;
  - whether the statement was made for a particular purpose;
  - whether the statement was made jointly with another person;
  - whether the evidence is presented as hearsay to prevent the court apportioning the appropriate weight to it.
- **Section 5** provides that the hearsay evidence of a legally incompetent witness is not admissible.
- **Section 6** allows, with the leave of the court, the admission of the previous statements of any witness called to give evidence.
- **Section 7(1)** makes admissions admissible; s 7(2) provides that the following documents are admissible as evidence of facts stated therein:
  - published works, for example histories, dictionaries or maps;
  - public documents including registers;
  - records such as court records, treaties and crown pardons.

Figure 9.1 is a summary diagram of the ways in which hearsay evidence may be admitted.

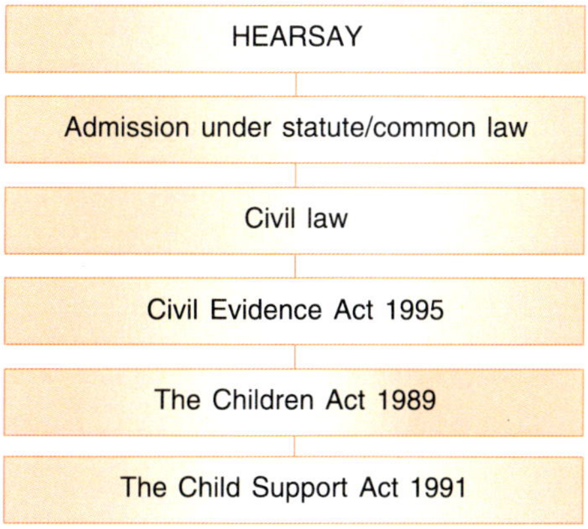

Figure 9.1 Summary diagram of the ways in which hearsay evidence may be admitted in civil cases

SUMMARY

The use of hearsay evidence in civil cases

In civil cases the attitude towards the admission of hearsay as evidence is far more relaxed than in criminal proceedings.

The Civil Evidence Act 1995 – s 1 CEA 1995

Section 1(1) of the CEA 1995 states that in civil proceedings 'evidence shall not be excluded on the ground that it is hearsay'. This means that evidence cannot simply be excluded because it is hearsay but suggests that procedural requirements set out in s 2 must be satisfied.

Section 2 CEA 1995

Any party wishing to rely on hearsay evidence must comply with the requirements of s 2 of the CEA 1995; that is, give notice of their intention to rely on such evidence and provide them with, if requested, details of the hearsay evidence so that they may overcome any practical difficulties that arise from the admission of it.

Section 3 CEA 1995

Section 3 allows the party against whom the hearsay evidence is tendered to call the witness to give evidence.

Section 4 CEA 1995

This provision allows the court to use its discretion to allocate appropriate weight to hearsay evidence, after considering any circumstances that may reasonably lead the court to infer that the evidence is unreliable or reliable. In doing so, the court will, under s 4(2), have regard to the following:

- how reasonable and practicable it was for the party tendering the evidence to produce the maker of the statement at court as a witness;
- how contemporaneously the statement was made in relation to the occurrence or matters stated;
- whether the evidence is multiple hearsay;
- whether anyone involved has a motive either to hide or conceal the matters contained in the evidence;
- whether the hearsay statement is a first-hand hearsay or an edited account;
- whether the statement was made jointly with another person;
- whether the statement was made for a particular purpose;
- whether the evidence is presented as hearsay to prevent the court apportioning the appropriate weight to it.

Section 5 CEA 1995

In civil proceedings, a hearsay statement made by anyone considered to be incompetent as a witness cannot be admitted.

SAMPLE ESSAY QUESTION

Consider the circumstances that must be taken into account when assessing the weight of hearsay evidence in civil proceedings.

Answer plan

Outline the considerations.
State that these include the ease by which the maker of the statement can be called to give evidence, i.e. they may be untraceable, the contemporaneousness of the statement with the events it describes, whether the statement involves multiple hearsay, whether it has been edited and any motive that the maker of the statement (or the person recording it) may have had to conceal, fabricate or misrepresent any of the matters stated.

Discuss what the evidence is admissible for.
Explore the fact that the evidence can be used to support or attack the credibility of the maker of the statement unless, under the rules of evidence, a denial would have been final (finality rule). This also means that collateral matters cannot be used to undermine the hearsay statement – this does not include the conviction of a crime, bias or previous inconsistent statements.

Further reading

Keane, A. and McKeown, P. (2012) *The Modern Law of Evidence*. Ninth edition. Oxford: Oxford University Press

Murphy, P. and Glover, R. (2011) *Murphy on Evidence*. Twelfth edition. Oxford: Oxford University Press

Other information

Chancery Guide (2016), chap 19: www.judiciary.uk/wp-content/uploads/2016/02/chancery-guide-feb-2016.pdf

Civil Procedure Rules 1998: www.justice.gov.uk/courts/procedure-rules/civil/rules/part01

Commercial Court Guide (2017) paras H1.7(c), H1.8 (p. 65) and J8.5 (p. 76) and Appendix 4 (p. 109): https://assets.publishing.service.gov.uk/government/uploads/system/uploads/attachment_data/file/672422/The_Commercial_Court_Guide_new_10th_Edition_07.09.17.pdf

Government Actuary's Department. *Compensation for injury and death (Ogden tables)*: www.gad.gov.uk/services/Other%20Services/Compensation_for_injury_and_death.html

Practice Direction 33 – Civil Evidence Act 1995 and Part 33 of the Civil Procedure Rules (Miscellaneous Rules About Evidence): www.justice.gov.uk/courts/procedure-rules/civil/rules/part33

10

Confessions and evidence obtained unlawfully

AIMS AND OBJECTIVES

By the end of this chapter you will be able to:

- understand the nature of confession evidence and discuss how the law historically developed;
- define confession evidence and its use through real case studies;
- understand the law regarding the admissibility and exclusion of confession evidence and discuss the risks associated with it;
- highlight the rules regarding illegally obtained evidence using case examples.

10.1 Introduction

This chapter focuses on confession evidence and evidence that is 'unlawfully' obtained. The discussion commences with the definition of a confession and moves on to its uses and the potential issues of admitting it as proof. The chapter concludes with a discussion on evidence that may have been obtained contrary to the law, for instance evidence obtained through an agent provocateur, or through a breach of the Police and Criminal Evidence Act 1984 (PACE) Codes of Practice.

10.2 The common law development of confession evidence

Admission
a statement by someone who is accused of committing a criminal offence that they committed it.

The English criminal law regards an informal **admission** that is relevant to guilt of the accused as a confession. For example, Mumtaz admits that she brutally murdered her husband, Ali. Confessions are important evidence and have long been exceptions to the hearsay rule in criminal cases. This area of the English law of evidence developed in the common law through concepts such as voluntariness (of one's own free will), and the now obsolete

DOI: 10.4324/9781003282433-10

Judge Rules (1964) often aided decisions of admissibility. In *Ibrahim v R* [1914] AC 599 Lord Sumner stated the test for admission.

JUDGMENT

'It has been long established . . . that no statement [made] by an accused is admissible as evidence against him unless it is shown . . . to have been a voluntary statement . . . that . . . has not been obtained from him . . . by fear of prejudice or hope of advantage exercised or held out by a person in authority.'

Lord Parker CJ added the terms 'in an oppressive manner' to this test. This was defined prior to the PACE 1984 coming into force in *R v Priestly* (1965) 51 Cr App R 1 as:

JUDGMENT

'. . . something which tends to sap, and has sapped . . . [the] free will which must exist before a confession is voluntary . . . the elements [of oppression] include such things as the length of time of any period of individual questioning, whether the accused person had been given refreshment or not, and the characteristics of the person who makes the statement'.

The common law rules have had a great impact on the admission of confession evidence and the rules that regulate it. The rules on admissibility only applied where there existed the 'fear of prejudice or hope of advantage exercised or held out by a person in authority': defined as persons that had, or that the accused reasonably thought had, some influence over their arrest, detention or prosecution. In short, this was someone from whom an inducement or a threat may indeed be credible.

The current position is regulated by s 76 of the PACE 1984 and Codes C and E of the Codes of Practice that accompany it. As a result of s 67(9) of the PACE 1984, the Codes apply to all organs of the State that are charged with investigating or charging offenders. This includes the police, customs officers and, more recently, Revenue Special Compliance Officers: see *R v Gill* [2004] 1 WLR 469. The *general rule* is that a confession obtained in breach of Code C will not automatically be rendered inadmissible. However, the breach will most definitely make it more difficult for the prosecution to argue for its admission. Code of Practice C lays down detailed procedural requirements that must be observed when detaining, interrogating and treating suspects not related to terrorism in police custody. For example, alongside s 58 of the Act, para 6 of Code of Practice C confers extensive rights to legal advice (see also Guidance note 6D, which stipulates that the only role of solicitors at the police station is to protect and advance the rights of their client). Section 60 regulated by Code of Practice E advances the authenticity of interviews through the requirement of tape recording. The most up-to-date versions of all PACE Codes of Practice are available to download at www.gov.uk/guidance/police-and-criminal-evidence-act-1984-pace-codes-of-practice.

10.2.1 Definition of a confession

Section 82(1) of the PACE 1984 provides a partial definition of a confession; it states that a confession is:

SECTION

'. . . any statement *which is* wholly or partly adverse to the person who made it, whether made to a person in authority or not and whether made in words or otherwise'.

At first glance this seems straightforward. However, this definition caused many interpretational difficulties in practice, see *R v Ward, Andrews and Broadley* [2001] Crim LR 316. What follows is an analysis of the requirements. First, s 82(1) clearly states that the statement may be wholly or partly adverse to the maker. This means that the effect of the statement need not be to wholly incriminate the accused and it is therefore enough if some of it does so. These statements are referred to as 'mixed statements'. Whether or not the statement is adverse is a question for the court. In *R v Sat-Bhambra* (1988) 88 Cr App R 55 the Court of Appeal held that the test to determine adversity should be applied to the time when the confession was made. Thus, it follows that if an accused's statement is favourable to them at the time at which they made it, it cannot become a confession if it later becomes incriminatory. In *Sat-Bhambra*, the court was of the opinion, although it did not form part of the judgment or ruling, that purely exculpatory statements did not fall within the meaning of s 82(1), *per* Lane LCJ, who stated:

JUDGMENT

'. . . the section is aimed at excluding confessions obtained by words or deeds that render them unreliable . . . *not at* statements containing nothing which the interrogator wished the defendant to say and nothing apparently adverse to the defendant's interests'.

This approach was confirmed in *R v Park* [1993] 99 Cr App R 270. Second, the incriminatory content in the confession must be unambiguous. In *R v Schofield* (1917) 12 Cr App R 191, the defendant on arrest shouted, 'Just my luck!' The court decided that this statement could not amount to a confession because it was too ambiguous. Third, the statement does not have to be made to a person in an authoritative position. It can be made to a police officer or a friend. For example, June confesses to Marcella that she murdered her wife, Tolu. Finally, the statement does not have to be in a particular form – this means that the prosecution can seek to establish any method that is used to communicate adverse information as amounting to a confession.

The courts confirmed in *R v Pearce* (1979) 69 Cr App R 365 that statements that are part admission and part exculpatory, if admissible, are admissible in their entirety. Thus, the prosecution cannot rely on the incriminating parts and exclude those that exculpate the defendant.

There are also situations in which the accused may remain completely silent. Silence cannot amount to a statement and thus a confession, and therefore this situation falls outside the scope of s 82(1). The position is, however, covered by the Criminal Justice and Public Order Act 1994, which provides for the drawing, in some instances, of adverse inferences from silence (see Chapter 5).

The discussion so far reveals that confessions are a valuable form of evidence. There are, however, a number of restrictions on their admission. Often, the police or the authority that is charged with the investigation of an offence will obtain the confession as a result of interrogation of the accused. Thus, if the confession is to comply with the rules on admissibility then PACE Codes of Practice C and E should be adhered to, so that the rights of the suspect are not infringed and are safeguarded. Code C provides the primary set of guidance, and Code E supports this with the additional requirement that all interviews are recorded whether by tape or other digital instrument. It is not always possible for this latter requirement to be satisfied as confessions are often made outside of the interview room. Where this occurs, non-recording does not render the confession inadmissible – as the discussion later in this chapter demonstrates, the confession may still be admissible.

The procedural safeguards provided by Code E ensure that the tape recording is an accurate reflection of what actually occurred in the interview and the transcript of that recording is subsequently agreed between the parties – this would undoubtedly be used in court. The cases of *R v Riaz, R v Burke* [1992] Crim LR 366 are authorities for the proposition that even if a transcript has been agreed, the tapes themselves can still be used. This may be a strategic ploy by the prosecution – it is far more powerful hearing a confession than to listen to one being read out. Where the prosecution wishes to rely on either the accused's significant statement or silence that had occurred outside of the interview, such as the accused's response when the tape is switched off, in these circumstances the police are required to mention the significant statement or silence to the accused in the next taped interview that they conduct and to invite a response.

ACTIVITY

When will a statement amount to confession?

Can a statement made by the accused that is initially favourable but later becomes adverse against them amount to a confession?

KEY FACTS

Confessions

A *partial* definition of a confession is outlined in s 82(1) of the PACE 1984. The requirements are as follows:

- The statement must be a wholly or partly adverse statement that incriminates the suspect.
- The incriminatory content must be unambiguous.
- The statement can be made to anyone, even those not in an authoritative position.
- No particular form is required for purposes of admissibility.

10.2.2 Admissibility

It is often useful to re-state, albeit as a useful reminder, the general rule on the admissibility of evidence, namely that evidence must be *relevant evidence* if it is to be *admissible*. The earlier discussion highlighted how the common law provided for the admission of confession evidence. Section 76(1) of the PACE 1984 also provides for the admission of confession evidence, but it does so in a far more regulated manner. Under this provision the court also has the power to exclude such evidence. Section 76(1) and (7) provides that where confession evidence is admitted, it is only admissible against the maker. For example, if Chanel and Graham are charged with murder and Chanel confesses to killing Janice then her confession, if it is admitted, is evidence only against her.

Individuals often confess to crimes for a variety of reasons, and this raises an interesting question, because of the potential risk of fabrication, is there a requirement for corroboration or support, by other evidence, of the confession. The answer to this question is no, confessions stand as evidence in their own right, as evidence that does not require corroboration. As discussed earlier in the book, there is no general requirement for corroboration in the English law of evidence. It is for the jury to determine how much weight they may wish to attribute to the confession, i.e., how believable is it in the circumstances. Thus, where a confession has been ruled admissible by the trial judge, it is the role of the defendant's counsel to raise such arguments before the jury. That may have the effect of reducing the weight that the jury may attach to the confession, even if the same arguments failed to dissuade the trial judge from excluding it in the first place. The arguments that the defendant can put forward include:

- a challenge to the factual basis of the confession;
- a dispute as to whether a confession was ever made;
- a dispute as to what is being represented as being a misrepresentation of what was actually said.

The effect of this is to undermine the confession evidence; the matter will then fall to the jury to decide what weight they should attribute to it. Take care to note that, where a tape recording of the confession exists, the last of the three arguments will be very difficult to prove. Additionally, grounds of appeal will not lie on the basis of the jury's view of an admissible confession, unless the confession evidence was ambiguous or where it could not have been reasonably taken to indicate that the defendant was guilty.

10.2.3 Exclusion: general

Burden
a rule of evidence that requires someone to prove something failing which the court will assume the contrary.

The **burden** of proving that a confession is admissible lies with the prosecution; the standard is beyond reasonable doubt – something that was long accepted at common law. If the confession is that of a co-accused the standard of proof the prosecution is required to satisfy is the balance of probabilities (as *per* s 76A, inserted into the PACE 1984 by s 128 of the Criminal Justice Act 2003). Where a judge concludes that a confession has been obtained in any of the ways proscribed by the law as being unlawful then the judge can exercise his or her discretion to exclude it, although you should note that he or she does not have to conclude that it was obtained in this way.

Section 76(2) of the PACE 1984 provides:

SECTION

'. . . if, in any proceedings where the Prosecution proposes to give in evidence a confession made by an accused person, it is represented to the court that the confession was or may have been obtained: (a) by oppression of the person who made it; or (b) in consequence of anything said or done which was likely, in the circumstances existing at the time, to render unreliable any confession which might be made by him in consequence thereof, the court shall not allow the confession to be given in evidence against him except in so far as the prosecution proves to the court beyond reasonable doubt that the confession (notwithstanding that it may be true) was not obtained as aforesaid'.

This means that confession evidence that is obtained by oppression, or is rendered unreliable by things said or done, is excluded. In addition, where the defence does not do so of its own volition, s 76(3) of the PACE 1984 allows the court to require the prosecution to prove that the confession evidence was not obtained by oppressive means or in circumstances that render it unreliable. Note: s 78 of the PACE 1984 also provides for a mechanism to exclude such evidence; this provides:

SECTION

'In any proceedings the court may refuse to allow evidence on which the prosecution proposes to rely to be given if it appears to the court that, having regard to all the circumstances, including the circumstances in which the evidence was obtained, the admission of the evidence would have such an adverse effect on the fairness of proceedings that the court ought not to admit it.'

CASE EXAMPLE

R v Mason [1988] 1 WLR 139

The police tricked the defendant into making a confession. There existed no oppression and thus the confession was reliable. The court excluded the evidence on the basis of s 78 (above).

10.3 Exclusion: specific

Sections 76 and 78 tend to appear in evidence assessments, and criminal lawyers are required to have a good understanding of both these provisions; what follows is a discussion in a little more depth. Where a defendant contends, or the court suggests under the power invested in it under s 76(3), that a confession was obtained in circumstances of oppression or unreliability, then the prosecution will bear the legal burden of disproving this allegation. The effect of this is to require the prosecution to prove beyond reasonable doubt that the confession was obtained without oppression and that it is reliable.

10.3.1 Section 76 and exclusion by reason of oppression

The term 'oppression' has caused difficulties in terms of interpretation and has been the subject of much debate. The common law did not adequately define what was meant by oppression. Similarly, the PACE 1984 does not provide a complete statutory definition of the instances in which a confession must be excluded under s 76(2)(a). Where oppression is alleged, then the law requires that the oppression *causes* the accused to make the confession. Section 76(8) partially defines oppression as including the following:

SECTION

'. . . torture, inhuman or degrading treatment . . . the use or threat of violence (whether or not amounting to torture) . . .'

It could be that a variety of behaviour is oppressive. However, the key factor of it is impropriety on the part of someone in a position of authority. The House of Lords in *A and Others v Secretary of State for the Home Department (No 2)* [2006] 2 AC 231 confirmed that any evidence that is obtained through the use of torture is inadmissible in English law. Section 76(8) left the courts to interpret the term 'oppression'.

CASE EXAMPLE

R v Fulling [1987] QB 426

A female suspect was informed that her partner was having an affair. This information caused her much distress and she made a confession to the police.

JUDGMENT

The Court of Appeal held that this was not in fact oppression under s 76(2)(a); it was the '. . . exercise of power in a burdensome, harsh or wrongful manner . . . unjust or cruel treatment of subjects . . . the imposition of unreasonable or unjust burdens'. The court also stated that the word oppression meant '. . . something above and beyond that which is inherently oppressive in police custody, and must import some impropriety, some oppression actively applied in an improper manner by the police'.

The Court of Appeal has indicated that treatment that falls short of oppression – for instance deliberate and harsh ill-treatment or behaviour that falls short of that but would have affected the suspect like that in *Fulling* – would fall under s 76(2)(b).

CASE EXAMPLE

R v Emmerson (1990) 92 Cr App R 284

The court decided that a police officer losing his temper and swearing at a suspect whilst questioning him did not amount to oppression.

CASE EXAMPLE

R v Miller, Paris and Others (1993) 97 Cr App R 99

The defendants were accused of murdering a prostitute. The police interviewed each of them for long periods of time. Miller, who had a very low mental age, was interviewed for over thirteen hours, and during this period he denied his involvement over 300 times. Apart from this fact, the tape recordings showed that he was subject to verbal bullying by the initial team of investigators. The subsequent team refused him access to legal advice, distorted the evidence they had against him and consistently pushed him to accept the police version of events. Miller finally confessed. The court ruled his confession inadmissible, because it was unreliable and obtained by oppression.

Considering this decision in a little more detail, the factors that bore on the court's consideration and subsequent decision in ruling that the confession was inadmissible were as follows:

- Miller's mental capacity;
- the length of the interviews being over thirteen hours long;
- the fact that he had made over 300 denials;
- the verbal bullying;
- the refusal of access to legal advice;
- the distortion of the evidence; and
- the constant badgering of Miller with the police version of events.

The Court of Appeal made the point that it would still have considered the tactics of the police to be oppressive even if Mr Miller had had a normal mental capacity. *Miller* adopts a far more lenient approach than that adopted in *Fulling*, and it is therefore unclear how far police questioning may go before it becomes oppressive.

Breaches of the PACE Codes of Practice will not automatically lead to the exclusion of a confession, but a breach of PACE Code C can lead to an exclusion of evidence under s 76 for being unreliable, see *Re Proulx*; *R v Bow Street Magistrates' Court ex parte Proulx* [2001] 1 All ER 57 and *R v Doolan* [1988] Crim LR 747.

10.3.2 Section 76 and exclusion by reason of unreliability

Section 76(2)(b) of the PACE 1984 provides for the exclusion of confession evidence, if anything said or done is likely, in the circumstances existing at the time, to render it unreliable. Therefore, under this provision the court will consider two points: first, *things said or done* and, second, those things within the context of the *circumstances that existed at the time*: see *R v Wahab* [2003] 1 Cr App R 232. The effect of this provision is to render unreliable a confession that was obtained by means falling short of oppression.

CASE EXAMPLE

R v Harvey [1988] Crim LR 241

H confessed to murdering someone in order to protect the other suspect, who happened to be her lesbian lover. The court confirmed that the test was whether a *confession that was made in the circumstances that existed was likely therefore to be unreliable*. H was, however, mentally retarded and the court excluded her confession by reason of its unreliability.

Unreliable
erroneous or misleading.

A confession will be excluded if it was made as a consequence of things said or done that are likely to render it **unreliable**. In *R v McGovern* (1990) 92 Cr App R 228, the Court of Appeal held the confession evidence of a defendant who had confessed to being involved in a murder to be inadmissible as being unreliable. At the time of making the confession McGovern was:

1. denied access to legal advice, contrary to s 58 of the PACE 1984;
2. of a low IQ level;
3. six months pregnant and in a highly distressed and emotional state.

The police had also failed to keep written notes of her initial interview:

JUDGMENT

'. . . this Court is clearly of the view that even if the confession given at the first interview was true, as it was later admitted to be, it was made in consequence of her being denied access to a solicitor and is for that reason in the circumstances likely to be unreliable. It follows that the prosecution has not in our judgment proved otherwise . . . if a solicitor had been present at the time this mentally backward and emotionally upset young woman was being questioned, the interview would have been halted on the very basis that her responses would be unreliable. It seems that the interview was held quickly and without the formalities prescribed by the Code of Conduct because the police were anxious to discover the missing girl, but this heightened the risk of the confession being unreliable.'

(Farquharson LJ)

McGovern is evidence that an initial interview that does not comply with the PACE 1984 or its Codes of Practice will mean any subsequent interview will be tainted, even though it may be compliant with the law:

JUDGMENT

'. . . we are of the view that the earlier breaches of the Act and of the Code renders the contents of the second interview inadmissible also. One cannot refrain from emphasising that when an accused person has made a series of admissions as to his or her complicity in a crime at a first interview, the very fact that those admissions have been made are likely to have an effect upon her during the course of the second interview. If, accordingly, it be held, as it is held here, that the first interview was in breach of the rules and in breach of section 58, it seems to us that the subsequent interview must be similarly tainted.'

(Farquharson LJ)

In *McGovern*, the court was unequivocal in excluding the confession. In *Fulling* (above), the court confirmed that, unlike s 76(2)(a), exclusion of a confession under s 76(2)(b) of the PACE 1984 does not require impropriety on the part of the investigative questioner to be shown, i.e. by police officers: see *R v Walker* [1998] Crim LR 211.

In considering the *circumstances existing at the time* under s 76(2)(b), the Act sets an objective test. For example, the question in Everett's case (below) would have been whether the defendant had a mental impairment. Consider the following scenario, Stacey is interviewed on the charge of low-value robbery. Unbeknown to the police, she is a heroin addict. Stacey confesses to the crime, thinking that she will be quickly released on bail, and then be able to satisfy her addiction. In *R v Goldenberg* (1989) 88 Cr App R 285 a case involving a similar situation, the court stated that s 76(2) does not apply where the *only* cause of the confession being unreliable is the suspect themselves. The decision in *Goldberg* was followed in *R v Crampton* (1991) 92 Cr App R 369. This decision should be distinguished from those where the court has taken into account individual characteristics, such as mental capacity: see *R v Blackburn* [2005] EWCA Crim 1349.

CASE EXAMPLE

R v Everett [1988] Crim LR 826

Everett, although aged forty-two, had a mental age of eight. On appeal it was held that the circumstance of his existing mental condition should have been taken into account when considering whether his confession to the commission of the offence was to be admitted.

The individual characteristics of a suspect may mean that certain behaviour will give rise to concern in relation to the suspect's vulnerability, even though the same behaviour may not have that effect in relation to another suspect; for example mental ability, threats or inducements. Section 76(2)(b) is wide enough to cover such situations, even those where it is the personal circumstances of the suspect that have led to unreliability. Finally, those things said or done, considered in the light of the circumstances existing at the time, must result in a confession being made.

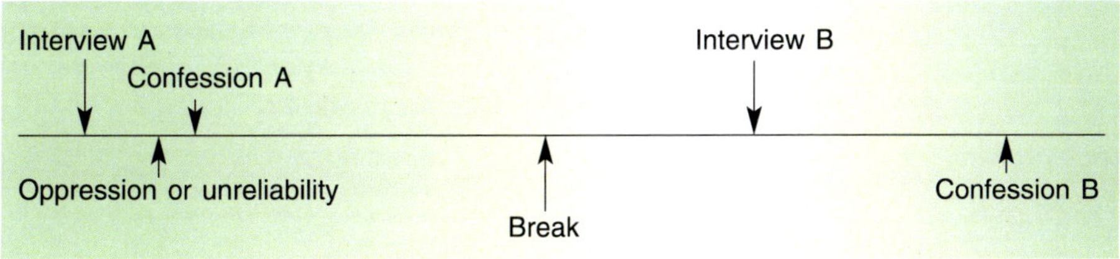

Figure 10.1 The exclusion of a confession: causation, unreliability and oppression

10.3.3 Causation

In order for confession evidence to be excluded, there must be a causal link between either the oppression or the unreliability and the making of the confession. This means that in instances where the effects of either the oppression or the unreliability have worn off at the point when the confession is made, then oppression or unreliability can be no ground to exclude the evidence. The diagram in Figure 10.1 summarises this point.

Figure 10.1 is purely for the illustration of the causal link; contemporaneity between the oppression or unreliability and the making of a confession will undoubtedly indicate that a causal link exists.

CASE EXAMPLE

R v Smith [1959] 2 QB 35

The court decided that Smith's confession, following threats from his commanding officer, was inadmissible. However, his confessions to investigating officers whilst in custody were admissible as the effects of the oppression/unreliability had worn off.

ACTIVITY

In what circumstances may a confession be excluded under s 76 of the PACE 1984?

Briefly outline what amounts to oppression under s 76(8).

When will a confession be unreliable under s 76?

KEY FACTS

Admissibility

The *general rule* is that only relevant evidence is admissible:

- The common law provided admissibility of confession evidence; now s 76 of the PACE 1984 regulates their admission.
- Section 76(1) and (7) provides that admissible confession evidence is only admissible as evidence against its maker.

- Confession evidence does not require to be corroborated or supported by other evidence.
- It is for the trier of fact (jury or magistrates) to decide how much weight to attach to a confession.

Exclusion

Section 76(2) of the PACE 1984 provides that confessions obtained through oppression or rendered unreliable because of things said or done are inadmissible:

- Section 76(2)(a) provides for the exclusion of confession evidence obtained by oppressive means; s 76(8) defines oppression as including treatment that is torturous, inhumane or degrading and the use or threat of violence.
- Section 76(2)(b) provides for the exclusion of confession evidence obtained as a consequence of something 'said or done' that is likely in the circumstances existing at the time to render it unreliable; impropriety on the part of the police is not required.

Causation

For exclusion under s 76 of the PACE 1984, there must be a causal link between the oppression or unreliability and the making of the confession.

10.4 Exclusion of evidence under s 78 of the PACE 1984

In addition to exclusion of confession evidence, and in spite of all the changes made to the law of evidence, judges have retained the general discretion to exclude any evidence, including a confession, under s 78 of the PACE 1984, which states that a court may exclude evidence where:

SECTION

'it appears to *it* that, having regard to all the circumstances in which the confession was obtained, that the admission of the *evidence* would have an adverse effect on the fairness of the proceedings *and therefore it should be excluded*.'

Section 67(11) of the PACE 1984 states that if any of the PACE Codes of Practice:

SECTION

'. . . appears to the court to be relevant to any question arising in proceedings, *then the Code should* be taken into account in determining it'.

There are a number of circumstances that fall within this provision. Therefore, PACE Act 1984 and its accompanying Codes of Practice give guidance on the treatment, detention and interrogation of suspects for fear of exclusion under s 78. The adherence to Codes C and E is of particular importance when it comes to s 78. The effect of this provision is not automatically to exclude evidence in the event of a breach of the Act or its Codes, as the Court of Appeal clearly stated in *R v Delaney* (1988) 88 Cr App R 338, *per* the Lord Chief Justices:

JUDGMENT

'. . . the flagrant breach of the Code, as the judge correctly described it, was the starting point of the submission made to the judge by counsel for the appellant that the confessions should be rejected . . . the mere fact that there has been a breach of the Codes of Practice does not of itself mean that evidence has to be rejected.'

In *Delaney* the Lord Chief Justice also thought it necessary to confirm that s 78 is not a disciplinary section, which means that when enacted it was not intended to be used as a method of disciplining the police for not following procedure:

JUDGMENT

'It is no part of the duty of the court to rule a statement inadmissible, simply in order to punish the police for failure to observe the Codes of Practice.'

It is, however, intended to promote the pursuance of the correct procedure. Non-compliance with the provisions, for example serious and substantial breaches of the Act or Codes, will result in the court exercising its discretion and thereby excluding the evidence. The practical importance of s 78 may in effect be the difference between a successful conviction and no conviction by reason of exclusion of the main evidence. For current examples, see *R v Keenan* [1989] 3 All ER 609; *R v Mason* [1988] 1 WLR 139, a case concerning trickery; and *R v Kwabena Poku* [1978] Crim LR 488, a case involving the innocent misleading of a defendant.

It would be correct to say that s 78 has caused a great deal of problems for the police and exists as a bright beacon of hope for an accused who has been treated unfairly. Section 58 of the PACE 1984 provides the suspect with the right to access legal advice, i.e. privately to consult with a solicitor, if they so wish. The only restriction on this right arises if the offence is a serious arrestable one and a police officer with the rank of at least superintendent authorises its suspension on the grounds under s 58(8).

Section 58(8) of the PACE 1984 states that:

SECTION

'. . . refusal of the suspect's right can be made on the basis that there exist reasonable grounds for believing that exercise of the suspect's right will (a) lead to interference with or harm to evidence connected with a serious arrestable offence or interference with or physical injury to other persons; or (b) will lead to the alerting of other persons suspected of having committed such an offence but not yet arrested for it; or (c) will hinder the recovery of any property obtained as a result of such an offence'.

In the case of *R v Samuel* [1988] 2 WLR 920, the Court of Appeal thought a refusal under s 58 would only be very exceptionally justified because solicitors are professionals, and therefore it is unlikely that their advice would give rise to the conditions of this provision being satisfied. The right to advice is considered to be a fundamental legal right, and on many occasions its refusal has led to confession evidence being excluded. There are, however, some contradictory cases, such as *R v Alladice* (1988) 87 Cr App R 380, where a refusal to allow a suspect access to legal advice was unreasonable. However, the suspect's confession was not excluded, because he was an experienced criminal who knew very well what his rights were and would therefore have been in a position to protect himself.

10.5 The effect of exclusion

The consequence of evidence being excluded is simple, and the general rule is as follows, the prosecution cannot use excluded confession evidence as part of their case against the defendant: see *R v Treacy* [1944] 2 All ER 229. This does not necessarily mean that the confession falls by the way, as s 76(4)–(5) allows the prosecution to extract certain evidence from the excluded confession. Section 76(4) of the PACE 1984 states that evidence is admissible if it relates to:

SECTION

'. . . any facts discovered as a result of the confession; or . . . where the confession is relevant as showing that the accused speaks, writes or expresses *themselves* in a particular way'.

This is often referred to metaphorically, as the 'fruit of the poisoned tree'. The effect of this provision requires some exploration. Consider this: Adele is charged with assault occasioning actual bodily harm. After a lengthy fifteen hours of interviews without comfort breaks and with persistent threats, she confesses and, in her confession, informs the police that the weapon is hidden in the cistern of her friend Ariana's lavatory. The police retrieve the evidence. The question here is whether it follows that if her confession is excluded by reason of oppression then any evidence that may have been obtained as a result of it is also excluded. Section 76(4)(a) allows for the admission of *any facts discovered as a result of the confession*. Therefore, such evidence is admissible, even where the actual confession from which it was derived is not. This poses an additional problem, whether the prosecution can refer to how the evidence was in fact discovered. The answer is that they cannot do so, as s 76(5) specifically prohibits the prosecution from referring to the fact that the evidence was discovered as a result of what the suspect said in their confession; that is, of course, unless the defence choose to refer to it. If the defence do refer to it then the prosecution is also then free to make such reference. The diagram in Figure 10.2 summarises the position.

Earlier it was discussed how confessions were an exception to the rule against hearsay and thus could be tendered as proof of the contents they contained. Another interesting question arises: whether the prosecution use a confession to prove something other than the truth of the contents therein. Section 76(4)(b) of the PACE 1984 allows the prosecution to use an excluded

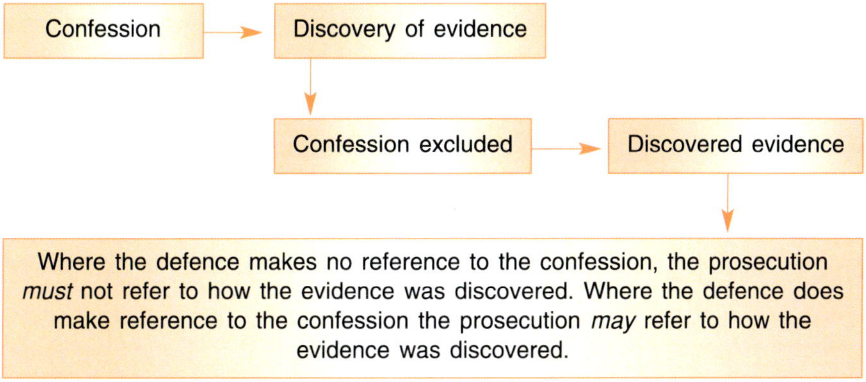

Figure 10.2 Using an excluded confession: s 76 PACE 1984

confession to prove something other than the truth of its contents, perhaps to prove that the defendant speaks or writes in a particular way. A good example of this is misspelling. For example, in a very popular television drama, an excluded confession was used to show that a murderer continuously misspelt the term 'murderer' as 'murdererr'.

Finally, it should be noted that a co-defendant may cross-examine the maker of an excluded confession on an inconsistency relevant to their own guilt: see *R v Rowson* [1986] QB 174. In *R v Myers* [1997] 3 WLR 552 (HL) (below), counsel argued that such cross-examination was not permitted where the confession was excluded by reason of oppression.

ACTIVITY

Outline the effect of exclusion on the subsequent use of a confession.

Summarise the status of evidence discovered as a result of a subsequently excluded confession.

KEY FACTS

Exclusion of evidence under s 78

The court may in the interests of justice exclude evidence that would have an adverse effect on the fairness of the proceedings.

The effect of exclusion

The *general rule* is that excluded confession evidence cannot be used by the prosecution as part of its case against the defendant. However, s 76(4)–(5) allows the prosecution to use any facts discovered as a result of the confession or to use it for a purpose other than to prove the truth of its contents, e.g. it may be relevant to show that the accused speaks, writes or expresses themselves in a particular way.

10.6 Presentation of confession evidence

Even where a confession is admissible, it will not usually be presented to the court in its 'raw' form. In effect, this means that not every word uttered by the defendant will be presented to the court. The most likely statement presented will consist of a mixture of incriminatory and exculpatory remarks. These will be remarks that point to the defendant's guilt or that are prejudicial to their case.

10.6.1 Remarks that are prejudicial to a defendant

Even though a confession represents an accurate reflection of what a defendant says, and the way in which it is said, it may be edited to remove remarks that are either inadmissible or prejudicial. Editing of this sort takes place only if, after the removal of the offending remarks, the remainder of the confession makes sense. An example of such editing is a reference in a confession to a defendant's previous antecedent history (prior convictions). This will be removed, as in *R v Knight* (1946) 31 Cr App R 52, unless one of the provisions of the CJA 2003 applies. If prejudicial remarks are put before the jury, then the only likely outcome is that the conviction will be rendered unsafe and therefore may be quashed on appeal.

10.6.2 Remarks that exculpate or incriminate a defendant

Remarks may be incriminatory or exculpatory and the distinction is of vital importance. It makes sense then that any incriminatory remarks in a confession are put to a jury, thereby providing a complete picture. What of exculpatory remarks, i.e. how a defendant has responded to exculpate or explain themselves? In the case of *R v Storey* (1968) 52 Cr App R 334, the court decided that such exculpatory remarks, made by a defendant to the police in a confession, were inadmissible because they amounted to proof of the truth of their contents. However, the same exculpatory remarks were admissible as part of the *res gestae* evidencing the defendant's reaction when accused. This approach was confirmed in *R v Donaldson* (1976) 64 Cr App R 65. The distinction that incriminatory remarks can be used as evidence of the truth of their contents and exculpatory remarks as evidence of reaction is often unclear. In *R v Duncan* (1981) 73 Cr App R 359, the court stated that the interests of fairness dictated that an entire response should be put to the jury with a direction from the trial judge to the effect that, whilst the incriminatory remarks are likely to be true, the remarks that exculpate the defendant are less likely to be so.

10.6.3 Remarks that incriminate a co-accused

The *general rule* is that a confession is admissible only against its maker and not anyone else that it may incriminate. This is because such evidence amounts to hearsay evidence of the guilt of the person implicated and is therefore inadmissible as against a person other than the maker of the statement: see *R v Spinks* [1982] 1 All ER 587. Editing such a reference is possible, but not usual in practice. Alternatively, it may be that the reference has little or no relevance to the allegations being made against the defendant, and therefore can be easily excluded.

It is important to remember that only relevant evidence is admissible, see *R v Rogers* [1971] Crim LR 413. In terms of prejudicial remarks that damage the case of a co-accused, such remarks can be edited out so long as they do not disadvantage the defendant, see *R v Lobban* [1995] 1 WLR 877. Where a confession made by defendant A is too prejudicial and results in unfairness to co-defendant B, but that unfairness is helpful to A's case, then, as is quite common, the confession will be used in its fuller form and a joint trial will be avoided – the indictment will be severed so that each defendant can be tried separately.

ACTIVITY

Why are confessions edited?

KEY FACTS

Remarks that are prejudicial to a defendant

Most confessions will be edited to remove remarks that are inadmissible or prejudicial.

Remarks that exculpate or incriminate a defendant

Incriminatory remarks will be put to a jury providing a fuller picture, even though these are tendered as proof of the truth of their contents. Exculpatory remarks cannot be tendered as proof of the truth of their contents but will normally be admissible because they are part of the *res gestae* – an exception to the rule against the admission of hearsay: see now the CJA 2003.

Remarks that incriminate a co-accused

The *general rule* is that a confession is admissible only against its maker and not anyone that it may incriminate.

10.7 Challenging and using confession evidence

There are two main points that need discussion at this stage. First, how confession evidence can be challenged to exclude it and, second, how an accused can use the confession of a co-accused. Let us begin with the former. Any challenges to the admissibility of confession evidence under s 76 or s 78 of the PACE 1984 are undertaken in a **voir dire**, the nature of which was discussed in Chapter 1: see *R v Oxford City Justices, ex p Berry* [1988] QB 507 and *R v Manji* [1990] Crim LR 512. If a challenge arises, then it is usual for a *voir dire* to be held in Crown Court cases. Whether or not it is practical in a magistrates' court case depends on whether the issue of admissibility can be dealt with at the time.

Voir dire
a trial that takes place within a trial to determine the admissibility of contested evidence.

Where an accused completely denies ever making a confession that the prosecution attributes to the accused this does not involve the reliability of the confession. No *voir dire* will be held in these circumstances. This is because the issue is a factual one of the credibility of the witness and therefore one for the jury: see *Ajodha v The State (Trinidad & Tobago)* [1982] AC 204.

A defendant can choose to give evidence in the *voir dire*. If they do, then he or she does not have to give evidence at the trial. Where a defendant gives evidence at the *voir dire*, an important issue arises. In terms of the answers they give and their use at trial, the *general rule* is that the prosecution at the trial may not use any evidence that emerges as a result of the *voir dire*, provided that the judge rules that the confession is inadmissible.

CASE EXAMPLE

Wong Kam Ming v R [1980] AC 247

The defendant W confessed to (a) being present at the scene of a crime and (b) attacking someone with a knife. Counsel on his behalf challenged the admissibility of the confession in a *voir dire* at which W admitted that he was both present and had participated. The trial judge ruled the confession inadmissible. Subsequently, at trial, the prosecution cross-examined W on the differences between his evidence to the jury and that which he had stated in the *voir dire*. The Privy Council (PC), on public policy grounds, held that it was inappropriate for the prosecution to have questioned W in the *voir dire* on the truthfulness of his statement and then used this incriminating evidence that had emerged in the *voir dire* at the trial before the jury. The PC also confirmed that such evidence could only have been used if the result of the *voir dire* was to include the confession; the prosecution would then have been free to cross-examine W on his inconsistencies.

A similar approach to *Wong* was adopted by the House of Lords in *R v Brophy* [1982] AC 476. The case concerned questioning in a *voir dire* that resulted in evidence of Brophy admitting that he was a member of the Irish Republican Army (IRA), the offence with which he was charged. The confession that was being challenged was ruled inadmissible by the trial judge. At the trial the prosecution was allowed to use evidence of his admission, which resulted in the defendant being convicted. The House of Lords held that this was wrong. Evidence relevant to an issue in a *voir dire* cannot later be the subject of cross-examination if the outcome of the *voir dire* is to result in the non-admission of a confession.

The rules that relate to the admissibility of confessions tended to focus on confession evidence that the prosecution sought to use against an accused. However, there is the additional situation where a co-accused may wish to make use of a confession that was made by the accused, perhaps as support for their own defence or as a means by which to cross-examine and discredit the accused by highlighting the inconsistency between their confession evidence and their oral testimony at court. Problems arose where a confession had been either excluded or the prosecution had chosen not to use it for some reason. The position of s 76 was to apply to confession evidence tendered by the prosecution. The issue for the co-accused was twofold: first, the inability to compel the accused to give evidence on his or her behalf and, second, the non-application of s 76. Thus, s 128 of the Criminal Justice Act 2003 inserted s 76A into the PACE 1984, states:

SECTION

'(1) In any proceedings a confession made by an accused person may be given in evidence for another person charged in the same proceedings (a co-accused) in so far as it is relevant to any matter in issue in the proceedings and is not excluded by the court in pursuance of this section.

(2) If, in any proceedings where a co-accused proposes to give in evidence a confession made by an accused person, it is represented to the court that the confession was or may have been obtained –
  (a) by oppression of the person who made it; or
  (b) in consequence of anything said or done which was likely, in the circumstances existing at the time, to render unreliable any confession which might be made by him in consequence thereof, the court shall not allow the confession to be given in evidence for the co-accused except in so far as it is proved to the court on the balance of probabilities that the confession (notwithstanding that it may be true) was not so obtained.

(3) Before allowing a confession made by an accused person to be given in evidence for a co-accused in any proceedings, the court may of its own motion require the fact that the confession was not obtained as mentioned in subsection (2) above to be proved in the proceedings on the balance of probabilities.

(4) The fact that a confession is wholly or partly excluded in pursuance of this section shall not affect the admissibility in evidence –
  (a) of any facts discovered as a result of the confession; or
  (b) where the confession is relevant as showing that the accused speaks, writes or expresses himself in a particular way, of so much of the confession as is necessary to show that he does so.

(5) Evidence that a fact to which this subsection applies was discovered as a result of a statement made by an accused person shall not be admissible unless evidence of how it was discovered is given by him or on his behalf.

(6) Subsection (5) above applies –
  (a) to any fact discovered as a result of a confession which is wholly excluded in pursuance of this section; and
  (b) to any fact discovered as a result of a confession which is partly so excluded, if the fact is discovered as a result of the excluded part of the confession.

(7) In this section "oppression" includes torture, inhuman or degrading treatment, and the use or threat of violence (whether or not amounting to torture).'

Thus, a co-accused can make use of the confession of an accused. The co-accused must prove that the confession is admissible on the balance of probabilities. The diagram in Figure 10.3 summarises the position.

CASE EXAMPLE

R v Myers [1997] 3 WLR 552 (HL)

Myers and her co-defendant were charged with the murder of a taxi driver. Both ran cut-throat defences, i.e. each blamed the other. Myers, whilst not under caution, made two confessions to the police to the effect that she had stabbed the taxi driver in order to rob and not to kill him. At the trial, the prosecution did not

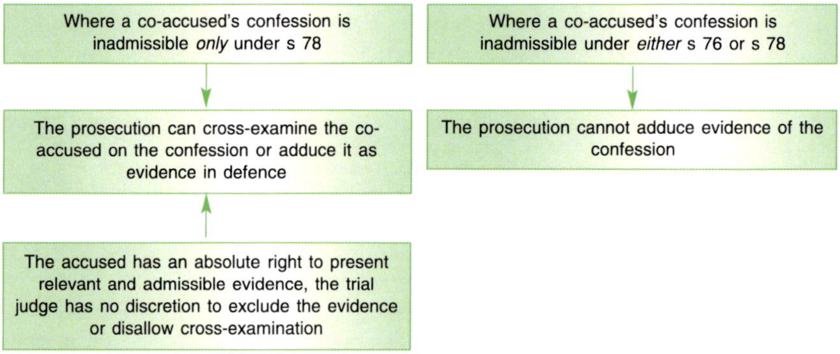

Figure 10.3 The co-accused and their use of the confession of the accused

adduce evidence of these confessions and Myers denied ever making them. Her co-defendant was eligible to adduce evidence of the confessions in defence and Myers was convicted. The House of Lords dismissed her appeal; her confession was relevant to the defence of her co-accused and therefore admissible.

JUDGMENT

'It seems to me that there is force in that comment despite Lord Bridge's anxiety that if confessions by third parties were admitted it would only be too easy for fabricated confessions to produce unjustified acquittals. Accepting Lord Bridge's view in *Blastland* that statements by third persons are not admissible there is a long line of authority showing that a defendant must be allowed to cross-examine a co-accused as to a previous inconsistent confession so long as the material is relevant to the defendant's own defence. In my opinion a defendant should also be allowed to put a co-defendant's confession to witnesses to whom the confession was made so long as the confession is relevant to the defendant's defence and so long as it appears that the confession was not obtained in a manner which would have made it inadmissible at the instance of the Crown under s 76(2) of the Act of 1984. There may be doubt as to whether the co-accused will be called (so that it may not be possible to put the confession to the co-accused directly) and not to allow the defendant to introduce it by way of cross-examination of prosecution witnesses could lead to great unfairness.'

(Lord Slynn of Hadley)

10.8 Confessions made by mentally handicapped persons

Section 77 of the PACE 1984 provides additional protection for people who are mentally handicapped. Where the prosecution case against such a person relies wholly or substantively on a confession that was not made in the presence of an independent person, who then is an independent person for the purposes of this provision? Section 77(3) of the Police Act 1996 specifically excludes police officers or those employed for police purposes, but includes lawyers i.e., solicitors. If such an instance arises, the court will direct the jury of the special need for caution before they decide to convict a mentally handicapped person on the basis of such a confession. Failure to comply with the provision will result in a conviction being quashed, as in *R v J* [2003] EWCA Crim 3309.

10.9 Other illegally obtained evidence

Section 78 of the PACE 1984 also applies to exclude prosecution evidence, the admission of which may have such an adverse effect on the fairness of the proceedings that it ought not to be admitted. The courts retained, as they do today, discretion under the common law to exclude confession evidence that was illegally, improperly or unfairly obtained where it considered that the prejudicial effect of the evidence outweighed its probative value: see *R v Sang* [1980] AC 402. An example of a situation that would fall under the common law discretion would be a confession obtained in breach of the PACE codes. The discretion is now preserved in s 82(3) of the PACE 1984 which states:

SECTION

'. . . nothing in this part of the Act shall prejudice any power of the court to exclude evidence (whether by preventing questions being put or otherwise) at its discretion'.

The discretion to exclude under s 78 is far wider than that under the common law. In contrast, this provision applies to all types of evidence on which the 'prosecution proposes to rely', and the court will consider all the circumstances, including the manner in which it was obtained. Section 78 applies prospectively and not retrospectively. For example, it cannot be used to withdraw evidence that has already been adduced in court. Three important points should be noted:

- The statutory power to exclude confession evidence is preferred over the common law discretion in practice.
- Section 78 only provides the trial judge with the power to exclude prosecution evidence and not relevant admissible evidence for a co-accused.
- The common law discretion allows a trial judge to direct a jury to disregard confession evidence if, after allowing its admission following a *voir dire* they subsequently decide, having heard all the evidence, that it should have been excluded.

Whether or not s 78 applies is a matter for the trial judge to decide, having considered the circumstances of the particular case. What is obvious is that its use is very much based on policy considerations. Strangely, the rules of evidence in jurisdictions such as the US or India operate to exclude evidence that is in breach of the law. In contrast, the rules of evidence in the UK render evidence inadmissible only on the basis of relevance and even then without the need to prove bad faith or deception.

CASE EXAMPLE

R v Mason [1988] 1 WLR 139

The police when investigating the commission of a minor offence blatantly lied and tricked both the defendant and his solicitor a number of times. Those lies and that deception were such that they had an adverse effect on the fairness of the proceedings and hence the evidence was excluded.

Although *Mason* (above) was a fairly straightforward case, it is obvious that investigators have problems where they act as agents provocateurs. The House of Lords in *Sang* (above) doubted that evidence obtained as a result of a crime instigated by an agent provocateur would be excluded. This rather oblique reasoning was challenged in *R v Edwards* [1991] Crim LR 45. In *R v Christou and Wright* [1992] 4 All ER 559 the police set up a fake jeweller's business and the defendants were arrested trying to sell stolen jewellery. Counsel for the defendants argued for the exclusion of this evidence by reason of the manner in which it had been obtained. The court decided that the evidence was relevant and therefore chose not to exercise its discretion to exclude it under s 78. In *Williams v DPP* [1993] 3 All ER 365, the police had loaded a 'bait' van with fake cigarette cartons and placed it in a vulnerable place. The defendants were arrested attempting to steal the cigarettes. In this case, the evidence was still admitted, even though no offence had been committed before the police had tricked the defendants – the evidence was lacking in assertions that pressure was brought to bear on the defendants to participate in an offence.

Much needed guidelines were laid down by the Court of Appeal in *R v Smurthwaite* [1994] 1 All ER 898. In this case, the defendant was convicted of soliciting a murder when he sought a contract killer and, unbeknown to him, in arranging it he had met with an undercover policeman and another, merely posing as a contract killer. Smurthwaite sought to have the evidence excluded on the basis that it had been improperly obtained by an undercover police officer. The court held that as the PACE 1984 required it to consider the circumstances in which the evidence was obtained, s 78 could operate to exclude evidence in cases of entrapment. The court stated that, in such cases, when considering exclusion the court should have regard to the following:

- whether the agent provocateur was encouraging the commission of a criminal offence that the defendant may not have otherwise committed;
- the means that the agent had used to entrap the defendant;
- the role the agent had played in entrapping the defendant;
- the strength of the evidence on what had actually occurred.

In *R v Latif* [1996] 1 All ER 353, a customs officer posed as a drug runner, thereby obtaining evidence which incriminated the defendant, Latif, who was convicted. In this case, counsel argued that where the agent provocateur plays an active and therefore arguably improper role, any evidence obtained thereby should be excluded, or the proceedings against the defendant stayed for an abuse of the courts' process – this latter claim may be the basis of future claims: see *R v Loosely* [2001] 1 Cr App R 29. Unfortunately for Latif his conviction was upheld. In doing so, the court stated that it will take into account the public interest.

In *R v Hall* [2002] EWCA Crim 1881, the police suspected that Hall had murdered his wife and in investigating the offence a policewoman, to whom he later confessed, initiated a romantic relationship with the defendant. In trying to ascertain whether he had in fact killed his wife, the policewoman asked him questions designed to elicit incriminatory information. This the trial judge held to be improper. In contrast, information obtained by the police through discreet surveillance will not necessarily be excluded; for example, evidence obtained through bugging a defendant's cell, as in *R v Bailey* [1993] 3 All ER 513, or bugging the home of the defendant's brother, as in *R v Khan* [1995] QB 27, even though the latter was done by trespassing.

In *Teixeira de Castro v Portugal* (1999) 28 EHRR 101 the European Court of Human Rights stated that:

JUDGMENT

'. . . the general requirements of fairness embodied in Article 6 of the European Convention on Human Rights apply to proceedings that concern all types of criminal offences . . . *the public interest cannot justify the use of evidence that was obtained as a result of incitement by the police*'.

Finally, the court confirmed in *Nottingham County Council v Amin* [2001] 1 WLR 1071 that the mere giving of an opportunity to break the law is not entrapment, and therefore evidence obtained as a result should not necessarily be excluded.

ACTIVITY

Summarise the effect of s 78 of the PACE 1984.

What is the position of the law on evidence obtained by reason of an investigator acting as an agent provocateur?

KEY FACTS

Other illegally obtained evidence

Section 78 of the PACE 1984 applies to exclude prosecution evidence, the admission of which may have an adverse effect on the fairness of the proceedings. The courts also retain a common law discretion to exclude confession evidence if obtained illegally, improperly or unfairly where its prejudicial effect outweighs its probative value. Exclusion under s 78 is wider than under the common law because it applies to all types of evidence on which the 'prosecution proposes to rely' and the court will consider all the circumstances, including the manner in which it was obtained.

SUMMARY

- Section 82(1) of the PACE 1984 provides a partial definition of a confession as a wholly or partly adverse statement containing unambiguous incriminatory content that incriminates the suspect.
- The statement can be made to anyone, even those not in an authoritative position and no particular form of words is required for purposes of admissibility.
- Confessions were admissible as exceptions to the rules against hearsay under the common law; s 76 of the PACE 1984 now regulates their admission.
- Section 76(1) and (7) provides that admissible confession evidence is only admissible as evidence against its maker.
- Confessions do not need to be corroborated.
- The trier of fact (judge or jury) will decide what weight to attribute to a confession.
- Sections 76(2)(a)–(b) and 76(8) of the PACE 1984 provide that confessions obtained through oppression or rendered unreliable because of things said or done are inadmissible.
- A confession will be excluded under s 76 of the PACE 1984 if there is a causal link between oppression or unreliability and the making of the confession.
- Section 78 of the PACE 1984 allows a court to exclude a confession in the interests of justice where its inclusion would have an adverse effect on the fairness of the proceedings.
- A confession is only admissible as evidence against its maker.
- The court also retains the common law discretion to exclude evidence if obtained illegally, improperly or unfairly where its prejudicial effect outweighs its probative value.

SAMPLE ESSAY QUESTION

Judges have a broader discretion to exclude evidence under s 78 of the Police and Criminal Evidence Act 1984 than under the common law. Discuss.

Answer plan

Outline the scope of the provision.
State that judicial discretion to exclude evidence lies in the common law (as preserved by s 82(3) of PACE 1984 and s 78 of the same Act). Highlight that it is often mooted that the latter provision had the effect of extending the common law judicial discretion to exclude (see *Matto v Wolverhampton Crown Court* [1987]) and that the discretion under s 78 was at least as wide as that in the common law (*Khan (Sultan)* [1997] AC 558).

Discuss the application of the law to evidence obtained unfairly and to that which the judge considers to have an adverse effect on the fairness of the proceedings.
Discuss the fact that one of the main differences between the two discretions is that the latter includes the exclusion of evidence on the basis of the manner in which it was obtained, and the common law exclusion applies to confessions and evidence retrieved from the accused after the offence had been committed – thus the discretion to exclude under s 78 is far greater. Outline that there have been cases where it has been suggested that s 78 included the discretion to admit inadmissible evidence (*Chalkley v Jeffries* (1998) 2 CrAppR 79) something that was quickly rebutted.

Highlight examples such as entrapment (agent provocateur).
Discuss that much of the case law surrounding s 78 concerns improperly obtained evidence. Analyse *Loosely* [2001] and *Hardwicke* [2000], which state that simply obtaining evidence in a particular method, for instance in breach of the PACE Codes of Practice, will not in itself be necessarily sufficient to warrant a judge exercising their discretion to exclude under s 78.

Further reading

Birch, D. 'Criminal Justice Act 2003: (4) hearsay – same old story, same old song?' (2004) Crim LR, Jul, 556–573

Mirfield, P. (1998) *Silence, Confessions and Improperly Obtained Evidence*, Oxford Monographs on Criminal Law and Justice, Oxford University Press

Munday, R. 'Convicting on confessional evidence in the complete absence of a corpus delicti' (1993) 157 JPJo 275

Munday, R. 'Adverse denial and purposive confession' (2003) Crim LR, Dec, 850–864

R v Delaney (1989) 88 Cr App R 338 – 'Case comment: evidence and the admissibility of a confession' (1989) Crim LR, Feb, 139–140

R v Goldenberg (1989) 88 Cr App R 285 – 'Case comment: admissions and confessions: words or acts of person making confession not included in matters affecting reliability' (1988) Crim LR, Oct, 678–679

Singh, C. (2014) *Beginning Evidence*. Oxford: Routledge

Internet links

PACE 1984 Codes of Practice: www.homeoffice.gov.uk/police/powers/pace-codes

11

Bad character evidence in criminal proceedings

AIMS AND OBJECTIVES

By the end of this chapter you will be able to:

- understand the various meanings of character at common law;
- analyse the modes of proving character, both good and bad;
- appreciate the effect of adducing evidence of good character;
- highlight the meaning of bad character under the Criminal Justice Act 2003.

11.1 Introduction

This chapter focuses on the definition of the expression 'character' in criminal proceedings. The common law definition of the term will be considered as well as the modes of adducing evidence of the defendant's character. Directions by the judge as to the proper treatment by the jury of the defendant's good character are of enormous importance and, to that end, the *Vye* directions will be considered. The common law notion of similar fact evidence will be analysed by reference to a number of illustrations. Finally, the definition of 'bad character' as laid down in the Criminal Justice Act 2003 will be explored.

11.2 Meaning of character evidence prior to the Criminal Justice Act 2003

There are two significant questions relating to character in a trial. These are:

(a) the meaning of the expression 'character evidence';

(b) the admissibility of character evidence in the proceedings.

The expression 'character evidence' has distinct connotations in criminal proceedings, depending on the context in which it is used. This varies with whether character is directly in issue or relates to credit of the relevant

DOI: 10.4324/9781003282433-11

individual (defendant or witness) and whether we are dealing with good or bad character.

There are three meanings that are attached to the expression 'character' in criminal proceedings. These are reputation, disposition, or either disposition or reputation evidence. Reputation evidence involves the general opinion of society concerning the witness. Indeed, the more popular the witness, the more likely that society will have an opinion of the witness. Disposition evidence involves specific incidents or separate acts of the witness, such as specific donations to charitable organisations, the previous convictions of the witness (including the accused) or background evidence. In other words, the expression means a tendency, propensity or inclination to do or omit from doing something connected to the proceedings.

At common law the meaning of character in criminal proceedings was restricted to the reputation of the witness. This rule was applicable to the admissibility of the accused's good character. In other words, prior to the Criminal Evidence Act 1898, a rule of law was developed to the effect that although the good character evidence of the accused was strictly irrelevant to the issue of guilt, he was nevertheless entitled to prove that, as a man of impeccable reputation, he was less likely to have committed the offence charged. The approach was based on a concession granted to accused persons who, at the time, did not have the capacity to testify. Such character witnesses called by the defendant were not allowed to testify as to specific acts of good conduct, but only as to the reputation of the defendant. Likewise, the prosecution was entitled to call rebutting evidence to challenge or dispute the good character of the accused. Again, such evidence was restricted to evidence of 'general reputation' only. This is known as the *Rowton* rule, derived from the case *R v Rowton* (1865) 11 LT 745.

CASE EXAMPLE

R v Rowton (1865) 11 LT 745

The accused, a headmaster of a boys' school, was charged with indecent assault on one of his pupils. The defence called character witnesses to testify on his behalf. The prosecution called rebutting evidence and the witness was asked the question, 'What is the defendant's general character for decency and morality of conduct?' The witness said, 'I know nothing of the neighbourhood's opinion, because I was only a boy at school when I knew him; but my own opinion, and the opinion of my brothers, who were also pupils of his, is that his character is that of a man capable of the grossest indecency and the most flagrant immorality.' It was held that this answer was inadmissible as it was a statement of disposition, not reputation:

JUDGMENT

'I am clearly of the opinion that when evidence in favour of the character of the prisoner has been given on his behalf, evidence of his bad character can be adduced upon the part of the prosecution to rebut the evidence so given . . . What is the meaning of evidence of character? It is laid down in the books that a prisoner is entitled to give evidence as to his general character. What does that mean? Does it mean evidence as to his "reputation" amongst those to whom his conduct and position are known? Or does it mean evidence of "disposition"? I think it means evidence of reputation only . . . The truth is, this part of our law is an anomaly. Although, logically speaking, it is quite clear that an antecedent bad character would form quite as reasonable a ground for the probability of guilt, as previous good character lays the foundation for the presumption of innocence, yet the prosecution cannot go into evidence as to the prisoner's bad character. The allowing of evidence of a prisoner's good character to be given has grown from a desire to administer the law with mercy as far as possible . . . I think that rebutting evidence must be of the same character and kept within the same limits; that while the prisoner can give evidence of general good character, so the evidence called to rebut it must be evidence of the same general description showing that the evidence which has been given to establish good reputation on the one hand is not true, because the man's general reputation is bad.'

(Cockburn J)

This principle was affirmed by the Court of Appeal in *R v Redgrave* (1982) 74 Cr App R 10. The charge was importuning men for immoral purposes contrary to s 32 of the Sexual Offences Act 1956, in that he noisily and violently performed acts of gross indecency in the presence of plain-clothes police officers at a urinal. The accused had wished to produce five bundles of love letters written to his girlfriends, and photographs, not being indecent, but of a heterosexual nature in order to rebut the inference of being of a homosexual disposition. The judge disallowed such evidence and the accused was convicted and appealed. The court dismissed the appeal and decided that the evidence was of disposition and inadmissible:

JUDGMENT

'. . . although disposition to commit the kind of offence charged was relevant, the law is as decided in *Rowton* (1865), viz., that the defendant could do no more than say, or call witnesses to prove, that he was not by general repute the kind of young man who would have behaved in the kind of way that the Crown alleged'.

(Lawton LJ)

The learned Lord Justice of Appeal continued by referring to the practice of the court to suspend or relax this rule in certain circumstances:

JUDGMENT

'It has long been the practice of judges to allow some relaxation of the law of evidence on behalf of defendants. Had this young man been a married man, or alternatively had he confined his relationship to one girl, it might not have been all that objectionable for him to have given evidence in general terms that his relationship with his wife or the girl was satisfactory. That would have been an indulgence on the part of the court.'

(Lawton LJ)

11.3 Good character

Before the Criminal Evidence Act 1898, evidence of the defendant's good character took the form of evidence of witnesses called by the defendant, as well as the cross-examination of witnesses on behalf of the defendant to bring out the good character of the defendant. Such evidence was restricted to the reputation of the defendant. Likewise, rebutting evidence adduced by the prosecution was restricted to evidence of the defendant's reputation in the community: see *R v Rowton* (above). Following the introduction of the 1898 Act, the defendant was allowed to testify on his own behalf and the court allowed the practice of permitting the defendant to testify as to his disposition, such as having done a number of good deeds or stressing the fact that he has led a good life. In practice, good character evidence of the defendant simply means that the defendant has no previous convictions. The defendant may testify to this effect or he may call witnesses to testify as to his good reputation. This remains the position today, although the 1898 Act has been replaced by the Criminal Justice Act 2003.

11.3.1 Directions as to good character

The courts have issued guidelines in *R v Vye* [1993] 3 All ER 241, as to the relevance of the good character of a defendant. The judge is required to consider whether to issue directions to the jury as to the use they may make of the evidence of the good character of the defendant and, if so, the contents of the direction.

- Good character may be relevant to the credibility of the defendant's testimony or pre-trial statements, i.e. whether the defendant is the sort of person who would tell the truth (first limb direction); a credibility direction.
- In addition, the judge is required to direct the jury as to whether the defendant is a person likely to have committed the offence charged (second limb direction), i.e. a propensity direction.
- The 'two limbs' of the direction are required to be given even where the defendant does not testify, provided that he had made pre-trial statements to the investigating authorities or other persons.
- Such directions are to be given even where the defendant of good character is jointly tried with a defendant of bad character.
- The judge is entitled to tailor his directions to the particular circumstances of each case.
- There is no rule in favour of separate trials for defendants of good and bad character.

JUDGMENT

'It is now an established principle that, where a defendant of good character has given evidence, it is no longer sufficient for the judge to comment in general terms. He is required to direct the jury about the relevance of good character to the credibility of the defendant. Conventionally, this has come to be described as the "first limb" of the character direction. In our judgment, when the defendant has not given evidence at the trial but relies on exculpatory statements made to the police or others, the judge should direct the jury to have regard to the defendant's good character when considering the credibility of those statements . . . Clearly, if a defendant of good character does not give evidence and has given no pre-trial answers or statements, no issue as to his credibility arises and a first limb direction is not required.'

[As to the 'second limb' direction, Lord Taylor CJ considered the leading authorities and continued:] 'We have reached the conclusion that the time has come to give some clear guidance to trial judges as to how they should approach this matter. It cannot be satisfactory for uncertainty to persist so that judges do not know whether this court, proceeding on a case-by-case basis, will hold that a "second limb" direction should or need not have been given. Our conclusion is that such a direction should be given where a defendant is of good character.

'Does the need for a "second limb" direction still exist when the defendant has not given evidence? We can see no logical ground for distinguishing in regard to a "second limb" direction between cases where the defendant has given evidence and cases where he has not.

'Having stated the general rule, however, we recognise it must be for the trial judge in each case to decide how he tailors his direction to the particular circumstances. He would probably wish to indicate, as is commonly done, that good character cannot amount to a defence. Provided that the judge indicates to the jury the two respects in which good character may be relevant, i.e. credibility and propensity, this court will be slow to criticise any qualifying remarks he may make based on the facts of the individual case.

'In our judgment, a defendant A of good character is entitled to have the judge direct the jury as to its relevance in his case even if he is jointly tried with a defendant B of bad character.

'To summarise, in our judgment the following principles are to be applied. (1) A direction as to relevance of his good character to a defendant's credibility is to be given where he has testified or made pre-trial answers or statements. (2) A direction as to the relevance of his good character to the likelihood of his having committed the offence charged is to be given, whether or not he has testified, or made pre-trial answers or statements. (3) Where defendant A of good character is jointly tried with defendant B of bad character, (1) and (2) still apply.'

(Lord Taylor CJ)

In *R v Aziz* [1995] 3 All ER 149, the House of Lords approved of the approach in *Vye* regarding the two-limbed direction. In addition, the court decided that the judge has a residual discretion to add words of qualification concerning other proved or possible criminal conduct of the defendant that has emerged during the trial, so as to place a fair and balanced picture before the jury. In the limited case where the defendant's claim to good character, other than his lack of previous convictions, was so spurious that it would make no sense to give the general character direction, the judge could exceptionally dispense with the direction in its entirety; for example where the defendant has been guilty of dishonesty concerning his employer but has not been charged with an offence.

In this case, A, Y and T were jointly charged with income tax and VAT frauds. A had no relevant previous convictions and Y and T had no previous convictions. A did not testify but relied on self-serving exculpatory statements made during interviews with customs officers. Y and T testified and denied committing the offences. The judge directed the jury to the effect that Y and T were entitled to be treated as persons of good character for the purpose of deciding whether their evidence was to be believed and A was to be treated as a person of good character for the purpose of considering whether he had the propensity to commit the offence. All three defendants were convicted and successfully appealed to the Court of Appeal. The House dismissed the prosecutor's appeal on the ground that all three defendants were entitled to full, good character directions (both limbs), notwithstanding that Y admitted to making a false mortgage application and to having lied to customs officers during interview. T admitted to not having declared his full income to the Inland Revenue:

JUDGMENT

'The certified question, although phrased in very general terms, was intended to raise the problem whether a defendant without any previous convictions may "lose" his good character by reason of other criminal behaviour. It is a question which was not directly before the court in *Vye*. It is a complex problem. It is also an area in which generalisations are hazardous. Acknowledging that a wide spectrum of cases must be kept in mind, the problem can be illustrated with a commonplace example. A middle-aged man is charged with theft from his employers. He has no previous convictions. But during the trial it emerges, through cross-examination on behalf of a co-defendant, that the defendant has made dishonest claims on insurance companies over a number of years. What directions about good character, if any, must the judge give? A good starting point is that a judge should never be compelled to give meaningless or absurd directions. And cases occur from time to time where a defendant, who has no previous convictions, is shown beyond doubt to have been guilty of serious criminal behaviour similar to the offence charged in the indictment. A sensible criminal justice system should not compel a judge to go through the charade of giving directions in accordance with *Vye* in a case where the defendant's claim to good character is spurious. I would therefore hold that a trial judge has a residual discretion to decline to give any character directions in the case of a defendant without previous convictions if the judge considers it an insult to common sense to give directions in accordance with *Vye*.

'The residual discretion of a trial judge to dispense with character directions in respect of a defendant of good character is of a limited variety. *Prima facie* the directions must be given. And the judge will often be able to place a fair and balanced picture before the jury by giving directions in accordance with *Vye* and then adding words of qualification concerning other proved or possible criminal conduct of the defendant which emerged during the trial. On the other hand, if it would make no sense to give character directions in accordance with *Vye*, the judge may in his discretion dispense with them.

'Subject to these views, I do not believe that it is desirable to generalise about this essentially practical subject which must be left to the good sense of trial judges. It is worth adding, however, that whenever a trial judge proposes to give a direction, which is not likely to be anticipated by counsel, the judge should follow the commendable practice of inviting submissions on his proposed directions.'

(Lord Steyn)

In *R v McCarthy (Stacie)* [2014] EWCA Crim 1963, the Court of Appeal decided that a good character direction by a trial judge was capable of leading to confusion and could have been couched in clearer terms. However, as the misdirection had no bearing on the issues in the trial the conviction was safe. In this case, the defendant was charged with causing death by careless driving. She was driving along a main road and turned right into a side road colliding with a pedestrian who later died. The defendant said she had not seen the pedestrian because she was blinded by the setting sun. The defendant had a clean driving record and was of good character. She relied *inter alia* on witness statements from individuals who had previously been passengers in cars driven by her. These statements were to the effect that she was a careful and prudent driver. The trial judge in directing the jury on her good character told them to ignore the witness statements as they did not deal with the issue as to her prudent driving in the trial. Later he told the jury that the defendant's good character meant that she was less likely to have committed the offence. She was convicted and appealed on the ground of a misdirection concerning her good character. The Court of Appeal dismissed her appeal on the ground that the misdirection had no bearing on the ultimate issue before the court, namely whether the defendant ought to have seen the pedestrian in time to avoid the collision. The direction should have been couched in terms that were explicitly consistent. That consistency could have been achieved by directing the jury as to the weight of the good character evidence rather than its admissibility.

JUDGMENT

'The jury were left with contradictory directions as to the effect of the evidence that the appellant was a prudent and careful driver. On the one hand, they were to ignore the evidence or to give it no weight; on the other, the appellant's good character, which included her driving record, might make it less likely that she had committed the offence. We do not consider that the appellant's good character, including her careful and competent driving record, could properly have had any bearing on the resolution of [the] issue [before the court]. Thus, this court has to ask whether the capacity of the full direction to cause confusion undermines the safety of the jury's verdict. In our view, the verdict was safe.'

(Pitchford LJ)

The trial judge is not shackled in the choice of the formulation of a good character direction. Provided that he conveys to the jury the requisite elements of the test laid down in *R v Vye* and *R v Aziz* (credibility and propensity), the appellate courts will very rarely interfere with his direction. However, in *R v Dillon* [2013] EWCA Crim 122, the judge had used inappropriate expressions in directing the jury on the defendant's good character. This case involved charges of assault and affray, which were denied by the defendant, a person of good character. The judge's good character direction was to the effect that the defendant had not previously been 'caught out' in anything dishonest or 'knocking a woman about'. The defendant was convicted and appealed *inter alia* on the ground of a misdirection. The Court of Appeal allowed the appeal and decided that the good character direction was defective. The statement by the judge implied that the defendant may have committed previous offences and, if so, had not been caught. In addition, the direction ought to have originated from the judge himself, rather than being expressed in the form of an argument that the defendant may have been entitled to say. Moreover, the direction as to propensity was also inadequate. It was true that the defendant had no previous convictions for 'knocking a woman about', but the principal issue was that he had no previous convictions for violence, and that had not been stated by the judge.

JUDGMENT

'In our view the direction is defective in four respects.

1. The judge three times states that the appellant has not been "caught out" committing offences. That carries the clear implication that the appellant may have committed offences but, if so, he has not been caught.
2. The direction should be expressed as coming from the court. It is not sufficient to state what the appellant was "entitled to say".
3. There is no clear statement that the jury should take the appellant's good character into account when deciding whether they believe his evidence. The oblique reference to "assessing" the appellant is not sufficient.
4. The direction in respect of propensity is insufficient. It is certainly true that the appellant does not have any previous convictions for "knocking a woman about" but that is not the limit of the matter. The appellant has no previous convictions for violence or any other offence. That fact may mean that the appellant was less likely to commit the offence that is now alleged.

In our view, if the judge had given a proper good character direction, it is possible that the jury would have not convicted. We regard the appellant's conviction as unsafe.'

(Jackson LJ)

Definitive guidelines by the Court of Appeal in R v Hunter

The Court of Appeal, constituted of five judges, considered a conjoined appeal in *R v Hunter and Others* [2015] EWCA Crim 631. In each of the appeals from convictions of sexual offences, the appellants had previous convictions, but none for sexual offences. All of the defendants chose to adduce their bad character evidence in an attempt to show that they had no propensity for the sort of crime with which they were now charged. The appeals were brought on the ground that the judge had misdirected the jury concerning the defendants' good character. The appeals were dismissed and the court took the opportunity to review the voluminous appeals on good character directions and issued guidelines on the subject. The two-limbed (credibility and propensity), good character directions laid down in *R v Vye* and *R v Aziz* were endorsed and the court noted that good character directions are no longer rules of practice but principles of law. But the court recognised that the law on good character directions had moved on since *Vye* and *Aziz*. The Criminal Justice Act 2003 significantly re-structured the law relating to the admissibility of bad character evidence. Section 98 of the 2003 Act defines 'bad character' as 'evidence of, or a disposition towards misconduct on [the part of the defendant or non-defendant]'. One of the gateways for the admissibility of the defendant's bad character involves the defendant's propensity to commit offences of the kind with which he is charged: see ss 101(1)(d) and 103(1) of the 2003 Act. This procedure will usually be adopted by the prosecution. However s 101(1)(b) of the Act entitles defence counsel to adduce the bad character of his client. This may be done where the conviction is old and unrelated to the charge with the intention of gaining a tactical advantage by requiring the judge to issue a modified good character direction concerning the absence of propensity. By way of illustration of this defence technique, see *R v Ahmed (Aneela)* [2015] 1 Cr App R 21. The defendant was charged on two counts of converting criminal property contrary to s 327(1)(c) of the Proceeds of Crime Act 2002. The appellant's brother was a convicted drug dealer. It was alleged that she helped him to convert drug-dealing proceeds using his funds to purchase expensive cars in her name under hire purchase agreements, which were subsequently paid off early. Five years before the alleged offences, and whilst a teenager, the defendant had been cautioned for theft, which she disclosed in her testimony. The trial judge decided to issue a good character direction but left it to the jury to decide whether the defendant was a person of good character. Following her conviction she appealed. The Court of Appeal allowed the appeal and quashed the conviction on the ground that it was a misdirection to invite the jury to reach their own conclusion as to whether the defendant was of good character. This was a question of law for the judge to decide including the terms of the directions. The weight to be attached to the direction was for the jury to decide. In his discretion the judge would have been entitled to dispense with a good character direction.

In *Hunter and Others* the Court of Appeal laid down the following propositions:

(1) In a number of authorities the law on good character directions has been unjustifiably extended beyond the principles laid down in *Vye* and *Aziz*. The Court of Appeal in *Vye*, and the House of Lords in *Aziz*, were dealing with defendants who did not have previous convictions, not defendants with previous convictions or implausible backgrounds. The consequence was that defendants with doubtful assertions as to good character have been successful in claiming entitlement to good character directions. Accordingly, many judges felt that they were obliged to give absurd or meaningless directions or ones that are far too generous to a defendant. Fairness to the defendant and the public did not require a judge to give a good character direction to a man whose claim to a good character is spurious.

(2) A judge's ruling and consequent directions on good character relate to the law not the facts.

(3) After re-iterating the principles laid down in *R v Vye* and *R v Aziz* (see earlier) the court asserted that *Vye* and *Aziz* did not decide:

   (a) that a defendant with no previous convictions is always entitled to a full good character direction whatever his character;
   (b) that a defendant with previous convictions is entitled to good character directions;
   (c) that a defendant with previous convictions is entitled to the propensity limb of the good character directions on the basis he has no convictions similar or relevant to those charged;
   (d) that a defendant with previous convictions is entitled to a good character direction where the prosecution do not seek to rely upon the previous convictions as probative of guilt;
   (e) that the failure to give a good character direction will almost invariably lead to a quashing of the conviction.

(4) Once evidence of bad character is admitted, a judge cannot ignore it and give directions to a jury that would make no sense.

(5) Good character means far more than not having previous convictions. A defendant who has no previous convictions may nevertheless have a bad character under section 98 of the CJA 2003. The issue of cautions and

reprehensible conduct on the part of the accused contribute to his bad character.

(6) The court introduced the following categories of character evidence as guidance to judges in order to promote consistency and fairness in trials:

(a) 'Absolute good character' i.e. a defendant who has no previous convictions or cautions recorded against him and no other reprehensible conduct alleged, admitted or proved. Such a defendant is entitled as of right to both limbs of a good character direction. The weight to be given to each limb is a matter for the jury.

(b) 'Effective good character' i.e. a defendant who has previous convictions or cautions recorded that are old, minor and have no relevance to the charge. The judge, in his discretion, is required to determine whether the defendant may be treated as a person of effective good character and, if so, he is required to issue a good character direction to the jury. In deciding the first question (whether the defendant is of effective good character) the judge is required to consider all the circumstances concerning the offence and the offender and fairness to all the parties concerned, including the public. Once the judge decides this question in favour of the defendant he has no choice and is required to give a good character direction (both limbs).

(c) 'Previous convictions and cautions adduced by the defendant under s 101(1)(b) Criminal Justice Act 2003' i.e. defendants frequently adduce evidence of previous convictions and cautions that are not in the same category as the offence charged in the hope of achieving a good character propensity direction from the judge. In these circumstances the judge has a discretion to determine whether to give any part of the good character direction and, if so, on what terms. The defendant does not have an entitlement to a good character direction.

(d) 'Bad character adduced by the Crown under s 101 of the Criminal Justice Act 2003', i.e. where a defendant has no previous convictions or cautions, but evidence is admitted and relied upon by the Crown of other misconduct, the judge is obliged to give a bad character direction. In addition, in the interests of fairness, the judge may include a modified form of good character direction subject to the limitation of absurdity.

(e) 'Bad character adduced by the defence but not relied on by the Crown', i.e. defendants with no previous convictions but the defence admits reprehensible conduct, not relied on by the Crown as probative of guilt. In these circumstances, the trial judge has a discretion as to whether to issue a good character warning. *Prima facie* the judge ought to issue such a warning unless it would defy common sense to do so.

(f) 'Joint trials – one accused with a good character and the other a bad character'. It is incumbent on the judge to issue a good character direction concerning the accused with a good character.

(7) The court dispelled the notion that whenever a judge misdirects the jury on good character, the conviction will be quashed as a matter of course. Each case will depend on its own facts. The appellate court will be required to analyse the impact of the error on the safety of the conviction.

More recently, in *R v B (E)* [2017] EWCA Crim 35 the Court of Appeal stated that the entitlement to be treated as a person of effective good character is dependent on the circumstances. In this case the defendant had been bound over to keep the peace, and therefore the bind over and the circumstances that led to it were also relevant considerations.

11.4 Disposition evidence of bad character of the defendant at common law (similar fact evidence)

As distinct from reputation evidence, the prosecution was allowed to adduce evidence of the disposition of the accused in order to prove that he committed the offence with which he had been charged. This is known as evidence of the propensity of the defendant to commit crimes of a similar nature. This is the position even though the evidence will have the incidental effect of presenting the accused in a bad light. In other words, where the specific acts of the accused are admissible to prove his guilt, the ancillary effect of admitting such circumstantial evidence may involve bringing out the accused's bad character. Such evidence was loosely called 'similar fact evidence'. The test of admissibility involved eschewing a chain of forbidden reasoning to the effect that the evidence establishes only that the accused is a person likely to have committed the offence charged. Indeed, the prosecution is required to go further and establish that the prejudicial evidence manifests a high degree of relevance.

The classic test of admissibility was stated by Lord Herschell in *Makin v AG for New South Wales* [1894] AC 57, thus:

JUDGMENT

'It is undoubtedly not competent for the prosecution to adduce evidence tending to show that the accused has been guilty of criminal acts other than those covered by the indictment, for the purpose of leading to the conclusion that the accused is a person likely from his criminal conduct or character to have committed the offence for which he is being tried. On the other hand, the mere fact that the evidence adduced tends to show the commission of other crimes does not render it inadmissible if it be relevant to an issue before the jury, and it may be so relevant if it bears upon the question whether the acts alleged to constitute the crime charged in the indictment were designed or accidental, or to rebut a defence which would otherwise be open to the accused.'

In this case, the two accused persons, husband and wife, were charged with the murder of a baby that they had in care for adoption. The child had died and its corpse was found buried in the garden of their home. Their defence was that the child died from natural causes or died accidentally. The prosecution was allowed to adduce evidence that the remains of a total of twelve other babies were found buried in gardens of houses occupied by the two accused, the Makins, over the years; these children were in the care of the Makins at the time of their deaths. The purpose for admitting the evidence was to rebut the defence of death from natural causes or accident.

In *Boardman v DPP* [1975] AC 421, Lord Hailsham explained the approach laid down by Lord Herschell in *Makin* thus:

JUDGMENT

'It is perhaps helpful to remind oneself that what is not to be admitted is a chain of reasoning and not necessarily a state of facts. If the inadmissible chain of reasoning is the only purpose for which the evidence is adduced as a matter of law, the evidence itself is not admissible. If there is some other relevant, probative purpose than the forbidden type of reasoning, the evidence is admitted, but should be made the subject of a warning from the judge that the jury must eschew the forbidden reasoning.'

In *R v P* [1991] 3 All ER 337, the House of Lords reiterated the *Makin/Boardman* principle and declared that an essential feature of the evidence requires that its probative force is sufficiently great to make it just to admit the evidence despite its prejudicial effect on the accused:

JUDGMENT

'. . . what has to be assessed is the probative force of the evidence in question, the infinite variety of circumstances in which the question arises demonstrates that there is no single manner in which this can be achieved. Whether the evidence has sufficient probative value to outweigh its prejudicial effect must in each case be a question of degree.'

(Lord Mackay)

The Criminal Evidence Act 1898 made the accused a competent witness in his defence for the first time. It was clear that if the accused had testified and was treated as an ordinary witness, he would have been unduly favoured on the one hand and unfairly disadvantaged on the other. The accused would have been unduly favoured in the sense that he would have been entitled to claim a privilege against self-incrimination and would have been entitled in cross-examination to refuse to answer questions relating to the facts in issue. This potential privilege was withdrawn by s 1(2) of the Criminal Evidence Act 1898. On the other hand, but for s 1(3), the accused would have been unduly prejudiced had he been subject to cross-examination like any ordinary witness. His previous convictions or bad character would have been admissible in order to discredit him as a witness. Undoubtedly, this would have had a discouraging effect on an accused with a criminal record. Accordingly, a compromise was reached in s 1(3). The accused was afforded protection from undue prejudice by being granted a 'conditional shield'. The shield involves a prohibition on the questioning of the accused to show that he 'had committed or been convicted of or been charged with' an offence other than the subject of the charge or is of 'bad character'. Subject to the discretion of the judge, this 'shield' or protection will be lost under one or more of the provisos laid down in s 1(3). This view was expressed by Lord Sankey in *Maxwell v DPP* [1935] AC 309:

JUDGMENT

'When Parliament by the Act of 1898 effected a change in the general law and made the prisoner in every case a competent witness, it was in an evident difficulty, and it pursued the familiar English system of compromise. It was clear that if you allowed a prisoner to go into the witness box, it was impossible to allow him to be treated as an ordinary witness. Had that been permitted, a prisoner who went into the box to give evidence on oath could have been asked about any previous convictions with the result that an old offender would seldom, if ever, have been acquitted. This would have offended against one of the most deeply rooted and jealously guarded principles of our criminal law . . . Some middle way, therefore, had to be discovered, and the result was that a certain amount of protection was accorded to a prisoner who gave evidence on his own behalf. As it has been expressed, he was presented with a shield and it was provided that he was not to be asked, and that if he was asked he should not be required to answer, any question tending to show that he had committed or been convicted of or been charged with any offence, other than that wherewith he was then charged, or was of bad character. Apart, however, from this protection he was placed in the position of an ordinary witness. . . .'

The Act contains no definition of 'character' but its meaning has been treated as including both 'reputation' and 'disposition' evidence. Indeed, in *R v Dunkley* [1927] 1 KB 323, the Court of Appeal decided that it was much too late in the day to change the meaning of 'character' under the 1898 Act to accord to the common law meaning of 'reputation'. The practice of the court is to accord to the expression 'character' a wide meaning including both reputation and disposition:

JUDGMENT

'It is apparent that within the space of a very few lines [of the Act] the word "character" is used in this part of the section no fewer than four times . . . Nevertheless, when one looks at the long line of cases beginning very shortly after the passing of the Criminal Evidence Act 1898, it does not appear that the argument has ever been so much as formulated that the "character" which is spoken of is the character which is so well known in the vocabulary of the criminal law – namely general reputation of the person referred to. The argument was formulated yesterday. One can only say that it is now much too late in the day even to consider that argument, because it could not now prevail without the revision, and indeed to a great extent the overthrow of a very long series of decisions.'

(Lord Hewart)

11.5 Abolition of the common law rules and the Criminal Evidence Act 1898

The Law Commission in its report on 'Evidence of Bad Character in Criminal Proceedings', No 273, October 2001, stated:

CLAUSE

'The present law suffers from a number of defects . . . In summary, however, they constitute a haphazard mixture of statute and common law rules which produce inconsistent and unpredictable results, in crucial respects distort the trial process, make tactical considerations paramount and inhibit the defence in presenting its true case to the fact-finder whilst often exposing witnesses to gratuitous and humiliating exposure of long forgotten misconduct.'

The Government's White Paper, 'Justice for All', published in 2002, summarised the current rules and indicated its preference in this area:

CLAUSE

'The current rules of evidence . . . are difficult to understand and complex to apply in practice. There has been growing public concern that evidence relevant to the search for truth is being wrongly excluded . . . We favour an approach that entrusts relevant information to those determining the case as far as possible. It should be for the judge to decide whether previous convictions are sufficiently relevant to the case, bearing in mind the prejudicial effect, to be heard by the jury and for the jury to decide what weight should be given to that information in all the circumstances of the case . . . Under this approach, where a defendant's previous convictions, or other misconduct, are relevant to an issue in the case, then, unless the court considers that the information will have a disproportionate effect, they should be allowed to know about it. It will be for the judge to decide whether the probative value of introducing this information is outweighed by its prejudicial effect.'

Section 99(1) of the CJA 2003 abolished the common law definition of character, save for one exception: the *Rowton* rule (see above) was retained in s 118(1). In addition, several statutory provisions that permitted the use of bad character evidence, including s 1(3) of the Criminal Evidence Act 1898, were repealed (see Sch 37 to the 2003 Act). The Criminal Justice Act 2003 introduces an all-encompassing definition of bad character in s 98 (see below).

Section 99 of the 2003 Act provides that:

SECTION

'(1) The common law rules governing the admissibility of evidence of bad character in criminal proceedings are abolished.

(2) Subsection (1) is subject to s 118(1) in so far as it preserves the rule under which . . . a person's reputation is admissible for the purposes of proving his bad character.'

11.6 Definition of bad character

Section 98 of the Criminal Justice Act 2003 identifies the types of evidence; admissibility is determined by the statutory regime. The issue concerns the 'bad character' of the accused and other persons. The 2003 Act completely reversed the pre-existing general rule that existed at common law and specific statutory provisions such as the Criminal Evidence Act 1898. Thus, evidence of bad character is admissible if it satisfies certain criteria (see s 101(1)), this approach departed from the historical position which was one based on inadmissibility, subject to exceptions.

The explanatory note to the Criminal Justice Act 2003 declared:

CLAUSE

'The intention is that this Part of the Act will provide a new basis for the admissibility of previous convictions and other misconduct. Accordingly, s 99 abolishes the common law rules governing the admissibility of such evidence. This abolition does not extend to the rule that allows a person's bad character to be proved by reputation . . .'

Section 98 of the Criminal Justice Act 2003 (CJA) enacted as follows:

SECTION

'References . . . to evidence of a person's "bad character" are to evidence of, or of a disposition towards, *misconduct* on his part . . .'

This definition applies to all aspects of bad character evidence governed by the CJA 2003. Thus, the definition is applicable to the admissibility of evidence of the bad character of non-defendants as well as the accused in criminal trials. The section also applies to misconduct both before and after the offence with which the accused is charged, but obviously does not include the facts concerning the commission of the offence charged. This last point is dealt with below: see s 98(a) and (b).

Misconduct

'Misconduct' is defined by s 112(1) of the CJA 2003 and means 'the commission of an offence or other reprehensible behaviour'. The subsection includes the commission of an offence but implicitly excludes the subject matter of the charge. Thus, the expression 'commission' must be taken to mean the commission of other offences that are not currently before the court. At the same time there is no requirement that the accused must have been convicted of the offence. If there is a conviction of the offence, then by virtue of s 6 of the Criminal Procedure Act 1865 and s 74 of the Police and Criminal Evidence Act 1984, the convicted person is treated as having committed the offence, until the contrary is proved.

If a conviction does not exist, it does not follow that no inference could be drawn that he committed the offence. At common law the fact that the accused was charged with an offence and was acquitted did not preclude the prosecution from establishing that he committed those offences. The test, however, is based on the relevance of the facts surrounding the charges that led to the acquittal and the facts underpinning the current charge, i.e. the defendant's guilt of the current charge may be overwhelming by virtue of the evidence of a number of similar incidents. This would be the position where a number of witnesses are willing to come forward and, without collusion, give a similar account of the defendant's behaviour that was denied by the defendant. In *R v Z* [2000] 2 AC 483, the defendant was charged with the rape of a young woman, C, in 1998. The defendant did not dispute that he had had sexual intercourse with the complainant, but his defence was that she consented, or that he believed she had consented to intercourse. Prior to this charge, the defendant had faced four separate allegations of rape of different young women, which resulted in four separate trials. In three of these trials the defendant was acquitted. In the fourth trial he was convicted. In each of the trials the defendant did not dispute that sexual intercourse had taken place, but alleged that each complainant had consented, or that he believed that each complainant had consented to intercourse with him. In the current trial, the House of Lords ruled that the Crown was allowed to call the four complainants involved in the previous trials in order to testify against the defendant on the issue of consent or to negate the defendant's claim that he believed the victims had consented. There was a considerable degree of striking similarity between the defendant's conduct, as alleged by C, and the reports of the other four complainants.

The Court of Appeal in *R v Edwards (Stewart)* [2006] 1 WLR 1524 considered four separate appeals concerning the admissibility of bad character evidence. In one of the appeals the court decided that on charges of rape and gross indecency a stay of proceedings concerning earlier allegations made on different occasions may be referred to by prosecution witnesses. The grounds for justifying such a principle were that *prima facie* all evidence that was relevant to the issues in the trial is admissible; and there was no reason in principle why evidence relating to allegations that had never been tried, because of a stay of proceedings for abuse of process, should not be admissible. The fundamental assumption that is required to be made is that the evidence is true, although the truth or falsity of the evidence is for the jury to decide.

In *R v Bovell* [2005] 2 Cr App R 401, the Court of Appeal decided that it was doubtful whether the mere making of an allegation as an end in itself was capable of being evidence of bad character within s 100(1) of the 2003 Act. Doubts concerning the reliability of such an assertion were increased where that allegation was withdrawn by the person who made it. If such an allegation was admitted in court it would have given rise to an excursion into 'satellite' matters, which was precisely the sort of excursion a trial judge should be discouraged from embarking upon. Thus, on a charge of wounding with intent contrary to s 18 of the Offences Against the Person Act 1861, the Court of Appeal decided that an application by defence counsel to admit an allegation against the complainant involving a s 18 charge, which was subsequently withdrawn by the victim, had little probative value.

The concept of 'reprehensible behaviour' is not defined by the Act and has been kept vague to avoid collateral arguments about whether conduct that does not result in a charge or conviction should be treated as misconduct. Undoubtedly, the concepts of 'misconduct' and 'reprehensible behaviour' are required to be judged objectively. This would include activities that are contrary to the criminal law (convictions) and other immoral conduct, whether or not resulting in a charge, prosecution or conviction. Pre-2003 examples are *R v Marsh* [1994] Crim LR 52, cross-examination of a rugby player on his bad disciplinary record, or a warning to or dismissal of an employee for misconduct at work. Likewise, an acquittal of an offence may amount to reprehensible behaviour: see *R v Z* above. Difficulties with the definition might arise in cases where there is no definitive measure for judging a person's conduct such as lack of courtesy, drunkenness or excessive swearing. May such conduct be treated as reprehensible? In *R v Renda* [2005] EWCA Crim 2826, the Court of Appeal stated that there must be some element of culpability or blameworthiness before conduct could be treated as reprehensible. In *R v Manister* [2005] EWCA Crim 2866 the Court of Appeal held that the trial judge had been wrong in concluding that reprehensible behaviour included a 34-year-old man instituting a sexual relationship with a girl aged 16. In this case, the evidence was still admissible at common law as it demonstrated that Manister had a sexual interest in teenage girls.

An analogy may be drawn between 'reprehensible behaviour' under the Criminal Justice Act 2003 and 'imputations' on the character of prosecution witnesses within s 1(3)(ii) of the Criminal Evidence Act 1898 (now repealed). There have been many decisions concerning the interpretation of the expression 'imputations', and not all these decisions are consistent. In *R v Rouse* [1904] 1 KB 184, it was decided that calling the prosecutor a liar from the witness box was not an imputation on the character of the prosecutor. It was decided that the statement amounted to no more than a plea of not guilty put in emphatic language. However, someone charged with receiving stolen goods may cast imputations if he makes allegations as to the morality of the prosecutrix: see *R v Jenkins* (1945) 31 Cr App R 1. Similarly, on a charge of burglary, an allegation by the accused that the complainant had a homosexual relationship with him amounted to casting imputations: see *R v Bishop* [1975] QB 274. Likewise, imputations were cast when the defence suggested that a confession was obtained by threats or bribes: see *R v Wright* (1910) 5 Cr App R 131; and that successive remands were obtained by the police to enable them to fabricate evidence: see *R v Jones* (1923) 17 Cr App R 117. On the other hand, on a charge of robbery the allegation that the prosecutor was a habitual drunkard did not amount to casting imputations on the character of the prosecutor: see *R v Westfall* (1912) 7 Cr App R 176.

In *R v Edwards* [2006] 2 Cr App R 4, it was decided that, in a drugs case, the judge was wrong to allow a defendant to be cross-examined about his legal possession of an antique, but functional, Derringer firearm. Such legitimate possession of the gun could not be treated as evidence of misconduct:

JUDGMENT

'It is difficult to see how evidence of lawful possession of an antique firearm can amount to evidence of, or a disposition towards, misconduct. The judge did not prevent questioning on it, but doubted its relevance. In our view it was not evidence of bad character and therefore no question of admissibility under s 101 arose.'

(Scott Baker LJ)

In *R v Weir* [2006] 2 All ER 570, in a consolidated appeal, the Court of Appeal decided that on a charge of a sexual offence on a thirteen-year-old girl, a thirty-nine-year-old defendant who had a three-year consensual sexual relationship with a girl (B) who had been sixteen at the commencement of the relationship, and a suggestive remark made to the fifteen-year-old sister of the complainant did not, *per se*, constitute evidence of 'misconduct'. The position may have been different had there been some peculiar feature in the case, such as grooming, parental disapproval or particular immaturity of the complainant, but the contraction of an odd but lawful relationship by the defendant was insufficient to make it reprehensible, and was not evidence of bad character:

JUDGMENT

'In our combined view, the judge was wrong to conclude that the sexual relationship between the appellant and B, without more, amounted to "evidence of, or a disposition towards, misconduct on his part" and therefore evidence of "bad character" for the purposes of s 98 . . . of the 2003 Act. The definition of "misconduct" is very wide. It makes it clear that behaviour may be reprehensible, and therefore misconduct, though not amounting to the commission of an offence. The appellant was significantly older than B. But there was no evidence . . . of grooming of B by the appellant before she was 16, or that the parents disapproved and communicated their disapproval to the appellant, or that B was intellectually, emotionally or physically immature for her age, or that there was some other feature of the lawful relationship which might make it "reprehensible".'

(Kennedy LJ)

The court decided that the evidence was nevertheless relevant and admissible at common law to demonstrate that the defendant had a sexual interest in girls of the complainant's age:

JUDGMENT

> '. . . once it is decided that evidence of the appellant's sexual relationship with B did not amount to "evidence of bad character", the abolition of the common law rules governing the admissibility of "evidence of bad character" by s 99(1) did not apply. We have no doubt that evidence of the relationship was admissible at common law, in the particular circumstances of this case, because it was relevant to the issue of whether the appellant had a sexual interest in A [the victim]. It was capable of demonstrating a sexual interest in early- or mid-teenage girls, much younger than the appellant, and therefore bore on the truth of his case of a purely supportive, asexual interest in A. It was not in our judgment unfair to admit the evidence (see s 78 of PACE 1984).'
>
> (Kennedy LJ)

In *R v Osbourne* [2007] EWCA Crim 481, it was decided that on a charge of murder the fact that the defendant became verbally aggressive if he failed to take his medication for schizophrenia was not reprehensible behaviour.

In *R v Fox* [2009] EWCA Crim 653, the Court of Appeal quashed convictions on charges involving sexual offences where, *inter alia*, the trial judge admitted evidence of extracts from the defendant's notebook of 'dirty' sexual thoughts, for such a document was not evidence of reprehensible behaviour within the meaning of the 2003 Act.

In *R v Saleem* [2007] EWCA Crim 1923, on charges of causing grievous bodily harm with intent contrary to s 18 of the Offences Against the Person Act 1861, the defendant admitted his presence along with three others at the time of the assault but denied taking part. The trial judge admitted a file of photographs depicting violence and rap lyrics as evidence against the defendant. On conviction, the appeal was dismissed. The photographs and rap lyrics were relevant to rebut the case of innocent presence put forward by the defendant. However the rap lyrics were not sufficiently connected in order 'to do with the alleged facts of the offence' under s 98 of the 2003 Act, as there was insufficient connection in time with the facts of the offence. Although the evidence did not go to show propensity to commit the offence, it was relevant to show that the defendant's presence at the attack was not innocent. The real issue was the reason for the defendant's presence at the attack and it would have been clear to the jury that the photographs and rap lyrics evidence was relevant as it went to disprove innocent presence.

It would appear that the notion of reprehensible behaviour is not dependent on the legality of the conduct involved. Likewise, conduct that may be regarded as irritating, inconvenient and upsetting on its own, without a sufficient element of culpability or blameworthiness (such as insisting on speaking to a disinterested stranger) may not be regarded as reprehensible behaviour: see *R v S* [2009] EWCA Crim 2457. Instead, reprehensible behaviour may be based on activity that may be frowned upon by a significant section of society, such as a teacher making inappropriate, suggestive remarks to his pupils.

11.6.1 Exclusion from the definition of bad character

Section 98 of the CJA 2003 creates two exceptions to the definition of bad character. These exclusions or exceptions to bad character evidence are outside the statutory rules and, when they apply, the evidence may be admissible because of its obvious relevance. In short, bad character evidence within s 98 may be admissible without going through any of the gateways within ss 100 and 101 of the 2003 Act, but the general safeguards of relevance and fairness will be exercisable by the judge. The Law Commission identified the reasoning behind the exclusions enacted in s 98. These are occasions when the Crown may wish to adduce evidence of the defendant's misconduct, not in respect of the offence charged, but as part of the transaction connected with the offence. In short, evidence that may be intimately connected with the commission or investigation of the offence, if admissible prior to the introduction of the 2003 Act, will continue to be admissible. These occasions are:

SECTION

'. . . evidence which

(a) has to do with the alleged facts of the offence with which the defendant is charged, or

(b) is evidence of misconduct in connection with the investigation or prosecution of that offence.'

Section 98(a) relates to facts or matters that are directly relevant to the offence. These are facts that, at common law, would have been admissible to prove the prosecution's case, such as similar fact and background evidence, for example evidence of an assault that had been committed in the course of a burglary as evidence to do with the facts of the offence. Such facts are required to be sufficiently linked with the charge to demonstrate his guilt of the offence. This is based on the test of relevance. The effect is that, under the Criminal Justice Act 2003 statutory regime, such evidence within s 98(a) does not have to pass through any of the gateways in s 100 (non-defendants) or s 101 (defendants). The phrase 'has to do with' is not the clearest that Parliament could have selected but the policy behind the subsection involves the situation where the charge against the defendant cannot be proved without establishing the additional prejudicial evidence of the defendant; for example on a charge of driving whilst disqualified, proof of the defendant's prior conviction and disqualification is not within the bad character definition but is admissible within s 98(a).

In *R v Edwards* [2006] 3 All ER 882, Scott Baker LJ said:

JUDGMENT

'Often the first inquiry is whether it is necessary to go through the "bad character" gateways at all. In this regard, s 98 is not to be overlooked. It excludes from the definition of bad character evidence which "has to do with the alleged facts of the offence or evidence of misconduct in connection with the investigation or prosecution of that offence". While difficult questions can arise as to whether evidence of background or motive falls to be admitted under those exclusions in s 98 or requires consideration under s 101(1)(c), it does not follow that merely because the evidence fails to come within the s 101 gateways it will be inadmissible. Where the exclusions in s 98 are applicable the evidence will be admissible without more ado.'

Likewise, in *R v Machado* [2006] All ER (D) 28, the prosecution alleged that the defendant had engaged in a conversation with the victim and then robbed him, but the defendant denied this allegation and contended that the victim had offered to supply drugs to him and had said that he (the victim) had taken an ecstasy tablet before. The Court of Appeal decided that this was not evidence of the victim's bad character governed by s 100 of the Criminal Justice Act 2003. The disputed evidence related to the very circumstances in which the offence had allegedly occurred. The evidence was contemporaneous with, and closely associated with, the alleged facts of the offence. It was therefore not bad character evidence.

Similarly, in *R v Malone* [2006] All ER (D) 321, the Court of Appeal decided that, on a charge of murder, evidence of a private investigator's report that was forged by the defendant as part of his plot to prove that the victim, his wife, was unfaithful was properly admitted to establish evidence of a matrimonial dispute and a build-up of hostility. The evidence could also have been admitted under s 101(1)(d) of the Criminal Justice Act 2003:

JUDGMENT

'There is no dispute that the document constituted evidence of bad character. It was, at the least, reprehensible behaviour (see s 112(1)). In our judgment, evidence of this sort was capable of being admitted under s 98(a). The prosecution case was based on circumstantial evidence. Its case was that the matrimonial difficulties between the appellant and his wife caused him to flare up and kill her . . . As such evidence of matrimonial difficulties, the intensity and effect of these difficulties on the appellant and how he dealt with them before she disappeared could, in our judgment, have been admissible as evidence going directly to show with other circumstantial evidence that he had committed the offence. As such it was capable of being evidence "to do with the alleged facts of the case" in the same way as evidence to show a conspiracy or a joint venture would be admissible under s 98(a).'

(Gage LJ)

A distinction is drawn between 'evidence which has to do with the alleged facts of the offence' and evidence that is relevant to proof of the offence. Evidence within s 98(a) involves acts that the defendant committed at the same time and place as the main offence charged, including preparatory acts (which may be insufficient to constitute attempts) in respect of the offence charged. In *R v Machado* [2006] EWCA Crim 837, the defendant was charged with robbery and wished to use evidence that the victim had taken an ecstasy tablet just prior to the incident and had offered to supply the defendant with drugs shortly before he was attacked. The Court of Appeal held that these matters were within s 98(a) and therefore outside the test of bad character. Whereas, in *R v Tirnaveanu* [2007] EWCA Crim 1239, there was an insufficient link in time between the evidence and the offences charged. In this case, the charges involved elements of fraud in that it was alleged that the defendant held himself out as a solicitor (which was false) in order to dishonestly represent immigrants seeking to enter the UK, and also to provide them with forged entry documents. The prosecution had argued that the evidence was central to the prosecution case in proving that the defendant was the person who committed the offences. The court rejected this argument and decided that the defendant's dealings with other would-be immigrants were not within s 98(a), although the evidence was admissible under s 101(1)(d) of the Act. The test was laid down thus:

JUDGMENT

'The basis on which it was contended before us by the prosecution that the evidence which they sought to adduce was "to do" with the facts of the alleged offence was that it was evidence which was central to the case in that it related to proving that the appellant was the person who had committed the offences charged in the various counts. We do not accede to that submission. As counsel for the prosecution accepted, if his submission was right, then in any case, where the identity of the defendant was in issue (including, by way of example, cases of sexual misconduct), the prosecution would be able to rely on this exclusion to adduce evidence of misconduct on other occasions which helped to prove identity. It seems to us that the exclusion *must be related to evidence where there is some nexus in time* between the offence with which the defendant is charged and the evidence of misconduct which the prosecution seek to adduce.' (emphasis added)

(Thomas LJ)

In *R v Hussain (Roshan Ara)* [2013] EWCA Crim 2053, the Court of Appeal remarked that a temporal connection is not a requirement in order to establish that the evidence 'has to do' with the alleged facts of the offence. In this case, the defendants were charged with attempting to pervert the course of justice. There had been an investigation as to a carousel fraud and one of the defendants, M, was found in possession of £47,000 of cash in carrier bags. His explanation was that the sum of money was a bonus payment authorised in a board meeting. A document was later produced as a copy of the minutes. The prosecution alleged that the document was executed some months after the arrest and was false. Co-defendant B stated that she created the document on the instructions of the defendant, but did not realise that it was in pursuance of a dishonest scheme. The defendant denied instructing B to create the false minutes. B's counsel applied for leave to cross-examine the defendant about her involvement in the fraud and whether she had cheated the Revenue. The trial judge ruled in favour of B and decided that the proposed questions related to issues within s 98(a). In the alternative, the questions were permitted under s 101(1)(e) of the 2003 Act. The defendant was convicted and appealed. The Court of Appeal dismissed the appeal and decided the judge was correct in his ruling on s 98(a), because the evidence showed that the defendant's misconduct took the form of a fraudulent act to cover up her actions on charges of attempting to pervert the course of justice. But the judge had erred in deciding that the questions were permissible under ss 101(1)(e) and 104(1). The evidence may have established that the defendant was lying, but did not establish a propensity to be untruthful.

JUDGMENT

'The very nature of the charge faced by both defendants impliedly posed the question: what was the justice that they sought to pervert? The prosecution case was that under the pressure of investigation into a massive VAT fraud by the companies that employed them, the defendants sought to represent the cash payment to one of the conspirators as a normal bonus entitlement. In our judgment, evidence of the motive to conceal the real purpose of the payment was, on the facts of the present case, evidence that had to do with the facts of the attempt to pervert the course of justice. Evidence that tended to establish either complicity by the appellant in the underlying misconduct, or such closeness to the conspirators that she shared their need for a cover-up, is undoubtedly evidence which has to do with the facts of the attempt to pervert the course of justice.

'The purpose of the cross-examination intended was to demonstrate that the appellant was lying upon the central issue between the defendants, but it was not to establish that the appellant had a propensity for telling lies.'

(Pitchford LJ)

Section 98(b) may concern evidence that exists after the alleged commission of the offence, such as evidence that the defendant tried to intimidate a prosecution witness or lied during the interrogation by police officers. Likewise, evidence of misconduct by a police officer in attempting to extract a confession from the accused would not constitute evidence of bad character but would be subject to the common law rules. In *R v Apabhai* [2011] EWCA Crim 917 (see Chapter 12), the Court of Appeal decided that the exception to the definition of bad character laid down in s 98(b) of the Act is not restricted to evidence of misconduct by the police and prosecuting authorities. The broad s 98(b) is capable of extending to the conduct of witnesses or co-defendants 'connected with' the prosecution or investigation of the offence. Accordingly, an allegation by a defendant that a co-defendant attempted to blackmail him in connection with the offence charged may be outside the bad character provisions.

The judge has an important role to play in deciding, in his discretion, whether the evidence satisfies the test of relevance to the offence charged. Provided that he approaches this question in a judicial manner, giving appropriate weight to significant facts and focusing on the nexus of the facts with the charge, the appellate courts will rarely interfere with his decision.

A further exception is enacted in s 99(2) of the CJA 2003, which preserves the common law in criminal proceedings concerning a person's reputation being admissible to prove his bad character. This is the *R v Rowton* exception: see above.

In conclusion, the Criminal Justice Act 2003 marked a radical change in the law of admissibility of evidence of bad character. It codified a set of provisions and the old law concerning evidence of bad character that existed as a historic edifice of rules that were developed over centuries. Hughes LJ in *R v Chopra* [2007] 1 Cr App R 16, summarised the court's approach to the changes introduced by the Criminal Justice Act 2003, thus:

JUDGMENT

'The right way to deal with the new law is not first to ask what would have been the position under the old. In saying that, we do not doubt that some, perhaps many, of the familiar considerations of relevance and fairness which confronted courts before the 2003 Act in cases of multiple allegations where they were said to be of a similar kind will continue to confront them dealing with such cases afterwards. Nor do we doubt that the answers may be the same. There has, however, been a sea change in the law's starting point.'

SUMMARY

- The common law definition of character was restricted to evidence of reputation by reference to the *Rowton* principle.
- The prosecution was entitled to adduce evidence of the defendant's disposition or propensity, but only where such evidence was capable of proving that the accused committed the offence. This was referred to as similar fact evidence.
- Before the Criminal Evidence Act 1898 the accused did not have the capacity to testify. But evidence as to his good or bad character was admissible through witnesses.
- The *Rowton* principle involves evidence of 'good' and 'bad' character.
- The Criminal Evidence Act 1898 empowered the defendant to testify in his defence. He was entitled to testify as to his good character by reference to disposition evidence. Rebutting evidence of the same nature was admissible in appropriate circumstances.
- Judicial directions on the defendant's good character involves two limbs known as the *R v Vye* directions. These are reputation and disposition evidence.
- Such directions are required to be given where the defendant is jointly tried and he is a person of good character and his co-defendant has a bad character.
- In exceptional circumstances, where an allegation of the defendant's good character will be spurious, the judge may dispense with the *Vye* directions.
- The common law rules concerning the defendant's bad character have been abolished by s 99 of the Criminal Justice Act 2003, except with regard to reputation evidence under the *Rowton* principle.
- The concept of bad character has been defined in 98 of the Criminal Justice Act 2003 as involving evidence of misconduct.
- Misconduct has been defined in s 112(1) as the commission of the offence or other reprehensible behaviour.
- Bad character is admissible under the 2003 Act with reference to a non-defendant (s 100) and the defendant (s 101).
- In addition, evidence 'which has to do with' the facts of the offence or misconduct in connection with the investigation or prosecution of the offence are excluded from the bad character provisions, but may be admissible at common law: see s 98(a) and (b).

ACTIVITY

Self-test questions

1. What meanings were attached to character evidence in criminal proceedings at common law?
2. What forms did good character evidence take in criminal proceedings, prior to the introduction of the Criminal Justice Act 2003?
3. What directions must the judge give in respect of the good character of a defendant in criminal proceedings?

4. What was meant by 'similar fact evidence' before the introduction of the Criminal Justice Act 2003?
5. What is meant by 'bad character' under the Criminal Justice Act 2003?

SAMPLE ESSAY QUESTION

The definition of bad character evidence, as laid down by the Criminal Justice Act 2003, involves a complex web of statutory provisions detached from the law that existed before the passing of the 2003 Act. Discuss.

Answer Plan

The pre-2003 law on bad character evidence has been abolished except in respect of evidence of a person's reputation; see s 99 of the 2003 Act.

The definition of 'bad character' is laid down in s 98 of the Act as evidence of or disposition towards misconduct.

'Misconduct' is defined in s 112(1) as meaning the commission of an offence or other reprehensible behaviour.

The expression 'commission' of an offence involves evidence that suggests the guilt of an offence, whether or not the defendant had been charged with or convicted of the offence.

The expression obviously includes facts supporting a conviction, but the underlying facts concerning a previous acquittal of an offence may also be included in the definition; see *R v Z*.

Likewise, facts supporting charges which have been stayed as an abuse of process may be included in the definition; see *R v Edwards*.

But the expression does not include an arrest following suspicion and release without a charge; see *R v Weir*; and where an allegation has been withdrawn; see *R v Bovell*.

The expression 'reprehensible behaviour' has not been defined but requires an element of culpability or blameworthiness; see *R v Renda*.

The expression requires the judge to exercise an element of moral judgment, such as sexual approaches to vulnerable women by a priest in a church; see *R v Weir*; or possession of a considerable number of offensive photographs; *R v Saleem*.

The test for reprehensible behaviour seems to be, in the opinion of the judge, whether the action may be viewed by society as so anti-social, albeit not illegal, that it bears a special relevance to the charge.

Excluded from the definition of bad character and its admissibility under the various gateways are the provisions in s 98(a) and (b).

These provisions involve admissibility of the evidence at common law based on the special test of relevance and include misconduct of someone other than the defendant; see *R v Machado*. Included are allegations of misconduct of police officers in planting evidence on the accused or the intimidation of potential witnesses.

CONCLUSION

Further reading

Branston, G. 'A reprehensible use of cautions as bad character evidence' [2015] Crim LR 594

Ho, H. 'Similar facts in civil cases' (2006) 26 Oxford Journal of Legal Studies 131

Hoffmann, L. 'Similar facts after Boardman' (1975) 91 LQR 193

Law Commission Report, Law Com No 273 (2001) 'Evidence in criminal proceedings: previous misconduct of a defendant'

Monaghan, N. 'Reconceptualising good character' [2015] E&P 190

Munday, R. 'What constitutes a good character?' [1997] Crim LR 247

Munday, R. 'What constitutes "other reprehensible behaviour" under the bad character provisions of the Criminal Justice Act 2003?' [2005] Crim LR 24

Munday, R. 'Cut-throat defences and the "propensity to be untruthful" under Section 104 of the Criminal Justice Act 2003' [2005] Crim LR 624

Munday, R. 'Misconduct that "has to do with the alleged facts of the offence with which the defendant is charged" . . . more or less' [2008] Crim L 214

Redmayne, M. 'The relevance of bad character' [2002] CLJ 684

Singh, C. (2014). *Beginning Evidence*. Oxford: Routledge.

Spencer, J. 'Evidence of bad character – where we are today' [2014] Arch Rev 5

Spencer, J. 'Cautions as character evidence: a reply to Judge Branston' [2015] Crim LR 611

Stone, J. 'The rule of exclusion of similar fact evidence: England' (1932) 46 Harvard LR 954
Tapper, C. 'The Criminal Evidence Act 2003: evidence of bad character' [2004] Crim LR 533
Waterman, A. and Dempster, T. 'Bad character: feeling our way one year on' [2006] Crim LR 614

12

Admissibility of bad character evidence of witnesses and defendants

AIMS AND OBJECTIVES

By the end of this chapter you will be able to:

- outline the occasions under s 100 of the Criminal Justice Act 2003 when bad character evidence of persons, other than the defendant, is admissible;
- highlight the various gateways for admitting the bad character evidence of the defendant in criminal proceedings;
- discuss the contents of the directions that are required to be given by the judge;
- understand the notion and significance of contaminated evidence;
- outline the procedure concerning the adduction of bad character evidence by the prosecution;
- set out the miscellaneous statutory provisions authorising the admissibility of bad character evidence of the defendant;
- understand the use of bad character evidence in civil cases.

12.1 Introduction and outline of the scheme of the Act

The statutory regime for the admissibility of evidence of bad character is laid down in s 100 of the Criminal Justice Act 2003 (CJA) for non-defendants and in s 101 for defendants. These provisions have been qualified by ss 102–106 of the CJA 2003. Safeguards and the procedure governing the admissibility of bad character evidence are laid down in ss 107–111 of the Act.

The effect is that Part 11, Chapter 1, ss 98–112 of the CJA 2003 codified the law relating to evidence of bad character in criminal proceedings. The courts have interpreted the provisions with reference to the old law very sparingly.

DOI: 10.4324/9781003282433-12

12.2 Grounds for admitting bad character evidence – non-defendant's bad character

Credit
involves the extent of the witness speaking the truth.

At common law, a witness other than the accused could be cross-examined on matters related to facts in issue as well as **credit**. As far as facts in issue are concerned, the witness's answer is not final and the cross-examiner is entitled to contradict the witness's answer. On matters related to credit or collateral issues the witness's answers are final, subject to a number of exceptions (see earlier). This rule was applicable to prosecution and defence witnesses, other than the accused: see Sankey LJ's judgment in *Hobbs v Tinling* (1929) (Chapter 6). There were few restrictions on the nature of the questions relating to credit that could be asked of such witnesses. Important restrictions included the discretion of the judge to intervene on grounds of oppression as well as ss 41–43 of the Youth Justice and Criminal Evidence Act 1999. The Law Commission was of the view that a more structured approach ought to be introduced with regard to the bad character of persons other than the defendant, in order to encourage such persons testifying and to restrict offensive cross-examination. The effect was the introduction of s 100 of the CJA 2003.

Section 100 is expressed in positive, inclusionary language in the sense that such evidence is admissible 'if and only if'. The section is also referable to 'evidence . . . of persons other than the defendant'. This is taken to mean witnesses and non-witnesses. Non-witnesses may include a third party who is alleged to have committed the offence. In addition, non-witnesses may possibly include deceased persons, such as the deceased victim of the offence. Witnesses include those called for the prosecution as well as the defence, other than the defendant. Moreover, although the sub-section refers to 'evidence' that is admissible, it is a fair assumption to make that the evidence refers to both evidence of bad character that is admissible as well as questions asked in cross-examination, for it would be odd otherwise.

Section 100(1) enacts three alternative criteria for the admissibility of the evidence, as follows:

SECTION

'In criminal proceedings evidence of the bad character of a person other than the defendant is admissible if and only if –

(a) it is important explanatory evidence,
(b) it has substantial probative value in relation to a matter which –
 (i) is a matter in issue in the proceedings, and
 (ii) is of substantial importance in the context of the case as a whole, or
(c) all the parties to the proceedings agree to the evidence being admissible.'

Section 100(1)(a) is identical to s 101(1)(c) that is applicable to the accused and will be discussed later when dealing with the admissibility of the defendant's bad character.

Section 100(1)(b) enacts a number of pre-conditions for the admissibility of the evidence. These are:

(a) that the evidence has 'substantial probative value'; and
(b) relates to a 'matter in issue' in the proceedings; and
(c) 'is of substantial importance in the context of the case as a whole'.

The notion of 'substantive probative value' relates to the enhanced quality that the evidence is required to possess. The word 'substantial' means that the evidence concerned has something more than trivial probative value but it is not necessarily of conclusive probative value. Ordinary relevance of the non-defendant's bad character to a matter in issue may not be sufficient, for the evidence is required to meet an 'enhanced relevance' test to be determined by the judge. Thus, evidence that is only marginally relevant to an issue will not be admissible. Section 100(3) lays down a number of factors that the judge is required to take into account when evaluating the 'probative value' of the evidence, including the nature, repetition of events, similarities and dissimilarities between the evidence of misconduct. These factors are by no means comprehensive or exclusive. This is an exercise by the judge of fact-sensitive judgment rather than discretion. In addition, s 109(1) enacts that the 'probative value' of the evidence is determined by reference to its relevance on the assumption that it is true, unless no court or jury may reasonably find it to be true: s 109(2). Thus, despite defence contention that the complainant's allegation against him is a tissue of lies, the *prima facie* rule guiding the judge is that the complainant's bad character is such that it does not impact on his assertion, the subject matter of the charge.

The significance of cautions as evidence of bad character was explored by the Court of Appeal in *R v Braithwaite (Stephen)* [2010] EWCA Crim 1082. A factor that is inherent in a caution is an admission of having committed an offence. The caution forms part of an offender's antecedents and an official record will be retained by the police for future use. It may also be disclosed in a court in any future proceedings. The question in issue is whether a caution imposed on a person may be introduced in court as part of that individual's bad character. The solution is that a caution will be treated as equivalent to a low level conviction and may be introduced as part of that individual's bad character. In *R v Braithwaite* the trial judge and the Court of Appeal drew a distinction between (a) conduct resulting in convictions and cautions and (b) material contained in police crime reports (CRIS) indicating that some third party had made an allegation against an individual (perhaps a witness) or that the individual had been investigated in respect of some offence. The latter category of allegations is likely to have insufficient weight to warrant its admissibility. In *R v Braithwaite*, the charge was murder by stabbing following an argument in the street. The defendant raised the defence of self-defence on the ground that the victim was a member of a group that had been aggressive and confrontational towards him. The prosecution relied significantly on evidence from other members of the victim's group. The defendant applied for leave to introduce evidence of the bad character of those witnesses under s 100(1)(b) of the CJA 2003. The trial judge ruled that the evidence of their bad character was potentially relevant to their propensity to act aggressively in the street and to their credibility, and admitted much of the evidence. However, he drew a distinction between conduct resulting in convictions, cautions and penalty notices, and material in police crime reports (CRIS reports) that indicated that a third party had made an allegation or that the witness had been investigated in respect of some offence. The latter was not admissible. Following his conviction the defendant appealed to the Court of Appeal on the ground of the wrongful exclusion of relevant evidence. The Court of Appeal dismissed the appeal and decided that the judge had correctly directed himself on the issues within s 100(1)(b). The evidence of disorder or violence in relation to the witnesses was potentially relevant to the issues of their propensity to act aggressively in the street and their credibility. That was central to the defence that the defendant had been the victim of unprovoked aggression. It was doubted whether the unsubstantiated allegations that the defendant wanted to put before the jury had substantial probative value in relation to that issue.

JUDGMENT

'We are quite satisfied that the judge was right in his ruling that the material from the CRIS reports, in which no conviction, caution or penalty notice had ensued, could not be adduced because they did not have substantial probative value. Indeed, for the most part, they had no probative value at all.

'A conviction is by statute evidence that the person convicted committed the offence. A caution involves a distinct admission. The position with regard to a penalty notice was not in issue before the judge because the Crown agreed to evidence of such notices being adduced, and accordingly it does not fall for decision by us either. A penalty notice may result from a distinct admission but it does not necessarily do so.'

(Hughes LJ)

On a charge of alleged rape where the material issue in the trial is consent, evidence that the complainant made a false allegation of sexual misconduct against another person, shortly before the alleged rape, may have substantial probative value in relation to the complainant's credibility and the determination of consent. The Court of Appeal so decided in *R v S* [2009] EWCA Crim 2457. In this case, the defendant was charged with rape. The material issue in the trial involved consent. The defendant was disallowed by the trial judge from adducing two pieces of evidence: one from H, to the effect that the complainant had harassed her to support her allegation of rape; and the second from D to the effect that the complainant falsely alleged inappropriate sexual advances on his part and leaving faeces on her doorstep. On conviction the defendant appealed. The Court of Appeal allowed the appeal and quashed the conviction. H's evidence did not constitute reprehensible behaviour on the part of the complainant and was not bad character evidence and was irrelevant. But the evidence of D had substantial probative value in determining the issue of the complainant's credibility and consent.

JUDGMENT

'Evidence is only admissible in a criminal trial if relevant. The only possible relevance of that evidence or any cross examination of the complainant relating to it would be to impugn the complainant's credibility. A judge has the power to prevent cross examination about a subject which can only go to the credit of a witness if the truth of the matter suggested would not, in his opinion, affect the credibility of the witness concerned.

'In our view, the trial judge in this case would have been bound to rule that this evidence concerning Ms H would not have affected the credibility of Ms FH [the complainant] in relation to the two charges of which the appellant was accused. Therefore he would have been bound to stop any cross examination of the complainant on those matters. It must follow that he would also have ruled that Ms H's evidence was irrelevant to the issues in the proceedings, so could not be introduced.

'In our view, the matters raised in Mr D's evidence cannot properly be characterised as "satellite litigation" in the sense that they were so divorced from the principal issue in the case, that they thereby lacked "*substantial probative value*" in the context of this case.

'The judge did not distinguish between the evidence of Ms H and that of Mr D. He did not, in our view, focus properly on the fact that, on Mr D's evidence and the CRIS reports, the complainant was making serious false allegations against him, in particular, she was making false allegations concerning conduct of a sexual nature. We have concluded that his evidence would have had substantial probative value in relation to a matter which was of substantial importance in the context of the case as a whole, *viz*. the central issue of the complainant's credibility and therefore consent.'

(Aitkens LJ)

In assessing the probative value of bad character evidence of the complainant the judge is required to maintain the focus on the matters in issue and avoid issues that may deflect the jury from the issues in the trial. Accordingly, on a trial of perverting the course of justice, the judge may be entitled to prevent the defendant from adducing evidence that the complainant had allegedly committed an offence of rape for which the complainant was not charged. In so doing, the judge may avoid significant delay and distraction from the main issue in the trial. In *R v Dizaei* [2013] EWCA Crim 88, the defendant, a commander in the Metropolitan Police, was charged with misconduct in public office and perverting the course of justice. He had arrested the complainant for allegedly a public order offence outside a restaurant. There was a history of animosity between the two individuals. The judge refused to allow the defendant to adduce evidence that the complainant had committed rape on his girlfriend and assaulted her in a nightclub. The defendant was convicted and appealed. The Court of Appeal dismissed the appeal and decided that despite s 109(1) assuming that the allegation was true the issue before the court was likely to be derailed if the jury was also required to consider whether the complainant committed a separate crime. This was a relevant consideration in determining the probative value of the evidence. The assault allegation may have some probative value in illustrating that the complainant was prone to violence but, in the circumstances of the case as a whole, the conviction was safe. In addition, once the conditions in s 100(1)(b) are satisfied the trial judge has no discretion to exclude the evidence.

JUDGMENT

'The pre-conditions to admissibility under s.100(1) are not automatically established, and, notwithstanding the evidential assumptions provided by s.109 at the admissibility stage, the bare fact of an allegation (even if assumed to be true) is not necessarily conclusive of the question whether it constitutes substantial probative evidence or evidence of substantial importance in the context of the case as a whole.

'A trial concerned with whether it is proved that the *defendant* has committed crime "A" is liable to be derailed if the jury is required to decide whether a *witness* has committed the distinct, separate crimes, "B" and "C". The evidential assumption in s.109 does not bind the jury, and the investigation of this evidence at trial may be liable to distract attention from the crucial issue which is whether the case against the defendant has been proved. If, in the context under discussion, the judge correctly directs the jury that they must not consider the alleged bad character evidence unless they are sure that it is true, two trials would be simultaneously in progress before the same jury. First, the trial of the defendant for the crime alleged against him by the prosecution; and secondly, the crime or misconduct alleged against the witness.

'In our judgment, these are relevant considerations bearing on the assessment of the probative value of the evidence sought to be adduced and its importance in the overall context of the case. When it is assessing the probative value of the evidence in accordance with s.100(1)(b) and 100(3), and consistently with s.100(2), among the factors relevant to the admissibility judgment the court should reflect whether the admission of the evidence relating to the bad character of the witness might make it difficult for the jury to understand the remainder of the evidence, and whether its understanding of the case as a whole might be diminished. In such cases the conclusion may be that the evidence is not of substantial probative value in establishing the propensity in or lack of creditworthiness of the witness, or that the evidence is not of substantial importance in the context of the case as a whole, or both. If so, the pre-conditions to admissibility will not be established.'

(Lord Judge LCJ)

The expression 'matter in issue' has not been defined by the statute and, despite the sharp distinction at common law between facts in issue and credit, there is some evidence to suggest that the expression is taken to mean matters directly in issue and the creditworthiness of a witness.

In *R v Weir* [2006] 2 All ER 570, Kennedy LJ said:

JUDGMENT

'Although couched in different terms from the provisions relating to the introduction of the defendant's bad character, in our view, s 100(1) does cover matters of credibility. To find otherwise would mean that there was a significant lacuna in the legislation with the potential for unfairness. In any event, it is clear from the explanatory notes that the issue of credibility falls within the section.'

Paragraph 362 of the Explanatory Notes to the Criminal Justice Act 2003 declares as follows:

CLAUSE

'Evidence is of probative value to a matter in issue where it helps to prove that issue one way or the other. In respect of non-defendants, evidence of bad character is most likely to be probative where the question is raised about the credibility of a witness (as this is likely to affect the court's assessment of the issue on which the witness is giving evidence). The evidence might, however, be probative in other ways. One example would be to support a suggestion by the defendant that another person was responsible for the offence.'

In addition, the expression 'matter in issue' is required to be of 'substantial importance' in the case as opposed to only trivial importance. Thus, the issue for the judge to decide, on an application to cross-examine a witness on his previous convictions, will be whether the matter is one of 'substantial importance in the case as a whole'. Professor J. R. Spencer in his book *Evidence of Bad Character*, second edition (Hart, 2009), draws a distinction regarding the probative value of two forms of convictions that may be sought to be within s 100 of the 2003 Act. On the one hand are convictions that bear on the credibility of the witness directly, because they provide a reason for doubting the truth of the particular evidence the witness has given in this particular case; for example, if the alleged victim of an assault claims that the defendant was the aggressor, the jury may be less inclined to believe him when they discover that he has five previous convictions for acts of violence himself. On the other hand, previous convictions may bear on credibility only indirectly, by inviting the jury to reason that a person who would do something like that is not a person whose word can be trusted. Such convictions are not directly linked to the question of whether the witness may be testifying truthfully in court, but it does indicate that his honesty cannot be taken for granted. In the latter case the judge may be justified in refusing leave to admit the evidence under s 100 of the 2003 Act.

The approach of the courts to the requirements of s 100(1)(b) is based on a two-part test referred to by Pitchford LJ in *R v Brewster* [2011] 1 WLR 601. The first question is whether the witness's credibility is a matter in issue and of substantial importance in the case. If yes, the second question is whether the bad character of the person other than the defendant is of substantial probative value to that issue:

JUDGMENT

'The first question for the trial judge under section 100(1)(b) is whether creditworthiness is a matter in issue which is of substantial importance in the context of the case as a whole. This is a significant hurdle. Just because a witness has convictions does not mean that the opposing party is entitled to attack the witness's credibility. If it is shown that creditworthiness is an issue of substantial importance, the second question is whether the bad character relied upon is of substantial probative value in relation to that issue. Whether convictions have persuasive value on the issue of creditworthiness will, it seems to us, depend principally on the nature, number and age of the convictions. However, we do not consider that the conviction must, in order to qualify for admission in evidence, demonstrate any tendency towards dishonesty or untruthfulness. The question is whether a fair-minded tribunal would regard them as affecting the worth of the witness's evidence.'

(Pitchford LJ)

In *R v Hussain (Mohammed)* [2015] EWCA Crim 383, on a charge of rape where contrasting accounts were given by the complainant and the defendant, a material issue was whether the complainant's testimony was to be believed. The Court of Appeal decided that the trial judge had erred in refusing the defendant permission to cross-examine her as to her previous convictions. In this case, the defendant was charged with rape. The prosecution alleged that the complainant was raped at a house party. She had fallen asleep on a bed and was awoken to find the defendant having sexual intercourse with her. The defendant denied rape, gave no account to the police and, in his defence statement served at the case management hearing, alleged that it was the complainant who committed acts of indecency on him. The defence application to cross-examine her as to her previous convictions for robbery, burglary, theft and assault was refused on the ground that, although the complainant's credibility was a matter of substantial importance in the case as a whole, the defendant was not alleging that she concocted the story but that she was mistaken in her assertions. He was convicted and appealed. The Court of Appeal dismissed the appeal but decided that the judge had erred in defining the issue too narrowly. The judge should have ruled that her convictions were so numerous, varied and recent that they were of substantial probative value on the issue of whether her accusation was worthy of belief, but the conviction was safe in view of the other evidence:

JUDGMENT

'We are persuaded that, having correctly ruled that the complainant's general creditworthiness was central to the case, the judge should also have ruled that the convictions were so numerous, varied and recent that they were of substantial probative value upon the issue of whether her accusation against the appellant was worthy of belief. It was for the jury to judge whether in the particular factual context of the present case her general bad character was of any assistance to them in resolving who was telling the truth. In our judgment, the bad character on which the appellant relied paled in significance beside a careful examination of the evidence that emerged: of the complainant and appellant respectively, the evidence of other occupants in the house at the time of the complaint, the scientific and medical evidence and the evidence of the police officers to whom the complaint and the complainant's first account were given.

We consider that the jury would have been quite unable to conclude that the frequency and nature of the complainant's misbehaviour in the past provided any ground for rejecting her present complaint against the appellant.'

(Pitchford LJ)

The Court of Appeal in *R v Stapleton* [2014] EWCA Crim 1983 affirmed the decision of the trial judge on a refusal to consider the defendant's late application under s 100 to cross-examine the complainant as to her bad character. It appeared that the defence's late application was made partly in response to the judge's ruling granting leave to the prosecution to cross-examine the defendant. In this case, the defendant was charged with causing grievous bodily harm with intent on his partner. Both parties had quite a lot of alcohol to drink and started a heated argument. According to the complainant the defendant assaulted her, by hitting her repeatedly in the face, punching her in the stomach and kicking her while she was on the floor. She had suffered broken ribs, a collapsed lung, an injury to her stomach and extensive bruising to her face, including two black eyes. She was admitted to hospital. The defendant denied that he was the aggressor and raised the defence of self-defence. Before the trial the prosecution applied in writing for leave to adduce the defendant's extensive and relevant previous convictions for offences of violence. After the ruling by the judge in favour of the prosecution, the defendant, without notice in writing, applied for leave to adduce evidence of the complainant's bad character under s 100. The complainant had an old conviction for robbery when she was 17 years old. The trial judge rebuked defence counsel for his late application and refused to allow the complainant's bad character to be admitted. On conviction the defendant appealed. The Court of Appeal dismissed the appeal on the grounds that the complainant's convictions were merely peripheral and without substantive probative value in relation to the matter in issue. In addition, the Court of Appeal criticised counsel for making the late application without notice in writing:

JUDGMENT

'At the very least, the point should have been raised with both counsel for the Crown and the judge at the outset of the trial, and before the complainant gave evidence. Indeed, proper written notice of a potential intention to make such an application should first have been provided before trial. It seems odd, to say the least, that the consequence of the appellant's own convictions being adduced in evidence having been caused by his own conduct of the trial, he should then seek to build on that by trying to adduce the bad character of the complainant. It is particularly unsatisfactory in circumstances where, as we see it, the complainant's previous convictions, such as they were, were on the face of it peripheral to the true issues to be decided at the trial.'

(Davis LJ)

Where it is highly likely that the jury may be given the wrong impression of the complainant, but for the defence questioning as to his bad character, the judge is required to take this into consideration, along with the other evidence, in determining whether there is substantive probative value between the bad character and the matters in issue. The possibility of raising satellite issues may be avoided by the judge in the ground rules and appropriate case management. In *R v O'Donnell* [2014] EWCA Crim 1779, the defendant's conviction for assault was quashed by the Court of Appeal when the trial judge in error inhibited the cross-examination of the complainant as to his bad character. In this case, the defendant, Lisa, and her partner, Wallace, were charged with assault occasioning bodily harm. The complainant, Mr Elliott, a neighbour of the defendants, presented himself in court as a man of good character. He was in the navy and before that was in the army; and he wore his service blazer (with the coat of arms) in court. He alleged that Wallace inflicted injuries to his eye, nose and lumbar region and Lisa struck him a blow resulting in a split lip. Wallace raised the defence of self-defence and Lisa denied involvement. The defendants sought leave to adduce Mr Elliott's previous convictions for theft, that he had lied about his previous convictions when attempting to obtain criminal injuries compensation, he had lied to the police about his convictions by giving an incorrect date of birth. The defendants alleged that Mr Elliott had exaggerated the extent of his injuries and produced photographs that he was fit for work, despite his allegations to the contrary. Mr Elliott claimed that he was wrongly convicted of those offences. The trial judge refused the defendants' application on the grounds that the convictions were old and capable of leading to satellite litigation. The defendants were convicted and Lisa appealed. The Court of Appeal allowed the appeal and quashed Lisa's conviction. The court decided that, given the link between the convictions, the alleged lies and the alleged offence, and the way Mr Elliott would have appeared to the jury, the convictions were relevant and potentially probative to important matters in issue between the parties. Further, extensive satellite litigation was not inevitable:

JUDGMENT

'By Mr Elliot's appearance in the witness box wearing his blazer with the crest and with the defence forbidden to mention his background, as counsel confirmed, Mr Elliot would have appeared to the jury as a law-abiding, upstanding member of the community and the injured party. Mr Finch would have faced an uphill battle in attacking his credibility.

Given the link between the convictions, the alleged lies and the alleged offence and given the way Mr Elliott would have come across to the jury, we are satisfied the convictions were relevant and potentially probative to important matters in issue between the parties. By asking about the previous convictions there was not an inevitability about extensive satellite litigation. Properly controlled, the questions could have been limited to a series of questions with some, but not much, amplification to deal with the fact that Mr Elliot wished to assert that he had been wrongly convicted.'

(Hallett LJ)

In cross-examining a police officer in respect of alleged improper conduct, the issue may be governed by s 100 of the Criminal Justice Act 2003 and some guidance may be discerned from pre-2003 decisions.

CASE EXAMPLE

R v Busby (1981) 75 Cr App R 79

The defendant was charged with burglary and handling stolen goods. He was alleged to have made certain damaging remarks to the police when interviewed. He alleged that these were fabricated by the police. At his trial, two police officers were cross-examined to establish that the defendant did not make the remarks and also that one officer, in the presence of the other, had intimidated a potential witness for the defence to stop him testifying. Both officers denied that they had threatened the potential witness for the defence. The defence was not allowed to call the defence witness and, following conviction, the defendant appealed. The Court of Appeal allowed the appeal on the ground that the evidence was admissible to show that, if true, the prosecution was prepared to go to improper lengths to secure a conviction:

JUDGMENT

'It is not always easy to determine when a question relates to facts which are collateral only, and therefore to be treated as final, and when it is relevant to the issue which has to be tried . . . We are of the opinion that the learned judge was wrong to refuse to admit the evidence. If true, it would have shown that the police were prepared to go to improper lengths in order to secure the accused's conviction. It was the accused's case that the statement attributed to him had been fabricated, a suggestion which could not be accepted by the jury unless they thought that the officers concerned were prepared to go to improper lengths to secure a conviction.'

(Eveleigh LJ)

CASE EXAMPLE

R v Edwards [1991] 1 WLR 207

It was held that a police officer could be questioned as to any relevant criminal offences or disciplinary charges found proved against him. However, charges that had not yet been adjudicated on should not be put to the officer in cross-examination. Such questions would have no probative value. Where a police officer had allegedly fabricated an admission attributed to a different defendant in a different trial and who was acquitted, he may be cross-examined to make the jury aware that the officer's evidence in the previous case was disbelieved. Where, however, the previous acquittal did not necessarily indicate that the officer had been disbelieved, such cross-examination was not allowed:

JUDGMENT

'The test is primarily one of relevance, and this is so whether one is considering evidence in chief or questions in cross-examination. To be admissible questions must be relevant to the issue before the court.

'Issues are of varying degrees of relevance or importance. A distinction has to be drawn between, on the one hand, the issue in the case upon which the jury will be pronouncing their verdict and, on the other hand, collateral issues of which the credibility of the witnesses may be one. Generally speaking, questions may be put to a witness as to any improper conduct of which he may have been guilty, for the purpose of testing his credit.

'The limits to such questioning were defined by Sankey LJ in *Hobbs v Tinling & Co* [1929] 2 KB 1:

"The court can always exercise its discretion to decide whether a question as to credit is one which the witness should be compelled to answer . . . in the exercise of its discretion the court should have regard to the following considerations: (1) Such questions are proper if they are of such a nature that the truth of the imputation conveyed by them would seriously affect the opinion of the court as to the credibility of the witness on the matter to which he testifies. (2) Such questions are improper if the imputation which they convey relates to matters so remote in time, or of such a character, that the truth of the imputation would not affect, or would affect in a slight degree, the opinion of the court as to the credibility of the witness on the matter to which he testifies. (3) Such questions are improper if there is a great disproportion between the importance of the imputation made against the witness's character and the importance of his evidence."

[After referring to two decisions, namely *Harris v Tippett* (1811) 2 Camp 637 and *R v Shaw* (1888) 16 Cox CC 503, his Lordship continued:] 'The result of those two decisions seems to be this. The acquittal of a defendant in case A, where the prosecution case depended largely or entirely upon the evidence of a police officer, does not normally render that officer liable to cross-examination as to credit in case B. But where a police officer who has allegedly fabricated an admission in case B, has also given evidence of an admission in case A, where there was an acquittal by virtue of which his evidence is demonstrated to have been disbelieved, it is proper that the jury in case B should be made aware of that fact. However, where the acquittal in case A does not necessarily indicate that the jury disbelieved the officer, such cross-examination should not be allowed. In such a case the verdict of not guilty may mean no more than that the jury entertained some doubt about the prosecution case, not necessarily that any witness was lying.'

(Lord Lane CJ)

If the evidence of misconduct of the person other than the defendant 'has to do with the alleged offence with which the defendant is charged' within s 98(a), the evidence will not be subject to the requirements of s 100. Instead, the evidence will be subject to the common law test of admissibility based on relevance to facts in issue. Accordingly, where it is alleged that in order to prove the defendant's guilt of the offence charged, it is necessary to prove that a person other than the accused was guilty of an offence, the application will be made under s 98(a); for example in *R v Pigram* [1995] Crim LR 808, on a charge of handling it is essential for the prosecution to prove that the goods were stolen. Thus, it would be admissible to prove the commission of the theft by another.

On the other hand, the defendant may wish to elicit evidence of the bad character of a witness or non-witness for a variety of reasons. This may be to suggest that someone else committed the offence with which the defendant is charged: see *R v Blastland* [1986] AC 41, or to bolster up a defence such as self-defence or duress: see *R v Randall* [2004] 1 Cr App R 375.

12.3 Requirement of leave

The leave requirement is a pre-condition to admissibility of the bad character of a person other than the defendant.

Section 100(4) of the 2003 Act enacts as follows:

SECTION

'Except where subsection (1)(c) applies, evidence of the bad character of a person other than the defendant must not be given without leave of the court.'

The exclusion of the leave requirement from s 100(1)(c) is self-explicit in the sense that all the parties had agreed to the admissibility of the evidence.

The subsection does not indicate the grounds on which the judge is entitled to grant leave, but s 100(3) identifies some of the factors the judge is required to take into account in deciding on the 'probative value of the evidence' when the application is made under s 100(1)(b). These factors may act as guidance to the judge in deciding whether leave may be granted. Of course, if the allegation is that the evidence of misconduct has to do with the facts of the offence or the investigation or prosecution of that offence within s 98(a) or (b), the bad character provisions or gateways are not relevant and the leave of the judge is not required; for example an allegation by the defendant that a prosecution witness or another person committed the offence or that the police fabricated a material part of the evidence of the prosecution does not fall within s 100.

The requirement of leave to cross-examine a witness other than the defendant on his bad character has the effect of modifying the common law, subject to the restrictions imposed by ss 41–43 of the Youth Justice and Criminal Evidence Act 1999, concerning cross-examination of the complainant on his or her sexual behaviour. It is believed that when the cross-examination is permitted under s 41, the leave requirement under s 100(4) would automatically be satisfied. Likewise the discretion to exclude evidence under s 78 of the Police and Criminal Evidence Act 1984 (duty to ensure a fair trial) will be taken into account by the judge when considering whether to grant leave or not.

In *R v S* [2006] EWCA Crim 1303, the defendant appealed against his conviction for indecent assault. The complainant (C) was a prostitute and heroin addict and alleged that the defendant had indecently assaulted her. The defence was that C had consented to perform sexual acts in return for a specified sum but that she had then demanded more money, threatened to accuse the defendant of rape if he did not pay and tried to take his gold chain. The defendant applied for, and was refused, leave to cross-examine C pursuant to s 100 of the 2003 Act in relation to her previous convictions for offences of dishonesty, namely going equipped for theft, handling stolen goods and a residential burglary, the latest of which was four years before the events at issue. The Court of Appeal allowed the appeal but declared that C's offences of dishonesty would only have been likely to demonstrate a propensity for untruthfulness if, in relation to those earlier offences, she had been shown to have told lies in pleading not guilty and giving an account which must have been disbelieved. However, C had pleaded guilty to the relevant offences, and none had involved false representations. On the other hand, her previous convictions for offences of dishonesty had substantial probative value in relation to another 'matter in issue' in the proceedings, namely whether she had a propensity to act dishonestly:

JUDGMENT

> 'The defendant's case was to the effect that the complainant demanded money with menaces and tried to take his property. Her persistent criminal record of offences of dishonesty, notwithstanding their antiquity, might in our judgment very well be said to possess substantial probative value upon this issue: did she have a propensity to act dishonestly? The judge, as we have indicated, was not faced with an application put on that basis. Had he been, we consider that it would have been proper for him to accede to it. The evidence of propensity thus described would have been a matter of some importance for the jury's consideration. We consider the fact that the jury proceeded in ignorance of it renders the conviction unsafe.'
>
> (Laws LJ)

In contrast to the approach as stated above, in *R v Brewster* [2011] 1 WLR 601, the Court of Appeal decided that in order to evaluate the evidence of bad character, the test is whether the evidence in question is capable of assisting the jury in determining the reliability of the evidence. In this case two defendants were charged with kidnapping. The defence case was that the complainant's claim to have been coerced and threatened by the defendants had been fabricated for the complainant's own purposes. Both defendants applied for leave to cross-examine the complainant in relation to her previous convictions for burglary, theft, manslaughter and possession of drugs. The judge refused the application. The defendants' appeal against conviction was allowed on the ground that the words 'substantive probative value', in the context of s 100(1)(b), did not require the applicant to establish that the bad character relied on amounted to proof of a lack of credibility of the witness when credibility was an issue of substantial importance, or that the convictions demonstrated a tendency towards untruthfulness. The test was whether the evidence of the previous convictions or bad behaviour was sufficiently persuasive and may be regarded by the jury as bearing on the issue of the creditworthiness of the witness:

JUDGMENT

'It seems to us that the trial judge's task will be to evaluate the evidence of bad character which it is proposed to admit for the purpose of deciding whether it is reasonably capable of assisting a fair-minded jury to reach a view whether the witness's evidence is, or is not, worthy of belief. Only then can it properly be said that the evidence is of substantial probative value on the issue of creditworthiness. It does not seem to us that the words "substantial probative value", in their section 100(1)(b) context, require the applicant to establish that the bad character relied on amounts to proof of a lack of credibility of the witness when credibility is an issue of substantial importance, or that the convictions demonstrate a tendency towards untruthfulness. The question is whether the evidence of previous convictions, or bad behaviour, is sufficiently persuasive to be worthy of consideration by a fair-minded tribunal upon the issue of the witness's creditworthiness.'

(Pitchford LJ)

KEY FACTS

Evidence of bad character of persons other than the defendant

- Admissibility under s 100.
- Bad character – s 98.
- Person other than defendant – not statutorily defined but includes witnesses and non-witnesses for the prosecution or defence.
- Admissibility under three criteria – s 100(1)(a), (b) and (c).
- Section 100(1)(a) – important explanatory evidence defined in s 102.
- Section 100(1)(b) – evidence has substantial probative value – defined in s 100(3): see *R v S, R v Brewster*.
- Section 100(1)(c) – all parties agree.
- Leave of the court – s 100(4).

12.4 Bad character evidence of the defendant

The common law rules and the principles laid down in the Criminal Evidence Act 1898 governing the admissibility of evidence of the bad character of the defendant have been repealed and replaced by the provisions enacted in s 101 as supplemented by other provisions. The grounds on which bad character evidence of the defendant may be admitted in a trial are laid down in s 101 of the Criminal Justice Act 2003. There are seven 'gateways' enacted in s 101(1), which declares as follows:

SECTION

'In criminal proceedings evidence of the defendant's bad character is admissible if, but only if –

(a) all the parties to the proceedings agree to the evidence being admissible,
(b) the evidence is adduced by the defendant himself or is given in answer to a question asked by him in cross-examination and intended to elicit it,
(c) it is important explanatory evidence,
(d) it is relevant to an important matter in issue between the defendant and the prosecution,
(e) it has substantial probative value in relation to an important matter between the defendant and a co-defendant,
(f) it is evidence to correct a false impression given by the defendant, or
(g) the defendant has made an attack on another person's character.'

12.4.1 Gateway (a) – s 101(1)(a) – 'agreement between parties'

Very little may be said of the subsection for it is the subject of an agreement between the parties. The purpose for which the evidence may be used would be identified by the terms of the agreement and may be the subject matter of a formal admission.

12.4.2 Gateway (b) – s 101(1)(b) – 'evidence adduced by the defendant'

This gateway may be non-contentious and may be resorted to for tactical reasons. The subsection involves the defendant testifying and declaring his bad character in the witness box or/and cross-examining witnesses with a view to bringing out the defendant's bad character. The leave of the judge is not required, for the admissibility of the evidence concerns a waiver by the defendant and a conscious decision to admit the evidence. This may be the case where the prosecution has been allowed to adduce evidence of the defendant's bad character and such evidence has already been admitted in the trial. In addition, the defendant may feel that for tactical reasons he ought to 'come clean' with his bad character and volunteer the information to the court, rather than allow it to be 'dragged' out of him. In *Jones v DPP* [1962] AC 635, on a charge of murder, the defendant, having given a false alibi at a police interview, explained at the trial why he lied as to his whereabouts at the time of the murder. The explanation involved the defendant 'being in trouble with the police before'.

If, alternatively, the defendant's bad character is revealed unintentionally through witnesses under cross-examination, perhaps because the witness volunteers the information without being asked, the evidence is inadmissible. Accordingly, the judge is required to direct the jury to ignore the evidence or, exceptionally, discharge the jury and order a retrial.

12.4.3 Gateway (c) – s 101(1)(c) – 'important explanatory evidence'

Section 102 of the 2003 Act defines 'important explanatory evidence' thus:

SECTION

'(a) without it, the court or jury would find it impossible or difficult properly to understand other evidence in the case, and

(b) its value for understanding the case as a whole is substantial.'

The test of important explanatory evidence is this 'double-barrelled' requirement that involves highly relevant but prejudicial evidence, not of the facts in issue but significant in understanding the background evidence. If the facts of the case or evidence is understandable on its own without recourse to other material, then the evidence is not admissible under this head. Paragraph 360 of the explanatory note accompanying the Act declares as follows:

CLAUSE

'The term "explanatory evidence" is used to describe evidence which, whilst not going to the question of whether the defendant is guilty, is necessary for the jury to have a proper understanding of other evidence being given in the case by putting it in its proper context. An example might be a case involving the abuse of one person of another over a long period of time. For the jury to understand properly the victim's account of the offending and why they did not seek help from, for example, a parent or other guardian, it might be necessary for evidence to be given of a wider pattern of abuse involving that other person.'

Such background evidence existed at common law and includes in exceptional circumstances the motive of the accused:

JUDGMENT

'Evidence of motive necessarily goes to prove the fact of the homicide by the accused, as well as his "malice aforethought" in as much as it is more probable that men are killed by those that have some motive for killing them than by those who have not.'

(Atkinson J in *R v Ball* [1911] AC 47)

In *R v Fulcher* [1995] 2 Cr App R 251, the defendant was charged with the murder of his infant son. The issue was the identity of the assailant. There were three possible suspects: the defendant, the defendant's wife and the defendant's mother-in-law, with whom the family was living. In order to prove that the defendant committed the crime, the prosecution was allowed to adduce evidence that the child had suffered injuries that were likely to cause the child to cry. The defendant became extremely irritable when the child cried. The defendant was found guilty and appealed. The Court of Appeal dismissed the appeal and decided that the evidence was admissible to show 'motive'. In view of the fact that the defendant was one of only three potential killers of the child, the evidence was highly probative of the identity of the offender.

Similarly, in *R v Phillips (Alun)* [2003] 2 Cr App R 35, the defendant was charged with the murder of his wife. It was held that the judge had correctly admitted evidence that the marriage had broken down to rebut his claim of a happy marriage and to demonstrate a motive for killing her.

The test of background evidence at common law was that, without the evidence, the account to be placed before the court would be incomplete and incomprehensible. This would be the position even though the evidence may have established that the defendant was guilty of an offence of which he was not charged.

In *R v Sawoniuk* [2000] 2 Cr App R 220, the defendant was convicted on two counts of the murder of Jews in Belarus in 1942 contrary to the War Crimes Act 1991. Two witnesses testified that they saw the defendant commit the offences charged. In addition, the court allowed two other witnesses to testify as to the defendant's participation in a 'search and kill' operation against Jewish survivors of an earlier massacre for which the defendant was not charged. On conviction the defendant appealed. The Court of Appeal dismissed the appeal on the ground that the evidence was important explanatory material:

JUDGMENT

'Criminal charges cannot fairly be judged in a factual vacuum. In order to make a rational assessment of evidence directly relating to a charge it may often be necessary for a jury to receive evidence describing, perhaps in some detail, the context and circumstances in which the offences are said to have been committed. This, as we understand, is the approach indicated by this court in *R v Pettman*, May 2, 1985 (unreported): "Where it is necessary to place before the jury evidence of part of a continual background of history relevant to the offence charged in the indictment and without the totality of which the account placed before the jury would be incomplete or incomprehensible, then the fact that the whole account involves including evidence establishing the commission of an offence with which the accused is not charged is not of itself a ground for excluding the evidence." This approach seems to us of particular significance in an exceptional case such as the present, in which a London jury was asked to assess the significance of evidence relating to events in a country quite unlike our own, taking place a very long time ago in the extraordinary conditions prevailing in 1941 to 1942. It was necessary and appropriate for the Crown to prove that it was the policy of Nazi Germany first to oppress and then to exterminate the Jewish population of its conquered territories in Eastern Europe . . . It seems to us that evidence relevant to . . . these matters was probative and admissible, even if it disclosed the commission of criminal offences, other than those charged.'

(Lord Bingham CJ)

Similarly, in *TM et al* [2000] 2 Cr App R 266, the Court of Appeal relied on the approach advocated by Lord Bingham CJ and upheld the trial judge's admission, in a case of horrific sexual abuses by TM of his sister, of the fact that TM had been forced at an earlier time to watch and then take part in other acts of sexual abuse committed by older members of the family. Without this information concerning the way that TM and the other children were groomed, the jury could not have properly appreciated the significance of the other evidence in the case, in particular why the victim did not feel able to seek protection against her brother from the rest of the family.

It is imperative that the courts are alert to the notion that 'background' evidence does not comprise a magnet to allow in otherwise inadmissible evidence under a broad heading. This caution was heeded by the Court of Appeal in *R v Dolan* [2003] 1 Cr App R 18, on a charge of murder of his child by forceful shaking. The issue was the identity of the killer. There were two suspects, namely the parents. It was held that the fact that the defendant (father) had in the past vented his fury on inanimate objects was not admissible as background evidence:

JUDGMENT

'The fact that a man who is not shown to have a tendency to lose his temper and react violently towards human beings becomes frustrated with and violent towards inanimate objects is, we think, irrelevant.'

(Tuckey LJ)

Likewise, in *R v Beverley* [2006] EWCA Crim 1287, the Court of Appeal ruled that the application to admit the previous convictions of the defendant under s 101(1)(c) was unfounded. In this case the charge was conspiracy to import more than 1 kg of cocaine from Jamaica. It was held that the judge had wrongly admitted previous convictions of possession with intent to supply cannabis and possession of cannabis:

JUDGMENT

'[The Crown's] submission ignores the provisions of s 102, whose two parts at (a) and (b) are cumulative. We are entirely unable to see how the jury would have been disabled or disadvantaged in understanding any of the evidence allegedly connecting the appellant with the crime without having these convictions before them. The evidence was perfectly clear. It required no footnote or lexicon . . . There should never have been an application under s 101(1)(c) in this case nor should it have been supported here. The gateway at s 101(1)(c) was entirely unavailable.'

(Laws LJ)

In *R v Osbourne* [2007] Crim LR 712, on a charge of murder of a close friend, the judge allowed evidence to be given from a former partner of the defendant that when he failed to take medication that controlled his schizophrenia, he was capable of snapping and verbally abusing her. At the time of the incident the defendant did not take his medication. The judge ruled that the evidence was admissible under s 101(1)(c) of the 2003 Act. On appeal, it was decided that the earlier verbal abuse did not amount to 'reprehensible behaviour' and, in any event, did not amount to 'important explanatory evidence' within s 101(1)(c).

It should be noted that s 100(1)(a) introduced similar principles concerning bad character evidence of a person other than the defendant.

In *R v Yaxley-Lennon*, conjoined appeal with *R v Weir and Others* [2006] 1 WLR 1885, the Court of Appeal held that bad character evidence of a prosecution witness, a caution for the possession of cannabis, was inadmissible as it had occurred after the incident with which the defendant was charged (assault) and because the witness's credibility had not been challenged on the basis that it was affected by drug use.

12.4.4 Gateway (d) – s 101(1)(d) – 'relevant to an important matter in issue between the defendant and the prosecution'

Section 101(1)(d) of the 2003 Act has a self-contained code of what used to be called 'similar fact evidence' (see earlier) prior to the introduction of the Act. The gateway under s 101(1)(d) is only applicable to prosecution evidence of bad character (see s 103(6)) and makes provision for the admissibility of evidence going towards the guilt of the defendant as well as his credibility. To this extent the provision is much wider than the common law rules of similar fact evidence.

Under this gateway the prosecution is required to establish the following requirements:

1. That the bad character of the defendant is relevant.
2. That it satisfies the test of 'important matter in issue' between the defendant and the prosecution (as defined in s 103).
3. The judge is satisfied that the admissibility of the evidence would not have an adverse effect on the fairness of the trial (s 101(3)). In determining 'fairness', the judge is required to have regard to the length of time between the matters concerning the bad character of the defendant and the matters that form the subject of the offence charged: see s 101(4). In addition, the judge is required to consider exercising his discretion generally under s 78 of PACE 1984 and the common law.

In assessing 'relevance', s 109 enacts that the evidence is assumed to be true, unless the judge decides that no reasonable jury may so regard the evidence. Thus, an element of credibility is written into the notion of relevance except where the evidence is incredulous in the first place.

An issue is 'important' if it is of 'substantial importance in the context of the case as a whole': s 112(1). A 'matter in issue between the defendant and the prosecution' has been defined in s 103 as including the defendant's 'propensity to commit offences of the kind with which he is charged' or the defendant's 'propensity to be untruthful', i.e. facts in issue or credibility: see s 103(1) (a) and (b). The effect is that the matters in issue between the defendant and the prosecution are (1) whether the defendant committed the *actus reus* of the offence, (2) with the appropriate *mens rea* and (3) the relevance of any subsidiary issues related to defences raised by the defendant, such as provocation, self-defence, etc.

Propensity to commit offences – s 103(1)(a)

The expression 'propensity' has not been defined by the Act and an aspect of the test involves a propensity to commit offences of the kind with which the defendant is charged, *provided* that the admissibility of the evidence leads to the conclusion that the defendant had, more than likely, committed the offence charged. If the prosecution evidence establishes only that the defendant is *likely to have committed* the offence charged, this inference will be insufficient to establish the degree of relevance envisaged by the subsection: see s 103(1)(a). Such evidence may shed more heat than light. The approach may be illustrated by the common law case of *Makin v AG for New South Wales* [1894] AC 57. The defendants were charged with the murder of a baby, whose body was found buried in the garden of a house occupied by them. The defendants had adopted it in return for a sum of money. The defendants argued that the death was from natural causes. The prosecution was allowed to adduce evidence of some twelve other babies who died in their care, similarly adopted by the defendants, whose bodies were found buried in gardens of homes occupied by the defendants. Their conviction for murder was upheld by the Privy Council as establishing a system of committing the offence. Lord Herschell summarised the test for admissibility of similar fact evidence:

JUDGMENT

> 'It is undoubtedly not competent for the prosecution to adduce evidence tending to show that the accused has been guilty of criminal acts other than those covered by the indictment, for the purpose of leading to the conclusion that the accused is a person likely from his criminal conduct or character to have committed the offence for which he is being tried. On the other hand, the mere fact that the evidence adduced tends to show the commission of other crimes does not render it inadmissible if it be relevant to an issue before the jury, and it may be so relevant if it bears upon the question whether the acts alleged to constitute the crime charged in the indictment were designed or accidental, or to rebut a defence which would otherwise be open to the accused.'
>
> (Lord Herschell)

Although s 112(1) defines an 'important matter' as a matter of 'substantial importance in the context of the case as a whole', it is not necessary for the bad character evidence to be of substantial probative value as previously was the position at common law. On the other hand, the position is different in construing the equivalent provision for non-defendants under s 100 where the probative value is required to be substantial: see earlier. The reason for this higher threshold of relevance under s 100 is to safeguard against the unwarranted revelation of a non-defendant's character. The effect of s 101(1)(d) is that the threshold for admitting the defendant's bad character is satisfied if the evidence is merely *relevant* to an important issue between the prosecution and the defendant, unless, of course, it is unfair to do so in the exercise of the discretion of the judge.

Proof

A defendant's propensity to commit offences of the kind charged may be established ('without prejudice to any other way of doing so') by evidence that he has been *convicted* of an offence of the 'same description' or an offence of the 'same category' as the one charged: s 103(2). Section 103(4)(a) defines offences of the same description as offences with the same statements of offences as in the charges or indictments. Thus, on a charge of assault contrary to s 47 of the Offences Against the Person Act 1861, the fact that the defendant has a conviction for a s 47 assault is evidence within s 103(2)(a) that the defendant has a propensity to commit offences of the same description. The age of the conviction is required to be considered by the judge to determine whether it is sufficiently relevant to the charge: see s 101(4). In addition, two offences are the 'same category' if they belong to the same category of offences prescribed by the Secretary of State: s 103(4). Since October 2004, there are currently two types of offences that, by order, have been made the subject of offences of the same category. These are offences within the 'theft category' and 'sexual offences'. In deciding on the admissibility of the conviction, the judge is required to consider whether it would be 'unjust' to admit the evidence by reason of the length of time since the defendant was convicted or for any other reason.

In *R v Hanson, Gilmore and Pickering* [2005] EWCA Crim 824, Rose LJ said:

JUDGMENT

'Where propensity to commit the offence is relied upon there are . . . three questions to be considered:

(i) Does the history of conviction(s) establish a propensity to commit offences of the kind charged?
(ii) Does that propensity make it more likely that the defendant committed the offence?
(iii) Is it unjust to rely on the conviction(s) of the same description or category; and, in any event, will the proceedings be unfair if they are admitted?'

Accordingly, the first question for the court to decide under this gateway is whether the proposed bad character evidence goes to propensity to commit offences of the kind charged. Having done so, the court is required to identify the specific matter in issue between the parties to which the evidence of misconduct is relevant. Finally, the judge is required to consider whether the admissibility of the evidence may have an adverse effect on a fair trial.

A single previous conviction will seldom satisfy the test of relevance to an important issue between the defendant and the prosecution unless it demonstrates a high degree of relevance with the offence charged equivalent to the common law test of 'striking similarity'.

In *R v Hanson, Gilmore and Pickering* [2005] EWCA Crim 824, the Court of Appeal issued guidelines as to the principles of admissibility under this gateway:

JUDGMENT

'A single previous conviction for an offence of the same description or category will often not show propensity. But it may do so where, for example, it shows a tendency to unusual behaviour or where its circumstances demonstrate probative force in relation to the offence charged.'

(Rose LJ)

Thus, in *R v M* [2007] Crim LR 637, the Court of Appeal allowed an appeal on a charge of possessing a firearm with intent to cause fear and violence contrary to s 16A of the Firearms Act 1968. The trial judge had admitted a previous conviction, which was then twenty years old, of possessing a firearm without a licence. The court decided that the single conviction was too old and with insufficient unique qualities to justify its admissibility under s 101(1)(d). Likewise, in *R v Leaver* [2006] EWCA Crim 2988 on a charge of rape by continuing with sexual intercourse in a violent manner after the complainant had allegedly withdrawn her consent, the prosecution was allowed to adduce evidence of a conviction for indecent exposure that had not been accompanied by circumstances of violence. Following a conviction, the Court of Appeal allowed the appeal on the ground that the conviction did not relate significantly to the question before the jury, which was whether the defendant had reasonably believed that the complainant was consenting to intercourse.

However, in *R v Brown* [2012] EWCA Crim 773, the Court of Appeal upheld a trial judge's decision to admit a single conviction for dangerous driving that had been committed a number of years previously when he was attempting to flee from the police. The court reasoned thus:

JUDGMENT

'There is no rule of law precluding a single previous conviction giving rise to a conclusion of propensity. Obviously where there is only one previous conviction and especially where it is some time ago, then caution is needed where it is sought to rely upon that previous single offence in order to found a propensity argument. We do not read the observations of the Vice President in *Hanson* as going any further than that.'

(Gross LJ)

Similarly, in *Pickering*, on charges of rape and indecent assault on one of the defendant's daughters, the court admitted a conviction that was about a decade old for indecent assault on an eleven-year-old girl. The court decided that this was an 'unusual' type of offence and even a single, old conviction for an offence of the same category was highly probative of the charge.

The court in *R v Hanson, Gilmore and Pickering* also gave an indication of some of the factors the judge is required to consider in determining whether it would be 'just' to admit the previous convictions of the defendant under s 101(1)(d). The range of issues that are required to be considered by the judge include the similarity between the conviction and the offence charged, the gravity and age of the offence for which the defendant had been convicted, as well as the danger of distracting the jury by reference to 'satellite' litigation where events are disputed:

JUDGMENT

'When considering what is just under s 103(3), and the fairness of the proceedings under s 101(3), the judge may, among other factors, take into consideration the degree of similarity between the previous conviction and the offence charged, albeit they are both within the same description or prescribed category. For example, theft and assault occasioning actual bodily harm each embrace a wide spectrum of conduct. This does not, however, mean that what used to be referred as striking similarity must be shown before convictions become admissible. The judge may also take into consideration the respective gravity of the past and present offences. He or she must always consider the strength of the prosecution case. If there is no or very little other evidence against a defendant, it is unlikely to be just to admit his previous convictions, whatever they are . . . Old convictions, with no special feature shared with the offence charged, are likely seriously to affect the fairness of proceedings adversely, unless despite their age, it can properly be said that they show a continuing propensity. It will often be necessary, before determining admissibility and even when considering offences of the same description or category, to examine each individual conviction rather than merely to look at the name of the offence or at the defendant's record as a whole.'

(Rose LJ)

In *R v Beverley* [2006] Crim LR 1065 (above), the Court of Appeal decided that two convictions for possession of cannabis with intent to supply (five years before the current charge) and simple possession of cannabis (two years prior to the current charge) were wrongly admitted under s 101(1)(d) to prove the guilt of the defendant on a charge of conspiracy to import cocaine. The previous convictions were too old, were of a different character, involved a different type of drug and were less serious than the current charge.

The extent of the similarity of the circumstances shared by the conviction and the charge may establish a high degree of probative value to justify the admissibility of the conviction. In *R v Smith* [2006] EWCA Crim 1355, the defendant was charged with domestic burglary, having tricked an elderly woman into letting him into her home by telling her that he was from the water company. The defendant's previous convictions for burglary and attempted burglary in entering houses of elderly people by deception and then stealing or attempting to steal from them were admitted under s 101(1)(d). The probative value of the convictions were found in the rather similar details of the circumstances surrounding the convictions.

Further, there is no requirement that the prosecution is first required to establish a direct link between a material fact supporting the charge and a material fact supporting the conviction, before evidence of the conviction may be established. Section 101(1)(d) does not contain such a precondition. The subsection is not directed at evidential sufficiency but instead principally concerns the relevance of the evidence that the prosecution proposes to introduce. Accordingly, the evidence focuses attention on the issue of whether the bad character evidence will throw light on the real issue or issues in the case. Thus, in *R v Bowman* [2014] EWCA Crim 716, on charges of *inter alia* complicity in possessing a firearm with intent to endanger life, the Court of Appeal decided that a trial judge was entitled to admit an earlier conviction, of approximately seven years old, for a firearms offence to establish that the defendant was prepared to carry and discharge a loaded firearm in public, and he behaved in an entirely reckless and violent manner, with no attempt to hide his identity. The conviction also established that the defendant had ready access to firearms and that he was willing to use them in connection with other criminal activity.

JUDGMENT

'When resolving whether the evidence is to be admitted as relevant to an "important matter in issue" the court does not, as a discrete question, need to satisfy itself as to the strength of the prosecution's case as regards the particular "matter". We are fortified in this conclusion by the decision in *Hanson*, in that the court in that case only considered the consequences of evidential weakness in the context of applying sections 101(3) and 103(3) rather than when addressing section 101(1)(d).'

(Fulford LJ)

In *R v Gillings (Keith)* [2019] EWCA Crim 1834 the Court of Appeal issued guidance on the age of previous convictions:

JUDGMENT

'Taking Hanson and McGarvie together, the following points are clear:

(1) The age of the convictions is not in itself a bar to their admissibility, but it is a factor which needs to be carefully considered, particularly in the case of very old convictions.

(2) The age of the convictions is relevant for two purposes. The first is that it is necessary to consider whether convictions many years beforehand are capable of constituting evidence of a continuing propensity. This is a question of law to be determined by the judge. If they are capable of doing so, the question whether they do in fact demonstrate such a propensity and, if so, the extent to which that assists in determining a defendant's guilt is a matter for the jury. The second question is whether, given that the convictions are capable of constituting evidence of propensity, the admission of old convictions is likely to cause greater prejudice to a defendant than is justified by the probative value of that evidence.

(3) The answer to both questions, propensity and prejudice, is likely to depend on the particular facts of each case and the issue which the jury have to determine. If there is no relevant similarity between the facts of the offence giving rise to the previous convictions and the events and issues of the instant case, the mere fact of old convictions even for the same or similar offences may be incapable of constituting evidence of propensity and, even if it is capable of doing so, any probative effect they may have is likely to be outweighed. However, if there are relevant similarities, it may be open to the trial judge to conclude that the convictions are capable of constituting evidence of propensity and that they ought to be admitted.

(4) If it is open to the judge, as a matter of law, to conclude that the convictions are capable of constituting evidence of propensity and if he exercises his discretion taking due account of the age of the convictions, this court is unlikely to interfere. It will do so only if the exercise of discretion by the judge is outside the broad range which is open to him.'

(Males LJ)

Section 103(2) enacts 'without prejudice to any other way' of proving the bad character of the defendant concerning his propensity to commit offences of the kind with which the defendant is charged. Other methods of proof of misconduct other than by way of conviction include:

- previous acquittals in the exceptional circumstances decided in *R v Z* (see earlier);

- other counts in the indictment where these are cross-admissible: see *DPP v P* (1991) 93 Cr App R 267;
- an offence where the defendant received a caution or was taken into consideration: *R v Nicholson* (1948) 32 Cr App R 98;
- previous, similar acts even though the defendant was not charged: *R v Smith* (1916) 11 Cr App R 229 (the 'brides in the bath' case).

Propensity to be untruthful – s 103(1)(b)

The principle here is that the defendant's bad character is relevant and admissible as part of the prosecution case to prove that the defendant has a propensity to be untruthful. Although this is a departure from the common law, the justification for the provision is that in some trials the accuracy or truth of the defendant's version of events is in itself an important issue. This is likely to be the case where the defendant's explanation of the events in the current trial is not dissimilar to the explanation that was not believed by the jury on a different occasion: see *Jones v DPP* [1962] AC 635.

The explanation for this provision was expressed in the Explanatory Notes accompanying the Act in para 374:

CLAUSE

'Section 103(1)(b) makes it clear that evidence relating to whether the defendant has a propensity to be untruthful (in other words, is not to be regarded as a credible witness) can be admitted. This is intended to enable the admission of *a limited range of evidence such as convictions for perjury or other offences involving deception* . . . as opposed to the wider range of evidence that will be admissible where the defendant puts his character in issue by for example, attacking the character of another person. *Evidence will not be admissible under this head where it is not suggested that the defendant's case is untruthful in any respect*, for example, where the defendant and prosecution are agreed on the facts of the alleged offence and the question is whether all the elements of the offence have been made out.'

In *R v Hanson, Gilmore and Pickering*, Rose LJ explained the operation of this provision thus:

JUDGMENT

'As to propensity to untruthfulness, this, as it seems to us, is not the same as propensity to be dishonest. It is to be assumed, bearing in mind the frequency with which the words honest and dishonest appear in the criminal law, that Parliament deliberately chose the word "untruthful" to convey a different meaning, reflecting a defendant's account of his behaviour, or lies told when committing an offence. Previous convictions, whether for offences of dishonesty or otherwise, are therefore only likely to be capable of showing a propensity to be untruthful where, in the present case, truthfulness is an issue and, in the earlier case, either there was a plea of not guilty and the defendant gave an account, on arrest, in interview, or in evidence, which the jury must have disbelieved, or the way in which the offence was committed shows a propensity for untruthfulness, for example, by the making of false representations.'

In *R v Campbell* [2007] 1 WLR 2798, the Court of Appeal considered how the jury ought to be addressed on the distinction in s 101(1)(d) between propensity to commit offences of the type charged and propensity to be untruthful. The court decided that juries must be given assistance as to the relevance of the defendant's bad character that is tailored to the facts of individual cases. Once the evidence is admissible under s 101 the jury is entitled to consider that it is supportive of any purpose for which it is relevant. It would be unrealistic and unsatisfactory for the judge to direct the jury to have regard to the relevance of the evidence for a specific purpose and to disregard it for other purposes; in other words, it may be confusing and futile to draw a distinction between propensity to commit an offence and propensity to be untruthful. If a jury is aware that the defendant's bad character is relevant to his propensity to commit the offence it is implicit that the jury may conclude that the defendant is less likely to be speaking the truth. Propensity for untruthfulness will not, of itself, go very far in establishing committal of criminal offences. In this case, the defendant was charged with false imprisonment and assault occasioning actual bodily harm. The victim was his ex-girlfriend and alleged that one day he gained entry to her house, kicking the door down and imprisoning her in her bedroom. She managed to escape to a friend's house but the defendant found her, dragged her by her hair, banged her head against a wall and tried to strangle her. At his trial he denied each of these incidents. In addition to the victim's testimony the prosecution was given leave to adduce evidence of two of the defendant's previous convictions under s 101(1)(d) of the CJA 2003. The convictions were for assault occasioning actual bodily harm on a former girlfriend and for battery of his then current girlfriend, in which his conduct had included hair pulling, grabbing by the throat and strangulation. The trial judge directed the jury that the convictions were related to propensity to commit the offences charged and propensity to be untruthful. The defendant was convicted and appealed. The Court of Appeal dismissed the appeal. The defendant's previous convictions for violence to women were of a similar nature to that alleged and gave cogent support to the victim's evidence. Whilst the trial judge followed the Judicial Studies Board specimen directions, these were not tailored to the facts of the case and were unlikely greatly to have assisted the jury, but the convictions were safe.

JUDGMENT

'Once the evidence has been admitted through a gateway it is open to the jury to attach significance to it in any respect in which it is relevant. To direct them only to have regard to it for some purposes and to disregard its relevance in other respects would be to revert to the unsatisfactory practices that prevailed under the old law.

'What should a jury's common sense tell them about the relevance of the fact that a defendant has, or does not have, previous convictions? It may tell them that it is more likely that he committed the offence with which he is charged if he has already demonstrated that he is prepared to break the law, the more so if he has demonstrated a propensity for committing offences of the same nature as that with which he is charged. The extent of the significance to be attached to previous convictions is likely to depend upon a number of variables, including their number, their similarity to the offence charged and how recently they were incurred and the nature of his defence.

'In considering the inference to be drawn from bad character the courts have in the past drawn a distinction between propensity to offend and credibility. This distinction is usually unrealistic. If the jury learn that a defendant has shown a propensity to commit criminal acts they may well at one and the same time conclude that it is more likely that he is guilty and that he is less likely to be telling the truth when he says that he is not.

'The question of whether a defendant has a propensity for being untruthful will not normally be capable of being described as an *important* matter in issue between the defendant and the prosecution. A propensity for untruthfulness will not, of itself, go very far to establishing the commission of a criminal offence. To suggest that a propensity for untruthfulness makes it more likely that a defendant has lied to the jury is not likely to help them. If they apply common sense they will conclude that a defendant who has committed a criminal offence may well be prepared to lie about it, even if he has not shown a propensity for lying whereas a defendant who has not committed the offence charged will be likely to tell the truth, even if he has shown a propensity for telling lies. In short, whether or not a defendant is telling the truth to the jury is likely to depend simply on whether or not he committed the offence charged. The jury should focus on the latter question rather than on whether or not he has a propensity for telling lies.'

(Phillips LJ)

Additional ways of establishing relevance

The matters in issue relating to bad character evidence of the accused within the gateway enacted in s 101(1)(d) are not restricted to those laid down in s 103 (concerning propensity to commit offences and be untruthful). Section 103(1) uses the expression 'include' to refer to propensity evidence. This does not exclude the common law that preceded the introduction of the Criminal Justice Act 2003:

JUDGMENT

'Section 103(1) prefaces s 103(1)(a) and (b) with the word, "include". This indicates that the matters in issue may extend beyond the two areas mentioned in the subsection.'

(Lord Woolf CJ in *R v Highton* [2005] 1 WLR 3472, HL)

In *R v Barrington*, the Court of Appeal decided that, under the pre-2003 law, the evidence need not be in respect of a conviction provided that it exhibited high probative value.

CASE EXAMPLE

R v Barrington [1981] 1 All ER 1132

The charge was indecent assault on three young girls at his mistress's (accomplice) house. The prosecution alleged that he had lured the girls to the house on the pretext that they were required as babysitters. In reality he needed them for his own sexual purposes. Once the girls arrived at the house he showed them pornographic pictures, asked them to pose for photographs in the nude and then indecently assaulted them. The victims gave evidence to this effect. The defendant contended that the evidence was a tissue of lies and each victim had her own private motive for concocting a story. In order to show that the girls were telling the truth, the prosecution applied for and was granted leave to call three other young women to show that they too had been lured to the house, had been shown pornographic pictures and asked to pose in the nude. None of them alleged that they had been assaulted by the defendant. The defendant appealed against his conviction. The Court of Appeal dismissed the appeal on the ground that the evidence had a high degree of probative value in proving the guilt of the defendant:

JUDGMENT

'. . . the judge had taken into account the following six factors which he left to the jury as capable of constituting similar fact evidence. First, the baby sitting proposition. Second, the boasting claims to the girls about his position as a scriptwriter of well-known television programmes and a friend of stars. Third, his mistress and accomplice was described as a professional photographer. Fourth, the evidence of the £200 prize for nude photographs. Fifth, the evidence that all the girls were shown pornographic pictures and sixth, the technique that was employed to try to get the girls to strip eventually for nude photographs . . . That the evidence of the three girls did not include evidence of the commission of offences similar to those with which the appellant was charged does not mean that they are not logically probative in determining the guilt of the appellant. Indeed, we are of the opinion that taken as a whole they are inexplicable on the basis of coincidence and that they are of positive probative value in assisting to determine the truth of the charges, in that they tended to show that he was guilty of the offences with which he was charged.'

(Dunn LJ)

A similar result was reached under the 2003 Act in *R v Saleem* [2007] EWCA Crim 1923. On a charge of assault, the court admitted evidence that the defendant had violent rap lyrics and photographs stored on his computer, not to demonstrate a propensity to commit serious offences of violence, but because such evidence undermined his defence that he had been an innocent bystander with no prior knowledge of the attack. His store of photographic images of victims of violent assaults, accessed a few days before the attack, demonstrated an interest in such images. This supported the prosecution's allegation that the defendant had recorded the attack with the camera attached to his mobile phone. Moreover, the alteration of a number of rap lyrics by the defendant was suggestive of his knowledge of a plan to commit the assault on the defendant's birthday.

In evaluating the quality of the evidence of previous misconduct the judge is required to proceed with considerable caution. He is required to be convinced that the extent of the evidence of misconduct bears a strong likelihood of establishing the guilt of the defendant in respect of the matters charged. He must determine that if the allegations of prior misconduct have not given rise to any previous investigation, the evidence is liable to be stale and incomplete. The likelihood that the defendant may also be prejudiced in trying to dispel it owing to a lapse of time and place may result in such allegations being hard to rebut and the jury may be left thinking that there is no smoke without fire. Where the judge admits such evidence of bad character he is also required to consider how to deal with it in his summing up in a way that is fair and does not give undue prominence to the bad character evidence. Provided that the judge has taken all relevant factors into consideration the appeal courts will be slow in interfering with his decision. These points were advocated by the Court of Appeal in *R v McKenzie* [2008] EWCA Crim 758. In this case, the defendant was charged with causing death by dangerous driving. At a junction the defendant had allegedly driven his van across the line of travel of the victim, a motor cyclist, causing his death. Evidence was given from two credible and independent eyewitnesses who implicated the defendant. In support of the prosecution case the judge allowed two further witnesses to be called, Miss Wakefield and Miss Stokes. Miss Wakefield was the defendant's driving instructor five years before the fatal accident, who testified that the defendant generally drove in an aggressive and over-confident manner. Miss Stokes, the ex-girlfriend of the defendant, testified that approximately three years prior to the accident the defendant had a tendency to drive aggressively and took dangerous chances. The defendant was convicted and appealed. The Court of Appeal dismissed the appeal but decided that the evidence of Miss Wakefield was inadmissible as based on evidence of general bad character and was too remote. Although many judges may have taken a different view of Miss Stokes's evidence they would not have admitted it because of the risk of the trial and the summing up becoming unduly complicated by collateral issues. However, in view of the strong evidence from the eyewitnesses and the summing up to the jury, the conviction was safe:

JUDGMENT

'We do not consider that it can be said to have been wrong in principle or perverse to conclude that the evidence could be regarded as tending to show that the appellant had a propensity to drive in an aggressive and impatient manner which involved taking dangerous risks (so as to fall within s.103) and that the evidence was relevant to an important matter in issue between the parties, i.e. whether the prosecution's version of the facts resulting in the fatal accident was to be accepted (so as to be admissible under s.101(1)(d)). Nor do we think that a court was bound to conclude that the admission of the evidence would have such an adverse effect on the fairness of the proceedings that the court ought not to admit it (under s.101(3)). In reaching these conclusions we are applying the principle established by this court in *Hanson* that it will not interfere with a ruling as to admissibility of evidence of a defendant's bad character unless the judge's judgment as to the capacity of prior events to establish propensity is plainly wrong or discretion has been exercised unreasonably in the *Wednesbury* sense.

'Without attempting to be definitive, but simply by way of a general indication, on the facts of this case the points which needed to be covered were these. The prosecution had called evidence about his alleged bad driving on previous occasions in order to try to establish that he was a person who characteristically took dangerous risks, because it was the prosecution's case that the fatal accident was caused by him taking a dangerous risk, and the evidence that he did so was more likely to be correct if such behaviour was characteristic of him. But the jury had to be very cautious before using evidence about his driving on other occasions in deciding whether he was guilty of the offence charged.'

(Toulson LJ)

Danger of jury distraction

The trial judge is duty bound to guard against the danger of jury distraction on multiple collateral issues during the trial and to enforce a strict case management regime. Accordingly, the enforcement of a fair set of ground rules will be a factor to take into consideration in deciding on whether to permit the prosecution to adduce evidence of the defendant's bad character. In *R v O'Dowd* [2009] EWCA Crim 905, the Court of Appeal issued a strong message of case management for the judge to consider in determining whether the defendant's prior misconduct may be adduced as prosecution evidence. The danger of collateral or satellite issues may have the tendency, not only to prolong the trial, but also to complicate the issues that may be put before the jury. In this case the defendant was charged with rape, sexual assault, false imprisonment and threats to kill. Following a pre-trial hearing the Crown was given permission under s 101(1)(d) of the Act to introduce bad character evidence concerning three previous allegations of rape under similar circumstances. The allegations resulted in a conviction (about seventeen years old), acquittal and a stay of proceedings. These allegations were denied by the defendant. The total length of the trial was six-and-a-half months due to a variety of factors not related to the prosecution. The defendant was convicted and appealed. The Court of Appeal allowed the appeal and quashed the conviction on the ground that the trial judge had erred in admitting evidence of the bad character of the defendant. He had not adequately considered the cumulative effect of the introduction of the three separate contested issues on the overall length of the trial and on the jury.

JUDGMENT

'There was only a single conviction. In the light of what this court stated in *Hanson* that it is normally difficult to show propensity from a single conviction in itself. It is only where the conviction shows a tendency to unusual behaviour or where its circumstances demonstrate probative force in relation to the offence charged that a single conviction may show propensity.'

'It was known at the time the Crown's application to adduce the bad character evidence was first considered that all the facts of the allegations by the three women were contested. Accordingly, particularly in the case of the allegations that did not result in a conviction, proof of the previous alleged misconduct would require the trial of three collateral or satellite issues as part of the trial of the applicant for the offences with which he was charged.

'It is incumbent upon a judge considering the application to try to project forward to see the problems which might later arise in the trial as a result of the disputed bad character evidence being admitted before ruling on the application. This is because, once the evidence is admitted, unless it has been contaminated (and s.107 applies) the question is of its weight. The judge will then only have limited remedies open to deal with problems that arise thereafter.

'While recognising the difficult task that the judge had in this case, we have concluded that he fell into error in his consideration of the s.101(3) matters. This is because he did not or did not adequately consider the cumulative effect of the introduction of three separate contested issues into the trial on its overall length and on the jury, or how the evidence might be timetabled or truncated. The ruling that evidence of the three bad character allegations could be adduced led to an estimate that the trial would last for four months. That in itself should have rung warning bells to the judge when undertaking the balancing process under s.101(3), especially since this was a trial of a single defendant concerning a single complainant.'

(Beatson J)

Directions by the judge

The judge is required to direct the jury as to the use it may make of the bad character of the defendant. The issues to be included in a direction were considered by the Court of Appeal in *R v Hanson, Gilmore and Pickering*, by Rose LJ. These issues are:

1. The judge should warn the jury against placing undue reliance on previous convictions and/or prior misconduct.
2. The jury should not conclude that the defendant was guilty or untruthful merely because he had the convictions and/or prior misconduct.
3. Although the convictions and/or misconduct might show propensity, that did not mean that the defendant committed the offences of being untruthful in respect of the current charge.
4. Whether the convictions and/or misconduct in fact show a propensity was for the jury to decide.
5. The jury is required to take into account what the defendant said about his previous convictions and/or misconduct.
6. Propensity may be only one relevant factor and the jury should assess its significance in the light of all the other evidence in the case.

12.4.5 Gateway (e) – s 101(1)(e) – 'important matter in issue between the defendant and the co-defendant'

The policy regarding the admissibility of bad character evidence of an accused under gateway (e) is that it has 'substantial probative value' in respect of an 'important matter' in issue between the defendant and the 'co-defendant'. The expression 'probative value' is determined on the assumption that *prima facie* the evidence is true (see s 109(1)) and an 'important matter' is defined in s 112(1) as a matter of substantial importance in the case. Thus, trivial or insignificant issues would not activate the subsection. The expression 'co-defendant' is defined in s 112(1) as a person charged In the same proceedings as the defendant. The co-defendant need not be charged with the same offence but is required to be jointly tried on the same indictment. In this respect the judge retains a discretion to decide whether the indictment ought to be severed; the test was considered in *Ludlow v MPC* [1970] 2 WLR 521. The House of Lords decided that for counts to be joined on an indictment, in addition to expediency, a loose nexus between the offences sufficient to constitute a series of offences would be sufficient.

The underlying issue under this gateway is that the defendant alleges that the co-defendant's bad character has substantial probative value in respect of an important matter in issue between the defendant and the co-defendant. When may this arise? There are two occasions when this gateway may be activated.

- The first is when the bad character of the co-defendant has *substantial probative value* to establish that he (the co-defendant) is more likely, as compared with the defendant, to have committed the offence, i.e. propensity to commit offences. This may be treated as an *important matter in issue between himself and the co-defendant*. The important matter in issue is considered in the context of the case as a whole. It involves the defendant running a 'cut-throat' defence, blaming the co-defendant for the commission of the crime; for example on a charge of murder committed after a violent struggle, the defendant, A, alleges that his co-defendant, B, has several convictions for violent assault and is more likely to have committed the offence on his own.

- The second occasion of evidence of *substantial probative value* on an *important matter in issue* between the defendant and the co-defendant involves the credibility of the co-defendant, i.e. the bad character of the co-defendant relates to his *propensity to be untruthful* and the co-defendant has attempted to *undermine the nature or conduct of the defence* of the defendant: see s 104(1). For example, on a charge of burglary the defendant (A) raises the defence of duress held out by the co-defendant (B). The co-defendant (B) alleges that the defendant (A) is a liar and that B did not make any threats to A. A alleges that B has a number of previous convictions for dishonesty, perjury and assault.

In addition, this gateway may only be utilised by the defendant and not by the prosecution, and the methods of raising the issue are through testimony of the co-defendant or a witness cross-examined by the co-defendant: see s 104(2).

Section 104(2) enacts:

Subject to the requirements laid down in s 101(1)(e), the defendant's bad

SECTION

'Only evidence –

(a) which is to be (or has been) adduced by the co-defendant, or
(b) which a witness is to be invited to give (or has given) in cross-examination by the co-defendant, is admissible under s 101(1)(e).'

character evidence may take the form of his previous convictions or allegations of reprehensible behaviour where the co-defendant and/or his witness testifies to this effect, or through cross-examination by the co-defendant. The effect of the evidence may be to establish the guilt of the defendant or to establish the defendant's propensity for untruthfulness. In *R v Musone* [2007] EWCA Crim 1237, two inmates were charged with the murder, by stabbing, of a third prisoner. Each defendant ran 'cut-throat' defences blaming the other. One of the defendants was permitted to adduce evidence of a conversation with the other defendant, who indicated that he had committed an earlier murder. The purpose was to submit that he was more likely to have committed the murder with which they were charged. The court decided that the evidence had substantive probative value with regard to an important matter in issue between the two defendants and was admissible under s 101(1)(e).

The decision of the Privy Council in *Lowery v R* [1974] AC 85, although a pre-2003 decision, illustrates how the two tests for admissibility under this gateway may be satisfied. K's testimony that L was aggressive, sadistic and that he (K) was in fear of L was relevant to the issue of propensity to commit the offence. The italicised words, concerning the testimony of Professor Cox (below) indicate that the test laid down in s 104(1) – propensity to be untruthful – may also be satisfied today.

CASE EXAMPLE

Lowery v R [1974] AC 85

Two defendants (L and K) were charged with a vicious and sadistic murder. It was clear from the evidence that only one of them committed the crime. Each blamed the other for the commission of the crime. L testified to the effect that he was not the sort of man to commit such a brutal crime and claimed that he had tried his best to stop K from committing the crime. K denied committing the offence and alleged that at the time he was under the influence of drugs and incapable of carrying out the deed or preventing L from committing the offence. K was allowed to call a psychologist to testify that, having examined the two defendants, K was immature and easily led, but L was aggressive and sadistic. His view was that K was less likely to have committed the offence. L was convicted and appealed. The Privy Council dismissed the appeal and decided that, since the issue was which one of the defendants committed the crime, K was entitled to call rebutting evidence to determine that L was more likely to have committed the offence:

JUDGMENT

'Lowery and King were each asserting that the other was the completely dominating person at the time Rosalyn Nolte was killed: each claimed to have been in fear of the other. In these circumstances it was most relevant for King to be able to show, if he could, that Lowery had a personality marked by aggressiveness, whereas he, King, had a personality which suggested that he would be led and dominated by someone who was dominant and aggressive. In support of King's case, *the evidence of Professor Cox was relevant if it tended to show that the version of the facts put forward by King was more probable than put forward by Lowery*. Not only, however, was the evidence which King called relevant to this case: its admissibility was placed beyond doubt by the whole substance of Lowery's case. Not only did Lowery assert that the killing was done by King and not only did he say that he had been in fear of King, but . . . he set himself up as one who had no motive whatsoever in killing the girl and as one who would not have been interested in the sort of behaviour manifested by the killer. While ascribing the sole responsibility to King he was also in effect saying that he himself was not the sort of man to have committed the offence. The only question now arising is whether in the special circumstances above referred to, it was open to King in defending himself to call Professor Cox to give the evidence that he gave. The evidence was relevant to and necessary for this case which involved negativing what Lowery had said and put forward: in their Lordships' view . . . the evidence was admissible.'

(Lord Morris)

Section 109(1) of the 2003 Act declares that 'substantial probative value' is measured on the assumption that that the evidence is true except where by reference to all the circumstances 'no court or jury could reasonably find it to be true' (s 109(2)). The word 'substantial' is taken to mean that the evidence has something more than trivial probative value, but it need not necessarily achieve conclusive probative value. The Law Commission, in its Report 'Evidence of Bad Character in Criminal Proceedings' (2001) Law Com No 273, adopted the term 'substantial probative value' to describe a form of enhanced relevance to prove or disprove a fact in issue. The purpose was to avoid the risk of unfairness to the co-defendant by having prejudicial evidence being put to the court for no reason other than that it may be of some marginal relevance, or relevant to some marginal issue. In addition, the evidence admitted on behalf of the defendant is required to satisfy the test of being an 'important matter in issue between the defendant and the co-defendant'. The judge is required to make an assessment as to whether the co-defendant's bad character is 'a matter of substantial importance in the context of the case as a whole' (see s 112(1)). The issue may well be propensity to commit the offence or propensity to be untruthful. This assessment by the judge is fact-sensitive and is taken in conjunction with other probative evidence that is directed to the issue. In *R v Phillips* [2012] 1 Cr App R 25 the point was expressed in the following manner:

JUDGMENT

'The important matter in issue in a "cut-throat" case may be the issue whether either or both defendants committed the offence and, accordingly, whether one is falsely (expressly or by implication) blaming the other. The evidence which the defendant wishes to deploy may be probative in the sense that it tends towards establishing the co-accused's propensity for similar criminal behaviour or for untruthfulness. The judge is required to evaluate the capacity of the evidence to establish the relevant propensity. Where there is already before the jury evidence which has the same probative effect, the judge is entitled to assess whether further evidence has substantial probative value in relation to the same issue. A judgment may be required as to whether, in the light of more probative evidence already before the jury the further disputed evidence has substantial probative force. It is our judgment that the judge is not required, when assessing whether the probative value of the evidence is substantial, to examine each piece of evidence going to the same effect in isolation from the rest of the evidence . . . So, where a defendant seeks to adduce evidence of his co-accused's behaviour on several other occasions, the judge is entitled to assess the probative value of the evidence in respect of each incident in the context of the other evidence which has been admitted or which the judge proposes to admit.'

(Pitchford LJ)

Evidence of propensity to commit the offence charged under s 101(1)(e)

Where (1) the important issue between the defendant and the co-defendant is which one of them committed the offence charged, the defendant may establish, (2) through evidence led by the defendant or cross-examination of prosecution witnesses, that the co-defendant's bad character has (3) substantial probative value in establishing that he is more likely to have committed the offence. In these circumstances, s 101(1)(e) admits the propensity evidence of commission of the offence irrespective of the nature of his defence, unlike propensity to establish untruthfulness (see below). In short, this test is outside s 104 of the Act.

An example of the way that s 101(1)(e) may operate may be gleaned by reference to a pre-2003 case, *R v Randall* [2003] UKHL 69. It is submitted that the result may be the same today. In this case the defendant and his co-defendant were jointly charged with murder. The prosecution case was that they either jointly or independently attacked and killed the victim. Each testified and blamed the other. Each had previous convictions and their respective counsel cross-examined each other on their bad character. The defendant had relatively minor convictions for driving offence and disorderly behaviour, whereas the co-defendant had more serious convictions for robbery and aggravated burglary. The trial judge directed the jury to the effect that the bad character evidence was relevant only to the credibility of the defendants and the co-defendant's convictions were irrelevant to the likelihood of him attacking the victim. The jury convicted the defendant for manslaughter and acquitted the co-defendant. The Court of Appeal allowed the defendant's appeal and the prosecution's appeal to the House of Lords was dismissed on the ground of a misdirection by the judge. The propensity evidence as to violent crimes was relevant to the facts in issue. Lord Steyn demonstrated the relevance of propensity evidence of disposition in the following extract:

JUDGMENT

'Postulate a joint trial involving two accused arising from an assault committed in a pub. Assume it to be clear that one of the two men committed the assault. The one man has a long list of previous convictions involving assaults in pubs. It shows him to be prone to fighting when he had consumed alcohol. The other man has an unblemished record. Relying on experience and common sense one may rhetorically ask why the propensity to violence of one man should not be deployed by the other man as part of his defence that he did not commit the assault. Surely such evidence is capable, depending on the jury's assessment of all the evidence, of making it more probable that the man with the violent disposition when he had consumed alcohol committed the assault. To rule that the jury may use the convictions in regard to his credibility but that convictions revealing his propensity to violence must otherwise be ignored is to ask the jury to put to one side their common sense and experience. It would be curious if the law compelled such an unrealistic result.'

(Lord Steyn)

The operation of s 101(1)(e) was considered by the Court of Appeal in *R v Phillips (Paul)* [2012] 1 Cr App R 25. In this case the accused and co-accused were charged on several counts with conspiracy to cheat the Revenue by paying a workforce without the deduction of tax and National Insurance and failing to account for tax and National Insurance. Both parties accepted that a fraud had been perpetrated but each denied responsibility. At the trial the defendant sought to adduce evidence of his co-defendant's (Thomas Scragg) bad character. This took the form of (a) previous convictions for conspiracy to defraud and (b) threatening behaviour, and (c) previous investigations implicating him in Revenue fraud. This evidence related to the period of the conspiracy charges. In addition the defendant wanted to adduce evidence of the co-defendant's implication in CIS fraud, for the post-indictment period. The trial judge only admitted the convictions for conspiracy to defraud and refused to admit the other evidence. On conviction the defendant appealed. The Court of Appeal dismissed the appeal, but decided that, in determining whether the probative value was substantial, the trial judge was not required to consider each piece of evidence in isolation. The evidence in (c) above had substantial probative value and ought to have been admitted, but the judge was correct in refusing to admit the other evidence. Further, once the statutory criteria had been satisfied the judge does not have a discretion to exclude the evidence:

JUDGMENT

'It is our judgment that the judge is not required, when assessing whether the probative value of the evidence is substantial, to examine each piece of evidence going to the same effect in isolation from the rest of the evidence. What evidence is of substantial probative value should be judged in a fact-sensitive manner in the context of the trial as it appears at the time the application is made. So, where a defendant seeks to adduce evidence of his co-accused's behaviour on several other occasions, the judge is entitled to assess the probative value of the evidence in respect of each incident in the context of the other evidence which has been admitted or which the judge proposes to admit.

'The main issues between the defendants at trial were whether the appellant was recruited by Thomas Scragg to perpetuate an existing fraud and, if so, whether he was recruited as an innocent front man. These were issues of substantial importance in the context of the case as a whole. It seems to us, as it did to the judge, that the evidence undoubtedly amounted to evidence of substantial probative value in relation to the issue whether Scragg was, in the months preceding the present fraud, engaged with others, including his nephew Paul, in the fraudulent use of a CIS6 certificate.'

(Pitchford LJ)

In *R v Land* [2006] EWCA Crim 2856, the Court of Appeal decided that, on charges of conspiracy to pervert the course of justice and misconduct in a public office, the co-defendant's bad character for violence was not substantially probative in relation to the defendant's defence of duress. The defendant, a CPS prosecutor, had allegedly unlawfully supplied his co-defendant with sensitive information. The defendant's application for leave to adduce the co-defendant's previous convictions and bad character was rejected and he was convicted. On appeal the Court of Appeal dismissed the appeal and decided that the statutory criteria laid down in s 101(1)(e) were not satisfied. In the context of the case as a whole the evidence was not substantially probative in relation to an important matter in issue, namely, duress. There was other material to support the defendant's case that the co-defendant was violent and, in any event, the evidence supporting duress was very weak.

In *R v Apabhai* [2011] EWCA Crim 917, the Court of Appeal decided that the exception to the definition of bad character laid down in s 98(b) of the Act (see Chapter 11) is not restricted to evidence of misconduct by the police and prosecuting authorities. The broad s 98(b) is capable of extending to the conduct of witnesses or co-defendants 'connected with' the prosecution or investigation of the offence. On this basis the ordinary test of relevance will apply and the gateways in admitting character evidence may not be activated. As an alternative, a defendant is entitled to establish that the co-defendant's bad character may be admissible under s 101(1)(e). In this case the defendant and co-defendant were charged with conspiracy to cheat the Revenue. The prosecution alleged that the defendants had participated in a large VAT fraud. The defendant complained to the police that his co-defendant tried to blackmail him into paying £125,000 to the co-defendant. The defendant refused, and he alleged that this furnished the motive for implicating the defendant. At the trial the defendant wanted to cross-examine the co-defendant about the blackmail allegation under s 98(b) but the judge refused. On conviction the defendant appealed. The Court of Appeal dismissed the appeal as the conviction was safe, but decided that the evidence was admissible under s 98(b). Alternatively, the evidence was capable of falling within s 101(1)(e). The defendant was willing to testify about the blackmail incident and, if he was able to convince the jury about the incident, this would have been more than of trivial probative value:

JUDGMENT

'In our view the judge was entitled to find that the evidence did fall within the scope of section 98(b). It can be said that the evidence is "connected with" the prosecution or investigation of the offence. There is no doubt that, prior to the 2003 Act, evidence of intimidation or blackmail by a co-accused would be admitted, notwithstanding that it might reveal bad character of, and perhaps criminal conduct by, that defendant. The evidence in this case was not sought to be admitted specifically because it was evidence of bad character, raising in a general way issues of credibility or propensity, but because in the particular context surrounding the alleged misconduct, and in particular the fact that the appellant then went to the police to complain about the conduct, it casts light in a more immediate way on particular aspects of the case as being presented to the jury and, in particular, the reliability of the evidence of Mr Amani [the co-defendant]. The fact that the evidence demonstrates bad character is not the central feature justifying its admission. Its principal purpose is to demonstrate a motive for Amani putting the appellant in the frame, and the fact that the evidence also demonstrates bad character is incidental.

'It would be strange if the effect of the 2003 Act, which was intended to allow evidence of bad character to be admitted more readily than had formerly been the case, was to restrict the admissibility of bad character in these circumstances unless it was able to pass through gateway (e).

'We accept that a mere assertion cannot be evidence of bad character, but we agree with Mr Blaxland [the counsel for the prosecution] that that is not the situation here. Mr Apabhai is not simply asserting; he also indicated, at least by inference, that he was willing to give evidence about this particular incident. Indeed, he said there were witnesses to the incident. Whether they might have been called or not had this evidence been allowed to be adduced, we are not in a position to say."

(Elias LJ)

On a separate point an issue that may arise concerns the effect of the admissibility of the bad character evidence against the co-defendant and the direction of the judge. On the assumption that the bad character evidence is admissible by the defendant against the co-defendant under s 101(1)(e) as evidence of the propensity to commit the offence, the question that may arise is whether the prosecution may benefit from this cross-examination in order to establish guilt of the offence. Although the prosecution is not entitled to utilise the gateway under s 101(1)(e), once the evidence is admitted in the trial, Lord Steyn in *R v Randall* (2003) considered that in the interests of consistency and to avoid legal gymnastics by the jury, the direction by the judge may indicate that the evidence is related to the guilt of the co-defendant and therefore support the prosecution's case against the co-defendant:

JUDGMENT

'For the avoidance of doubt I would further add that in my view where evidence of propensity of a co-accused is relevant to a fact in issue between the Crown and the other accused it is not necessary for a trial judge to direct the jury to ignore the evidence in considering the case against the co-accused. Justice does not require that such a direction be given. Moreover, such a direction would needlessly perplex juries.'

(Lord Steyn)

Propensity to be untruthful under s 101(1)(e)

Section 101(1)(e) permits the co-defendant to introduce bad character evidence of the defendant concerning his credibility if the evidence has *substantial probative value* and relates to an *important matter in issue* between the defendant and the co-defendant. This is qualified by s 104(1) where the evidence is relevant to the defendant's *propensity to be untruthful* and the nature or conduct of the defendant's defence is such as to *undermine* the co-defendant's defence.

Section 104(1) enacts as follows:

SECTION

'Evidence which is relevant to the question whether the defendant has a *propensity to be untruthful* is admissible on that basis under section 101(1)(e) only if the nature or conduct of his defence is such as to *undermine the co-defendant's defence.*'

The expression 'undermine' has not been defined by statute, but the expression had been referred to under the pre-2003 law in interpreting s 1(3)(iii) of the Criminal Evidence Act 1898. The expression 'giving evidence against' the co-defendant in s 1(3)(iii) of the 1898 Act means evidence 'which supports the prosecution's case in a material respect or undermines the defence of the co-accused'. This test was applied objectively and not simply subjectively in accordance with a hostile intent, for it was the effect of the evidence upon the minds of the jury that matters and not the state of mind of the defendant: see *Murdoch v Taylor* [1965] AC 574. However, s 104(1) deals only with undermining the co-defendant's defence. If, therefore, the evidence of the defendant only supports the prosecution's case without undermining the co-defendant's defence the section is not activated. The pre-2003 test was whether the defence of the co-defendant, X, would, if believed, leave the defendant without an effective defence or increase the risks of the defendant being found guilty of the offence. A mere denial by the co-defendant, X, may be insufficient to have this effect. In *R v Varley* (1982) 75 Cr App R 242, the defendant was jointly charged with the co-defendant, X, on two counts of robbery and one count of possession of a firearm at the time of the robbery. Both defendants had previous convictions. At the trial, X said that they had both taken part in the robbery but that he acted under duress imposed by the defendant. The defendant testified to the effect that he was not there at all and that X was lying. X's evidence was clearly against the defendant and X was cross-examined by the defendant's counsel. The judge allowed the defendant to be cross-examined as to his previous convictions under s 1(3)(iii). The defendant was convicted and appealed. The court dismissed his appeal and decided that the defendant had given evidence against the co-defendant on the ground that, if the defendant's evidence was believed, X would have been left as a participant on his own volition and not acting under duress. Perhaps the provision under the 2003 Act may be interpreted in the same way as before the passing of the 2003 Act.

The Court of Appeal in *R v Lawson* [2007] 1 Cr App R 11 decided that the expression 'propensity to be untruthful' under s 104(1) is to be construed differently from a similar expression used in s 103(1)(b) in qualifying the s 101(1)(d) gateway – important matter in issue between the defendant and the prosecution. Section 103(1)(b) is required to be construed cautiously so as not to offend the overriding principle of fairness in the proceedings: see earlier. As between the prosecution and the defendant, the judge is entitled to exercise his discretion in the interests of fairness and disallow bad character evidence on an application by the prosecution. This may be the case where there is a serious risk that the jury may incorrectly construe the evidence as going towards propensity to commit the offence. On the other hand, once the criteria for admissibility are satisfied under s 101(1)(e), the bad character evidence is admissible and the judge does not retain a discretion to exclude the same:

JUDGMENT

'Particular attention has to be paid if the evidence is suggested to be relevant only to truthfulness or credit, to the danger that the jury may even subconsciously and despite careful direction be influenced by the evidence on the question of propensity to offend and thus directly as to guilt. Whether upon examination of the test of relevance under gateway (d), or on application of the discretion under section 101(iii), it remains essential that a cautious test of admissibility should be applied to applications made by the Crown in relation to the character of the defendant who is on trial. But it remains nevertheless wholly rational that the degree of caution which is applied to a Crown application against a defendant who is on trial when considering relevance or discretion should not be applied when what is at stake is a defendant's right to deploy relevant material to defend himself against a criminal charge. It is quite apparent from the shape of this Act that although it uses the expression "propensity to be untruthful" in both section 103(1)(b) in relation to prosecution applications and in section 104(1) in relation to applications by co-defendants, it addresses the various different occasions on which bad character may arguably be admissible separately and provides a different framework of rules for each situation.'

(Hughes LJ)

The material elements underlying the application under s 101(1)(e) are whether the bad character of the defendant has substantive probative value concerning an important matter between him and the co-defendant to such an extent that his propensity to be untruthful undermines the co-defendant's defence. Although there is an element of overlap concerning these issues the trial judge is required to consider these issues separately. In addition, it must be borne in mind that not necessarily all the defendant's convictions or bad character may be the subject of cross-examination by the co-defendant but only those aspects that impact on the defendant's propensity to be untruthful such as conduct that involves an element of deception, perjury and the like. But in *R v Lawson* (2007) the court decided that a conviction of L for violence is capable of showing that he was unscrupulous and unreliable. In *R v Lawson* [2007] 1 Cr App R 11, the Court of Appeal decided that material inconsistencies between the defences of the defendant and co-defendant entitled the co-defendant to adduce evidence of the defendant's bad character in order to establish the defendant's credibility as to truthfulness, provided that the evidence had substantive probative value. In this case, three defendants were charged with manslaughter by drowning. The victim was a forty-four-year-old mentally handicapped man with a mental age of an eight-year-old. He wandered onto a lakeside pontoon where he sat with his feet in the water. The three defendants, Q, L and K, approached him and Q pushed him into the lake causing his death. Q pleaded guilty but L and K pleaded not guilty and alleged that they did not encourage Q to push the victim into the water. They raised defences incriminating each other as to their intentions. K was a person of good character but, between the date of the charge and the trial, L had been convicted of unlawful wounding. Counsel for K cross-examined L as to his previous conviction and L was convicted and appealed *inter alia* on the ground that the judge had erred in allowing K to cross-examine L on his bad character. The Court of Appeal dismissed the appeal and decided that an important issue in the trial was to determine who was telling the truth. The evidence given by L undermined the defence of K (s 104(1) of the Criminal Justice Act 2003) and had substantial probative value in relation to the issue of L's truthfulness (s 101(1)(e)):

JUDGMENT

'It is apparent that there is an element of overlap between the questions whether there arose an important matter in issue between the defendants, whether the defence of Lawson undermined that of King and whether the proposed evidence had substantial probative value. This, as it seems to us, will often be the case but it remains necessary for the questions to be addressed seriatim.

'The evidence given by Lawson did undermine King's defence. It was an important part of King's defence that he had never contemplated touching Watts, that he had only gone near out of curiosity, that he had done no more than offer him the kindness of a cigarette and that it was Lawson who had spoken of pushing him in whilst he, King, was simply an innocent bystander. If accepted, Lawson's evidence, however qualified, that King had made the remark alleged undermined that defence. We are satisfied that it did not cease to undermine it for either of the two reasons which we have previously analysed.'

(Hughes LJ)

No discretion to exclude bad character evidence under gateway (e)

Prior to the introduction of the 2003 Act, the judge did not have a discretion to exclude 'evidence given against' the co-defendant under s 1(3)(iii) of the Criminal Evidence Act 1898, the reason being that the court has always been reluctant to interfere with a case presented by the defendant, including the co-defendant. In short, fairness to one defendant may be perceived as unfairness to another defendant in the same trial:

JUDGMENT

'. . . a trial judge has no discretion whether to allow an accused person to be cross-examined as to his past criminal offences once he has given evidence against his co-accused. [Section 1(3)] in terms confers no such discretion and in my opinion, none can be implied.'

(Lord Donovan in *Murdoch v Taylor* [1965] AC 574)

Likewise, in *R v Randall* [2004] 1 Cr App R 375, Lord Steyn repeated the view of Lord Donovan:

JUDGMENT

'The discretionary power to exclude relevant evidence which is tendered by the prosecution if its prejudicial effect outweighs its probative value, does not apply to the position as between co-accused. In a joint criminal trial a judge has no discretionary power at the request of one accused to exclude relevant evidence tending to support the defence of another.'

Under similar provisions enacted in s 101(1)(e) of the Criminal Justice Act 2003, the courts have affirmed that there is no judicial discretion to prevent one defendant from adducing evidence of the co-defendant's bad character whenever such evidence has substantial probative value:

JUDGMENT

'Once evidence of a defendant's bad character is admissible under s 101(1)(e) the section confers no express power on a court to exclude such evidence on grounds of unfairness, let alone imposing any obligation to do so. Nor is there any power under s 78(1) of the Police and Criminal Evidence Act 1984 to exclude the evidence since it is not evidence on which the prosecution propose to rely. Admissibility under s 101(1)(e) depends solely on the quality of the evidence. The judge had no power under that section to exclude the evidence on the grounds of unfairness.'

(Moses LJ in *R v Musone* [2007] 2 Cr App R 29)

Similarly in *R v Phillips (Paul)* [2012] 1 Cr App R 25 (see earlier), Pitchford LJ reiterated the underlying limitation to the effect that once the criteria for admissibility under s 101(1)(e) has been met, the judge has no discretion to disallow the cross-examination by the defendant.

JUDGMENT

'It is settled that, while the statutory criteria must be met to their full effect, once they are met there is no discretion under s.101(3) or (4) or any other statutory provision, such as s.78 of the Police and Criminal Evidence Act 1984 (because the application is made by a defendant and not the prosecution), to exclude it on the grounds of unfair prejudice or some other unfairness. The underlying assumption is that if the statutory test of enhanced probative value upon a matter of substantial importance is met the scope for unfairness is removed.'

(Pitchford LJ)

12.4.6 Gateway (f) – s 101(1)(f) – 'correct a false impression given by the defendant'

This provision was introduced by s 101(1)(f) of the Criminal Justice Act 2003 with the object of admitting the bad character evidence of the defendant in order to correct a false impression given by the defendant. Thus, it is the defendant's action in creating a false impression that entitles the prosecution to adduce the bad character evidence. There is some similarity between this provision and the repealed s 1(3)(ii) of the Criminal Evidence Act 1898 that involved the defendant putting his character in issue and thereby subjecting him to cross-examination on his bad character. Of course, s 101(1)(f) is much broader than its predecessor in that the admissibility of bad character evidence under the 2003 Act is not restricted to the defendant testifying at the trial.

Modes of creating a false impression

Section 105(1) defines when the defendant may create a false impression. This would be the position if the defendant is:

SECTION

'(a) . . . responsible for the making of an express or implied assertion which is apt to give the court or jury a false or misleading impression.'

Only the prosecution is entitled to utilise this gateway in order to admit evidence of the defendant's bad character: see s 105(7). Thus, in joint trials with more than one defendant and where a co-defendant has given evidence creating a false or misleading impression, the defendant is not entitled to adduce bad character evidence under s 101(1)(f), but may do so if the circumstances warrant the admissibility of such evidence under s 101(1)(e): see earlier.

An express assertion that is false may be made by the defendant if he alleges that he is a man of 'good character' when in reality there are several previous convictions recorded against the defendant: see *R v Ullah* [2006] EWCA Crim 2003. Likewise, in *R v Spartley* [2007] EWCA Crim 1789, on charges of conspiracy to import a large quantity of ecstasy tablets and possession of cannabis with intent to supply, the accused pleaded not guilty and in his police interview had asserted that he had never been in trouble with the police and knew nothing about the ecstasy or the cannabis found at his house. Evidence was admissible under s 101(1)(f) of a record of an interview by the defendant with Dutch police some seven years earlier in which he admitted that he had smuggled 35 kg of cannabis from Holland to Spain. Moreover, the subsection endorses 'implied assertions' made by the defendant. This will include assertions made from the defendant's conduct or behaviour to the extent that it may be implied that the defendant is a person of good character. In this respect, s 105(4) declares that:

SECTION

'where . . . a defendant, by means of his conduct (other than the giving of evidence) in the proceedings, is seeking to give the court or jury an impression about himself that is false or misleading, the court may, if it appears just to do so, treat the defendant as being responsible for the making of an assertion which is apt to give that impression.'

Section 105(5) declares that:

SECTION

'conduct includes appearance or dress'.

Illustrations of this principle include on a charge for theft an assertion by the defendant that in the past he had restored lost property to its owners: see *R v Samuel* (1956) 40 Cr App R 8. In *R v Robinson* [2001] Crim LR 478, the Court of Appeal doubted whether the defendant's holding of a copy of the Bible in his hands whilst testifying amounted to an assertion of good character. Today, it is arguable that it is the impression that is required to be misleading, not the assertion, and Mr Robinson may reasonably be treated as attempting to convey the image of an honest and truthful individual whilst testifying. At the same time, it is obvious that some limit will be imposed on this provision, for it would be unjust for the judge to allow in bad character evidence on the ground that the defendant had recently changed his appearance by growing a beard or shaving his head at the time of the trial.

In effect, the following methods have been envisaged by the provisions for making assertions, by or on behalf of the defendant:

- the testimony of the defendant: s 105(2)(a);
- an assertion made on behalf of the defendant who does not testify: s 105(2)(a);
- an assertion made by the defendant on being questioned under caution, before charge and admitted in court: s 105(2)(b)(i);
- an assertion made by the defendant on being charged with the offence or officially informed that he might be prosecuted and admitted in court: s 105(2)(b)(ii);
- an assertion made by a witness called by the defendant: s 105(2)(c);
- in response to any answer given by any witness in cross-examination on behalf of the defendant and intended to elicit the assertion: s 105(2)(d);
- the assertion was made by any person out of court and endorsed and admitted by the defendant: s 105(2)(e).

Withdrawal of assertion

Section 105(3) of the 2003 Act enacts that a defendant may be allowed to 'withdraw or disassociate' himself from an assertion with the effect that he will not be treated as making the assertion. There are a number of issues with this provision: first, whether the withdrawal/disassociation will be sufficiently clear to convince the court that the defendant has made a genuine withdrawal; second, what constitutes the court for these purposes – the judge or the judge and jury? It is not clear from the Act what method(s) of withdrawal or disassociation will be effective for this purpose. At the same time, the defendant is a competent but not compellable witness for himself; it would be against his constitutional rights to require him to testify in order to disassociate himself from an assertion. It would appear that the defendant's legal representative may be entitled to communicate the defendant's withdrawal from the assertion in the presence of the judge on a *voir dire*. Indeed, s 105(3) permits a partial withdrawal and to that extent is treated as not making an assertion. In this respect it is important that the court is clear as to the assertions that are still being made by the defendant. In *R v Renda* [2006] 1 WLR 2948, Judge LJ issued a note of caution thus:

JUDGMENT

'There is a significant difference between the defendant who makes a specific and positive decision to correct a false impression for which he is responsible, or to disassociate himself from false impressions conveyed by the assertions of others, and the defendant who in the process of cross-examination is obliged to concede that he has been misleading the jury. A concession extracted in cross-examination that the defendant was not telling the truth in part of his examination-in-chief will not normally amount to a withdrawal or disassociation from the original assertion for the purposes of section 105(3).'

Rebuttal evidence

Section 105(6) enacts that the rebutting evidence may not be excessive but is restricted to the specific issue of rebutting the assertion creating the false impression. Section 105(6) declares as follows:

SECTION

'Evidence is admissible under section 101(1)(f) only if it goes no further than is necessary to correct the false impression.'

Thus, the prosecution is only entitled to adduce evidence of the defendant's misconduct that has probative value in correcting the false impression for which the defendant was responsible.

As distinct from the pre-2003 law (see *R v Winfield* [1939] 4 All ER 164), bad character evidence is not indivisible but is required to deal with the specific assertion for which the defendant is responsible. This involves a specific test of relevance in that the evidence deals with only the assertion that creates the false impression. This may require a certain amount of editing of the evidence by the judge.

In addition, s 105(1)(b) declares that the rebutting evidence is required to be of probative value. Thus, the quality of the evidence will be determined by the judge. Section 105(1)(b) enacts as follows:

SECTION

'Evidence to correct such an impression is evidence which has probative value in correcting it.'

Discretion to exclude

Since the prosecution alone is allowed to adduce rebutting evidence to correct a false impression created by the defendant, the judge has a discretion under s 78 of the Police and Criminal Evidence Act 1984 to refuse to admit evidence that would otherwise have 'an adverse effect on the fairness of the trial'. This approach is encouraged under s 112(3)(c).

In *R v Weir* [2006] 1 Cr App R 303, Kennedy LJ said:

JUDGMENT

'We note that the provisions of section 101(3) do not apply to subsection (1)(f), and we see no reason to doubt that section 78 of the 1984 Act should be considered where section 101(1)(f) is relied upon.'

12.4.7 Gateway (g) – s 101(1)(g) – 'attack on another person's character'

The principle under this gateway bears a similarity to the old 'tit-for-tat' principle enacted in s 1(3)(ii) of the Criminal Evidence Act 1898 ('the nature or conduct of the defence is such as to involve imputations on the character of the prosecutor or witnesses for the prosecution or the deceased victim of the offence'). Under the new provision enacted in s 101(1)(g) of the 2003 Act the prosecution will be entitled to adduce evidence of the defendant's bad character if he (defendant) has made an attack on any other person's character, and it is irrelevant that the defendant has chosen to give or not to give evidence. The rationale of the provision is not to protect the character of others but to provide evidence to the jury to balance any attack that the defendant has made. Lord Pearce, in *Selvey v DPP* [1970] AC 304, stated the rationale for the repealed s 1(3)(b) thus:

JUDGMENT

'The practical justification for [s 1(3)(b)] is the "tit-for-tat" argument. If the accused is seeking to cast discredit on the prosecutor, then the prosecution should be allowed to do likewise. If the accused is seeking to persuade the jury that the prosecutor behaved like a knave, then the jury should know the character of the man who makes these accusations, so that it may judge fairly between them instead of being in the dark as to one of them . . .'

The old law involved the concept of casting 'imputations', whereas the new provision introduced the concept, 'attack on another person's character'. The provisions under the 2003 Act are much broader than their nineteenth-century equivalent. When does a defendant make an attack? Section 106(2) enacts as follows:

SECTION

'. . . evidence attacking the other person's character means evidence to the effect that the other person –

(a) has committed an offence (whether a different offence from the one with which the defendant is charged or the same one), or

(b) has behaved, or is disposed to behave, in a reprehensible way; and "imputation about the other person" means an assertion to that effect.'

There are a number of points that need clarification. First, the provision is not restricted to persons who testify in the trial; indeed, the person attacked need not be named. It may involve the defendant alleging that such a person committed the offence charged or a different offence or in some way misconducted himself. In *R v Bishop* [1975] QB 274, it was decided that, under the pre-2003 law, suggesting that a prosecution witness had a homosexual relationship with the defendant was treated as casting imputations on the character of the witness, whereas in *R v Westfall* (1912) 7 Cr App R 176, calling the prosecutor a habitual drunkard did not have this effect. Likewise, in *R v McClean* [1978] Crim LR 430, an allegation that the complainant was intoxicated and swearing did not justify adducing evidence of the defendant's bad character. In *R v Weir* [2006] 1 Cr App R 303, on a charge of rape, an allegation by a Hindu priest that the complainant conspired with others to fabricate the complaint was treated as an attack. Similarly, in *R v Renda* [2006] 1 WLR 2948, comments by the defendant that suggested that the complainant would consent to sexual intercourse with anyone amounted to an attack. In *R v Nelson* [2006] EWCA Crim 3412, a suggestion that a neighbour and the victim conspired to fabricate evidence against the defendant amounted to an attack on the character of a non-witness.

Second, there is no requirement that the attack should be untrue or unfounded. Accordingly, if the attack is an integral part of the defence, in theory the defendant's bad character may be admitted. Of course this is subject to the discretion of the judge to disallow the defendant's bad character evidence within s 101(3) of the 2003 Act or s 78 of the Police and Criminal Evidence Act 1984, where the admissibility of the evidence may have an adverse effect on the fairness of the trial. In *R v Singh (James Paul)* [2007] EWCA Crim 2140, on a charge of robbery an allegation by the defendant that the complainant was smoking crack cocaine and had fabricated his evidence amounted to an attack on the character of the complainant. Hughes LJ explained the discretion of the judge thus:

JUDGMENT

> '. . . it may be relevant to the exercise of discretion if an attack on the complainant is an entirely gratuitous one. Gateway G is, however, not limited to such cases and the question is not relevant to whether the gateway is passed. The purpose of gateway G is to enable the jury to know from what sort of source allegations against a witness (especially a complainant but not only a complainant) have come . . . This court will not interfere with the exercise of the judge's discretion under s 101(3) any more than it would under section 78 of the Police and Criminal Evidence Act 1984 or similar provisions unless the judge has either misdirected himself or had arrived at a conclusion which is outside the legitimate band of decisions available to him.'

A similar view was expressed by Keene LJ in the earlier case, *R v Nelson* [2006] EWCA Crim 3412:

JUDGMENT

> '. . . we must emphasise that the trial judge still has a discretion as to whether the jury should hear about a defendant's bad character when he has merely made imputations about the character of a non-witness. Not only does he have such a general discretion under s 78 of the Police and Criminal Evidence Act 1984, but section 101(3) of the 2003 Act specifically provides that: "the court must not admit evidence under subsection (1)(d) or (g) if on an application by the defendant to exclude it it appears to the court that the admission of the evidence would have such an adverse effect on the fairness of the proceedings that the court ought not to admit it."

'How the trial judge exercises that discretion is a matter for him or her, but it seems to this court that it would be unusual for evidence of a defendant's bad character to be admitted when the only basis for so doing was an attack on the character of a non-witness who is also a non-victim. The fairness of the proceedings would normally be materially damaged by so doing.'

In *R v Rouse* [1904] 1 KB 184, a plea of not guilty, even in forcible language, did not involve casting imputations; but if the defendant, in his defence, makes an allegation that goes beyond a mere denial of the charge, his bad character may become admissible. This would be the position where the defence alleges that the police had fabricated evidence attributed to the defendant: see *R v Britzmann and Hall* [1983] 1 All ER 369. In *Selvey v DPP* [1970] AC 304, the defendant was charged with committing buggery with the complainant. He pleaded not guilty and alleged that the complainant was a male prostitute, had told the defendant that he had submitted himself to buggery earlier on the same day of the incident with another person and was paid £1, and was willing to offer himself to the defendant for £1. The defendant refused this offer and alleged that the complainant in a fit of pique planted indecent photographs in the defendant's flat. The court decided that these allegations amounted to casting imputations on the character of the complainant. Viscount Dilhorne postulated four guidelines relevant to s 1(3)(ii), thus:

JUDGMENT

'1. The words of the statute must be given their ordinary meaning.
2. The section permits cross-examination of the accused as to character both when imputations on the character of the prosecutor and his witness are cast to show their unreliability as witnesses independently of the evidence given by them and also when the casting of such imputations is necessary to enable the accused to establish his defence.
3. In rape cases, the accused can allege consent without placing himself in peril of such cross-examination.
4. If what is said amounts in reality to no more than a denial of the charge, expressed, it may be, in emphatic language, it should not be regarded as coming within the section.'

The methods by which the defendant may make an attack on another person's character, both in and out of court, are stated in s 106(1) as follows:

SECTION

'(a) he adduces evidence attacking the other person's character,
(b) he (or any legal representative appointed under s 38(4) of the Youth Justice and Criminal Evidence Act 1999 to cross-examine a witness in his interests) asks questions in cross-examination that are intended to elicit such evidence, or are likely to do so, or
(c) evidence is given of an imputation about the other person made by the defendant –
  (i) on being questioned under caution, before charge, about the offence with which he is charged, or
  (ii) on being charged with the offence or officially informed that he might be prosecuted for it.'

Thus, the definition of attacking a person's character under gateway (g) is similar to the general definition of 'bad character' in s 98 and includes facts relating to the offence charged as well as the investigation and prosecution of the offence. These allegations or attacks may be made by the defendant in person, or through defence witnesses or by cross-examination of witnesses.

Evidential value of the bad character evidence

Once evidence of the defendant's bad character has been admitted in court, the judge is required to direct the jury as to the value of such evidence. The Act does not give an indication, but the courts have declared that such evidence is admissible as to the credibility of the defendant and his propensity to commit the offence. In *R v Highton* [2006] 1 Cr App R 125, Lord Woolf CJ said:

JUDGMENT

'Once the evidence is admitted, it may, depending on the particular facts, be relevant not only to credibility but also to propensity to commit offences of the kind with which the defendant is charged.'

A similar view was expressed by Hughes LJ in *R v Singh (James Paul)* [2007] EWCA Crim 2140:

JUDGMENT

'We think that it is perfectly plain that, once admitted under gateway G, bad character evidence does go to the credibility of the witness in question. That accords with common experience. It is, among other things, the obverse of the reason why a defendant is entitled to plead his own good character in support of his claim that he should be believed. The reason why he is entitled to do that is because ordinary human experience is that people of proven respectability and good character are, other things being equal, more worthy of belief than those who are not. Conversely, persons of bad character may of course tell the truth and often do, but it is ordinary human experience that their word may be worth less than that of those who have led exemplary lives. Once gateway G is passed the consequence of the defendant's bad character falls to be weighed with all the other evidence when the jury decides whether or not he has been proved to be guilty, and in doing so it may think him less worthy of belief because of his history.'

In *Highton* the court held that bad character evidence admitted under one gateway can be used for any purpose for which it might be relevant. This principle has been followed in *R v Johnson* [2019] EWCA Crim 1025 and *R v Campbell* [2007] EWCA Crim 1472 (see below). However, it may be necessary in such cases expressly to direct the jury in relation to why the evidence is being adduced for example credibility, and the basis upon which they can consider it relevance other matters i.e., propensity.

12.5 Warning by judge

Although there is no legal requirement for the judge to issue a warning to the defendant (in the absence of the jury) that his defence or allegation may expose him to a risk of revealing his bad character, it is submitted that it is good legal practice to issue such a warning in appropriate cases. Failure to issue such a warning may not be fatal to a conviction but involves the exercise of judicial discretion to disallow evidence in order to ensure a fair trial. A similar principle existed before the 2003 Act was passed: see Viscount Dilhorne in *Selvey v DPP* [1970] AC 304:

JUDGMENT

'It is desirable that a warning should be given when it becomes apparent that the defence is taking a course which may expose the accused to cross-examination [as to his bad character]. That was not given in this case but the failure to give such a warning would not, in my opinion, justify in this case the allowing of the appeal.'

12.5.1 Sparing use of bad character provisions

In one of the first Court of Appeal decisions to consider the new character provisions the court, in *R v Hanson* [2005] EWCA 824, expressed the view that parties in criminal proceedings are best advised to use the character provisions sparingly, after careful consideration of their relevance. Rose LJ stated that:

JUDGMENT

'The starting point should be for judges and practitioners to bear in mind that Parliament's purpose in the legislation, as we divine it from the terms of the Act, was to assist in the evidence-based conviction of the guilty, without putting those who are not guilty at risk of conviction by prejudice. It is accordingly to be hoped that prosecution applications to adduce such evidence will not be made routinely, simply because a defendant has previous convictions, but will be based on the particular circumstances of each case.'

In *R v Eyidah* [2010] EWCA Crim 987, it was unfortunate that this warning was not taken on board. The defendant was charged on two counts with making an untrue statement for the purpose of obtaining a passport, contrary to s 36 of the Criminal Justice Act 1925. The prosecution successfully applied to admit, as evidence of bad character, numerous documents, including rent arrears letters, loan demands and council tax overdue notices. On conviction the Court of Appeal allowed the appeal and quashed the convictions on the ground that the jury should not have been deluged with a mass of prejudicial and irrelevant material.

12.5.2 Directions by the judge

In *R v Campbell* [2007] 1 WLR 2798, Lord Phillips CJ issued guidance on the summing up to the jury of the defendant's bad character. Where such evidence has been introduced in the trial, the jury should be given assistance by the judge as to its relevance that is tailored to the facts of the individual case, rather than the gateway under which the evidence is admitted. He needs to warn the jury against attaching too much weight to previous convictions, for such convictions do not by themselves prove the defendant's guilt of the offence charged. The judge will be required to explain to the jury why they have heard of the defendant's bad character and, above all, how such evidence becomes relevant to the charge.

JUDGMENT

'Once the evidence has been admitted through a gateway it is open to the jury to attach significance to it in any respect in which it is relevant. To direct them only to have regard to it for some purposes and to disregard its relevance in other respects would be to revert to the unsatisfactory practices that prevailed under the old law.

'The summing up that assists the jury with the relevance of bad character evidence will accord with common sense and assist them to avoid prejudice that is at odds with this.

'What should a jury's common sense tell them about the relevance of the fact that a defendant has, or does not have, previous convictions? It may tell them that it is more likely that he committed the offence with which he is charged if he has already demonstrated that he is prepared to break the law, the more so if he has demonstrated a propensity for committing offences of the same nature as that with which he is charged. The extent of the significance to be attached to previous convictions is likely to depend upon a number of variables, including their number, their similarity to the offence charged and how recently they were incurred and the nature of his defence.

'In considering the inference to be drawn from bad character the courts have in the past drawn a distinction between propensity to offend and credibility. This distinction is usually unrealistic. If the jury learn that a defendant has shown a propensity to commit criminal acts they may well at one and the same time conclude that it is more likely that he is guilty and that he is less likely to be telling the truth when he says that he is not.

'The question of whether a defendant has a propensity for being untruthful will not normally be capable of being described as an *important* matter in issue between the defendant and the prosecution. A propensity for untruthfulness will not, of itself, go very far to establishing the commission of a criminal offence. In short, whether or not a defendant is telling the truth to the jury is likely to depend simply on whether or not he committed the offence charged. The jury should focus on the latter question rather than on whether or not he has a propensity for telling lies.

'If the jury is told in simple language and with reference, where appropriate, to the particular facts of the case, why the bad character evidence may be relevant, this will necessarily encompass the gateway by which the evidence was admitted.

'In the rare case where evidence of bad character has been admitted because the question of whether the defendant has a propensity to be untruthful is an important matter in issue between the defendant and the prosecution, the direction should always explain the relevance of the evidence with reference to the particular facts which make that matter important.'

(Lord Phillips CJ)

KEY FACTS

Admissibility of bad character evidence of the defendant

- The pre-2003 rules concerning the admissibility of the defendant's bad character were abolished by the Criminal Justice Act 2003.
- Bad character evidence is admissible under seven gateways as laid down in s 101(1) of the 2003 Act.
- Section 101(1)(a) – admissibility by agreement between the parties. This is self-explicit.

- Section 101(1)(b) – admissibility by the defendant in chief or under cross-examination. This may be resorted to by the defendant for tactical reasons.
- Section 101(1)(c) – admissibility as important explanatory evidence. Such background evidence existed at common law. The evidence is relevant in order to understand other evidence in the case.
- Section 101(1)(d) – admissibility as a relevant matter in issue between the defendant and the prosecution. This is the statutory equivalent of similar fact evidence that existed at common law.
- Section 101(1)(e) – admissibility as a matter of substantial probative value between the defendant and the co-defendant. This gateway is triggered when the defendant alleges that the co-defendant's bad character is relevant to an important issue in the trial.
- Section 101(1)(f) – admissibility to correct a false impression given by the defendant. This gateway is relevant where the defendant has created an alleged false impression and the bad character evidence goes no further than to correct the false impression.
- Section 101(1)(g) – admissible when the defendant has attacked another person's character. This is the statutory equivalent of the old 'tit-for-tat' principle where the defendant has cast aspersions on another person's character.

12.6 Contaminated evidence

Section 107 introduces a special principle to protect a defendant whose bad character may be admitted under s 101(1)(c)–(g) and who may be prejudiced where such evidence has been contaminated to the extent that a conviction may be unsafe: see s 107(1). This power of the court is additional to the court's power to order an acquittal or to discharge the jury: see s 107(4). But in *R v Renda* [2006] 1 WLR 2948, Judge LJ declared that the power of the trial judge to stop the case within s 107 will not be construed generously for this function is reserved for the appeal courts.

JUDGMENT

'Section 107 deals with a particular situation where the evidence of "bad character" has been admitted and proves to be false or misleading in the circumstances described in s 107(5). Unless the case falls squarely within that statutory provision, the Court of Appeal, Criminal Division is the appropriate court in which the correctness of the judge's decision should be questioned.'

The expression 'contamination' has been defined in s 107(5) as follows:

SECTION

'. . . a person's evidence is contaminated where –

(a) as a result of an agreement or understanding between the person and one or more others, or

(b) as a result of the person being aware of anything alleged by one or more others whose evidence may be, or has been, given in the proceedings,

the evidence is false or misleading in any respect, or is different from what it would otherwise have been.'

The contamination may originate from bribery of or threats to a witness, potential or otherwise, to adjust or colour his evidence, or the modification may have been brought about inadvertently. If the judge rules that the evidence has been contaminated as enacted in s 107(1), then s 107(2) and (3) specifies what orders the judge is required to issue – this may amount to an acquittal of the charge or any alternative charges or a discharge of the jury and a retrial.

In *R v C* [2006] 3 All ER 689, the Court of Appeal made the following observations:

1. Contamination may arise from deliberate collusion, the exercise of improper pressure, through inadvertence or innocently.
2. The section required the judge to make what was in effect a finding of fact after the admission of the evidence (based on an assessment as to whether the evidence of a witness was false or misleading, or different from what it would have been, had it not been contaminated).
3. The purpose of the section is to reduce the risk of conviction based on over-reliance on evidence of bad character and the provision acknowledges the potential danger that, where evidence is contaminated, the evidence of bad character may have a disproportionate impact on the evaluation of the case by the jury.
4. Although the duty to stop the case does not arise unless the judge is satisfied that there has been an important contamination of the evidence, if he is so satisfied, he has no discretion and he must stop the case (whether or not there would, on a conventional approach, be a case to answer).
5. An order for retrial, rather than a direction to acquit, would not normally be susceptible to a subsequent application based on an asserted abuse of process since, without something fresh emerging, that would amount to an appeal of the order for a retrial.
6. Where the prosecution make an application to adduce evidence of the defendant's bad character at the start of the trial and the defence make a responsible submission that there is material in the prosecution case to suggest that there was or may have been witness contamination, it would normally be sensible for the judge to postpone a decision on the application until the allegedly contaminated evidence has been examined in the trial; by doing so, the judge will have well in mind the precise details of the evidence actually given, rather than anticipated, with such weaknesses and problems as may have emerged.

In this case, the charge was sexual assault on a child under the age of thirteen. There was evidence that the complainant's mother had told the complainant what to say and had told the complainant that she (the mother) had suffered sexual abuse. The trial judge ruled that the defendant's previous convictions for sexual offences with children were admissible. The defendant was convicted and his appeal was allowed under s 107 and the conviction quashed. At some stage before the complaint the child had acquired more information from another source, which suggested that the child's evidence was different from what it would otherwise have been.

In the pre-2003 case, *R v H* [1995] 2 AC 596, the House of Lords decided that where there is an issue of contamination raised by the defence, and the trial judge leaves the issue with the jury, the judge is required to issue a direction to the jury not to accept the allegedly contaminated evidence, unless they are satisfied that it is reliable and true.

Inadmissible bad character evidence

Occasionally, the prosecutor may inadvertently and unlawfully refer to the defendant's bad character during the trial. In these circumstances, the issue involves an element of damage limitation to be exercised by the judge. In the interests of fairness, the trial judge will have to make a positive decision as to the appropriate course to take concerning the trial. Much will depend on the extent and weight of the bad character that has been partially disclosed to the jury and the conduct of the judge in his attempt to mitigate the scope of the damage to the defendant. The test that will be applied by the appellate court will be taking all the circumstances of the trial into account, whether there is a real possibility that the jury would have arrived at a different verdict. On this issue the appellate courts will hesitate to interfere with the trial judge's ruling on the admissibility of bad character evidence of the accused, or person other than the accused, provided that the judge had properly directed himself on the issue. In *R v Renda* [2006] 1 WLR 2948, Sir Igor Judge declared:

JUDGMENT

> 'The circumstances in which this court will interfere with the exercise of a judicial discretion are limited. The principles need no repetition. However, we emphasise that the same general approach will be adopted when the court is being invited to interfere with what in reality is a fact-specific judgment . . . the trial judge's "feel" for the case is usually the critical ingredient of the decision at first instance which this court lacks. Context therefore is vital . . . This legislation has now been in force for nearly a year. The principles have been considered by this court on a number of occasions. The responsibility for their application is not for this court but for the trial judge.'
>
> (Sir Igor Judge P)

In *R v Kelly* [2015] EWCA Crim 500, the Court of Appeal decided that the prompt action by the trial judge in preventing the prosecution from referring to the defendant's inadmissible bad character evidence in cross-examination avoided the risk of prejudicial evidence being admitted. In this case the defendant was charged with murder. The victim, who was known to the defendant and co-defendant, was savagely beaten and was discovered in the co-defendant's flat. All three individuals were regular users of class A drugs. The defendant admitted the killing but ran the defence of loss of control. The trial judge had earlier ruled as inadmissible the defendant's previous convictions for assault and a forensic psychiatrist's report that the defendant was prone to violence when dealing with conflict. During cross-examination of the expert the prosecution asked the witness whether the defendant had 'any established patterns of behaviour'. The trial judge intervened and, in the absence of the jury, reminded the prosecution to respect the ruling against the admissibility of bad character evidence. A similar question was asked in respect of another expert witness and, in like circumstances, the judge intervened and rebuked the prosecutor in the absence of the jury. The judge dealt with the issue as fairly as possible in his summing up to the jury. The defendant was convicted and appealed. The Court of Appeal dismissed the appeal and decided that, owing to the judge's quick action, the safety of the conviction was not compromised.

JUDGMENT

'The quick action of the judge resulted in no harm being done. In our judgment, the judge dealt with this problem admirably. We note that no submission was made to the judge that more should be done in respect of this matter, or that any harm had arisen in consequence of this undoubted lapse by prosecution counsel.'

(Burnett LJ)

12.7 Duty to give reasons

Section 110 enacts that on certain occasions, called 'relevant rulings', the judge is required to state in open court, in the absence of the jury, the reasons for relevant rulings. In the magistrates' court, relevant rulings and reasons are required to be entered on the register of court proceedings. The relevant rulings to which this provision applies are identified in s 110(2) of the Act as follows:

SECTION

'(a) a ruling on whether an item of evidence is evidence of a person's bad character;
(b) a ruling on whether an item of such evidence is admissible under section 100 or 101 (including a ruling on an application under section 101(3));
(c) a ruling under section 107.'

Thus, the trial judge is required to make rulings, giving reasons, on whether an item of evidence is within the definition of bad character, rulings on questions of admissibility of the bad character of non-defendants and defendants, and decisions to withdraw a case from the jury on grounds of contamination.

12.8 Rules of court

Section 111 authorises the making of rules for the prosecution to give notice (fourteen days after committal) and particulars to the defendants if it proposes to adduce evidence of the defendant's bad character or to elicit evidence from a witness in cross-examination: see s 111(2). These rules have been made and are referred to as the Criminal Procedure Rules 2005, Part 35. Similar rules may be made where a party wishing to raise bad character evidence is the co-defendant. The rules may also prescribe the circumstances when the notice requirements may be dispensed with: see s 111(3).

In *R (on the application of Robinson) v Sutton Coldfield Magistrates' Court* [2006] 2 Cr App R 13, the Divisional Court considered the policy behind the notice procedure and the approach of the courts towards applications for extensions. In this case the charge was assault and was tried summarily. At the pre-trial hearing the prosecution orally indicated that it would seek to introduce the defendant's bad character. However, written notice was not served on the defendant until the eve of the trial. This was well out of the time limit, and the prosecution applied for leave to introduce the defendant's previous convictions. The defence objections were rejected by the magistrates and the defendant was convicted and appealed. The Divisional Court dismissed the appeal and decided that, in the circumstances, there was no prejudice to the defendant:

JUDGMENT

'The first point to be made is that the time limits must be observed. The objective of the Criminal Procedure Rules "to deal with all cases efficiently and expeditiously" depends upon adherence to the timetable set out in the rules. Secondly, Parliament has given the court a discretionary power to shorten a time limit or to extend it even after it has expired. In the exercise of that discretion the court will take account of all the relevant considerations, including the furtherance of the overriding objective . . . In my view a court would ordinarily wish to know when the relevant enquiries had been initiated, and in broad terms why they have not been completed within the time allowed. Any application for an extension will be closely scrutinised by the court. A party seeking an extension cannot expect the indulgence of the court unless it clearly sets out the reasons why it is seeking that indulgence. But importantly, I am entirely satisfied that there was no conceivable prejudice to the claimant, bearing in mind that he would have been well aware of the facts of his earlier convictions; secondly, that he was on notice on April 14 [the date of the pre-trial hearing] that there could be such an application; and thirdly there was no application [from the defendant's legal adviser] for an adjournment on June 16 [the eve of the trial] from which it is to be inferred that the claimant and his legal advisers did not consider their position to be prejudiced by the short notice.'

(Owen J)

12.9 Other statutes admitting evidence of the bad character of the defendant

A miscellany of other statutory provisions have allowed the defendant's previous convictions to become facts in issue admissible by the prosecution as part of its case. In other words, specific statutory provisions have created specific instances of the defendant's character as constituent elements of the relevant offence or the means of proving an element of the offence, such as *mens rea*.

Section 21 of the Firearms Act 1968:

SECTION

'It is an offence for a person who has been sentenced to imprisonment for a term of three years or more, to have a firearm or ammunition in his possession.'

The effect of s 21 is that a sentence of imprisonment of at least three years following a conviction for an offence is an essential prerequisite to the commission of the offence. The judge is required to direct the jury that the conviction is an essential part of the crime and has no probative value in respect of the charge under the Firearms Act.

Section 27(3) of the Theft Act 1968:

SECTION

'[On a charge of] handling stolen goods (but not for any offence other than handling stolen goods) . . . the following evidence shall be admissible for the purpose of proving that he knew or believed the goods to be stolen –

(a) evidence that he has had in his possession, or has undertaken or assisted in the retention, removal, disposal or realisation of stolen goods from any theft taking place not earlier than 12 months before the offence charged; and

(b) provided that seven days' notice in writing has been given to him of the intention to prove the conviction) evidence that he has within the five years preceding the date of the offence charged been convicted of theft or of handling stolen goods.

The policy of s 27(3) was designed to assist the prosecution in discharging the legal burden of proof that the defendant had the relevant *mens rea* in relation to the handling charge. This may be done by showing that the defendant had goods in his possession (the subject of a different charge) which were stolen twelve months before the offence charged (s 27(3)(a)) or that he was convicted of theft or handling stolen goods within five years preceding the date of the offence charged. In other words, Parliament was of the view that the bad character evidence, in the circumstances specified by the Act, has a tendency to show that the defendant knew that the goods (the subject of the current charge) were stolen. The cogency of such evidence will depend on the frequency of such occurrence and the circumstances surrounding the event, including the similarity between the previous occasions and the current charge. Merely adducing evidence of the 'fact' of possession without considering the circumstances surrounding the previous occasion has the effect of reducing the impact of the section: see *R v Bradley* [1980] Crim LR 173.

In *R v Bradley*, the defendant was charged with handling stolen goods contrary to s 21(1) of the Theft Act 1968 in that it was alleged that he received a diamond ring knowing or believing it to be stolen. The prosecution relied on s 27(3)(a) and adduced evidence that the defendant on another occasion had handled another ring within the twelve months preceding the offence. The thief was called and gave detailed evidence of the theft and transactions with the defendant. The summing up of the judge included a direction on the doctrine of recent possession, but following defence objection, the direction was withdrawn tersely. The defendant was convicted and appealed. The Court of Appeal allowed the appeal and quashed the conviction on the ground that s 27(3)(a) ought to be construed strictly and did not allow the prosecution to render details of the possession or theft on the earlier occasion that is not the subject matter of the present charge.

If the defendant does not admit the conviction, the prosecution may prove the same under s 73 of the Police and Criminal Evidence Act 1984 (PACE). This may allow in court some of the details of the offence such as the substance, etc., of the charge and the conviction: see s 73(2) of the PACE 1984. In *R v Hacker* [1995] 1 All ER 45, the defendant was charged with handling stolen goods – the body shell of a Ford Escort RS Turbo motor car. The prosecution was allowed to adduce evidence of the defendant's previous conviction for handling a Ford Escort RS Turbo motor car by reference to a certificate of conviction under s 73 of the Police and Criminal Evidence Act 1984. Thus, the substance of the previous conviction was revealed and this related to similar goods to those involved in the charge. The stated purpose of admitting the evidence was to determine whether the defendant knew or believed that the goods (the subject matter of the current charge) were stolen, the subject of a direction by the judge, and not that the defendant had a propensity to commit this sort of crime.

In addition, the judge has a discretion, under s 78 of the PACE 1984, to refuse to admit evidence under s 27(3) of the Theft Act 1968, if the adduction of such evidence would be of minimal probative value in relation to the charge. In short, the judge is required to consider whether the probative value of admitting the evidence would outweigh the prejudicial effect of admitting the evidence: see *R v Perry* [1984] Crim LR 680.

12.10 Bad character of defendants in civil cases

The rule in civil cases is that disposition evidence of the bad character of a party is admissible provided that it is relevant to a fact in issue. There are no special rules that are peculiar to parties in civil proceedings. Such parties are treated like any other witness. Thus, a defendant with a previous conviction, like an ordinary witness, may be subjected to cross-examination about his record, subject to the provisions within the Rehabilitation of Offenders Act 1974.

Likewise, other occasions of misconduct may be admitted in court if they are relevant to an issue in the case. In *Mood Music Publishing Co Ltd v De Wolfe Publishing Ltd* [1976] 1 All ER 463, the claimants and defendants were both music publishers. The claimants brought an action for alleged infringement of copyright. The defendants admitted the similarity of the musical work owned by the claimants but contended that the similarity stemmed from sheer coincidence. To rebut this contention, the claimants were allowed by the trial judge to adduce evidence of other works ostensibly produced by the defendants but bearing a marked similarity to works in which other persons owned the copyright. The defendants appealed to the Court of Appeal against the judge's ruling. The Court of Appeal dismissed the appeal on the ground that the evidence was relevant to an issue in the case and was not oppressive or unfair:

JUDGMENT

'In civil cases, the courts will admit evidence of similar facts if it is logically probative, that is, if it is logically relevant in determining the matter which is in issue: provided that it is not oppressive or unfair to the other side: and also that the other side has fair notice of it and is able to deal with it.'

(Lord Denning MR)

In *Berger v Raymond & Son Ltd* [1984] 1 WLR 625, a case involving allegedly fraudulent share transfers, Warner J amplified the principle in *Mood Music*, by referring to the burden on the defendant of adducing evidence, the possibility of lengthening the trial, and the undesirability of re-litigating issues disposed of in previous proceedings, as factors militating against admission.

The test of admissibility of similar fact evidence in civil cases is much broader than the common law test that was applicable in criminal cases. In criminal cases, the common law test was based on a degree of enhanced probative value that outweighs the prejudicial value of admitting the evidence. In civil proceedings the test of admissibility is based on relevance only, namely, that evidence to be adduced is potentially probative of an issue in the action. Where this test is satisfied, the judge will then consider whether to admit the evidence, having regard to the overriding objective of fairness to all the parties. In doing so, the judge will assess the potential significance of the evidence in the context of the case as a whole, weighing its potential probative value against its capacity both to cause unfair prejudice and to increase disproportionately the length and complexity of the trial. These principles were laid down in the definitive House of Lords case, *O'Brien v Chief Constable of the South of Wales Police* [2005] 2 WLR 1038. Here, the claim for damages was against the defendants' officers for malicious prosecution for murder and misfeasance in public office by putting pressure on the claimant to make false admissions. He wished to adduce evidence that the same officers had been involved in similar misconduct on two other occasions. The claimant had spent eleven years in prison before his conviction was quashed. His claim to adduce similar fact evidence was allowed at a case management hearing, prior to the trial. The House of Lords decided that the evidence was properly allowed in the trial. The court advocated a two-stage test for the admissibility of the evidence. The first stage involved satisfying the test of relevance, and the second stage involved considering factors that are significant in maintaining a fair balance between the parties:

JUDGMENT

'In a civil case such as this the question of admissibility turns, and turns only, on whether the evidence which it is sought to adduce, assuming it (provisionally) to be true, is in Lord Simon's sense probative. If so, the evidence is legally admissible. That is the first stage of the inquiry. The second stage of the inquiry requires the case management judge or the trial judge to make what will often be a very difficult and sometimes a finely balanced judgment: whether evidence or some of it . . . which *ex hypothesi* is legally admissible, should be admitted. For the party seeking admission, the argument will always be that justice requires the evidence to be admitted; if it is excluded, a wrong result may be reached. In some cases, as in the present, the argument will be fortified by reference to wider considerations: the public interest in exposing official misfeasance and protecting the integrity of the criminal process; vindication of reputation; the public righting of public wrongs. These are important considerations to which weight must be given. But even without them, the importance of doing justice in the particular case is a factor the judge will always respect. The strength of the argument for admitting the evidence will always depend primarily on the judge's assessment of the potential significance of the evidence, assuming it to be true, in the context of the case as a whole.'

(Lord Bingham)

SUMMARY

- The bad character of non-defendants is admissible under three gateways laid down in s 100 of the 2003 Act.
- 'Bad character' is defined in s 98 of the 2003 Act: see Chapter 11.
- The first gateway in s 100(1)(a) is that the evidence is admissible as 'important explanatory evidence'.
- 'Important explanatory evidence' is defined in s 100(2) of the 2003 Act.
- Section 100(3) identifies the factors that must be taken into account by the judge in deciding the question of 'important explanatory evidence'.
- The second gateway enacted in s 100(1)(b) admits bad character evidence of a non-defendant where it has substantial probative value on a matter in issue in the proceedings and is of substantial importance in the trial.

- A number of factors are laid down in s 100(3) that are required to be considered before deciding whether the evidence has substantial probative value.
- The probative value is based on the assumption that the evidence is true: see s 109.
- Leave of the court is required to admit evidence under these two gateways: s 100(4).
- The third gateway, as enacted under s 100(1)(c), is self-explicit in that all the parties agree to the evidence being admissible.
- The admissibility of bad character evidence of the defendant under the Criminal Justice Act 2003 is governed by s 101, creating seven gateways.
- The first gateway enacted in s 101(1)(a) is self-explicit in that all the parties to the proceedings agree to the admissibility of the evidence.
- The second gateway is enacted in s 101(1)(b) in that the defendant volunteers evidence of his bad character for tactical reasons. This may be done by way of the defendant giving evidence in chief or through cross-examination of witnesses.
- The third gateway, as enacted in s 101(1)(c), enacts that the defendant's bad character is admissible as 'important explanatory evidence'. This concept is defined in s 102 and requires two conditions to be satisfied to demonstrate a high degree of relevance. At common law such background evidence was admissible in exceptional circumstances. A similar provision is enacted in s 100(1)(a) concerning bad character evidence of a person other than the defendant.
- The fourth gateway is enacted in s 101(1)(d), where the defendant's bad character is relevant to an important issue between the defendant and the prosecution. This comprises a self-contained code of similar fact evidence and is admissible only on behalf of the prosecution. The aim is that the evidence manifests a high degree of relevance to indicate that the strong likelihood that the defendant committed the offence with which he is charged.
- The fifth gateway is enacted in s 101(1)(e) to the effect that the defendant's bad character has substantial probative value in an 'important matter in issue between the defendant and the co-defendant'. This gateway may only be utilised by the defendant and not the prosecution and in appropriate cases the judge does not have a discretion to exclude such evidence.
- The sixth gateway enacted in s 101(1)(f) involves the defendant's bad character being admissible to 'correct a false impression given by the defendant'. Only the prosecution is entitled to utilise this provision by adducing rebutting evidence.
- The seventh gateway is enacted in s 101(1)(g) and involves an attack by the defendant on another person's character. The policy here is that where the defendant attempts to discredit another person, irrespective of whether he testifies or not, the prosecution is entitled to do likewise. It is also immaterial that the attack is an integral part of the defence, although this may be a matter that concerns the exercise of the discretion of the judge.
- Following an application for leave to admit bad character evidence, the judge is required to make a ruling, giving reasons in open court in the absence of the jury, as to whether such evidence is admissible.

- It is desirable, not amounting to a rule of law, that the judge warns the defendant that his defence or allegation may expose him to the risk of revealing his bad character.
- When bad character evidence is admitted in court the judge is required to give a direction to the jury that is tailored to the facts of each case. The purpose of the direction is to explain to the jury, in simple language, what use may be made of the defendant's bad character.
- Other statutory provisions provide for the admissibility of bad character evidence.
- In civil cases the admissibility of bad character evidence is subject to the common law principle of relevance.

SAMPLE ESSAY QUESTION

Have the provisions in s 101(1)(g) of the Criminal Justice Act 2003 substantially modified the pre-2003 law?

Answer plan

The bad character provisions in gateway s 101(1)(g) bear a resemblance to the old provisions enacted under s 1(3)(ii) of the Criminal Evidence Act 1898 (imputations on the character of prosecution witnesses or the deceased victim of the offence).

Section 101(1)(g) is much broader than the equivalent provision under the 1898 Act. The new provisions are not restricted to prosecution witnesses but are applicable to 'another person's character', whether a witness or not, and may include the co-defendant.

'Character' bears the same meaning as laid down in s 98.

Section 106(2) defines 'attacking the other person's character' as evidence that the other person has committed the offence or behaved in a reprehensible manner.

Section 106(1) enacts how such an attack may be mounted and this may be by the adduction of evidence by or on behalf of the defendant, in cross-examination intended to elicit such evidence or by out-of-court assertions in interview.

In *R v Hanson* the Court of Appeal observed that the old law as to imputations will continue to apply when 'attacking another person's character' in so far as it is not inconsistent with the 2003 Act.

Under the old law, the following allegations amounted to imputations: an allegation against a police officer that a confession attributed to the defendant was dictated by one officer to another (*R v Clarke*); aspersions on the morality of the prosecutrix

(*R v Jenkins*); an allegation of a homosexual relationship with the complainant (*R v Bishop*); attacks within the 2003 Act are made when a priest alleged that the complainant conspired with others to fabricate a complaint of rape (*R v Weir*); comments by the defendant that the complainant would have a sexual relationship with anyone (*R v Renda*); a suggestion by the defendant that the complainant and a neighbour had conspired to fabricate evidence implicating the defendant (*R v Nelson*); an allegation by the defendant that the complainant was smoking cocaine and fabricated evidence against the defendant (*R v Singh*).

The evidential effect of introducing evidence of the defendant's bad character in response to casting imputations on the character of a prosecution witness, etc., in the pre-2003 era, was that the evidence went to the credibility of the defendant. This was based on the old 'tit-for-tat' policy. However, Lord Woolf in *R v Highton* declared that the evidential effect of introducing bad character evidence of the defendant under s 101(1)(g) relates to both his propensity to commit the offence charged and his credibility in a way similar to s 101(1)(d). This view was endorsed by Lord Phillips CJ in *R v Campbell*.

The view of Lords Woolf and Phillips have been criticised on the ground that s 101(1)(d) permits bad character evidence only when it is relevant to an important issue in the proceedings, whereas no such requirement exists under s 101(1)(g). To equate the two provisions would have the effect of dispensing with the relevance in issue test. It is arguable that the evidential effect of evidence admitted under s 101(1)(g) should be restricted to the credibility of the defendant, but this does not represent the current law. However, in *R v Nelson* the court decided that it is improper.

On a minor point, s 101(3) and (4) deals with the judge's discretion to exclude evidence specifically under s 101(1)(d) and (g) on the application of the defendant. Although the wording is similar to s 78 of the Police and Criminal Evidence Act 1984 it is assumed that in any event s 78 may be triggered whether on the application of the defendant or not.

CONCLUSION

ACTIVITY

Self-test questions

1. How many gateways exist to adduce evidence of the bad character of a person other than the defendant in criminal proceedings?
2. What is meant by 'important explanatory evidence' under s 100(1)(a) of the CJA 2003?
3. What factors determine whether evidence has reached the test of 'substantial probative value' under s 100(1)(b) of the CJA 2003?
4. How many gateways exist to admit the bad character evidence of the defendant under s 101 of the CJA 2003?
5. What safeguards exist to ensure that no miscarriages of justice take place as a result of admitting the bad character evidence of the defendant?

Further reading

Brevis, B., Jackson, A. and Stockdale, M. 'Bad character evidence and potential satellite litigation' [2013] J Crim L 110

Ho, H. 'Similar facts in civil cases' (2006) 26 Oxford Journal of Legal Studies 131

James, J. 'Good character directions and blemished defendants' [1996] 2 Web JCLI

Jones, I. 'A problem of the past? The politics of "relevance" in evidential reform' [2012] Contemporary Issues of Law 277

Lloyd Bostock, S. 'The effects on juries of hearing about the defendant's previous criminal record: a simulation study' [2000] Crim LR 734

Mackie, J. 'A question of character' [2012] SJ 156(6), 7

Mirfield, P. 'Bad character and the Law Commission' (2002) 6 E&P 141

Mirfield, P. 'Character, credibility and truthfulness' [2008] LQR 1

Mirfield, P. 'Character and credibility' [2009] Crim LR 135

Munday, R. 'What constitutes a good character?' [1997] Crim LR 247

Munday, R. 'What constitutes "other reprehensible behaviour" under the bad character provisions of the Criminal Justice Act 2003?' [2005] Crim LR 24

Munday, R. 'Cut-throat defences and the "propensity to be untruthful" under section 104 of the Criminal Justice Act 2003' [2005] Crim LR 625

Munday, R. 'Case management, similar fact evidence in civil cases, and a divided law of evidence' (2006) 10 International Journal of Evidence and Proof 81
Munday, R. 'The purposes of Gateway (g)' [2006] Crim LR 300
Munday, R. 'Single-act propensity' [2010] J Crim L 128
Redmayne, M. 'Recognising propensity' [2011] Crim LR 117
Roberts, A. 'Evidence – non-defendant's bad character' [2011] Crim LR 58
Roberts, A. 'Evidence: bad character of defendant – attack on prosecution witness – Criminal Justice Act 2003 s 101(1)(g) – test for admissibility' [2011] Crim LR 642
Singh, C. (2014). *Beginning Evidence*. Oxford: Routledge.
Smith, E, and Stockdale, M. 'Bad character evidence as evidence of identity' [2015] J Crim L 12
Tapper, C. 'Criminal Justice Act 2003: evidence of bad character' [2004] Crim LR 533
Waterman, A. and Dempster, T. 'Bad character: feeling our way one year on' [2006] Crim LR 614

13

Corroboration, lies, care warnings and identification evidence

AIMS AND OBJECTIVES

By the end of this chapter you will be able to:

- comprehend how the courts handle suspicious evidence through hypothetical and real case studies;
- understand the nature and purpose of corroboration evidence through a brief historical overview;
- highlight how corroboration and care warnings are used through a discussion on the related rationale that underpins them;
- outline the importance and significance of Lucas directions and Turnbull warnings through an analysis of their respective functions.

13.1 Introduction

The discussion in this chapter focuses on care warnings. These are directions by the judge for the jury to take care when dealing with certain pieces of evidence: corroboration evidence (supporting evidence) and identification evidence – the latter includes lies that an accused may have told. These topics refer to the rules of evidence that relate to what is commonly regarded as 'suspicious evidence'. The discussion starts with corroboration, then moves on to focus on care warnings and finally explores evidence of identification.

13.2 Corroboration

Unlike other jurisdictions (i.e., the US) in the English law of evidence there has never existed a general requirement for corroborative evidence, subject to two exceptions: corroboration that is required as a matter of law or practice. Traditionally, judges retained discretion in terms of whether they gave a warning to the jury in relation to certain types of evidence and, if

DOI: 10.4324/9781003282433-13

they did, what form it should take. The Court of Criminal Appeal was established in 1907 and those same practices became often very rigid rules of law. The rules on corroboration were one of the areas that rapidly developed and as a result they became quite complex. Alongside these rigid rules there developed a system of informal warnings that should be given to the jury if the witness might be unreliable if their evidence did not fall into any of the categories to which the stricter rules were of application. The Criminal Justice Act 1988 (CJA) and s 32 of the Criminal Justice and Public Order Act 1994 (CJPOA) largely abolished these common law rules. You should note that the Court of Appeal confirmed in *R v Makanjuola* (1995) and *R v Stone* (2005) that the body of case law relating to corroboration had not survived the abolition of the substantive common law rules. Thus, the discussion that is presented lends context to corroboration warnings.

Corroboration means to confirm or support and there is very little technicality in this definition where the law of evidence is confirmed. Looking for evidence to confirm or support a statement commonly occurs in the course of everyday life; this is often what a belief in a statement is based upon. Reading LCJ stated in *R v Baskerville* [1916] 2 KB 658 that: 'It would be in high degree dangerous to attempt to formulate the kind of evidence which would be regarded as corroboration, except to say that corroborative evidence is evidence which shows or tends to show that the story of the **accomplice** that the accused committed the crime is true, not merely that the crime has been committed, but that it was committed by the accused.' On this basis corroboration evidence could be defined as admissible and independent evidence that supports or confirms that a defendant committed the offence with which he is charged. Therefore three elements required satisfaction: admissibility, independence of the evidence and support or confirmation that the defendant committed the offence.

Accomplice
someone who aids, abets, advises or encourages another to commit a criminal offence.

Lord Morris in *DPP v Hester* [1973] AC 296 stated:

JUDGMENT

'The essence of corroborative evidence is that one creditworthy witness confirms what another creditworthy witness has said. Any risk of the conviction of an innocent person is lessened if the conviction is based upon the testimony of more than one acceptable witness. Corroborative evidence in the sense of some other material evidence in support, implicating the accused, furnishes a safeguard which makes a conclusion more sure than it would be without such evidence . . . The purpose of corroboration is not to give validity or credence to evidence which is deficient or suspect or incredible but only to confirm and support that which as evidence is sufficient and satisfactory and credible: and corroborative evidence will only fill its role if it itself is completely credible evidence . . .'

Lord Reid echoed this in *DPP v Kilbourne* [1973] AC 729, when he stated:

JUDGMENT

'There is nothing technical in the idea of corroboration. When in the ordinary affairs of life one is doubtful whether or not to believe a particular statement one naturally looks to see whether it fits in with other statements or circumstances relating to the particular matter; the better it fits in the more one is inclined to believe it. The doubted statement is corroborated to a greater or lesser extent by the other statements or circumstances with which it fits in . . .'

Weight
the measure of how credible evidence is.

The rationale here was quantitative, the greater the amount of corroborative evidence presented, the better the chances of success because more **weight** will be attached to the case. The English law of evidence is not known for its concern for corroboration and much was determined without its use. In contrast, convictions without corroboration were considered to be of greater risk – this led to some criminal offences actively requiring it.

ACTIVITY

What is corroboration evidence?

What criteria must be satisfied for evidence to amount to corroboration evidence?

Outline the effect of s 32 of the Criminal Justice and Public Order Act 1994.

Summarise the effect of *R v Makanjuola*.

KEY FACTS

Corroboration

This can be defined as evidence that is admissible, independent and confirms or supports that a defendant committed the offence with which he or she is charged (see *R v Baskerville* [1916] 2 KB 658). The following should be noted:

- The general rules on relevance and admissibility apply.
- The evidence must be independent and it must support or confirm that the defendant committed the offence.

13.2.1 Admissible and independent evidence

All evidence that is tendered has to satisfy the general rules on relevance and admissibility. The same was the case for corroboration evidence. Where the evidence was admissible, the prosecution was required to prove that it came from a source that was independent from the evidence that it was due to corroborate. Statements made by the victim to other witnesses and then repeated by the witnesses, although often admissible in criminal cases as previous consistent statements, could not amount to corroboration evidence. In the case of *R v Whitehead* [1929] 1 KB 99 the defendant was charged with sexually assaulting a young girl, who had complained of this to her mother a few months later. The court held that this evidence from the mother was not corroboration evidence because it did not have an independent source – it came from the young girl (the witness) herself.

Hewart LCJ in this case confirmed the need for corroborative evidence to be independent of the witness, stating that:

JUDGMENT

'. . . any such inference as to what the girl had told her mother could not amount to corroboration of the girl's story, because it proceeded from the girl herself; it was merely the girl's story at second hand. In order that evidence may amount to corroboration it must be extraneous to the witness who is to be corroborated. A girl cannot corroborate herself; otherwise it is only necessary for her to repeat her story some twenty-five times in order to get twenty-five corroborations of it.'

This meant that the status of a complaint from A to B about something that they had suffered did not amount to corroboration evidence. However, B could give evidence of the distress that A had suffered. The position after Whitehead was that the girl's mother would have been able to give evidence of her daughter's distress as an independent observation as percipient evidence – something that in itself could amount to corroboration.

CASE EXAMPLE

R v Redpath (1962) 46 Cr App R 319

The defendant was charged with indecently assaulting a seven-year-old girl. The girl stated that whilst playing on the moor with her two friends, Redpath pulled her to the ground and indecently assaulted her. The girl's mother stated in her evidence that the girl had come home in a terrible state and had immediately complained of the indecent assault to her. This was a case in which corroboration evidence was required, albeit the story that the girl had told her mother was a consistent one. At the time of the indecent assault a Mr and Mrs Hall were near the edge of the moor and witnessed two important things: first, a parked car; and, second, a man whom they claimed was Redpath walking towards the girl. The same couple witnessed the man return and drive off. Mr Hall gave evidence that the little girl was terribly white and almost on the brink of tears, at which point the little girl burst into tears and thus they accompanied her home. The defendant was convicted and appealed. In dismissing his appeal, the Court of Appeal stressed that in order for distress to amount to corroboration, it must not be faked:

JUDGMENT

'So far as any question of indecent assault is concerned, the learned judge told the jury that her distressed condition observed by Mr Hall and the fact that he had spoken to her was capable of being corroboration. The point in this appeal is whether that is so. Counsel for the defence has argued that the distressed condition of the complainant is no more corroboration than the complaint, if any, that the complainant makes, and that while the latter merely shows that the story is consistent and is not corroborative, so the distressed condition is not corroborative. This Court is quite unable to accept that argument. It seems to this Court that the distressed condition of a complainant is quite clearly capable of amounting to corroboration. Of course, the circumstances will vary enormously, and in some circumstances quite clearly no weight, or little weight, could be attached to such evidence as corroboration. Thus, if a girl goes in a distressed condition to her mother and makes a complaint, while the mother's evidence as to the girl's condition may in law be capable of amounting to corroboration, quite clearly the jury should be told that they should attach little, if any, weight to that evidence, because it is all part and parcel of the complaint. The girl making the complaint might well put on an act and simulate distress. But in the present case, the circumstances are entirely different . . .'

(Parker LCJ)

CASE EXAMPLE

R v Chauhan (Ramesh) (1981) Cr App R 232

Chauhan was accused of indecently assaulting a woman with whom he had been left in a room. The woman had managed to get away and had run off to the company lavatory in tears. When asked by a fellow employee what had happened she complained that Chauhan had assaulted her. At the trial, the judge directed the jury that evidence of her distress could amount to corroboration evidence, if tendered through an independent witness. The defendant was convicted and appealed. In upholding his conviction the Court of Appeal confirmed this principle stating that:

JUDGMENT

'. . . there may be cases (e.g. *Redpath* (1962) 46 Cr App R 319) where there can be no suggestion that the distress was feigned. In normal cases, however, the weight to be given to distress varies infinitely, and juries should be warned that, although it may amount to corroboration they must be fully satisfied that there is no question of it having been feigned.'

(Lord Parker C.J.)

Widgery LCJ stated that:

JUDGMENT

'In the present case there is no doubt, whatever view one may take of the correctness of the trial judge's direction to the jury, that it was extremely carefully prepared; it was beautifully phrased and it was of outstanding clarity. It starts, after he has given a very full and accurate warning, yet nevertheless concise, on the dangers inherent in this type of allegation of indecent assault, and a very clear direction on the reasons for the desirability of corroboration . . .'

In summary, it would appear that:

(a) provided that there was sufficient evidence of identity i.e., that the accused had been shown to have been implicated in the alleged crime;

(b) the 'distressed condition' of the complainant was capable of potentially corroborating her testimony if it is proved not to have been simulated i.e., if it is proved that her condition was genuine.

Circumstantial evidence
evidence that may allow a judge or jury to deduce a fact from other facts that have been already proven.

13.2.2 Supporting or confirming the commission of the criminal offence by the defendant

In addition to this the corroborative evidence was required to either directly or **circumstantially** support or confirm that it was the accused that committed the offence alleged. Therefore, this evidence was required to have been such that it implicated the defendant.

CASE EXAMPLE

James v R (1970) 55 Cr App R 299

The defendant, James, was charged on indictment of having sexual intercourse with a woman without consent. The allegation was that he did so whilst armed with a gun and knife. He was convicted and sentenced to ten years' imprisonment and twelve strokes to be given by an approved instrument (lashes). He appealed on the grounds that the trial judge had misdirected the jury by telling them that medical evidence of recent sexual intercourse was corroborative evidence that the defendant had raped the complainant. The Privy Council agreed. Such medical evidence proved nothing more than the fact that sexual intercourse had occurred. It also stated that in order for such evidence to amount to corroboration evidence, it must confirm two things; first, that sexual intercourse with the defendant had taken place, and second, that it had taken place without the woman's consent.

ACTIVITY

Define with an example what is meant by evidence from an independent source.

KEY FACTS

Independence

Admissible corroboration evidence required an independent source.

Statements by witnesses, although admissible in criminal cases, could not amount to corroboration evidence.

Support or confirmation

The corroboration evidence was required to directly or circumstantially support or confirm that it was the accused that committed the offence with which he was charged, thereby implicating him or her.

13.3 Corroboration: as a matter of law or practice

The prosecution was required to provide evidence of corroboration as a matter of law where a statute so required. The effect of its failing to do so was often considered unjust because it would result in the trial judge directing the jury (trier of fact) to acquit the accused of the offence with which they stood charged, and any conviction would have to be set aside on appeal. Here are some examples of instances in which corroboration was required: corrupt electoral practices, perjury, sexual offences and speeding. Prior to its abolition by the Statute Law Revision Act 1875, s 1 of the Treason Act 1848 required, for successful conviction, the oaths of two lawful and credible witnesses that corroborated the act of treason. There are two main instances in which corroboration or care warnings still apply; these are perjury and speeding.

Corroboration as a matter of law

Section 13 of the Perjury Act 1911 (still in force as at 1 February 2022) states:

SECTION

'. . . a person shall not be liable to be convicted of any offence against this Act, or of any offence declared by any other Act to be perjury or subornation of perjury, or to be punishable as perjury or subornation of perjury, solely upon the evidence of one witness as to the falsity of any statement alleged to be false'.

Section 89(2) of the Road Traffic Regulation Act 1984 states:

SECTION

'. . . a person prosecuted for such an offence shall not be liable to be convicted solely on the evidence of one witness to the effect that, in the opinion of the witness, the person prosecuted was driving the vehicle at a speed exceeding a specified limit'.

Corroboration as a matter of practice

This exception consisted of cases that developed over a number of years, on the basis that where statute did not require corroboration as a matter of law then a judge should, as a matter of good practice, direct the jury on the risks of convicting an accused where the evidence is uncorroborated – this direction was mandatory even though the terminology suggests it to be discretionary. However, you should note that the jury was still entitled to convict the accused on the basis of uncorroborated evidence. Generally, the mandatory direction was given in three instances: in relation to the uncorroborated evidence of an accomplice, of complainants in cases involving sexual offences, and that of young children. This 'rule' was rejected in *R v Makanjuola* but it was suggested that some direction should still be given in the instances outlined.

CASE EXAMPLE

R v Makanjuola (Oluwanfunso) [1995] 2 Cr App R 469

Makanjuola and another were convicted of indecent assault. They made an application to appeal on the ground that, although s 32 of the Criminal Justice and Public Order Act 1994 had removed the requirement that the judge give a corroboration warning, the trial judge had failed to exercise his discretion to warn the jury about the dangers of convicting the defendants, in the case of a sexual offence, on evidence that was not corroborated. The defendants argued that the judge had, in his failure, given retrospective effect to the provision that had only come into force after they had been charged and committed for trial on indictment but before the trial. Dismissing the applications, the court held that following the repeal of s 32 the judge could choose to exercise, or not, his discretion to give a warning that he considered appropriate in respect of such a witness. The court stressed that the decision to give the warning and the terms in which the warning would be given were matters for the judge to decide on the basis of the circumstances of the case, the issues raised and the quality of the witness's evidence.

Both *R v Makanjuola* (1995) and *R v Easton* [1995] 1 WLR 1348 involved appeals against convictions for indecent assault on the basis that the common law rules, albeit abolished, could not be eliminated overnight. The Court of Appeal took this opportunity to lay down the common law rules to settle this argument, stating that any attempt to reinvigorate the rules would fail. In its conclusions the court held that:

- s 32 of the CJPOA 1994 formally revokes the requirement for the trial judge to give a direction in respect of a complaint relating to a sexual offence just because the witness falls into this category;
- it is a matter of discretion for the judge whether they do or do not give a direction, although in some cases it may be appropriate to warn the jury to exercise care before they act on the unsupported evidence of a witness;
- counsel should settle any argument regarding the need for a direction with the trial judge in the jury's absence before final speeches;
- directions, where given, should be part of the judge's summing up; and
- where a warning is given, it is for the trial judge to decide the terms and strength of it.

The Court of Appeal took the opportunity to also summarise these principles in *R v Stone* [2005] EWCA Crim 105.

13.4 The development of corroboration warnings

As far as certain offences were concerned, the courts were of the view that it was undesirable to convict a defendant without corroboration evidence and, by the same token, corroboration evidence was considered to be fraught with issues concerning fabrication, and thus validity. *R v Baskerville* [1916] (above) highlighted the categories in which a care warning should be given to the jury. The attempted extension to these categories can be found in the judgment of Edmund Davies J in *R v Prater* [1960] 2 QB 464, who suggested that warnings should also be given where an individual may have their own purpose to serve. It is widely accepted that Edmund Davies J was referring to corroboration warnings. However, the courts were unwilling to accept this as a new instance in which a care warning should be given because it was inherently difficult to define it. The case of *R v Bagshaw* [1984] 1 WLR 477 is a good example where a full direction was given to the jury.

13.4.1 The evidence of an accomplice

Fabrication
an account that is deliberately false or improbable.

Many argue that given the risk that an accomplice may concoct or **fabricate** their evidence, perhaps this is an instance in which their evidence should require corroboration or at the very least should a care warning be given to the jury. Consider this, Usha and Bo conspire to attack and murder Stephanie, and they carry out their plan one night in August. After a lengthy investigation both Usha and Bo are charged with murder. They then turn against one another, each running cut-throat defences that in essence blame the other for murdering Stephanie. The evidence of an accomplice is considered with care and suspicion, and quite rightly so, for each may have a vested interest in proving that they were least involved in the commission of the offence, and possibly even argue that the other was entirely to blame. Cases such as *R v Hills* (1988) 86 Cr App R 26 and *R v Barnes* [1940] 2 All ER 229 only exemplify this issue. The law suggests that some direction should be given to the jury, warning them or asking them to take care when approaching the evidence of an accomplice, especially where the accomplice has turned Queen's evidence. It is within a judge's discretion to give a warning where an accomplice merely gives some evidence that implicates a co-accused.

CASE EXAMPLE

Davies v DPP [1954] AC 378

A group of six young men, who included Davies, attacked a second group of young men. During a fistfight one of the young men from the second group was stabbed and subsequently died. Davies and five other men from his group, including one known as 'L', were charged with murder. At the trial, no evidence was offered against L and three others and not guilty verdicts were entered for the remaining two. At Davies's trial, L gave evidence against him, which resulted in Davies being convicted. Davies appealed on the basis that L and one of the other witnesses were his accomplices and, thus, the judge had failed to give the jury a warning as to the risk of accepting their evidence without corroboration. Davies's appeal was dismissed. The House of Lords confirmed that L was not an accomplice, because at the time he gave evidence he had been acquitted. Just because the group had attacked with their fists did not mean that the rest of the men became associated when one used a knife and the others had no knowledge of this. Hence, in Davies 'L' was unaware of the knife and thus could not be considered to be an accomplice.

The question is whether the trial judge should give the jury a warning to take care when handling such evidence. Prior to the enactment of s 32 of the Criminal Justice and Public Order Act 1994, this would have been standard procedure – the provision abolished this requirement. What follows is a discussion of the provision itself in s 32(1) of the Criminal Justice and Public Order Act 1994:

SECTION

'. . . any requirement whereby at a trial on indictment it is obligatory for the court to give the jury a warning about convicting the accused on the uncorroborated evidence of a person merely because that person is: (a) an alleged accomplice of the accused, or (b) where the offence charged is a sexual offence, the person in respect of whom it is alleged to have been committed, is hereby abrogated.

'[Subsection] . . . (2) In section 34(2) of the [1988 c 33] Criminal Justice Act 1988 (abolition of requirement of corroboration warning in respect of evidence of a child) the words from "in relation to" to the end shall be omitted.

'[Subsection] . . . (3) Any requirement that (a) is applicable at the summary trial of a person for an offence, and (b) corresponds to the requirement mentioned in subsection (1) above or that mentioned in section 34(2) of the Criminal Justice Act 1988, is hereby abrogated.'

It should be noted that the term 'abrogate' here means to repeal or abolish.

13.4.2 The evidence of children

Prior to the enactment of the Criminal Justice Act 1988 (CJA), corroboration warnings, where sworn or unsworn evidence of a child was tendered, were routine occurrences – this requirement was also abolished by the CJA 1988. Currently, the evidence of children over the age of fourteen is given under oath i.e., it is sworn evidence; the evidence of a child under that age may be given unsworn. Where the evidence of children is involved, the trial judge may consider that the evidence tendered gives cause for concern in relation to the ability of the child to differentiate between what is fact and what is fiction. In such a case, the trial judge may consider exercising their discretion and issue a care warning instead.

13.4.3 The evidence of a victim of a sexual offence

This is an interesting but sensitive topic in the English law of evidence. This substantiates how the requirements for corroboration evidence have diminished substantially over time. The alleged victim of a crime of a sexual nature will in most cases make allegations against the person he or she alleges has committed the offence, rebuttal of which can be a difficult task. In addition, allegations may be fabricated for a number of reasons including anger, jealousy or shame. Hence, the law previously required a corroboration warning to be given to the jury. The case of Burgess highlights this.

CASE EXAMPLE

R v Burgess (Bertram Fraser) **(1956) 40 Cr App R 144**

The defendant was convicted of indecent assault on an adult male in a cinema. Unbeknown to Burgess, the male was a police officer. Burgess appealed. No corroboration evidence of the police officer's evidence had been tendered, and the jury had not received a care warning. In addition, Burgess contended that the officer was a willing participant in the acts. His conviction was quashed; the case concerned an indecent assault by one adult male upon another and, thus, the jury should have been warned of the desirability of having some corroboration evidence in a case such as this. The position was also altered by s 32 of the Criminal Justice and Public Order Act 1994, which abolished this requirement.

ACTIVITY

Is the judge required to give a corroboration warning where an accomplice has given evidence against a defendant?

Are there any instances in which the law requires corroboration evidence?

KEY FACTS

Corroboration as a matter of law

Where a statute requires corroboration evidence, then it must be provided. A failure to do so will result in the trial judge having to direct the trier of fact to acquit the defendant of the charge.

Corroboration as a matter of practice

The law as it stands suggests that some direction should be given in relation to the uncorroborated evidence of an accomplice, of complainants in cases involving sexual offences, and that of young children.

The courts have been unwilling to extend corroboration warnings to categories outside those stated in *R v Baskerville* [1916].

13.5 Care warnings

The discussion so far has highlighted how the majority of the requirements for corroboration that were built up over many years have been abolished, and the fact that judges do not have to give corroboration warnings. In the absence of this, the judge may prefer to give a care warning instead. This is a warning given to the jury in relation to the evidence of an accomplice, a child, a complainant in a case involving a sexual offence or a witness who may have a grudge against the defendant, e.g. malicious fabrication, or suffers from mental illness or is handicapped. Reference to this was made throughout the preceding text.

CASE EXAMPLE

DPP v Hester [1973] AC 296

Hester was charged with indecently assaulting a 12-year-old girl, contrary to s 14(1) of the Sexual Offences Act 1956. Although the complainant (A) gave evidence on oath, her nine-year-old sister (B) was permitted to give unsworn evidence under s 38 of the Children and Young Persons Act 1933. The trial judge directed the jury that the unsworn evidence of B could amount to corroboration of the sworn evidence of A. Hester was convicted and appealed. Quashing the conviction, the Court of Appeal stated that the unsworn evidence of B could corroborate the sworn evidence of A only if it satisfied the proviso that '. . . in the present case the complainant's sworn evidence could corroborate that of her sister and the sister's

> evidence that of the complainant provided that the jury after suitable adequate guidance and warning were satisfied that each child was a truthful and satisfactory witness . . . but that the appeal should be dismissed on the ground that the conviction was unsafe and unsatisfactory'.

Although the evidence of children was considered to be unreliable in the past, the contemporary approach is different. These days, such evidence is considered more reliable and, thus, relevant statutory assistance exists to facilitate the court in receiving it: see s 55(2) of the Youth Justice and Criminal Evidence Act 1999.

Judicial discretion
the power given to a court or judge, by law, to select two or more alternatives from those that are lawful.

A trial judge has the **discretion** to give a care warning where the evidence against an accused emanates from a witness who could potentially hold a grudge against the defendant, for example a co-accused. In terms of a co-accused the trial judge may also feel it necessary and proper to direct the jury that the evidence of an accomplice should be treated carefully because accomplices often have an agenda of their own, to reduce the case against themselves. In *R v Knowlden* (1981) 77 Cr App R 94 the trial judge considered it unnecessary to give the jury a warning where the defendant's family members tendered evidence that implicated one another. In contrast to the rules on corroboration, where a co-defendant turns Queen's evidence there is still no requirement that a care warning be given to the jury. However, the trial judge will be obliged to direct the jury to take care when handling such potentially unreliable evidence as the witness may have an ulterior motive.

Where the evidence of the mentally ill or handicapped is concerned s 77 of the Police and Criminal Evidence Act 1984 requires a trial judge to give a care warning in relation to a mentally handicapped defendant who has confessed to the commission of a crime without the presence of an appropriate adult. In most other cases, the trial judge retains the discretion as to whether or not to give the jury such a warning: see *R v Bagshaw* [1984] 1 WLR 477 and *R v Spencer* [1987] AC 128. Generally, a warning will be given by reason of the dangers that exist in manipulation of witnesses with such disabilities, manipulation that could lead to unsafe convictions that are later quashed.

Where the prosecution's case depends wholly or in part on the identification evidence of a witness then a Turnbull warning will be given to the jury – this is the focus of the following discussion.

ACTIVITY

When is there a need for the judge to issue a care warning to a jury?

KEY FACTS

Care warnings

A trial judge no longer has to give a corroboration warning. They may prefer to give a care warning where the evidence tendered is that of an accomplice, a child, a complainant in a case involving a sexual offence or a witness who may have a grudge against the defendant, i.e. malicious fabrication, or be mentally ill or handicapped.

Section 38(1) of the Children and Young Persons Act 1933 originally contained a requirement for the unsworn evidence of children to be corroborated by 'some other material evidence'; however, this requirement was removed by s 34(1) of the Criminal Justice Act 1988. Similarly s 33 of the Criminal Justice and Public Order Act 1994 removed the requirement for corroboration in relation to sexual offences. Requirements for corroboration in relation to corrupt electoral practices under the Representation of the People Acts 1949 and 1983 have also long since been abolished.

13.6 *R v Turnbull* guidelines

There was a public outcry concerning several convictions that were miscarriages of justice based on visual identification evidence, and because of this the Devlin Committee was set up in 1976 to investigate and report on the matter. On conclusion of this investigation it made a number of strong recommendations to the Home Secretary. Shortly after the report was published, the Court of Appeal in *R v Turnbull* [1977] 3 All ER 549 (CA) took the much-needed opportunity to refine the law on identification evidence, so much so that Parliament no longer needed to adopt the recommendations of the Committee.

CASE EXAMPLE

R v Turnbull [1977] 3 All ER 549 (CA)

Turnbull and others were convicted of conspiracy to burgle. The defence was based on a mistaken identification. Four separate appeals were made from separate trials and dealt with by the court; all the appeals were based on the quality of the identification evidence upon which the convictions were based. The court allowed two of the appeals but dismissed the remaining two. In *Turnbull* the court established guidelines for the courts that largely reflected the recommendations of the Devlin Committee on how to handle evidence of witnesses that purports to identify the accused as the perpetrator of the crime. The reasoning that lies behind the need for such dogmatic guidance to be given by the judge to the jury is due to the generally unreliable nature of identification evidence.

13.6.1 Guideline 1

Whenever the prosecution's case is based wholly or substantially on identification evidence that the defence claims to be mistaken, the jury should be warned of the need for caution and the reasons for such caution (factors taken into account):

JUDGMENT

'The judge should direct the jury to examine closely the circumstances in which the identification by each witness came to be made. How long did the witness have the accused under observation? At what distance? In what light? Was the observation impeded in any way, as for example by passing traffic or people? Had the witness ever seen the accused before? How often? If only occasionally, had he any special reason for remembering the accused? How long elapsed between the original observation and the subsequent identification to the police? Was there any material discrepancy between the description of the accused given to the police by the witness when first seen by them and his actual appearance?'

(Lord Widgery CJ in *R v Turnbull*)

13.6.2 Guideline 2

JUDGMENT

'Recognition, on the other hand, is potentially more reliable than identification of a stranger for the first time, but even when the witness is purporting to recognise someone whom he knows, the jury should be reminded that mistakes in recognition of close relatives and friends are sometimes made . . .'

(*per* Widgery CJ in *R v Turnbull*)

'Recognition' evidence involves identifying a person who has previously been known to the witness – in short, an acquaintance of the witness – whereas 'identification' evidence involves selecting an individual from features that had been observed previously. The length and clarity of the observation will vary with the facts of each case. The point is that recognition evidence may potentially carry more weight than identification evidence. At the same time, the witness may be mistaken in his recognition of a person known to him.

CASE EXAMPLE

R v Walshe (1982) 74 Cr App R 85 (CA)

The defendant was charged and convicted of obtaining property on forged prescriptions. Two of the prescriptions were presented to the same chemist on two separate occasions. At an identification parade, the shop's proprietor and his daughter both identified the defendant as the person who presented the prescription. The proprietor had served the man four times previously and his daughter had done so twice. Each time, the man had waited in the well-lit shop for about ten minutes for the prescription to be filled. The prosecution's case depended on the identification. The defendant claimed that the identification was mistaken. An application was made to the judge to hold a trial within a trial to determine whether the evidence was admissible. The judge granted the application and ruled that the evidence was admissible. (From the report, it was not clear whether the judge gave a warning. Presumably there was one.)

On appeal, the Court of Appeal held that:

1. The *voir dire* was an inappropriate procedure to hear such evidence, as the Crown did not have a specific legal burden on this issue.
2. In the circumstances, the evidence was admissible – identifications were made on more than one occasion in circumstances well suited for identification.

JUDGMENT

'It is unnecessary to go through the catalogue of the matters which will be relevant when considering the quality of the identification. Here there could be no basis for stopping the case on the ground that the quality was inferior. The identifying witnesses had seen the man on more than one occasion in circumstances well suited to accurate observation and identification and for a period of time which put this case well outside those where the identification depended on but a fleeting glance which was made in difficult conditions . . .'

(Boreham J)

In *R v Bentley* (1994) 99 Cr App R 342, Taylor LCJ explained the need for caution even in respect of recognition evidence:

JUDGMENT

'The recognition type of identification . . . [cannot] be treated as straightforward or trouble-free . . . Each of us, and no doubt everyone sitting in this court, has had the experience of seeing someone in the street whom we know, only to discover later that it was not that person at all. The expression, "I could have sworn it was you" indicates the sort of warning which the judge should give, because that is exactly what the witness does. He swears that it was the person he thinks it was.'

13.6.3 Guideline 3

When the identification evidence is poor, the judge should withdraw the case from the jury unless there is other evidence that supports the identification – not necessarily in the strict sense of corroboration but any evidence that may make the jury feel sure that there has been no mistaken identification:

JUDGMENT

'When, in the judgment of the trial judge, the quality of the identifying evidence is poor, as for example when it depends solely on a fleeting glance or on a longer observation made in difficult conditions, the situation is very different. The judge should then withdraw the case from the jury and direct an acquittal unless there is other evidence which goes to support the correctness of the identification. This may be corroboration in the sense lawyers use that word; but it need not be so if its effect is to make the jury sure that there has been no mistaken identification . . .'

(Lord Widgery in *R v Turnbull*)

13.6.4 Guideline 4

Where the quality of the identification is good, the jury may be left to assess the weight of the evidence but should be given a warning of the need for caution. If there is any supporting evidence of identification, the judge should say so (i.e., tell this to the jury).

JUDGMENT

'The trial judge should identify to the jury the evidence which he adjudges is capable of supporting the evidence of identification. If there is any evidence or circumstances which the jury might think was supporting when it did not have this quality, the judge should say so. A jury, for example, might think that support for identification evidence could be found in the fact that the accused had not given evidence before them. An accused's absence from the witness box cannot provide evidence of anything and the judge should tell the jury so. But he would be entitled to tell them that when assessing the quality of the identification evidence they could take into consideration the fact that it was uncontradicted by any evidence coming from the accused himself . . .'

(Lord Widgery CJ in *R v Turnbull*)

13.7 Voice identification or earwitness evidence

The jury may be asked to compare a recording of the offender's voice with the voice of the accused. If there is a dispute as to whether the offender's voice is that of the defendant, expert evidence may be admissible to assist the jury. In *R v Roberts* [2000] Crim LR 183, the court received expert evidence to the effect that voice recognition is more likely to be mistaken compared with visual identification evidence. Thus, it is appropriate for a judge to issue a warning to the jury analogous to a visual identification warning but adapted to the circumstances: see *R v Hersey* [1998] Crim LR 281 and *R v Gummerson* [1999] Crim LR 680.

13.8 Failure to follow guidelines

A failure to follow the guidelines would invariably lead to a conviction being quashed: see *R v Hunjen* (1979) 68 Cr App R 99. However, each case is decided on its own facts and, in particular, on the strength of the evidence.

In exceptional circumstances, a failure to issue a Turnbull warning concerning identification evidence may not lead to the conviction being quashed. In *R v Shand* [1996] 1 WLR 67, the Privy Council decided that despite a failure on the part of the judge to issue a Turnbull warning, the conviction was safe. Two eyewitnesses recognised the defendant in daylight from 300–400 feet away, respectively. There was nothing to suggest that the witnesses were mistaken and the recognition evidence was very good. In addition, there was evidence before the jury that the defendant had confessed his guilt.

In addition, it would appear that the evidence of more than one independent and credible identification witness would have the effect of supporting each other. It is the duty of the judge to point this out to the jury, subject to the appropriate warning. In *R v Weeder* [1980] Crim LR 645 (CA), the defendant was charged with wounding with intent contrary to s 18 OAPA 1861, following a street attack on the victim. He was struck from behind on the back of the head and fell to the ground under a lamp post. The streetlamp provided a bright light and he had a good look at W, the defendant. Another witness, X, looked out of the window during the attack and saw W's face. She was acquainted with him. The victim identified W at an identification parade. The judge In his summing up, inter alia, told the jury that one identification witness may support the identification of the other or another and issued a clear warning that even honest witnesses could be mistaken. On appeal the Court of Appeal dismissed the appeal and held that there was no misdirection.

CASE EXAMPLE

R v Shelton & Carter [1981] Crim LR 776 (CA)

S and C were convicted of robbery in that S drove a Triumph motor car and they both robbed A. The evidence in dispute was of identification. A detective constable, Hodgson, had seen a Triumph motor car half an hour before the incident and had recognised both S and C in it. A week earlier another police officer, Bennett, had seen the same car and had recognised S in it. Both S and C denied having any connection with the car. The judge allowed the evidence to be put to the jury, subject to a warning of the danger of relying on inaccurate identification evidence. Both the defendants were convicted and appealed.

The Court of Appeal held that the evidence was correctly admitted on the grounds that (i) the evidence of the officers was of 'recognition' rather than 'identification', which was potentially more reliable; (ii) in the alternative, relying on *R v Weeder*, even if the evidence of each officer taken separately was not very strong, as a matter of common sense and taken collectively, the evidence of two credible witnesses who identified the accused on independent and separate occasions was sufficient to rebut the suggestion that the accused persons were victims of an incorrect identification.

The voir dire is an inappropriate procedure to deal with disputed identification evidence: see *R v Flemming* (1988) 86 Cr App R 32 (CA):

JUDGMENT

'It is quite unnecessary to hold a trial within a trial for this purpose. The normal procedure in identification cases is clearly laid down in *Turnbull* . . . In the normal way, the trial judge will make his assessment either at the end of the prosecution case or after all the evidence has been called. There may be exceptional circumstances where the position is so clear on the depositions . . .'

(Woolf LJ)

In *R v Willoughby* (1989) Cr App R 91 (CA), the victim of a sexual assault testified that her attacker, whom she saw briefly, had spots on his face, and identified him on this basis. At the trial the accused had spots on his face, which he developed whilst waiting for trial, and was convicted. The Court of Appeal quashed the conviction on the basis that the identification was poor and was inadmissible.

In *R v McInnes* (1989) 90 Cr App R 99, on a kidnapping charge, the victim gave a detailed, accurate description of the inside of the defendant's car, including sweet papers and a rip in the upholstery of the car. It was decided that such knowledge was independent corroborative identification evidence.

13.9 Dispensation with a warning

If the judge is in doubt as to whether he or she should issue a Turnbull warning, then they should proceed prudently and err on the side of caution and issue the warning. In certain exceptional circumstances a Turnbull warning is unnecessary. These are, first, where the defendant admits they were present at the scene of the crime and there is no possibility of mistaken identity, because of the distinctive quality of the defendant. In *R v Slater* [1995] 1 Cr App R 584, on a charge of assault in a nightclub, the defendant admitted that he was present in the club. He was six feet six inches tall and extremely large and there was evidence that no one else with his height was in the club. The trial judge did not issue a warning and the Court of Appeal dismissed his appeal against conviction. There was no possibility of a mistaken identity.

Second, a Turnbull warning is not necessary where the issue is not whether there is a possibility of mistaken identity, but whether the witness is telling the truth. In short, the issue involves the veracity of the witness. In *R v Courtnell* [1990] Crim LR 115, the defence was alibi. It was alleged that the witness had known the defendant for a week and claimed to recognise that the defendant was fabricating the evidence. The judge issued no warning and, following a conviction, the Court of Appeal dismissed the appeal and decided that a Turnbull direction would have confused the jury.

Third, where the witnesses merely provide a description of the defendant that matches their appearance, there is no need to issue a Turnbull direction. Thus, in *R v Constantinou* (1989) 91 Cr App R 74, the witness provided a description of the defendant and a photo-fit picture was admitted to the court and was consistent with the appearance of the defendant; a warning was not required to be issued. In *R v Gayle* [1999] 2 Cr App R 130, following the theft of a handbag, a caretaker at a school described seeing a man on the premises. The description was that the man was stocky, black and wearing a bomber jacket with a distinctive logo. The defendant matched the description, was acting suspiciously and was discovered near the stolen item. The trial judge did not issue a warning and the Court of Appeal dismissed the appeal.

Fourth, a Turnbull warning is unnecessary with regard to the identification of motor vehicles: see *R v Browning* (1991) 94 Cr App R 109. The reason is that motor vehicles, unlike individuals, do not change their shape in the sense that each is not unique in appearance. The judge, however, is duty bound to direct the jury on the witness's ability to distinguish makes of cars and their characteristics.

Fifth, a Turnbull warning is unnecessary where the jury is asked to make an identification from photographs or video recordings, etc. In *R v Blenkinsop* [1995] 1 Cr App R 7, photographs and video footage were taken at the scene of a violent demonstration. The question was whether the photographic evidence was of the defendant taking part in the demonstration. The court held that it was not necessary for a Turnbull warning to be issued.

ACTIVITY

Self-test questions

Why is there a need for the judge to issue a care warning to a jury when considering visual identification evidence?

When is a *Turnbull* warning required to be issued to the jury and what is the effect of failure to issue such a warning?

When may a *Turnbull* warning be dispensed with concerning identification evidence?

When would the judge be required to issue a *Lucas* direction?

13.10 Accused conduct: lies told by the accused (in or out of court)

The Court of Appeal clarified the law in this respect in 1981. The rule is that lies told by the accused, generally, are incapable of corroborating the evidence of a prosecution witness. However, if the lie was

(a) deliberate, and

(b) relates to a material issue, and

(c) the motive for the lie had been the realisation of guilt, and

(d) the statement of the accused is clearly shown to be a lie by the evidence from an independent witness (other than the accomplice who required corroboration) (these are complementary, not competitive, criteria),

it is capable of being corroborative evidence and the judge is required to direct the jury accordingly.

CASE EXAMPLE

R v Lucas [1981] 2 All ER 1008 (CA)

The accused, Ruth Lucas, and A were charged and convicted on two counts of importing cannabis contrary to the Misuse of Drugs Act 1971 – count (1) related to an offence committed at Heathrow airport and count (2) took place at Gatwick airport. Defendant A pleaded guilty on both counts. The accused pleaded 'guilty' to the Heathrow count but 'not guilty' on count (2).

The main prosecution witness, B, had pleaded guilty and was sentenced, and testified, implicating both accused. It was proved by B that the accused, A, had lied out of court about the events and the judge told the jury that this was capable of amounting to corroboration. The defendant appealed to the Court of Appeal.

It was held that since the accused's lies were only proved by an accomplice, the lies did not corroborate the prosecution witness's testimony. In this respect, there is no distinction between lies told out of court and in court. The appeal was allowed and the conviction was quashed:

JUDGMENT

'Statements made out of court, e.g. statements to the police which are proved or admitted to be false may in certain circumstances amount to corroboration . . . It accords with good sense that a lie told by a defendant about a material issue may show that the liar knew that if he told the truth he would be sealing his fate . . . To be capable of amounting to corroboration the lie told out of court must first of all be deliberate. Secondly, it must relate to a material issue. Thirdly, the motive for the lie must be a realisation of guilt or fear of the truth. The jury should in appropriate cases be reminded that people sometimes lie, e.g. in an attempt to bolster up a just cause, or out of shame or out of a wish to conceal disgraceful behaviour from their family. Fourthly, the statement must be clearly shown to be a lie by evidence other than that of the accomplice who is to be corroborated i.e., by admission or by evidence from an independent witness . . . Providing that the lies told in court fulfil the four criteria we are unable to see why they should not be available for the jury to consider in just the same way as lies told out of court . . .'

(Lane LCJ)

This test is known as a Lucas direction and was approved by the Court of Appeal in *R v Burge and Pegg* [1996] 1 Cr App R 163. In this case, the accused were charged with murder. They burgled the seventy-four-year-old victim's flat, having forced their way into the flat, wearing masks and carrying sticky tape and cord. They gagged and bound the victim and stole from his flat. The left the victim tied up and he died from asphyxia. In interview, each blamed the other. At the trial they claimed that a neighbour of the deceased who lived upstairs had killed the deceased after they had left the flat. The judge gave the jury a warning as to the significance of lies told to the police. The accused were convicted and appealed. The Court of Appeal dismissed the appeal and decided that the direction was correct. The jury was told of the proper significance of the lies:

JUDGMENT

'. . . it may be helpful if we conclude by summarising the circumstances in which, in our judgment, a *Lucas* direction is usually required. There are four such circumstances, but they may overlap:

1. Where the defence relies on alibi.
2. Where the judge considers it desirable or necessary to suggest that the jury should look for support or corroboration of one piece of evidence from other evidence in the case, and amongst that other evidence draws attention to lies told, or allegedly told, by the defendant.
3. Where the prosecution seek to show that something said, either in or out of the court, in relation to a separate and distinct issue was a lie, and to rely on that lie as evidence of guilt in relation to the charge which is sought to be proved.
4. Where although the prosecution have not adopted the approach to which we have just referred, the judge reasonably envisages that there is a real danger that the jury may do so.

'If a *Lucas* direction is given where there is no need for such a direction (as in the normal case where there is a straight conflict of evidence), it will add complexity and do more harm than good. Therefore, in our judgment, a judge would be wise always, before speeches and summing up in circumstance number four, and perhaps also in other circumstances, to consider with counsel whether, in the instant case, such a direction is in fact required, and, if so, how it should be formulated. If the matter is dealt with in that way, this court will be very slow to interfere with the exercise of the judge's discretion . . .

'. . . The direction should, if given, so far as possible, be tailored to the circumstances of the case, but it will normally be sufficient if it makes the two basic points:

1. that the lie must be admitted or proved beyond reasonable doubt, and;
2. that the mere fact that the defendant lied is not in itself evidence of guilt since defendants may lie for innocent reasons, so only if the jury is sure that the defendant did not lie for an innocent reason can a lie support the prosecution case.'

(Kennedy LJ)

It follows that a Lucas direction is not appropriate where the lie told by the defendant related to the central issue in the trial – whether the defendant is guilty of the crime or not: see *R v Ball* [2001] Lawtel, 5 January 2001.

SUMMARY

- Corroboration is defined as evidence that is admissible, independent and confirms or supports that a defendant committed the offence with which he or she is charged (see *R v Baskerville* [1916] 2 KB 658).
- Corroboration evidence must be independent and it must support or confirm that the defendant committed the offence.
- Where a statute requires corroboration evidence, then it must be provided as a matter of law; any failure would result in an acquittal.
- The uncorroborated evidence of accomplices, complainants in cases concerning sexual offences and young children should be accompanied by a judicial direction as a matter of good practice.

SAMPLE ESSAY QUESTION

Mistaken eyewitness identification evidence is often the root cause of wrongful convictions. Do Turnbull directions and PACE Code D provide adequate protection?

Answer plan

Outline the protection available: R v Turnbull *(1977) and PACE Code D.*
The Court of Appeal in *R v Turnbull* established guidelines that apply where the case of the prosecution depends substantially or wholly on the correct identification of an accused. PACE Code D governs identification procedures.

Discuss the adequacy of a Turnbull *direction.*
State that a *Turnbull direction* must be given where the risk of misidentification is greater, for instance where a witness has caught only a fleeting glance of the accused. Analyse the stages that the

court must follow: warning the jury of the special need for caution, informing them why a warning is needed, directing the jury to closely examine the circumstances in which the identification was made, and whether any other evidence supports the identification. Point out that where the judge summarises the identification evidence then he or she should also highlight the strengths and weaknesses in it and any evidence that supports or undermines it. State that a *Turnbull* direction provides very strong protection.

Highlight the inadequacy of PACE Code D when compared to the Turnbull *direction.*
Discuss the fact the failure to follow a procedure will not result in the evidence being excluded, and how para 3.12 of the Code provides that a procedure should be held unless impracticable and thus in effect reverses the House of Lords decision in *R v Forbes* (2001), which held that a procedure was mandatory. State that, unlike in an identification parade procedure, an accused is far more vulnerable in terms of a video identification parade because he or she cannot withdraw their consent to participate in it where an image has already been provided.

Further reading

Birch, D. 'Corroboration: goodbye to all that?' [1995] Crim LR 524

Hartshorne, J. 'Corroboration and care warnings after Makanjuola' (1998) 2 E&P (1) 1–12

Jackson, J. 'Insufficiency of identification evidence based on personal impression' [1986] Crim LR 203

Mirfield, P. 'Corroboration after the 1994 Act' [1995] Crim LR 448

Murphy, P. and Glover, R. (2011) Murphy on Evidence. Twelfth edition. Oxford: Oxford University Press

Ormerod, D. 'Sounds familiar? Voice identification evidence' [2001] Crim LR 595

Singh, C. (2014) Beginning Evidence. Oxford: Routledge

14

Opinion, documentary and real evidence

AIMS AND OBJECTIVES

By the end of this chapter you will be able to:

- highlight the different types of opinion evidence through a discussion of how the law developed;
- explore expert and non-expert opinion evidence through case and hypothetical examples;
- outline who qualifies as an expert through a discussion of the criterion and the rationale under which it developed;
- highlight the status of opinion evidence in the criminal and civil cases through a discussion of case examples;
- discuss real and documentary evidence through a discussion of its classification;
- set out the forms of documentary evidence, i.e. primary and secondary, through a discussion of their classification and hypothetical examples.

14.1 Introduction

In this chapter you will learn about three categories of evidence: opinion, real and documentary evidence. Our discussion will begin with a brief introduction to the background to opinion evidence and then turn more specifically to expert and non-expert opinion evidence, its importance and the rules governing its admission, after which the discussion focuses on real and documentary evidence and the rules on relevancy and admission.

14.2 Opinion evidence

The general rule is that witnesses should only give evidence of facts that they have perceived themselves without speculating, drawing conclusions

DOI: 10.4324/9781003282433-14

and inferences or giving their opinion. There is a distinction between the role of a witness in giving evidence of facts and the court in coming to conclusions; therefore, when giving evidence, the witness should not usurp the role of the court or jury. The 'opinion rule' in the English law of evidence excludes the opinion evidence of **lay witnesses** by reason that the witness may be unreliable or inexperienced in giving evidence and hence there exists a greater risk of such evidence lacking probative force. The further opinions of lay witnesses are simply irrelevant. The court will determine its opinion in relation to the facts that are in issue and counsel and the court will object to questions that seek to elicit witness opinion.

Lay witness
any witness who does not testify in court as an expert.

In summary, opinion evidence is excluded. However, there are three exceptions to the rule; opinion evidence may be admissible if it is:

- expert opinion;
- opinion evidence of general reputation;
- the opinion of an eyewitness.

What follows is a discussion of each of these.

14.2.1 Expert opinion

There are notable occasions where the court is required to adjudicate on a case involving complex and technical issues that are beyond its experience or competence. In an ideal world the presiding judge would be an expert in the discipline with which the case is concerned; in reality the majority of the time this is not true. In such cases the court will seek the assistance of experts or expert witnesses who will be better equipped to express their opinion and make conclusions from the facts; for example, on the time relative to the decomposition of a corpse, handwriting analysis (s 8 of the Criminal Procedure Act 1865), **facial mapping** where closed circuit television (CCTV) is in question (*R v Grey* [2003] EWCA Crim 1001 and *R v Atkins and Atkins* [2009] EWCA Crim 1876), or auditory, acoustic or biometric voice identification (the identification of a suspect via their voice: see *R v O'Doherty* [2003] 1 Cr App R 161). The general rule is well established; in *Folkes v Chadd* (1782) 3 Doug KB 157 the court allowed an engineer to give his opinion on the causes of silting in the harbour of the defendant port owner.

Facial mapping
the process by which the unique facial characteristics of an individual are distinguished.

Like any exception, before such evidence can be admitted it must satisfy a series of conditions; in relation to expert evidence these are that:

- the witness's opinion is beyond ordinary experience and competence; and
- the witness is a qualified 'expert'.

In addition, admission of such evidence is subject to a series of procedural requirements.

Witness expertise

The court will only hear the opinion evidence of a person who is *qualified* to form an opinion on the matter concerned; for example, a professor of haematology in relation to blood-clotting or a forensic scientist on dismemberment of a body and its decomposition. Although the witness does not need to have a formal qualification because their skill and experience is enough, having such qualifications will undoubtedly demonstrate competence and expertise.

CASE EXAMPLE

R v Silverlock [1894] 2 QB 766

The court permitted the evidence of a solicitor on handwriting even though he had only studied and researched handwriting and had no formal qualification in relation to it.

Where the evidence is admitted, then the actual level of skill, experience and expertise demonstrated by them will affect the weight of it. Contrast these cases:

CASE EXAMPLE

R v Oakley (1979) 70 Cr App R 7

An officer of the police was permitted to give opinion evidence on road traffic accidents due to his extensive amount of experience in the matter concerned.

CASE EXAMPLE

R v Inch (1989) 91 Cr App R 51

A medical orderly was not permitted to give opinion evidence on medical matters due to his inexperience in the matters concerned.

The full text judgment of both these cases is available on Westlaw, LexisNexis and other reputable legal resource databases. This area of the law is always changing, especially with the advents of new methods and technologies designed to capture data. This raises an interesting issue: what if the witness's evidence requires the use of a new or developing skill, for example a new method of facial mapping, lip reading or voice identification, namely evidence of which the reliability is still being rigorously contested? The court will not automatically accept the evidence as being an expert opinion. Before this can be done, the court will first adjudicate on whether the discipline qualifies as a recognised expertise, and then whether the witness can be considered to be an expert: see *R v Luttrell* [2004] 2 Cr App R 31 and *R v Robb* (1991) 93 Cr App R 161.

The party instructing the expert witness does not own the evidence to be given by them. The court in *Harmony Shipping v Saudi Europe Line Ltd* [1979] 1 WLR 1380 held that there can be 'no property' in an expert witness, which means the witness, regardless of whoever has instructed or called them, will be an independent witness of the court:

JUDGMENT

'. . . so far as witnesses of fact are concerned, the law is as plain as can be. There is no property in a witness. The reason is because the Court has a right to every man's evidence. Its primary duty is to ascertain the truth. Neither one side nor the other can debar the Court from ascertaining the truth either by seeing a witness beforehand or by purchasing his evidence or by making communication to him. In no way can one side prohibit the other side from seeing a witness of fact, from getting the facts from him and from calling him to give evidence or from issuing him with a subpoena. That was laid down by the Law Society in their Guide to the Professional Conduct of Solicitors. It was affirmed and approved in 1963 by the then Lord Chief Justice and the Judges . . . that principle is established in the case of a witness of fact: for the plain, simple reason that the primary duty of the Court is to ascertain the truth by the best evidence available. Any witness who has seen the facts or who knows the facts can be compelled to assist the Court and should assist the Court by giving that evidence.

'The question in this case is whether or not that principle applies to expert witnesses. They may have been told the substance of a party's case. They may have been given a great deal of confidential information. On it they may have given advice to the party. Does the rule apply to such a case? Many of the communications between the solicitor and the expert witness will be privileged. They are protected by legal professional privilege. They cannot be communicated to the Court except with the consent of the party concerned. That means that a great deal of the communications between the expert witness and the lawyer cannot be given in evidence to the Court. If questions were asked about it, then it would be the duty of the Judge to protect the witness (and he would) by disallowing any questions which infringed the rule about legal professional privilege or the rule protecting information given in confidence – unless, of course, it was one of those rare cases which come before the Courts from time to time where in spite of privilege or confidence the Court does order a witness to give further evidence. Subject to that qualification, it seems to me that an expert witness falls into the same position as a witness of fact. The Court is entitled, in order to ascertain the truth, to have the actual facts that he has observed adduced before it and to have his independent opinion on those facts. It is interesting to see that it was so held in Canada in *McDonald Construction Co Ltd v Bestway Lath & Plastering Co Ltd* (1972) 27 DLR (3d) 253 . . . it seems to me . . . that the expert witness is in the same position when he is speaking as to the facts he has observed and is giving his own independent opinion on them, no matter by which side he is instructed.'

(Lord Denning)

The effect of this is to render the opinion neutral, i.e. either party to the proceedings may use it. The judgment outlines the exception to this rule, and although legal and professional privilege is discussed in Chapter 4, there are a few salient points that you should note at this stage. Consider this question: is privileged information that which does not need to be disclosed? Information is privileged if it involves communications between a lawyer and a client in the normal course of litigation or communications between a lawyer, a client and a third party – for our purposes the expert witness, where the dominant purpose in litigation does not need to be disclosed. This information, subject to certain limitations, may only be disclosed where the client receiving it waives the privilege, i.e. their right. The position of the law can be summarised as shown in Figure 14.1.

Privileged communication obtained with a dominant purpose of litigation	Not privileged where privilege waived or if communication not obtained with a dominant purpose of litigation
Use: only by party instructing expert	Use: by any party to the proceedings

Figure 14.1 Opinion evidence of an expert witness

CASE EXAMPLE

R v R (1994) *The Times*, 2 February

The court held that both the opinion and sample of an expert witness who had carried out testing on the defendant's DNA sample were privileged because they had been created in connection with contemplated legal proceedings where the dominant purpose was litigation.

As the status of the expert witness is one of an independent witness the court can validly reject their evidence: see *R v Lanfear* [1968] 2 QB 77. In *Anderson v R* [1972] AC 100 the court stated that where the expert opinion evidence is clear and not contradicted, then it should not be disregarded.

ACTIVITY

What is expert opinion evidence?

KEY FACTS

Opinion evidence

The *general rule* known as the *opinion rule* prohibits the admission of opinion evidence as it may be unreliable, it may lack probative force and the opinion of a witness is irrelevant, unless it is:

- the opinion of an expert;
- evidence of general reputation;
- eyewitness opinion.

Expert opinion

The established principle in *Folkes v Chadd* (1782) 3 Doug KB 157 is to the effect that the opinion of an expert is admissible as evidence if:

- the witness's expert opinion is beyond ordinary experience and competence, for example matters that are complex or technical;
- the witness is a qualified expert, although a professional qualification is not required;
- certain procedural conditions are satisfied.

Property in expert witness evidence

In *Harmony Shipping v Saudi Europe Line Ltd* [1979] 1 WLR 1380 the court held that there can be 'no property' in the evidence of an expert witness, which means the expert is classified as an independent witness of the court whose evidence can be utilised by another party subject to the law on privilege.

Subject matter of expertise

An expert witness will only be called to give evidence on matters that are beyond *normal* experience or expertise. If the matter falls within the capabilities of the jury, then the expert witness's opinion becomes redundant and therefore will be unnecessary. There are a number of examples that are commonly cited where the opinion evidence of an expert witness has become redundant and unnecessary. They include:

- defences: provocation (*R v Turner* [1975] QB 834);
- personality disorders (*R v Weightman* [1991] Crim LR 204);
- the general truthfulness of witnesses (*R v MacKenney* (1981) 76 Cr App R 271).

CASE EXAMPLE

R v Land [1999] QB 65

L was charged with possession of indecent photographs of a child (unidentified). The prosecution sought to adduce the opinion of an expert paediatrician in relation to the issue of the child being under 16 and therefore underage. The Court of Appeal held that this was unnecessary as the jury were just as competent as the paediatrician to ascertain the child's age.

In contrast, the courts have decided that expert evidence can be validly adduced where the following defences are raised: insanity (*R v Holmes* [1953] 1 WLR 686), diminished responsibility (*R v Bailey* (1977) 66 Cr App R 31) and automatism (*R v Smith* [1979] 1 WLR 1445). In *R v Lowery* [1974] AC 85 two defendants were charged with a murder; from the evidence it was obvious that one or both of them must have committed it. The court allowed the prosecution to adduce the opinion evidence of an expert witness to show which one of the two defendants was more likely to have committed it, as *per* Lord Herschell, partly quoting the decision of the Court of Criminal Appeal:

JUDGMENT

'. . . "it is, however, established by the highest authorities that in criminal cases the Crown is precluded from leading evidence that does no more than show that the accused has a disposition or propensity or is the sort of person likely to commit the crime charged"; and further, "It is, we think, one thing to say that such evidence is excluded when tendered by the Crown in proof of guilt, but quite another to say that it is excluded when tendered by the accused in disproof of his own guilt. We see no reason of policy or fairness which justifies or requires the exclusion of evidence relevant to prove the innocence of an accused person."

'The evidence of Professor Cox, as will have been seen, was not as such evidence in regard to the character of Lowery and King but rather was evidence as to their respective intelligences and personalities . . . Lowery and King were each asserting that the other was the completely dominating person at the time when Rosalyn Nolte was killed: each claimed to have been in fear of the other. In these circumstances it was most relevant for King to be able to show, if he could, that Lowery had a personality marked by aggressiveness whereas he, King, had a personality which suggested that he would be led and dominated by someone who was dominant and aggressive. In support of King's case the evidence of Professor Cox was relevant if it tended to show that the version of the facts put forward by King was more probable than that put forward by Lowery. Not only, however, was the evidence which King called relevant to this case: its admissibility was placed beyond doubt by the whole substance of Lowery's case. Not only did Lowery assert that the killing was done by King and not only did he say that he had been in fear of King but, as previously mentioned, he set himself up as one who had no motive whatsoever in killing the girl and as one who would not have been likely to wreck his good prospects and furthermore as one who would not have been interested in the sort of behaviour manifested by the killer. While ascribing the sole responsibility to King, he was also in effect saying that he himself was not the sort of man to have committed the offence . . . the evidence was relevant to and necessary for his case which involved [negating] what Lowery had said and put forward . . . the evidence was admissible.'

It should be noted that this precedes the changes to admission of character evidence rules brought in by the Criminal Justice Act 2003.

More generally, expert witnesses will be called to give evidence on matters that are complex, scientific or technical. In modern criminal justice evidence has become far more sophisticated and, as a result, evidence of a forensic nature may carry much weight and therefore an expert's opinion would normally be required to meticulously examine exhibits. Other areas where experts are instructed include detailing professional or trade practice, proving foreign law and examining handwriting. *Lowery* (above) highlights the nature of opinion evidence and its potential use, although it has been distinguished in *R v Rimmer* [1983] Crim LR 250 on the basis of its peculiar or special facts.

The ultimate issue rule

In general terms, in criminal cases, an expert should only give their opinion in evidence on matters that are not directly in issue; this is known as the ultimate issue rule. *Lowery* (above) provides a good example, where the psychiatrist gave evidence on which defendant was more likely to have murdered the victim and not whether or not they actually had committed the crime. The ultimate issue rule seeks to prevent experts from usurping the function of the trier of law and fact, namely the judge and jury, for it is for them to decide on those matters. More recent case law – see *DPP v A & BC Chewing Gum Ltd* [1968] 1 QB 159 – shows that judges in criminal cases are not too strict where it comes to policing the rule and will allow an expert to give their opinion in evidence on an ultimate issue so long as the jury does not attribute excessive weight to it. In civil cases the position is slightly more relaxed, and expert witnesses can give evidence on any matter that is relevant: see s 3 of the Civil Evidence Act 1972.

Expert opinion as hearsay evidence

Generally, expert opinion evidence can be presented to a court either orally or in writing in the form of a report. Consider this question: what if the expert worked alongside other scientists in their scientific work and therefore has personal knowledge of some but not all the facts? When assessed on a technical basis, such a report would be classified as an inadmissible hearsay statement of opinion. We will discuss the position in criminal cases in a moment, but the position with regard to civil cases is far simpler – such hearsay statements of opinion are permissible under s 1 of the Civil Evidence Act 1995, which in effect means that the expert making the report does not need to give oral evidence themselves. As *ES v Chesterfield and North Derbyshire NHS Trust* [2004] Lloyds Rep Med 90 shows, the Civil Procedure Rules 1998 encourage the use of expert reports where necessary, the result of which is a saving in court resources and time taken to adjudicate. In this case, Brook LJ stated that:

JUDGMENT

'. . . *judges* have a . . . responsibility under the CPR to . . . restrict expert evidence to that which is reasonably required to resolve the proceedings'.

In criminal cases the agreed use of expert statements of opinion in the form of reports is permissible under s 30 of the Criminal Justice Act 1988: see *Jackson* [1996] 2 Cr App R 420. Once again the evidence is admissible regardless of whether the experts themselves give oral evidence; however, leave of the court to adduce the reports will be required if they do not. Where the court seeks to grant leave it will consider the following:

- the contents of the report;
- the reason for the expert not testifying;
- any risk of unfairness that may result from the expert not testifying because, in effect, the evidence will be uncorroborated;
- all the circumstances of the case.

Where the report is not controversial and is uncontested, then the court is likely to allow it to be adduced; if the opposite is true, then the expert should give evidence along with the admissible report. In criminal cases the issue of admissibility of such evidence was based on the negative views of hearsay held by others; the problems with the admission of expert reports was rectified by Part 24 of the Criminal Procedure Rules and the Criminal Justice Act 2003. First, s 114(1)(b) of the CJA 2003 preserves expert reports as evidence of facts stated therein; second, s 127(3) states that where such evidence is admitted it must be treated as 'evidence of what it states' and the court retains the power to make an order against the use of it where the interests of justice so require, thereby safeguarding the rights of the party against whom the evidence is being adduced. In making an order the court will take into account the costs, practicalities and summoning of the expert witness upon whose opinion the report is based so that they may be cross-examined on it. In summary, expert reports, namely hearsay opinion statements, are admissible in both civil and criminal cases, with the latter being subject to certain conditions.

ACTIVITY

How is expert opinion evidence presented in court?

KEY FACTS

The ultimate issue rule

The *general rule* in criminal cases is that a common law expert should only give their opinion in evidence on matters that are not directly in issue so that they do not usurp the function of the trier of fact.

Expert opinion as hearsay evidence

Where an expert does not give oral evidence, their opinion, for example a report, can be technically classed as an inadmissible hearsay statement; however:

- s 1 of the CEA 1995 and the CPR encourage the use of such statements in civil proceedings;
- s 30 of the CJA 1988 made their use permissible subject to the leave of the court, a problem rectified by s 114(1)(b) and s 127(3) of the CJA 2003 and the CPR.

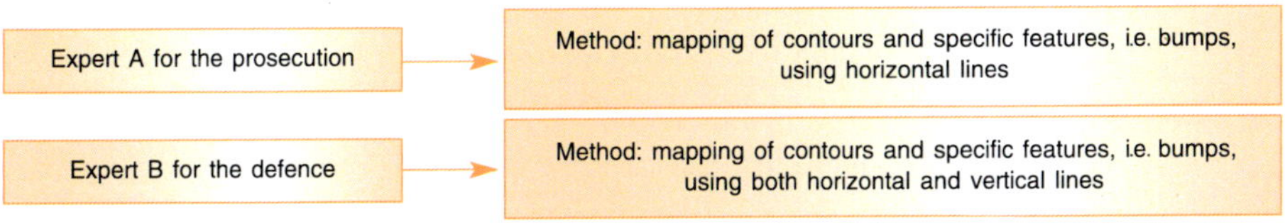

Figure 14.2 The presentation of expert opinion evidence in court

The presentation of expert opinion evidence

Oral evidence
the testimony of a witness given in court.

Most experts will have been experienced in writing reports and giving **oral evidence** (testifying). Normally the expert will work closely with the instructed advocate so that they can develop and present the report in court in the most effective manner. The advocate will normally question the expert on how they formulated their conclusions because this will most probably be the line of questioning pursued by the opposition when seeking to undermine it. Let us look at an example: two facial mapping experts each instructed by opposing parties to assess some low-quality CCTV footage consisting of the part of the face of an individual dressed in a hoodie committing a crime.

The methods of each of the experts were slightly different. Expert A had twenty-five years' experience using a 'traditional' method of facial mapping. In contrast, expert B had only ten years' experience but used a newer method of facial mapping. The evidence of expert A only indicated that the person in the CCTV footage and the defendant were 'likely' to be the same person. Expert B claimed that the person on the CCTV footage and the defendant were not the same person. The evidence of expert A was contradicted in cross-examination by counsel because he could not give a valid enough reason why he had rejected the use of the 'newer' method. The outcome was that the jury could not decide whom to believe and therefore could not return a verdict; the case had to be retried with a new jury.

In *English Exporters (London) Ltd v Eldonwall Ltd* [1973] Ch 415 the court outlined the extent to which an expert may refer to the hearsay data that they used to formulate their opinion when writing the report. The case at hand concerned the valuation of leases; the court confirmed that, although an expert could express their opinion based on matters that may not be within their personal knowledge, they cannot testify as to those facts unless they have actual personal knowledge of them.

CASE EXAMPLE

R v Abadom [1983] 1 WLR 126

The defendant was charged with robbery. The evidence of an expert witness showed that the glass that was found on his shoes was very likely the same as that of the window that had been broken during the commission of the offence. The broken glass had the same refractive index which, according to Home Office statistics, was only found in around 4 per cent of all glass samples. The defendant appealed, arguing that the statistics were technically hearsay and that the expert should not have been allowed to refer to them.

The Court of Appeal disagreed: the expert could refer, in the course of his testimony to research of which he had personal knowledge because the details of the research, although not directly evidence themselves, added weight to his evidence.

Proceedings	Reason for disclosure and source for reference
Civil	Part 31 of the Civil Procedure Rules requires the parties to comply with pre-trial disclosure in compliance with the overriding objective: to reduce costs, save time and increase efficiency in the way in which the case proceeds, i.e. clarification of the issues. The rules are available to download at: https://www.justice.gov.uk/courts/procedure-rules/civil/rules/part31
Criminal	The Crown Court (Advance Notice of Expert Evidence) Rules 1987 govern disclosure of opinions and any test or observation used to formulate it (rule 3(1)). A failure to follow these rules will result in the evidence being inadmissible unless the court grants leave for it to be adduced. See: https://www.justice.gov.uk/courts/procedure-rules/criminal

Figure 14.3 How expert reports are disclosed

The current position is neatly outlined by the courts in *H v Schering Chemicals Ltd* [1983] 1 WLR 143, where it was stated that medical or research reports that are technically hearsay statements if used by an expert to formulate their opinion can be referred to when assessing the weight of the expert's evidence.

Issues of disclosure

Figure 14.3 summarises how expert reports are disclosed.

14.3 Non-expert opinion evidence

The focus of the discussion now moves on to the opinion evidence of non-experts or lay witnesses. In civil cases the position is clarified by the Civil Evidence Act 1972; s 3(2) states that where the testimony of a witness is of their opinion in conveying the perception of facts by them, then that evidence is admissible as evidence of what they perceived. The effect of this is to render admissible the evidence of a witness that expresses a common-sensical observation or opinion of their perception. In criminal cases, although such clarity has not yet been achieved by statute, it is likely that the position is the same.

The next question, logically, concerns the subject matter upon which a non-expert can give evidence. Commonly cited and accepted facts upon that a non-expert can give evidence of perception include:

- the intoxication of the defendant, i.e. she was drunk;
- identification;
- the common value of an item other than a rare antique, i.e. that an iPod Nano is worth about £100;
- the speed of travel of a car, i.e. they were driving very fast;
- the physical fitness of a defendant.

Where non-expert evidence is concerned, the issue of such evidence being classified must be kept in mind because the opinion of a non-expert is irrelevant. In civil cases the notice procedure discussed earlier applies.

ACTIVITY

In civil cases, is non-expert opinion evidence admissible?

KEY FACTS

Non-expert opinion evidence

Generally, the opinion of non-expert witnesses is in civil cases admissible under s 3(2) of the CEA 1972 so long as it purveys their perception of facts.

In criminal cases the position is not clear; however, the jurisprudence of the courts suggests that it is essentially the same.

14.4 Opinion evidence of reputation

In civil cases the position generally accepted is that evidence of reputation is admissible, without giving notice, under s 7 of the CEA 1995 to show pedigree, good or bad character, or public right. In addition to this, evidence of opinion is also admissible, as already discussed. In criminal cases the Criminal Justice Act 2003 (CJA) governs evidence of bad character; this is discussed in Chapter 11, but you should note that there also exist a variety of rules that impact on reputation which are discussed throughout this book.

14.5 Previous judgments – hearsay?

Res judicata
an issue already judicially determined.

In certain instances a party may wish to rely on a previous judgment because it is factually relevant to their cases. It could be argued, technically, that such evidence is hearsay and therefore the argument against the use of previous judgments centres on the risk of prejudice; for example, there is a risk that court A will be prejudiced after learning of the opinion of court B on a factual issue. Exclusion of such evidence would result in unnecessary and repetitious arguments being pursued, not to mention the inconsistency in judgment; it is therefore important that in some situations evidence of this type be admissible with limitation. The principle of ***res judicata*** has the effect of debarring the same parties to an action from re-opening the same issue in subsequent proceedings. Think about this: Jane sues her plumber for negligence and loses; she is not happy and decides she would like to sue him again, and again until she wins. This would be an absurd situation. The current position of the law is as follows: an estoppel operates to bar subsequent actions based on the same issue(s).

14.6 Common law rule: *Hollington v Hewthorn*

The salient question concerns previous position at common law. On the issue of using previous judgments as evidence in subsequent civil cases, the common law frequently shifted between admission and exclusion. The matter was finally ambiguously settled in *Hollington v Hewthorn* [1943] KB 587, where the court decided that reference to previous judgments should be excluded. In this case the claimant, at that time referred to as the plaintiff, was the victim of alleged negligent driving on the part of the defendant's employee. The Court of Appeal decided that the employee's previous conviction for driving without due care and attention was inadmissible because the opinion of the previous court could not match the opinion of the High Court in a contested personal injury action.

The effect of the decision was to prevent previous judgments being used as evidence in a subsequent case; this was inconvenient and resulted in much inequity. The rule was somewhat reversed by the Civil Evidence Act 1968 (CEA), which provides exceptions to the rule in the form of ss 11–13, which respectively provide for the use of criminal convictions, findings of adultery and paternity and convictions for defamation as evidence in civil cases.

In *Ward v Savill* [2021] EWCA Civ 1378 the court held that the rule also covers declarations made by a previous court, a decision that was later confirmed by the Court of Appeal. In *Crypto Open Patent Alliance v Wright* [2021] EWHC 3440 (Ch) the court took the opportunity to review the authorities relating to the principle from *Hollington v Hewthorn*.

ACTIVITY

To what extent, if any, are the judgments of a previous court admissible as evidence in a subsequent case?

Summarise the extent to which criminal convictions may be used as evidence in civil cases.

KEY FACTS

Previous judgments

Generally, the arguments centring on the inadmissibility of previous court judgments focus on the risk of prejudice in the opinion of the current court based on something decided by a previous court, duplicity and inconsistency in judgment.

- In civil cases:
  - The principle of *res judicata* has the effect of *estopping* a party to an action from subsequently re-opening the same issue in subsequent proceedings.
  - The *common law rule* in *Hollington v Hewthorn* [1943] KB 587 meant that reference to previous civil judgments was excluded; this was partially reversed by ss 11–13 of the CEA 1968, which provide for reference to criminal convictions, findings of adultery and paternity and convictions for defamation.
- In criminal cases:
  - The use of previous criminal convictions as evidence is admissible under the CJA 2003 and s 74 of PACE 1984.

14.6.1 Section 11 CEA 1968

The discussion begins with s 11, which provides for the use of previous criminal convictions in civil cases.

Section 11(1) of the CEA 1968 states that:

SECTION

'. . . in any civil proceedings the fact that a person has been convicted of an offence by or before any *UK* court or by a court-martial *in the UK* or elsewhere shall be admissible in evidence for the purpose of proving, where relevant to any issue in

> those proceedings, that *they* committed that offence, whether *they were* so convicted upon a plea of guilty or otherwise and whether or not *they are* a party to the civil proceedings; but no conviction other than a subsisting one shall be admissible as evidence by virtue of this section.'

Section 11 contains a statutory persuasive presumption, which means that the court will *presume* the offence was committed by the defendant unless they can show otherwise: see *Wauchope v Mordecai* [1970] 1 WLR 317. The effect of s 11(1) is to allow the use of a criminal conviction in a *subsequent* civil action; one of the main underlying reasons for this includes the fact that the burden of proof on the prosecution in criminal cases (beyond reasonable doubt) is far higher than that in civil actions (on the balance of probabilities). Therefore, if a particular point has been proven to the judge and jury's satisfaction at the higher standard of proof, it makes sense to accept it as having satisfied the lower one. Most interestingly, the conviction does not need to be a conviction of a party to the action but it must be relevant to an issue. The following question arises: if a criminal conviction is admissible in evidence in subsequent civil actions, is, then, a finding in a civil case admissible as evidence in a criminal case? The provision only deals with convictions and does not state anything in respect of this situation and hence must be read as not having that effect.

The condition for admissibility, apart from relevance, is that the conviction must be one by a UK court or court martial or court martial under the authority of the British Forces. A conviction by a foreign court will not suffice; for example a Spanish conviction for careless driving could not be used as evidence of careless driving in the UK. The use of the conviction does not depend on whether the defendant pleaded guilty or not guilty; however, it must exist without a lodged appeal. If the conviction is being appealed, then the civil action must be adjourned or continued without that evidence.

The conviction will be proof of the fact that the person convicted committed the offence unless they can prove the contrary (s 11(2)); that does not mean a re-opening of the case but it may mean that there was an error on the record of the court convicting or the conviction was successfully appealed and quashed. The burden of proving that the conviction does not represent the true facts is on the party asserting that. Discharging this burden is difficult. Remember, the decision is one of twelve jurors who have been satisfied so that they are sure that the defendant committed the offence. In *Stupple v Royal Insurance Co* [1970] 3 All ER 230, Paull J stated:

JUDGMENT

> '. . . for at least the best part of 1,000 years it has been the law of England that it was not for a lawyer or for lawyers in any case of serious crime to pronounce whether an accused person was guilty of the crime and should be punished accordingly. Lawyers can pronounce that a man charged is not guilty if there is not sufficient evidence upon which his fellow citizens can properly find him guilty, or can pronounce that a summing up by a judge was not a satisfactory summing up; but once there is proper evidence, and the law and the facts have been satisfactorily explained to the accused's fellow citizens, it is for his fellow citizens, and for no one else, to pronounce whether he is guilty or not.'

Burden
a rule of evidence that requires someone to prove that which they contend and a failure to do so results in the contrary being assumed by the court.

In effect the party discharging this burden is arguing that the decision of the jury was wrong or mistaken; therefore, the discharge of this **burden** must be evidenced by the provision of convincing supporting evidence: see *Taylor v Taylor* [1970] 1 WLR 1148. The Court of Appeal in *Stupple* outlined how difficult this requirement could be, even though it was divided as to whether the conviction gave rise to a presumption or the very fact of the conviction was a factor that would be taken into account when considering whether the standard of the balance of probabilities had been satisfied.

14.6.2 Sections 12–13 CEA 1968: adultery, paternity and defamation

The discussion now moves on to specific instances in which 'findings' in other judgments can be used subsequently. Section 12 of the CEA 1968 provides that where a UK court, in matrimonial or other relevant proceedings, has made a finding of adultery or paternity, then that finding can be taken as evidence of adultery or paternity. It is obvious that adultery or paternity must be relevant to an issue in the subsequent proceedings. The effect of s 12 is to create a statutory presumption, on the person disputing the earlier finding, placing a legal burden of proof on them to prove the alternative.

Section 13 of the same Act provides that in defamation cases, the fact that a person has been convicted by a UK court or court martial of a criminal offence, where it is relevant to the subsequent proceedings, is conclusive evidence that they have committed the offence. This presumption was amended by the Defamation Act 1996, allowing the presumption in relation to the conviction of a non-party, i.e. a witness, to be rebutted.

14.6.3 Issues in the use of ss 11–13 CEA 1968

The party seeking to rely on s 11 or 12 must plead that they are seeking to rely on the conviction as part of their case in their particulars of claim; this is not necessary in those situations falling within s 13. All three provisions apply to criminal convictions, therefore criminal acquittals, i.e. where the person is not convicted and the charge is discontinued against them, are not covered because there would be no way of ascertaining what fact the person was acquitted is attempting to prove and what the probative value of such evidence would be. For example, Hannah cannot plead that James was tried for a criminal offence but acquitted and thereby assert that circumstantially there must be some truth in the allegation because charges were levied although unproven.

14.7 The use of previous criminal convictions in criminal cases

The law on the admissibility of a previous criminal conviction as evidence proving that an offence was committed by the person convicted in criminal cases is contained in the Criminal Justice Act 2003 (CJA) and s 74 of the Police and Criminal Evidence Act 1984 (PACE). The CJA 2003 is discussed in depth in Chapter 11; therefore, our discussion in this chapter will be limited to s 74 of the PACE 1984. Both provisions make previous criminal convictions admissible, within constraints, as evidence proving that the person convicted committed the offence. A major difference between the two provisions is that s 74 distinguishes between the criminal convictions of the accused and those of other persons, i.e. witnesses.

Section 74(1) PACE 1984 states that:

SECTION

'In any proceedings the fact that a person other than the accused has been convicted of an offence . . . shall be admissible evidence for the purpose of proving, where it is relevant to any issue in those proceedings, that that person committed that offence, whether or not any other evidence of his having committed that offence is given.'

In addition, s 74(2) PACE 1984 provides that the conviction, unless proven to the contrary, is proof that the person convicted committed the offence. The outcome here is similar to that under s 11 of the CEA 1968; let us take a look at a criminal law example. Sharon and Sunny are respectively charged with handling stolen goods and theft. Sunny is convicted of theft and sentenced to imprisonment. At Sharon's trial for the handling offence the prosecution may wish to adduce as evidence Sunny's conviction for theft; the effect of this is to prove that the goods were stolen.

The life of s 74 has not always been so easy; the provision has encountered other problems. What if the 'guilt' of the other person is not relevant to an element of the offence that the defendant is charged with but implicates them? In this instance the use of the previous conviction is likely to be excluded under s 78 PACE 1984. An interesting point to note concerns the meaning of conviction within the provision; does it mean conviction after a plea of guilty and hence no trial, or does it mean a conviction after a plea of not guilty and therefore after trial? Section 74 refers to a finding of guilt after a plea of not guilty being entered and the trial having taken place. Furthermore, once the person has been convicted, proof of the conviction can be used straight away; the party seeking to adduce it does not need to wait until the person has been sentenced: see *R v Golder* [1987] QB 920.

CASE EXAMPLE

R v O'Connor (1987) 85 Cr App R 298

A was charged with conspiring with B to defraud C. Even though B had been convicted after having pleaded guilty, hence no trial had taken place, the trial judge allowed for B's conviction to be adduced at A's trial. The Court of Appeal stated that the judge had erred; he should have excluded the evidence because of the greater likelihood of prejudice to A, i.e. of the jury thinking that if B had admitted it, then A must have done it. The Court declined to comment on the technicalities of s 74.

In contrast to the decision of the Court of Appeal in *O'Connor*, a differently constituted Court of Appeal (different judges) in *R v Robertson* [1987] QB 920 decided that s 74 was not so restricted. In *Robertson* the Court of Appeal held that the provision applied so long as the conviction of the other person was relevant to any issue in the subsequent proceedings. However, the judge should be careful when directing and summing up to the jury.

CASE EXAMPLE

R v Curry [1988] Crim LR 527

A was convicted of allowing his credit card to be fraudulently used. The Court of Appeal held that the use of his conviction in the trial of B would have resulted in unfairness. Although the conviction was technically admissible it was excluded on the ground that 'where the evidence expressly or by . . . inference imported the complicity of the accused it should not be used'.

CASE EXAMPLE

R v Warner (1993) 96 Cr App R 324

A was accused of supplying drugs (heroin). The police had witnessed a number of people visiting the premises and speaking to the defendant, after which he would run to his car to collect small packages to give to them. Of the visitors at least eight were known drug dealers with previous convictions for such offences. The prosecution sought to admit these previous convictions as part of their case against A under s 74. The defence objected on the basis that the evidence was hearsay; the court thought otherwise. The evidence was not hearsay because the purpose in tendering it was not to prove what was either said or done or both, nor was it to prove the intention of the visitors. The convictions allowed a circumstantial inference as to the reason for the visits to be drawn by the jury.

R v Warner supports the idea that convictions with a wider relevance can be admitted under s 74. You should refer to the recommended additional reading at the end of this chapter for further information on the topics discussed so far.

ACTIVITY

Summarise the extent to which civil findings may be used as evidence in criminal cases.

14.8 Documentary and real evidence

We now turn to two other types of evidence, documentary and real evidence, the latter of which is widely used in the dramatisation of crime.

14.8.1 Documentary evidence

Documents are an important type of evidence because they may be direct evidence, for example in the form of a contractual agreement that evidences the existence of the agreement or admissible hearsay – evidence pointing to the truth of a particular statement under either the CJA 2003 or the Civil Evidence Act 1995. Interestingly, a document is not evidence in its own right when used as an *aide-memoire*, i.e. a memory-refreshing document; however, in order for it to be used as evidence the document must be admissible.

Our first question focuses on the legal classification of a document. In modern-day colloquial terms, i.e. everyday language, a document is something that contains and conveys information that can be viewed and understood.

This has a wider meaning today because of the advances in technology, such as email, fax, etc. Previously, s 10(1) of the Civil Evidence Act 1968 had stated that documents included films, photographs, tape recordings, soundtracks and other methods of recording data, such as Dictaphones, and this will most likely expand as new and novel forms of evidence are created.

The common law required the party that seeks to rely on a document to produce the original version of it; a copy was unacceptable. The reason for this was the extent of fraud in hand-copied documents, an issue largely reduced as a result of modern copying methods and newer forms of document, such as DVDs. The current position is different; the courts are not as stringent with this requirement. Ackner LJ and Woolf J confirmed this in *Kajala v Noble* (1982) 75 Cr App R 149, stating that:

JUDGMENT

> '. . . the old rule, that a party must produce the best evidence that the nature of the case will allow, and that any less good evidence is to be excluded, has gone by the board long ago. The only remaining instance of it is that, if an original document is available in one's hands, one must produce it; that one cannot give secondary evidence by producing a copy. Nowadays we do not confine ourselves to the best evidence. We admit all relevant evidence. The goodness or badness of it goes only to weight, and not to admissibility: *Garton v Hunter* [1969] 1 All ER 451, per Lord Denning MR at 453e . . . in our judgment, the old rule is limited and confined to written documents in the strict sense of the term, and has no relevance to tapes or films.'

The case of *Augustien v Challis* (1847) 1 Exch 279 is a good example as to how important an original document (primary evidence) could be. In this case the court refused to accept other documents (secondary evidence) as evidence as to the terms of a lease. This rule does not apply where the purpose of the document is to establish that a lease exists and not the terms it contains. It should be noted that other statutes contain rules for the admission of other types of documentary evidence, for example s 71 of the PACE 1984 allows the contents of a document to be evidenced by an authenticated microfilm copy of the document. The CJA 2003 and the Civil Evidence Act 1995 govern the admissibility of documentary hearsay. What follows is an in-depth discussion of the differences between primary and secondary documentary evidence.

A good example of primary documentary evidence is an original document, for example a lease, a contract or a receipt. If, for some reason, only a copy of a document was given to the person, then they must produce all copies, i.e. when you submit your assessments, the assessment office normally will return to you a carbon copy of the front slip as proof that you have submitted it – you would need to produce more than that carbon copy for the document to amount to primary evidence. What if the document is one that was purposefully duplicated so that each party signed all copies that were thereafter distributed amongst them, such as a tenancy agreement? Then that agreement is enough. Where the person no longer has the original copy because they have had to submit it somewhere e.g., deeds to a bank or a contract to a court, then an official copy produced by the body where it is submitted will count as primary evidence.

Reason	Admissibility of secondary evidence in lieu
The original has been lost or destroyed	Reasonable effort to locate or trace the original after which secondary evidence can be received by the court.
Production of the original is impossible	If it is impossible or difficult to produce the original then the court may receive secondary evidence.
The document is a part of a bankers' book, i.e. accounts	The Bankers' Books Evidence Act 1879 allows the use of copies of the book if the book is used in the custody of the bank and is used in the ordinary course of its business. Proof will be required that the copy was inspected alongside the original.
Someone who is not party to the litigation refuses to produce the original	Where someone that is not party to the litigation possesses the document and is entitled to refuse production, then the court may receive secondary evidence unless they can be compelled by the court to produce it.
A party fails to produce the original after having been given notice to do so	Party A can serve party B with a notice requiring them to produce the original document in their possession failing which secondary evidence can be received by the court.

Figure 14.4 Requirements for admissibility

In contrast, secondary evidence can come in a number of forms; it can be oral or written. For the majority of the time, secondary evidence will be inadmissible unless:

- the original has been lost or destroyed;
- production of the original is impossible;
- the document is a part of a bankers' book;
- someone who is not party to the litigation refuses to produce the original;
- a party fails to produce the original after having been given notice to do so.

The diagram in Figure 14.4 summarises the requirements for admissibility where one of the above reasons applies.

A collateral issue concerns facts that can be presumed from documentary evidence. Documentary evidence will be proof of primary facts so long as it is over twenty years old and is produced by appropriate authority. A good example is the production of paper deeds in unregistered land proving ownership (subject to the rules contained within the Land Registration Acts). Secondary facts that can be presumed from the production of a document include the date on which it was executed, such as the date upon which a contract came into force.

14.8.2 Real evidence

The final topic for discussion is real evidence. This is evidence that can be tangibly put before the court and which the court can observe and draw inferences from. Examples of real evidence include:

- objects, e.g. a knife, gun or hacksaw;
- physical appearance of persons, for example bruises, responses and behaviour;

- physical appearance of animals, such as emaciation;
- video recordings including CCTV footage;
- photographs or film; and
- views, where the court may relocate, as in the UK's Soham murders case, where the jury visited the site itself.

It is common for the court to come across real evidence, whether it is the bloodstained axe with which someone was killed or seeing the post-attack victim in court. Real evidence must be authentic; if there is any doubt or if it is of low quality, then it will be excluded: see *R v Stevenson* [1971] 1 WLR 1.

ACTIVITY

Give examples of what amounts to documentary evidence for the purpose of the law.

Define real evidence; give three examples.

KEY FACTS

Documentary evidence

Documents can be direct evidence or hearsay.

- A *document* is something that contains or conveys information that can be viewed and understood, including emails, tape or video recordings, DVD, Blu-ray and fax.
- *Generally* the law requires the primary document to be produced, for example the original contract. Secondary evidence, e.g. a copy of a lease, falls into the provisions of the CJA 2003, the CEA 1995 or PACE 1984.

Real evidence

This is evidence that can be tangibly put before the court and which the court can observe and draw inferences from, e.g. the knife used to dismember a body.

SUMMARY (INCLUDING EXAMINATION TIP)

In this chapter we have discussed two important types of evidence: evidence that can make the difference between proving and disproving a claim or allegation. These topics tend, very rarely, to appear as questions in their own right; therefore, you can rest assured that these topics will usually pervade other questions; hence, it is important to have a practical grasp of the issues we have discussed.

OPINION EVIDENCE

Witnesses should only give evidence of facts that they have perceived themselves without speculating, drawing conclusions and inferences or giving their opinion. The English law of evidence excludes the opinion evidence of witnesses because they may be unreliable or inexperienced in giving evidence and hence there exists a greater risk of such evidence lacking probative force. Opinion evidence is excluded unless it is:

- expert opinion;
- opinion evidence of general reputation;
- the opinion of an eyewitness.

EXPERT OPINION

Expert opinion evidence is used where the court requires assistance on matters beyond its competence or experience, i.e. complex and technical issues. Expert witnesses are better equipped to express their opinion and make conclusions from the facts, for example on the time relating to the decomposition of a corpse or facial mapping. The court will receive expert evidence where the witness's opinion is beyond ordinary experience and competence and they are a qualified expert.

WITNESS EXPERTISE

The court will only hear the opinion evidence of a person who is *qualified* to form an opinion on the matter concerned, for example a professor of haematology. The person need not have a formal qualification because their skill and experience is enough, although the level of skill and expertise will affect the weight attributed to the evidence.

SUBJECT MATTER

An expert witness will only be called to give evidence on matters that are beyond *normal* experience or expertise.

THE ULTIMATE ISSUE RULE

The ultimate issue rule states that in a criminal case at common law an expert should only give their opinion in evidence on matters that are not directly in issue, even though in practice they may do so. In civil cases the expert witness can give evidence on any matter that is relevant.

EXPERT OPINION AS HEARSAY EVIDENCE

The opinion of an expert can be presented to a court orally or in writing in the form of a report. A report could be classified as a hearsay statement of opinion. In civil cases such hearsay statements of opinion are permissible and in fact encouraged under s 1 of the Civil Evidence Act 1995. In criminal cases the use of expert statements of opinion in the form of a report is permissible under s 30 of the Criminal Justice Act 1988.

NON-EXPERT OPINION EVIDENCE

In civil cases the Civil Evidence Act 1972, s 3(2) states that where the testimony of a witness is of their opinion conveying the perception of facts by them, then that evidence is admissible as evidence of what they perceived.

The effect of this is to render admissible the evidence of a witness that expresses a commonsensical observation or opinion of their perception. In criminal cases such clarity has not yet been achieved; it is likely that the position is the same.

Non-experts can give evidence of their perception, e.g. the intoxication of the defendant, i.e. she was drunk.

OPINION EVIDENCE OF REPUTATION

In civil cases the position generally accepted is that evidence of reputation is admissible, without giving notice, under s 7 of the Civil Evidence Act 1995 to show pedigree, good or bad character, or public right. In criminal cases evidence of bad character is governed by the Criminal Justice Act 2003.

COMMON LAW RULE: *HOLLINGTON V HEWTHORN*

In *Hollington v Hewthorn* [1943] KB 587 the Court of Appeal decided that reference to previous judgments in civil cases should be excluded. The employee's previous conviction for driving without due care and attention was inadmissible because the opinion of the previous court could not match the opinion of the High Court in a contested personal injury action. The effect of the decision was to prevent previous judgments being used as evidence in a subsequent case; this was inconvenient and resulted in much inequity. The rule was partially reversed by the Civil Evidence Act 1968, which provides exceptions to the rule in ss 11–13. In summary, s 11 provides for the use of criminal convictions, s 12 for findings of adultery and paternity and s 13 for convictions for defamation.

THE USE OF PREVIOUS CRIMINAL CONVICTIONS IN CRIMINAL CASES

The law on the admissibility of a previous criminal conviction as evidence proving that an offence was committed by the person convicted in criminal cases is contained in the Criminal Justice Act 2003 and s 74 of the PACE 1984. Both provisions make previous criminal convictions admissible, within constraints, as evidence proving that the person convicted committed the offence.

DOCUMENTARY EVIDENCE

Documents are an important type of evidence because they may be direct evidence in the form of a contractual agreement that evidences the existence of the agreement and the form it takes, i.e. the terms and conditions. Documents are things that contain and convey information that can be viewed and understood. There are two forms of documentary evidence: first, primary documentary evidence – this is an original document, for example a lease, a contract or a receipt. In contrast, secondary evidence can come in a number of forms; it can be oral or written. The common law requires the party that seeks to rely on a document to produce the original version of it; a copy is unacceptable. The courts are not as stringent with this requirement.

REAL EVIDENCE

Real evidence is evidence that can be tangibly put before the court and that the court can observe and draw inferences from, such as a knife, gun or hacksaw.

SAMPLE ESSAY QUESTION

Po Yang is charged with the murder of his neighbour Xilai Bo. The prosecution alleges that Po beat Xilai to death. Po's defence is one of diminished responsibility, and that Xilai was blackmailing him, stating that Po had threatened to tell Po's wife Chang of his homosexual relationship if he did not give him £100,000. Po wishes to adduce an expert report by Dr Singh which describes Po's distress at being blackmailed, the fact that he loved his wife and that, in the expert's opinion, this could lead to a violent outburst. Discuss whether Po can adduce any of these. Dr Singh highlights that his opinion is based on the research of other experts.

Answer plan

Outline the main issues relating to murder.
State that diminished responsibility is a defence contained in s 2 of the Homicide Act 1957 and that it is up to Po to prove he has the defence under this provision. Mention *Dix* (1982), where the court held that the provision makes it necessary to have medical evidence in support if the accused is to run this defence.

Explore the admissibility of Dr Singh's report.
Highlight that the report relates to Po's reaction to the blackmail and the fact that he loves his wife dearly. Also state that it is unclear from the facts as to how Dr Singh came to his conclusions: did Po tell him or did he make a medical assessment? Argue that it seems this evidence would be inadmissible where Dr Singh was repeating what Po had said to him, as this would be hearsay. Additionally, outline that Po's reaction, namely the distress, would be admissible.

Analyse the expert's opinion on violent reaction.
State that the question that would be posed here is whether the jury would need the assistance of a psychiatrist to help them determine the matter at issue. Explore whether Dr Singh is of that opinion himself or whether he accepts what others are saying – if it is his own then the argument for the admission of that which he contends in his report will be far stronger – refer to the case *Abadom* (1983). Finally, state that where the judge considers that all Dr Singh's report does is describe ordinary human reactions then it is unlikely to be admitted because it would not assist the jury.

Further reading

Blom-Cooper QC, Sir L. 'Witness immunity: the argument against' (2006) 156 (7232) NLJ 1088–1089
Chippindall, A. C. 'Expert evidence and legal professional privilege' (2003) JPI Law, Jan, 61–70
Gooderham, P. 'Witness immunity: the argument in favour' (2006) 156 (7232), NLJ 1086–1087
Jackson, J. D. 'The ultimate issue rule – one rule too many' [1984] Crim LR 75
Keane, A. and McKeown, P. (2012) *The Modern Law of Evidence*. Ninth edition. Oxford: Oxford University Press (Chapter 18 has an excellent discussion on both expert and non-expert evidence)
Munday, R. (2011) *Evidence*. Sixth edition. Oxford: Oxford University Press (Chapter 8 of this text has a very good discussion on opinion evidence including an interesting discussion on the use of psychologist and psychiatrist opinion)
Singh, C. (2015). *Q&A Evidence 2013–2014*. Oxford: Routledge
Singh, C. (2015). *Quis custodiet ipsos custodies? Should justice beware: a review of the debate surrounding the reliability of voice identification evidence in light of advances in biometric voice identification technology*. International Commentary on Evidence. Volume 11: 1–28. Germany and the USA: De Gruyter

Index

Note: Page numbers in *italic* refer to figures on the corresponding page.